PUBLICATIONS OF
THE DUGDALE SOCIETY

Under the General Editorship of

JOAN LANE

M.A., Ph.D., F.S.A.

VOLUME XXXVI

THE DUGDALE SOCIETY

THE DUGDALE SOCIETY, named after Warwickshire's distinguished antiquary, Sir William Dugdale (1605–86), was founded in 1920 with the objects of publishing original documents relating to the history of the County of Warwick, fostering interest in historical records and their preservation, and generally encouraging the study of local history and its sources.

The Society publishes as frequently as its resources and circumstances permit and so far thirty-five volumes in the Main Record Series have appeared as well as thirty-four Occasional Papers.

Volumes which are in active preparation include *Records of Coventry Priory*, *The Diaries of Sanderson Miller*, *The Correspondence of Sir Roger Newdigate* and *The Coventry Muster Rolls*.

Membership of the Society is open to any person, library or corporate body interested in promoting the objects of the Society. The annual subscription is at present £10.00, due on 1 January. Members receive a free copy of all publications issued. An Annual Meeting takes place in the autumn at which a paper is presented and a summer social event is usually held.

Applications for membership are welcome. They should be sent to the Honorary Secretary of the Dugdale Society, c/o The Shakespeare Centre, Stratford-upon-Avon, Warwickshire, CV37 6QW, England.

THE GREAT FIRE
OF WARWICK
1694

THE RECORDS OF THE COMMISSIONERS
APPOINTED UNDER AN ACT OF
PARLIAMENT FOR REBUILDING THE
TOWN OF WARWICK

EDITED BY

MICHAEL FARR
M.A., F.S.A., F.R.Hist.S.

Warwickshire County Archivist 1967–1989

The Dugdale Society

Email:
dugdale-society@hotmail.co.uk

Website:
www.dugdale-society.org.uk

PRINTED FOR THE DUGDALE SOCIETY
BY STEPHEN AUSTIN AND SONS LTD, HERTFORD
1992

ISBN 0 85220 069 2

*Text set by Joshua Associates Ltd, Oxford and
printed in Great Britain
for the Dugdale Society
by Stephen Austin and Sons Ltd
Hertford*

CONTENTS

CONTENTS

ILLUSTRATIONS

Between pages 284 and 285

STREET DIAGRAMS

MAP OF WARWICK

FOREWORD

The records in this volume are published by kind permission of the former Borough Council and their successors the Town Council of Warwick, and of the Warwickshire County Council regarding a document in the Warwick Castle archives.

The editor of the volume wishes to acknowledge his indebtedness to the late A. C. Wood, the former County Archivist from whom he inherited the project, for much background material and advice. He would also like to express his gratitude to his colleagues in the Record Office for many references passed on over the years, to Mr Stephen Wallsgrove for information from the St Mary's commoners' rolls, and to Mrs Rosemary Booth for undertaking the map and street diagrams. Thanks are also due to Peter Coss for his help and encouragement during the time that he was General Editor.

The Council of the Dugdale Society is most grateful to the Trustees of the Charity of King Henry VIII in Warwick, to the British Academy and to the Marc Fitch Fund for generous grants towards the costs of publication.

INTRODUCTION

The records of the Warwick Fire Commissioners span the decade 1694–1704, during which they exercised the powers given them by the *Act for Rebuilding the Town of Warwick*.[1] They and their officers made and received documents of several classes which run parallel, and cannot be arranged consecutively; some are in any case undated. It is therefore necessary to get an idea of the sequence of the events to which they relate.

Warwick before the Fire

In 1694 Warwick was still largely a medieval town of narrow streets and timber-framed houses, with only a few larger buildings of stone or brick. The population was about 3,500.[2] Most of the houses fronting the principal streets were tiled, but there were also a great many buildings down the crofts or back gardens,[3] including barns, stables, malthouses, workshops, pigsties and privies, and most of these were thatched, as were many dwelling houses in the poorer quarters.[4] Thatch had long been recognized as a fire hazard. Stratford-upon-Avon corporation ordered as early as 1583 that all houses should be roofed with tiles, but such orders were hard to enforce, and Stratford suffered four serious fires between then and 1641, when it was said that all the fires had their beginnings in poor tenements and cottages which were thatched with straw.[5] The Warwick court leet ordained in 1628 that kilns for drying malt should be tiled and their fires should be out by 8 o'clock at night, and in 1648 forbade householders to store combustible furze or broom,[6] presumably used as fuel for bread-ovens. By 1694 the town possessed a 'large ingeon for the exstinguishing of fire',[7] and fire buckets were kept by the two trade companies and by a saddler, who may have made them of leather.[8] The engine was kept in the church, which also had three fire-hooks on long poles, and a fire bell, recast in 1670 and hung in a frame for sounding the alarm.[9] There was no fire brigade as such, but in 1692–3 the corporation paid a body of thirty-four men for beating down a fire in the back lane; they also paid water carriers and men to watch afterwards,[10] which makes it appear that fire-fighting was to some extent organized. Fire insurance had been available in London since 1680 with

---

[1] *See* p. 133.

[2] *Victoria History of the County of Warwick* (*V.C.H. Warws*), Oxford, 1969, viii, p. 418.

[3] The masons' and carpenters' survey distinguishes front and back bays of building, *see* pp. 135–43.

[4] *Cf.* the survey of thatch in the unburnt streets, pp. 271–83.   [5] *V.C.H. Warws.*, iii, p. 223.

[6] Warwickshire County Record Office, CR 1618/W.11/3; *V.C.H Warws.*, viii, p. 513.

[7] *See* p. 229.   [8] *See* pp. 166, 202, 203.   [9] DR 133/16.

[10] W.C.R.O., CR 1618/W.13/5.

Nicholas Barbon's Fire Office, which grew into the Phoenix Fire Office,[1] but it had not yet reached Warwick.

The Fire

The fire broke out at two o'clock in the afternoon of the fifth of September, probably in a back building behind the last house on the south side of the High Street, near Saunders Row. Field, relating a popular tradition, says 'as a person was crossing a lane, with a piece of lighted wood in his hand, a spark flew from it, and fell on the thatch of an adjoining house, which was soon in flames'.[2] The fire, aided by a strong south-west wind, reached the High Street at the Quakers' meeting house, tenanted by George Harris, which was half burnt,[3] and proceeded up the street, crossing over after a short distance to burn both sides as far as the Cross. From here it continued along the north side of Jury Street, where 'it stopped at a large house belonging to the Archers of Umberslade, where the burnt ends of the timbers testified the dreadful escape it had had from the fury of the flames'.[4] This was a stone house, now incorporated in the Lord Leycester Hotel. The south side of Jury Street was not affected, though the Mayor's Parlour on the corner of Castle Street was slightly damaged. The fire spread northwards, as described in the letter to the bishop of Worcester and in the brief,[5] presumably taking a direct line through the thatched buildings in the crofts, until it had burnt Church Street, Northgate otherwise Sheep Street, two sides of the Market Place, and poorer houses at the top of the Butts and in Joyce Pool, finally crossing the Saltisford to end with five houses where Northgate House now stands. The tower, nave and transepts of St Mary's church were destroyed, according to Field because goods moved into the church were smouldering and so set fire to the fabric,[6] though it is perhaps more likely that the flames leapt the narrow gap between the houses in Canon Row and the church tower, where it was noted that the extreme heat melted the bells.[7]

Fire-fighting was successful at the Shire Hall, which was saved by a team of thirty men[8] and suffered only minor damage; it was used to house prisoners from the gaol next door,[9] which was burnt down.[10] Four men were also paid by James Fish, *custos* of St Mary's, for putting out the fire 'at chapel',[11] presumably the Beauchamp Chapel, which may have been

---

[1] *Chartered Insurance Institute Journal*, 11, part 3, Aug. 1987, p. 185.
[2] Rev. William Field, *An historical and descriptive account of ... Warwick*, Warwick, H. Sharpe, 1815, p. 10.   [3] *See* p. 136.
[4] Rev. Thomas Ward, *Collections for the Continuation of the History and Antiquities of Warwickshire by Sir William Dugdale ... to the present year 1830*, B.L. Add. MS 29264, f. 38ᵛ.
[5] *See* pp. 1, 116-7.   [6] Field, *loc. cit.*
[7] St Nicholas parish register, W.C.R.O., DR 181/1.   [8] *See* p. 412.
[9] *See* p. 255.   [10] *See* p. 237.   [11] *See* p. 412.

preserved by their efforts. These teams probably used buckets and water, but elsewhere attempts to stop the fire were by pulling down houses to create fire breaks. Six houses in different parts of the town are reported to have been wholly or partly demolished for this purpose. Of these, two had only the tiles thrown off their roofs, one was 'untiled and the roof took down', two were part burnt and part pulled down, and only one 'untiled and the timber frame thereof cutt down'. This last house, occupied by Nathaniel Gilstrop, stood on the corner of the Butts at the Eastgate, and although Dr William Johnson, the owner of a newly re-fronted mansion two doors away at the top of Smith Street, was held responsible,[1] its demolition may have been part of a considered plan to halt the fire then advancing up the High Street. At the fire of London, there was at first reluctance to demolish houses before the fire reached them, but by the third day whole rows of houses were being blown up with gunpowder on the orders of the King and Duke of York to make effective fire breaks.[2] In Warwick, the authority of the mayor, Joseph Blissett, was sought, but it was doubtful whether Dr Johnson was acting on his orders for the good of the town, or was trying to preserve his own property.[3] The house of Timothy Norbury, half way down Jury Street on the south side, was unroofed on the mayor's orders well ahead of the fire, but demolition presumably stopped when the fire failed to cross Castle Street. The house belonging to James Cook's guardians on the other corner of the Butts opposite Gilstrop's house, was also untiled on Dr Johnson's initiative, plainly with the sound idea of widening the bottom of the Butts on both sides, but the fire, although it started down the north side of Jury Street, stopped unexpectedly at the Archer mansion about 120 yards away, making this piece of fire prevention unnecessary.

One of the houses 'part burnt and part pulled down' belonged to Mrs Mann on the north-east side of the Market Place. Enough of this house remained for her tenant John King to attempt to live and trade on the ground floor until the chimney and upper floor fell, nearly killing him and his family.[4] However, the adjoining houses were wholly or partly burnt, so this demolition can hardly have been effective in arresting the fire, which continued on into Joyce Pool. The house of George Chinn in Swann Lane, on the other hand, also part burnt and part pulled down to stop the fire, may have saved the King and Queen's Head next door,[5] and prevented the fire from spreading further northwards there. About fifteen other houses on the fringes of the burnt area are described as 'part burnt', but it is not clear whether these were saved by human endeavour. Watchmen were set that night to see that the fire did not break out again.[6] No people were killed in

---

[1] See pp. 374-5.
[2] John Bedford, *London's Burning*, Abelard-Schumann, 1966, pp. 39, 118.
[3] See p. 49 and n.   [4] See pp. 355-6.
[5] See p. 341.   [6] See p. 412.

the fire,[1] probably because it occurred in daylight from two until about eight p.m., but at least a dozen pigs perished in their sties in High Street and Church Street.

The Fire Committee

Sir Henry Puckering described the first steps towards recovery in a letter on 27 September to the earl of Northampton, the Lord Lieutenant.

> ... The next day after the fire, many gentlemen comeing in to bemoane and view the yet smoakeing and unextinguished ruines of the forgoeing day, wee all together, with my Lord Brooke, withdrew, to consider of some speedy course, whereby best to provide for the subsistence and present reliefe of such as having lost all they had, had neither bread to eate, tools to worke, or bedd to lay on; when presently a subscription was made before we parted, of two or three hundred pounds for that purpose, which by cursory letters sent by two trusty persons severally into every hundred, recommending to theire charityes the present necessityes of our sufferers, in a short time brought in a very seasonable and liberall contribution (besides what provisions for the mouth came from some neighbouring townes) which every day since encreas'd to a considerable summ, as your lordship may perceive by th'enclosed paper; of which, what first came in, was then impartially distributed, to such, as by consent of all were judged to have the greatest need of it, though tenn pounds was the greatest summ allowed to any one. A further equall distribution will I suppose be made next weeke by the Justices when they meete at their sessions, as likewise a strict computation of all such losses as every person shall justly claim to have suffered by the fire, either in goods or houses, which valuations will be delivered upon oath, the goods by that of the owners, the houses by the judgement and valuation of eight able and sufficient masons and carpenters imploy'd to make such estimate upon oath, that thereupon an address may bee made, with a certificate from the bench, to my Lord Keeper, for a breife, which our Mayor and Corporation, and all of us humbly begg that your Lordshipp upon occasion will countenance and assist, as also the procuring of an Act of Parliament for rebuilding the Towne, when it shall come before the Lords at theire next sitting, where your favour, and knowne interest, will bee of very great use. The computation of the losses is not yett ready, or else I would also send it. ...[2]

Lord Brooke was the recorder of Warwick and Thomas Newsham, the

---

[1] The St Mary's parish register (W.C.R.O. DR 447/1) has a gap of six months immediately before the fire, which probably indicates that it was written up at intervals from rough notes, lost on this occasion.

[2] Compton Papers at Castle Ashby, 1321. (W.C.R.O. microfilm M1.167/7).

town clerk named in the new borough charter of 1693,[1] was one of the gentry who joined with him to form a relief committee,[2] but the others were almost all county justices of the peace, not members of the Warwick corporation as one might have expected. The county justices at Quarter Sessions had much experience of the procedure described in Sir Henry Puckering's letter. In the decade before 1694 they had received petitions, backed up by certificates of losses, on nine occasions, and had issued letters of request for charitable collections in particular hundreds once, country-wide seven times, and had sent their own certificate to the lord chancellor for letters patent for a nation-wide brief for a larger fire at Gaydon in 1684.[3] They must also have been accustomed to hearing briefs for other 'sudden and lamentable' fires read from the pulpits of their parish churches,[4] and grown used to the language of disaster, which by now had become stereo-typed. On this occasion the committee of gentry sent out letters of request to the four hundreds within the county on 6 September, as well as con-tributing themselves, and two days later ordered a list to be made of those most in need; they also appointed treasurers and ordered books to be kept recording their actions. One of the treasurers, William Tarver, was a profes-sional, since he was the county treasurer, appointed despite being himself a major sufferer by the fire. A first distribution of £523 to 143 people was made on 10 September, and on 13 September contributions from the bishop of Worcester and from the Worcester city parishes arrived, and a second distribution was made on 17 September. During this time the mayor and aldermen of the borough had ordered sufferers to bring in their estimates of losses by 14 September. A survey of burnt properties by four masons and four carpenters was completed by the 27th, and on the strength of it Quarter Sessions were able to send their certificate to the lord chancellor for a brief on 2 October.[5] The letters patent which formed the text of the brief are dated 8 December, but the bill for the Act of Parliament took rather longer; first read on 14 December, it did not receive the royal assent until 11 February, 1695.[6] Thomas Newsham the town clerk and John Mitchener his assistant were rewarded for their great pains in Chancery and in both Houses of Parliament, where they were assisted by William Colmore, one of the members for Warwick borough. John Smith, a bar-rister, later a baron of the Exchequer, was paid five guineas for drafting the Act,[7] which is modelled very closely on the London rebuilding Acts of 1667

---

[1] Joseph Parkes, *The Governing Charter of the Borough of Warwick*, London, 1827, p. xx.

[2] *See* p. 2.

[3] Warwick County Records, viii, p. 115 and viii and ix, *passim*.

[4] E. L. Jones, S. Porter and M. Turner, *A Gazetteer of English Urban Fire Disasters, 1500–1900*, Historical Geography Research Series, No. 13, Norwich, 1984.

[5] *See* pp. 1–9.

[6] *Calendar of State Papers Domestic 1695*, p. 295; *House of Lords Journals* xv, p. 488.

[7] *See* pp. 410–13.

and 1670,[1] apart from the clause establishing the court of record, which follows a similar clause in the 1676 Northampton Act.[2] Substantial passages in the Warwick Act are taken verbatim from the London examples. However, the directions for four classes of houses with detailed specifications in the London Act of 1670 were not copied, but instead the houses in Warwick were to be limited to two storeys with garrets, and a third storey was only to be allowed if there were good reason for it. John Smith, whose native place was Frolesworth (Leics.), must have relied on Thomas Newsham, William Colmore or even Lord Brooke for local knowledge regarding the particular streets in Warwick to be altered or widened.

The brief money began to come in to the two designated London banks, Child's and Hoare's, in February 1695. The Warwick brief contained two features normally reserved for major catastrophes, first that it was a 'walking brief', not only to be read in pulpits but also to be taken by churchwardens and ministers from house to house,[3] and second that the distribution or 'laying' of the briefs and the return of the money collected was to be carried out by the archdeacons,[4] to avoid the expense of professional agents. The archdeacons were expected to charge 6*d*. per brief, but were urged by the members of Parliament concerned to forego their fees.[5] An agent, Daniel Eyre of Clerkenwell, was in fact appointed to disperse the briefs and collect the money in Herefordshire at 4*d* per parish and in Wales at 6*d*.[6] Recognizing that charity must be timely to be effective, the brief required churchwardens within ten days to pay the money collected to their parson or minister, who should in turn within another ten days pass it to the archdeacon, who within twenty days more should return it to Child's or Hoare's banks in London. The brief was valid for two years. It is not known how long it took to distribute the briefs, but the speed of return was variable. The London city parishes seem to have paid their collections promptly into the banks direct, and Dr Thomas Plume, archdeacon of Rochester, dutifully brought in collections as they reached him in seven instalments in 1695 and 1696,[7] but others were more laggardly. Money was still coming in as late as 1700 and some, like Dr John Cawley, archdeacon of Lincoln, had to be sued for withholding collections.

The Fire Court

Immediate relief had been funded by the local worthies and by money raised from letters of request within the county, administered by the

---

[1] 19 Car. II, c. 2 and 3; 22 Car. II, c. 9; in Joseph Keble, *Statutes at Large*, London, 1681, pp. 1328, 1329, 1378.
[2] 27 Car. II, Keble, *op. cit.*, p. 1472.
[3] W. A. Bewes, *Church Briefs*, 1896, pp. 48–9.
[4] *See* p. 118.
[5] *See* pp. 12–13.
[6] W.C.R.O., CR 1618/WA.4/192.
[7] *See* pp. 510–15, 518.

committee of gentry, many of whom became trustees of the brief money. All the trustees named in the brief then became commissioners under the Act of Parliament, either specifically named, or *ex officio* as county justices. The commissioners were henceforth responsible for all allocations of money. They first met on 29 April 1695, nearly eight months after the fire, took the required oath, and formed themselves into a court of record, with John Mitchener as registrar. The commissioners had the example of the London fire court, and also the advice of the Northampton town clerk regarding the procedure adopted there.[1] The extent of the disaster was by now fairly well defined. The masons and carpenters counted 144 buildings wholly or partially destroyed, while the book of estimates, based on the returns of the sufferers themselves, made it 156, with 295 sufferers of whom about 180 were probably heads of families. The corporation gave two barns and fitted them up in 1695 as tenements for 28 poor people made homeless by the fire,[2] but most had presumably found places to live in the unburnt parts of the town. The value of the losses in the book of estimates, though not added up by its compilers, comes to some £60,000 before reduction by the team of assessors, which is less than the £100,000 or £90,000 claimed in the letter to the bishop or in the brief.

At their second court, held on 3 May, the commissioners at last embarked on their main task, that of regulating the rebuilding of the town. They decreed the new building lines of Jury Street, High Street, Church Street and Sheep Street, as staked out, and on 13 May that no one was to begin to build until the ground had been set out by Samuel Dunckley, a Warwick mason, and that his stakes marking the building lines were to be driven firmly into the ground, and not moved under threat of dire punishment. On 22 May Samuel Dunckley, Thomas Masters, a carpenter, and James Fish the elder, parish clerk, were appointed surveyors to see the orders of the court carried out. Similar officials had been appointed by the London fire court who were to be 'discreet and intelligent persons in the art of building', to act as supervisors.[3] In Warwick, Samuel Dunckley continued as a surveyor, but his fellows were changed in July to John Phillips, a carpenter from Broadway (Worcs.), and William Smith, bricklayer.[4] Also in July, the commissioners ordered the new street opposite the church, proposed in the Act, to be made into a new square, with a road leading from it to New Street,[5] taking in part of Pebble Lane, and later continuing on to the Market Place, as allowed for in the Act;[6] the rest of Pebble Lane was closed off. Attempts to widen Swan Lane leading to the market met

[1] *See* p. 15.
[2] *A brief Description of the Collegiate Church and Choir of St Mary in the Borough of Warwick*, printed by J. Sharp, Warwick, n.d., p. 53, from a charity board in the church. The date is probably a mayoral accounting year, beginning 1 Nov. 1694.
[3] Keble, *op. cit.*, p. 1330.
[4] *See* p. 26.
[5] *See* p. 33.
[6] *See* p. 123.

opposition from those interested in the site of the Swan at the south end, and in the Red Lion, unburnt at the north end; only a limited widening at the Red Lion took place at this time.[1] Compensation was paid to house owners for ground taken to enlarge the streets, at varying rates, and to make the new square. The largest piece of ground taken into the square was owned by Fulke Chernock, who made no claim for a burnt building; it may already have been an empty site.[2]

Distributions of small sums of money to large numbers of sufferers continued until the seventh distribution on 20 May 1695, but then on the 27th twelve 'discreet and substantial inhabitants'[3] were appointed to reduce and regulate the estimates of losses, a difficult task; their 'book of reductions' was not handed in until 1 July. Houses were valued at twenty years purchase, that is, twenty times the actual or estimated rent, with the value of the toft or burnt site deducted. Goods were also reduced if the claims were judged overrated. It was now decided that sufferers who were ready to rebuild should receive 4s. in the pound of their reduced estimates, to be paid when the ground floor was laid, and a list of twenty-seven names was produced.[4] It must be remembered that most houses in Warwick were leasehold at this time, and it was not always clear whether the owner or the tenant was better able to rebuild. In fact, of these first twenty-seven, all were house-owners apart from one, John Burton, who was tenant of the Kings Arms at the corner of New Street and Pebble Lane, owned by his brother-in-law Thomas Lean or Lane. Thomas Lean 'went a soldier into Flanders', leaving a will, and had not returned by the time of the fire. Burton rebuilt a house on part of the site without delay, having regard for the rights of his wife and her sisters, who were Lean's heirs, but Lean returned in 1697 and they agreed that Burton should pay him for the land and hand over all charity money. Lean unfortunately died the next year, and the commissioners passed a decree to settle the affair.[5] Decrees were sometimes used to determine disputes between parties, but most often to confirm doubtful titles and reinforce conveyances, so giving a reluctant rebuilder confidence to go ahead.

At the same time in July 1695, a distribution of 2s. 6d. in £1 was ordered to about 128 sufferers, who were either householders still trying to gather the capital to rebuild, and might claim the additional 1s. 6d. in £1 when they were ready, or people whose only losses were goods. One such was John Howell, a harpist, who with his companion Beverley Bedoes was lodging at the Bear on the north side of the High Street.[6] The finery listed in Howell's inventory, and the amount of gold he was carrying, show that he was someone with an extraordinary position to keep up. He may very

[1] See pp. 28, 326–7, 354.   [2] See p. 72.
[3] See p. 21.   [4] See p. 27.
[5] See pp. 268, 311, 351–2, 400–2.   [6] See pp. 150–1.

likely be identified with the singer John Howell, a counter tenor, appointed
to the Chapel Royal in 1691 and confirmed in his place in 1695; a harpist
would be expected to sing.[1] Beverley Bedoes may have had a similar background, but there is no contemporary record of him. A harpist named
Thomas Bedoes was performing at court in 1634 and was in a nobleman's
retinue in Anglesey in 1644; Beverley may have been a descendant.[2] These
two have no apparent connection with Warwick, but seem to have had the
misfortune to be passing through at the time of the fire. On 8 July 1695 the
commissioners ordered that in cases between parties the court could only
be addressed by means of petitions in writing, in the form used by
Chancery.

Rebuilding the Town

Thought had been given to the provision of bricks and tiles as early as 15
October 1694, when leading inhabitants of St Mary's parish gave permission for brickmakers to set up their works on more than one part of St
Mary's commons; this permission was included in the Act.[3] Brick making
was in active progress by November 1695, when the commoners complained that the brickmakers were injuring their cows in driving them from
the brickworks, where the cows were eating the thatch on their hovels or
drying sheds, which were to be fenced and roads to the brick kilns staked
out.[4] Timber was provided by private enterprise. Edward Priest, writing to
his brother, probably at Knowle, just after the fire, said

> The fire you saw on Wensday night last was at Warwick and began the
> next house to Richard Sharpes, and his house the 2nd howse that was
> burnt and Mrs Overtons the 3rd or 4th house. . . . Yesterday I had sever-
> all chapmen from Warwick for timber and doe not know how to have
> sawers. . . .[5]

An appeal to the Crown in February 1695 for a thousand tons of timber
from Whittlewood forest (Northants.) and £400 a year from the excise fell
on deaf ears, as did similar appeals for timber from Needwood (Staffs.) and
in January 1696 from the Forest of Dean.[6] To clear the ground, the commissioners made many orders about removing rubbish from the streets and
burnt sites. Finally in October 1695 they appointed Moses Robinson as
'surveyor and director of all earth and rubbish', which was to be deposited

---

[1] A. Ashbee, *Records of English Court Music*, ii, Snodland, 1987; E. F. Rimbaut, *The Old Cheque-book of
the Chapel Royal*, London, 1872. I am indebted to Peter Holman, M.Mus., ARAM, for these references.

[2] Peter Holman, 'The Harp in Stuart England', in *Early Music*, xv (1987), p. 196; Dafydd Wyn Wiliam
in *Allwedd y Tannau*, 46 (1987), p. 69. Dr Roy Saer of the Welsh Folk Museum, St Fagans, very kindly
provided these references.

[3] *See* pp. 11–12, 130.   [4] *See* p. 50.   [5] W.C.R.O., CR 2855/box 4.

[6] *Calendar of Treasury Papers*, vol. i, 427–8; *Calendar of Treasury Books*, vol. x part iii, p. 1280.

in hollows which may have been former quarries in the Butts, on the Saltisford Rock and lastly in the brickmakers' clay pits when they were disused.
At this time they ordered the removal of the High Cross with its pump; the
stones were to be carried to the churchyard as if for re-use, but it was never
re-erected. It was said to be an open canopy on eight pillars, surmounted by
a cross.[1] In May 1695 the commissioners had directed that the three corner
houses at the Cross should have a third storey and be of equal height, and
in August they ordered that they should have modillion cornices 'answerable the one house to the other', and that the cornices should be continued
all round the houses.[2] The modillion cornice was not a new feature in the
town. When Roger Hurlbut contracted to re-front Dr Johnson's house
below the Eastgate in 1692, its roof was to have 'carved canteleivers and
cornishes in all respects as good as Mr Blissett's', the front to be cased with
'good brick and stone with rustick quines of stone' and to have a pair of
doors 'in the same form as Mr Blissett's' with mouldings of Shrewley stone.[3]
The model may have been Joseph Blissett's house next to the Swan in High
Street, or more likely Robert Blissett's on the corner of Church Street and
Jury Street, one of these three houses at the Cross.

Apart from dictating the style of these prominent houses, the commissioners took no part in the rebuilding process beyond the distribution of
charity money to encourage the builders and payments to compensate
them for ground taken to widen streets. They did, however, settle disputes
as they arose, and it is only when a bill for lime remained unpaid and the
supplier petitioned the court, that we learn that the builder of William
Tarver's new house let to Devereux Whadcock at the Cross, on the corner
of High Street and Church Street, was Solomon Bray.[4] Building agreements
are sometimes mentioned, as that of Thomas Masters and William Smith
with Fulke Weale, to build the house adjoining the corner house on the
south side of the High Street, 'according to the draught then agreed on',
but unfortunately not now extant.

One building contract for a post-fire house has, however, survived
among family papers, and is probably typical of many. Thomas Mann of
Kenilworth had bought from Thomas Archer, esq., the sites of two houses
on the south side of the High Street formerly inhabited by George Smith,
barber, and Charles Harrison, saddler. The adjoining site westwards had
been bought from Richard Green of Abingdon and rebuilt by George

---

[1] Ward *op. cit.*, f. 38ᵛ, *and see* p. 47. Sewer works in Jury Street in 1989 revealed a deep well in the
centre of the road, slightly to the east of the Court House door, presumably once served by this pump.
Robert Blissett's house, on the corner of Jury Street and Church Street, was probably set back from the
building line before the fire by reason of the Cross, which accounts for ground being taken from the
street and added to his house site, instead of the reverse. *See* p. 24.

[2] *See* pp. 18, 34, 36.

[3] W.C.R.O., CR 1618/WA.6/116, articles of agreement and elevation for re-fronting Landor House.

[4] *See* p. 319.

Chinn, carpenter[1] and that to the east had been rebuilt by the original owner, Edmund Wilson. Thomas Mann now entered into articles of agreement dated 26 September 1696 with Richard King of Warwick, carpenter, and John Cooke of Harbury, mason,[2] that for £180 they should 'in a strong, fashionable and workmanlike manner' before 10 March next ensuing

> erect, build and finish, turne key and go[3] . . . two houses or tenements on a certaine plott of ground scituate in the High Street . . . betweene a new house there lately erected by Edmund Wilson and another new house lately erected by George Chinne and containing in front 28 foote . . . and to build the same in depth 33 foote or so farre as the said Mr Wilsons new house extends in depth (and according to a moddell or draught thereof now remaining in the hands of the said Thomas Man and according as the late Act of Parliament for the Rebuilding the Towne of Warwicke directs) and shall and will bring up, sinck and finish in each of the said two houses one cellar under the back front 13 foote square within and shall bring up the said houses water table high with good, sound Warwick stone and the rest with good, well burnt brick, and tyle in the same with good, sound well burnt tyle, and all the timber therein to be of good sound well seasoned oke boards (except the garrett floores which are to be laid with good, sound well seasoned elme boards and joysts) and to build up the same in all points as well as Mr Wilsons house is built (the balcony and shell over the doore and sash windowes only excepted) together with all front doores and other doores, shop windowes and other windowes, and shall and will finde all stone, timber, boards, brick, lime, tyles, lead, glass, casements, colouring, nailes, lath and all other necessary materialls whatsoever for the compleating and finishing of the said two houses (washing only excepted). . . .

The builders were to pave the two cellars and two shops with bricks or quarries, and pay for the party walls on both sides. Payment was to be by four instalments, but the agreement is in fact endorsed with seven receipts between 3 October 1696 and 10 April 1697, making up the total agreed. Thomas Mann then claimed the 1s. 6d. in the pound from the commissioners, but Richard King had to be ordered by the court to pay George Chinn for his party wall in September 1697. The two houses are unfortunately not now standing, but have been replaced by the Midland Bank.

Building accounts for another pair of post-fire houses are preserved among the family papers of the Webbs of Sherbourne, whose circumstances were rather different. Elias Webb *alias* Morrell was a landowner with tenants in Sherbourne, Warwick, Claverdon, Butlers Marston and elsewhere. He had married Mary, daughter of William and Mary Wagstaffe

[1] *See* p. 301.   [2] W.C.R.O., CR 556/364/21.
[3] This expression is still used locally in the construction trade, *ex inf.* Mr John Hodgetts of Warwick.

in 1685, but his wife had died in 1690, leaving him with a son Thomas. William Wagstaffe, her father, was also dead, but Mary Wagstaffe, his mother-in-law, was living and owner for life, under the marriage settlement of Elias and Mary, of two houses lived in by John Butler and Thomas Rush opposite the Shire Hall in Sheep Street.[1] Elias obtained a decree of the burnt site at the court held 9 March 1696, and began keeping accounts of the rebuilding on 24 March. After consulting with workmen on three separate occasions, he began by bringing his own wagon team to carry away the ruins of the old houses, saving 'the old floors', meaning presumably the paving stones or quarries, and the better bricks and tiles. He then bought forty loads of 'parpen' and ashlar stone from Richard Williams at the Humbridge Down quarry in the north part of Coten End in Warwick for £3. 6s. 8d., giving a shilling in earnest and a shilling more to the quarry men. More stone was bought from Mr Keene and Henry Winn. Bargains were struck with Richard Bromley, mason, and George Hawkes for building the cellar walls and the stonework up to the water table, with Richard Bromley for all the brickwork of the front building, and with John Hope for all the carpenter's work there. Lime was bought from William Smith the lime-man, about 50,000 bricks from William Phillips the brickmaker, 5,000 tiles with gutter and crest tiles from William Tranter, and 6800 tiles more from William Phillips. On 29 July 1696 Richard Bromley was paid for seventy-nine perch of stonework from the foundations up, at 20d. the perch. £20-worth of timber was obtained from 'Esquire Archer's bailiff', probably at Umberslade, as well as heart lath. More heart and sap lath came from John Kallaway of Lapworth, and 4100 [feet of] oak boards were bought from Richard Hews and had to be fetched from Beoley (Worcs.). Doors, windows and casements were painted in oil by Samuel Acock. The halls of the two houses were paved with stone brought by Elias Webb's team from Bearley. By January 1697 work was proceeding on the back buildings, including horse racks and mangers in the stables, and a tobacco hogshead was bought from Mr Whadcock to make window bars. The final bills were paid in May 1697, when it appeared that the total charge of the two houses was £323. 2s.[2] Mrs Wagstaffe had received a distribution of £5 and a further £5 to bring this up to 2s. 6d. in the pound of her loss, and Elias Webb was now ordered £8. 12s. 6d., being the 1s. 6d. in the pound as the rebuilder, based on the reduced estimate of £115 for the two houses, which seems very much less than the actual cost of replacement.[3]

Loans of charity money were available to potential rebuilders able to name approved securities,[4] or to mortgage houses already rebuilt. George

---

[1] See pp. 337–8. The implied dispute was probably collusive, in order to obtain the decree of the court for Elias Webb. See also p. 56.
[2] Nottinghamshire Record Office, Edge of Strelley, DDE/117/1.
[3] See pp. 57, 70, 250.   [4] See p. 54.

Chinn, carpenter, was able to apply for a succession of loans by mortgaging his new houses rebuilt in Swan Lane, then moving on to ground acquired on the south side of the High Street, before undertaking part of the site of the Bear Inn. Thomas Masters did likewise, ending with the Swan ground. But others, like James Fish the elder, the parish clerk, one of the first re-builders, had difficulty repaying when their loans were called in. James Fish died in 1702 still owing a small sum to be repaid by his son.[1] John Hancox and his wife, with a house of only one bay in the Butts 'have rebuilded theire house soe far as possible they could, but they haveing sold all as they had and cannot make noe further shift for to finish their house;' they applied to the court for further assistance, which was apparently not forth-coming. Widow West's petition to Quarter Sessions following a separate fire, probably in 1695, which destroyed her malt house and malt to the value of nearly £400, had already been turned down by the commissioners, but was returned to them with no action taken.[2]

The Great Recoinage

On 9 September 1695 Mrs Anne Palmer, the absentee owner of Robert Taylor's house in Church Street, was ordered to be paid £13. 10s. for ground taken to enlarge the street, which she claimed was less than she was entitled to, 'and that shee must take it in small clipt money with a great deal of unpassable naughty brasse mony amongst it and guineas at thirty shillings apeece, which your peticioner looks upon to be very hard measure'.[3]

There were two kinds of silver coinage current in England in 1694: first the old hammered money produced by placing a blank between two dies and striking the upper one by hand with a hammer, and second the milled coins which succeeded them in 1663, but without the old money being called in. The new coin blanks were punched out mechanically from metal sheets rolled to a uniform thickness in horse-operated rolling mills, then struck in powerful screw presses and edged by a secret machine which imprinted the legend DECUS ET TUTAMEN on the larger denominations, an effective safeguard against clipping. The hammered coins, which varied in thickness and were often not struck centrally, lent themselves to clipping and, in their worn state, to counterfeiting in inferior or 'coarser' alloys. By 1695 they were reduced on an average to barely 50 per cent of their proper weight, and almost 20 per cent were counterfeit. Guineas had been minted since 1663, at first for the Africa trade with a value of 20s., but circulated at home at between 21s. and 22s., along with other more exotic gold coins. Gold passed by weight, so there was no advantage in clipping. The standard of silver in the hammered and milled coins was the same, but the

---

[1] *See* p. 464.   [2] *See* p. 359.   [3] *See* p. 350.

milled coins in their perfect state were sometimes worth more as bullion abroad than their face value at home, and although melting or exporting them was illegal, most were hoarded or melted down, and few were in circulation by 1695. By then, hammered silver was no longer accepted at its face value, and guineas rose accordingly. In William Tarver's bill for the fire commissioners, 5 guineas paid to Mr Middleton for the brief was set down as £7 in May 1695, while another 5 guineas to John Smith Esq. for the Act, not more than two months later, came to £7. 10s.[1] The recoinage and demonetization of the hammered money was finally announced by a proclamation of 19 December 1695, which set the dates after which clipped money of various denominations should not pass in markets, with later dates up to which it would be accepted in payment of taxes or in loans to the Exchequer at its face value. The limits were extended by an *Act for Remedying the Ill State of the Coin of the Kingdom* in January 1696, under which clipped coin remained current for payment of taxes until 4 May 1696 and for loans to the Exchequer until 24 June. A later Act set the rates at which hammered money would be received at the Mint by troy weight as bullion, coming down to 5s. 2d. per ounce after 1 December 1696. There were no arrangements for ordinary people to exchange their hammered money locally. The effect of these measures was that the old money became unpassable from the date of the Proclamation, because nobody wanted to be left with it on his hands.[2] The work of recoinage began at the Mint in the Tower of London in January 1696, where additional machinery had been installed, with the temporary assistance of five provincial mints as they were set up. Sir Isaac Newton was sworn in as Warden of the Mint in May, and saw the operation through to its conclusion in 1699 with his customary efficiency. Unfortunately the old error continued: the new silver coins were still worth more as bullion than their face value, and most of them could not be kept long in circulation before disappearing into the melting pot. Guineas were not left to find their own level, but were reduced by Parliament in stages to 22s. from April 1696.[3] This may account for the strange transaction in May 1696 at Hoare's bank, where Thomas Newsham on the commissioners' instructions withdrew 552 guineas as £828 (at 30s.) on the 26th, and paid them in again on the 27th as £607. 4s. (at 22s.), an apparent loss of £221.[4] By June 1703 guineas were being received at Hoare's bank at 21s. 6d.,[5] which must have been their natural level.

John Newsham of Chadshunt, the brother of Charles the J.P. and father of Thomas, all active members of the fire court, was also receiver general of

---

[1] *See* p. 413.

[2] Lord Macaulay, *History of England*, London, 1863, vii, p. 272.

[3] Ming-Hsun Li, *The Great Recoinage of 1696-9*, London, 1963, *passim*; Sir John Craig *The Mint*, Cambridge, 1953, chapter XI; Richard S. Westfall, *Never at Rest, a Biography of Isaac Newton*, Cambridge, 1980, pp. 551-67.

[4] *See* pp. 516, 518.   [5] *See* p. 463; Macaulay, *op. cit.*, vii, p. 273.

taxes for the county, and therefore a regular carrier of cash to the Exchequer. On 3 February 1696 the court desired him to carry up the money 'in bank', meaning that stored in a chest in the Castle, and pay it into the Exchequer on loan, and on 27 April following Sir Francis Child and Mr Richard Hoare, the two London bankers named in the brief, were instructed to do likewise.[1] This money would have been accepted at its face value until 24 June, but there is no record of tallies[2] purchased until after that date. Brief money was still coming in for at least another year, and there was an added difficulty that much of it could not be transmitted by bill of exchange. Griff: Reignolds, a collector employed by the commissioners' agent Daniel Eyre, wrote to him from Hereford in December 1695, to say that after paying in £100 to Sir Francis Child's in gold, he still had £46 'the one half whereof is bad money and the rest soe small and clipt, that I cannot return it from hence by any of our tradesmen, therefore I desire you to let me know how it shall be sent up, for it must come *in specie* ...'.[3] A copy of the commissioners' order of February 1696 was attached to a receipt made out to John Newsham from Hoare's bank for thirty bags of old hammered money weighing more than six hundredweight avoirdupois, twenty-eight of which were paid into the Exchequer in May 1697,[4] more than a year later. The commissioners' account with Child's bank also shows large amounts paid in by weight for Exchequer tallies as advances on the three shilling aid, and withdrawn a year later with interest at seven or eight per cent.

John Newsham, in his role as receiver general of taxes, had to answer at the Treasury in January 1697 to charges brought by Sir Richard Newdigate regarding the acceptance or refusal of clipped money for taxes and private exchanges of gold for half-crowns in which John Mitchener, 'the receiver general's man' was also implicated. The hearing was inconclusive.[5] John Newsham died the following March, and Thomas Newsham, his son and executor, was appointed to wind up his taxation accounts, which took several years.[6]

---

[1] *See* pp. 54, 58.
[2] The Exchequer was still issuing receipts in the medieval form of notched wooden hazel sticks, called tallies.
[3] W.C.R.O., CR 1618/WA.4/194.
[4] W.C.R.O., CR 1618/WA.4/39 and 95.
[5] *Cal. Treas. Bks.*, xi, pp. 347-9; *Cal. Treas. Papers 1557-1696*, pp. 561-2 (the writer confuses Thomas Newsham with his father John, and is wrong to infer that John Newsham was dismissed; he simply died).
[6] *Cal. Treas. Bks.*, xii, p. 99; xiv, p. 409; xv, p. 205; xvii, pp. 318-19; xviii, p. 467.

The Church[1]

Celia Fiennes rode into Warwick in 1697

> ... the town of Warwick by means of a sad fire about 4 or 5 year since that laid the greatest part in ashes, its most now new buildings which is with brick and coyn'd with stone and the windows the same; there still remains some few houses of the old town which are all built of stone; the streetes are very handsome and the buildings regular and fine, not very lofty being limited by act of parliament to such a pitch and size to build the town; the ruines of the Church still remains, the repairing of which is the next worke design'd; the Chancel stands still in which was all the fine monuments that were preserv'd from the fire. . . .[2]

Hitherto the commissioners had concerned themselves with regulating and encouraging the efforts of others to rebuild the town; now they set about actively rebuilding the church, paying the workmen out of the charity money. The chancel had been saved by its stone vault, although the timber roof above it was burnt off, and immediately after the fire an agreement was made with carpenters to protect the stonework with a temporary wooden roof.[3] The corporation, who were responsible for the chancel as lay rectors, were allowed £100 in May 1695 towards making it ready for public service.[4] In December 1695 the commissioners ordered that a thousand load of stone should be quarried in preparation for rebuilding, and that a trial pit should be dug in the north part of the churchyard;[5] in June 1696 bills were paid for getting stone in the churchyard quarry and from the site of a house owned by St Mary's in Church Street. Lead and bell metal had been collected from the ruins of the church and refined on the spot into pigs and ingots.[6] Sir Christopher Wren was probably consulted during these preliminaries. A 'draught of the Town and Church' were sent to him in February 1695, and it seems probable that these are the outline plan of the town and the plan and elevation of the old church, perhaps then a shell, which are in the Wren Collection at All Souls, Oxford.[7] A payment of £3. 15s. was made to 'Sir Christopher Wren's gentleman' in May

[1] See Philip B. Chatwin, 'The Rebuilding of St Mary's Church, Warwick', in *Birmingham Arch. Soc. Trans.*, lxv, 1949. Mr Chatwin (d. 1964) was for many years consultant architect to the church. His article is based on the building accounts in the Duke Collection deposited in the Birmingham Reference Library in 1932, and his own knowledge of the building.

[2] Christopher Morris (ed.), *The Journeys of Celia Fiennes*, London, 1949, pp. 114–15.

[3] *See* p. 8.   [4] *See* p. 19.   [5] *See* p. 52.

[6] *See* p. 308. That church bells melted and ran was observed during the fire of London (Bedford, *op. cit.*, p. 46). A temperature of 1000°C. is possible in a house fire. Bronze melts at about 1020°C., but becomes red hot and soft enough to pick up impurities at above 800°C. (*ex inf.* Mr Stedman Payne of the museum of John Taylor and Co., bellfounders, Loughborough).

[7] *See* p. 410; All Souls, Oxford, Wren Collection vol. IV no. 35; *ibid.* no. 37, published in *The Wren Society*, x, 1933, pl. 14. The town plan (no. 35) does not show the new square, decided on in July 1695. All Wren's drawings for St Mary's are published in *The Wren Society*, vol. x.

1695,[1] and Nicholas Hawksmoor received ten guineas for 'Coppy designes and papers by Sir Christopher Wren's order for the use of Warwick Church' in 1697.[2] An undated entry of £11 'to Sir Chr: Renn's man for Ch: work' probably refers to this same payment, and there is a further undated entry of £10 'to Sir Christopher Wren for the Church'.[3] These later payments were probably for copies of the tentative drawings by Wren for St Mary's now in the All Souls collection. They appear to be sketches for more than one possible scheme, but none bears any resemblance to anything actually built at Warwick.

The remains of the old tower had been pulled down and removed by November 1695,[4] and in November 1697 William Smith and Samuel Dunckley were instructed to pull down the old walls of the church, dig out the foundations down to the rock, and lay new foundations 'according to the draught made and left by Sir William Wilson'.[5] On 23 February 1698 the masons, William Smith, Samuel Dunckley and Francis Smith, all of Warwick, agreed with the commissioners to build the body or nave of the church, the side and cross aisles and tower according to Sir William Wilson's designs, the side aisles to rise even with and the same height as the lady chapel, and the nave and cross aisles to rise so high as to range even in height with the chancel; the tower to be 98 ft high from the ground to the top of the battlements, and to make the four pinnacles on the top of the tower[6] and all other pinnacles, cornices, mouldings, doors, windows, portico, etc., and to face the stairs of the tower with Wilmcote stone, and to take down 'that dead wall that is att the entrance into the chancel carefully', all for £2,300, to be paid as Sir William Wilson shall order, proportionable to the work done. The masons were to have the old stone, but to pay for the new stone now lying in the churchyard, and to have liberty to quarry in the churchyard on the north side. Sir William Wilson might order any defective work to be taken down and done again. On completion, if the commissioners thought the work well done, the masons were to have £50 more.[7]

On 30 March 1698 Thomas Masters of Warwick, a carpenter, agreed to provide timber of all sizes to be used in rebuilding the church and tower, as Sir William Wilson, surveyor of the work, and the undertakers of the stonework should direct. The commissioners or Sir William might reject defective timber. Thomas Masters also agreed to provide 7,000 ft of oak

---

[1] See p. 411.

[2] Howard Colvin, *A Biographical Dictionary of British Architects 1600–1840*, London, 1978, pp. 926–7.

[3] W.C.R.O., CR 1886/9134 A. This is an abstract of the commissioners' accounts made by James Fish in about 1708 in support of a Chancery case against the treasurers. It appears to quote in part from an early account book now lost, but gives no dates.

[4] See pp. 16, 49.   [5] See p. 84.

[6] It may have been intended at one time that the tower should be surmounted by a cupola; *see* p. 94n.

[7] W.C.R.O., CR 1618/WA.4/13.

boards to cover the timber roof to lay lead on, and for the tower floors, and oak planks for the church doors as Sir William should approve.[1] On the same day Nicholas Paris of Warwick and William Marshall of Henley-in-Arden, blacksmiths, agreed to provide and make all the iron work for the church and tower of all sorts and sizes as laid down in a schedule annexed, or as Sir William Wilson or the masons should direct, at a cost of £1. 12s. 6d. per hundredweight, paid as the work progressed; the schedule gives specifications of hinges, window bars, iron bands for the tower, etc.[2] In May 1698 'because there will be great occasions to pay workmen and buy materials', loans to sufferers and house builders amounting to £900 were called in by the commissioners.[3] On 9 June 1698 the carpenters John Phillips of Broadway and Thomas Masters undertook to make and frame all the timbers for the roof of the church, with cross and side aisles, according to a model or draft annexed to their agreement, the sizes and scantlings to be as in Thomas Masters' contract for providing the timber. The carpenters were to lay boards on the timbers ready for the lead, let joists into the roof beams to hold up the 'braggetting' of the ceilings, and put in beams, joists and boards for the tower floors, paid at the rate of 16s. per 100 square feet of roof or floor completed. The model or draft, now detached, is merely a rough cross-section, altered in pencil, of the columns of the church and the roof trusses of the nave and side aisles. The new square was ordered to be levelled for the carpenters to frame and work up the timber for the church roof there.[4] On 25 November 1698 Richard Lane, then mayor of the borough, agreed to take all the lead belonging to the church, new and old, refined or unrefined, and deliver the same quantity of sheet lead of an agreed weight, later set at 8–9 lbs per square foot, and lay it on the roof and cornice, for £3 for every fodder of sheet lead, counting $22\frac{1}{4}$ hundredweight to the fodder.[5] On 26 November 1698 Francis Badson of Binton, mason, undertook to pave the aisles with 2,000 feet of blue and white Wilmcote stone in sixteen inch squares laid 'orrice way', set in good lime mortar 'with as good stone and in as good manner of work as the Hall floore at Warwick Castle is laid with', paid at $5\frac{1}{4}d.$ per foot as the work advanced. A further 500 ft were to be provided by William Smith of Bearley and two or three thousand feet by James Walker of Wilmcote at $5\frac{1}{2}d.$ per foot in June 1699.[6] Glazing of the windows with the best sort of Stourbridge glass was assigned to William Hyron and Richard Hancox of Warwick and Hugh Canter of Coventry, glaziers, though it appears from the accounts

---

[1] W.C.R.O., CR 1618/WA.4/14.
[2] W.C.R.O., CR 1618/WA.4/15.
[3] *See* p. 86.
[4] W.C.R.O., CR 1618/WA.4/18, 19; *and see* pp. 86-7.
[5] W.C.R.O., CR 1618/WA.4/20; *and see* p. 94n.
[6] W.C.R.O., CR 1618/WA.4/21, 21A, 22.

that the work was in fact done by Richard Hancox and Richard Lane.[1] Also in 1699 William Marshall undertook to make a good and substantial iron screen with a pair of doors, to be put up between the church and chancel, in every particular according to the draft or model shown to the commissioners, finished and erected as should be approved by Lord Digby, for £110 and £5 more 'if Lord Digby shall think it deserves the same'.[2]

The rebuilding proceeded until January 1700, when a setback occurred. The tower, which was to have been ninety-eight feet high to the battlements, was carried on two pillars within the nave and two in the west wall, with a portico opening into the new square. It had reached twenty-nine feet above the body of the church, with twenty-four feet still to go,[3] when alarming vertical cracks, still visible today, appeared in the two nave pillars. On 10 January messengers were sent to Sir William Wilson and to many of the commissioners, calling them to a consultation on 25 January with 'Mr Strong, a surveyor from London' about the failure in the pillars of the tower. This was Edward Strong, one of Wren's master masons at St Paul's, who came with his son, also Edward; they were paid ten guineas and two guineas respectively for their report.[4] Wren had been having difficulties earlier with the piers supporting the dome of St Paul's,[5] but this was not common knowledge, and his advice, through the Strongs, was probably sought not so much for this reason, as because the commissioners wanted the authority of the Surveyor General for their decision. The tower had to be taken down to just above the arches. The stub of this tower remains in the roof space, with walls seven feet thick at the level where demolition stopped. Sir William Wilson does not seem to have been blamed for the failure, and it was the masons, whose contract required them to replace defective work, who suffered. A new and larger tower was designed and built 'according to Sir William Wilson's directions',[6] and the masons' bill had to be modified to allow for the part of the first tower and portico not built, set against the cost of the new work.[7] The verdict of the Strongs must have been that pillars of Warwick stone could not be relied on for such a weight. The new tower stands on piers, two in the west wall and two out in the square, which are of a harder sandstone from Shrewley, four miles

[1] *See* pp. 93–4, 437, 451.
[2] W.C.R.O., CR 1618/WA.4/26; *and see* p. 93.
[3] W.C.R.O., CR 1618/WA.4/109.
[4] *See* pp. 97, 441.
[5] *Wren Soc.*, xvi, 1939, pp. ix–x. The problem at St Paul's was in fact different. The columns or legs of the dome rested on wedge-shaped piers in the crypt below, which were faced with stone but had rubble cores; because the piers were larger than the columns, the weight came on the rubble, whose strength depended on the mortar binding it together. It showed signs of compression, causing some facing stones to split, which had to be replaced.
[6] British Library, C.45.K2, Dugdale's *Warwickshire*, 1765 edition, graingerized by William Hamper, vol. ii, p. 319.
[7] *See* pp. 106, 107n.; W.C.R.O., CR 1618/WA.4/40.

north-west of Warwick. An agreement for this was entered into in March 1700 with John Gardner, father and son, who were to dig 200 tons 'of the best palpin Shrewley stone' from their quarry at 4s. a ton, of sizes given by the workmen rebuilding the tower, to be collected by teams sent by the commissioners, each having two good and able men to load the stone.[1] About eighteen teams from Warwick took part.[2] In June 1700 the masons contracted to dig and lay foundations of Warwick stone for the new tower, and to build up good solid pillars of Shrewley stone thereon.[3] The 'trees of the water house', which were the underground wooden water pipes from the water tower in Sheep Street, had to be moved to run outside the tower.[4] The new tower stands 128 feet to the battlements and 155 feet to the top of the pinnacles.[5] By agreement made in June 1702, the bell metal was sent to Abraham Rudhall of Gloucester, the bellfounder, to be cast into eight good and substantial well-tuned bells for £60, and £6 per hundredweight for additional bell metal required.[6] Carriage was by road between Warwick and Stratford, and by water between Stratford and Gloucester.[7]

Inside the church, seating was provided by agreement dated 8 March 1699 by Thomas Masters and Nicholas Kington of Warwick, joiners, who were to construct pews of good, well-seasoned English oak according to an approved plan and model, the wood of the fronts to be well matched in colour, and those adjoining the middle aisle to have draw-outs, or benches drawn from under the seats for such as should sit in the aisle; the floors of the pews to have provision for raising them to allow for burials next to the middle aisle, and the seats to be of deal.[8] From 1704 onwards, life interests in the pews were sold to parishioners and their relatives in family groups at quite high prices, paid to the commissioners,[9] and gifts were received from notables towards finishing the church, including £100 from Lord Brooke and £30 from Lord Digby.[10] Also in February 1704 an application to Queen Anne was successful, and a warrant was granted for £1000 'towards finishing the church and relieving the sufferers at Warwick', to be paid to the corporation or their nominee by the Surveyor General of Woods on this side Trent. The corporation appointed Sir Richard Hoare to accept the money and pay it to the five trustees,[11] who received the final instalment in July 1706. The gift was recorded on a benefaction board in the church: 'Queen Anne of pious and glorious memory by the seasonable application

---

[1] W.C.R.O., CR 1618/WA.4/23.
[2] See pp. 444–5.   [3] See p. 98.
[4] W.C.R.O., CR 1618/WA.4/226.
[5] Ex inf. Mr Charles Brown, the present church architect.
[6] W.C.R.O., CR 1618/WA.4/27.
[7] See pp. 458, 504–5, etc.
[8] W.C.R.O., CR 1618/WA.4/16.
[9] W.C.R.O., CR 1618/WA.4/3; and see pp. 479 et seq.
[10] See pp. 470, 490.
[11] W.C.R.O., CR 1618/WA.4/43, 44; and see pp. 469, 496.

of the Rt Hon. William Bromley Esq. gave towards the Rebuilding of this Church, one thousand pounds.'[1]

In September 1704 the commissioners decided that the new pulpit with reading desk and clerk's seat should be set up in the middle of the centre aisle between the two pillars nearest the chancel, but should be movable.[2] This provision was included in a faculty for pewing in November 1704,[3] and another faculty was obtained in February 1705 for fixing it. The pulpit was constructed during 1705 by Masters and Kington, possibly to a drawing obtained by Henry Jephcott in London in 1701.[5] The elegant marble font was bought for £30 in May 1705 from John van Nost, a stone carver from Mechelen (now in Belgium) who had a yard in the Haymarket in London.[6]

The chancel, although it had previously been repaired for church services and was the responsibility of the corporation, was now included in the restoration. In July 1702 a bargain was struck with Francis Badson to pave the chancel in the same manner as the church.[7] New stalls and an altar piece were given by Lord Brooke.[8] The communion rails and balusters, bought elsewhere by Henry Jephcott and Mr Hurlbut, were installed by Masters and Kington.[9] Plaster work was carried out by Richard Huss, in addition to his much more extensive work in the church, and he was responsible for plaster repairs to the monument of Thomas Beauchamp I in the chancel, where the figures of the weepers have indeed been repaired in plaster.[10] Sir William Wilson was rightly indignant that work on the monument had not been entrusted to a stone carver.[11] On the outside, Samuel Dunckley was paid for the balustrade and urns, which were continued from the church along the side walls of the chancel,[12] and served to tie the old and new work together until removed in the 1880s restoration. Work on the chancel cost £200, to which the corporation contributed £50. The churchyard quarries, on the north, east and finally south sides of the church were filled in,[13] and the churchyard planted with yew trees, fetched from a distance, and fir trees from London.[14] Householders in the widened streets were required to 'pitch', that is pave, their frontages, including the ground taken from them, as far as the gutter, under the direction of the commissioners' surveyors.[15] For paving the extensive frontage of the church, and the roadway under the tower, James Green, a professional paviour, known as Old Green, was hired with his sons, and quantities of pebbles supplied to them, some from Norton Lindsey.[16]

---

[1] *A brief Description of the Collegiate Church . . .*, p. 55.
[2] *See* p. 110.   [3] W.C.R.O., CR 1618/WA.4/7.
[4] *See* pp. 482–4.   [5] *See* pp. 484, 489, 493.
[6] *See* p. 489; Rupert Gunnis, *Dictionary of British Sculptors, 1660–1851*, 1964, p. 279.
[7] *See* p. 457.   [8] *A brief Description . . .*, p. 49.
[9] *See* p. 497.   [10] *See* pp. 481, 508, etc.   [11] *See* p. 367.
[12] *See* pp. 489, 498.   [13] *See* pp. 436, 441, 474.   [14] *See* pp. 486, 489, etc.
[15] *See* p. 61.   [16] *See* pp. 472 *et seq.*

The commissioners were empowered under the Act to regulate noisome trades, and those perilous in respect of fire. They had excluded butchers from the five central streets in June 1696, and now at their last meeting on 8 November 1704 they banished tallow chandlers from Castle Street, High Street, Jury Street, Church Street and from the New Square.[1] Daniel Defoe saw Warwick in 1716:

> Warwick was ever esteemed a handsome, well-built town, and there were several good houses in it, but the face of it is now quite alter'd; for having been almost wholly reduc'd to a heap of rubbish, by a terrible fire about two and twenty years ago, it is now rebuilt in so noble and so beautiful a manner, that few towns in England make so fine an appearance. The new church is also a fine building. . . .[2]

The Final Reckoning

The powers of the fire commissioners under the *Act for Rebuilding Warwick* ceased in 1704 at the end of ten years. William Tarver, county Treasurer and, to start with, one of the more active treasurers of the brief money, was also the owner of the Swan Inn, the former Bell Inn and Mr Devereux Whadcock's house on the corner of High Street and Church Street, altogether valued with goods at £1940. However, the commissioners disallowed his estimate for goods lost, and in March 1704 ordered him to pay in £36 which he had retained in his own hands to compensate himself, and to hand over all his books and papers relating to the charity money:[3] he seems to have done neither.[4] This means that for the early part of the commissioners' term of office, there are only some subsidiary accounts, and a few statements taken from an account book which does not now exist. William Tarver was probably not thought of as disgraced; he was mayor of Warwick for the second time the following year, 1704–5. The later account book, kept by John Mitchener for Thomas Newsham, begins in 1698 after the work on the church had started. Mitchener, at first described as John Newsham's or Thomas Newsham's man, is recognized as the accountant for the trustees of the brief money by the end of the book, when he was made a present of the amount by which his accounts failed to balance. The accounts continued on from 1704 until 1711, during which time money was still coming in by repayment of monies loaned to sufferers and by Queen Anne's gift and other gifts to the church, and payments were made to a few late house builders as well as to workmen finishing the church. Mitchener became borough treasurer in 1697 and county treasurer in 1711.

[1] *See* pp. 62, 111, 130.
[2] Daniel Defoe, *A Tour through the whole island of Great Britain*, London, 1962, ii, p. 84.
[3] *See* pp. 105, 107, 111.
[4] W.C.R.O., CR 1886/9113 A, f. 1.

In about 1710 some of the sufferers put forward James Prescott and James Fish to inspect Mitchener's accounts on their behalf, and Fish was permitted by William Colmore to borrow Mitchener's book. He kept it for three-quarters of a year until Lord Digby ordered him to return it with his objections, in spite of which the trustees approved Mitchener's final accounts in September 1711. None the less a Chancery case was started in about 1713, by the Attorney General *ex relacione* John Cakebread and other sufferers against John Mitchener and others, in which a Master in Chancery reported, amongst other things, that Thomas Newsham and Mitchener had not sufficiently justified the expenditure on the chancel of the church, since the corporation had an estate in trust for that purpose. The case went on until about 1718, and in the meantime Mitchener's and Newsham's books were brought before a Master in Chancery, 'and the charges laid much closer to the defendants'. The accounts relating to the recoinage were now considered, and the sufferers claimed that delays by John Newsham, the receiver general, and Sir Richard Hoare in paying in the clipped and coarse money to the Exchequer had cost the sufferers hundreds of pounds. They even alleged that John Newsham 'having clipt and coarse money of his own and of his friends and relations, to defraud the sufferers he pretended the loans in the Exchequer were full in February 1695/6', so that some of the money 'lay dead in his hands till December 1696, when money went by weight'. The revaluation of guineas at Hoare's bank in May 1696[1] was regarded as a fraud on the sufferers perpetrated by Thomas Newsham and Sir Richard Hoare.[2]

However, in October 1718 John Watts and Alexander Nicholls, on behalf of the sufferers still involved in the case, produced a printed petition addressed to William Bromley, Esq. Although they still believed in the merits of their plea, they besought him to join with Lord Digby and William Colmore in order to instruct Mr Groves, their attorney, how to proceed or how to compound the matters in dispute.[3] Proceedings were extremely slow. In May 1720 Lord Digby wrote to William Grove at Coventry:

> I have always had a great deal of compassion for the poor sufferers at Warwick and have endeavoured to serve them, but, as you say, they have been misled by their sollicitors.... They will be sure to find a great increase of charges and trouble, whatever the issue be. I have often try'd with some pains, and without effect, to bring this affair to an accommodation; and thô I was quite tired with it, I should not yet be sparing of my trouble, were there any good prospect of success....[4]

---

[1] *See* pp. 516, 518.
[2] W.C.R.O., CR 1886/9133 A, 9145 A.
[3] W.C.R.O., CR 1886/9155.
[4] W.C.R.O., CR 1886/box 608.

But finally Lord Digby wrote from Coleshill on 14 November 1720 to William Colemore at Warwick:

> ... You know I would not take upon me to make an absolute Award; but the terms of accommodation that I think reasonable to propose, are these. That Mr [Henry] Hoare do pay the ballance of his account which is forty nine pounds, and add to it thirty one pound on account of the loss sustain'd by guineas, which will make it just £80. That no costs shall be demanded of the sufferers, but each side shall bear their own charge.[1]

The sufferers must by now have been desperate regarding their legal costs, and this arbitration was evidently accepted. The account at Hoare's bank ends in May 1721 with a payment into the account by Henry Hoare of £30. 19s. 11d., and a payment out of £80 to William Colmore, which he no doubt passed on to the sufferers. And so the story ends. Dr Thomas, the continuator of Dugdale's *Warwickshire* and editor of the 1730 edition, sums it up:

> This church, as far as the choir, together with the greatest part of the town, was in the year 1694 consumed by fire; the loss sustained thereby was computed at ninety thousand six hundred pounds, towards which they gathered by a brief eleven thousand pounds, and Queen Anne gave them one thousand pounds more, with which they rebuilt their Church and Steeple, and very little came to the relief of the poor Sufferers.[2]

THE DOCUMENTS

Provenance of the Documents

The Warwick fire committee at its second meeting ordered that a book of receipts and disbursements should be kept, also a receipt book which every sufferer receiving money should sign, and a book in which memorials and orders concerning the fire should 'be fairly entered'.[3] There seems little doubt that the order book on paper published here is that last-mentioned book, continued by the fire commissioners, though it was not quite one of the 'parchment books' which the Act required them to keep and to sign.[4] It appears to be a fair copy, written up after each court from the rough minutes, and presented at the next court for those who had been present to sign. The vellum book in Thomas Newsham's earliest account, bought 'to record the Decrees of the Court in',[5] may be this volume in spite of the

---

[1] W.C.R.O., CR 1886/9149 A.

[2] Sir William Dugdale, *Antiquities of Warwickshire*, second edition, *revised augmented and continued . . . by Wm Thomas, D.D.*, London, 1730, p. 439.

[3] *See* pp. 3, 4.   [4] *See* p. 132.   [5] *See* p. 411.

confusing terminology, since the existing order book contains no actual decrees, though plenty of orders that decrees should be made. There was, however, a parchment book bought by John Mitchener from Mr Teonge 'to enter orders and decrees', whose pages were stamped.[1] This would have been suitable for entering and signing decrees on which titles to burnt properties were often founded, and may have been the book carried to several commissioners for them to sign regarding the title to part of the church land,[2] and also the 'Decree Book' sent to London for Lord Brooke's signature.[3] Unfortunately no stamped book has survived, and the only record of the decrees are some imperfect drafts. The early account books have also perished.

The commissioners were required by the Act to deposit their books with the Warwick Borough records and evidences, and this was probably done in September 1711 after the treasurer's accounts were closed. But in about 1713 the records were inspected by a Master in Chancery in the course of the action started by a group of former sufferers, and were retained and numbered as a Chancery Master's Exhibit (Master Tinney [C.104], bundle 97) until returned to Warwick under an order of the Master of the Rolls dated 18 August 1955. They are now reunited with the Warwick Borough archives in the County Record Office (CR 1618/WA.4).

Three bundles of petitions and draft decrees, however, did not go to London but remained with the Borough archives (CR 1618/W 10). A separate small group of accounts and papers relating to the church was in the hands of Henry Eyres Landor, a Warwick lawyer and antiquarian, in the early nineteenth century. Landor lent them to the Birmingham antiquary William Hamper, who returned them in 1823 after transcribing many of them into his graingerized copy of the 1765 edition of Dugdale's *Warwickshire*, now in the British Library (c. 45. k2), whereupon Landor made him a present of one of the original documents, a copy in the hand of James Fish jun. from Mitchener's account book, which he inserted in the second volume at p. 319. The rest of this group descended in the Landor family of Rugeley to the Revd R. E. H. Duke, whose executors fortunately added them to his bequest of deeds to the Birmingham Reference Library in 1932, where they now form part of the Duke Collection and were published in part by Philip Chatwin in the *Transactions of the Birmingham Archaeological Society*, vol. LXV.

The original letters patent for the brief found their way into the Warwick Castle archives (CR 1886/6928), now in the County Record Office, and another group of papers in the same collection (CR 1886/9131 A–9150 A, 9152–9155) derives from the Chancery case later brought by the sufferers; it includes copies of documents in the hand of James Fish similar to some in the Duke Collection. Whether all these papers were once together in the

---

[1] *See* p. 502.   [2] *See* p. 342.   [3] *See* pp. 484–5.

Borough muniment room, or whether they came directly from the descendants of the sufferers is unclear. One further group in the Castle archives (CR 1886/7526-7537) is catalogued as records of the fire; it relates to the chief rents of the manor, which the commissioners were empowered to reduce or remit where they related to burnt properties, and to an Exchequer case brought by the lord of the manor, William Bolton, for those rents claimed from Fulke Weale.[1] These papers presumably came into the Castle muniments when Lord Brooke acquired the manor from the heirs of the Bolton family in 1742.

Description of the Documents

The Commissioners' Order Book (CR 1618/WA.4/1) is a paper book, 29.5 × 19.0 cm., in a vellum binding with remains of ties and contemporary pagination 1-328 followed by 87 blank leaves; inscribed on the spine 'Booke Orders Fire', and numbered on the front cover (225).[2]

　　The rough minute books (CR 1618/WA.4/2, 3) quoted in footnotes and on pp. 110-2, are (*a*) a paper book 19.0 × 15.0 cm. approx., crudely sewn into a limp parchment cover with projecting flap and attachment for a tie, 70 leaves unnumbered with an additional gathering of 28 leaves sewn in later, the whole book formerly rolled up, covering dates 28 April 1695-17 March 1698/9. (*b*) a paper book 31.2 × 20.6 cm. in a stiff parchment binding, 80 leaves of which 18 at the front and 12 at the end are used; at the back (book reversed) a valuation of seats in the church. The minutes cover 21 March 1698/9-8 Nov. 1704. Inscribed on the spine 'Seates in the Churche'.

The Bishop's Letter (CR 1618/W10/bundle 1) is a document 31.5 × 19.5 cm., printed in roman and italic type.

The Brief (CR 1618/WA.4/29) is a broadside 47.0 × 37.0 cm. approx., printed in roman and italic type.

The Act of Parliament (CR 639, deposited on loan in 1960 by Mr S. M. Duke) is printed in roman, italic and black-letter on paper 30.0 × 19.5 cm. approx., not cut square, sewn into a coarse grey paper cover by stabbing through, inscribed 'Warwick fire act', paginated 3-18, damaged by damp and folding.

The Masons' and Carpenters' Survey (CR 1618/WA.4/128) is a paper book made up of one sheet of paper folded to give 2 leaves 33.0 × 20.5 cm. and two sheets folded to give four leaves 30.5 × 19.5 cm., roughly sewn into a paper cover.

The Estimates of Losses (CR 1618/WA.4/267) are loose papers forming an original bundle enclosed in a parchment wrapper inscribed 'The Bills

---

[1] *See* pp. 334-5.

[2] Numbering of this kind on the documents is probably the work of a Chancery clerk; it appears to be haphazard.

of Losses given in by the Sufferers by the Late Fire in Warwick which happened the 5th of September 1694', and numbered (178). The estimates are on paper of many different sizes, but mostly on half foolscap or foolscap, 32.5 × 20.5 cm. approx., in many handwritings. Most have holes in the centre from filing on a lace or spike. They were later folded to a width of about 5.5 cm. and docketed with the sufferer's name and value of the loss in houses and goods, then arranged in packets by streets and numbered within each street in series starting at (1), but with some numbers intentionally repeated, to indicate losses in the same house, or houses with the same landlord. The arrangement by streets is unreliable: corner houses may appear in one street or the other, and in the packet labelled 'The Butts', estimates numbered 1–3 are in the Saltisford, 4–20 are in Joyce Pool, 21 and 22 are in the Butts, 23 is in the Saltisford and 24–38 are in the Butts again.

THE BOOK OF ESTIMATES (CR 1618/WA.4/10) is a tabulated digest of the original estimates, following the same arrangement. It consists of a paper gathering of ten leaves 31.0 × 20.0 cm., of which the last is blank, sewn into a cover of thicker paper 33.0 × 20.7 cm. inscribed 'The Booke of Estimates of the Loss by Fire' and numbered (167).

THE BOOK OF REDUCTIONS (CR 1618/WA.4/11) is a paper book of six leaves of which one is blank, 33.0 × 21.0 cm. approx., sewn into a re-used coarse grey paper cover inscribed 'Reductions of Losses in Houses and Goods', and 'For Mr Geo. Teonge, Books[eller] in Warwicke', and numbered (166).

THE PETITIONS AND OTHER PAPERS LAID BEFORE THE COURT are in two bundles (CR 1618/W10/2, 3), not in order, on paper of many shapes and sizes and in a variety of handwritings. Many have central holes from filing on a lace or spike, nearly all are docketed with the petitioner's name, some are numbered and some are also lettered, usually M but sometimes N, R or B, the significance of which is obscure.

SIR WILLIAM WILSON'S LETTER (CR 1618/WA.4/66) is a single sheet of paper 32.2 × 20.0 cm., written on one half only, and originally folded to 12.0 × 7.0 cm., sealed, and stabbed through, possibly for a sealing thread; numbered (38).

THE DRAFT DECREES OF THE COURT (CR 1618/W10/bundle 1) are mostly on paper of double foolscap size, folded once to produce two leaves 30.0 × 19.0 cm. approx. In one case printed sheets 38.0 × 30.0 cm. of blank land tax receipts for the year 8 Wm III have been re-used, and in three cases printed sheets 59.0 × 48.0 cm. of blank land tax warrants for the same year, probably left over from John Newsham's last year as receiver general of taxes.

THE COLLECTION ON THE BRIEF IN COTHERIDGE, WORCS. (CR 1618/WA.4/31) is a folded sheet of paper making two leaves 31.5 × 19.3 cm. numbered (188).

THE ACCOUNT FOR LETTERS PATENT AND THE ACT (CR 1618/WA.4/74) is a
folded sheet of paper giving two leaves 30.5 × 19.2 cm., of which only the
first side is used; numbered (191). MR FALL'S BILL (CR 1618/WA.4/84) is
similarly a sheet folded to give two leaves 23.0 × 18.0 cm., of which only
the first side is used; numbered (192).

WILLIAM TARVER'S OCCASIONAL PAYMENTS (CR 1618/WA.4/130) is a single
sheet folded to give two leaves 33.0 × 21.2 cm., numbered (218).

THE DISTRIBUTIONS TO SUFFERERS (CR 1618/WA.4/130) is a narrow paper
gathering, sewn in the centre, of eleven leaves 30.5 × 10.2 cm., the pen-
ultimate leaf cut out leaving a stub with the word 'To . . .' repeated thirty-
eight times, indicating a missing page of payments, the last leaf blank,
numbered (15).

THE STATEMENT OF THE TREASURER'S ACCOUNTS (CR 1618/WA.4/65) is a
single sheet of paper 30.0 × 19.2 cm., with one corner torn away when
folded, not affecting the writing, numbered (77).

THE ORDER TO MAKE UP PAYMENTS TO 4S. IN £1 (CR 1618/WA.4/34) is a
single sheet of paper folded to give two leaves 33.0 × 21.2 cm., of which
only the first side is used, numbered (89).

JAMES FISH'S BILL FOR SURVEYING (CR 1618/WA.4/210) is a single sheet of
paper folded to give two leaves 30.4 × 19.0 cm., of which only the first
side is used, numbered (112).

THE TREASURER'S ACCOUNT BOOK (CR 1618/WA.4/4) is a paper book 28.8
× 18.0 cm. in a rigid parchment binding with vellum ties, modern
pagination 1-184, of which pages 126-59 are blank, inscribed on the
spine '. . . Brief Money', numbered (1).

HOARE'S BANK ACCOUNTS (CR 1618/WA.4/131) are a copy on four sheets
of thin paper folded and roughly sewn together to give eight leaves 35.5
× 29.8 cm., written in a bold hand with flourished capitals, as the original
bank ledgers.

CHILD'S BANK ACCOUNTS (CR 1618/WA.4/62) are a copy on one folded
sheet giving two leaves 42.0 × 16.5 cm. of which one is blank, numbered
53; this copy stops in December 1695. Another copy in the Warwick
Castle MSS (CR 1886/9151), in the same format but badly damaged,
continues to the end of the account in 1703.

Editorial Method

The documents selected for publication include the most substantial of the
commissioners' records. In addition, some minor reports and accounts have
been chosen for their human interest or because they fill gaps left by missing records. The draft decrees and some petitions have been calendared,
mostly by omitting repetitions and legal common form; omissions are
indicated by dots. Original spelling has been reproduced, but capital letters

and punctuation have been modernized. Some of the manuscripts are fair copies, but others are rough drafts, often by writers who were almost illiterate. Every effort has been made to present the documents as the writers intended them to be read, and cancellations, insertions, overwritings and other alterations have not been noticed unless they indicate a significant change of mind. Square brackets are used to enclose words supplied by the editor. Attention has not usually been drawn to errors in arithmetic, which are frequent, and it will be realized that many totals of money are unreal, due to the changes in value of the coinage. The original accounts of the treasurer and of the two banks are arranged with receipts and payments on facing pages; since the columns are of unequal length, this resulted in much unused blank paper. To save space, the columns of receipts and payments with their original page totals have been transcribed consecutively.

Documents among the commissioners' records not published here, nor mentioned in the Introduction, include many duplicate and overlapping statements of account and distribution lists, but mainly relate to the rebuilding of the church and tower. 'An Abstract of John Mitchener's account . . .' made in 1711 (CR 1618/WA.4/5), derived from the published treasurer's account book, shows the payments relating to the church arranged ledger-fashion under the names of workmen and craftsmen; and hundreds of original bills and vouchers (CR 1618/WA.4/268–276), in packets partly arranged under workmen's names, illustrate the work in immense detail. A list is available in the County Record Office of the entire collection.

THE COMMISSIONERS' ORDER BOOK

MEMORIALS OF AND ORDERS MADE TOUCHING ALL MATTERS PUBLICK
AND OF MOMENT RELATEING TO THE LATE DREADFULL FIRE WHICH HAP-
PENED IN THE TOWNE OF WARWICK ON THE FIFTH DAY OF SEPTEMBER
1694

September the 6th 1694

At a meeting of the Right Honourable the Lord Brooke, Sir John Mordaunt, Bart., Sir Charles Holt, Bart., Sir Henry Puckering, Bart., Sir Thomas Wagstaff, Kt., Henry Parker, Esq., Wm Colemor, Esq., Charles Newsham, Esq., and divers other gentlemen, to consider of ways and meanes to releive and support the distressed sufferers by the late fire, it was thought expedient that the Letter of Request following should be sent to all townes in the County to gather and excite the charitable benevolence of good and well-disposed people, toward the speedy and present releif of the said sufferers:

Whereas by a sudden fire, which broake out about two of the clock in the afternoon on the fifth of this instant September, in the western part of the towne of Warwick, which by the violence of the wind was soe swiftly carried through the principall parts of the same that noe opposition could be made to hinder the feirceness of its progress, till it had in few hours consumed almost all the Highstreet, the Church Street and the Sheepstreet intirely, part of the Jury Street, Newstreet, and many buildings about the Market House, together with the great and antient church of St Maryes and severall other buildings in other parts of the towne, and with them a very great part of the goods of the inhabitants, not onely those whose houses were wholly ruined, but many others, whose houses were adjoyning thereunto, the loss by which calamity is soe greate as cannot presently be computed, and the necessityes of great numbers of the sufferers such, as need speedy releife, they haveing lost with their goods the meanes of their livelyhood, and nothing left for theire support in this theire deplorable condicion, but the charity of well disposed Christians. We therefore whose names are subscribed, under the deep sence of this theire misery, doe earnestly commend this theire sad estate to your pious charity; desireing you by the most speedy and effectual meanes, to assist the said poor sufferers with such supplyes as God shall enable you to afford them for theire present releife, who to our knowledge are under great necessity; and what contribucions you shall soe raise and collect, to send by the hands of the bearers hereof ———
Mr Richard Grimes, Mr Richard Lane, Mr Thomas Roberts, Mr Stephen

Nicholes, Mr Wm Nicholls, Mr Samuell Paxton, Mr Henry Harper, Mr Richard Wigley, Mr Richard Hands, malster, and Mr John Davis, or any two of them, who are approved by us. And we doe hereby promise to use our utmost care to see the said money applyed according to their respective necessityes, and the said moneys so collected are hereby appointed to be paid into the hands of the Rt Honourable Fulke Lord Brooke and the present Maior of Warwick to be issued out accordingly.

Brooke	Richard Verney	H. Puckering
Jo. Mordaunt	Tho. Wagstaffe	Hen. Parker
C. Holt	Geo. Lucy	Char. Newsham
		Wm. Colmore[1]

At the same time, for the more immediate support of the poor sufferers, and to excite and hasten the charity of others, the summs under written by the persons then present, were endorsed on the said letter and three copies of it, as followeth:

Brooke	£40	Char. Newsham	£5
Jno. Mordaunt	10	Jno. Newsham	5
C. Holt	10	Tho. Newsham	5
Hen. Puckering	10	Dr Wm. Johnson	2
Rich. Verney	10	Tho. Ferne	0 10s.
Tho. Wagstaffe	10	Jno. Smith	1
Geo. Lucy	10	Hen. Holden	0 10s.
Hen. Parker	5	Jo. Vere	0 10s.
Wm. Colmore	10		

And Ordered that the persons appointed in the letter above written to collect the said charities, be dispatch'd (viz.) Two of them with a letter into each of the four Hundreds, to gather for the use of the poor sufferers, the charitable contribucions of every parish in their respective Hundreds, which was accordingly performed.

Upon complaint made at the same time, that many persons takeing advantage of the distractions of the inhabitants, had stol'n and carried away their goods, several warrants of search sign'd and seal'd by the Justices then present (viz.) Sir Jno. Mordaunt, Sir Richard Verney, Henry Parker, Esq., and Charles Newsham, Esq., were issued out into all the neighbouring townes, and ordered to be carried by one or more substantiall and honest inhabitants of this town, to the constables of each place, and to attend the execution thereof.

---

[1] The names of the signatories to the letter were copied by the clerk, and are not original signatures.

September the 8th 1694

Ordered by the Maior, the Right Honourable the Lord Brooke, Sir Henry Puckering, Wm. Colemor, Esq., etc., that the persons following (viz.) Henry Heath, gent., Mr Nicholas Wrothwell, Mr Jno. Smith at the Cross, Mr Jno. Watson farrier, Mr Jno. Davies, Mr Thomas Eedes, Mr Wm. Roe, Mr Thomas Masters, Mr Samuell Dunkley, Mr Wm. Wilson and Mr Wm. Smyth, inhabitants of this town, and who have been no sufferers by the late fire, doe on the 10th of this instant September, haveing taken a survey of the whole, bring in and lay before the Maior, the Rt. Honourable the Lord Brooke and such gentlemen as should then meet at the Maior's Parlour, a list of all such sufferers as in their judgements they should think fitt objects of charity, and need present releife, and what summ each person and family should require for present subsistence and enable them, in some measure, to carry on theire respective trades.

Joseph Blissett, Mayor	Wm. Colmore	Brooke
John Newsham	Wm. Bolton	H. Puckering
Robert Boyse[1]		

Ordered alsoe that Mr Maior, Mr Thomas Newsham, Mr Wm. Tarver and Mr Jemmat be the Treasurers or Receivers of all moneys contributed and brought in for the end aforesaid.

		Brooke
Jo. Stanton	J. Bagshaw	J. Mordaunt
Wm. Bolton	Aar. Rogers	H. Puckering

Ordered that for preventing mistakes and for the farther satisfaccion of the severall persons and towns contributing, the said Treasurers doe give a receipt for each summ soe given, and two of the said Treasurers at the least to sign each receipt.

Jo. Stanton	J. Bagshaw	Brooke
Wm. Bolton	Edward Heath	J. Mordaunt
		H. Puckering

Ordered that a book be prepared and a fair entry made of the receipts of all such contribution money, with the names of the persons or towns soe contributing. And alsoe an entry of all disbursements and distribucions that shall be made, the summs and persons names to whom given.

Jo. Stanton	J. Bagshaw	Brooke
Wm. Bolton	Edw. Heath	J. Mordaunt
		H. Puckering

[1] The names at the foot of this and subsequent entries, and later at the foot of each court, are original signatures. The order on the page does not indicate the sequence of signing, which presumably took place at the next meeting. Lord Brooke, if present, appears to have signed first.

Ordered that a booke be prepared in which every sufferer who receives any of the charitie moneys, shall sign a receipt of the summs given to him.

		Brooke
Jo. Stanton	J. Bagshaw	J. Mordaunt
Wm. Bolton	Edw. Heath	H. Puckering

Ordered that a book be prepared in which the memorials of, and orders made concerning all matters publick and of moment, that have been transacted relateing to the late dreadfull fire in Warwick, be fairly entred

		Brooke
Jo. Stanton	J. Bagshaw	J. Mordaunt
Wm. Bolton		H. Puckering

September the 9th.

To a letter brought by a messenger, written by order of the Lord Bishop of Worcester, desireing an account of the late fire in this Burrough, the answer following sign'd by the Right Honourable the Lord Brooke, Sir Henry Puckering, Wm. Colemore Esq., the Mayor, Aldermen, etc., was sent to the Bishop by the same messenger:

My Lord,

The greate amazement and confusion, into which the late sudden and dreadfull fire in our Burrough hath put all persons who were eye witnesses of that dismal scene, and out of which we are not yet soe much recovered, as to adventure to give your Lordshipp any estimate or satisfactory account, of the losses thereby sustained, hath hitherto prevented us from certifying or applying to your Lordship (our Diosecan) in the behalf of the great numbers of familyes utterly ruined and impoverished by the same. The best account we are yet able to give, your Lordship may be pleased to take as follows. About two of the clock in the afternoone, on the fifth of this instant September, a fire broke forth in the western part of the town of Warwick, which by a violent and tempestuous wind then blowing from the south west, was soe swiftly carried through the principal and cheif tradeing parts of the town, that within the space of half an hour, severall places, and farr distant from each other, were all in flames at once, soe that all endeavours that could be used to hinder the fiercness of its progress, the same were vaine and ineffectual, and within the space of four or five hours it had wholly consumed (except two or three houses) all the High-street, Sheep-street and Church-street entirely, part of the Jury-street, Newstreet, and many buildings about the market place, together with (the most to be lamented loss) the great and antient Church of Saint Maryes and severall lanes and buildings in other parts of the town, and with them a very great part of the goods of the inhabitants, not onely of those, whose houses were wholly ruined, but many others whose houses were adjoyning thereunto. The mighty losses by which calamity are soe great, as are not easily to be imagined, much less at present with any certainty to be computed, but cannot, we judge, be estimated at less then one hundred thousand pounds, and the necessities of great numbers of sufferers, such as requires a speedy reliefe, they haveing lost with their habitacions and goods, all means of subsistence, and nothing left for their support, but the charity of well disposed people, which it hath pleased God already to move and stirr up, even beyond our hopes, as your Lordshipp by a list of the contributors under written may more particularly see, and which all the just care imaginable shall be taken to employ and distribute, according to the present exigences and pressing necessities of the poor sufferers.

The truth of this to the best of our knowledg we whose names are under written doe attest, who are

Your Lordships most humble servants,

Joseph Blisset, Mayor	Brooke
Aaron Rogers	H. Puckering
Wm. Tarver, etc.	Wm. Colemor, etc.[1]

September the 10th 1694

1st Distribucion[2]

At a meeting of the Right Honourable the Lord Brooke, Sir Henry Puckering, etc., in the Mayor's Parlour, and a list presented to them by the persons in the preceeding order appointed of such whose necessities required a present support, the said list of persons, and summs given, being read over and after some alteracions and amendments made, approved of, amounting to five hundred twenty eight pounds and ten shillings.[3] Ordered that notice be given thereof to the said sufferers to whome the said summs are allotted, and that the Treasurers appointed of the said charityes, doe out of the charity moneys lying and being in their hands, make a distribucion pursuant to the said list, and enter the same in their booke of disbursements.

	Brooke
Joseph Blissett, Mayor	H. Puckering
John Newsham	Wm. Colmore
Robert Boyse	Wm. Bolton

---

[1] These names are not original signatures.

[2] This heading inserted in the margin in another hand.

[3] 'Memorandum the summs paid in the particulars amount to but £523 10s. od.' inserted in the margin in another hand.

September the 13th 1694

To the letter sent to the Bishop, his Lordshipp's answer directed to Mr Mayor with a particular of the contribucions from the Bishop, Church and Citty of Worcester, as followeth

Sir,

I have been extreamly concerned for the distressed condicion of those whoe have suffered so much by the late dreadfull fire among you, and I have used my best endeavours to get in what supplyes I could, in this short time, towards their releife. What I have been able to procure by my self, or others hereabouts, I have now sent for a present supply, and I find the same persons will be ready to contribute more when Letters Patents are obtained for a generall collection. But I know that all such things will fall short of a sufficient reparacion of the losses sustained, and therefore I heartily pray to Almighty God, to support the minds of those, who have suffered by this sad and amazeing providence, and to make up their losses in some measure by patience under them, and to give them an abundant recompence in better and more certain riches in another world. I was heartily glad to find by the account which I received that so many of your neighbours have been soe kind and charitable; I pray God increase their number and enlarge the hearts of those, whoe are att a greater distance. I hear that the Chancell of your great Church will in a little time be made ready for publick service, which I am very glad of, that you may not want a place to serve God in, in the midst of your ruins. I pray God to send his blessing among you.

I am your most faithfull friend
and servant, Edward Wigorn.

City and Cathedral Church of Worcester   13th September 1694[1]

The voluntary contribucions towards the relief of the distressed sufferers by the late dreadfull fire at Warwick the 5th September instant

	£	s.	d.
Given by the Rt. Revd. Father in God Edwd. Lord Bishop:	20	0	0
more:	14	10	0
In his Lordship's family:	13	10	0
Procured by his Lordship from friends:	34	10	0
Given by the Dean and Chapter of the Cathedral:	20	0	0
Given by others in the precincts of the Colledge:	14	3	1
Given alsoe in the parishes of St Helen and St Alban:	18	8	3

[1] This adjunct to the bishop's letter has been moved from a later page in the MS.

St Andrew:	8	19	5½
St Clement:	10	18	8
St Martin:	15	8	o
St Nicholas:	22	9	9½
All Saints:	21	6	1
St Peter:	12	16	8½
St Swithin:	36	16	10
St Michael:	9	11	o
St John:	5	o	4
and given in small summs from private hands:	o	14	6
The whole summe	279	2	8

September the [   ][1]

Ordered that Mr Newsham doe cause the following to be put into the London Gazett

Warwick Sept. 5th
About two of the clock this afternoon, a fire suddenly broke forth in the western part of the towne, which by a violent tempestuous wind then blowing from the south west instantly gott head and burnt soe quick and furious that within the space of half an hour the town was on fire at the same time in severall places farr distant from one another, the swiftness of which was such that noe opposition could be made, soe that in few hours space it consumed severall streets in the principal trading part of the town with most of the inhabitants goods, together with the great Church and many other buildings in other parts of the town. The manner of it was soe dreadfull as is not easily to be imagined and the loss soe great as cannot yet be computed.

September the 17th[2] 1694

2d Distribucion[3]
At a meeting of the Right Honourable the Lord Brook, Sir Henry Puckering, Sir Charles Shughburg, etc., to consider farther, of the wants and necessityes of the poor sufferers and supplyes for their reliefe, Ordered that a farther distribucion of the summ of fifty six pounds and ten shillings[4] of the charitye moneys be made according to a list then brought in and that the Treasurers doe pay the same pursuant thereunto and enter

---

[1] The day of the month left blank.
[2] Altered from '18th'.
[3] This heading inserted in the margin in another hand.
[4] 'Memorandum there is paid on this order but £54 10s. od.' inserted in the margin in another hand.

the names of the sufferers, and the summs given them into their booke of disbursements.

Joseph Blissett, Mayor   Brooke
John Newsham   Wm. Bolton
Wm. Colmore   Robert Boyes
                               H. Puckering

September the [   ]¹

Ordered that the advertisement following be sent by Mr Newsham to be inserted into the London Gazett, and that he be repaid the charges thereof:

Information being given and complaint made that divers lewd and disorderly people wandering about in severall countys pretending themselves to be inhabitants of, and ruin'd by the late dreadfull fire in Warwick, and to have testimonials or passes from the Mayor and other justices of the said towne, these are to certifie that due care is taken and provision made for all the sufferers, by a weekly distribucion of the charityes sent in for their relief, and that all such testimonials or passes are counterfeit, and the persons producing them, to be punished, as vagrants and common cheats.

September the [   ]²

An agreement being made with Roger Hurlbutt and Thomas Masters, carpenters, for the summ of twenty nine pounds to cover the chancell with a roof of boards and poles of oake, which are to be and remaine for the use of the Corporacion, Ordered that Mr Newsham draw articles pursuant to the said agreement.

Certificate from the Generall Quarter Sessions holden for the County of Warwick of the losses sustained by the late fire within this Borough, as followeth:

To the Right Honourable Sir John Summers Knt. Lord Keeper of the Great Seale of England

We their Majesties justices of the peace for the County of Warwick, doe certifie your Lordshipp that at their Majesties Court of Generall Quarter Sessions of the Peace holden at Warwick for the said County of Warwick on Tuesday the second day of this instant October, it did then and there appear unto us the said justices, sitting in open court as well upon the oaths of Samuell Dunkley, Richard Bromley, Thomas Adams and Job Burch,

---

¹ Day of the month left blank. The following undated entries are not necessarily in chronological order.
² Day of the month left blank.

masons, and John Hope, Roger Hurlbutt, Thomas Masters and George Perkins, carpenters, as alsoe upon the oaths of Mr Joseph Blissett, Mayor of the
said towne, Wm. Tarver, gent., and John Lanyon, gent., three of the most
substantial inhabitants of the town of Warwick within the County of Warwick, that on Wensday the fifth day of September last past between two
and three of the clock in the afternoone of the same day, a sudden and
dreadfull fire did break forth at the said town of Warwick which by reason
of the fury and violence thereof, within the space of six hours, burnt downe
and consumed the dwelling houses, malting houses, barns, stables and outhouses of above two hundred and fivety familyes of the inhabitants of the
said towne, together with their malt, corn, hay and most of their severall
goods of trade and houshould stuff, together with the great church of Saint
Maryes and other publick buildings, and that the whole loss sustained
thereby did amount unto the summ of ninety thousand and six hundred
pounds and upwards, soe that the said inhabitants with their familyes are
totally impoverished and are noe wayes able to subsist, but must necessarily
perish, unless they shall be timely relieved by the charitable benevolence of
well disposed people. We doe therefore humbly pray, that the same may be
recomended by your Lordship to their Majesties for their gracious Letters
Patents, throughout the Kingdom of England, Dominion of Wales and
towne of Berwick upon Tweed on behalf of the poore distressed sufferers.
Dated under our hands and seales at the sessions abovesaid, we remain—
my Lord,

Your Lordshipps most humble servants—

Tho. Rawlins	Rich. Verney	Basill Fielding
John Mordaunt	Regin. Forster	Hen. Parker
Cha. Shugberg	Wm. Underhill	Wm. Palmer
Ri. Newdigate	John Clopton	

September the [　　]¹ 1694

At a meeting of the Mayor, Aldermen, etc., of this Borough for ascertain-
ing the estimates of the severall losses by the late fire, and in order to prepare matters for the obtaining a certificate to the Lord Keeper, from the
justices of the peace at the Generall Quarter Sessions for this County, the
following order was made and published in and throughout the whole
Borough.

For the more speedy ascertaineing the losses sustained by the severall
sufferers, in and by the late dreadfull fire in this Borough, and that the same
may be in a readiness to be certifyed at the next Generall Quarter Sessions
of the peace, to be held for this County, in order to the obtaineing their

¹ Day of the month left blank.

Majesties Letters Patents for a generall brief, it is this day ordered by the Mayor, Aldermen, etc., that each particular sufferer by the said fire, doe bring in writeing under their hands, the present yearly rents of their houses, with an estimate in particular of their severall losses, in houses, goods or otherwise, such as they will answer upon their severall oaths at the said next Generall Quarter Sessions. And this they are required to doe on Friday the fourteenth of this instant September at two of the clock in the afternoone at the Mayor's Parlour, that soe the accounts of the said losses may be examined, and if upon due enquiry and examinacion thereof, it shall appear that any of the said sufferers, doe or shall falsly represent their losses, such persons shall loose the benefitt acruing by the contribucions and charity collected and to be distributed for their present relief.

Charles Hicks   Wm. Tarver   Joseph Blisset, Mayor
Stephen Nichols   Devereux Whadcock   Aaron Rogers[1]

September the [   ][2] 1694

The petition of the severall innkeepers, sufferers by the late fire, was signed and sent to the Honourable the Commissioners of their Majesties Excise, as followeth

To the Honourable their Majesties Commissioners of the Excise. The humble peticion of John Williams, John Stoaks, George Watts, Sarah Hicks, Sarah Bunter, Robert Taylor, John Atterbury, Thomas Arpes, Samuel Parsons, Richard Hadley, Ann Harris, Elizabeth Whinnick, Matthew Busby, John Burton, Timothy Simpkins, Charles Emes, George Flower, Benjamin Bowers, Judith Farr, Job Roades, Thomas Rush and James Rainbow, innkeepers within the Borough of Warwick, humbly sheweth,

That, whereas your poore peticioners haveing not onely lost their houses and the greatest part of their goods by the late dreadfull fire which happened in the said towne on the fifth of this instant September, but alsoe their whole stock of ale and beer, as well that which hath been pay'd for, as that which hath not, and thereby left debtors to their Majesties for their excise, due from the last sitting before the said fire, and being very much impoverished, are not in a capacity at present to pay their said duty, doe therefore hope to find favour and compassion from the honourable Board, that the debts due for their excise before that time, may at least be remitted, that soe your peticioners may by help of friends, endeavour to pursue their said calling, as God shall enable them, for which singular clemency your distressed peticioners shall be continually bound to pray for your [   ].[3]

---

[1] These names are not original signatures.
[2] Day of the month left blank.
[3] Word omitted.

October the 15th 1694

3d Distribucion[1]

At a meeting of the Rt. Honourable the Lord Brooke, Sir John Mordaunt, Baronett, Sir Henry Puckering, Baronett, William Colemor, Esq., Edward Heath, Thomas Newsham, Aaron Rogers, etc., trustees amongst others for the management and disposall of the charity moneys given for the present relief of the poor sufferers by the late fire in Warwick, Ordered that the Treasurers, out of the charity moneys lying and being in their hands, doe pay to the severall persons whose names and the summs allotted to them were sett down in a paper subscribed by the said trustees, the severall summs therein contained and expressed amounting in the whole to one hundred fourty and six pounds and ten shillings, and that they enter the said summs into their book of disbursements and take receipts for the same.

Severall brickmakers haveing undertaken to furnish this Borough with good bricks at the rate of fourteen shillings per thousand, provided they might have ground to make them withall, rent free, it was thought expedient by the principall inhabitants of the same, and to be for the common benefitt of all rebuilders, that they should have some parcels of ground on the common grounds allotted to them for that purpose, but the said brickmakers being interrupted in the said work, by some evill disposed people, it was thought fitt, that a paper expressing and declaring their consent, should be subscribed by all those, who have right of common in the said grounds, which was as followeth

Whereas the ground called Monsieur Hill and the Greens Hill,[2] lying neer to the Borough of Warwick, and in which the inhabitants of the parish of Saint Maryes and others[3] in the said borough or the greatest part of them, have right of common for depastureing their cattle, are by experience found to be a proper soile and earth for the makeing of good brick and tyle, and whereas severall brickmakers doe propose at much easier rates than heretofore hath been known, to furnish the said town with brick and tyle, provided they may have soe much of the ground of the said common as shall be assigned them for that purpose, rent free and without charge, wee whose names are underwritten, inhabitants of the said parish of Saint Maryes and others[3] and who have right of common grounds above mencioned, conceiveing the said proposal to be for the publick benefitt of the said parish of St Maries, and very much to contribute to the more speedy, cheap and easy rebuilding the houses thereof demolished by the late

---

[1] This heading inserted in the margin in another hand.
[2] It is not known where these places are.
[3] 'and others' inserted over a caret.

dreadfull fire, which happened within the said parish, doe therefore hereby severally consent promise and agree, soe farr as in us lyes, that such brick-makers as shall be allowed and approved of by the Mayor and Aldermen of the Borough aforesaid, shall and may for the use of the said parish, and not otherwise, without any interrupcion or disturbance by us to be given, have free leave and liberty, in such places and parts of the said commons as shall be allotted and marked out to them for the purpose aforesaid, to digg and throw up clay, and the same to make into bricks and tyles, and from thence to carry and deliver to any parts of the said parish, at the rates that[1] shall be agreed upon between them and the said Mayor and Aldermen. In witness whereof we have hereunto set our hands, the twenty second day of October in the sixth year of their now Majesties reigns annoque domini 1694.

<table>
<tr><td>Joseph Blissett, Mayor</td><td>Henry Puckering</td></tr>
<tr><td>Henry Heath</td><td>Wm Colemar</td></tr>
<tr><td>Wm Tarver</td><td>Wm Bolton</td></tr>
<tr><td>Stephen Nichols, etc.</td><td>Jn Staunton[2]</td></tr>
</table>

Whereas[3] their Majesties were graciously pleased to grant their Letters Patents, bearing date the 8th day of December last, to the sufferers by the late dreadfull fire in Warwick, the Trustees and Treasurers appointed by the said Letters Patents (to avoid the charges extraordinary in takeing out duplicates of the same) doe desire all ministers to accept such printed copies thereof as shall be sent to them by the registers of their respective archdeaconries, to read the same and hasten their collections, assureing them that the utmost care is taken to prevent all frauds in the same, and that the money soe collected shall be justly and equally distributed among the poor sufferers according to the true intent of the said Letters Patents.

Reverend Sir,
    The breifs for the town of Warwick being now sent down to the severall registers in the diocesses of England and Wales in order to be dispersed by their apparitors to the severall ministers and the archdeacons being directed by the said briefs to receive the money collected upon them within their respective archdeaconryes we earnestly recomend it to you in behalf of the poor sufferers whose condicion is most deplorable that you will to your utmost promote soe great a charity and take the most effectual care you can to prevent any fraud or failure in the collecting and returning the money which shall arise out of your archdeaconry and that both the laying the breifs and returning the money may be with the least charge and deduction that shall be possible, some have undertaken to doe both for six

---

[1] 'at' altered from 'as', 'the rates that' inserted over a caret.
[2] These names are not original signatures.
[3] Preceded by 6 blank leaves.

pence a parish and others we have reason to believe will be soe kind as to doe it gratis, the loss is soe much greater then can be repaired by a breife that we are desirous to save all we can for the poore sufferers and doubt not of your concurrence in soe good a work.

We desire a speedy answer directed to one of us at the house of Commons.

Your humble servants,

Digby   W. Bromley   Wm Colmore[1]

Warwick Burrough.[2]

At the Maior's Parlour in the Burrough aforesaid the 29th day of Aprill 1695 annoque regni Gulielmi tertii Anglie etc. regis septimo.

The Rt. Honourable the Lord Brooke, the Rt. Honourable the Lord Leigh, the Rt. Honourable the Lord Digby, the Honourable Francis Grevile, Esq., Sir Henry Puckering, Sir John Burgoyne, Barts., Sir Thomas Wagstaffe, Kt., Charles Hicks, Mayor of the Burrough of Warwick, Richard Newdigate, William Peytoe, William Palmer, William Colemore, William Bolton, John Newsham and Thomas Newsham, Esqs., being Commissioners or Judges appointed by an Act of Parliament entituled an Act for Rebuilding the Town of Warwick and for determining differences touching houses burnt or demolished by reason of the late dreadfull fire there, did then and there take the oath mencioned and directed in the said Act before Sir Reginald Forster, Bart., and Sir John Clopton, Kt., two of his Majesties justices of the peace of the county of Warwick.

Memorandum at the same time and place Sir Reginald Forster, Bart., and Sir John Clopton, Kt., being Commissioners or Judges appointed by the Act aforesaid did then and there take the oath mencioned and directed in the said Act before William Palmer, Esq., and Richard Newdigate, Esq., 2 of his Majesties justices of the peace of the county aforesaid.

The said Commicioners doe agree and order that the stile of the Court of Record erected by the said Act shall be ———
The Court of Record holden by vertue of[3] an Act for the Rebuilding the Town of Warwick and for determining differences touching houses burnt or demolished by reason of the late dreadfull fire there.

The Rt. Honourable the Lord Brook, the Rt. Honourable the Lord Leigh, the Rt. Honourable the Lord Digby, the Honourable Francis Grevile, Esq., Sir Henry Puckering, Bart., Sir John Burgoyne, Bart., Sir Reginald Forster, Bart., Sir John Clopton, Kt., Sir Thomas Wagstaffe, Kt., Charles Hicks,

---

[1] These are not original signatures.
[2] Preceded by 20 blank leaves. The hand now changes.
[3] 'vertue of' inserted over a caret.

Mayor of the Burrough of Warwick, Richard Newdigate, William Peytoe, William Palmer, Wm. Colemore, Wm. Bolton, John Newsham and Thomas Newsham, Esqs., doe elect John Mitchener register of the said Court.

Ordered by the Commissioners or Judges then present that Friday next be appointed for the Court to be holden at the Mayor's Parlour by nine of the clock in the morning.

Charles Hicks, Mayor	Brooke
Ri. Newdigate	Leigh
Wm. Peyto	W. Digby
Will. Palmer	F. Grevile
Wm. Bolton	H. Puckering
John Newsham	Jo. Burgoyne
Tho. Newsham	John Clopton
Reg. Forster	Tho. Wagstaffe

Warwick Burrough

At the Court of Record[1] held before the Commicioners or Judges appointed by an Act of Parliament for Rebuilding the Towne of Warwick and for determining differences touching houses burnt and demolished by reason of the late dreadfull fire there att the Mayor's Parlour on Friday the 3d day of May 1695

Present: the Rt. Honourable the Lord Brook, the Honourable Francis Grevill, Esq., Sir Henry Puckering, Bart., Sir John Burgoyne, Bart., Sir Tho. Wagstaffe, Kt., Charles Hicks, Mayor, William Colemore, Esq., William Bolton, Esq., John Newsham, Esq., Thomas Newsham, Esq.

By vertue of the powers to the Commicioners by the said Act given for regulateing the foundacions of the streets to be built, Ordered that the line drawne from the house of Andrew Archer Esq. in the Jury Street, to the corner house of Mr Blissett in the said street, and from Mr Whadcock's house at the corner of the High Street on the north side thereof, to the house late of Mrs Chernock on the same side in the same street, as it is now staked out, And that the line drawn from the house of John Bradshaw apothecary being the corner house on the south side of the high Street, to the house of George Harris on the same side in the said street, as now staked out, being fourty and three feet broad in the cleer from one end of the said street to the other, And that the line drawn from the corner of Mr Rainsfords his house to the corner whereon stood the house of Richard Harris, and which is already staked out.

---

[1] The style of the court which follows is repeated exactly at the head of each subsequent court, where in this transcription it has been omitted for the sake of brevity. All courts are held at the Mayor's Parlour.

And the line drawn from the ground whereon stood the parson's house, to the County hall in the Sheepstreet, and from the said hall to the corner house of Robert Watts, senior, on the same side of the said street and which is staked out, the north end of the said Sheepstreet containing in breadth sixty foot and the south end of the said street fourty seven foot and nine inches,

And that the line drawn from the house of Mr Whadcock on the north side of the High Street to the house of Mrs Murcott as it is already staked out, Be the lines by which all builders along the severall streets above mencioned are to be governed and that whoever presumes to build or lay his foundacions farther into the said streete or backward from the said streets, then the said lines as above laid, the foundacions soe laid[1] and building thereon erected shall be deemed a common nusance and proceeded against as contrary to the said Act.

Ordered that Mr Samuel Dunkley view the ground of Mr Savage whereon stood the house of Mr Bradshaw, and the ground whereon stood the house of Mrs Dorothy Weale widdow, and to make his report to this Court on Munday next what quantity of ground is taken from each of them and what sufficient recompence may be made to them for the same.

Ordered that three guineas being the summ of three pounds fiveteen shillings be given to Mr Lee, town clerk of Northampton, as a gratuity to him for his free comunicateing the proceedings in the Court[2] erected there for rebuilding the said towne and the methods and rules observed by the Commissioners relateing thereunto.

Ordered that this Court be holden in this place on Munday next by nine of the clock in the morning.

Wm. Bolton	Brooke
John Newsham	F. Grevile
Charles Hicks mayor	H. Puckering
Tho. Newsham	Tho. Wagstaffe
	Wm. Colmore

Warwick Burrough
At the Court of Record held . . .[3] on Munday the sixth day of May 1695.

Present: the Rt. Honourable the Lord Brook, the Honourable Francis Grevile, Esq., Sir Henry Puckering, Bart., Sir Thomas Wagstaff, Kt., Charles Hicks, Mayor, Richard Newdigate, Esq., Wm. Colemore, Esq., Wm. Bolton, Esq., John Newsham, Esq., Thomas Newsham, Esq.

[1] 'the foundacions soe laid' inserted over a caret.
[2] 'in the Court' inserted over a caret.
[3] See p. 14, n. 1.

Whereas Samuell Dunkley hath (by an order of the last Court) view'd the ground of Mr Savage and the ground of Mrs Dorothy Weale and reported the same to this Court, Ordered that fourteen foot of ground in length and three foot nine inches in depth containeing in measure fifty and four foot be taken from the ground of Mr Savage for the enlargement of the High Street, and that there be taken from the ground of Mrs Dorothy Weale to make good the ground of Mr Savage four foot and a half long and twelve foot deep, containeing in the whole fifty four foot, and alsoe that there be taken away from Mrs Weale fivety six foot of ground in length and three foot in breadth at one end and nothing at the other fronting the High Street, containeing in the whole eighty four foot; in the whole taken away from Mrs Weale one hundred thirty eight foot.

Ordered that there be taken away from the ground of Mr Cooke next adjoyning to Mrs Weales, and added to the ground of the said Mrs Weale four foot and nine inches in length and thirty four foot deep containing in the whole one hundred fivety and seven foot which ground soe taken away is an equivalent to make good the ground of Mrs Weale. Ordered that Mr Cooke be allowed and paid twelve pence per foot for every foot soe taken away as aforesaid.

Whereas by the said Act, the outsides of all walls to be erected within the said Borough are to be with brick or stone, or brick and stone together, Ordered that notice be given by Richard Hadley to the severall persons, who presume to build outside walls with frames of timber, or otherwise, contrary to the intent of the said Act, that the walls soe built shall and will be deemed a common nusance, and the builders thereof incurr the penalties inflicted by the said Act.[1]

Ordered that Solomon Bray on or before the one and twentieth day of this instant May doe remove and carry away the rubbish and ruins of the late tower of St Maries Church and dispose of the same according to his agreement with the said Commicioners and that on default or neglect thereof, workmen be forthwith employ'd to remove and dispose of the said rubbish and be allowed and paid for the same out of the monies contracted for with the said Solomon Bray, for the doeing and performing the same. And that all persons, whose houses rainged with the streets as they are now sett and staked out, and whose rubbish is not already removed, doe on or before the day abovesaid, clear the streets before, and the foundacions of, their respective houses, from the rubbish lying thereon in order to the better distinguishing of the said foundacions and settleing the property of each particular person concerned therein as they will answer the contrary at

[1] The rough minute book adds 'And that there be an Order placed up att the County Hall and the Cross, to prevent any such building contrary to this Order, for the future.'

their perils. And that notice to be given of these orders by affixing copies therefore of the walls of the County Hall, Markett House and Mayor's Parlour within this Borough.

Ordered that Mr Samuel Dunkley view the lines of the streets as they are now staked out by the Commicioners and make his report to this Court on Munday next what ground is to be taken away from the severall persons who had houses rainging along the said lines, and what ground may be given them in lieu thereof or other recompence made.

The Commicioners now present doe make choice of Richard Hadley to attend constantly this court, serve the orders thereof, impanell juries and summon persons to appear at this Court.

Ordered that five guineas, being at this time the summ of six pounds and five shillings, be given to Mr William Middleton as a reward to him for services done in sending out the briefs for this towne, and that Mr Tarver doe pay him the same out of the charity monies being in his hands.

Ordered that Munday in every week be the constant Court day appointed for the future and that nine of the clock in the morning be the hour for persons summoned to appear, unless upon especial occasions this Court shall think fitt to alter the day.

	Brooke
Wm. Bolton	F. Grevile
John Newsham	H. Puckering
Charles Hicks, Mayor	Tho. Wagstaffe
Tho. Newsham	Wm. Colmore

Memorandum that Andrew Archer, Esq. one of the Commicioners or Judges appointed by the Act for Rebuilding the Town of Warwick, etc., did on the ninth day of this instant May take the oath mencioned in the said Act before Wm. Palmer, Esq. and Richard Newdigate, Esq. two of his Majesties justices of the peace for the county of Warwick at the house of Samuell Barber within the said towne.

Warwick Borough
At the Court of Record held . . . on Munday the thirteenth day of May 1695

Present: Charles Hicks, Mayor, the Rt. Honourable the Lord Brook, the Honourable Francis Grevile, Esq., Sir Henry Puckering, Bart., Sir Thomas Wagstaff, Kt., William Colmore, Esq., William Bolton, Esq., John Newsham, Esq., Thomas Newsham, Esq.

Ordered that Samuel Dunkley and Thomas Masters doe view the Red Lyon Inn and the ground belonging to it, and make their report to this Court on

Wensday sevenight, how much of the said house and ground is necessary to be taken away, in order to the opening, enlarging and makeing streight the Swan Lane, leading from the High Street into the Markett Place, and to give in an estimate of the charge in rebuilding and makeing good the said inn to rainge with the lane as now design'd.

For preventing disputes that may arise betwixt proprietors concerning the limits and bounds of their severall grounds, Ordered that noe person shall remove any old foundacion or open ground to lay a new one, or in any wise begin to build, untill the ground soe to be built upon be first view'd and sett out by Mr Dunkley.

Item that Mr Dunkley doe cause the stakes by which the severall streets are now sett out, to be driven fast into the ground, leaving them noe more than one foot above the surface; and that if any person presume without good authority to remove any of the said stakes, and shall be thereof legally convicted by the oath of one witness other than the informer, to be taken before the Mayor or Justices of the towne, that then the Mayor or Justices shall or may send such offender to the Common Goale of the towne, there to remaine for the space of one month without baile or mainprize, unless he pay or cause to be paid for the publick uses of the said towne the summ of twenty shillings ——
and that where such offender shall be adjudged unable to pay the said penalty, the said Mayor and Justices shall cause such offender to be openly whipped neer to the place where the offence shall be comitted.

Ordered that the corner house late of Mr Whadcock, the corner house late of Mr Bradshaw and the corner house late of Mr Blissett be built of equal height, the two first stories ten foot each, the third story eight foot high, the garretts as shall hereafter be appointed and directed by the Commicioners.

For the better convenience of qualifying those Commissioners who have not yet taken the oath to put the said Act into execution,
Ordered that Wednesday sevenight being the twenty second of this instant May, and time of the Generall Quarter Sessions for this County, be the day appointed for this Court to be held in this place by nine of the clock in the morning.

	Brooke
H. Puckering	Wm. Bolton
Tho. Wagstaffe	John Newsham
Wm. Colmore	Tho. Newsham

Warwick Burrough
At the Court of Record held ... on Wensday the two and twentieth day of May 1695

Present: the Rt Honourable the Lord Brook, the Rt. Honourable the Lord Leigh, Sir Henry Puckering, Bart., Sir John Burgoine, Bart., Sir John Clopton, Kt., Sir Richard Verney, Kt., Sir Thomas Wagstaff, Kt., Wm. Bromley, Esq., Andrew Archer, Esq., Bazil Feilding, Esq., Wm. Colemore, Esq., Wm. Bolton, Esq., Charles Newsham, Esq., Simon Biddolph, Esq., John Newsham, Esq., Thomas Fetherston, Esq., Thomas Newsham, Esq.

Memorandum that William Bromley, Esq., Charles Newsham, Esq., Simon Biddulph, Esq. and Thomas Fetherston, Esq., being Commicioners or Judges appointed by the said Act, did then and there take the oath mencioned and directed in the said Act before Sir Richard Verney, Kt., and Basill Feilding, Esq., two of his Majesties justices of the peace of the County of Warwick.
Memorandum at the same time and place Sir Richard Verney, Kt., and Basill Feilding, Esq., being Commicioners or Judges appointed by the said Act, did then take the oath mencioned in the said Act before William Bromley, Esq., and Charles Newsham, Esq., two of his Majesties justices of the peace of the County aforesaid.

Ordered that there be taken from Mr Watts in the High Street and added to that of Thomas Dadley six foot of ground as the same is sett out by Samuel Dunkley.

The Court being this day acquainted that the chancel of St Maries Church has suffered much by the late fire, and that the Corporacion as impropriators are of right to repaire the same and it appeareing they are already considerably in debt, having[1] sustained great losses by the said fire in several buildings given to charitable uses which they are oblig'd at their own proper charges to rebuild, and their revenues much impaired thereby, it is therefore Ordered that for the more speedy repaireing of the dammage done to the said chancell of St Maries Church by the late fire and makeing it ready for publick service, the Corporacion in this Borough be allowed the summ of one hundred pounds to be employed towards[2] the use abovesaid.

Agreed and resolved that a distribucion of the summ of six hundred pounds be made out of the charitie monies now lying in the hands of Mr William Tarver, and in order thereunto the Commicioners by the said Act liveing in this Burrough are desired to prepare and bring in a list of the names of such sufferers as purpose and intend speedily to begin to rebuild their houses, and what summs will be proper to be given to each of them, and to lay the same before this Court on Munday next, that an order may then be made for the said distribucion.

That the regulacions of the foundacions of the severall streets already made and others which shall hereafter be made, and the orders of this Court

---

[1] 'have' in MS.   [2] '-wards' inserted over a caret.

touching the measureing of ground be better observed, and that all builders may the better be confined within the rules of the said Act and the orders of this Court touching building, the Commicioners now present doe make and appoint Samuell Dunkley, mason, Thomas Masters, carpenter, and James Fish, senior, Surveyors to execute all orders of this Court relateing to the said office and to represent from time to time all irregularities and breaches of such rules and orders to this Court.

Ordered that Samuel Dunkley, Thomas Masters and James Fish doe make enquiry and inform themselves the best they may of the numbers of the sufferers who are able or intend to begin forthwith to rebuild their houses burnt down by the late fire, and lay a list of such persons before this Court on Munday next.

Ordered that Robert Watts be allow'd ten shillings for twelve foot of ground taken from him on the back of his front ground adjoyning to the goale and that he be paid the same out of the charitie monies in Mr Tarver's hands, and that liberty be given for two lights or windows to be made in the wall of the said goale adjoyning to the said Robert Watts provided the bottoms of the said lights be sett at least six feet high from the ground.

Ordered that Mr Tarver have and be allowed the whole plott or parcell of the poors ground consisting of three hundred eighty and seven foot lying between the said Mr Tarver's ground and the ground of Thomas Dadley, in lieu of the ground taken from him to enlarge the Church Street, and that nineteen pounds seven shillings be allow'd and paid for the same to the poors use.

Leigh	Brooke
H. Puckering	Tho. Fetherston
Tho. Wagstaffe	Wm. Colmore
W. Bromley	Wm. Bolton
	John Newsham
	Tho. Newsham

Warwick Burrough

At the Court of Record held . . . on Munday the twenty seventh day of May 1695

Present: the Rt Honourable the Lord Brook, the Rt Honourable the Lord Leigh, Sir Henry Puckering, Bart., Sir Thomas Wagstaffe, Kt, William Bromley, Esq., William Palmer, Esq., William Colemore, Esq., Charles Hicks, Mayor, William Bolton, Esq., John Newsham, Esq., Thomas Fetherston, Esq., Thomas Newsham, Esq.

Whereas informacion hath been given to this Court, that severall of the bills of losses both in houses and goods given in by the respective sufferers by the late fire, require a farther adjustment and regulacion, it is Ordered by the Commicioners now present in Court that Aaron Rogers, Richard Hands and Richard Lane gent., William Lingham, Edward Norton, Thomas Hicks, John Watson, Henry Heath, William Wilson, Thomas Roberts, John Davies and John Rogers gent., twelve of the most discreet and substantiall inhabitants of the said Borough, be desired to meet tomorrow at such time and place as they shall think most convenient, then and there to consider of and examine the severall bills and estimates given in by the said sufferers, and to reduce and regulate the same where they shall find cause according to the best of their judgments, and to make their report of what regulacion they shall think fitt to be made of the said bills to the next Court or soe much as they can have finished of the same by that time, that the Commicioners being thereby well apprized of the true valuacions of the severall losses may be the better enabled, to make such distribucion of the said charitie monies as shall best answer the necessities and losses of the said sufferers and the ends for which the said monies were given.

It appeareing to this Court that the ground call'd the poor's ground in an order of the last Court, is the ground of John Weale, gent., and the tenement lately standing thereon the house of the said John Weale lett att the rent of three pounds and seven shillings per annum, and the rent charge on the same to the use of the poor but two pounds twelve shillings per annum, it is Ordered that the said Mr Weale have his proporcion out of the nineteen pounds seven shillings given to the poor by order of the last Court being four pounds thirteen shillings and four pence.[1]

The Commicioners desired at the last Court to prepare and bring in a list of such sufferers as doe intend speedily to begin to rebuild their houses burnt down by the late fire, requireing farther time for the doeing the same, by reason of the many difficulties they meet with in the enquiries they have made, Ordered that farther time be given and that they be desired to bring in such a list soe soon as conveniently they may.

Agreed and resolved that according to the account brought in by Samuel Dunkley, of what ground is taken away from or added to the severall proprietors on the south side of the High Pavement the same be settled and confirmed by an order of the next Court.

Ordered that the summ of one hundred pounds given by an order of the last Court to the Corporacion in this Borough for the speedy repaireing of the chancell of Saint Maries Church, be paid by Mr Tarver out of the

---

[1] This sum is worked out in the margin.

charity monies lying in his hands to the present Mayor of this Borough, to be disposed of by him according to the intent and direccions of the said order.

H. Puckering
Tho. Wagstaffe
Wm. Colmore
Wm. Bolton

Brooke
John Newsham
Tho. Fetherston
Tho. Newsham

Warrwick Burrough
At the Court of Record held ... on Munday the third day of June 1695.

Present: The Rt. Honourable the Lord Brook, Sir Henry Puckering, Bart., William Colemore, Esq., William Bolton, Esq., John Newsham, Esq., Tho. Newsham, Esq., Charles Hicks, Mayor.

According to the schem or draught brought in by the Surveyors of the quantitys of ground taken away from or added to the severall proprietors of the houses rainging on the south side of the High Street, it is Ordered by this Court as followeth, that in pursuance of a former order for laying the lines and fixing the stakes on the south side of the said street, there be taken away from the street ground lying before the late house of Mr William Cook sixty four foot and six inches and that the same be added and given to the said William Cook; and that there be taken away from the street ground lying before the late house of Mr Edmund Wilson one hundred and fourteen foot and nine inches and that the same be added and given to the said Edmund Wilson, and that there be taken from the ground of the said street lying and being before the front of the late house of Thomas Archer, Esq., one hundred and fourteen foot and nine inches and that the same be added and given to the said Thomas Archer, and that there be taken from the ground of the said street lying and being before the front of the late house of Mr —— Green, ninety two feet and six inches, and that the same be laid to and given to the said Mr —— Green, and that there be taken from the ground of the said street lying and being before the front of the late houses of Mr Prescott three hundred seventy six foot and six inches, and that the same be added to and given to the said Mr Prescott, and that there be taken away from the ground of the said High Street fronting the late house of Mr Welton five hundred and tenn foot, and that the same be added to the ground of Mr Welton. And that there be taken from the ground of Mr Welton whereon stood his house to enlarge Fox his lane lying on the west side of the said house and adjoyning to it, five hundred seventy and five foot, and that the said Mr Welton be recompensed for the same according to the value thereof by the Commicioners out of the monies now lying in Mr Tarver's hands, and that there be taken away from the ground of Mr Tomkins to enlarge the High Street, twelve foot and six inches, and that there be taken away from the ground of the High Street fronting a house late belonging to this Corporacion, Thomas Gibbs tenant, twenty eight foot, and that the same be added to the Corporacion ground there, and that there be taken away from the ground of the said street fronting the late house called the White Lyon Inn, George Watts tenant, two foot, and that the same be added to the ground of the said inn, and that there be taken from the ground whereon stood the house late of Thomas Dixon fronting the High Street, to enlarge the same, fourty one foot and eleven inches, and that there be taken from the front ground whereon stood two houses belonging to Mr Weale, Humphrey Carter and widow Rider tenants, one hundred and fivety foot and four inches, to enlarge the said street, and that there be taken from the ground whereon stood a house late belonging to this Corporacion, George Harris tenant, one hundred fivety and eight foot to enlarge the said street, and alsoe that there be taken from the front ground of the widow Lucas one hundred and twelve foot to enlarge the said street, and that the severall proprietors of the ground taken away as aforesaid[1] to enlarge the said street, be allowed for the same according to the value thereof by the Commicioners out of the money lying in Mr Tarver's hands.

The Commicioners desired by the two last Courts to bring in a list of such sufferers as intend speedily to begin to rebuild their houses for the same reasons as in the said order alledged, requireing yet a farther time for the doeing the same, Ordered that a farther time be given to them, and that they be desired to hasten and perfect the same and to lay it before this Court soe soon as done.

The twelve persons desired by an order of the last Court to inspect, reduce and regulate the bills of losses given in by the sufferers by the late fire, haveing made some progress therein, requireing a farther time to perfect and finish the same, Ordered that a farther time be given and that they make report thereof to this Court soe soon as with convenience they may.

Ordered that William Tarver, Stephen Nicholls, Joseph Blissett, John Williams and William Roe, gent., be added to the twelve persons desired by the last Court to inspect, examine, reduce and regulate the bills and estimates of losses given in by the severall sufferers by the late fire, and that they be desired to joyne with, and assist them in the regulacion that shall be made and with them to make their report soe soon as conveniently they may.

	Brooke
Charles Hicks, Mayor	H. Puckering
John Newsham	Wm. Colmore
Tho. Newsham	Wm. Bolton

[1] 'as aforesaid' interlineated over a caret.

Warwick Burrough
At the Court of Record held ... on Munday the 17th[1] day of June 1695.

Present: The Rt. Honourable the Lord Brook, the Honourable Francis Grevile, Esq., Sir Henry Puckering, Bart., Charles Hicks, Mayor, William Colemore, Esq., John Newsham, Esq., Tho. Newsham, Esq.

Upon reading the peticion of Robert Cole to be relieved against John Hicks of this Borough, blacksmith, it is referred to the next Court to be considered of, and Ordered that summons goe forth to summon John Hicks to answer the contents of the peticion.

Ordered that according to the scheme and draught brought in by the Surveyors, of the quantityes of ground taken away from and added to the severall proprietors of the ground fronting the north side of the Jury Street, there be taken from the ground of Mr Ward one hundred thirty seven foot to enlarge the said street, and that there be taken from the ground of Nicholas Paris one hundred ninety and four foot to enlarge the said street, and that there be taken from the towne ground lying betwixt the ground of Nicholas Paris and that of Thomas Wall to enlarge the said street, one hundred twenty and six foot, and that there be taken from the ground of Thomas Wall one hundred thirty two foot to enlarge the said street, and that there be taken from the ground of the said street lying and being before the late house of Mr Blissett, one hundred and fourteen foot, and that the same be added to the ground of the said Mr Blissett.

Whereas all persons whose houses rainged with the streets as they are now sett and staked out, and whose rubbish was not then removed, were obliged by an order of this Court of the sixth day of May last to clear the same on or before the one and twentieth day of the same month, and wheras many of the said persons have neglected to clear their foundacions and the streets fronting their said houses of and from the rubbish lying thereon in contempt of the said order, it is therefore this day Ordered, that if the said rubbish and ruins be not carryed away and disposed of before the first day of July next, that labourers be forthwith employed and sett on work by the Treasurers of the charity monys to remove and carry away the same, and that they be paid for their said work out of the proporcions of the charity monys which, upon devidend to be made, shall be allotted to the respective sufferers who shall neglect to remove the same within the time hereby limited, and that notice be given of this order by affixing coppies thereof to the walls of the County Hall, Markett house and Mayor's Parlour.

Charles Hickes, mayor	H. Puckering
Tho. Newsham	Wm. Colmore
	John Newsham

[1] Interlineated over a caret above a word, probably 'tenth', struck out.

Warr' Burr'

At the Court of Record held ... on Munday the 24th day of June[1] 1695.

Present: Sir Henry Puckering, Bart., Sir John Burgoyne, Bart., Charles Hicks, Mayor, Wm. Colemore Esq., Wm. Bolton Esq., Tho. Fetherston Esq., John Newsham Esq., Tho. Newsham Esq.

O[rdered][2]

Warr' Burr'

At the Court of Record held ... on Munday the first day of July 1695

Present: The Rt. Honourable the Lord Brook, the Rt. Honourable the Lord Leigh, Sir Henry Puckering, Bart., William Bromley, Esq., Charles Hicks, Mayor, William Colemore, Esq., Henry Parker, Esq., Geo. Lucy, Esq., William Bolton, Esq., John Newsham, Esq., Tho. Newsham, Esq.

Memorandum that George Lucy, Esq. one of the Commicioners or Judges appointed by the said Act did then and there take the oath mencioned and directed in the said Act befor William Bromley, Esq. and Henry Parker, Esq., two of his Majestie's justices of the peace of the County of Warwick.

Ordered that Richard Kerby of this Borough pay to the four legatees in the will of Samuel Medley, viz. Margery Miller, Mary Lee, Faith Fowler, widow, and Humphrey Carter, the sum of twenty shillings each in full satisfaccion of twenty pounds, viz. five pounds a peice to each of them given and payable to them by the said will after the death of Jane Kerby, wife of the said Richard Kerby, out of the late messuage of the said Richard and Jane Kerby, charged with the payment of the said legacies, and that all persons interested therein joyn in conveying and assureing the toft whereon stood the said mesuage, to Edward Norton of this Borough, gent., in and for the consideracion of twenty pounds and one guinea by him paid to the said Richard and Jane Kerby, in full satisfaccion for the said toft; and that the purchase deed of the said messuage, and the said will of Samuel Medley, lye in this Court, to form and make a decree of this Court by, for the purpose aforesaid.

Ordered[3] by consent of all parties that Nicholas Paris and Thomas Wall paying to the Corporacion in this Borough, the summ of twenty five pounds, for the ground behind the stakes, lying betwixt the late houses of the said Nicholas Paris and Thomas Wall, the ground be assured to them

---

[1] Altered from 'July'.

[2] No business was entered for this court. The rest of the page and the next are blank. The rough minute book has an order that Mr Welton be lent £3.

[3] 'Stet' written in the margin against this order.

by decree of this Court, and that the Corporacion have a farther recompence out of the charity monies for the front part of the said ground staked and laid out into the Jury Street, to enlarge the same.

Whereas this Court is empowered by the said Act, to regulate the foundacions of the streets burnt downe by the late fire, and to open and enlarge others, and have the direccion and ordering of balconies and penthouses, and of the step or stepps out of the street into the first floor, and the building of garretts, with such roofs and lights as shall seem most commodious to them, for the better causeing the rules of building prescribed by the said Act to be observed, and putting in execution all such orders as have and shall be made touching measuring of ground, laying out the lines of the streets, makeing balconyes and penthouses, the stepps up into the houses, building of garretts, and other powers and authorities given by the said Act, they doe elect Samuell Dunkley, mason, John Phillips, carpenter, and William Smith, bricklayer, Surveyors of all buildings and other the premises to execute the said office, and from time to time to represent to this Court all irregularities and breaches of the rules of the said Act for building, and orders of this Court touching the premises; and they doe hereby vacate the order of the twenty second of May last makeing and appointing Samuell Dunkley, Tho. Masters and James Fish, senior, Surveyors.

Ordered that the Treasurers pay out of the charity monies lying and being in their hands the summ of one hundred and eighteen pounds fourteen shillings and six pence according to the list of sufferers and summs allotted to each of them by order of this Court, being the seventh distribucion made for the support of the sufferers by the late fire.

Ordered that the scheme or draught of the roofs of all houses to be rebuilt, and the manner of joyning the said houses together be the rules whereby all persons shall build their garretts and joyn their houses, and

Ordered that noe balconies or penthouses to be built and sett up, project from the respective houses more or less than three foot and six inches.

Whereas upon complaint made and informacion given, that many of the sufferers had overrated and given in immoderate estimates of their losses both in houses and goods, this Court did the twenty seventh day of May last desire several gentlemen of this Borough to inspect examine and reduce where they saw just reason the said estimates, and did joyn others to assist them on the third day of June last, and the said gentlemen haveing perus'd inspected and examined the said estimates and regulated and reduced the same according to the best of their skill and judgment, and given in to this court, subscribed with their names, a list of such persons as they thought fitt to reduce, together with the losses soe reduced, it is now ordered that the said regulacion and reducctions of losses be the rule whereby they govern themselves in the distribucions to be made to the severall and respective sufferers.

Whereas by an order of the twenty second day of May last, the Surveyors were required to inform themselves of the persons who did intend speedily to begin to rebuild, and by an order of the same Court, a distribucion was agreed to be made of the summ of six hundred pounds, to such persons as should begin to rebuild, and the Commissioners liveing within this Borough were desired to lay a list of such builders before the Court, and what summs were proper to be given to each of them; and it appearing by the list now brought in, that the said summ of six hundred pounds will not be a sufficient encouragement for such a number to induce them to build,

Ordered that such a summ be added to the six hundred pounds as with what they have already received will make up four shillings per pound to the severall sufferers whose names are hereunder written who purpose forthwith to begin to rebuild their houses, that the said monies be not paid them till the first floor of their respective houses be laid, or such security given for the laying out and disposeing the summs given in and towards their building as shall be approved of by order of this Court, and the intent and meaning of this order is that the proporcion of four shillings per pound is limitted to the loss of the house or houses only which they begin to rebuild, this being the eighth distribucion.[1]

John Prichard	James Fish	Tho. Dadley
Tho. Wise	Tho. Wall	Tho. Dixon
Richard Hadley	Nich. Paris	Mr Biker
Robert Watts	Tho. Clemens	Tho. Shatswell
Tho. Spencer	John Hicks	Bartlemew sen. and
Mrs Cawtherne	Widow Eles alias Williams	jun. and Edward Aston
Mr Jarvis	John Burton	John Tatnald
Mr Chesley	Mrs Mann	William Perks, baker.
Joseph Ainge	Mr Tho. Watts	

Ordered that a distribucion be made to the persons who are noe builders of such summs, which with what they have already received, will amount to two shillings and six pence in the pound, and that the Commissioners liveing within this Borough do prepare and bring in a list to the next Court of such sufferers, with the summs they have already received and what they are to receive to make up two shillings and six pence in the

---

[1] The names which follow are those of the sufferers in question.

pound and that theire names and the said summs be entered in the book of receipts and disbursements; this being the ninth distribucion.

	Brooke
Charles Hickes, Mayor	Wm. Colmore
Tho. Newsham	Wm. Bolton
H. Puckering	John Newsham

Warwick Borough
At the Court of Record held ... on Munday the 8th day of July 1695

Present: The Rt Honourable the Ld Brook, Sir Henry Puckering, Bart., Charles Newsham, Esq., Tho. Fetherston, Esq., William Bolton, Esq., John Newsham, Esq., William Colemore, Esq.

Ordered that noe matters in variance, or cause between party and party relateing to or within the cognisance of this Court, be admitted to be heard but by peticion in writeing directed to the Commicioners or Judges sitting in Court.

Ordered that the summ of one hundred fourty nine pounds five shillings and six pence be allowed out of the charity monies for removeing rubbish, casting lead, and buying the refiners proporcion of lead and bell mettall and other charges expended in and about the church of Saint Maries since the same was demolished by the late fire, the same appeareing unto us by the churchwardens bill to have been soe expended and that the Treasurers pay the same and place it to the account aforesaid.

Ordered that by consent of all parties, the severall parcells of Mr Cook's ground, lying next to Mrs Dorothy Weale's ground on the south side of the Highstreet, be conveyed and assured to the severall purchasers by decree of this Court, according to the draught or schem of the same delivered by Mr James Fish.

Ordered that the Surveyors view and sett out the street to be opened against the west end of St Maries Church, and alsoe the Swann Lane, as it is to be enlarged, and bring in a draught of the same at the next Court, in order to the haveing the said street and the said lane laid out, if the Commicioners shall approve the same.

Ordered that the examinacion of the distribution to be made of four shillings in the pound to the builders, and two shillings and six pence to the noe builders, as the same were cast up and brought into Court, this day be referred to the Treasurers to consider and adjust according to the losses of the respective sufferers, and the Treasurers haveing soe examined and adjusted the same, and obtained the hands in writeing of the Commissioners subscribed thereunto, are hereby empowred to distribute the said proporcions of four shillings in the pound and two shillings and six pence out of the charity monies lying in their hands.

Charles Hickes, Mayor	John Newsham
Geo. Lucy	H. Puckering
Wm. Bolton	Wm. Colmore
Tho. Newsham	

Warwick Borough
At the Court of Record held ... on Munday the 15th July 1695.

Present: Sir Henry Puckering, Bart., Charles Hicks, Mayor, William Colemore, Esq., George Lucy, Esq., William Bolton, Esq., Thomas Newsham, Esq.

Ordered that Mr Edmund Wilson, Samuell[1] Ainge and Richard Gibbard be entered into the list of builders, and have the encouragement given by an order of this Court of the first of July last, to builders.

That the consideracion of the petition of Stephen Nichols against Mr John Weale be referred to this[2] Court on Munday next.

Upon reading the peticion of Mrs Wagstaff, to be relieved against one William Gerrard of Henley, Ordered that summons goe forth to summon the said William Gerrard to appear at this Court on Munday next, to answer the contents of the peticion as prayed.

Upon reading the peticion of John Hicks, it is referred to the next Court to be considered of.

Upon reading the peticion of Richard Hands, it is ordered that summons goe forth to summon John Prichard to appear at this Court on Munday next to answer the contents of the peticion.

Ordered that a jury be impanelled to inquire into, and veiw the matter in difference between Mr William Tarver and Mr Foulk Weale, and give in their verdict of the same at this Court on Wensday next.

Ordered that the severall summs, given in an order for a distribucion of two shillings & six pence in the pound to the severall and respective sufferers who are noe builders, and alsoe in the distribucion of four shillings in the pound given to the present builders, be first paid out of the monys lying in the Treasurers' hands, as far as 'twill goe, and after they have paid out the monys lying and being in their hands, to pay the residue out of the monys

---

[1] Interlineated above 'Joseph' struck out.
[2] Altered from 'the next'.

lying in the chest at the Castle, and that the Treasurers doe state the accompt of what monies they have received and paid out to and for the use of the sufferers, and lay the same before the Commicioners at the next court, to be held on Wednesday next.

Memorandum that Mr Samuell Dunkley and Mr William Smith were then and there sworne, faithfully to execute the office of Surveyors, according to the contents of an order of Court made the first day of July instant according to the best of their skill and knowledge.

Ordered that Samuell Dunkley and William Smith doe take a view of all irregularities and breaches of the rules of the said Act and orders of this Court, touching building, that have been made, and give an account thereof at the next court.

Ordered that the payment of the summ of twenty six pounds and five shillings given to Elizabeth Carr and the summ of fifteen pounds twelve shillings and six pence given to Charles Emes in the distribucion of two shillings & six pence in the pound, be suspended till farther order of this Court; and that the payment of the summs given to Mr Biker, John Prichard and John Burton in the distribucion of four shillings in the pound, be alsoe suspended till farther order of this Court.

Charles Hickes, Mayor	H. Puckering
Tho. Newsham	Wm. Colmore
	Wm. Bolton

Warr' Borough
At the Court of Record held . . . on Wednsday the 17th July 1695.

Present: Sir Henry Puckering, Bart., William Colemore, Esq., Charles Hicks, Mayor, William Bolton, Esq., Thomas Newsham, Esq., John Newsham, Esq.

Ordered that the sum given to Thomas Shatswell in the distribucion made and ordered to be paid the first day of July be struck out of the said order of distribucion and that he receive only the summ of two pounds and twelve shillings given him in the distribucion of four shillings in the pound as a builder.

Whereas George Smith and his son George Smith haveing received in the first distribucion the summ of twenty shillings more than came to their share at the rate of two shillings and six pence in the pound, and George Barton twenty shillings less than his share, and the said George Smith haveing ten shillings allotted to him in the distribucion of two shillings and six pence in the pound, Ordered that the said George Barton have the said ten shillings, allotted to George Smith.

A jury being impanelled and sworne, according to an order of the last Court to try the matters in variance between William Tarver complainant and Fulke Weale defendant, touching the limitts and bounds of a parcell of ground lately purchased by the said Mr[1] Tarver of Thomas Dadley, by their verdict they find, the widness of the front of the said ground, takeing it from the rainge of a front wall of the said complainants next adjoyning, to be nine foot and nine inches, from the brick wall of Tho. Dadley his new building to the outside of the said complainants ground lately purchased of Thomas Dadley to be six foot and six inches and three quarters of an inch, as it is now staked out by the said jury with three stakes and nailes fixed on the same.

Ordered that the ground that the complainant purchased of Thomas Dadley be assured to him by decree of this Court, according to the verdict brought in by the jury impanelled to try the matters in variance between the said William Tarver and Fulk Weale touching the said ground.

Ordered that the Surveyors veiw and sett out the eastside of the Church Street and report the same to this Court on Munday next.

Charles Hickes, Mayor	H. Puckering
Tho. Newsham	Wm. Colmore
John Newsham	Wm. Bolton

Warwick Borough
At the Court of Record held ... on Munday the 22th of July 1695.

Present: The Honourable Francis Grevile Esq., Sir Henry Puckering, Bart., Sir Thomas Wagstaff, Kt., Charles Hicks, Mayor, William Bolton, Esq., William Colemore, Esq., Thomas Newsham, Esq.

Upon heareing the peticion of Tho. Dixon of this Borough, blacksmith, read, Ordered that summons goe forth to summon Dorothy Hopkins of Welsborne, widow, to appeare at this Court on Munday next come sevenight to answer the contents of the said peticion.

Upon heareing the peticion of John Ashwin read, Ordered that summons goe forth to summon Eleanor Peirce to appeare at this Court on Munday next come sevenight, to answer the contents of the said peticion.

Upon reading the peticion of Richard Hands of this Borough against John Prichard, setting forth that he had a mortgage of eighty pounds on the late house of the said John Prichard and praying he may have the proporcion of the charity allotted to the loss of the said house, the said John Prichard appeareing in Court, it was agreed between both partyes, that the peticioner

---

[1] 'Mr' interlineated over a caret.

should in consideracion of his mortgage money and interest, have the toft whereon the said house stood, and the share of charity monys that will fall to the said house, and thereupon Ordered by this Court, that the peticioner have the said toft discharged of all equity of redempcion, and the share of charity money, and the defendant be discharged of all covenants, bonds and agreements for the payment of the mortgage money and interest.

Upon reading the peticion of Mary Wagstaff, widow, of this Borough, and Elias Webb of Shirborne in the County of Warwick, gent., against William Gerrard of the City of Worcester, gent., Ordered that the defendant Gerrard, lessee to the said Mary Wagstaffe, be discharged of the covenants in his lease, and the lease be cancelled, he paying the arrears of rent due from the feast of St John Baptist 1694 to the fourth day of September following, and accounting to the lessor for the proffitts made by sheeppens on the premisses, from and after the late fire to this time.

It being agreed between the said Mary Wagstaffe, tenant for life in the messuage late in the occupacion of the said William Gerrard and alsoe in the messuage next adjoyning late in the possession of Thomas Rush, and the said Elias Webb who hath a remainder for life in both the said messuages, that the toft whereon the said messuages stood be assured to the said Elias Webb and his heirs forever, by decree of this Court; Ordered that the said Elias Webb, satisfying this Court that he hath the consent of all other persons interested in the premises, have the same assured to him accordingly, and that the rebuilding the said two messuages have the encouragement given to builders.

Ordered that the said William Gerrard have four pounds seven shillings and sixpence, being two shillings and sixpence per pound for his loss as it is now reduced to thirty five pounds, and that the loss of the said Mary Wagstaffe be reduced to fourscore pounds.

Ordered that the payment of the charity monies given to the widow Whinnick in the distribucion of two shillings and six pence in the pound be suspended till farther order be given for the same.

Ordered that William Mann the son of the peticioner Mary Mann, Thomas Mann and Robert Mann, sons of Thomas Mann by Alice Fox, and William Mann and John Hicks be summoned to appeare at this Court on Munday come sevenight, to answer the peticion of the said Mary Mann touching the property of the ground whereon she proposeth to build, that the same may be settled by this Court, and shee be encouraged with safety to proceed in the same.

Ordered that Alexander Nichols of this Borough, tallow chandler, be entered into the list of builders for the house wherein he[1] dwelt before the late fire, and have the encouragement given to builders.

Memorandum that John Phillips of Broadway in the County of Gloucester, carpenter, made one of the Surveyors by order of this Court of the first day of July last, was this day sworne to execute the office of Surveyor according to the directions given in the said order.[2]

Charles Hickes, Mayor	F. Grevile
Tho. Wagstaffe	H. Puckering
Tho. Newsham	Wm. Colmore[3]

Warwick Borough

At the Court of Record held ... on Tuesday the 30th day of July anno domini 1695.

Present: Sir Henry Puckering, Bart., Sir Richard Verney, Kt, Sir John Clopton, Kt, Sir William Underhill, Kt, Sir Thomas Wagstaffe, Kt, William Bromley, Esq., Henry Parker, Esq., Charles Newsham, Esq., William Palmer, Esq., William Colemore, Esq., George Lucy, Esq., William Bolton, Esq., John Newsham, Esq., Thomas Newsham, Esq.

Memorandum that Sir William Underhill, Kt., and Henry Parker, Esq., being Commicioners or Judges appointed by the said Act, did then and there take the oath mencioned and directed in the said Act, before William Bromley, Esq., and Charles Newsham Esq., two of his Majesties justices of the peace of the county of Warwick.

For the greater grace and ornament of the Church of Saint Maries, and convenience of this Borough, according to the powers and authority given by the said Act, this Court doth order a large and spacious place, square or street to be opened over against the west front of the said church, and from thence to be continued to the New Street in manner and form and according to the dimencions herein after expressed. That is to say, that according to the draught brought in and laid before the Commicioners, the said place, square or street containe in breadth seventy two foot from one end to the

[1] The rough minute book has 'his father and he'.

[2] The rough minute book has an additional paragraph: 'Ordered that Samuel Ainge bee entered as a builder, and have the encouragement of a builder.'

[3] The rough minute book has an additional court at this point:
'Warr' Borough
'At the Court of Record held ... on Monday the 29th of July 1695
'Present: The Honourable Francis Grevile, Esq., Sir Henry Puckering, Bart., William Bromley, Esq., Henry Parker, Esq., Charles Newsham, Esq., William Colemore, Esq., John Newsham, Esq., Thomas Newsham, Esq.
'Ordered that no person presume to lay any more rubbish in the holes before the front of the house of Mr Aileworth in the Butts.'

other and in length from the east end to the west end thereof, the dimencions and number of feet following (viz.) from the corner of the north side whereon stood the parsonage house to the west end on the same side, eighty foot, and from the corner whereon stood the house of Edward Chesley on the south side of the said street to the further end on the same side, ninety and five foot, and that the Surveyors stake out the said place, square or street according to the lines and number of feet aforesaid.

Alsoe ordered that according to the draught mencioned in the next preceeding order, the street to be opened at the west end of the said square and leading into the street called the New Street doe containe in breadth thirtysix foot from one end to the other and in length on the north side of the said street, one hundred and ten foot, (viz.) from the angle of the square to the angle nere Burtons corner, and in length on the south side of the said street (viz.) from the angle of the said square to Clemens his house, one hundred and ten foot, and that the Surveyors stake out the same accordingly.

| John Newsham | W.Palmer | H. Puckering |
| Tho: Newsham | Tho: Wagstaffe | Wm Colmore |

Warwick Borough
At the Court of Record held ... on Munday the 5th day of August 1695

Present: the Honourable Francis Grevile, Esq., Sir Henry Puckering, Bart., Charles Hicks, Mayor, Thomas Fetherstone, Esq., William Bolton, Esq., John Newsham, Esq., Thomas Newsham, Esq.

Ordered that the cornish of the three corner houses pointing upon the Cross be made of wood, with cantilavers, answerable the one house to the other, and that the cornish with the cantilavers doe project from the wall two and twenty inches.

Ordered that Mr Chernock be summon'd to appeare at this Court on Munday next, in order to the setting out his ground, and regulateing the square to be made before the front of the west end of Saint Maries Church, and settleing all other matters and disputes that shall arise concerning the same.

Memorandum that an order to Mr Tarver this day was signed, for the payment of one hundred pounds, given to the Corporacion by an order of this Court of the twenty second day of May last, toward the repaireing the chancel, and alsoe an order to Mr Tarver to pay the summ of four pounds thirteen shillings and four pence given to Mr John Weale by an order of the same Court.

Upon reading the peticionof the widow Mann against John Hicks and severall other persons in the said peticion mencioned, it is ordered by consent of both partyes that Mrs Mann paying to the said John Hicks the summ of fourty shillings, the said John Hicks be barr'd of all right and title which he claims or might have had in the messuage in the said peticion mencioned, and that the ground be assured to the said Mrs Mann, by decree of this Court.

Whereas Frances[1] Commander did put in a bill of her loss soon after the late fire which happened to be lost, it is ordered that the said Frances[1] Commander be admitted to put in a bill of thirty five shillings, and that she receive such proporcions of the charity monies as the commicioners shall think fitt.

Ordered that the widow Hopkins remove the rubbish out of the cellars of her house, late the White Lyon Inn, on or before Wensday next, and that if she neglect to doe the same, that workmen be imploy'd to carry away the same and the charges thereof to be deducted out of the share of the charitie monies to be allotted to her.

That upon reading the peticion of John Ashwin to be relieved against Elianor Peirce wife of Thomas Peirce, senior, of Harvington in the county of Worcester, and upon the appeareance of Thomas Peirce in the behalf of his wife, it is ordered by this Court by consent of parties, that Thomas Peirce receive out of the charity monies given to the widow Ashwin in the distribucion of two shillings and six pence per pound[2] the summ of seven pounds, and that the peticioner John Ashwin have the other part of the said charity monyes and that the toft[3] whereon stood the messuage in the peticion mencion'd, be assured to the said John Ashwin by decree of this Court, and that the said John Ashwin rebuilding the said house have[4] the encouragement as a rebuilder.

Ordered that the Treasurers be desired to meet at the Mayor's Parlour to morrow morning, to distribute the monies given to such sufferers who are noe builders in the distribucion of two shillings and six pence in the pound, and that the beedle give notice to the severall sufferers to appeare to receive the same accordingly.

Upon reading the peticion of William Perks against John Eld, ordered that

---

[1] 'Frances' inserted in a space previously left blank.
[2] 'per pound' interlineated over a caret.
[3] 'the toft' interlineated over a caret.
[4] 'have' altered from 'haveing'.

a jury be impanelled to veiw and try the matters in variance between the said parties on Munday next.

Charles Hickes, Mayor	Wm Bolton
F. Grevile	John Newsham
H. Puckering	Tho: Newsham

Warwick Borough
At the Court of Record held . . . on Munday the 12th day of August 1695

Present: the Honourable Francis Grevile, Esq., Sir Henry Puckering, Bart., Sir Thomas Wagstaff, Kt, Charles Hicks, Mayor, William Colemore, Esq., William Bolton, Esq., William Bromley, Esq., John Newsham, Esq., Thomas Newsham, Esq.

Ordered that Mrs Hannah Doolittle be allowed and paid two shillings and six pence in the pound according to her bill of loss given in of the summ of thirty five pounds and twelve shillings.

A jury being impannelled and sworne according to an order of the last Court, to try the matters in variance between William Perks complainant and John Eld defendant, touching a party wall between the said William Perks and the said John Eld, by their verdict they find, the complainant's ground[1] from the middle of the party wall between Mrs Palmer and the complainant's ground to the middle of the party wall between the complainant's and the said John Eld to be thirty one foot and an inch wide in the front next the Church Street, and the widness of the back front of the said ground takeing it from the middle of the same party walls to be thirty two foot and half an inch, as the same is now staked out by the said jury.

Ordered that the cornish of the three corner houses pointing upon the cross, be made of wood with cantilavers as in an order of the last Court and that the same to be continued, to project from the wall twenty two inches round the said houses.

Ordered that Mrs Marianna Duckett be allowed two shillings and six pence in the pound, according to her bill of losses given in of the summ of eight pounds.

Ordered that Samuel Barber be allowed three pounds and six shillings in full of his bill of loss given in of ten pounds, and that he be paid the same out of the charity monies.

Whereas by an order of the fifteenth day of July last, the summ given to John Burton in the distribucion of four shillings in the pound was

[1] 'complainant's ground' interlineated over a caret.

suspended till farther order of this Court, it is now ordered that the sus-
pencion be taken of, and he be paid the summ of thirty two pounds and ten
shillings allotted him in the said distribucion.[1]

Ordered that Mr Blissett pull down his upper row of lutherne lights, it
being judged built contrary to an order of this Court of the first day of July
last, and that noe person for the future build contrary to the schem or
draught brought in by Mr Phillips of the roofs of all houses to be rebuilt,
and that they put up one row of luthern lights and noe more in the fore
fronts of their houses.

Charles Hickes, Mayor	F. Grevile
Tho. Newsham	H. Puckering
Tho. Wagstaffe	Wm Colmore
	John Newsham

Warwick Borough
At the Court of Record held ... on Munday the 19th day of August 1695

Present: the Honourable Francis Grevile, Esq., Sir Henry Puckering, Bart.,
Charles Hicks, Mayor, William Colemore, Esq., Andrew Archer, Esq., William Bolton, Esq., John Newsham, Esq., Thomas Newsham, Esq.

Ordered that the widow Dickins be allowed more then what she have
already received in the distribucions hitherto made, one pound ten shillings
in full of her loss given in of five pounds.[2]

Ordered that the summ of twenty two pounds and tenn shillings given to
Mr Webb in the distribucion of two shillings and six pence per li.[3] be
suspended till farther order of this Court, and that he be desired to bring in
and lay before this court on Munday next a bill of the particulars of his loss
by the late fire.

Whereas Mr Edmund Wilson, Samuell Ainge and Alexander Nicholls were
ordered their full proporcion according to their losses in the distribucion of
two shillings and six pence in the pound, in an order of Court made the first
day of July last, and are since entered as builders in an order of Court made
the fifteenth day of July last and in another made the 22d day of the same
month, it is ordered that they receive the severall summs, sett against their

---

[1] Followed in the rough minute book by this additonal paragraph:
'Whereas informacion hath been given to this Court by Mr Dunkley one of the Surveyors, that Mr
Watts hath built his house adjoyning to the Gaole irregular and contrary to the Act of Parliament and
orders of this Court for building, it is ordered that Mr Watts be summon'd to appear att the next Court
to answer the same, and that in the mean time he proceed noe farther in building while the same be
settled by this Court.'
[2] Followed in the rough minute book by: 'Memorandum to see Mr Gibbs his lease, what rent and
what laid out in repaires.'
[3] 'per li.' inserted in a space at the end of a line.

severall names, in a list made and signed by the Commicioners this day, to make up what they were before ordered four shillings in the pound, and that Mr Richard Hands receive the summ sett against his name in the said distribucion for the loss of John Prichard his house in the Sheepstreet, and that the severall other persons in the same list, who were omitted in the severall distribucions heretofore made, doe receive the severall summs set against their respective names, amounting in the whole to one hundred and ten pounds nine shillings and six pence as by the said list and summs may appeare, this being the tenth distribucion.

Charles Hickes, Mayor   John Newsham
Tho: Newsham   Wm Colmore
F. Grevile   Wm Bolton
H. Puckering

Warwick Borough
At the Court of Record held . . . on Munday the 26th of August 1695

Present: the Rt Honourable the Lord Brook, the Honourable Francis Grevile, Esq., Sir Henry Puckering Bart., Sir John Burgoyne, Bart., Charles Hicks, Mayor, Wm Palmer, Esq., Wm Colemore, Esq., John Newsham, Esq., Thomas Newsham, Esq.

Upon reading the peticion of Mr Richard Gibbard to be relieved against Mrs Dorothy Weale touching a gutter of lead lying betwixt their houses, ordered that Mrs Weale be summoned to appeare and answer the peticion at three of the clock in the afternoon this day.

Order'd that Mrs Cawthern be allowed fifteen pounds being four shillings in the pound for the loss of her house in the Churchstreet of seventy five pounds, and that she receive for the loss of her three houses in the Sheep Street and two in the Butts being three hundred thirty nine pounds and ten shillings, out of which the fifteen pounds she hath already received being deducted at two shillings and six pence in the pound, she is to receive twenty seven pounds seven shillings and six pence, and for the loss of her goods of fourty pounds at two shillings and six pence in the pound, the summ of five pounds, to receive in the whole fourty seven pounds seven shillings and six pence[1] and to John Hicks twelve shillings for his loss in goods of 3 li.[2]

Richard Gibbard and Mrs Dorothy Weale appeareing in Court at the time appointed and comeing to noe agreement in the matters in controversie between them, it is ordered that the witnesses hereunder named on both

---

[1] The sum has been worked out in the margin.
[2] 'of 3 li.' inserted in a space at the end of a line.

sides be subpena'd to appear and give in their evidence touching the said matters at the next Court by eleven of the clock in the forenoone, to the end they may be there heard and determined.

Witnesses: for Mr Gibbard the complainant — Edward Scott, George Hawkes, George Coplin, Thomas Coplin and William Grey.
: for Mrs Weale the defendant — Edward Atkins, William Eborall, Robert Farmer, Thomas Smith, Hancox glazier, Thomas Masters.

Complaint haveing been made to this Court that great quantities of earth and rubbish have been lately carried and laid in the streets, lanes and passages in and about this towne to the prejudice of the said wayes and passages, it is ordered by this Court that for the time to come no person carry or lay or cause to be carried and laid any earth or rubbish in any publick or open part of the town, without the leave and direccions of the respective surveyors of the parish where it is intended to be soe laid, first had and given, except in a place called the Butts, in the hollow parts whereof, any persons have liberty to lay what quantities they please, without such leave and direccion.

Upon reading the peticion of Mrs Cawtherne, it is ordered that a jury be impanelled to veiw and try the matters in difference between Mr Fulk Weale and the peticioner concerning the setting out the bounds of the foundacions in dispute between them.

	Brooke
Charles Hickes, Mayor	H. Puckering
Tho: Newsham	F. Grevile
John Newsham	Wm Colmore

Warwick Borough
At the Court of Record held . . . on Munday the 2nd day of September anno domini 1695

Present: the Rt Honourable the Lord Brooke, the Honourable Francis Grevile, Esq., Sir Henry Puckering, Bart., Sir Thomas Wagstaff, Knt, Charles Hicks, Mayor, William Colemore, Esq., William Bolton, Esq., Thomas Peers, Esq., John Newsham, Esq., Thomas Newsham, Esq.

There[1] being an agreement made between Samuel Ainge and Thomas Leane for an exchange of some ground lying intermixed betwixt them, ordered that the parties delivering in their peticion for the same to this Court according to the draught now brought in by the Surveyors of the said

---

[1] 'Quere' in the margin against the beginning of this paragraph.

ground, a decree be formed to ratifie the said agreement and exchange pursuant thereunto.

The jury impanelled between Mrs Elizabeth Cawthern and Mr Fulk Weale doe find that from the middle of Mr Tarver his party wall to the middle of Mrs Cawthern her party wall in the front to the Church Street is twelve foot one inch and three quarters of an inch and the back front from the middle of the said party walls eleven foot and ten inches.

The jury impanelled to try the matters in variance between Richard Gibbard complainant and Fulk Weale defendant, concerning a gutter lying between the complainants house and the Signe of the Blew Bell, doe find that Mr Gibbard hath not encroached upon the house of Mr Weale, he being upon his own foundacion tho' he hath cutt into his sill, the sill butting inwards about two inches, and for the gutter they doe find it Mr Weale's in respect of his haveing repaired it, and they doe alsoe find that Mr Weale hath taken away the leade and that if the gutter is not laid speedily it must needs be a damage to the house of the complainant.

	Brooke
Charles Hickes, Mayor	Wm Colmore
F. Grevile	Wm Bolton
Tho. Wagstaffe	John Newsham

Warwick Borough
At the Court of Record held ... on Munday the ninth day of September anno domini 1695

Present: the Rt Honourable the Lord Brook, the Honourable Francis Greville, Esq., Sir Thomas Wagstaff, Kt., William Palmer, Esq., Andrew Archer, Esq., William Colemore, Esq., Thomas Peers, Esq., Charles Hicks, Mayor, William Bolton, Esq., John Newsham, Esq., Thomas Newsham, Esq.

Ordered that a day be appointed by the Treasurers for payment of the sums given to the severall sufferers by the late fire in the distribucion of four shillings and two shillings and six pence in the pound, and that they have notice to come and receive the same allotted to them as aforesaid.

The jury upon the valuacion of Mr Fulk Chernock his ground doe find by an estimate taken by the Surveyors that the same ground doth containe six thousand four hundred ninetey three foot or thereabouts, and doe judge and rate the same to be worth threescore and seven pounds and twelve shillings, and the said Mr Chernock to have all the materialls and rubbish that lye on and belong to the same.

Ordered that the sufferers who had ground taken from them on the south side of the High Street to enlarge the said street from Thomas Dixon's house to the widow Lucas her ground, be allowed nine pence a foot for every foot soe taken from them as aforesaid.

Ordered that Mr Williams be allow'd five pounds more then he is already allowed in the distribucion of two shillings and six pence in the pound, the five pounds that he received before being to be reconned as money given for the use of, and to secure, the felon prisoners.

Memorandum that Thomas Peirce, Esq., being a Commicioner or Judge appointed by the said Act, did then and there take the oath mencioned and directed in the said Act before Andrew Archer, Esq., and William Palmer, Esq., two of his Mayestyes justices of the peace of the county of Warwick.

Ordered that the widow Mann be allowed two shillings and six pence in the pound according to her loss out of the charity monys allotted her in the distribucion of four shillings in the pound, shee being entered as a builder in the said order of distribucion.

Upon reading the peticion of Timothy Norberry against Mr John Williams, ordered that the same be refered to the next Court to be considered of.

Ordered that eight pounds be allowed out of the charity monies to Mr James Fish, junior,[1] for draweing the survey of the town, attending this Court, and all other business that he hath been employed about by the Commicioners since the late fire.

Wm. Bolton	Brooke
John Newsham	F. Grevile
Tho. Newsham	Tho. Wagstaffe
	Wm. Colmore

Warwick Borough
At the Court of Record held ... on Munday the 16th day of September anno domini 1695.

Present: the Rt Honourable the Lord Brooke, the Honourable Francis Grevile, Esq., Sir Richard Verney, kt., Sir Thomas Wagstaffe, Kt, William Colemore, Esq., William Bolton, Esq., George Lucy, Esq., John Newsham, Esq., Thomas Peers, Esq., Thomas Newsham, Esq.

Upon heareing the peticion of William Bolton, Esq., read, ordered that summons goe forth to summon Mr Fulk Weale to appear att this Court on Munday next to answer the contents of the said peticion.

[1] Altered in the rough minute book from 'Mr Fish and his son ... that they have....'

Upon heareing the peticion of Richard Gibbard of this Borough, maulster, read, to be relieved against Mrs Dorothy Weale concerning a gutter of lead which was in dispute between them, and upon which a jury was impanell'd to veiw and determine the same, and they upon veiw and examinacion thereof did find the right of the said gutter to be in the said Mrs Weale and she to repair the same, it is therefore ordered that the said Mrs Weale doe lay the said gutter of lead and finish the same by Munday next pursuant to the said order, as she will answer the contrary at her perill.

It appeareing to this Court that Jane Dale wife of Phillip Dale did give in a bill of her loss by the late fire of the summ of sixteen shillings, which bill was lost, it is therefore ordered that the said Jane Dale be allowed the summ of ten shillings for her loss given in[1] as aforesaid.

Ordered that Mary Low be allowed nine shillings and six pence for her bill of loss given in of nineteen shillings, she being omitted in the distribucions hitherto made.

Ordered that Mr John Williams pay to Timothy Norberry his tennant the summ of four pounds toward the repaire of his house in the Jury Street damnified by the late fire, and the said Timothy Norberry to be allowed two shillings and six pence in the pound for the loss of the said house given in att eleven pounds, being 1 7 6d.[2]

Upon reading the peticion of Thomas Mayo of Rughby, to be relieved against Edward Aston of this Borough, ordered that summons goe forth to summon the said Edward to appeare in this Court on Munday next, to answer the contents of the said peticion.

According to the powers given to the Commicioners by the said Act, of setting the rates on bricks and tyles to be used within the said Borough, ordered that noe brick or tyle maker take or receive more then the summ of fourteen shillings per thousand for bricks or sixteen shillings per thousand for tiles, untill the same rate and prices shall be altered by order of this Court.

Ordered that Mr Jemmatt of St Nicholas, Warwick, being desired by the Commicioners to waite on the Bishop of Worcester to have his lordships direccions for the keeping a day yearly of humiliacion in memory of the late dreadfull fire here, be allowed eleven shillings and six pence for his charges for his said journey.

Ordered that Thomas Clemens be paid the twenty six pounds allotted him in the distribucion of four shillings in the pound, he [having] given security

[1] 'given in' interlineated over a caret.
[2] 'being 1 7 6d.' added in a space at the end of a line.

that he will lay the foundacions and the first floor of the front ground which he hath not yett built upon.

	Brooke
John Newsham	F. Grevile
Tho. Newsham	Tho. Wagstaffe
Wm Bolton	Wm Colmore

Warwick Borough
At the Court of Record held ... on Munday the twenty third day of September 1695.

Present: the Rt Honourable the Lord Brook, the Honourable Francis Grevile, Esq., Sir Henry Puckering, Bart., Sir William Boughton, Bart., Sir Richard Verney, Kt., Sir Thomas Wagstaff, Kt., William Bromley, Esq., Charles Newsham, Esq., William Colemore, Esq., George Lucy, Esq., William Bolton, Esq., John Newsham, Esq., Thomas Newsham, Esq.

Memorandum that Sir William Boughton, Bart., one of the Commicioners or Judges appointed by the said Act of Parliament did then and there take the oath mencioned and directed in the said Act before William Bromley, Esq., and Charles Newsham, Esq., two of his Majesty's justices of the peace for the county of Warwick.

Ordered that Mr Mayor, Mr Bolton and Mr Thomas Newsham, three of the Commicioners of this court, be desired to examine the matters in dispute between Roger Hurlbutt and Edward Chesley and give the Commicioners an account of the same at the next Court.

Upon appearance of Edward Aston of this Borough to answer the peticion of Thomas Mayo and upon veiw made by the Surveyors of the house now rebuilt since the late fire by the said Edward Aston, they doe find that he has not encroched upon any part of the ground next adjoyning to his house, and forasmuch as it appears to this court that the said house before the late fire was mortgaged to Mr [   ]¹ Lingham of this Borough with another house adjoyning to it by one Edward Mayo, who had noe right to mortgage the house in controversie and that the same was assigned over to Thomas Mayo of Rughby the now peticioner, ordered that the said Edward Aston enjoy the said house now rebuilt without any molestacion of him the said Thomas Mayo freed from all incumbrances and that the same be assured to him by decree of this Court.

Ordered that the matters in dispute between William Bolton, Esq., complainant, and Mr Fulk Weale defendant be referr'd to the Court to be held on the 7th of October next² to be considered of.

¹ A space not filled in.   ² Altered from 'the next Court'.

Ordered that Thomas Griffin be allowed to make up his loss with what he hath already received 4s. in the pound being[1] the summ of ten shillings

	Brooke
Tho. Newsham	F. Grevile
Tho. Wagstaffe	Wm Colmore
John Newsham	Wm Bolton

Warwick Borough
At the Court of Record held ... on Munday the 30th day of September anno domini 1695.

Present: the Rt Honourable the Lord Brook, the Honourable Francis Grevile, Esq., Sir Thomas Wagstaff, Kt., William Colemore, Esq., William Bolton, Esq., Thomas Newsham, Esq.

Ordered that what monies are yett wanting to make up four shillings in the pound to the tenements belonging to the surveyors of the highways[2] be paid to the said surveyors of the highways, to be disposed of for rebuilding the said two tenements that stood on their ground as they shall think fitt.

Ordered that the consideracion of the peticion of Roger Hurlbutt of the last Court be referr'd over to the next Court.

Ordered that what monies were allotted to Sarah Mayo, sempstress, and which were by mistake paid to another, she have the same allowed to her out of the charity monies.

Ordered that twenty shillings be given to Francis Woodhams for his attendance on this Court to this time

	Brooke
Tho. Newsham	F. Grevile
Wm Bolton	Wm Colmore
	Tho. Wagstaffe

Warwick Borough
At the Court of Record held ... on Munday the seventh day of October anno domini 1695.

Present: the Rt Honourable the Lord Brooke, the Honourable Francis Grevile, Esq., Sir Thomas Wagstaff, Kt., Simon Biddulph, Esq., George Lucy, Esq., William Colemore, Esq., William Bolton, Esq., Thomas Newsham, Esq.

---

[1] 'being' interlineated over a caret.
[2] i.e. the parish officers.

Ordered that one pound sixteen shillings be putt into the hands of the surveyors of the highwayes of St Maryes parish in this Borough to be given to Thomas Hancox or Edward Cornwell, which of them and what proporcion they think fitt, toward the rebuilding the two tenements given to the repaires of the high wayes, which summ makes up four shillings in the pound to the loss of the said two tenements.

Ordered that Mr Heath have leave to front his particion wall with coyns of stone and that the next builder pay the moiety of the charge of the said party wall, and that the said Mr Heath have liberty to make a breake in the front of his house projecting two inches and noe more beyond the ground table.

Ordered that Doctor Johnson[1] and Nicholas Paris be summon'd next Court to answer the peticion of Mr Edward Heath alderman of this Borough.

Ordered that Mrs Martha Clopton be summon'd to appeare in this Court this day fortnight to answer the peticion of Edward Clopton, Esq., her husband.

Ordered that Thomas Dadley, according to a resolucion of a former Court, pay one shilling and six pence per quarter to Judith Dunn for her interest in a chamber in the late house of the said Thomas Dadley.

Ordered that Mr Bolton have a coppy of Mr Weale's answer to his peticion in order to make his reply thereto the next Court.

Ordered that Mr Moses Robinson be surveyor and director of all earth and rubbish where it shall be laid, and that he acquaint this Court, where he shall find occasion, with all offences that shall be comitted by the carryers and layers of the rubbish, and that the said carriers levell the earth att the Butts with the high way on the west side of the said Butts, and lay none in the ditch betwixt the said Butts and Dr Johnson's garden

Ordered that the consideracion of Roger Hurlbutt's peticion be referred againe over to the next Court.

Ordered that nine pence per foot be paid to Nicholas Paris, Thomas Wall, Mr Ward and the Corporacion for the front ground taken from theire houses in the Jury Street and that the same be paid out of the charity mony.

| Geo. Lucy | Tho. Wagstaffe | Brooke |
| Wm Colmore | Wm. Bolton | F. Grevile |

---

[1] 'Johnson' interlineated over a caret.

Warwick Borough

At the Court of Record held ... on Munday the 14th day of October anno domini 1695.

Present: the Rt Honourable the Lord Brook, Sir Henry Puckering, Bart., Sir John Mordaunt, Bart., Sir Richard Verney, Kt., Sir Thomas Wagstaffe, Kt., William Colemore, Esq., Charles Newsham, Esq., Charles Hicks, Mayor, William Bolton, Esq., John Newsham, Esq., Thomas Newsham, Esq.

Memorandum. It appeareing that the number of feet of ground taken away from Mr Cook and given to Mr Weale by order of the sixth day of May last was not right cast up, being by that order but one hundred fifty and seven feet, ordered that the same be rectified, and that Mr Cook be allowed for one hundred sixty and one foot, twelve pence per foot, and that the Receivers pay the same.

Ordered that Doctor Johnson have time given him to put in his answer to the peticion of Mr Heath till next Court.

That Mr Bolton have time given him to reply to the answer of Mrs Weale till the next Court.

Ordered that one hundred and sixteen pounds, being four shillings in the pound for the loss of the gaole given in, be paid by the Receivers to Mr Williams for the use of the county, according to an order of the justices at the last Generall Quarter Sessions of the county.

John Newsham	Wm Colmore	Brooke
H. Puckering	Wm Bolton	Tho. Wagstaffe

Warwick Borough

At the Court of Record held ... on Munday the one and twentieth day of October anno domini 1695

Present: the Rt. Honourable the Lord Brook, the Rt. Honourable the Lord Digby, the Honourable Francis Grevile, Esq., William Bromley, Esq., Sir Henry Puckering, Bart., Sir Thomas Wagstaffe, Kt., Andrew Archer, Esq., William Palmer, Esq., George Lucy, Esq., William Colemore, Esq., William Bolton, Esq., John Newsham, Esq., Thomas Newsham, Esq.

Ordered that the Chamberlains[1] and the Surveyors be desired to view the foot way in a ground called the Pigwells next the Pryory Lane, and stake out a way for carts to bring and carry bricks and tiles and other materialls through the same that will prove least prejudiciall to the tenant of the said Pigwells, and to estimate what damage the said way will be to Mr Prichett

[1] Sc. of St Mary's Commons.

tenant of the said ground, and report the same to this Court on Munday morning next.

Ordered that the business depending between Mr Edward Heath and Doctor Johnson be referred to the Court to be held at the Mayor's Parlour this day three weeks and that both partyes have notice to have their witnesses ready at that time.

Ordered that the building called the High Cross scituate in the center of the towne be taken downe and the pump removed before the next Court, and that Mr Dunkley forthwith employ workmen to take down the same and carry the stons soe taken downe into the church yard and the rubbish to the Butts.

This Court doth think fitt to make choice of Mr Mayor of this Borough for the time being, Mr Edward Heath, Mr Jemmat vicar of Saint Nicholas and Mr Thomas Newsham Treasurers of the breif money collected and to be collected for the use of the poor sufferers by the late fire within this Borough.

Ordered that every man remove his rubbish from before his doors in the burnt streets, the Church Street to be cleared of the same fourty foot wide, the Sheepstreet the same, the High Street to be cleared to the scaffolds, and that Solomon Bray be treated withal to open the passage against the church according to his old agreement, and on the performance of such agreement as shall be made by the Commicioners to be discharged of his former agreement, and that Mr Robinson be the surveyor and director of the streets soe to be cleared, and represent all negligences therein and defaults to this Court.

Ordered that a jury be impannelled, etc., to view and sett out the dimencions, meets and bounds, on all parts, of the late messuage of Mrs Dorothy Weale, widow, which messuage before the late fire stood on the south side of the High Pavement between a messuage then of Mr Boyce and in the occupacion of John Bradshaw, apothecary, on the east side thereof, and a messuage then of William Cooke of London, apothecary, and in the occupacion of Thomas Tippin, cutler, on the west side thereof, and a true verdict thereof to make to this Court, without proceeding to any farther inquiry whether the same were copyhold or freehold.

This Court being informed that Richard Good of this Borough, tallow chandler, is now building a house for makeing candles in the Jury Street neer the house of Andrew Archer, Esq., and which is adjudged will be an annoyance to the same, ordered that he have notice to disist from goeing on therewith, and that he attend this Court on Munday next touching the same.

	Brooke
John Newsham	F. Grevile
Wm. Bolton	H. Puckering
Tho. Newsham	W.Palmer
	Tho. Wagstaffe

Warwick Borough
At the Court of Record held ... on Munday the 28th of October anno domini 1695.

Present: the Rt Honourable the Lord Brook, Sir Henry Puckering, Bart., William Palmer, Esq., George Lucy, Esq., William Colemore, Esq., William Bolton, Esq., John Newsham, Esq., Thomas Newsham, Esq.

Ordered that a jury be impanelled touching matters in variance betwixt Mr Heath and Doctor Johnsons and summoned to appear at this Court on this day fortnight.

Ordered that the Chamberlains and the Surveyors, according to the order of the last Court, report the matters in variance between John Prichett and William Holmes to this Court on this day fortnight.

Ordered that the Surveyors order all persons to cover their wells, houses of office, cellars and other places of danger by to morrow night.

Ordered that Mrs Weale have notice to answer the complaint of Mr Savage, touching the gutter of lead betwixt their two houses.

Ordered that William Colemore, Esq., and Mr William Tarver be added to the number of Treasurers appointed by an order of this Court of the twenty first day of October last for the brief money.

	Brooke
John Newsham	F. Grevile
Wm Colmore	H. Puckering
Tho. Newsham	Wm Bolton

Warwick Borough
At the Court of Record held ... on Munday the eleventh day of November anno domini 1695

Present: the Rt Honourable the Lord Brook, the Honourable Francis Grevile, Esq., Sir Henry Puckering, Bart., Sir Richard Verney, Kt., William Colemore, Esq., William Bolton, Esq., John Newsham, Esq., Thomas Newsham, Esq.

A jury being impanelled to sett out the meets and bounds of Mrs Dorothy Weale her house and the said jury appeareing here in Court, ordered that the same be suspended till farther order of this Court.

It appeareing to this Court that John Atterbury hath bought lately of John Eld of Killenworth and Thomas Carr of Berkswell, executors of Elizabeth Carr, the toft whereon lately stood the house of the said Elizabeth Carr lying and being in the Church Street betwixt the ground whereon stood the late house of one Hemming belonging to the Corporacion on the north side thereof, and the ground of William Perks on the south side thereof, and by agreement was to give thirty six pounds and ten shillings for the same, Ordered by consent of both parties that the same be assured to the purchaser by decree of this Court.

The jury impanelled and sworn this day to try the matters in variance between Edward Heath, gent., complainant, and William Johnson, doctor of phisick, defendant, touching the pulling down of a house of the said Mr Heath att the time of the late fire then in possession of Nathaniel Gilstrop nere the east chappell in the said Borough, doe find the house to be pulled down by order of the said Doctor Johnson, and that the damage done to the house by the pulling of it downe amounted to twenty pounds.[1]

Ordered that Solomon Bray be paid by Mr Tarver the remainder of his money for pulling down the tower of the late Church of Saint Maries and carry away the ruins and rubbish of the same, and that Mr Tarver discount for soe much as he hath already received.

Ordered that the Surveyors doe bring in the severall draughts of the church on Munday morning next and to bring in their estimates of the said draughts of the said church.

Ordered that two shillings and six pence per the pound be allowed to all sufferers, builders, who have not had any shares in the charity money out of the monies ariseing out of the briefe.

The jury inpanelled to try the matters in varriance betwixt Mr William Savage, complainant, and Fulk Weale, defendant, doe order that Mr Fulk Weale doe cause a spout to be made to carry the water from Mr Weale's

---

[1] The rough minute book contains the evidence of several witnesses. Among those for Mr Heath, the complainant, 'Mr Samuell Jematt sais that Dr Johnson standing in the street call'd to him and complained that he did offer $\frac{1}{2}$ a crown for pulling down the house and did say he would rebuild the same and would give some men that stood by $\frac{1}{2}$ crown each' and 'Wm Hyron: goeing along the street Dr Johnson tooke him by the arme, bid him help him down with the house, he would give them $\frac{1}{2}$ crown, he with others stript the house and Dr Johnson promised to save them harmless, Nicholas Paris bid them make hast to pull it down'. Among those for Dr Johnson, the defendant, 'Nicholas Paris: Dr Johnson's man sais that his master bid him if the fire was goeing down the street, to goe to the Mayor and gett men to pull down the house to stopp the fire. Dr Johnson said to Mr Mayor he could gett noe men to pull down the house and he said for god sake doe you gett some men to pull it downe.'

leaden spout to the wooden pipe of Mr Savage that goes down the corner of his house att Mr Weale's own charge two foot under the windows, and they find Mr Weale's wall goes six foot and ten inches from the corner of his house.

The jury impanelled and sworne betwixt Thomas Watts, complainant, and Thomas Dadley, defendant, doe find the gutter between the said Thomas Watts his house and the house of the said Thomas Dadley to be noe nusance to Mr Watts.

Ordered that Mr Savage have the ground he bought of Mr Boyce assured to him by decree of this court.

Ordered that William Holmes, brickmaker, doe bring and lay four pounds in the hands of William Bolton, Esq., within four dayes, as a pledge for the indemnifieing John Prichard for the way he carts over in the Pigwells, and upon his refusall and neglect of the same to have the said way stopped up.

On complaint made to this Court by severall commoners, that their cows have been dangerously maimed and wounded, which they suspect to have been done by brickmakers or their servants in drieving them from their works and from eating and pulling the thacking from their hovells, and that the commons are endamaged much by carts being driven carlessly over more ground than need to have been, Ordered that the severall brickmakers hedge and fence in their severall hovells and thatch buildings to secure them from cattle by this day sevenight, under the penalty of haveing their hovells and buildings pulled downe, and that the Chamberlains stake out the ways to and from their brickilns over the commons, and that whoever transgresses the bounds soe staked out on complaint and proof made of the same to suffer such punishment as this Court may by the said Act inflict, and that the Chamberlaines have one coppy and the brickmakers another of this order.

Upon reading the peticion of Mr William Tarver, Ordered that the matters therein contained be referr'd to the next Court.

Ordered that the severall sufferers on the west side of the Church Street have nine [pence] per foot for the ground taken away from them, except those persons who have had an euquivaluent or consideracion already given them.

F. Grevile	Wm Bolton
H. Puckering	John Newsham
Wm Colmore	Tho. Newsham

Warwick Borough

At the Court of Record held . . . on Munday the sixteenth day of December anno domini 1695

Present: the Honourable Francis Grevile, Esq., Sir Henry Puckering, Bart., Sir John Clopton, Kt., Sir Thomas Wagstaffe, Kt., William Colemore, Esq., William Bolton, Esq., John Newsham, Esq.

Whereas there hath been received of Sir Francis Child and Mr Richard Hoar by way of return by Mr John Newsham out of the brief monies by them received, the summ of four thousand pounds and the sum of six hundred pounds, part thereof being paid to Mr William Tarver, one of the Treasurers of the monies ariseing by the said brief, and the remainder of the said summ being three thousand and four hundred pounds lodged in the chest att the Castle by Mr Newsham and there remaineing untold, it is ordered that the Treasurers of the said brief monies be desired to tell over the same to morrow being the seventeenth of this instant December.

Whereas there hath been a peticion this day offered in Court by William Johnson, doctor of physick, against Mr Joseph Blissett, it is Ordered that the said Mr Blissett have a coppy of the said peticion delivered to him and that he be summoned to appear at the next Court to answer the contents of the same.

Ordered that the severall sufferers who are allowed two shillings and sixpence in the pound (according to their losses) in an order sign'd this day and directed to the Treasurers of the brief monies, have notice to come to the Mayor's Parlour on Thursday next, there to receive the severall summs given them as aforesaid, and alsoe to the sufferers who are allowed nine pence per foot for their ground taken away on the west side of the Church Street.

F. Grevile	John Newsham
John Clopton	Wm Bolton
Wm Colmore	

Warwick Borough

At the Court of Record held . . . on Munday the twenty third day of December anno domini 1695

Present: the Honourable Francis Grevile, Esq., Sir Henry Puckering, Bart., Sir John Clopton, kt., Sir Thomas Wagstaff, kt., William Palmer, Esq., John Combs, Esq., William Colemore, Esq., Thomas Peers, Esq., William Bolton, Esq., John Newsham, Esq., Thomas Newsham, Esq., Devereux Whadcock, Mayor.[1]

---

[1] The Mayor's name has been inserted in a space alongside the list of those present.

Memorandum that John Combs, Esq., and Mr Devereux Whadcock, Mayor of the Borough of Warwick, being Comicioners or Judges appointed by the said Act, did then and there take the oath mencioned in the said Act before Sir John Clopton, Kt., and William Palmer, Esq., two of his Majestyes justices of the peace of the county of Warwick.

Whereas severall orders for the distribucion of the charity monies to the severall sufferers by the late fire have been made by this Court, many of whom have not received the proporcions allotted to them by the said orders, it is therefore this day ordered that Thursday and Friday next be the days appointed for the Treasurers to pay the same, and they are hereby desired to meet for that purpose att nine of the clock in the morning of each day at the Mayor's Parlour, and that the said sufferers have notice thereof by the beedle his goeing to their respective houses to acquaint them therewith, and if it shall appeare to this court any of the said sufferers have had due notice given them of the said dayes for the receipt of their monies, and they refuse or neglect to goe or send to receive the same, they be excluded the benefitt of the said orders of distribucion.

It being thought necessary for and towards the more early beginning in the spring to rebuild the Church of St Maries ruined by the late fire, that materialls be provided for the same this winter, Ordered that one thousand load of stone fitt for such a use be contracted for with workmen and labourers to be forthwith began to be digged and laid in places convenient for working up the same.

Ordered that a pitt of three or four yards square be opened and sunk on the north side of the church yard of St Maryes adjoyning to the walls of Mr Rainsford and Mr Colemore for a tryall whether the stone that shall be dugg therein will be fitt to be used toward the rebuilding of the said church, and that the said pitt be pall'd round for the security of passengers from danger.

Ordered that whilst any matters in variance[1] are by the Comicioners debateing in Court, all partyes concerned therein doe withdraw dureing the said debate.

Ordered that the Treasurers be desired to bring in a state of all monies by them received and paid for the use of the poor sufferers by the late fire, whether voluntary monies or monies received upon the account of the brief, and lay the same before this Court on Munday next.

Ordered that six baggs of one hundred pounds each be taken out of the chest att the Castle by the Treasurers, and that two shillings in the pound

---

[1] 'in variance' interlineated over a caret.

of the bad monys lately sent from the Receivers in London, be mixed and distributed to all the sufferers who have not yet received their shares and allottments upon any orders of distribucions that have been hitherto made.

The peticion of Doctor Johnson preferr'd the last Court against Mr Joseph Blissett being defective both in matter and form, Ordered that the said Doctor Johnson exhibite in writeing to the next Court the particulars, grounds and reasons of his complaint against the said Mr Blissett.

Upon reading the peticion of Edward Heath, gent., of this Borough, desireing the decree of this Court for the payment of twenty pounds, being the summ found by the jury to be the damage done to his house pull'd downe at the time of the late fire by the order of Dr William Johnson, it is Ordered that the summ be decreed to be paid to him by the said Dr Johnson before the first Munday after Candlemas day next.[1]

Dev. Whadcock, Mayor	Wm Bolton
F. Grevile	John Newsham
Wm Colmore	Tho. Newsham

Warwick Borough
At the Court of Record held ... on Munday the 27th of January anno domini 1695/6.

Present: the Honourable Francis Grevile, Esq., Devereux Whatcoate,[2] Mayor, William Colemore, Esq., William Bolton, Esq., John Newsham, Esq., Thomas Newsham, Esq.

Upon heareing the peticion of Mr Elias Webb alias Morrell read, Ordered that the persons who are mentioned therein be summon'd to appear at this Court on Munday next.

Upon reading the peticion of William Phillips, brickmaker, against William Perks, baker, Ordered that the matters in dispute between the said partyes be referr'd to the next Court.

Upon reading the peticion of John[3] Woods of Claverdon, it is Ordered that the contract between the said peticioner and Mary Mann, widow, appeareing to this Court, the said peticioner have the said toft mencioned in the said peticion assured to him by decree of this Court.

Ordered that any sufferer by the late fire who hath occasion to borrow money to carry on their building and will give such security for the same as

[1] 'Decree'd accordingly' inserted in the margin against this paragraph.
[2] *Sic.*
[3] 'John' inserted above 'Richard' struck through.

shall be approved by 5[1] Commicioners, be furnished out of the charity monies with such summs as shall be thought fitt by the said Commicioners.

Ordered that Samuel Dunkley employ workmen to open a quarry in the church ground and a quarry in the church yard according to a late order of this Court for digging one thousand load of stone.

Ordered that Joseph Hemming have the share of charity mony that was due to Elizabeth Carr for her loss.

Ordered that Mr Biker have four shillings in the pound for the house he has built, and two shillings and six pence in the pound for the loss of his houses unbuilt.

Ordered that Mrs Ann Webb have soe much paid her as makes up two shillings and six pence per pound for her loss, being one pound ten shillings.

Ordered that teams be hyred to carry away the rubbish of the church, that Mr Robinson oversee the work and bargaine for teems and horses, and that the said rubbish be carryed to Saltisford Rock or the Butts.

Ordered that John Hicks be summon'd to appear the next court to answer the peticion of Charles Emes.

| Dev. Whadcock, Maior | F. Grevile | John Newsham |
| Tho. Newsham | Wm Colmore | Wm Bolton |

Warwick Borough
At the Court of Record held ... on Munday the third day of February anno domini 1695/6.

Present: the Honourable Francis Grevile, Esq., William Colemore, Esq., Devereux Whadcock, Mr John Newsham, Mr Thomas Newsham.

Resolved that the securityes given in by the persons who borrow mony, as follows, viz. Mr Tarver and Mr Whadcock, Mr Nicholls and Mr Norton, Mr Norton and Mr Nicholls, Mr Blissett and his son, Mr Tomkis and his son, Mr Fish and his son, Mr Heath and [   ][2] are approved of.

The sufferers haveing desired the trustees, and this Court, that the monies in bank be paid into the Exchequer on loane, and that Mr Newsham the Receiver Generall be desired to carry up the same, Ordered that Mr Newsham be desired to carry up the same with the King's taxes and pay it in accordingly.

---

[1] '5' inserted above 'the' struck through.   [2] A blank has been left for a further name.

Ordered that Mr Mayor, Mr John Newsham and Mr Thomas Newsham be desired to view the ground Mr Blissett is goeing to build in the Markett Place, and sett out the same.

That they likewise view a quarry of stone by Mr Smith's house in the New Street in his petition mencioned, and report what damage is done to Mr Smith's garden by the said quarry, and that Mr Gibbard, one of the said quarriers, be summon'd to appear next Court to answer the said peticion.

Ordered that the ground of Mr Thomas Stratford be decreed to William Cockbill, who had a mortgage of fifty pounds on it and the benefitt of the charity monies for the future, and that the same be transferr'd to Solomon Bray according to the contract betwixt the said Cockbill and the said Sollomon Bray.

Ordered that Edward Chesley have four shillings in the pound, he giveing his owne and son's bond for it that he will build.

Ordered that the toft in dispute between John Hicks and Charles Emes be decreed to Charles Emes, that John Hicks have fifteen pounds for his moity of the ground and half all charitie monies belonging to the same, that Charles Emes have the other half.[1]

Ordered that George Chinn, giveing security of his three houses, have one hundred pounds lent him and twenty pounds more if the Court hereafter shall think the former security sufficient.

Ordered that George Chinn have his monie already allotted him made up four shillings in the pound.

Dev. Whadcock, Mayor	John Newsham
Wm Colmore	Tho. Newsham

Warwick Borough

At the Court of Record held ... on Munday the ninth day of March anno domini 1695/6

Present: William Colemore, Esq., Thomas Peers, Esq., William Bolton, Esq., John Newsham, Esq., Thomas Newsham, Esq.

Ordered that the foundacions of the walls of Mr Smith's house in the New Street, next to Mr Gibbard's quarry, be view'd by the Surveyors, and the foundacions of the said house, if prejudiced or in danger of receiveing any, be made good and secure as the Surveyors shall think fitt at the costs of the said Mr Gibbard, the same to be done within a month and the garden of

---

[1] 'Decreed' inserted in the margin against this paragraph.

the said Mr Smith to be made good from the copeing of the said quarry, and fences to be put up againe, within the same time.

Upon reading the peticion of Andrew Parker, carpenter, to be relieved against William Perks, baker, Ordered that the said William Perks be summon'd to appeare at the next Court to answer the contents of the said peticion.

Ordered that Mr Elias Webb of Shirborn, being tenant for life in remainder of two messuages in the Sheepstreet, of which Mrs Wagstaff was at the time of the fire the immediate tenant for life, paying to Joshuan Fox the wife of Joseph Fox, and their heirs, the summ of thirty pounds, in case the said Elias Webb and his son Thomas Webb dye before the said Thomas attaine the age of twenty one years, or without issue, the toft whereon the said messuages stood to be decreed to the said Elias Webb for his life, the remainder in tayle to Thomas his son, with the last remainder to the right heirs of the said Elias Webb, and that the said Elias Webb rebuild the said messuages, and have all the monyes given for encouragement of rebuilders.[1]

Wm Bolton	John Newsham
Wm Colmore	Tho. Newsham
Tho. Peers	

Warwick Borough
At the Court of Record held ... on Munday the twenty third day of March 1695/6.

Present: the Rt Honourable the Lord Brook, Sir Henry Puckering, Bart., Devereux Whadcock, Mayor, William Bolton, Esq., John Newsham, Esq., Thomas Newsham, Esq.

Order'd that the Treasurers draw up a full state of the account, of what moneys they have received and paid toward the reliefe of the poor sufferers by the late fire in Warwick, and lay the same before this Court on Munday next.

Ordered that Mr Welton have three pence per foot, for 575 feet of ground taken from him to enlarge Foxes Lane in the High Street, being the summ of seven pound three shillings and nine pence, and that the Surveyors stake out the whole ground of the said Mr Welton.

Ordered that Mr Weale doe putt up the gutter in dispute between him and Mr Savage, before the thirtyeth day of this instant March.

---

[1] 'Q. if decree, [? then], not to be writt' added in the margin against this paragraph.

Ordered that Mrs Wagstaff be paid the summ of five pounds, it being the residue of the money allow'd her in the distribucion of two shillings and six pence in the pound.

Whereas by an order of Court of the one and twentyeth day of October last, it was ordered that a jury be impannelled to sett out the metts and bounds of the late messuage of Mrs Dorothy Weale, now it appeareing to this Court that the said Mrs Weale was then noe party to the controversie, it is Ordered that a jury be empannelled to sett out the dimencions,[1] meets and bounds of the late house of Mr Fulk Weale, draper.

Dev. Whadcock, Mayor	Brooke
John Newsham	H. Puckering
Tho. Newsham	Wm. Bolton

Warwick Borough
At the Court of Record held ... on Munday the thirteenth day of Aprill anno domini 1696.

Present: Sir Henry Puckering, Bart., William Colemore, Esq., William Bolton, Esq., John Newsham, Esq., Thomas Newsham, Esq., Devereux Whadcock, Mayor.

Ordered that George Chinn have one hundred pounds lent him, he giveing security by mortgage of his houses in the Swann Lane lately purchas'd of Mr Thomas Stanton.

Ordered that Richard Hadley have the liberty of a breake in his house in the Sheepstreet[2] to project into the street as farr as Mr Heath's, haveing the consent of the Lord Brooke and Sir Henry Puckering thereunto.

Ordered that the ground in the Butts, purchased of William Reevs, be assured to Mr Colemore by decree of this Court.

Ordered that the Surveyors stake out the ground of the late house of John Prichard lately decreed to Mr Richard Hands, maulster.

Upon readeing the peticion of William Holmes, carpenter,[3] and Edward Reading to be relieved against William Perks, baker, it is Ordered by consent of all partyes that the matters in controversie betwixt them be referr'd to Mr Jephcott to be determined by him.

Dev. Whadcock, Mayor	Wm. Bolton
Tho. Newsham	Wm. Colmore
	John Newsham

---

[1] 'dimencions' interlineated over a caret.
[2] 'Sheepstreet' interlineated over a caret above a word struck out.
[3] 'carpenter' interlineated over a caret above 'brickmaker' struck out.

Warwick Borough
At the Court of Record held . . . the 20th day of Aprill anno 1696.

Present: Sir Henry Puckering, Bart., Devereux Whadcock, Mayor, William Colemore, Esq., William Bolton, Esq., John Newsham, Esq., Thomas Newsham, Esq.

Ordered that William Pestle have one pound and ten shillings allowed him for his loss of three pounds and three shillings and that Mr Tarver pay the same.

Ordered that Mr Thomas Newsham be paid fifteen shillings (viz.) ten shillings for putting in an advertisement into the Gazett to the archdeacons and registers, five shillings being the half charge of an advertisement for describing one Churchley[1] who was a counterfeiter of deputacions for collecting briefs.

Ordered that Mrs Eades be paid one pound, being a particular gift of my Lady Peirpoint to her out of the ten pounds given to the sufferers by the late fire in Warwick.

Dev. Whadcock, Mayor	Tho. Newsham
Wm. Colmore	John Newsham
Wm. Bolton	

Warwick Borough
At the Court of Record held . . . on Munday the twenty seventh day of Aprill anno domini 1696.

Present: Devereux Whadcock, Mayor, George Lucy, Esq., William Colemore, Esq., William Bolton, Esq., John Newsham, Esq., Thomas Newsham, Esq.

Order'd that the jury summon'd to appear here this day between Mr William Bolton and Mr Fulk Weale be referr'd to another Court.

Order'd that the monies now lying and being in the hands of Sir Francis Child and Mr Richard Hoare be paid by them into his Majestie's Receipt of Exchequer upon the surest fond they can, and that will be most advantagious to the sufferers.

	Brooke
Dev. Whadcock, Mayor	John Newsham
Geo. Lucy	Tho. Newsham
Wm. Colmore	Wm. Bolton

---

[1] 'Cruchley' in the rough minute book.

Warwick Borough
At the Court of Record held ... on Munday the fourth day of May anno domini 1696

Present: The Rt Honourable the Lord Brooke, the Honourable Francis Grevile, Esq., Sir Henry Puckering, Bart., Devereux Whadcock, Mayor, William Colemore, Esq., John Newsham, Esq., Thomas Newsham, Esq.

Ordered that George Chinn have one hundred and forty pounds lent him, he giveing security by mortgage of his two houses in the Swan Lane, and alsoe of the peice of ground he hath lately bought of Mr Green in the High Street.

Ordered that the Surveyors stake out the Swan Lane by the next Court, that they drive in the stakes as nere as they can to the places first staked out by order of the Commicioners.

Upon reading the peticion of William Smith of this Borough, shoomaker, to be relieved against Richard Gibbard of the same Borough, maulster, it is resolved that the difference between the said partyes is within the cognisance of this Court, and that this Court will proceed to heare and determine the same.

Whereas the difference betwixt Roger Hurlbert, Elizabeth his daughter and Edward Cheseley hath been examined by William Bolton, Esq., Mr Thomas Newsham and Mr Charles Hicks, three Commicioners desired by an order of this Court of the twenty third day of September last to examine the same, it is Ordered that the controversie betwixt the said parties be fully ended and determined, and resolved that the note given by Roger Hurlbert under his hand to the said Edward Chesley for the summ of six pounds is and shall be hereby cancelled, and the accounts examined by the Commicioners aforesaid between the said partyes fully ballanced.

Ordered that Richard Hadley[1] have the liberty of makeing a break in the front of his house in the Sheep Street, the same to extend into the street as farr as Mr Heath's house in the Church Street.

Dev. Whadcock, Mayor	Brooke
Tho. Newsham	F. Grevile
H. Puckering	Wm Colmore
	John Newsham

Warwick Borough
At the Court of Record held ... on Munday the eleventh day of May anno domini 1696

[1] 'Sergt. Hadley' in the rough minute book.

Present: The Rt Honourable the Lord Brooke, the Honourable Francis Grevile, Esq., Sir Henry Puckering, Bart., Devereux Whadcock, Mayor, Sir John Clopton, Kt., George Lucy, Esq., William Colemore, Esq., William Bolton, Esq.

Ordered that a jury be impanelled to appear here this day fortnight to view and enquire into all controversies sett forth in a peticion preferred by William Smith of this Borough, shoomaker, against Richard Gibbard of the same Borough, maulster, on Munday the fourth day of this instant May, and that both partys have notice to appeare then, and that the said Richard Gibbard doe stopp all proceedings at law in any other court, as he will answer the contrary at his perill.

Dev. Whadcock, Mayor	Brooke
H. Puckering	F. Grevile
Geo. Lucy	Wm Colmore
	Wm Bolton

Warwick Borough
At the Court of Record held . . . on Munday the 25th day of May 1696.

Present: The Rt Honourable the Lord Brooke, the Honourable Francis Grevile, Esq., Sir Henry Puckering, Bart., Sir Thomas Wagstaffe, Kt., Devereux Whadcock, Mayor, Simon Biddolph, Esq., William Palmer, Esq., George Lucy, Esq., William Colemore, Esq., William Bolton, Esq., John Newsham, Esq.

Upon reading the peticion of William Holmes, brickmaker, it is Ordered that the said peticion be referred to the next Court to be considered of.

Upon reading the peticion of John Burford, it is Ordered that the same be referred to the next Court to be considered of.

It appeareing by the jury impanelled and sworn this day to view and sett out the dimencions, meets and bounds of the late house of Mr Fulk Weale, draper, according to an order of Court of the twenty third day of March last, that they went according to their oaths to the house of the said Mr Weale in order to view and sett out the same, but were, contrary to the said order and in contempt of this Court, utterly denyed by the said Fulk Weale and his mother to enter into the said house, or make any view or sett out the meets and bounds according to the said order, the said Fulk Weale att the same time denying the jurisdiccion of this Court. It is therefore resolved and agreed by all the Commicioners present that the said denyall is in contempt of this Court and that this Court will proceed farther into the same on Munday next.

The jury impanelled and sworne this day to try the matters in variance between William Smith of this Borough, shoomaker, complainant, and Richard Gibbard of the same Borough, maulster, defendant, doe find that the said William Smyth hath not made any encrochment upon the said Richard Gibbard by building upon any part of his ground, or that the building sett up by the said William Smith is any encrochment whatsoever upon the said Richard Gibbard.

	Brooke
Wm. Colmore	F. Grevile
Wm. Bolton	H. Puckering
John Newsham	Geo. Lucy
	Symon Biddulph

Warwick Borough
At the Court of Record held ... on Munday the first day of June anno domini 1696

Present: The Rt Honourable the Lord Brooke, the Honourable Francis Grevile, Esq., Sir Henry Puckering, Bart., William Petoe, Esq., Simon Biddulph, Esq., George Lucy, Esq., William Colemore, Esq., William Bolton, Esq., John Newsham, Esq., Thomas Newsham, Esq.

Whereas some of the proprietors of the west side of the Churchstreet as alsoe in other streets refuse to pave that part of their ground which is laid into the said streets to enlarge the same, it is Order'd that the said proprietors haveing had extraordinary allowances made them by the Commicioners for the ground taken away from them to enlarge the said streets, that in consideracion of the said allowances, they be obliged to pave the breadth of their respective houses from the said houses to the gutter or channell, and they are hereby obliged and ordered to pave the same accordingly as they will answer the contrary at their perills.

Whereas some of the pavements before the new buildings are laid very irregular and unequall, by reason of which the streets are made inconvenient for passengers and carrying off the water, it is Ordered that noe proprietors of any of the new buildings pave or cause to be paved the streets before the houses without direccion of the Surveyors first had. And it is ordered that the said Surveyors doe report to this Court on Munday next, what the descents in the severall streets are, and how much fall is required from the houses to the channell, that the same may be made into an order for all proprietors in paveing before their houses to govern themselves by.

Ordered that the Chamberlains and the Surveyors goe and view the cart way in the Pigwells made by William Holmes, brickmaker, by carrying bricks and tyles through the same, and assess what damage the said carriage hath done to the said ground, and report the same to this Court on Munday next, to the end the said William Holmes may have the overplus of his money now lying in the hands of William Bolton, Esq., if any due.

Upon reading the peticion of William Lattimore and Edward Bloxwich against William Holmes, brickmaker, it is ordered that the said William Holmes be summoned to appeare and answer the said peticion on Munday next.

According to the powers and authorityes given to this court by the said Act, it is resolved that the following and exerciseing the trade of a butcher, in the five streets, call'd the High Street, Church Street, Castle Street, Jury Street and Sheep Street is a publick annoyance, and soe judged to be by this court and to be proceeded against and punished accordingly.

Wm. Bolton	Brooke
Tho. Newsham	F. Grevile
John Newsham	H. Puckering
	Wm. Colmore

Warwick Borough
At the Court of Record held ... on Munday the eigth day of June anno domini 1696.

Present: The Rt Honourable the Lord Brook, the Honourable Francis Grevile, Esq., Sir Henry Puckering, Bart., John Marriott, Esq., Thomas Peerce, Esq., William Colemore, Esq., William Bolton, Esq., John Newsham, Esq., Thomas Newsham, Esq.

Whereas William Holmes did contract by articles with William Lattimore and Edward Bloxwich the peticioners, that the said William Lattimore and Edward Bloxwich should have six shillings per thousand for two hundred thousand of tyles for makeing and burning the same, and whereas the said William Holmes hath not provided fewell for the burning the same, nor a hovell or place for keeping them dry, and fifty thousand, part of the said two hundred thousand, to the detriment of the peticioners, lye unburnt, it is Ordered that the said Holmes pay and allow to the said William Lattimore and Edward Bloxwich four shillings per thousand for soe many as are made, which summ with what has been already paid amounts to five pound twelve shillings and eleven pence, the same to be paid when the said tyles are chisel'd and ready for burning; and that the said Lattimore and Bloxwich be discharged of the covenants in the said articles and that the said Holmes alsoe pay the peticioners eight shillings for the days work done for him by the said peticioners.

Ordered that Mr Newsham have liberty to lett the cornish of his house project in the whole twelve inches, and that the pedestals of the pilasters project three inches beyond the ground table.

Upon view made by the Surveyors by order of the last Court of the descents to be made along the severall streets and from the houses to the gutters, it is Ordered that the descents from Mr Aings his house to the corner of Mr Blissett's house against the Court House be twenty two inches, and that the pavement at the corner of Mr Blissets new building against the Court House be layd eighteen inches above the gutter which now is, and from thence to be carried on with an equall descent to Nicholas Paris his entry doore, and that the shopp floor of the said Mr Blissett be laid fourteen inches above the top of the said pavement.

It is farther ordered that the pavement before Mr Tarvers house att the corner be taken lower then now it is nine inches.

	Brooke
Wm. Colmore	H. Puckering
John Newsham	Dev. Whadcock, Mayor
Wm. Bolton	Tho. Newsham

Warwick Borough
At the Court of Record held . . . on Munday the fifteenth day of June anno domini 1696.

Present: The Rt. Honourable the Lord Brooke, the Honourable Francis Grevile, Esq., Sir Henry Puckering, Bart., Devereux Whadcock, Mayor, William Colemore, Esq., John Newsham, Esq., Thomas Newsham, Esq.

Ordered that the Treasurers bring and lay the account of all receipts and disbursments before the Commicioners on Wednesday morning next at the Court House of all monys received and disburst on account of the charity.

The Chamberlains according to order haveing [viewed] the damage done in the Pigwells to John Prichard tenant thereof, by carting over the same, and reported that the damage amounts to two pounds fifteen shillings, Ordered that William Holmes, for whose use the cart way was made, allow to the said John Prichard the said summ of two pounds fifteen shillings, and it is farther Ordered that Mr William Bolton, in whose hands four pounds was laid as a pledge by the said William Holmes for makeing good the said way and ground, doe pay to the said John Prichard out of the said £4, £2–15s., restoreing the overplus to William Holmes.

Upon reading the peticion of Elizabeth Martin of this Borough, widow, to be relieved against Richard Martin of London her son, it is Ordered that a letter be writt and sent to London to the said Richard Martin, requireing him to appeare in this Court to answer the peticion of his said mother, and shew cause why the toft of the said house in the peticion mencioned should not be sold, that a house may be rebuilt.

Resolved that an order, requireing all persons who have back buildings in the Jury Street, Castle Street, etc., according to the rules and directions of the Act of Parliament, and which yet remains unthatched, be made forthwith to tyle the said back buildings, and that the said order be hung up publickly to notifie the same.

Ordered that Mr Robinson goe and view all new thatcht buildings within this towne and report to this Court what buildings have been thatched since the fire.

Upon reading the peticion of John Parker preferred in this Court on the 23rd day of December last against Solomon Bray, and upon examineing both partyes and heareing what could be alledged on both sides, and it appeareing by the peticion prefer'd that there was due to the said John Parker for work done by him and his son for the said Solomon Bray six pounds thirteen shillings and three pence, but this Court haveing duly considered thereof doe think the said worke over rated one pound three shillings and three pence, and doe agree that the same shall be reduced to the summ of five pounds and ten shillings, and the said Solomon Bray is hereby Ordered to pay the same, except it appears by Mr Tarvers books that he hath paid more in money to the said John Parker then he owns to have received.

Ordered that the severall proprietors who had houses burnt down by the late fire and whose rubbish is not yet removed from the ground of such houses soe burnt downe, but remains yet to be carryed away, that for the future all such proprietors doe carry the same to the commons, and lay it in the severall pitts out of which the brickmakers have dugg their clay, in order to fill up the same.

Ordered that the 2 bills brought into Court by the Surveyors for getting the stone in the church yard quarry and on the church ground in the Church Street, amounting to the summ of twenty four pounds fourteen shillings, be paid out of the brief monies, and that the summ of three pounds seven shillings and six pence be alsoe paid to Thomas Masters out of the brief moneys, for three pullies by him made for drawing up the stone out of the said quarrys.

Ordered that if it appeare to this Court that William Holms hath purchased the ground of the Black Raven, and given security for the same as is accepted, that he be allowed for 208 foot taken away to enlarge the Sheep-street six pence per foot.

H. Puckering
John Newsham

Brooke
F. Grevile
Wm. Colmore
Dev. Whadcock, Mayor

Warwick Borough
At the Court of Record held . . . on Munday the twenty second day of June 1696.

Present: The Rt. Honourable the Lord Brooke, the Honourable Francis Grevile, Esq., Devereux Whadcock, Mayor, William Colemore, Esq., William Bolton, Esq., John Newsham, Esq.

Ordered that Mr Blissett have liberty of makeing pilasters at the corner house against the Court House, the pedestalls of the same to come out into the street, not to exceed eight inches beyond the water table, besides the projecture of the mouldings, the said pedestals not to exceed seven foot high from the ground.

Wm. Bolton
Dev. Whadcock, Mayor
John Newsham

Brooke
H. Puckering
Wm. Colmore

Warwick Borough
At the Court of Record held . . . on Munday the twenty ninth day of June 1696.

Present: The Rt. Honourable the Lord Brook, Sir Henry Puckering, Bart., William Bolton, Esq., William Colemore, Esq., John Newsham, Esq.

Upon reading the peticion of Hannah Tuckey, widow, and Samuel Tuckey her son, setting forth that she the said Hannah was at the time of the late fire in this Borough, seized of an estate for life in a messuage or tenement scituate in the Church Street late in the posession of Thomas Lean, barber, haveing the messuage of Edward Heath, gent., on the north side thereof, and that the said Samuell Tuckey was seized of the reversion and inheritance of the said messuage, that the said messuage was burnt down by the said fire, that neither of them being able to rebuild the same, the said peticioners humbly pray'd that for the consideracion of the summ of twenty five pounds, the toft whereon stood the said messuage might be assured to him the said Thomas Lean and his heirs by the decree of this Court, it is Ordered that the said toft be assured to the said Thomas Lean and his heirs by the decree of this Court according to the prayer of the said peticion, he the said Thomas Leane to pay the yearly rent of eight pence to William Bolton, Esq., lord of the mannor of Warwick, his heirs and asigns.

Wm. Bolton
John Newsham

Brooke
H. Puckering
Wm. Colmore

Warwick Borough
At the Court of Record held ... on Munday the sixth day of July anno domini 1696

Present: Sir Henry Puckering, Bart., Sir John Burgoin, Bart., Devereux Whadcock, Mayor, William Colemore, Esq., John Newsham, Esq., Wm. Bolton, Esq.

Upon reading the peticion of John Browne and Thomas Lewis, masons, setting forth that one Joseph Martin, carpenter, had articled with William Perks, baker, to build a mault house on the back ground of the said William Perks in the Church Street, that the said peticioners had articled with the said Joseph Martin to build all the brick and stone work belonging to the same, that the said peticioners had done work in and about the said mault house to the value of about thirty pounds, and had received of the said Martin but eleven pounds and ten shillings, that the said Martin was runn away, and the peticioners, conceiving that the said William Perks had not paid to the said Martin soe much money as the said work soe done will amount unto, humbly pray'd the said Court that the said work might beview'd and estimated by the Surveyors, it is therefore Ordered that William Smith and Samuel Dunkley, Surveyors, view the said work, and a true estimate thereof make according to the rates agreed on, and report the same to this Court on Munday next.

It appeareing to this Court that Stephen Glendall hath given security for William Holmes, brickmaker, to make good the ground of the common that the said Holms should break up for the makeing brick, it is Ordered that the said Stephen Glendall have full power to burn the said bricks of the said Holms now lying on the said common, and to have the benefitt of the said brick after burnt and the hovell now standing on the said common to make good the ground of the same, and the over plus after the said ground is soe made good (if any) be restored to the said William Holmes or otherwise as this Court shall think fitt.

Dev. Whadcock, Mayor
John Newsham

H. Puckering
Wm. Colmore
Wm. Bolton

Warwick Borough

At the Court of Record held . . . on Munday the thirteenth day of July anno domini 1696

Present: The Rt. Honourable the Lord Brook, Sir Henry Puckering, Bart., Devereux Whadcock, Mayor, William Bromley, Esq., William Colemore, Esq., William Bolton, Esq., Thomas Newsham, Esq.

Ordered that Charles Emes and John Hicks have one shilling and sixpence in the pound to make up what they have already received four shillings in the pound, for the loss of the house in the Market Place rebuilt by Charles Emes.

Ordered that the Treasurers meet at the Mayor's Parlour on Wednesday next, then and there to make up their accounts of all moneys by them received and paid for the use of the sufferers by the late fire.

Ordered that Joseph Fenix, carpenter, make it appear on Munday next by the oath of two witnesses, that he hath bought and paid for the timber he alleadgeth to have bought of Joseph Martin lying within this Borough.

Ordered that William Phillips, brickmaker, be summoned to appeare here next court, to answer the takeing away the cole of Stephen Glendall lying upon the common, the same being layd there in order to burn the bricks of William Holmes according to an order of the last Court.

Ordered that Joseph Martin his creditors be summon'd to appear here next Court.

	Brooke
Wm Bolton	H. Puckering
Tho. Newsham	Wm Colmore

Warwick Borough

At the Court of Record held . . . on Munday the twentyeth day of July anno domini 1696

Present: The Rt. Honourable the Lord Brook, Sir Henry Puckering, Bart., Devereux Whadcock, Mayor, Thomas Fetherston, Esq., William Colemore, Esq., William Bolton, Esq., John Newsham, Esq., Thomas Newsham Esq.

Ordered that Joseph Fenix, carpenter, goe with George Perkins and John Hope, carpenters, and shew them every peice of timber that he proves to have bought of Joseph Martin within this Borough for the summ of twenty pounds, upon the place where the said timber then lay or is since removed, and that the said George Perkins and John Hope doe make a true estimate of the said timber at the true value thereof and report the same to this Court on Munday next.

Upon complaint made to this Court by John Bradshaw of this Borough, apothecary, in behalf of William Savage of Tachbrooke, gent., against Mrs Dorothy Weale and Fulk Weale her son, that they or one of them did discharge and disturb the said William Savage his workmen from working on the wall of him the said William Savage next adjoyning to the backside of the said Mrs Weale or Fulk her son, and upon view thereof made by William Bolton and Thomas Fetherston, Esqs., two of the Commicioners of this Court desired to view the same and upon their report made to this Court, that building upon the said wall and raiseing it two foot higher then now it is will be noe prejudice or damage to the said Mrs Weale or Fulk her son, it is Ordered that the said Mr Savage have liberty of raiseing the said wall two foot higher then now it is and noe more.[1]

Ordered that the Surveyors doe sett out the bounds of the Pibble Lane and the ground called Okens ground next adjoyning thereto, and take the true dimencions thereof and lay the same before this Court on Monday next.

Ordered that Abigall Rider be allowed one shilling and six pence in the pound to make up what she hath already received four shillings in the pound according to her loss given in by the late fire.

Upon reading the peticion of the inhabitants of St Marys parish in this Borough, it is ordered that a jury be impanelled to view and sett out the church ground in the Church Street next adjoyning to the house of John Atterberry, and alsoe to view the building of the said John Atterberry and according to their evidence to find whether the said John Atterberry hath made any incrochment by building upon any part of the said church ground.

	Brooke
John Newsham	H. Puckering
Tho. Newsham	Wm. Colmore
	Wm. Bolton

Warwick Borough
At the Court of Record held . . . on Munday the twenty seventh day of July anno domini 1696

Present: The Rt Honourable the Lord Brook, Sir Henry Puckering, Bart., William Colemore, Esq., Devereux Whadcock, Mayor, William Bolton, Esq., John Newsham, Esq., Thomas Newsham, Esq.

The jury impanalled to appear here this day to view and sett out the church ground in the Church Street and to view the building of John Atterberry

---

[1] The rough minute book adds: '. . . in order to build a roome over the house of office.'

next adjoyning thereto, doe find that the said John Atterberry hath encroched and built upon the said church ground in breadth twelve inches, and in length twenty foot, that the widness of the said church ground from Mr Tarvers brick wall towards John Atterberrys house, is fourty four foot and one inch; that the wideness of the said ground by Mr Tarvers brick wall is sixty eight foot, and that the length of the said ground from Mr Tarver his wall between it and Mr Okens land to the Church Street, is one hundred fifty six foot, and the wideness of the same in the front to the street is fifty two foot and three inches.

Whereas there have been severall complaints made to this Court by severall of the creditors of Joseph Martin[1] against Joseph Fenix, carpenter, who bought timber of the said Martin for twenty pounds lying upon the ground of Mrs Cawthern in the Sheep Street, and whereas by an order the last Court, George Perkins and John Hope were ordered to estimate the timber which the said Joseph Fenix should shew them, whether upon the said ground or otherwise disposed of, the said Perkins and Hope haveing made an estimate thereof and given it in to this Court, viz. the timber now lying on the ground of Mrs Cawthern, the house of John Watts and in Kerbys Close, it is ordered that noe person presume to take away any of the said timber soe estimated except by order of this Court.

Ordered that Mr Fulk Chernock be forthwith sent to, to acquaint him that upon cleering his ground against the church in order to the makeing a new square, he shall receive the moneys the said ground was valued at by the jury.

Whereas the house in the Church Street given for the repaires of St Mary's Church is not likely to be rebuilt unless by the assistance of the charity monies, ordered that (the same being given for soe pious and charitable use) the summ of twenty pounds be given out of the brief money, for and towards the rebuilding of the said house, and converting it to the use abovesaid.

Ordered that a new survey of the Church Street be made by the Surveyors of all ground taken away from the severall proprietors of the ground in the said street taken away to enlarge the same.

Ordered that one hundred and fifty pounds be lent to Mr Robert Blissett out of the moneys comeing in by the brief, he giveing his own and his father Mr Joseph Blissett his bond for the same.

Ordered that George Chinn be allow'd one shilling and six pence in the pound for the loss of Mr Green's house in the Highstreet as reduced to

---

[1] The rough minute book includes notes of statements by William Miles 'undertaker from Martin of Watts his house att 50s. per square he judged it to be, but agreed in the whole for £30 ...' and of William Egerton 'undertaker to Miles, he undertook to make some garrett windows att 9d. a peice ...'.

£170 being £12 15s. od., and that he giveing security of his two houses in the Swann Lane, have twenty pounds lent him, the same to be made up one hundred pounds when he hath paid Mr Green for his ground in order to give a security for the same.

Ordered that Mr Webb of Sherborne be paid one shilling and six pence in the pound for the loss of Mrs Wagstaffe her house in the Sheepstreet as reduced to one hundred and fifteen pounds being £8 12. 6.

Upon readeing the peticion of Mr Boyce of Welsborne, it is Ordered that Mr Edwards of Hampton on the Hill be summon'd to appear to answer the same next Munday.

Dev. Whadcock, Mayor	Brooke
John Newsham	H. Puckering
	Wm. Colmore
	Wm. Bolton

Warwick Burrough

At the Court of Record held . . . on Munday the 24th August anno domini 1696.

Present: Sir Henry Puckering, Bart., Devereux Whadcock, Mayor, William Colemore, Esq., Wm. Bolton, Esq., Thomas Newsham, Esq.

Ordered that the inheritance of the toft of ground whereon stood the house of Mrs Green of Abbingdon scituat in the Highstreet within this Borough be decreed to Thomas Mander, late lessee of the said messuage, Richard Green, Elizabeth his wife and Samuel Green their eldest son haveing given their consent to the same.

Dev. Whadcock, Mayor	H. Puckering
Wm. Colmore	Tho. Newsham
Wm. Bolton	

Warwick Burg'

At the Court of Record held . . . on Munday the 31st of August anno domini 1696

Present: William Palmer, Esq., Charles Newsham, Esq., Devereux Whadcock, Mayor, John Newsham, Esq., Thomas Newsham, Esq.

Upon reading the peticion of Saunders Nicholls, chandler, to be relieved against William Perks, baker, it is Ordered that a jury be impanelled to try the matters in variance between the said parties and summoned to appear here at two of the clock this afternoone.

Ordered that Richard Hurst be allowed according to his loss one shilling and six pence per pound to make up what he hath already received four shillings in the pound.

The jury impanelled to appear here by two of the clock this afternoon to try the matters in variance between Saunders Nicholes, complainant, and William Perks, defendant, doe find that the said William Perks hath incroched upon the ground of the said Saunders Nicholls by building the wall of his malt house thereon over against the well 24 foot in length and 18 inches in breadth.

Ordered that Richard Hancox, paying for the ground he hath lately bought of Elizabeth Martin and Mary Martin, wife of Richard Martin of the Citty of London, silkweaver, on which before the late fire stood a messuage nere the pillory in the Markett Place, the summ of fourty five pounds (viz.) two third parts thereof to the said Mary Martin for the use of Richard Martin her husband, and one third part to the said Elizabeth Martin, he have the same assured to him by the decree of this Court. Whereas the loss of the said messuage burnt downe by the said fire was valued at £170, for which the said Elizabeth Martin hath received twenty one pounds and five shillings being 2s. 6d. in the pound for the same, Ordered that the said Elizabeth pay to Mary Martin wife of Richard Martin two third parts of the said twenty one pounds and five shillings, being fourteen pounds three shillings and four pence, and that she the said Elizabeth have liberty to deduct out of the said £14 3s. 4d. the summ of ten pounds being money oweing to her by bond from the said Richard Martin.[1]

Warwick Burg'
At the Court of Record held . . . on Munday the seventh day of September anno domini 1696

Present: The Rt. Honourable the Lord Brooke, George Lucy, Esq., William Colemore, Esq., William Bolton, Esq., John Newsham, Esq., Thomas Newsham, Esq., Devereux Whadcock, Mayor.

Ordered that Elizabeth Martin, widow, be allowed and paid two shilling and six pence in the pound for the loss of her goods given in at thirteen pounds.

Ordered that the severall proprietors of the ground taken away and laid into the new square be allow'd 2½d. per foot for every foot of ground soe taken away as aforesaid.

---

[1] There are no signatures at the end of this court.

Memorandum the ground taken away is

	£	s.	d.
From Edward Chesley 448 foot att 2½d. per foot	4	13	4
From Mr Chernock allow'd for his ground per jury 6493 foot	67	12	0
From the parsonage ground 4233 foot at 2½d. per foot	44	1	10½
From Mr Okens ground 1845 foot at 2½d. per foot	19	4	4½
From the Pebble Lane 477 foot att 2½ per foot	4	19	4½
	140	10	11½

Dev. Whadcock, Mayor
Tho. Newsham

Brooke
Wm. Colmore
John Newsham
Wm. Bolton

Warwick Burg'
At the Court of Record held ... on Munday the twelfth day of October anno domini 1696

Present: the Rt Honourable the Lord Brooke, Devereux Whadcock, Mayor, William Colemore, Esq., Thomas Peers, Esq., William Bolton, Esq., John Newsham, Esq., Thomas Newsham, Esq.

Ordered that John Averne be allowed and paid 1s. 6d. in the pound for the loss of his house and goods as reduced to £105 2s. 6d. being £7 15s. 6d.

That Mr Alderman Hands be allowed and paid 1s. 6d. in the pound for the loss of John Prichard his house burnt down in the Sheep Street, as the same is reduced to £150 according to a decree of this Court beareing date the 4th of May last being £11 5s. 0d.

That William Bolton, Esq., be allowed and paid 1s. 6d. in the pound for the loss of Brooks his house and barn in the Butts, as reduced to £50 being £3 15s 0d.

Upon reading the peticion of James Cook an infant against William Johnson, doctor of physick, it is Ordered that summons go forth to summon the said Doctor Johnson to appear in this Court on Munday next to answer the contents of the said peticion.

Upon reading the peticion of Mr Job Rainsford, Ordered that Mr James Prescott be summoned to appeare in Court to answer the contents of the said peticion.

Ordered that Moses Robinson have five pounds allowed him out of the charity moneys, for his pains in takeing care and overseeing the removeing the rubbish of the church, and disposeing the rest of the rubbish of the towne.

Ordered that the bill brought in by Samuel Dunkley for digging stone in the quarry in the church yard, being thirteen pounds fourteen shillings, be paid out of the charitie monyes.

Ordered that Mr Job Rainsford be allowed and paid 1s. 6d. in the pound for the loss of the house he lived in before the fire in the Sheepstreet as the same is reduced to £80, being six pounds as an encouragement for rebuilding the same. Ordered that Mr James Prescott be allowed for the said loss of £80, two shillings and six pence in the pound being tenn pounds.

Wm. Bolton	Brooke Ri. Hands, Mayor[1]
Tho. Newsham	Wm. Colmore

Warwick Burg'
At the Court of Record held . . . on Munday the 19th day of October anno domini 1696

Present: The Rt. Honourable the Lord Brooke, William Palmer, Esq., Charles Newsham, Esq., George Lucy, Esq., Devereux Whadcock, Mayor, William Colemor, Esq., Wm. Bolton, Esq., John Newsham, Esq., Thomas Peers, Esq.

Whereas Mr Fulk Chernock hath according to a former order of this Court taken care to dispose of and remove the brick and stone and other materialls lying on the ground against Saint Maryes Church taken away to enlarge the new square, it is Ordered that he be paid the summ of sixty seven pounds and twelve shillings out of the charity monies, being the summ given him by a jury empanell'd to sett a price upon the said ground.

Tho. Newsham	Brooke Wm. Colmore
W. Palmer	Wm. Bolton

Warwick Burg'
At the Court of Record held . . . on Munday the 26th day of Aprill anno domini 1697

---

[1] Richard Hands was in fact mayor elect. He became mayor on 1 November.

Commissioners present: The Rt. Honourable the Lord Brooke, Richard Hands, Mayor, William Colemore, Esq., William Bolton, Esq., Thomas Newsham, Esq.

Ordered: That Mr Welton be allowed and paid 1s. 6d. in the pound for the loss of his house burnt down in the Highstreet as the same is reduced to £280 being £21.[1]

That John Atterbury be allowed and paid 1s. 6d. in the pound for the loss of Elizabeth Carrs house in the Church Street burnt down by the said fire (he haveing rebuilt the same) as it is reduced to £110, being £8 5s. 0d.

That Richard Good, chandler, be allowed and paid 1s. 6d. in the pound for the loss of Mr Ward's house in the Jury[2] Street burnt down by the said fire as the same is reduced to £55, being £4 2s. 6d.

That Mr Richard Lane and Thomas Masters be allowed and paid 1s. 6d. in the pound for the loss of Mr Prescott house in the Highstreet burnt down by the said fire (they haveing rebuilt the same) as reduced to £280, being £21.

That Mr Mann of Killenworth be allowed and paid 1s. 6d. in the pound for the loss of Mr Archer's house burnt down in the Highstreet (he haveing rebuilt the same) as it is reduced to £120, being £9.

That Mr Job Rainsford be allowed and paid 1s. 6d. in the pound for the loss of the Black Raven house in the Sheepstreet (he haveing rebuilt the same) as it is reduced to £120, being £9.

That George Flower be allowed and paid 1s. 6d. in the pound for the loss of Mr Blisset's house in the Markett Place as the same is reduced to £170, he haveing rebuilt the same, being £12 15s. 0d.

That William Cockbill *alias* Deason of Barford be paid 1s. 6d. in the pound for the loss of Mr Stratford's house in the Highstreet as the same is reduced to £105, being £7 17s. 6d.

That Alexander Nicholls be paid 1s. 6d. in the pound for the loss of Mrs Palmer's house in the Churchstreet as the same is reduced to £170, being £12 15s.

Whereas by the said Act it is enacted that in case the proprietors or owners of the houses demolished by the said fire, their heirs, executors or assigns shall not within the space of two years next ensueing the said fire lay their foundacions of their houses to be rebuilt and shall not within the time to be

[1] The final sum of money is repeated in the margin against this and the following paragraphs.
[2] 'Jury' interlineated over a caret above 'Church' struck out; the rough minute book has 'Castle Street'.

limitted by the said Court rebuild and finish the same, that upon such default the said Court shall have power and authority by their order and decree to dispose of and assigne all the estate and interest of the said owners, and of the ground and soyle thereof and of all yards, backsides, gardens, orchards and other appurtenances thereto belonging, to such person and persons who shall give security to rebuild the same in such time as the said Court shall direct, and whereas many tofts and peices of burnt ground whereon messuages before the said fire stood remaine unbuilt and noe foundacions yet laid, it is this day Order'd in Court that notice be given by affixing copies of this order to the most publick places of this Borough, that from and after three weeks hence next ensueing,[1] the said Commissioners at every Court will be ready to grant and dispose of any part of the burnt ground remaineing then unbuilt, pursuant to the direccions of the Act abovesaid.

Whereas by the said Act of Parliament for rebuilding the town of Warwick, etc., it is enacted that there shall be party walls and party piers sett out equally upon each builders ground to be built up by the first beginner of such building, and that this Court may and shall ascertaine and sett a price upon the said partye walls (viz.) what the last builder shall reimburse the first builder for the moiety of the charges of the same, it is therefore upon due consideracion had of the premises Ordered by this Court that the first builders of such party walls shall be allowed and paid by the latter builder four pounds eighteen shillings per rod for every rod soe built, and soe proporcionably for a greater or lesser quantity.

Whereas severall of the streets and lanes within this Borough have been enlarged and made wider then before the fire by reason of the ground taken away by order of this Court to enlarge and widen the same, it is therefore this day Ordered that the Surveyors bring in and lay before this Court a draught of the ground soe taken away from the severall proprietors and owners thereof in the severall streets and lanes on Munday next.

Upon reading the peticion of Dorothy Hopkins of Charlecoate, widow, James Neale of the Borough of Warwick, shoemaker, and Mary his wife and John Sumner of Charlecoate aforesaid and Rebecca his wife, setting forth that by agreement had and made by and between the peticioners and Thomas Masters of the Borough aforesaid, carpenter, the said Thomas Masters was for the consideracion of the summ of thirty pounds to have the moiety or one half part of the ground whereon before the late fire the White Lyon Inn stood and $\frac{1}{2}$ of the materialls lying thereupon to be conveyed to him and his heirs, the peticioners therefore pray that the said Thomas Masters may be summon'd to appeare in court and the said agreement be confirmed by decree of this Court. It is therefore Ordered that the

---

[1] 'hence next ensueing' interlineated over a caret.

said Thomas Masters be summon'd to appear and the said agreement be confirmed by the decree of this Court.

Ordered that Mr Job Rainsford have the decree of this Court for the Black Raven ground purchased of William Holmes paying the reserved rent of 4d. to the lord of the mannor of Warwick.

Ordered that John Prichard have 2s. 6d. in the pound for the loss of the Corporacion ground in the Sheep Street as the same is reduced to £150 unless the Corporacion of this Borough shew cause to the contrary at the next Court.

Ordered that the bill brought in by William Smith and Samuell Dunckley, Surveyors, dated the 22d of March 1696 for getting stone in the church yard be paid, being £27 5s. 5d.

Wm. Bolton	Brooke
Tho. Newsham	Ri. Hands, Mayor
	Wm. Colmore

Warwick Burg'
At the Court of Record held . . . on Munday the 31st day of May 1697.

[Present:] The Rt Honourable the Lord Brooke, Richard Hands, Mayor, Thomas Peerce, Esq., William Bolton, Esq., Thomas Newsham, Esq., George Lucy, Esq., Wm. Colmore, Esq.

Ordered that Mr Savage, junior, of Tachbrooke be allowed and paid 1s. 6d. in the pound for the loss of Mr Boyce his house in the possession of Mr Bradshaw, apothecary, burnt down by the late fire (he haveing rebuilt the same) as it is reduced to £220, being £16 10s. 0d.[1]

Ordered that Samuell Acock be lent £60[2] out of the brief monies, he giveing security by mortgage of his house in the High Street.

Ordered that the Surveyors be allowed and paid the summ of ten pounds (viz.) four pounds to William Smith and six pounds to Samuel Dunkley for their care and pains in the said office.

Ordered Mr William Weale be allow'd and paid as a gratuity to him for his draught of the church of Saint Maryes four guineas.

Ordered that a jury be impanelled and summon'd to appeare here next Court, to view and sett a price upon a certaine plott, peice or parcell of ground taken out of the back part of the ground called the church ground in the Churchstreet next adjoyning to Mr Tarvers brick wall and now in the

---

[1] This sum of money is repeated in the margin.
[2] Altered probably from '£40'.

possession of John Atterberry, and alsoe that the jury at the same time sett a price upon the 12 inches of ground in breadth and 20 feet in length which was found by a jury on the 27th day of July to be encroch'd and built upon by the said John Atterberry.

Ordered that a jury be impanelled and summon'd to appear here next Court to assess such recompence and satisfaccion as they upon their oaths shall think to be awarded and paid to the owners and proprietors of a certaine toft or peice of burnt ground now lying on the north side of the High Street, on which before the late fire stood a messuage or tenement call'd or known by the name of the Dolphin and for the yards, backside and appertenances thereto belonging, and a true verdict thereof give to this Court according to the best of their judgements.[1]

	Brooke
Wm. Bolton	Ri. Hands, Mayor
Tho. Newsham	Wm. Colmore

Warwick Burg'

At the Court of Record held . . . on Munday the 23d day of August anno domini 1697

[Present:] The Rt Honourable the Lord Brooke, Richard Hands, Mayor, John Combs, Esq., William Colemore, Esq., Thomas Newsham, Esq.

Upon heareing the peticion of Thomas Dixon read, it is Ordered that Richard King, carpenter, be summon'd to appeare here next Court to answer the contents of the said peticion.

Upon heareing the peticion of George Chinn read, it is Ordered that Richard King, carpenter, be summon'd to appear here next Court to answer the contents of the said peticion.

---

[1] The rough minute book has the following additional items at this court: 'Order'd . . . that George Harris have 1s. 6d. per lib. for the loss of his house in the Highstreet as the same is reduced.'
'Ordered that Nicholas Paris be allowed and paid his bill for mending the great engine being £5 10s. od. burnt by the said fire.'
'Memorandum that upon mocion made this day in Court by Moses Robbinson for purchasing a peice of ground part of the church ground in the Church Street, the summ of £20 as a price sett upon the said ground by the Commissioners, the said purchasers to have the ground in case they will pay for the party walls.'
'Ordered that John Foster have £5 lent him upon good security.'
'Ordered that the ground of Mr Bromwich be cleared in the street leadeing to the Pillory and other ground lying in the said street, and alsoe that the rubbish be cleared in all other streets enlarged.'
'Ordered that Samuell Roberts *alias* Burford have an allowance of 1s. 6d. per lib. for the loss of the house he bought of John Sale in the Horse Cheeping.'
'Ordered that Wm. Perks be summon'd to appear next Court to answer the complaints of John Atterbury his wife relateing to a party wall, and that Mr Perks be ordered not to trouble the said John Atterbury for the money for the said party walls.'
'Ordered that Thomas Lean be summon'd to answer the complaint of Samuell Ainge att the next Court.'

Upon heareing the peticion of Thomas Lean, barber, read praying he might be allowed 1s. 6d. per lib. for the loss of Mrs Tucky's house in the Church Street, he haveing purchased the burnt ground thereof and rebuilt the same, it is Ordered that Mr Joseph Blissett in behalf of Mrs Tucky be summon'd to appear here next Court to satisfie this Court whether there be any agreement to the contrary by and between the said peticioner and the said Mrs Tuckey.

Ordered that Mr Moses Robinson doe view the new buildings in this Borough, and report to this Court what thatch'd buildings or other buildings he shall find built contrary to the Act of Parliament.

Ordered that the church wardens of St Maryes parish be summon'd to appear next Court to shew cause why the church ground in the Church Street should not be sold to Moses Robbinson.

Ordered that Richard Hancox be allow'd and paid 1s. 6d. per lib. for the loss of Mrs Martins house in the Markett Place as reduced to £170, being £12 15s. 0d.

Ordered that Mr Cook be paid the £8 1s. according to a decree dated the 14th day of October 1695.

Ordered that the Surveyors bring in a survey of the Church Street and to lay the lines of the descents in the same, in order to the better paveing the said street.

Upon reading the peticion of John Burton, it is Ordered that John Davies and William Eborall be summon'd to appear here next Court to answer the contents of the said peticion.

Ordered that workmen be employ'd by Moses Robbinson to remove the rubbish now lying before Mr Bromich his ground near the pillory, and alsoe to remove the rubbish lying before the church ground in the Churchstreet.[1]

| Wm. Colmore | Brooke |
| Tho. Newsham | Ri. Hands, Mayor |

Warwick Burg'
At the Court of Record held ... on Munday the sixth day of September anno domini 1697.

---

[1] The rough minute book has the following additional items at this court: 'Ordered that James Fish appear next Court and that a jury be empanelled upon the peticion of the feoffees of Mr Oken.'
'Order'd that Widow Tuckey appear next Court to know whether T. Leane shall have the 1 6d. per pound.'
'That the Surveyors deliver in a draught of Mr Chesleys ground taken from him in the Churchstreet seperate from that taken away and added to the square.'

Commissioners then present: The Rt. Honourable the Lord Brooke, Richard Hands, Mayor, Sir Thomas Wagstaffe, Kt., George Lucy, Esq., William Colemore, Esq., William Bolton, Esq., Thomas Newsham, Esq., Thomas Peerce, Esq.

Upon Richard Kings appeareing in Court this day according to summons of the last Court, it is Ordered that he pay George Chinn for his party walls with interest for the same according to the said Act.

Upon reading the peticion of the widow Palmer, it is Order'd that the same be refered to the next Court.

Upon reading the peticion of severall joyners and carpenters, freemen and inhabitants of this Borough, complaineing that many forreign joyners and carpenters haveing noe settlement within the said Borough, doe exercise their respective trades of makeing shop goods and workeing in and upon the building not consumed by the late fire there, to the prejudice of the trade and contrary to the priviledges of the said freemen and inhabitants, it is resolved and agreed by the said Court that noe[1] forreign joyners or carpenters as aforesaid are authorized by the Act of Parliament for the rebuilding of the Town of Warwick, etc., to make shopp goods for sale and to sell them within this Borough, or to work in and upon any old building within the said Borough farther then they might or could have done before the said Act commenced.

Upon reading the peticion of John Burton and upon William Eboral and John Davis appeareing in Court, it is ordered that the matters in controversie be referr'd till farther time.

Ordered that Samuel Ainge have fifty pounds lent him out of the brief monies, he giveing security by mortgage of his house in the Church Street.

Ordered that Mr Robbinson employ labourers to remove the stone now lying upon the ground of the new square, and lay the same in a heap in the church yard.

Upon reading the peticion of Edward Kitchin of Alveston and Thomas Whitacre of Welsborne to be relieved against John Avern of this Borough, tayler, he the said John Avern haveing bought of the said peticioners boards amounting to £4 17s. 6d. and hath not paid for the same, it is Ordered that if any monies be hereafter order'd to the said John Avern towards his loss by the late fire, the same be paid to the peticioners towards paying for the said boards.

Ordered that Edward Chesley be allow'd and paid nine pence a foot for 64 feet of ground taken from him to enlarge the Church[2] Street, being

---

[1] 'noe' interlineated.   [2] Altered from 'High'.

£2 8s. od., and that he be allowed and paid 2½d. per foot for 384 feet of ground taken from him to enlarge the new square, being four pounds.

Ordered that Thomas Lean have 1s. 6d. in the pound for the loss of Mr Tuckeys house in the Church Street, he haveing rebuilt the same, as reduced to £60, being £4 10s. od.

Upon reading the peticion of Thomas Mayo of Rughby in the county of Warwick, yeoman, setting forth that Edward Mayo of the said Borough, carpenter, being seized of two messuages or tenements before the late fire scituat neer the Joyce Poole in the said Borough, did on the 19th day of January 1691[/2] for the consideracion of the summ of £20 mortgage the same to William Lingham of this Borough, gent., that the said William Lingham did on the 18th day of January 1692[/3] in consideracion of the above mencioned summ of £20 assign the said mortgage over into the said peticioner, that the said two messuages were burnt down by the said fire and the same remained unbuilt, by reason whereof the disposall of the same is now in the hands of this Court. It is therefore Ordered that the toft whereon the said two messuages stood be decreed to the said Thomas Mayo and his heirs in consideracion of the said mortgage soe assign'd as aforesaid.

The jury impanelled and sworn this day to assess and sett a price upon a certein toft or peice of burnt ground whereon before the late fire stood a messuage or tenement called or known by the name of the Dolphin Inn, and to award what recompence and satisfaccion the party who would undertake to rebuild the same should pay unto the severall owners and proprietors of the said ground for their interests in the same, doe find the said ground to containe 7020 feet, and doe award the summ of thirty six pounds to be given for the said ground[1], and it appeareing that Edward Clopton of Bridge Town in the parish of Old Stratford in the county of Warwick, Esq., and Martha his wife are the owners of the said ground, and that the said Edward Clopton is willing to purchase his said wife's interest in the said ground and to rebuild the same, it is Ordered that he paying the summ of nine pounds to his said wife Martha shall have the said ground decreed to him and his heirs for ever, and the said Martha by the said decree be barr'd of all claime and demand of, in and unto the premises or any part thereof.

The jury impanelled and sworn this day to sett a price upon the peice of ground taken out of the back part of the church ground in the Church Street next adjoyning to Mr Tarvers brick wall in possession of John Atterberry's widow,[2] according to an order of the last Court, and to sett a price upon the 12 inches of ground in breadth and 20 feet in length which was

---

[1] Followed by 'and the said jury' erased.   [2] ''s widow' inserted and interlineated.

found by a jury to be encroched and built upon by the said John Atterbury, doe by their verdict find the said ground in possession of John Atterberrys widow to be worth the summ of five pounds, and the summ of two shillings and six pence to be paid for the incrochment.[1]

	Brooke
Wm. Bolton	Ri. Hands, Mayor
Tho. Newsham	Wm. Colmore

Warwick Burg'

At the Court of Record held ... on Munday the eleventh day of October anno domini 1697

Commissioners present: The Rt Honourable Lord Brooke, Richard Hands, Mayor, William Colemore, Esq., William Bolton, Esq., Thomas Peers, Esq., Thomas Newsham, Esq.

Upon reading the peticion of John Williams, carpenter, it is Ordered that Mr Tomkys be summon'd to appear next Court to answer the same.

Ordered that the Surveyors bring in a survey of the street leading from the pillory into the new square with an account of what ground is taken away from the severall proprietors and owners of ground in the said street.

Ordered that Mr Aileworth of Welsborn have one shilling and six pence in the pound for the loss of his house burnt down in the Butts as the same is reduced to £18, being £1 7s. od.

Ordered that the feoffees of Thomas Oken, gent., deceased, have £150 lent them out of the brief mony upon mortgage of the new house on the west side of the Church Street in the possession of Mr Thomas Newsham.

Upon reading the peticion of James Fish to be relieved against Edward Chesley, it is Ordered that the said Edward Chesley pay to the said James Fish the summ of two pounds fifteen shillings in full for the charge and interest of the party wall built by the said James Fish for the said Edward Cheseley.

Ordered that John Watts be allow'd and paid one shilling and six pence in the pound for the loss of his houses burnt down on the east side of the Sheepstreet as the same is reduced to two hundred and fifty pounds, being eighteen pounds fifteen shillings.

---

[1] The rough minute book has the following additional items at this court: 'Order'd that the Corporacion shew cause why John Prichard should not have the 2s. 6d. in the pound for the loss of the house in Sheep Street.'
'Ordered that Thomas Wall be lent £60 out of the brief monies upon security of his house in the High Street now the Bare.'

Ordered that the said John Watts have fifty pounds lent him out of the brief monies, he giveing security for the same such as this Court shall approve.

Ordered that George Chinn have £40 lent him out of the brief monies upon mortgage of his new built house in the Swann Lane.

Ordered that Mr Richard Lane and Thomas Masters be summon'd to appear here next Court to answer the petition of George Chinn.

Ordered that George Chinn, paying to Mr William Tarver the summ of fourty seven pounds four shillings, have the inheritance of a certaine peice or plott of ground lying in the Swan Lane, being part of the Bell ground assured to him and his heirs by decree of this Court subject to the yearly payment of three pence to William Bolton, Esq., lord of the manor of Warwick.

Ordered that the Treasurers state and make up their accounts of all monies by them received and paid for the use of the sufferers by the late fire in Warwick, and lay the same before this Court with all convenient speed.

Ordered that John Prichard be allowed and paid 2s. 6d. in the pound for the loss of the Corporacion house on the west side of the Sheep Street as the same is reduced to £150, and that he be alsoe allow'd 1s. 6d. in the pound more for the said loss when he hath laid the foundacion of the said house in order to rebuild the same, and that he paying to the Corporation of this Borough the summ of twenty pounds have the inheritance of all that ground, whereon before the late fire stood a messuage then in possession of the said John Prichard, assured to him and his heirs by decree of this Court.

	Brooke
Wm. Bolton	Ri. Hands, Mayor
Tho. Newsham	Wm. Colmore

Warwick Burg'
At the Court of Record held . . . on Munday the twenty fifth day of October anno domini 1697

Commissioners present: The Rt Honourable the Lord Brooke, Richard Hands, Mayor, William Colmore, Esq., William Bolton, Esq., Thomas Newsham, Esq.

Ordered that Moses Robbinson employ workmen to lower the ground in the new square, and that he give notice to the severall proprietors in the Sheepstreet that they and every of them cleer and carry away the dirt and rubbish lying before their doors in the said street.

Ordered that Serjeant Hadley be lent sixty pounds out of the brief monies upon his own and Mr Alderman Young's bond for the payment of the same.

Ordered that William Perks be lent sixty pounds out of the brief monies upon mortgage of his house in the Church Street.

Whereas John Ashwin of Bretforton in the county of Worcester hath by agreement sold unto Samuel Burford of this Borough, inkeeper, a certaine toft, peice or parcell of burnt ground lying and being in the Sheepstreet on the north side of the Black Raven, for the consideracion of the summ of fifteen pounds to be by him the said Samuel Burford in hand paid to the said John Aswin or his assigns, and the summ of fifteen pounds more within six months after the said agreement made, it is Ordered that, for the consideracions aforesaid, the said ground be decreed to the said Samuel Burford and his heirs, together with the benifitt of one shilling and six pence in the pound given towards the rebuilding the same.

Ordered that Moses Robbinson employ workmen to[1] remove the rubbish lying in the new street leading from the pillory.

Upon review of a former order of this Court for skirting the luthern lights with lead, it is order'd that the severall builders in the Sheepstreet have notice to skirtt there luthern lights with lead according to the said order.

Ordered that the bill brought in by William Smith and Samuel Dunkley, Surveyors, for takeing down and putting up the Red Lyon wall in the Swann Lane be paid out of the brief monies, being £7 3s. 6d.[2]

Tho. Newsham
Rich. Hands, Mayor

Brooke
Wm. Colmore
Wm. Bolton

Warwick Burg'
At the Court of Record held . . . on Munday the 8th day of November anno domini 1697

Commissioners present: The Rt Honourable the Lord Brooke, Sir Henry Puckering, Bart., Sir John Clopton, Kt., Richard Grimes, Mayor, William Palmer, Esq., Andrew Archer, Esq., William Colmore, Esq., William Bolton, Esq., Thomas Peirce, Esq., Thomas Newsham, Esq.

Ordered that Joseph Ainge give bond for £20 formerly lent him, being the gift of my lord Guildford, and that the same be placed to account by the Treasureres of the brief monies.

[1] 'employ workmen to' interlineated over a caret.
[2] Followed in the rough minute book by an additional item: 'That Samuell Dunkley and Mr Smith view the wall in dispute between George Chinn and Mr Lane and Thomas Masters, and report the same to this Court.'

Memorandum that Richard Grimes, Mayor of the said Borough, did then and there take the oath mencion'd and directed in the said Act before William Palmer and Andrew Archer, Esqs., two of his Majestie's justices of the peace for the county of Warwick.

Ordered that Moses Robbinson give notice to Mrs Cawthern and Richard Hadley, that they remove the robbish from before their doors in the Sheepstreet.

Ordered that Mr Wills be paid £20 toward carrying on the informacion against archdeacons and registers, who have not made return of what monies they received upon the brief monies according to the direccion of the said brief.

Ordered that Sir Henry Puckering be paid 4s. in the pound for one bay of building, part of 3 bay of building mencion'd in the book of reductions as reduced to £6 the same being rebuilt   £ 1   4s.   od.
That he be paid 2s. 6d. in the pound for £12 being the loss of the[1] other 2 bay of building   £ 1   10s.   od.
That he be paid 4s. in the pound for the loss of a barn as reduced to £40 being rebuilt   £ 8   os.   od.
That he be paid 4s. in the pound for the loss of Angraves house as reduced to £100   £20   os.   od.
That he be paid 4s. in the pound for the loss of widow Harris house as reduced to £60 being   £13   os.   od.
That he be paid 2s. 6d. in the pound for the loss of Bromfield's house as reduced to £20 being   £ 2   10s.   od.

                                     £46   4s.   od.

Memorandum it is this day agreed with William Smith and Samuel Dunkley, that the said Smith and Dunkley pull down the old walls of the church of Saint Maryes left standing on the north and south side of the said church, and the cross arch between the cross isles and the body of the church, and digg up the old foundacions of the said church to the rock and bring up the same from the said rock with square stone, part of the stone dugg out of the quarry in the churchyard, even with the surface of the ground according to the draught made and left by Sir William Wilson, kt., and that the said Smith and Dunkley shall be paid two pence three farthings a foot for every solid foot contained in the said work, they finding lime, sand and workmanshipp.

[1] 'loss of the' interlineated over a caret.

Ordered that Mr Richard Lane be desired to enquire out the prizes of timber and lead to be used in and about the rebuilding of the church of Saint Maryes, and report the same to this Court.

	Brooke
Tho. Newsham	Rich. Grimes, Mayor
Tho. Peers	Wm. Bolton
	Wm. Colmore

Warwick Burg'

At the Court of Record held . . . on Munday the 17th day of January anno domini 1697/8

[Present:] The Rt. Honourable the Lord Brook, Sir Henry Puckering, Bart., Richard Grimes, Mayor, William Colmore, Esq., William Bolton, Esq., Thomas Newsham, Esq.

Ordered that Wm. Smith and Samuel Dunckley take care to remove the stone belonging to the Church of St Maryes from off the church ground in Church Street.[1]

Ordered that they likewise take care that all the bones of dead corps that shall be dugg up by digging the foundacions of the Church of St Maryes, be laid in the bone house.

Ordered that the two shopp windows att the upper end of the Swann Lane be taken downe, and that the same when putt up againe be placed soe as to extend noe farther then the Act of Parliament doth allow of.

Ordered that Mr Aaron Rogers be paid three guineas for three jorneys (viz.) two to Worcester and one to Leicester to Mr Serjeant Wright, upon the bussiness and by order of this Court.

	Brooke
Wm. Colmore	H. Puckering
Tho. Newsham	Rich. Grimes, Mayor
	Wm. Bolton

Warwick Burg'

At the Court of Record held . . . on Munday the sixteenth day of May anno domini 1698

Commissioners then present: The Rt. Honourable the Lord Brooke, Sir John Mordaunt, Bart., Sir Henry Puckering, Bart., Sir Thomas Wagstaffe, Kt., Richard Grimes, Mayor, William Bolton, Esq.

---

[1] The rough minute book refers to 'stone lying now upon the ground bought by Mr Cook in Church Street and Mrs Robbinson'. ['Mrs' in error for 'Mr'.]

Whereas there have been severall summs of money lent, out of the monies given to and for the use of the sufferers by the late fire within this Borough, to the severall persons hereunder named, sufferers amongst others by the said fire (viz.)

Unto Mr Tomkys the summ of	£100
To Mr Nicholas the summ of	£100
To Mr Tarver the summ of	£150
To Mr Norton the summ of	£100
To Mr Blissett the summ of	£100
To Mr Fish the summ of	£ 50
To Mrs Weale and her son	£100
And to Mr Heath the summ of	£200
In all amounting unto the summ of	£900

And whereas there is and will be great occasions for monies to pay workmen and to buy materialls to be used in and about the rebuilding of the Church of Saint Maryes, it is therefore ordered that the severall persons abovemencioned have notice to provide the severall summs sett against their names, and to pay in the same to the Treasurers of the said monies on or before the twenty fourth day of June next.

Ordered that the Treasurers of the monies given to and for the use of the sufferers by the late fire within this Borough, doe state and make up their accounts of all monies by them received and paid by order of this Court since the stateing of the last account on the 30th day of October anno domini 1697, and that they lay the same before the Comissioners at the next Court.

<table>
<tr><td></td><td>Brooke</td></tr>
<tr><td>Wm. Bolton</td><td>J. Mordaunt</td></tr>
<tr><td>Rich. Grimes, Mayor</td><td>H. Puckering</td></tr>
<tr><td></td><td>Tho. Wagstaffe</td></tr>
</table>

Warwick Burg'
At the Court of Record held . . . on Saturday[1] the 25th day of June 1698

Commissioners present: Sir Henry Puckering, Bart., William Palmer, Esq., Richard Grimes, Mayor, William Colmore, Esq., Thomas Peers, Esq., William Bolton, Esq., Thomas Newsham, Esq.

Ordered that Moses Robbinson employ men to lower and levell the ground in the New Square over against the Church of Saint Maryes, in order for the undertakers to frame and work up the timber for the roof of the said

---

[1] 'Saturday' written after 'Munday' struck out.

church, and alsoe that the said Moses Robbinson take care to have an arch of stone turn'd over the well now being in the said square.

Ordered that Mr Cole of Tachbrooke pay Mr Job Rainsford for his party walls on the north side of his house in the Sheepstreet, he the said Mr Cole haveing begunn to build on the same, within two months next ensueing the date hereof, with interest after the rate of £6 per cent per annum, according to the direccion of the Act of Parliament.

Ordered that Samuell Acock be allowed and paid 9d. per foot for 74 foot of ground taken away from him on the north side of the Highstreet to enlarge the said street.

Ordered that Sir William Wilson, Kt., be paid twenty pounds in farther part of the summ to be paid him for surveying the building of the Church of Saint Maries, he haveing before received twenty two pounds for the same use.

Ordered that John Watts be allowed and paid six pence per foot for 45 feet of ground taken away from him to enlarge the Sheepstreet at the White Lyon.

Ordered that a jury be impanelled and sworn at the next Court to view a building and party wall in dispute between John Phillips, carpenter, and John Watts, flax dresser, belonging to the goale lying on the backside of the said John Watts his house in the Sheepstreet, and report to this Court whether the said John Watts ought to pay for the same as a party wall or not.

Whereas a considerable part of the burnt ground in severall streets within this Borough remains unbuilt, to the great prejudice of the trade and publick weale of the said Borough, for the encouragement of the more speedy rebuilding the same, it is agreed and resolved by this Court, that unless the late proprietors of the said ground doe on or before the 25th day of July next beginn to lay the foundacions or give security to this Court to rebuild the said ground within such time as shall be agreed on, that then any person who will undertake to build the said ground or any part thereof, may come in and purchase the same at the price of one penny per foot.[1]

It is also agreed that all person or persons who have already built or shall hereafter rebuild any house or houses within this Borough, that shall neglect to make their lights in the roofe or roofes of the said houses fronting the streets with pediment windows skirted with lead and good wrought

[1] The rough minute book adds: 'And that the owners and proprietors of ground who live att some distance from this Borough have notice given them of this order.'

cornish of wood, the same alsoe skirted with lead, shall loose the benefitt of 12d. per pound the next distribucion if any.

Wm Bolton	H. Puckering
Tho. Newsham	Richard Grimes, Mayor
Tho. Peers.	Wm. Colmore

Warwick Borough
At the Court of Record held ... on Tuesday[1] the ninth day of August anno domini 1698

Commissioners present: Sir Henry Puckering, Bart., Richard Grimes, Mayor, William Colmore, Esq., William Bolton, Esq., Thomas Newsham, Esq.

Ordered that the Treasurers make up and state their account of all monies by them received and paid for the use of the sufferers by the late fire in Warwick, and lay the same before the Commissioners at the next Court.

Ordered that the bussiness in dispute between John Burton, William Eborall and others relateing to the house built by the said John Burton be referr'd till the next Court to be held to morrow morning.

Ordered that a jury be impanelled to sett out the meets and bounds of the ground whereon before the late fire stood a house belonging to the feoffees of Thomas Oken deceased, then in possession of Matthew Busbie call'd the Signe of the Peacock, and give in the same at the next Court.

Ordered that the jury order'd to be impanelled the last Court to view a wall in dispute between John Phillips, carpenter, and John Watts, flaxdresser, be summon'd to appear here next Court.

| Wm. Colmore | H. Puckering |
| Tho. Newsham | Rich. Grimes, Mayor |

Warwick Borough
At the Court of Record held ... on Wednesday the tenth day of August anno domini 1698

Commissioners present: Sir Henry Puckering, Bart., Richard Grimes, Mayor, William Colemore, Esq., William Bolton, Esq., Thomas Newsham, Esq.

Upon the complaint of Mary Dadley, widow, it is ordered by this Court that Mr Fulk Weale, draper, and Thomas Marriott, shooemaker, doe make up their mounds betwixt their back ground and the back ground of the said

[1] 'Tuesday' altered from 'Munday'.

widow Dadley on the south side of the High Street in possession of Francis Bickley, on this side and before the 24th day of this instant August.

The jury impanelled and sworn this day according to an order of the last Court to sett out the meets and bounds of the burnt ground belonging to the feoffees of Thomas Oken, gent., deceased, on which before the late fire stood a messuage or tenement in possession of Matthew Busbie, doe find the ground lying in a streight line from the first antient post now standing in the mound of and belonging to the feoffees of Mr Oken to the corner of Mr John Williams his barn fronting the street, to be part of and to belong to the said Mr Oken's land.

The jury impanell'd and sworen this day to view a wall in dispute between John Phillips, carpenter, and John Watts, flaxdresser, doe find the same to be a back partition wall belonging to the goale lying on the back part of the said John Watts his shopp, extending in length to the little window in the said shopp, and that the said wall is built eighteen inches thick without any toothing left in the same.

Upon heareing of severall matters in dispute between John Burton, William Eborall and Alice Mattson, daughter of Edward Lane deceased, relateing to the severall interests of the said persons to a new house lately built by the said John Burton in the new street leading to the pillory, and considering the interest of the said Alice Mattson in the premises, this Court doe think fitt and soe order that the said John Burton pay unto the said Alice Mattson the summ of four pounds and ten shillings out of the summ of money to be by him paid for the ground whereon he hath built his said house, which summ of four pounds and ten shillings this Court doth award in full satis-faccion of her right, tytle, claime or interest in and too the premises or any part thereof.

Wm. Colmore	H. Puckering
Tho. Newsham	Rich. Grimes, Mayor

Warwick Burg'

At the Court of Record held ... on Munday the fifteenth day of August anno domini 1698

Commissioners present: Sir Henry Puckering, Bart., Richard Grimes, Mayor, William Colmore, Esq., William Bolton, Esq., Thomas Peers, Esq., Thomas Newsham, Esq.

Whereas Doctor John Cauley hath received severall summs of money which have been collected by vertue of his Majesties gracious letters patents for relief of the sufferers in the late dreadfull fire at Warwick, and hath offer'd to give three severall bonds for payment of the same to the use of the said sufferers, the first whereof is to be for payment of one hundred pounds in November next, and the second for payment of one hundred pounds more in February next, and the third for payment of the residue of the said summ in Easter term next, it is this day order'd by this Court by the advice of Mr Edward Wills as the most safe and expedicious way, that the said three bonds be accepted of and be taken in the names of the Right Honourable the Lord Brooke, Sir Henry Puckering, Bart., William Colmore, Esq., and Thomas Newsham, Esq.

Tho. Newsham	H. Puckering
Ri. Lane, Mayor[1]	Wm. Colmore
	Tho. Peers

Warwick Burg'
At the Court of Record held ... on Munday the sixteenth day of January anno domini 1698/9

Commissioners present: Sir Henry Puckering, Bart., Richard Lane, Mayor, William Peyto, Esq., William Colmore, Esq., Thomas Peers, Esq., William Bolton, Esq., Thomas Newsham, Esq.

Ordered that Moses Robbinson employ labourers to remove the rubbish and dirt now lying against the church wall in the Churchstreet.

Ordered that the severall proprietors of the ground taken away and laid into the street leading to the pillory be allowed five pence per foot for every foot of ground soe taken away as aforesaid (viz.)

From Thomas Lea 160 feet att 5d. per foot	£3 6s. 8d.
John Burton 147 feet att 5d. per foot	£3 1s. 3d.
James Wilson 48 feet att 5d. per foot	£1 0s. 0d.
Richard Hancox 32 feet att 5d. per foot	£0 13s. 4d.
	£8 1s. 3d.

Upon reading the peticion of George Chesley, taylor, it is ordered that Mr Edmund Wilson be summon'd to appear here next Court to answer the contents of the said peticion.

Upon reading the peticion of Mr Fulk Weale, draper, it is order'd that the consideracion of the said peticion be referr'd to the next Court to be considered of.

Ordered that there be ballasters placed over the windows of the Church of Saint Maryes with a wall with[2] mouldings round the topp of the said

---

[1] Richard Lane did not become mayor until 1 Nov. 1698.
[2] 'a wall with' interlineated over a caret.

church, according to the draught this day laid before the Commissioners, and that William Smith, Samuel Dunkley and Francis Smith be allowed and paid twenty five pounds for such extraordinary work more then att first agreed for.

Ordered that the severall proprietors of the ground taken away and laid into the street called the Sheepstreet be allowed six pence per foot for every foot soe taken away to enlarge the said street.

Tho. Newsham
Ri. Lane, Mayor

H. Puckering
Wm Colmore
Tho. Peers

Warwick Burg'
At the Court of Record held . . . on Tuesday the twenty eigth day of February anno domini 1698/9

Commissioners present: Sir Henry Puckering, Bart., Richard Lane, Mayor, William Colmore, Esq., Thomas Peers, Esq., Thomas Newsham, Esq.

Ordered that an order be drawn upon Mr Hoar, one of the Treasurers of the brief monies in London, for the summ of four hundred pounds to be by him paid out of the said brief monies, and return'd to Warwick for the use of the sufferers there.

Ordered that all sufferers who have had money lent them out of the brief monies have notice to pay in the same, and that upon their refusall soe to doe their bonds and securityes will be sued.

Ordered that Mr Aaron Rogers and Mr Jephcott be desired to take an account of the weight of the old lead of the Church of Saint Maryes, and alsoe of the new lead to be laid and used on and about the said church.

Whereas the bill this day given in by Thomas Masters for the timber used in roofing the Church of St Marys amounts to the summ of £296 12s. 6d., and the bill given in by John Phillips and Thomas Masters for working up and frameing the said timber being 143 square 89 cts att 16s. the square to the summ of £115 2s. 3d., and whereas the said Thomas Masters hath received of Mr William Tarver the summ of £305, and the said John Phillips and Thomas Masters have received of John Mitchener the summ of £90, it is ordered that the summ of £16 14s. more be paid to the said John Phillips and Thomas Masters in full of the said 2 bills.[1]

Ordered that Thomas Masters be paid the summ of five pounds and ten shillings in full for covering the tower and church walls of St Mary's to preserve the same from frost and weather.

[1] These sums are worked out in the margin.

Ordered that £5 17s. 4d. be allowed and paid to John Phillips and Thomas Masters for the workmanshipp in braggetting[1] the first arch in the Church of Saint Maryes, and that for the remainder of the said braggetting work they be paid after the rate of eight shillings per square.

Ordered that a jury be impanelled and summon'd to appear here next Court to sett a value upon the ground taken away and laid into the Swan Lane.

Ordered that the consideracion of the peticion of Mr Fulk Weale, draper, be referr'd to the next Court.

Ordered that the consideracion of the peticion of George Chesley be referr'd to the next Court.

Whereas a considerable quantity of ground hath been taken away from the ground call'd Okens ground lying att the upper end on the north side of the New Square, over against the west end of St Maryes Church, and laid into the said square, soe that the remainder of the said ground now unbuilt is left in soe narrow a compass that the Corporation, owners of the said ground, cannot sett the same to be rebuilt, it is ordered that the party wall built by John Foster adjoyning to the said ground be paid for out of the brief monies, for an incouragement towards rebuilding the same.

Ordered that Mr Jephcott be desired to make enquiry of the rates for glaseing the windows of the Church of St Maryes.

Ri. Lane, Mayor
Tho. Newsham

H. Puckering
Wm Colmore
Tho. Peers

Warwick Burg'
At the Court of Record held ... on Wednesday the eighth day of March anno domini 1698/9

Commissioners present: Sir Henry Puckering, Bart., Richard Lane, Mayor, Sir John Clopton, Kt., William Palmer, Esq., Thomas Peers, Esq., William Colmore, Esq., Thomas Newsham, Esq., John Andrews, Esq.

Memorandum that John Andrews, Esq., one of the Commissioners or Judges appointed by the said Act of Parliament as a justice of the peace for the time being,[2] did then and there take the oath mencion'd and directed in the said Act before Sir John Clopton, Kt., and William Palmer, Esq., two of his Majesties justices of the peace for the county of Warwick.

[1] Bracketing, in preparation for plaster mouldings.
[2] 'as a justice of the peace for the time being' interlineated over a caret.

Ordered that an agreement be drawn between the Commissioners and William Marshall for makeing an iron skreen and paire of doors to be putt between the church and chancel of Saint Mary's Church, according to the modell now lying before the Commissioners, he the said William Marshall to be paid the summ of one hundred and ten pounds for the same, and five pounds more if the Lord Dighby shall think he deserves the same.

Tho. Newsham	H. Puckering
Ri. Lane, Mayor	Wm Colmore
	Tho. Peers

Warwick Burg'

At the Court of Record held . . . on Friday the seventeenth day of March anno domini 1698/9

Commissioners present: Sir Henry Puckering, Bart., Richard Lane, Mayor, William Colmore, Esq., Thomas Peerse, Esq., Thomas Newsham, Esq.

Ordered that John Prichard have a decree for the Corporacion ground in the Sheepstreet according to an order of Court of the eleventh day of October 1697.

Ordered that Mr Fish pay to the Treasurers the summ of fourty pounds, being with ten pounds received before[1] in full of the fifty pounds lent to him by bond dated the 3d day of February 1695/6, viz. the summ of twenty pounds part thereof within one week after Lady day next, and the summ of twenty pounds the residue thereof on or before Midsummer next, and that upon his neglect or refusall soe to doe his bond to be sued.

Tho. Peers	H. Puckering
Ri. Lane, Mayor	Wm Colmore

Warwick Burg'

At the Court of Record held . . . on Tuesday the 21st day of March anno domini 1698/9

Commissioners present: Sir Henry Puckering, Bart., Richard Lane, Mayor, William Colmore, Esq., Thomas Newsham, Esq., Thomas Peers, Esq.

Memorandum it is this day agreed by and between the Commissioners now present and William Hyron and Richard Hancox of the Borough aforesaid and Heugh Canter of the Citty of Coventry, glaziers, as followeth——
Imprimis the said William Hyron, Richard Hancox and Heugh Canter doe agree to glaze the windows of Saint Marys Church with the best sort of Stourbridge glass and a lead according to and as good as the sample

---

[1] 'with ten pounds received before' interlineated over a caret.

presented this day to the Commissioners, the same to be well cemented and soddered in substantiall and workmanlike manner, the bands to be substantiall and strong proporcionable to the said work, and to doe the same in such proporcion as hereafter is expressed, that is to say that he the said William Hyron shall doe one third part of the said glazeing, Richard Hancox one third part and the said Heugh Canter one other third part. Item they doe agree to doe and finish all the said glazeing in good workmanlike manner as aforesaid on or before the 1st day of September next ensueing. In consideracion of which said work to be done and finished as aforesaid, the said Commissioners doe agree to pay unto the said William Hyron, Richard Hancox and Heugh Canter 5½d. per foot for every foot of glasswork to be done as aforesaid.[1]

Warwick Burg'

At the Court of Record held . . . on Tuesday the fourth day of Aprill 1699

Commissioners present: Sir Henry Puckering, Bart., Richard Lane, Mayor, Mayor, William Palmer, Esq., William Colmore, Esq., Thomas Newsham, Esq., John Andrews, Esq., Charles Newsham, Esq.

The[2] jury impanelled and sworn this day to view and determine the difference between George Chesley, tayler, and Edmund Wilson, gent., relateing

---

[1] There are no signatures at the end of this court. In the rough minute book it is followed by notes for an additional court, viz.
'Warr' Burg'. At a Meeting att the Mayor's Parlour on Munday the 3rd day of April 1699.
'Commissioners present: Sir Henry Puckering, Bart., Richard Lane, Mayor, William Colmore, Esq., Thomas Newsham, Esq.
'Severall things to be considered of:
'1. To order the plaistering the church: Ordered that William Smith agree with workmen to doe the plastering of the church att the cheapest rates he can, and that he be supervisor of the said work, the Commissioners giveing him such gratuity as they shall think fitt.
'2. To order the remainder of the paveing: Ordered that Smith, Walker and Hemming be sent for and treated with about the remainder of the paveing.
'3. To order the church walls.
'4. To order the allowance by drossy lead in the bone house: For 6 tun 10 c. 2 qrs 11 lb. of drossy lead, Mr Mayor is to deliver 5 tun 12 c. of sheet lead.
'5. To enquire what has been done about thatch'd building ordered to be tyled.
'6. To consider the paveing belonging to the church in the Church Street.
'7. To order the iron in the bone house: Mr Rogers and Mr Jephcott to weigh out the iron.
'8. To consider the height of the tower and cupulo.
'9. To consider the size of the lead for the church: The size to be betwixt 8 and 9 pound to a foot square upon the flatt.
'10. To order the foundacions of the church.
'11. To order one to receive the lead from Mr Mayor and see the same weigh'd and enter it.'
[2] The rough minute book has the following additional items at the start of this court: 'Memorandum Samuell Fox, currier, liveing in a house in the Castle Street some part of the back building thereof being thatch'd, he hath promised to tyle it before the 1st of August next.
'William Fouks hath promised that he will either pull down a thatch'd building belonging to his house in the Castle Street or tyle the same before the 1st day of August next.
'Captain Williams hath promised to tyle his back building in the Jury Street, Timothy Norberry tenant, when the Kingshead buildings are tyled.'

to the repaireing of part of the mound wall lying between the garden ground of the said George Cheseley belonging to his house on the south side of the Highstreet and the garden ground of the said Edmund Wilson in possession of Mr Henry Rogers, apothecary, being the lower part of the said mound, doe find the said lower part of the said mound to belong unto the said George Chesley and he to repaire the same.

The said jury sworn this day to assess and sett a price upon the ground taken away from the proprietors of the ground in the Swann Lane, doe find that according to the survey of the said lane, there is taken from the ground of Mr William Tarver 1710 feet in measure, and doe assess the price of $2\frac{1}{2}$d. per foot to be paid for the same, being £17 16s. 3d.

The said jury doe find 264 feet of ground in measure to be taken from Mr Tho. Hicks and added to the Swann Lane, and doe assess the price of $2\frac{1}{2}$d. per foot to be paid for the same, being £2 15s. 0d.

The said jury doe find according to the survey of the said Swan Lane that there is taken from the said lane and added to the ground of George Chinn and George Taylor 216 feet of ground in measure, and doe assess the price of $2\frac{1}{2}$d. per foot to be paid by them for the same, being £2 5s.

The said jury doe find 1697 feet of ground to be taken from the church ground in the Church Street and added to the ground called Oken's ground next adjoyning in possession of Mr Thomas Newsham, and doe assess the price of one penny half penny per foot to be paid for the same, being £10 12s. $1\frac{1}{2}$d.

The said jury doe alsoe find that there is taken from the front of the ground called the church ground and added to the ground aforesaid called Oken's ground 72 feet of ground or thereabouts, and doe assess the price of $2\frac{1}{2}$d. per foot to be paid for the same being 15s.

It is agreed and order'd by this Court that the seats and pews to be erected and sett up in the Church of Saint Maryes be fixed according to the first draught to the north and south side walls of the said church, and that the middle isle of the said church be made to be betwixt eleven and twelve feet wide betwixt the said seates.

Ri. Lane, Mayor　　　　　　　　　　　H. Puckering[1]

[1] Followed in the rough minute book by an additional court:
'Warr' Burg'
'At the Court of Record held ... on Wednesday the 19th day of Aprill 1699.
'Commissioners present: William Colmore Esq., Richard Lane, Mayor, William Palmer, Esq., Basill Feilding, Esq., Thomas Newsham, Esq.
'Whereas by a former order of this Court of the 26th of April '97 it was ordered that notice should be given to all persons who had a mind to rebuild any house or houses within this Borough upon any part of the burnt ground which should remaine unbuilt by the space of 3 week next ensueing the date of the

Warwick Burg'

At the Court of Record held ... on Wednesday the second day of August 1699

Commissioners present: The Rt. Honourable the Lord Digby, William Colmore, Esq., John Marriott, Esq., John Combs, Esq., Thomas Peers, Esq., Thomas Newsham, Esq.

Ordered that the severall owners and proprietors of houses fronting the principall streets within this Borough, that have any outhouses and buildings thereunto belonging now thatched, have notice that they forthwith unthatch the said buildings and tyle or slatt the same according to the direccion of the aforesaid Act of Parliament on this side and before the 29th day of September next ensueing, upon the penalty of being indicted and suffering the penaltys in the said Act inflicted.

Ordered that the widow Bucknall tyle or slate her back buildings in the Markett Place according to the Act aforesaid, and that she lay out and expend towards doeing the same (she being tenant for life) the summ of ten pounds, and it is order'd that the remaineing part of the charge in finishing the tyleing or slateing of the said back building, over and above the said summ of ten pounds, be charged upon [   ]¹ Bucknall her son, he being tenant in reversion, and that he allow and pay the same accordingly.

Warwick Borough

At the Court of Record held ... the fourth day of October anno domini 1699

Commissioners present:²

Whereas the jury impanelled and sworn the tenth day of August in the year of our Lord 1698, according to an order of this Court of the 16th day of said order, that the said Commissioners att every Court would be ready to grant and dispose of any part of the said burnt ground, and whereas by a subsequent order of the 20th day of June last it was ordered that any person who had a mind to come in and purchass any part of the said burnt ground to rebuild any house or houses thereon might purchass the same att the price of one penny per foot, and whereas notwithstanding the said two orders a considerable part of the burnt ground remains still unbuilt to the great prejudice of the trade and publick weale of the said Borough, for the encouragement of the more speedy rebuilding the same, it is agreed and resolved by this Court that any person who will come in and purchass any part of the said burnt ground within this Borough may come in and purchass the same att the price of one half penny per foot, and that any person or persons who will come in and purchass the ground lying unbuilt att the upper end of the new square over against the Church of St Maryes to rebuild a house on the same shall have liberty to purchass one half of [the] garden called the Swan Garden to accommodate the said house att the same rate, and upon purchaseing any part of the said ground as aforesaid the partyes soe purchaseing shall have the Decree of this Court for the same.

[signed in the margin:] Wm Colmore'

¹ Blank not filled in.
² Names not filled in; the Commissioners sign in the left-hand margin.

May 1698 and a subsequent order of the ninth day of May 1698, to view a wall in dispute between John Phillips, carpenter, and John Watts, flaxdresser, did by their verdict find the same to be a back particion wall belonging to the County Goale lying on the back part of the said John Watts his shopp and that the same was built eighteen inches thick, and it appeareing to this Court that the said John Watts hath made use of the said wall by laying timber into the same and by building up thereto, it is now therefore agreed and resolv'd by this court that the said wall shall be and is hereby adjudged to be a party wall, and this court doe hereby order that the said John Watts pay unto the said John Phillips the summ of five pounds and ten shillings, being the summ cast up by the Surveyors as appears by a note under their hands, for the said John Watts to pay for the same after the rate of four pound eighteen shillings per rod, being the price settled by a former order of this Court, with interest according to the aforesaid Act of Parliament.

W. Palmer   Hen. Parker   J. Mordaunt

Warwick Burg'
At the Court of Record held ... on Thursday the 25th of January anno domini 1699[1700]

Commissioners present: Sir Henry Puckering, Bart., George Lucy, Esq., William Colmore, Esq., Thomas Peers, Esq., Thomas Newsham, Esq.

Upon reading the peticion of William Edes, vicar of the Church of Saint Mary's within this Borough, for an allowance to be made to him for the damage he hath sustained by reason of the digging stone in the church yard of the said church, it is ordered that the said William Edes be allow'd and paid the summe of five pounds in full recompence and satisfaccion of the damage he hath already and may sustaine for the future, by reason of the digging of stone and laying rubbish in the said church yard for the use of the said church in rebuilding and finishing the same.

Order'd that Mr Strong be paid the summ of ten guineas and his son the summ of two guineas for their jorney from London to view the tower of the Church of Saint Mary's, and for the report made as to the failure in the pillars of the said tower.

Tho. Newsham   H. Puckering

Warwick Burg'
At the Court of Record held ... on Munday the seventeenth day of June anno domini 1700

Commissioners present: The Rt. Honourable the Lord Brooke, the Rt. Honourable the Lord Digby, Sir Henry Puckering, Bart., Sir William

Boughton, Bart., Andrew Archer, Esq., George Lucy, Esq., Thomas Peers, Esq.

Memorandum: It is agreed by and between the Commicioners then present and William Smith, Samuel Dunckley and Francis Smith as follows (viz.) it is agreed that they the said William Smith, Samuel Dunckley and Francis Smith shall digg and lay a foundacion of Warwick stone well squared and bedded att the west end of Saint Mary's church, in order to build a new tower there according to the draught now lying before the Commissioners, and that they shall and will att their own propper costs and charges remove and carry away all rubbish that shall be digged out of the ground in order to lay the foundacions of the said tower.

And alsoe it is agreed that they the said William Smith, Samuel Dunckley and Francis Smith shall build good solid pillars of Shrewley stone above the ground on the foundacions aforesaid in order to carry the said tower, and find all lime and workmanship about the said pillars, they the said Commissioners finding all Shrewley stone and carriage thereof to Warwick.

And the said Commissioners doe agree and order that they the said William Smith, Samuel Dunckley and Francis Smith shall in consideracion of digging and laying the foundacions aforesaid and carrying away the said rubbish, be paid two pence three farthings per foot for every foot square of worke contained in the said foundacion when the same shall be laid as aforesaid, and alsoe four pence per foot for every solid foot of work which shall be contained in the said pillars of Shrewley stone when built as aforesaid.

And it is further order'd that Mr Aaron Rogers be desired to agree with men for the carriage of the stone from Shrewley quarry to the church of Saint Mary's in Warwick.

Memorandum there was this day[1] an order drawne on Sir Francis Child for one hundred pounds made payable to Mr Richard Lane or order, being to buy lead for the use of the Church of Saint Mary's in Warwick.

	Brooke
Tho. Peers	Digby
	H. Puckering

Warwick Burough
At the Court of Record held ... on Munday the 19th day of August anno domini 1700

Commissioners present: The Rt. Honourable the Lord Brooke, the Rt. Honourable the Lord Digby, Sir John Mordaunt, Bart., Sir Henry Pucker-

---

[1] 'this day' interlineated over a caret.

ing, Bart., John Hollyoake, Mayor, Thomas Peers, Esq., Thomas Newsham, Esq.

Ordered that the center of the arch for the new tower shall spring from the topp of the architrave that now is att the west end of the church and the architrave, friz and cornish to runn round the outside and inside of the new tower.

Order'd that the rubbish now lying within side of the Church of Saint Mary's be forthwith cleer'd and carry'd away by the workmen.

Order'd that the glaziers have notice that they forthwith make ready the glazeing work for the windows of the Church of Saint Mary's in order to putt up the same.

Order'd that Mr Lane have notice to gett ready and put up the leaden spouts att the north and south sides of the church.

Ordered that Thomas Masters forthwith goe about makeing and frameing the timber roof to be laid on that part of the west end of the church now lying open, and put up the same with all expedicion he can, and that Mr Lane have notice to gett ready the lead to cover the same.

Order'd that the cases be pull'd down that are round the great pillars within side of the church in order to finish the said pillars.

Upon complaint made by Thomas Lea against John Burton relateing to the payment for the party wall between the said Thomas Lea's house in the possession of Joseph Batteson and the said John Burtons house, it is ordered that the said John Burton doe pay unto the said Thomas Lea the summ of five pounds one shilling and two pence for the said party wall (the same being measured by the Surveyors) with interest for the same according to the Act of Parliament for rebuilding the said towne, on or before the ninth day of September next, according to the said John Burton's own agreement this day in Court.

Order'd that William Smith enquire out the prizes of hinges for the seates for the Church of Saint Mary's.

	Brooke
Tho. Newsham	H. Puckering
	John Holioake, Maior

Warwick Burg'
At the Court of Record held ... the fourteenth day of September 1700

Commissioners present: The Rt. Honourable the Lord Brooke, Sir Henry Puckering, Bart., William Colmore, Esq., John Holyoake, Mayor, Thomas Newsham, Esq.

It is order'd and agreed that George Chinn, carpenter, shall have the ground on which before the late fire stood the Bear Inn, scituate on the north side of the Highstreet within the said Borough, att the price of one penny per foot for every foot square the said ground shall containe and amount unto, and alsoe that he the said George Chinn shall have the benefitt of the one shilling and six pence in the pound for the loss of the said Bear Inn as the same is reduced, and it is alsoe order'd that the said George Chinn have £70 lent him out of the breif monys upon security of his new built house in the Swann Lane, with a covenant in the said security that he the said George Chinn shall repay the said summ within one month after the same shall be demanded of him, and alsoe that the said ground for the consideracion aforesaid be assured unto him by the decree of this Court.

Ordered that Mr Lane be paid for four fudder of lead to be used about the Church of Saint Maryes after he hath bought the same.

Order'd that Mr Rogers, Mr Jephcott and John Mitchener doe see and take an account what monies has been paid to the severall workmen about the Church of St Mary's, and soe farr as att present may be, to see what the severall sorts of work comes too, and state the said accounts and make report thereof to this Court.

It is order'd and agreed that Mr Aaron Rogers, Mr Henry Jephcott and John Mitchener doe take to their assistance such workmen as they shall think fitt, to view the laying of the paveing in the Church of Saint Maryes, and that they see the same laid according to the articles made with the persons who were agreed with to provide the paveing stone for the said church.

Order'd that a dore case[1] be made in the south isle of the said church to answer that in the north isle.

Order'd that Thomas Masters and Nicholas Kington be allow'd 15s. per yard for the church doors to be made according to the draught presented to the Commissioners, the same to be measured pole measure as the seates of the church are to be measured.

Order'd that Mr Rogers, Mr Jephcott and John Mitchener doe see the orders of this and the last court relateing to the church putt in execution.

Brooke

H. Puckering

Wm. Colmore[2]

Tho. Newsham

John Holioake, Maior.

---

[1] The rough minute book has 'a shamm door'.

[2] After this court the rough minute book has the following entry:

'September the 24th 1700

'Memorandum that Sir William Wilson was paid twenty pounds for carving in and about the Church of St Mary's by the hands of John Mitchener this day.

'Per order of Sir Henry Puckering, William Colmore, Esq., Tho. Newsham, Esq.'

Warwick Burg'
At the Court of Record held ... the second day of July anno domini 1702

Commissioners present: George Webb, Mayor, William Palmer, Esq., William Colmore, Esq., Thomas Peers, Esq., Thomas Newsham, Esq.

Ordered that the proprietor or proprietors of the ground adjoyning in the Highstreet to the house now in possession of Mr Venor, baker, which remaines now unbuilt upon, being late the ground of the widow Overton, have notice to build upon the said ground according to the Act of Parliament aforesaid, or else to shew cause att the next Court why the Commissioners may not proceed to sell the same.

Ordered that Madam Beaufoy be summoned to appear here next Court, to shew cause why the chief rent upon the ground in the above order should not be abated.

Ordered the Serjeant Hadley doe appear here next Court to answer the peticion of John and George Watts relateing to a watercourse, and alsoe that a jury be impanelled to view, enquire into and settle the same.

Upon reading of the peticion of Thomas Clements, baker, it is ordered that the matters therein mencioned be referr'd to the jury in the above order mencioned.

Upon reading the peticion of Francis Smart against Mr Nicholas Wrothwell, it is order'd that the said Mr Wrothwell be summon'd to appear here next Court, and that the matters in the said peticion contain'd be referr'd to the jury above mencion'd, and they to enquire into the same.

Whereas Richard Hands, joyner, hath built upon the ground of Thomas Clements mencioned in his peticion, it is order'd that the jury abovesaid have notice that this Court sold unto the said Hands the ground next adjoyning for a half penny per foot.

Order'd that the severall persons who have had monies lent them out of the brief monies have notice to pay in the same forthwith.

Upon reading the peticion of Mathew Busby, Edward Deacon and Joseph Averne to be relieved as to a water course going out of the back parts of the ground of their severall houses, order'd that the jury abovesaid doe view and settle the same.

W. Palmer
Wm. Colmore

Warwick Burg' [1]

At the Court of Record held . . . the tenth day of August anno domini 1702

Commissioners present: The Rt. Honourable the Lord Willowby de Broake, Sir John Mordaunt, Bart., Sir John Clopton, Kt., Sir Henry Parker, Kt., Sir William Underhill, Kt., Heugh Brawn, Esq., Hercules Underhill, Esq.

Whereas the jury impanelled and sworn the tenth day of August in the year of our Lord 1698, according to an order of this Court of the 25th day of June 1698 and a subsequent order of the 9th of August 1698, to view a wall in dispute between John Phillips, carpenter, and John Watts, flaxdresser, did by their verdict find the same to be a back particion wall belonging to the County Goale lying on the back part of the said John Watts his shopp and that the same was built eighteen inches thick, and it appeareing to this court that the said John Watts hath made use of the said wall by laying timber into the same and by building up thereto, it is now therefore agreed and resolved by this court that the said wall shall be and is hereby adjudged to be a party wall, and this court doe hereby order that the said John Watts pay unto the said John Phillips the summ of five pounds and ten shillings being the summ cast up by the Surveyors, as appears by a note under their hands for the said John Watts to pay for the same after the rate of four pounds eighteen shillings per rod, being the price settled by a former order of this court, with interest according to the aforesaid Act of Parliament.

John Clopton	Willughby de Broke
W. Underhill	John Mordaunt
Her. Underhill	Hen. Parker
Hugh Brawne	

Warwick Burg'

At the Court of Record held . . . the eighth day of Aprill anno domini 1703

Commissioners present: Edward Norton, Mayor, John Marriott, Esq., John Combs, Esq., William Colmore, Esq., Thomas Newsham, Esq., Thomas Peers, Esq.

Ordered that the matters relateing to the abatement of the chief rent upon the ground in the Highstreet late the ground of the widow Overtons be referr'd to the next Court.

Ordered that all persons that have had att any time monies lent them out of the brief monies, and that have not paid in one half of the monies lent, have notice that they pay in forthwith one half of their monies by them borrowed, and that they pay in the other half on or before the four and

---

[1] This court is written by a different hand.

twentyeth day of June next upon penalty of being sued for the same upon each default.[1]

Ordered that the severall verdicts of the[2] jury impanelled and sworne this day be confirmed by the decree of this Court, being as follows:

Imprimis they doe find that there is noe water course running into the ground of Richard Hadley from the messuage or tenement of John Watts now in the possession of Henry Smith, the messuage or tenement of George Watts called the White Lyon Inn, nor from the messuages or tenements of Mr Elias Webb in the possession of Edward Angrave and Thomas Rush, nor from any or either of them.

The said jurors doe also find that there has been taken from the ground of Thomas Clements and added to that of Richard Hands, joyner, six hundred and twenty foot, and doe assess and rate the summ of two pence half penny per foot to be paid for each foot of the same.

The said jurors doe alsoe find and agree that the mound wall to be built between the ground of Thomas Clements and the ground of Richard Hands, shall be built from the corner of Edward Scambler's stable next Thomas Clements his ground to the corner of the said Edward Scambler's pales, and from thence to returne to the corner of a leantoo of Robert Grey, the said wall to be built seven foot high from the ground att the charge of the said Richard Hands, he the said Thomas Clements to have liberty to sett a building upon the said wall and likewise he the said Thomas Clements to repaire the same after it is built as aforesaid, that the said Richard Hands shall build the said wall in workmanlike manner nine or ten inches thick.

Ordered that William Smith, Samuell Dunckley and Francis Smith be paid the summ of one hundred pounds upon the account of their work done and to be done in and about the church and tower of Saint Maryes.

Ordered that Mr Abraham Ruddhall, bellfounder, be paid the summ of seventy pounds towards the bell mettall he shall find and provide for the bells for St Mary Church and towards casting the same.

> Jo. Mariett   Wm. Colmore
> John Combe   Tho. Peers
>   Tho. Newsham

[1] 'upon each default' interlineated over a caret. This entry is followed in the rough minute book by: 'Memorandum Mr Biddulph gave in tyles which repaired the County Hall and not mencioned in the accounts.'

[2] 'severall verdicts of the' interlineated over a caret.

Warwick Burg'

At the Court of Record held . . . the sixth day of October anno domini 1703

Commissioners present:[1]

Whereas the jury impanelled and sworne the tenth day of August in the year of our Lord 1698, according to an order of this Court of the 25th day of June 1698 and a subsequent order of the ninth day of August 1698, to view a wall in dispute between John Phillipps, carpenter, and John Watts, flax-dresser, did by their verdict find the same to be a back partition wall belonging to the goale, lying on the back part of the said John Watts his shopp, and that the same was built eighteen inches thick, and whereas it appears to this Court that the said John Watts hath made use of the said wall by laying timber into the same and by building up thereto, and whereas by an order of this Court of the tenth day of August 1702 the said wall was adjudged to be a party wall, and then ordered that the said John Watts shjould pay unto the said John Phillipps the summ of five pounds and ten shillings for the same with interest, according to the aforesaid Act of Parliament, and whereas it now appears to this Court that Joseph Fenix, carpenter, was a partner with the said John Phillips in rebuilding of the goale aforesaid, and that he the said Joseph Fenix hath right to one half of the party walls thereto belonging, it is now therefore hereby order'd by this Court that the said John Watts doe pay or cause to be paid unto the said John Phillipps and Joseph Fenix the full summe of five pounds and ten shillings, being the summ cast up by the Surveyors according to the rates order'd by this Court, and alsoe interest for the said party wall after the rates appointed by the Act of Parliament aforesaid.

Wm. Colmore	J. Mordaunt
Jo. Mariett	Hen. Parker
Hugh Brawne	John Clopton
Geo. Lucy	

Warwick Burg'

At the Court of Record held . . . on the thirtyeth day of March anno domini 1704.

The jurors sworne this daye doe find the water course....[2]

---

[1] Blank not filled in.

[2] The entry breaks off at this point. The rest of the page and the page following are blank, but a paper is enclosed here, docketed 'Verdict of Jury 30th March 1704, to be confirmed by decree.' It reads as follows:

'Warwick Burg'. 30th March 1704.

'Names of the jury sworn in matters relateing to disputes following, viz. upon petition of Matthew Busby v. Deacon et al., Robert Blissett v. Thomas Wall, Francis Smart v. Nicholas Wrothwell.

'Willelmus Fetherston, gen., jur.; Stephanus Cumberlidge, Edwardus Makepeace, Thomas Jones, sadler,

Warwick Burg'

At the Court of Record held ... on the thirtyeth day of March anno domini 1704 and on the one and thirtyeth day of the same month.

Commissioners present: The Rt. Honourable the Lord Brooke, the Rt. Honourable the Lord Digby, Joseph Blissett, Mayor, William Palmer, Esq., Simon Biddulph, Esq., William Colmore, Esq., Thomas Newsham, Esq.

Whereas Mr William Tarver of this Borough being appointed one of the Treasurers of all the monyes which should be brought in on account of charityes to the sufferers by the late fire, and haveing kept and retained in his hands att the makeing up of his Treasurer's account thirty six pounds seventeen shilling and six pence of the said charity moneys, on account of a bill of losses given in to the persons appointed to take the same, and it not appeareing to this Court that the said Mr Tarver, after severall examinacions made into that matter, did bring in a bill of his losses of goods att the Swan amounting unto the summ of £295 within the time limitted for all the sufferers to bring in their estimates of their losses, this Court doth not think fitt to admitt of the said bill, but doe hereby order him the said William Tarver to pay unto John Mitchener, Receiver of the brief monyes, the said £36 17s. 6d. that the same may be applyed to the use first intended on or before the tenth[1] day of May next ensueing, and in default thereof that such course in law be taken for the recovering the same as shall be thought most adviseable.

Whereas[2] there is a parcell of ground[3] the ground of George Cheseley remaineing unbuilt in the square att the west end of Saint Maryes church, which by a former order of this Court ought to be built, this Court to encourage the building of the same for the better uniformity and ornament of the said square, doe order him the said George Chesely the summ of five

Willelmus Howe, jur.; Thomas Lea, Willelmus Roe, Alexander Nicholles, Moses Robinson, jur.; Oliver Fleetwood, Timothy Norberry, Johannes Williams, Johannes Cater, jur.; Johannes Atkins, Thomas Ward, Petrus Miller jun., Willelmus Crow, jur.; [Johannes Bacon *struck out*].

'The said jurors doe find the water course from the pigstye in Matthew Busby's backside to goe in a close surf through the backside of the house in possession of Barnaby Ashby, and from thence through the backside of Edward Deacon, and then through the backside of Joseph Avern, and from thence through the passage or ground of Nicholas Wrothwell lately purchased by him from Thomas Masters, and then through the ground of the said Thomas Masters, and from thence along by the corner of Mr Perquott's wall and soe into the ground of Mr Joseph Blissett, being the ancient water course.

'The said jurors do find that the window made in the new erected building of Mr Wrothwell upon part of the ground formerly the Swan garden, att the east end of the said building, is a nusance to Francis Smart and the other neighbors that are the owners of the houses and garden ground thereabouts in the Church Street.

'The said jurors doe find the leantoo or building in dispute between Mr Robert Blissett and Thomas Wall to be a nusance and damage to the building of the said Mr Blissett.'

[1] 'tenth' written in a space previously left blank.
[2] 'a decree to be made' written in the margin against this paragraph.
[3] Preceded by 'burnt' struck out.

and twenty pounds[1] for and towards the building of the same, viz. the summ of six pounds[1] when the foundacions shall be laid, the summe of ten pounds[1] when one story is built and the summe of nine pounds[1] when the whole messuage is regularly built and finished answereable to the houses next adjoyning, the foundacions to be laid before midsummer next, the whole to be compleately finished on this side and before the first day of October next, and in default of soe building, the ground and buildings thereon not built according as this order directs, to be sold to the best purchasser.

Whereas Mr Fulk Weale of this Borough haveing not built his burnt ground in the High Street according to the direccions of the Act for Rebuilding the Towne of Warwick or within the time limitted by the said Act, it is order'd att this Court that the said Mr Weale doe, on or before the twelfth day of May next, give good and sufficient security to William Colmore, Esq., Mr Joseph Blissett, Mayor of this Borough, or Thomas Newsham, Esq., three of the Commissioners appointed by the said Act, and such as they shall approve, that he will rebuild the said burnt ground fronting the said street, filling the vacant place and joyning the house soe to be rebuilt to the next adjacent houses regularly and according to the direccions of the said Act and orders by the said Court formerly made for rebuilding the said towne, and in default of giveing or tendring such security within the time limitted as abovesaid, that then this court will within twenty dayes after the said twelfth day of May proceed to order the said ground to be sold to such person or persons who shall bid and offer most for the same, pursuant to the powers given them the said Commissioners by the said Act.

Ordered that nine coates of armes be cutt in stone and placed up in the blank table in the tower under the loop holes, and that William Smith, Samuell Dunckley and Francis Smith be allow'd and paid eight pounds for to doe and finish the same.

Order'd that the persons aforesaid doe likewise fill up the windows in the bell roome in the tower according to the draught brought in, and that they be paid for the same according to the value.

Order'd that William Smith, Samuell Dunckley and Francis Smith be paid the summ of one hundred and forty pounds in full ballance of all accounts between the Commissioners and them, relateing to the rebuilding and finishing the church and tower of Saint Maryes and other matters according to the account stated, and that the same be paid by the Treasurer.

Order'd that Serjeant Hadley be paid six pence a foot for 273 foot of ground taken away from him to enlarge the Sheepstreet.

[1] These sums of money are inserted in spaces left for the purpose.

Order'd that Mr Young be sued for sixty pounds formerly lent unto Serjeant Hadley, he being surety for the same, except he shew reason to the contrary att the next Court.

Order's that John Phillips one of the Surveyors sworne formerly by this Court be paid thirty shillings for his attendance att this Court.

Ordered that Mr Tarver deliver into the hands of the Comissioners, all papers and books relateing to the charity moneyes, briefe and Commissioners, or touching or relateing to the fire which he has in his hands, before the last day of April next, the Commissioners giveing a sufficient discharge for the same.

Ordered that the severall verdicts of the jury that are given in now att this Court be confirmed by the decree of this Court.

Order'd that Moses Robbinson be paid three guineas for his extraordinary attendance upon this Court, goeing jorneys upon severall occasions, ordering rubbish to be removed about the church, and other matters by him done.[1]

	Brooke
Wm. Colmore	Digby
Tho. Newsham	Will. Palmer
Joseph Blissett, Mayor	Symon Biddulph

Warwick Burough

At the Court of Record held ... on Thursday the twenty first day of September 1704

Commissioners present: The Rt Honourable the Lord Digby, the Honourable John Smith, Esq., one of the Barons of her Majesties Court of Exchequer, William Palmer, Esq., Simon Biddulph, Esq., Joseph Blissett,

---

[1] The rough minute book includes the following additional item at this court:

'Upon veiwing the account of William Smith, Samuell Dunckley and Francis Smith, masons, of all their work about rebuilding and finishing the church and tower of St Maryes, it appears to this Court that the whole demands of the said masons amounts to the summe of   4689 4 5½

And that they have been paid in money   4244 12 5

And that the deduccion for that part of the tower att first building that was not built (by the masons consent) comes to   169 5 —   } 4413 17 5

Soe then it appears that the summ demanded by them as a ballance is   275 7 0½

But this Court haveing truly considered the whole matter doe think reasonable and soe order that the summ of £120 7s. 0½d. be deducted out of the said summ of 275 7 0½, being part of the loss sustained by that part of the first tower that was built above the roof of the church and pull'd downe againe before the present tower was begun, and the summ of £15 for a portego which was design'd att the west end of the church in case the first designe of the tower had stood, being in the whole 135 7 0½   135 7 0½

And we doe hereby order that the summe of   140 0 0

being the ballance of all accounts between the Commissioners and the masons be paid to the said workmen.'

Mayor of the said Burough, William Colmore, Esq., John Marriott, Esq., John Combs, Esq., Thomas Newsham, Esq.

Upon considering of the chief rent upon the ground scituate lying and being in the High Street now unbuilt upon, being the ground on which before the late fire stood a messuage or tenement then in the possession of the widow Overton, now the wife of William Jeacocks of Lightorn, being twenty shillings per annum, and for apportioning of the same, it is thought fitt and soe order'd by this Court, that for incouragement of the rebuilding of the said ground the said chief rent of twenty shillings per annum be reduced to the yearly rent or summe of two shillings upon rebuilding the same, and that all the arrears unpaid since the said fire be discharged and abated.

Whereas Mr Fulk Weale of this Borough, draper, the reputed owner and proprietor of a certaine toft or peice of burnt ground scituate lying and being on the south side of the High Street within the said Borough on which before the late fire stood two messuages or tenements in the posses-sion of [   ]¹ Carter and Sarah Rider; and William Jeacocks and Mary his wife the reputed owners or proprietors of a toft or parcel of burnt ground on the north side of the said street on which before the said fire stood a messuage or tenement in the possession of the said Mary; and Francis Smith the reputed owner of the ground att the upper end of the Sheepstreet adjoyning to the house of the said Francis Smith, have neglected to lay the foundations on their said ground within the time limitted in the Act of Parliament for rebuilding the said towne and have not yet begun to rebuild their said ground, notwithstanding severall orders have been made by this Court for the proprietors of the severall parcells of burnt ground yett unbuilt upon for to rebuild the same, it is now therefore agreed and resolved that the said Mr Fulk Weale, William Jeacocks and Mary his wife, and the reputed owners and owners of the said ground in the Sheepstreet, have notice that if they do not effectually proceed to rebuild their said parcells of ground before the twenty first day of October next according to the said Act and orders of this Court touching building, that then this Court will imediately after the said day proceed to sell the said ground to any such person as will bid the summe of five shillings or more for each parcell of the said ground, and that such person or persons who shall become purchaser or purchasers thereof shall for their further encouragement be allowed the one shilling six pence² in the pound accord-ing to³ the losses sustained in the houses burnt down by the said fire towards rebuilding the same.

¹ Space left for the first name not filled in.
² 'six pence' interlineated over a caret.
³ 'according to' interlineated over a caret above 'for' struck out.

Ordered that all peticions relateing to the abatement of chief rents be referr'd to the next court.

Ordered that Barnaby Ashby, Edward Deacon, Joseph Avern, Nicholas Wrothwell, Thomas Masters and all persons concerned in repaireing the watercourse from the pigstye of Matthew Busby into the ground of Mr Joseph Blissett according to the verdict of the jury att the last Court, have notice that they repaire the said watercourse belonging to each of them on this side and before the twenty first day of October next.

Ordered that Mr Wrothwell have notice that he remove the window or light mencioned in the verdict of the jury att the last Court on this side and before the twenty first day of October next.

Ordered that Thomas Wall remove the building found by the jury att the last Court to be a nusance to Mr Blissett on or before the twenty first day of October next.

Upon reading the peticion of Francis Smith, mason, it is order'd that he be allow'd ten pounds, being the proporcion of the one shilling and six pence in the pound for that part of the ground by him built according to the loss of the houses burnt downe in the late fire which was standing on the ground late of Mr Cauthorn, and alsoe six pence per foot for soe many foot of ground as shall appear to be taken away in the Sheepstreet to enlarge the same soe farr as the new house goes.

Upon reading the peticion of Thomas Roberts, innholder, it is order'd that the charges of pitching[1] soe much of the ground as was taken away from the Red Lyon Inn and added to the Swann Lane to enlarge the same, be first[2] paid for out of the publick money, and the remainder att the charge of the owner or occupier of the said Red Lyon Inn, and all the whole ground soe taken away to be for the future (after the first pitching) repaired by the said owner or occupier of the said inn or such other person who shall by contract with such owner or occupier agree to repaire the same.

Ordered that all the proprietors of houses in the New Square against the west end of the tower of the Church of Saint Marys and street leading towards the pillory soe farr as the corner of Thomas Clements his house, doe pay for the pitching only fifteen foot wide from their respective house or houses att the rate of two pence half penny per yard,[3] and that the pibbles and all other charges be paid for out of the publick moneys, and that likewise all the pitching and other charges in and about pitching of the middle of the said square and the ground above and below the church, soe

---

[1] 'the charges of pitching' interlineated over a caret.
[2] Followed by 'pitched out' struck through.
[3] 'yard' written after 'foot' struck out.

farr as the gutters are already sett out adjoyning to the church yard the full length of the new walls, be paid out of the publick moneys and that the same be for the future repaired by the whole parish of Saint Maryes.

Ordered that the new pulpitt, reading desk and clerk's seat to be made and sett up in the Church of Saint Maryes be placed in the middle of the middle isle between the two pillars next the chancel, the same to be moveable.

Ordered that Thomas Clements sett forth his matters of complaint in a peticion against the next Court, and that all persons concerned therein have a coppy of the said peticion delivered to them before the said Court.

Ordered that Robert Taylor be allow'd one shilling and six pence in the pound for the loss of his house burnt down in the late fire then in possession of Henry Wilson, if the same has not been already paid.

Ordered that pursuant to the consent in writeing delivered in of the major part of the sufferers, William Smith, Samuel Dunckley and Francis Smith be allow'd and paid forty pounds in full payment and satisfaccion of the fifty pounds referr'd to the Comissioners in the articles of agreement made with the said William Smith, Samuel Dunckley and Francis Smith for building the church and tower of Saint Maryes.

<table>
<tr><td></td><td>W. Palmer</td></tr>
<tr><td>Jo. Mariett</td><td>Symon Biddulph</td></tr>
<tr><td>John Combe</td><td>Wm Colmore</td></tr>
</table>

Peticioners att the Court held November 8th 1704[1]

George and John Watts to be relieved in their water course.
Mr Venor for allowance of money for his loss more than 20s. received.
Mr Norton: chief rent.
Mr Tarver's chief rent.
Tim. Roberts and Tho. Wall —— about chief rent.
Richard Hands about chief rent.
Memorandum about 30s. John Burton sayes is due to him over and above £5 already paid him for pulling down and towards rebuilding a stack of chimneys.[2]
Tho. Clements prayes he may be discharged of legacys mencioned in his father's will.
Mayo business and alsoe 1s. 6d. in the pound.
William Smith and Samuell Dunckley prayes an allowance for their service

---

[1] This court is recorded only in the rough minutes. After some notes of agenda, it begins with the formal style of the court, and is signed towards the end by the Commissioners present, giving it the status of a court in the order book. The Commissioners perhaps realised that this was their final meeting, and that there would be no later opportunity to sign any formal record.
[2] 'Mr Dunckly' inserted in the margin against this item.

done in surveying and agreeing with workmen to plaister the church and paveing streets and other matters by order of this Court.

Memorandum about papers and accounts in Mr Tarver's hands.

Memorandum Mr Smith's bill and Mr Dunckley.

Memorandum Mr Acock's bill.

Memorandum Mr Paris bill.

Memorandum Mr Fish desires to have a gratuity or allowance for measureing ground, surveying the same, etc.

Warr' Burg'

At the Court of Record held before the Commissioners or Judges appointed by an Act of Parliament for Rebuilding the Town of Warwick, etc., the 8th day of November 1704

Commissioners present: Sir John Clopton, Knt., George Lucy, Esq., Heugh Brawne, Esq., John Marriott, Esq., John Combs, Esq., William Colmore, Esq., Thomas Newsham, Esq.

Whereas the melting of tallow and making candles neer the fronts of the —— streets, cause noysome and offensive smells which may tend, etc.

This Court doth Order and Decree that noe tallow chandler or other chandler melt any tallow or make any candles in any of the roomes or cellars of any house or houses fronting the Castle Street, High Pavement, Jury Street, Church Street or New Square against the Church of St Mary's, and if any chandler or other person doe melt any tallow or make any candles in any of the roomes or places fronting any of the said streets or places above mencioned, such melting tallow and makeing candles shall be and is hereby decreed and adjudged to be a common nusance and may be proceeded against and punished accordingly.

Whereas it was agreed and resolved at the last Court, held the 21st day of September last, that the ground unbuilt of Mr Fulke Weale on the south side of the High Pavement, and the ground unbuilt of William Jeacocks and Mary his wife on the north side of the High Pavement, and the ground unbuilt of Mr Cawthorn or Francis Smith, mason, on the east side of the Sheepstreet at the upper end thereof, should be sold to any person who would give five shillings for any of the said 3 pieces of ground if the said Fulke Weale and William Jeacocks and Mary his wife and the said Francis Smith, upon due notice given, did not proceed effectually before the 21st day of October then next ensuing to rebuild the said ground, and whereas notice was given and they nor either of them have begun to rebuild the same, this Court therefore doth now order and decree, for the consideration of 5s. deposited in Court for the use of the said Fulke Weale, the inheritance of the said unbuilt ground of the said Fulke Weale to John

Mitchener[1] to the use of him, his heirs and assigns for ever, and the inheritance of the unbuilt ground of Francis Smith in the Sheepstreet for the consideracion of 5s. deposited in Court, to John Mitchener[1] to the use of him and his heirs, and the inheritance of the unbuilt ground of the said William Jeacocks and Mary his wife, the chief rent being apportioned to 2s., for the consideracion of 5s. deposited in Court for the use of the said Wm. Jeacocks and Mary his wife, to the said J. Mitchener[1] to the use of him and his heirs; and the said Jn. M. having offered Mr Thomas Newsham for his security that he will build the said grounds before mention'd within the space of four years, this Court doth accept the same, and doth order and decree the same.

Wm. Colmore	John Clopton
John Combe	Geo. Lucy
Tho. Newsham	Jo. Mariett
	Hugh Brawne

Att the Court aforesaid held the 8th of November 1704.

Upon reading againe the Peticion of Mr William Tarver preferred in Court on the 11th day of November 1695 relateing to the apportioning of a chief rent, order that Madam Beaufoy have notice that this Court will proceed upon that matter tomorrow att 9 of the clock.

Order'd that all arrears of chief rent due from any person to the lord or lady of the mannor of Warwick, from the time of the late fire to the time of rebuilding and inhabiting the messuages for which the same was payde, be and is hereby discharged.

Memorandum: Mrs Elizabeth Cawthern and Mr Richard Cawthern's lease for [a] year to Francis Smith of the ground att the upper end of the Sheepstreet is dated the 25th of November 1702. The release of them the said Elizabeth Cawthern and Richard Cawthern to Francis Smith of the same ground is dated the 26th day of November 1702.

---

[1] This name inserted in a space previously left blank.

THE BISHOP'S LETTER

To the Ministers and Church-Wardens of the several Parishes within my Diocess, concerning a Collection to be made for those who have suffered by the late Dreadful Fire at Warwick.

I Hope it will not be necessary to say much to stir up your Zeal upon so Sad an Occasion. The hand of God lies very heavy on many of our Brethren, who were lately in a plentiful Condition, and no Man knows how soon such a Calamity may befal him, and therefore every one ought to bestir himself to give, or procure such Relief as he would desire, if he were reduced to the like Misery. And I do earnestly recommend this good Work of Christian Charity to the Pious Care of my Brethren of the Clergy of my Diocess, beseeching and requiring them to use their utmost diligence to promote it in their several Stations; and in order to their doing it the more effectually, that they observe the following Directions.

I. Upon the next Lords day, in which you have as full a Congregation as you can ordinarily expect, you are to Read the Brief immediately after the *Nicene*-Creed, in your Church or Chappel, if you have only one in your Charge; but if you have more than one, in the other, on the Lord's day next following. And after you have Read the Tenor of the Brief, earnestly to exhort, perswade, and stir up your People to contribute freely and chear-fully towards the Relief of our poor distressed Brethren that have suffered so great a loss by this dreadful Fire.

II. On the Week days, next following after the Public Reading of the Brief, you are to go your self with the Church-Wardens, or to get some other of the Chief Inhabitants to go with them from House to House, there to make the Collection according to what is here given in Direction to the Church-Wardens.

III. On the next Lords-day after the making of the Collection, you are to see the Church-Wardens do their duty according to their Direction in the Second Article.

IV. Within Ten days after, at the farthest, you are to receive from the Church-Wardens, as well the Brief it self, as the Money collected upon it.

V. You are required (as you may see in the Brief) to send both that and the Money collected upon it, to your Arch-Deacon, subscribed with your Hands within Ten days after that, at the farthest. But because this may be hard for those Ministers that live at a great distance from their Arch-Deacons, for them it may suffice, if they return their Briefs and Collections to the Arch-Deacon at his next Visitation. And it would behove them for their own Security, both to take his Receipt for every Brief and Collection, and also to cause his Receipt to be entred into the Account-Book of their Parish Church or Chappel.

VI. As soon as a Copy of the Brief, with this Letter, shall come to your Hands, you shall give notice of the Receipt thereof to the Right Honourable the Lord *Brooke*, the Right Honourable the Lord *Digby*, or *William Colemore*, Esq. (Commissioners amongst others for disposing the Money that shall be given by Virtue and Means of the said Brief) at Sir *Francis Child*'s, or Mr. *Richard Hoar*'s, Goldsmiths in *Fleet-street, London*.

Directions to the Church-Wardens or Chappel-Wardens.

I. When the Brief has been read in your Parish, upon the Week-days next following, you, together with the Minister, or with such other of the Chief Inhabitants as he shall procure, are to go from House to House, where-ever they do not receive Alms, and at every such House you are to ask and receive from all the Parishioners, as well Masters, Mistresses, and Servants, as others in their Family, their Christian and Charitable Contributions, and to take in Writing the Names of all such as shall contribute any thing, and the Sum or Sums by them given respectively.

II. On the next Lords-day following, after such Collection is made, you are to call the Chief Inhabitants together, and in their presence you are to write down on the back of the Brief, both the Day of the Month, and the Name of your Parish or Chappelry, to gether with the whole Sum that has been gathered there upon this Brief; and then having set your Hands to it, you are to cause all that you have written to be fairly Copied into the Account-book of the Parish or Chappelry.

III. This being done, within Ten days after, at the farthest, you are to deliver the Brief, together with the Money you have collected, to the Minister of your Parish or Chappelry, to be sent by him to the Arch-Deacon; or if there be no Minister in your Parish, you are to bring or send both the Brief, and the Money collected upon it, to the Arch-Deacon.

In case either the Minister, or any of the Church-Wardens neglect their Duty herein, they must expect to be proceeded against by the Arch-Deacon at his next Visitation. And therefore it is hoped they will prevent any Trouble and Charge to themselves, as they easily may by observing these Directions.

Your Affectionate Brother,

EDW. WIGORN. [1]

---

[1] There is a similar letter over the printed signature 'W. COV. & LICH.'.

☛ *The several Arch-Deacons are desired to return the Briefs, with the Sums endors'd, to the abovmentioned Sir* Francis Child, *or Mr.* Richard Hoar, *with all convenient speed*

THE  BRIEF

WILLIAM and MARY, By the Grace of GOD King and Queen of *England*, *Scotland*, *France* and *Ireland*, Defenders of the Faith, etc. To all and singular Arch-bishops, Bishops, Arch-deacons, Deans, and their Officials, Parsons, Vicars, Curates, and all other Spiritual Persons: And also to all Justices of the Peace, Mayors, Sheriffs, Bayliffs, Constables, Church-Wardens, Chapel-Wardens, Headboroughs, Collectors for the Poor, and their Overseers: And also to all Officers of Cities, Boroughs, and Towns Corporate, and to all other Our Officers, Ministers and Subjects, whatsoever they be, as well within Liberties as without, to whom these Presents shall come Greeting:

Whereas the Sad and Deplorable Condition of many of Our good Subjects of Our ancient Borough of *Warwick*, in the County of *Warwick*, hath been represented to Us, by the Humble Petition of the Mayor, Aldermen, Burgesses, and other, distressed Inhabitants of Our said Borough; as also by a Certificate made at the General Quarter Sessions of the Peace, holden at the said Town of *Warwick*, on *Tuesday* the Second Day of *October* last, under the Hands and Seals of Our Trusty and Well-beloved *Thomas Rawlins*, Serjeant at Law, Sir *John Mordaunt*, Sir *Charles Shugburg*, Sir *Richard Newdigate*, Sir *Reginald Forster*, Baronets; Sir *Richard Verney*, Sir *William Underhill*, Sir *John Clopton*, knights; *Basill Feilding*, *Henry Parker*, and *William Palmer*, Esquires, Justices of the Peace of Our said County, That upon *Wednesday*, the Fifth Day of *September* last past, between Two and Three of the Clock in the Afternoon of the same Day, it pleased God that there broke forth a sudden, outragious, and most dreadful Fire in the said Town of *Warwick*, which being driven by the Violence and Fury of a tempestuous Wind then blowing, and carrying the Flames at the same time to several parts of it, far distant from each other, became quickly irresistable by all humane Aids; and in less than the space of six Hours, burnt to the Ground, and consumed the Dwelling Houses and Habitations of above Two hundred and fifty Families, many of which were the principal and chiefest Traders of the said Town, together with their Shops, and most of their Wares in their Shops; their Malt-houses, Stables, and other Out-houses, and the greatest part of their Goods, Housholdstuff, Malt, Corn, Grain, Hay, and other their Provisions. And also several publick Buildings, and the great and ancient Collegiate Church of St. *Mary*; into which, as a

Place of Safety, the distracted Inhabitants had thrown the most valuable Goods so short a time would permit them to remove. The Loss amounting in the whole to Fourscore and ten thousand six hundred Pounds and upwards, as appeared to Our said Justices, then sitting in open Court, by the Oaths of *Samuel Dunkley*, *Richard Bromley*, *Thomas Adams*, and *Job Burch*, Masons; and *John Hope*, *Roger Hurlbut*, *Thomas Masters*, and *George Perkins*, Carpenters, experienced and able Workmen, who had diligently and carefully examined, surveyed, and taken an Estimate of the Buildings so burnt down and consumed. As also by the Oaths of the most substantial Inhabitants of the said Town. Besides the Loss of many Persons Estates, Houshold Goods, and Goods of Trade, not included in the said Sum; by reason whereof, the greatest part of the distressed Inhabitants are become Objects of that Charity, which they themselves, on such like sad Occasions, were never wanting to bestow, and do not only labour under the present Wants of the common Necessaries of Life, but are wholly deprived of all Hopes and Means of a future Subsistence by their honest Labours and Endeavours, and must inevitably perish, unless timely Relieved by the Charitable Helps of well disposed Christians. And therefore have most humbly besought Us, that We would be graciously pleased to take into consideration their distressed and deplorable Condition, and to grant unto them Our Gracious Licence and Protection, under Our Great Seal of *England*, for a General Collection within this Our Kingdom of *England*, Dominion of *Wales*, and Town of *Berwick* upon *Tweed*.

We therefore being deeply affected with the Sence of the wretched and disconsolate Estate to which they are reduced, have condescended to their humble Requests, and do earnestly recommend the miserable Condition of the said poor Sufferers, to the Pious and Charitable Considerations of Our said Loving Subjects, desiring that a Regard and Observance to these Our Letters Patents, may be given, suitable to so sad and mighty a Calamity.

Know ye therefore, That of Our especial Grace, and Princely Compassion, We have given and granted, and by these Our Letters Patents, under Our Great Seal of *England*, do give and grant unto the said Poor distressed Sufferers, and to their Agents, and other Persons, who shall be lawfully Authorised on their Behalf, full Power, Licence, and Authority, to Ask, Gather, Receive, and Take, according to the Rules hereafter specified in these Presents, the Alms and Charitable Benevolence of all Our Loving Subjects, not only Housholders, but also Servants, Strangers, and others, within all and every the Counties, Cities, Boroughs, Towns Corporate, Priviledged Places, Parishes, Chapelries, Towns, Villages, Hamlets, and other Places whatsoever, in Our Kingdom of *England*, Dominion of *Wales*, and Town of *Berwick* upon *Tweed*, for, and towards the Support and Relief of the said poor and distressed Sufferers.

Wherefore We Require and Command all and singular the Arch-Bishops and Bishops of all and singular the Provinces and Dioceses within Our Kingdom of *England*, and Dominion of *Wales*, unto whose Pious and Paternal Care, We chiefly recommend the Conduct and Pursuit of these Our Letters Patents; that they, and every of them do give a particular Recommendation and Command to all Parsons, Vicars and Curates, of all and every the Parishes, and other Places, as well within Liberties as without, within their respective Dioceses, for the Advancement of this, so Charitable a Work; and the said Parsons, Vicars, and Curates, upon the next Lord's Day, after that the true Copies of these Our Letters Patents shall be delivered to them, shall deliberately and effectually publish and declare the Tenor of the same unto Our said Loving Subjects; and by powerful Inducements, earnestly perswade, exhort and stir them up, to Contribute freely and chearfully to the Losses of the said poor Sufferers.

And the Church-Wardens are hereby also required, upon the Week Days next following the Lord's Day, to go from House to House, to Ask and Receive from all the Parishioners, as well Masters, Mistresses, and Servants, as of others in their Families, their Christian and Charitable Contributions, and to take the Names of all such as shall Contribute thereunto, and the Sum or Sums by them given respectively; and after such Collection made, they are, together with their respective Parsons, Vicar or Curate, in the presence of the respective Inhabitants, on the next Lord's Day following, in their respective Parish Churches or Chapels, after Morning Service or Sermon ended, to Subscribe the whole Sum in Words at length, and not in Figures, upon the said Brief, under their Hands: And also in another Writing, to be signed in the like manner, to express the several Names and Qualities of the respective Donors and Benefactors, and the Sums by them given; and also to enter them severally into their Books of Accompts for the said Parishes and Chapelries respectively: And the Place where, and the Time when such Sums were Collected.

And the said Parsons, Vicars, or Curates, are to send the said Moneys, together with the said Briefs, and other Writings so signed, unto the respective Arch-Deacons, as is herein after directed; and the said Arch-Deacons are to enter, or cause to be entered, the Sums so received into the Registers of their respective Dioceses.

And for the better performance of this so Charitable a Work, the said Parsons, Vicars or Curates respectively, are desired, where conveniently they may, to accompany the Church-Wardens, in Asking and Receiving the Contributions, or procure some other of the Chief Inhabitants to do the same.

And that all Our Loving Subjects of this Kingdom may manifest their Zeal and Christian Charity to these their distressed Brethren, We do recommend it to all Heads and Governors of Colledges and Halls within Our Universities. And also to the Judges and Officers of all and every Our respective Courts at *Westminster*, and the Professors of the Law, both

Common and Civil. And to all Students of the Inns of Court and *Chancery*, by their several Bodies and Societies; that they, and every of them, will Contribute their Free and Charitable Benevolence therein.

And Our Will and Pleasure is, and We do hereby recommend unto the Care and Circumspection of all and singular the Arch-Bishops, and Bishops of the said respective Provinces and Dioceses, and the Arch-Deacons; that it be so ordered, that the Collection and Return of the said Moneys may be with the most Ease, and as little Charge and Deductions to be made out of the said Contributions as is possible. And also that the Church-Wardens of every Parish, where these Our Letter Patents shall be read, do Collect the Charity of each Parishioner in manner as aforesaid, and pay the same within ten Days unto the Parson, Vicar, or Curate of their respective Parishes; which said respective Parson, Vicar, or Curate, shall, within Ten Days of his Receipt of the said Money, make Return thereof to the respective Arch-Deacons; and where there is no Incumbent, that the Collector, or Collectors pay the said Money to the respective Arch-Deacons: And that the Arch-Deacons of the several Arch-Deaconries, do likewise return the said Collections within Twenty Days, next after the Receipt thereof, unto Sir *Francis Child*, near *Temple-Bar* in *Fleet-Street*, *London*, or *Richard Hoar*, at the *Golden Bottle* in *Fleet-Street*, *London*, Goldsmiths; or to such other Person or Persons, as by the Major Part of the Commissioners and Trustees herein after named shall be directed and appointed; whose Receiving thereof, together with their, or any of their Acquittances, shall be their sufficient Discharge for so doing.

And Our farther Will and Pleasure is, and We do hereby, for the better Advancement of this Charitable Work, and the more effectual putting in Execution the Powers and Duties herin before granted and enjoyned, and for the more Impartial and equal Disposal of the Alms and Charities that shall be given on this Account, Authorise and Appoint Our Trusty and Well-beloved, the Right Reverend Father in God, Edward Lord Bishop of *Worcester*, The Right Honourable *Fulk* Lord *Brooke*, The Right Honourable *Simon*[1] Lord *Digby*, of the Kingdom of *Ireland*, The Honourable *Thomas Coventry* Esq; Sir *John Mordaunt*, Sir *Henry Puckering*, Sir *John Burgoyne*, Sir *Clement Fisher*, Baronets; Sir *Richard Verney*, Sir *John Clopton*, Sir *Thomas Wagstaffe*, Knights; *William Bromley*, *Andrew Archer*, Esquires; *Thomas Rawlins* Serjeant at Law, *William Collmar*, *George Lucy*, *Francis Fisher*, *Charles Newsham*, Esquires; the Mayor of *Warwick* for the time being, *Thomas Newsham* Esq; and all Justices of the Peace for the County of *Warwick* for the time being, whom We do appoint to be Commissioners and trustees of all such Moneys as shall be given by Vertue and Means of these Our Letters Patents, with Power to them, or Seven, or more of them, to Dispose and Distribute the said Moneys in such proportion to the respective

---

[1] A mistake for *William*.

Losses and Necessities of the Sufferers, as to them shall seem most just and equal.

And Lastly, Our Will and Pleasure is, That no Person or Persons shall Receive the said Moneys of, or from the said Sir *Francis Child*, or *Richard Hoare*, or any other Person, but such as shall be Authorised and Appointed so to do by Deputation in Writing under the Hands and Seals of the said Commissioners and Trustees, or any Seven or more of them, whereof the Lord Bishop of *Worcester* for the time being, or the said *Fulk* Lord *Brooke* to be one.

In Witness whereof, We have caused these Our Letters to be made Patents, and to continue for the space of Two Years from the Day of the Date hereof, and no longer. Witnes Our Selves at *Westminster*, the Eighth Day of *December*, in the Sixth Year of Our Reign.

GOD Save the KING and QUEEN.   Fall.

In the *SAVOY*: Printed by *Edward Jones* for *William Fall* dwelling in *Weld-street*. 1694

[*Endorsed in MS:*]

Collected in Coften-Hackett[1] in the County of Worcester to fire in Warwick, Five pounds twelve shillings three pence.

5—12—3   by me, John Greene, churchwarden.

[*Endorsed in another hand, after folding:*]

Cotten[2] Hackett Brief with moneys received thereon.   68.

---

[1] Cofton Hacket, 6 miles N.E. of Bromsgrove, had 211 inhabitants in 1841.
[2] This spelling of the place-name is probably a misreading of the first endorsement.

THE ACT OF PARLIAMENT

Anno Sexto
Gulielmi III Regis
[1694/5]

An Act[1] for the Rebuilding the Town of *Warwick*, and for Determining Differences touching Houses Burnt or Demolished by Reason of the late Dreadful Fire there.

Forasmuch as the Principal Streets, and best Parts of the Ancient Borough of *Warwick*, together with the Fair and Ancient Church there, called St. *Mary's*, by reason of a most Dreadful Fire which hapned there upon the Fifth Day of *September* last past, were, in the compass of a few Hours, Burnt down and Destroyed: For the speedy Restauration and Rebuilding of the same, and for Removal of all Impediments which may Hinder or Obstruct so Good a Work, and for the better Regulation of such New Buildings there as shall be Erected, and for Preventing (as far as humane Providence, with Submission to the Divine Pleasure may) such Great and Outragious Fires for the future; Be it Enacted by the Kings most Excellent Majesty, by and with the Advice and Consent of the Lords Spiritual and Temporal, and the Commons in this present Parliament Assembled, and by the Authority of the same, That the Judges of Assize for the County of *Warwick*, and other the Justices of the Courts of Kings Bench and Common Pleas, and the Barons of the Coife of the Exchequer for the time being, the Justices of the Peace of the said County for the time being, and the Mayor of the said Town of *Warwick* for the time being, and the Right Honourable *Charles* Earl of *Dorset*, Lord Chamberlain of the Houshold, *George* Earl of *Northampton*, *Bazil* Earl of *Denbigh*, *Thomas* Earl of *Stamford*, *Robert* Earl of *Sunderland*, *William* Earl of *Craven*, *Lawrence* Earl of *Rochester*, *Charles* Earl of *Monmouth*, *Thomas* Lord Viscount *Weymouth*, *Henry* Bishop of *London*, *Edward* Bishop of *Worcester*, *Foulk* Lord *Brooke*, *Thomas* Lord *Coventry*, *Thomas* Lord *Leigh*, the Lord *Digby* of the kingdom of *Ireland*; the Honourable *Francis Grevill*; the Honourable *Thomas Coventry* Esquires, Sir *Charles Holt*, Sir *Clement Fisher*, Sir *Henry Puckering*, Sir *John Burgoyne*, Baronets; Sir *William Byshop*, Sir *Thomas Wagstaffe*, Knights; *Robert Burdett*, *William Bromley*, *Andrew Archer*, *George Lucey*, *Robert Somervile*, *William Colemore*,

---

[1] 6 Will. III cap. 1 (private). The original printing was in black-letter, roman and italic. This transcript in roman and italic preserves as far as possible the differentiation of the original; capital letters have been retained.

Francis Fisher, *Symon Bydolph*, *John Marryott*, *Thomas Fetherston*, *John Combes*, *Thomas Peeres*, *William Bolton*, *John Newsham*, and *Thomas Newsham*, Esquires; or any Five or more of them, Sitting at the same time together at the Mayors Parlour, or some other Place in the said Borough of *Warwick* to be Appointed by them, shall be, and are by the Authority aforesaid, Made and Constituted a Court of Record; and shall and may from time to time, with or without Adjournment, Summarily, and without the Formalities of Proceedings in Courts of Law or Equity, either by Verdicts or Inquisitions of Jurors, Testimony of Witnesses upon Oath, or Examination of Parties Interested, or by all or any of the said Ways, or otherwise at their Discretion, Hear and Determine all Differences and Demands whatsoever which have arisen, or may any way arise between Landlords, Proprietors, Tenants, Lessees, Under-tenants, or late Occupiers of any the Houses or Buildings Burnt, Pulled down, or otherwise Demolished, Defaced or Ruined by reason of the Fire aforesaid, or of any Courts, Yards, Gardens, or other Grounds or Appurtenances to the said Houses or Buildings, or any of them belonging, or of any Rents of Assize, Fee-farm Rents, Chief Rents, or other Rents Issuing out of, or Payable in the same, or between any other Person or Persons, their or any of their Heirs, Successors, Executors, Administrators or Assigns, Having or Claiming any Estate, Right, Title, or Interest in Law or Equity, Charge or Incumbrance of, or in the Premises, for, touching or concerning the Repairing, Building, or not Building of the said Houses or Buildings, Yards, Courts and Grounds, or for or concerning the Payment, Defalcation, Apportioning or Abatement of any Rent or Rents, other then Arrears of Rent, become due on or before the Fourth Day of *September*, in the Year One thousand six hundred ninety four; or for touching or concerning any Covenant, Condition or Penalty relating thereunto, or for touching or concerning the Prefixing or Limiting of any Time for such Repairs or New-buildings, or any Rate or Contribution to be paid thereunto by any Person or Persons, Bodies Politick or Corporate Interested in the Premisses, and all Incidents relating thereunto; And that the Judges of the said Courts shall and may Administer to any Person or Persons, such Oaths as are necessary for the Execution of the Power and Authority above mentioned, or any other Powers and Authorities hereafter given by this Act; And that the Difinitive Order or Decree of the said Court as aforesaid, shall bind all the said Parties, their Heirs, Successors, Executors, Administrators and Assigns, and all Claiming by, from, under, or after them, touching the Matter contained in such Order or Decree, from which there shall be no Appeal otherwise then as is hereafter Expressed.

And be it further Enacted by the Authority aforesaid, That the said Judges of Assize for the said County, and other the Justices of the Courts of Kings-Bench and Common-Pleas, and the Barons of the Coife of the

Exchequer for the time being, the Justices of the Peace for the said County for the time being, and the Mayor of the said Town for the time being; And the said Earl of *Dorset*, Earl of *Northampton*, Earl of *Denbigh*, Earl of *Stamford*, Earl of *Sunderland*, Earl of *Craven*, Earl of *Rochester*, Earl of *Monmouth*, Lord Viscount *Weymouth*, Bishop of *London*, Bishop of *Worcester*, Lord *Brook*, Lord *Coventry*, Lord *Leigh*, Lord *Digby*, *Francis Grevill*, *Thomas Coventry*, Sir *Charles Holt*, Sir *Clement Fisher*, Sir *Henry Puckering*, Sir *John Burgoyne*, Sir *William Byshop*, Sir *Thomas Wagstaffe*, *Robert Burdett*, *William Bromley*, *Andrew Archer*, *George Lucy*, *Robert Somervile*, *William Colemore*, *Francis Fisher*, *Simon Biddolph*, *John Marriot*, *Thomas Fetherston*, *John Combes*, *Thomas Peeres*, *William Bolton*, *John Newsham*, and *Thomas Newsham*, or any Five or more of them sitting together, as aforesaid, shall have Authority, and are hereby Impowered, where they shall judge it convenient, to Order the Surrendering, Encreasing, Abridging, Ceasing, Determining, Charging or Changing of any Estates in the Premises; or to order New or Longer Estates to be made of any the Premisses, by the Proprietors or Owners thereof, or other Persons Interested therein, to any Tenant, Sub-tenant, or late Occupier of the same, their Executors, Administrators, Successors or Assigns, at such Rent or Fine as they shall think fit, unless in such Cases, where the Laws of this Realm do forbid the Diminishing of Ancient and Accustomable Rent; all which Orders, according to the Tenors thereof, shall be obeyed by all Persons concerned therein respectively, and all other Persons whatsoever, Claiming by, from, under or after them, or any of them.

And because it is not only for the Ornament, but also for the common Convenience and Safety of the said Borough, That all publick Streets and Lanes therein should be of a convenient wideness, Be it further Enacted by the Authority aforesaid, That the said Court shall have Power to Enlarge and Widen the Lane called *Swan Lane*, leading out of the Street called *The High Street*, or *Pavement* into the Market-Place in such manner as they shall think meet, in order to make a Convenient Passage for Carts and Carriages through the same to the said Market-Place; and the said Court shall also have Power to Enlarge and Widen the Lane called *The Pebble Lane*, leading out of the Street called *The Sheep Street*, into the Street called *The New Street*, and from thence into the said Market-Place as they shall think fit, or to order the same to be Built upon, and stopt up, or otherwise used, and to appoint another Street in Lieu thereof, to be made and opened overagainst the West or Tower end of the said Church called *St. Mary's*, into the said Street called *New Street*, as they shall judge most Convenient; And the said Court shall and may appoint what Sum or Sums of Money shall be paid by the Person or Persons within the said Borough, who have or may have any Benefit by such Alterations, unto the Person or Persons who are Owners of, or Interested in the Ground that shall be laid into the said Lanes or Streets to be Enlarged or new Made, as aforesaid, or any Rent of Assize, Fee-Farm Rent, Chief Rent, or other Rent or Charge Issuing out of, or Payable for, or Chargeable on the same, and in case the Owners of, or Persons Interested in the said Ground, or any such Rent or Charge, will not, or by reason of any Disability by Nonage, Coverture, Intail, or other Impediment, cannot accept thereof, that in such Cases, the said Court are hereby Impowered to Impannel and Summon a Jury before them, which Jury (upon their Oaths to be Administred by the said Court) are to Assess such Damage to be given, and Recompence to be made to the Owners and others Interested in the said Ground Rent or Charge respectively for their respective Interests in the same, as they shall think Reasonable, and upon Payment of the said Money so Awarded, or tender and refusal thereof, the Interest of the said Persons in the said Ground Rent, or Charge, shall be for ever Devested out of them; And that the said Ground, and all other Ground that shall be laid into any Street or Lane by virtue of this Act, shall ever after remain to, and be actually Vested in the Person or Persons, who are or shall be Owner or Owners of the Soil and Ground of the Common Streets and High-ways within the said Borough, and if the Person or Persons receiving Benefit by the Alterations aforesaid, shall refuse to pay the Sum or Sums respectively Charged upon them by the Court, as aforesaid, after Demand thereof made by a Treasurer to be appointed by the said Court to Receive the same, that then the said Court shall and may by Warrant under their Hands and Seals, cause the same to be Levied by Distress and Sale of the Goods and Chattels of the Person or Persons Charged and refusing, as aforesaid, rendring the Overplus, after all charges of the said Distress and Sale, to the Party Distrained.

And forasmuch as the Passage of the Streets, called *Church Street* and *Sheep Street*, by the said Church called St. *Mary's*, and the Church-yard of the said Church is Narrow and Inconvenient, Be it therefore Enacted by the Authority aforesaid, That the said Court shall and may Widen and Enlarge the same, as they shall think most fit and convenient; And that the said Court shall and may Order and Direct in what Manner and Form the said Church called St. *Mary's* shall be Rebuilt, and that the Parishioners of the said Parish shall not be Obliged or Compellable to Rebuild the said Church in any other Manner or Form, then that which shall by the said Court be Directed and Appointed; Any Law or Usage to the contrary in any wise notwithstanding.

And for the Encouraging the speedy Rebuilding of the Houses demol-ished by reason of the Fire aforesaid, Be it further Enacted by the Authority aforesaid, That there shall be Party-Walls, and Party-Piers set out equally on each Builders Ground, to be built up by the first Beginner of such Building, and that convenient Toothing shall be left in the Front Wall or Walls, by the said first Builder, for the better Joyning of the next House or Houses that shall be built to the same; And that no man be permitted to build on, or to the said Party-Walls, or on his own Contiguous Ground, until he hath fully Reimbursed the first Builder the full Moyety of the Charges of the said Party-Wall and Pier, together with Interest for the same, after the rate of Six Pounds *per Centum per Annum* for the forbearance thereof, to be accounted from the beginning of the said first Building. And in case any difference shall arise between the first and latter Builders, concerning the true Values of the said Charge, That upon complaint made to the said Court, they, or any Five of them, shall and may ascertain the same, and their Order therein shall bind the said Parties, and all Claiming by, under or after them, from whence no Appeal shall be had, otherwise then as is hereafter mentioned; And in case the Proprietors or Owners of the Houses demolished, by, or by reason of the said Fire, or their Heirs, Successors, Executors, Administrators or Assigns, shall not within the space of Two Years ensuing after the said Fire, lay the Foundations of their Houses to be Rebuilt, and shall not within the time to be Limited by the said Court, Rebuild and Finish the same, that upon such Default the said Court shall have Power and Authority by their Order and Decree, to Dispose of, and Assign all the Estate and Interest of the said Owners and Proprietors of the said Houses so to be Rebuilt, and of the Ground and Soyl thereof, and of all Yards, Backsides, Gardens, Orchards, and other Appurtenances thereto belonging, to such Person or Persons who will give Security to Rebuild the same within such time as the said Court shall Direct and Appoint; And that the said Court shall and may Award what Sum of Money or other Satisfaction, the Party who Undertakes to be the Rebuilder, shall give for the same to the Proprietor or Proprietors, Owner or Owners, making Default, as aforesaid, and in case the said Person or Persons making Default, as aforesaid, will not, or by reason of Nonage, Coverture, Intail or other Disability, cannot accept thereof; that in such Case, the said Court are hereby Impowered to Impannel and Summon a Jury before them, which Jury upon their Oaths, to be Administred by the said Court, are to Assess such Recompence and Satisfaction, as they shall think fit to be Awarded and Paid unto the Person or Persons making Default in Rebuilding, for the said Houses to be Rebuilt, and the Ground and Soil thereof, and for the Yards, Backsides, Gardens, Orchards, and other Appurtenances thereto belonging, by the Person or Persons who Undertake to be the Rebuilder or Rebuilders, and upon Payment of the said Recompence and Satisfaction so Awarded or Tender and Refusal thereof, the said Person or Persons making Default in Building, his, her and their Heirs, Successors, Executors, Administrators, Assigns, and all other Persons shall be for ever Barred, and the said Houses to be Rebuilt, and the Ground and Soil, Yards, Backsides, Gardens, Orchards and other

Appurtenances thereof, so Assigned by the said Court unto the Undertaker or Undertakers to Rebuild the same, shall for ever be and Remain to the said Undertaker or Undertakers, in such manner as the said Court shall have Assigned and Appointed the same.

And for the more Regular and Uniform Rebuilding the Houses Demolished by the Fire, as aforesaid, Be it further Enacted by the Authority aforesaid, that all Houses Rebuilt, fronting the Street called *The High Pavement*, the Street called *The Castle Street*, the Street called *The Church Street*, the Street called *The Sheep Street*, the Street or Lane commonly called *The Swan Lane*, the Street or Lane commonly called *The Pebble Lane*, or the New Street to be made in Lieu thereof, as aforesaid, and the Street leading from the New Street to the Pillory, and also all Houses fronting the Booth-Hall, shall be of Two Stories high, besides Cellars and Garrets (unless where the said Court shall find good cause to Permit and Allow the Building another Story) and that the First Story shall be Ten Foot high from Floor to Cieling, and no more; the Second Story Ten Foot high from Floor to Cieling, and that the Garrets of the said Houses shall be Built in such manner and with such Roofs and Lights as the said Court shall direct and appoint, and that the thickness of the Party-Walls between every of the said Houses, as high as the First Story, shall be Eighteen Inches at the least, and thence upwards to the Wall-Plate of the thickness of Thirteen Inches at the least, and thence upwards to the top of the said Wall, which shall be carried to the Roof of the respective Houses, of the thickness of eight Inches at the least, save only where the said Court shall judge it Convenient to permit any Barn, Stable, or other Out-house, to be set fronting any of the said Streets or Lanes, they may be Built of such heights, and in such manner as the said Court shall appoint, any thing beforesaid to the contrary notwithstanding.

And be it further Enacted by the Authority aforesaid, That no House to be Rebuilt shall be set further into, or backward from the Streets or Lanes than the Ancient Foundations, save only that where it shall happen that the said Ancient Foundations are Irregular and Inconvenient towards the said Streets or Lanes, the said Court be, and are hereby Impowered to Regulate the same as they shall think most Convenient for the Buildings, and least Prejudicial to the said Streets or Lanes; And that the First Floor of all Houses fronting any of the said Streets shall be Fourteen Inches above the said Streets, and that there shall be such Step or Steps of Stone to lead up thereto, to be placed in the Street without the Building as the said Court shall Direct and Appoint, and that no Trap-Doors, or open Grates, be in any wise suffered to be made in any such Cellar without the Foundations of the Front, but that all Lights to be made into any of them, be henceforth made upright and not otherwise, and that no Bulks, Jetty's, Windows, Posts, Seats, or any thing of the like sort, be made or Erected in any the said

Streets or Lanes to extend beyond the Foundations of the Houses, save only that it shall and may be lawful to and for the said Court to Direct and Allow the making any Balconeys or Penthouses to their said Houses, and for the Trading Inhabitants to suffer their Stall-Boards, when their Shops and Windows are set open, to turn over and extend Twelve Inches, and no more, from the Foundations of their Houses into the Streets, for the Convenience of their Shops and Windows, and that the respective Builders and Owners of the said Houses may set a Pale or Palizado in the Street before their Houses, equal and along with the Step or Steps before their Houses, and no further.

And be it further Enacted by the Authority aforesaid, That if any Dispute shall arise between the respective Proprietors and Owners of Houses and Ground to be Rebuilt, as aforesaid, touching the Foundations, Bounds and Extent of their respective Houses and Grounds thereto belonging, or touching the Placing or Stopping up any Lights, Ways, Windows, Passages, Waters and Water-courses, Gutters, Easements and such like annoyances, upon Complaint thereof to the said Court made, they shall and may, in manner as is above directed, Inquire of, and Hear and Determine the same; and their Order and Determination therein, shall Bind all the said Parties, and all Persons claiming by, from, under, or after them, or any of them; from which Order and Determination no Appeal shall be had, otherwise then as hereafter mentioned.

And in regard that Building with Brick and Stone, and Covering with Tile, Slate or Lead, is not only most Comely and Durable, but also most Safe against future Perils of Fire, Be it therefore further Enacted, by, and with the Authority aforesaid, That all the outsides of the Walls of all Buildings hereafter to be Erected in the said Borough, be henceforth made of Brick or Stone, or of Brick and Stone together, except Door-Cases and Window-Frames, and the Breast, Summers, and other parts of the First Story to the Front between the Pires, which are to be left to the discretion of the Builder to use substantial Oaken Timber in stead of Brick and Stone, for convenience of Shops, and that all the Roofs of such Buildings be also Covered with Tile, Slate or Lead.

And Be it further Enacted by the Authority aforesaid, That if any Person or Persons shall presume to Build, in any wise, contrary to the Rules and Directions above given, and be Convicted thereof by the said Court, by the Oaths of Two or more Credible Witnesses, That then, and in such Case, the House so irregularly Built shall be deemed as a Common Nusance, and the Builder and Levyer thereof shall be Bound by Recognizance in such Sum as the said Court shall in their Direction Appoint, to abate the same in convenient time, or otherwise to amend the same according to the Rules and

Directions aforesaid; and in default of entring into such Recognisance, the said Court shall and may Commit such Offender to the Common Goal of the said Borough, there to remain without Bail or Mainprize, till he shall have abated, or otherwise amended the same, or such irregular House may be abated by Order of the said Court.

And forasmuch as the said Dreadful Fire was Principally occasioned by the Buildings Covered with Thatch and Straw, which happened to take Fire at divers Parts of the said Borough at the same time: For Preventing the like Danger for the future, Be it further Enacted by the Authority aforesaid, That all Buildings and Out-Houses, Parcel of, or belonging to any House Fronting the Remaining Parts of the *Castle Street*, the Remaining Parts of the *Jury Street*, the Remaining Parts of the *High Pavement*, the Remaining Parts of the Market-Place, which are now Covered with Thatch, Reed, or Straw, shall, on or before the Twenty fourth Day of *June*, One thousand six hundred ninety six, by the Tenants or Occupiers thereof, be Uncovered and Covered with Slate or Tyle. And the said Court shall and may Order, whether All, or what Proportion of the Charge of such New Covering, shall be Born by the several Immediate, or Mediate Landlords, if any such there be, according to their several and respective Interests and Estates, and according as the said Tenants or Occupiers, stand Obliged or not Obliged to the Repairs thereof. And that it shall and may be Lawful for the said Tenants or Occupiers, to Detain and Deduct out of their Rents, the Sums Charged by such Order upon their Respective Landlords; and such Deteiner and Deductions thereof, shall be Adjudged and Taken for Good Payment of so much of the said Rent or Rents, to all Intents and Purposes whatsoever. And if any of the said Buildings or Outhouses, shall from and after the said Twenty Fourth Day of *June*, Remain and be Covered with Thatch, Reed or Straw, they shall from thenceforth be Taken, and hereby Declared to be Common Nusances, and shall and may be Proceeded against as such.

And to the Intent that no Brick-maker, Tile-maker, Lime-Burner, Carpenter, Bricklayer, Mason, Plaisterer, Joyner, Plumber, or other Artificer, Workman or Labourer, may make the Common Calamity a Pretence to extort Unreasonable Prizes or Wages, Be it further Enacted, That in Case of Combination or unreasonable Exaction by Brick-makers, Tile-makers, and Lime-burners, it shall and may be Lawful for the said Court to Call before them such a Number of Brick makers, Tile-makers, and Lime-burners, Making or Burning Brick, Tile or Lime, at any Place within Ten Miles of the said Borough of *Warwick*, as they shall think fit, and upon Conference with them had, concerning the Premisses, if they will be Present, or else in their Absence, to Assess such Prices from time to time upon every Thousand of Bricks and Tiles, and every Quarter of the said Lime, and every Greater and Lesser Quantity, to be Delivered at the Kilnes, as may equally respect the Honest Profit of the said Brick-makers, Tile-makers, and Lime-burners, and the Necessity and Convenience of the Builder. And in Case of Combination or Exaction of unreasonable Wages, by Brick-makers, Tile-makers, Lime-burners, or any other of the Artificers, Workmen or Labourers above mentioned, or any of them, the said Court may Limit, Rate, and Appoint the Wages of the said Artificers, Workmen and Labourers, by the Day, Week, or otherwise, and what Wages every of the said Workmen shall have by the Great,[1] by the Foot, Yard, Rod or Pearch, or for any greater Quantity; which said Rate of Wages and Prices of Materials so Assessed, being set down in a Table, and Public Notice thereof given by Proclamation made in the open Market of the said Borough, If any Artificers, after notice by Proclamation, as aforesaid, shall refuse to Sell the said Materials for the Prices so Assessed, or if any of the said Artificers, Workmen and Labourers, shall either refuse to Work for the Wages so Assessed, or shall depart from his or their said Work, after he or they hath, or have undertaken to do the same, without Licence of such Person or Persons as employed him or them, and before it be finished, unless for Nonpayment of his or their Hire, or other just Cause to be allowed by the said Court; or if any Person or Persons whatso-ever, shall by any secret ways or means, Give or Covenant, Article or Agree to Give, directly or indirectly, by himself or any other for him, any other or greater Wages or Prices than shall be so Assessed, the said Offender or Offen-ders, being thereof Legally Convict by the Oath of One or more Credible Wit-ness or Witnesses, shall be by the said Court forthwith Committed to the House of Correction for the County of *Warwick*, there to receive such Pun-ishment as the said Court shall think fit to order, unless he shall Pay, or cause to be paid, for every such Offence, to the Treasurer to be appointed by the said Court to receive the same, such Fine as by the Discretion of the said Court shall be set upon such Offender, not exceeding Ten Pounds; out of which Fine the said Court shall, and may award to the Party injured, such Satisfaction as they shall Judge Reasonable, and the Residue thereof shall order to be paid towards the Rebuilding of the said Church, called St. *Mary's*, or other public Uses of the said Borough, as they shall think fit.

And be it further Enacted by the Authority aforesaid, That all Carpen-ters, Bricklayers, Masons, Plaisterers, Joyners and other Artificers, Work-men and Labourers, Fit and Convenient to be Imployed in the said Buildings, although they are not Freemen of the said Borough, during the space of Seven Years, and until the said Buildings are finished, shall, and may Work and be Imployed in the said Buildings, as well as the Freemen of the said Borough of the same Trades and Professions.

Provided always, and it is hereby Declared, That they shall not thereby gain any Settlement in the said Borough for themselves, their Wives,

[1] i.e. by contract for the whole.

Children or Servants; And if any such Artificer or other Person shall, within Seven Years next ensuing, for himself, and upon his own Account, Erect within the said Borough, any House of the Value of One hundred Pounds or more, every such Artificer and Person shall from thenceforth be a Free-man of the said Borough to all intents and purposes whatsoever, and shall and may Exercise any Trade within the said Borough, as well as if he were actually Admitted into, or made Free of any Company within the said Borough.

And forasmuch as the Soil of the Commons adjoyning and belonging to the said Borough, and commonly called and known by the Name of *The West Street, Common Mount, Sorrel Hill,* or *Green Hill,* and *Salsford Commons,* are fit and proper for making Brick and Tile, and may be used accordingly, with great Advantage to Builders in the said Borough, and with very little prejudice to the Commoners there; And for as much as the said Com-moners have given their Consent by Writing under their Hand, That the Mayor and Aldermen of the said Borough, for the time being, should License Persons to dig up such parts of the said Commons as they should think Convenient for making of Brick and Tile: Be it therefore Enacted, That the said Mayor and Aldermen shall and may License so many Persons as they shall think fit, to dig in such parts of the said Commons as they shall think most Convenient for the making of Brick and Tile; And if any the Persons so Licensed shall be Disturbed and Hindred in such their Work, by any Person or Persons whatsoever, if such Person or Persons so Hindring and Disturbing shall be thereof Convicted by the Court aforesaid, by the Oath of Two or more Credible Witnesses, the said Court shall and are hereby Impowered to Impose upon every such Offender, for every such Offence, such Fine as they shall think Reasonable, with respect to the Quality of the Offence, and the Ability of the Offender; And the said Court shall and may Commit such Offender to the Common Goal, there to remain, without Bail or Mainprize, till he shall have paid such Fine, and given Security by Recognizance in such Sum as the said Court shall think Reasonable, not to Offend in the like nature for the future.

And for as much as before the said Dreadful Fire divers Noysom Trades, and Perilous in respect of Fire, were Exercised in the Principal Publick Streets of the said Borough, to the great Annoyance and Dread of the Inhabitants there; For preventing the like Mischief for the future, Be it Enacted, That the said Judges of Assize, Justices, and other Persons Authorized, as aforesaid, or any Seven of them, shall, and may Order and Appoint, where and in what manner any such Noysom or Perilous Trade shall be Exercised within the said Borough; And if any such Trader shall at any time after Use and Exercise such Trade within the said Borough in any other manner than as by the said Order shall be Directed, every such

Trader shall be adjudged Guilty of setting up a Common Nusance, and shall and may be proceeded against and punished accordingly.

And be it further Enacted by the Authority aforesaid, That where any Order or Decree, as aforesaid, shall be made by a lesser Number of the said Judges of Assize, Justices, and other the Persons above Authorized than Seven, it shall be lawful for any Person agrieved by such Order or Decree, to present his Exceptions to the same in Writing, within Twenty days next after due Notice of any such Order or Decree made to one of the Judges of Assize for the said County of *Warwick* for the time being, or other the Justices of the Courts of Kings-Bench or Common-Pleas, or the Barons of the Coife of the Exchequer for the time being; And if One of them shall subscribe thereto, that he finds probable Cause of Complaint, Then it shall be Lawful to, and for any Seven or more of the Judges of Assize, Justices, and other persons Authorized, as aforesaid, that made not the said Order and Decree, Sitting together at the same time in the said Mayors Parlour, or other Place within the said Borough of *Warwick*, to Review the said former Order and Decree, and thereupon to Reverse or Alter any such Order and Decree, as in their Judgment they shall think fit, or to Affirm the same, and to Award Costs against such Appellants for their Vexation and Delay, and to cause the same to be Levied by Distress and Sale of the Appellants Goods, rendring the Overplus, if any such be, to the said Appellant.

Provided always, and it is hereby Declared and Enacted, That if such Appeals be not fully Finished and Determined within Three Months next following the Delivery of such Exceptions, as aforesaid, Then the said Appeals shall stand discontinued to all Intents and Purposes whatsoever; And the said Order and Decree Appealed against and Excepted to, shall stand absolute and be Final, from whence no other or further Appeal shall be had.

And be it further Enacted, That if upon any Controversie depending in the said Court, between Party and Party, touching their Estate or Interest in any House Demolished by the said Fire, or any Ground or Appurtenences to such House belonging, any Person shall be produced as a Witness to prove the Summons of any of the Parties concerned in such Controversie, or to prove their, or any of their Estates or Interest in such House, Ground, or any Appurtenances thereto belonging, and shall in his Testimony concerning any the matters aforesaid, Wilfully and Corruptly Forswear himself, such Person is hereby Declared Guilty of Perjury, and shall, and may for every such Offence be Indicted in any of His Majesties Courts of Record, and after his Conviction thereof, shall Incur such Forfeiture, and Receive and Have such Pains and Punishment as are Limited by the Statute made in the Fifth Year of the Reign of the late Queen Elizabeth, Entituled, *An Act for Punishment of such Persons as shall Procure, or Commit any willful Perjury.*

And for the better satisfaction of Builders, Purchasers, and others concerned, Be it further Enacted by the Authority aforesaid, That all and every Judgment, Order and Decree made, as aforesaid, shall be Good, Valid and Effectual, both in Law and Equity, to all intents and purposes, and shall be Obeyed by all Persons concerned therein, and shall Bind and Conclude Infants, *Feme Coverts*, Ideots, Persons of *Non sane* Memory, or beyond the Seas, Tenants in Taile, Bishops, and all other Ecclesiastical Persons, and all other Persons and Bodies Natural and Politick, their and every of their Heirs, Successors, Administrators and Assigns, whether Privies or Parties to the said Judgments, Orders and Decrees, or not; Any Law, Statute or Custom, or other Matter or Thing to the contrary notwithstanding; And that no Writ of Error, or *Certiorari*, shall lie or be for Reversal, or Removal of the same. And for the perpetuating the same to all Posterity, the said Judgments, Orders, and Decrees shall be fairly Entred into one or more Books made of Parchment, and be Subscribed with the Names of the Persons that made the same, except any of them shall happen to die before he shall have Subscribed the same: In which Case the Signing by the Survivor or Survivors, shall be sufficient and good, to all intents and purposes whatsoever; and the said Books shall be delivered in unto the Mayor and Aldermen of the said Borough of *Warwick* for the time being, to the intent the same may be disposed and kept among their Records and Evidences: And that all Persons concerned may have free liberty of Recourse to the said Books, to peruse the same from time to time, as occasion shall require, without paying any Fee or Reward for the same.

And be it further Enacted by the Authority aforesaid, That the said Judges of Assize, Justices, and other Persons Authorized, as aforesaid, by this Act, or any Seven of them, for a Reward of such Officer or Officers as they shall Judge necessary to be Imployed under them in the Execution of this Act, shall and may Order and Direct a Table of such reasonable Fees to be made, as may be a Competent Encouragement to such Officer or Officers, and may Carry on and Effect the Purpose and Intent of this Act, which shall be hung, or set up in some Publick Place by the Court, to the intent that every Person concerned may have and take Notice of the same.

And be it further Enacted by the Authority aforesaid, That where any person or persons, or Bodies Politick or Corporate shall be Ordered to Build, make any Estate, give any Security, or do any Matter or Thing by any Order or Decree in pursuance of this Act, It shall and may be Lawful to and for any person or persons, Bodies Politick or Corporate, concerned in the default thereof, by his Action upon the Case, in any of His Majesties Courts of Record at *Westminster*, to Recover his Damage for Non-performance thereof, or at his Election to have and maintain his Bill in Equity, for the performance thereof *in Specie*; And where any person or persons, or Bodies Politick and Corporate, shall be Ordered and Decreed by the said Court, to pay any Sum or Sums of Money, it shall be Lawful for the party or parties concerned, upon Non-payment thereof, to bring an Action at the Common Law for the Recovery thereof, and to give such Order or Decree in Evidence, to prove the same; In which Action no Essoign, Protection or Wager of Law shall be allowed, and the Plaintiff that Recovers shall have double Costs.

Provided always, and it is hereby Enacted, That all and every person and persons, before they Execute any of the Powers or Authorities above in this Act mentioned, shall take the Oath following, before any Two of the Justices of the Peace of the said County of Warwick for the time being, which the said Two Justices are hereby Impowered to Administer, and which follows, That is to say;

I Do hereby Swear, That I will Justly and Truly Execute the Powers and Authorities in this Act contained, according to the best of my Knowledge, without Favour or Affection to any the Parties concerned So help me God.

And be it Enacted, That the Powers and Authorities given and mentioned in this Act, shall continue for the space of Ten Years, and no longer; And that if any person or persons be Sued or Impleaded for any Matter or Thing done in Execution of this Act, or in pursuance thereof, he or they may plead the General Issue, and give the Special Matter in Evidence; and if the Plaintiff be Non-Suit, or a Verdict do pass against him, such Defendant shall Have and Recover his double Costs.

And forasmuch as the said Dreadful Fire did seize upon the Common Goal of the said County of *Warwick* with such violence and suddenness, that the Doors of the said Goal, for the preservation of the Prisoners Lives, were forced to be set open, by reason whereof some of the said Prisoners have Escaped out of Custody, which in a time of such Disorder and Confusion could not be prevented or avoided; Be it therefore Enacted by the Authority aforesaid, That neither the Sheriff of the said County, nor the Keeper of the said Goal, shall be Charged or Chargeable, either Criminally or Civilly, by or with any Suit or Action Whatsoever, for any Escape of any Prisoner out of the said Goal, occasioned by reason of the said late dreadful Fire only.

Provided always, and be it further Enacted by the Authority aforesaid, That the persons hereby Authorized to put this Act in Execution, shall not be liable, for, or by reason of such Execution, to any of the Penalties mentioned in an Act made in the Five and twentieth Year of the Reign of King *Charles* the Second [1673/4] Entituled, *An Act for the Preventing of Dangers which may happen from Popish Recusants*.

And for the better Encouragement of Gentlemen, and others, to Build and Reside in the said Town, Be it Enacted by the Authority aforesaid, That the Justices of the Peace for the County of *Warwick* from time to time being, who shall be Inhabitants within the said Town, may for ever hereafter Use and Exercise their said Office, to all intents and purposes, within the said Town, and Liberties thereof, and in the Sessions of the said Town to be held, as they may or can do in the said County at large, or in the Publick Sessions thereof; And that all other persons who from time to time shall be Justices of the Peace for the said County, shall for ever hereafter Use and Exercise the said Office within the said Town and Liberties thereof, during the time in which the Assizes, and Publick Sessions of the Peace for the said County shall be there kept.

FINIS

THE MASONS' AND CARPENTERS' SURVEY

The Survey of Building taken after the late Fire by Masons, etc.

September the 27 1694
A Sirvay of the Loss in Building consumed in the late fire hapned in Warwick and taken by Masons and Carpenters

Masons	Carpenters
Samuel Dunckley	Thomas Masters
Richard Bromley	Gorg Perkins
Job Birch	Roger Hurlburt
Thomas Adams	John Hope

	[Bays]	[Value]		
1. Mr Boyce landlord and Mr Brodshaw tenant, the front 4 bay and 1 bay backward	5 bay	350[1]	o	o
2. Mr Weale front 4 bay and a half, backward 2 bay, of Mr Oken land	7 bay ½	300	o	o
3. Mr Cook landlord, Baker Hands tenant, the front 4 bay and half, the back building 9 bay	13 bay	240[2]	o	o
4. Mr Willson landlord, Mr Rogers tenant, the front 2 bay and half, the back buildin 6 bay, of Mr Archer 1 bay	9 bay ½	300	o	o
5. Mr Archer landlord, Gorg Smith and har,[3] the front 2 bay and half, of back buildin 8 bay	10 bay ½	180	o	o
6. Mr Grene landlord, Mr Maunder tenant, front 2 bay, of back building 4 bay, Counceler Smith 6 bay, of barning 2 bay	14	312	o	o
7. Mis[4] Prescut landlord, Mis Ascoe and Mis Stemphford tenants, the front 5 bay, of back buildin 10 bay	15	340	o	o

[1] Altered from '280'.
[2] Possibly altered to '250'.
[3] Perhaps for 'Harrison'?
[4] For 'Mistress', and so throughout this document.

8. Mr Welton landlord, William Eabroll tenant, in the front 2 bay, backward 2 bay   4   292 10 0

9. Mr Welton landlord and John Langton tenant, the front 3 bay, of back building 7 bay, of barning[1]   12

10. Mr Tomkiss, the front 5 bay, the depth 7[2] bay the back building 8 bay   15   2000 0 0   8

073½   4294 10 0[3]

	Bays	Value
11. Corperation landlord, Thomas Gibbs tenant, the front 3[4] bay, the back building 3 bay, of molting rooms 8 bay	14	120 0 0
12. Widdow Hopkins landlord, Gorg Wats tenant, the front 5 bay, backward 5 bay, of molting rooms 15 bay and stabling	25	240 0 0
13. Thomas Dixon, in the front 3 bay, back building 1 bay	4	70 0 0
14. Mis Weale landlord, Humphry Carter tenant, front 3 bay, backwards 1 bay	4	160 0 0
15. Mis Weale landlord, Mis Rider tenant, front 2 bay, back building 4, of barning 2 bay	8	
16. Corperation landlord, Richard Bromly tenant, in the front 3 bay, back buildin 11 bay	14	80 0 0
17. Mis Lucus landlord, Richard Sharp tenant, the front 3 bay, back building 3 bay	6	50 0 0
18. Gorg Harris part of his burnt, with 6 bay of barning, in all	8	60 0 0
19. Mr Corpsen landlord, John Banbury 4 bay of back building	4	24 0 0
20. Mr Perks 7 bay of barning and part of his hous burnt	7	45 0 0
21. Mr Holioke landlord and Mr Veners tenant, the dwelling hous part burnt 2 bay and part of the back building	2	40 0 0
22. Mis Ovarton, in front 4 bay, the back building 15 bay	19	220 0 0

[1] Number of bays not filled in.
[2] Altered from '5'.
[3] The arithmetic seems very unreliable throughout.
[4] Altered from '6'.

23. Mr Clapton landlord, Mis Hix tenent, the front 4
bay and half, the back building 11 bay · · · · · · · · · · 15½ · 180 · 0 · 0
24. Mr Craine and Mis Bunter, front duble buildin 12
bay, the back building 19 bay · · · · · · · · · · · · · · 31 · 400 · 0 · 0
25. Mr Stratford, in the front duble building 5 bay,
the back building 7 bay · · · · · · · · · · · · · · · · 12 · 160 · 0 · 0

155 · 1799 · 0 · 0

	Bays	Value		
26. Mr Tarver landlord and Mr West, Mr Tongue, Mr Brierley, the front 5 bay, the back dwellings 19 bay, the stabling 8 bay ·	32	440	0	0
27. Mr Tarver landlord, Mr Stooks tenant, the front duble building 24 bay, the back building 10 bay, the new stable 8 bay, the back stable and leantoo 6 bay	48	1060	0	0
28. Mr Maior,[1] front 4 bay deep and 2 bay and half in the front, 10 bay, the brewhous 3 bay and 2 leanetoo 1 bay	16	450	0	0
29. Mr Grimes landlord, Thomas Moore and Gorg Tayler tenants, the front duble building 3 bay, the back building 10 bay	13	180	0	0
30. Mr Norton, the front duble building 8 bay, the kichin building 8 bay, and one bay more of Mr Grimes landlord	17	300	0	0
31. Mr Kerby, front duble building 2 bay, and 2 bay of back building	4	140	0	0
32. Mr Watts, the front duble building 4 bay, the back building 5 bay	9	200	0	0
33. Thomas Dadley, front duble building 3 bay	3	130	0	0
34. Mis Weale landlord, Thomas Dadly tenant, the front 2 bay	2	66	15	0
35. Mr Tarver landlord, Mr Whadkock tenant, front duble building 6 bay	6	370	0	0
	150	3336	15	0

[1] i.e. the mayor, Joseph Blisset.

The Church Street[1]

	Bays	Value		
36. Thomas Dadley landlord and John Hands tenant, the front duble building 3 bay	3	80	0	0
37. Mis Weale landlord, Henry Smith tenant, the front duble building 3 bay and half	$3\frac{1}{2}$	80	0	0
38. Mis Cauthrey landlord, Thomas Clarig tenant, the front duble building 4 bay $\frac{1}{2}$, of back building 1 bay	$5\frac{1}{2}$	100	0	0
39. Mr Weale landlord, Mr Nickols tenant, the front duble building 6 bay, the back building 14 bay	20	300	0	0
40. Mis Palmar landlord, Robert Tayler tenant, the front duble building 8 bay, the back building 9 bay	17	230[2]	0	0
41. Will Perks his front duble building in the front 5 bay, the back buildin 15 bay	20	220	0	0
42. Elizabeth Carr, front duble building 7 bay, the back building 6 bay	13	150	0	0
43. Church landlord, Joseph Hemins tenant, the front 8 bay, the back building 13 bay	21	150	0	0
44. Mr Oken[3] landlord, Mr Byker, the front 4 bay, the back buildin 11 bay	15	102	10	0
45. Mr Fish, 7 bay and a half	$7\frac{1}{2}$	120[4]	0	0
45.[5] Mr Chesley, in the front 4 bay and half, the back building 9 bay	$13\frac{1}{2}$	160	0	0
46. Mis Murcoot, in the front 6 bay, the back buildin 4 bay / Mr Fetherston hous 4 bay, the back buildin 2 bay	16	300	0	0
47. The parsnag hous, the front 4 bay, the back building 11 bay	15	180	0	0
48. Mr Oken landlord, John Atterbury tenant, the front 3 bay, the back buildin 4 bay	7	71	0	0
	177	2143	10	0

[1] This is the only street heading in the document. Houses before this are presumably in the High Street, but there is no break in the sequence (other than page totals) to show where Church Street or any subsequent street finishes.
[2] Altered from '200'.
[3] i.e. Oken's Charity.
[4] Altered from '130'.
[5] Sic.

	Bay	Value		
49. Mr Oken landlord, 6 alms houes, 6 bay	6	80[1]	o	o
50. Mr Oken landlord, widdow Mathews, the front 3 bay	3	50	o	o
51. Mr Oken landlord, widdow Wodward, front 4 bay, back building 1 bay	5	61	o	o
52. Thomas Clemens, the front 6 bay, the back building 8 bay and a half	$14\frac{1}{2}$	200	o	o
53. Thomas[2] landlord, Nicholas Kinton the front 3 bay	3			
54. Mis Sayle landlord, Edward Atkins, the front 5 bay, the back building 9 bay	14	200	o	o
55. John Haulks landlord, Mr Arps tenant, the front 3 bay, the back buildin 10 bay	13	200	o	o
56. Mis Ashwin landlord, Joseph Willis, front 4 bay, back buildin 4 bay	8	113	o	o
57. Mr Prichit, front duble buildin 7 bay	7	450	o	o
58. Corperation landlord, Mr Prichit, front 6 bay, back buildin 2 bay	[ ][3]			
59. The Sheir Hall damnified		34	o	o
60. The Jale, the front duble buildin 8 bay, the back building 21 bay and 3 bay of barning	32	700	o	o
61. Mr Watts landlord, the front 6 bay and half, the back building 4 bay, the cross buildin 3 bay	$13\frac{1}{2}$	200	o	o
62. The water hous deminished		102	o	o
	119	2390	o	o

	Bay	Value		
63. The Bridwell, front 6 bay	6	90	o	o
64. Mathew Busby, Mr Okens landlord, front 5 bay and half, the back buildin 4 bay	$9\frac{1}{2}$	105	o	o
65. The widdow Rogers, front 4 bay, the back buildin 2 bay	6	80	o	o
66. Mr Hadley landlord, Sam. Dunckley, 2 bay of building	2	20	o	o
67. Edward Wall, part of his hous burnt		20	o	o
68. John Sharley, 3 bay	3	25	o	o

[1] Altered from '60'.
[2] Surname omitted, presumably 'Clemens'.
[3] Total not filled in.

	Bay	Value		
69. John Tatnall, 1 bay and half	$1\frac{1}{2}$	15	0	0
70. Mathew Busby, 1 bay and a half	$1\frac{1}{2}$	15	0	0
71. Richard Hurst, 1 bay and a half	$1\frac{1}{2}$	15	0	0
72. Thomas Williams, 3 bay	3	25	0	0
[ ].[1] Jacob Dunckly, Thomas Grifin		10	0	0
73. Mr Bycker landlord, widdow Whinock, front 4 bay, back building 3 bay	7	100	0	0
74. Mr Bycker, landlord, William Mathews, front duble building 8 bay, back building 2 bay	10	80	0	0
75. Mr Bycker, landlord, Job Roods, the front 4 bay and half, the back buildin 3, of barning 2 bay	$9\frac{1}{2}$	84	0	0
76. Thomas Barthemalew 1 bay and half	$1\frac{1}{2}$	15	0	0
78.[2] Edward Aston, 1 bay and half	$1\frac{1}{2}$	15	0	0
[ ].[3] Widdow Maioh, front 2 bay, the back buildin 3 bay	5	30	0	0
79. Thomas Maioh, 1 bay	1	13	0	0
	$69\frac{1}{2}$	757	0	0

	Bay	Value		
80. Mr Boolton landlord, Thomas Shachwell, 1 bay and half	$1\frac{1}{2}$	20	0	0
81. Mr Ealworth landlord, Mathew Perry, 2 bay	2	30[4]	0	0
82. John Hancocks, 1 bay	1	11	0	0
83. William Cornwell, 1 bay	1	11	0	0
84. Richard Hadley, 1 bay	1	18	0	0
85. Gorg Francis, 1 bay	1	24	0	0
86. Mis Cauthrin, 3 bay	3	24	0	0
87. Mr Reeve, Thomas Mastars, 2 bay of barning	2	16	0	0
[ ].[5] Henry Stills		22	0	0
88. Mr Kinch[6] landlord, Mathew Perry, the hous 4 bay, barning 3 bay	7	64	0	0
89. Mis Ang landlord, 3 dwelling houses 3 bay	3	46	0	0
90. William Newburey, 2 bay	2	20	0	0
91. Henry Willson, 2 bay of housing, 1 bay of barning	3	33	0	0
92. Sir Henry Puckrin landlord, widdow Bromfield, 3 bay	3	20	0	0

[1] This entry inserted by the same hand in a darker ink, unnumbered.
[2] 77 omitted.
[3] This entry unnumbered.
[4] Altered from '20'.
[5] This entry inserted between the lines, unnumbered.
[6] Altered, reading doubtful.

93. Freckelton barn 5 bay	5	50	0	0
94. Sir Henry Puckrin landlord, Edward Angrove, the front 5 bay, the back buildin 12 bay	17	120	0	0
95. Sir Henry Puckrin landlord, widdow Haris, front 3 bay, back building 5 bay and 2 bay of barning	10	80	0	0
96. John Evets, 1 bay of hou[s]eing, 1 bay of barning	2	15	0	0
97. Mis Cauthrin, front 3 bay, the back buildin 13	16 ⎫			
98. Mis Cauthrin landlord, Martain Taylor, front 7 bay, back buildin 1 bay	8 ⎭	420	0	0
	$88\frac{1}{2}$	1040	0	0

	Bay	Value		
99. Sargen Hadley, front 9 bay, the back buildin 18 bay	27	450	0	0
100. Mis Wagstaf landlord, John Butler, front 2 bay and half, the back building 1 bay	$3\frac{1}{2}$ ⎫			
101. Mis Wagfstaf landlord, Thomas Rush, front 2 bay and half, the back buildin 1 bay	$3\frac{1}{2}$ ⎬	155	10	0
102. John Watts landlord, Sam. Parsons, front 7 bay, the back buildin 17 bay and a half	$24\frac{1}{2}$	297	10	0
103. John Watts landlord, John Burnill, the front 3 bay	3 ⎭			
104. Mr Wise, front 5 bay, the back building 3 bay	8	240	0	0
105. Mis Prescot landlord, Mr Rainsford, front 8 bay, the back buildin 4 bay	12	140	0	0
106. Mr Jarvis, the front of his own hous 6 bay	6 ⎫			
107. Mr Jarvis landlord, Mis Webb, the front 3 bay	3 ⎬	385	0	0
108. Mr Jarvis landlord, John Coole, the front 3 bay, the back building 1 bay	4 ⎭			
109. Mr Heath, the front duble building 10 bay, the back building 25 bay and half	$35\frac{1}{2}$	1200	0	0
110. Mis Tuckey landlord, Mr Lane, the front 3 bay, back building 2 bay	36[1]	85	0	0
111. Mr Ange, front 3 bay, the back building 10 bay	13	300	0	0
112. Mr Blisset, front duble building 7 bay, back buildin 3 bay	10	400	0	0
	189	3683	0	0

[1] *Recte* '5', but the writer was led into error by seeing '35' in the line above, and '36' is included in the page total.

	Bay	Value		
113. Mr Blisset landlord, Mr Webb, the front 3 bay and half	$3\frac{1}{2}$	80	0	0
114. Thomas Wall, front duble building 5 bay, back building 1 bay	6	160	0	0
115. Corperation landlord, Richard Good, front duble building 3 bay, back buildin 3 bay	6	95	0	0
116. Nicholas Paris, front 5 bay, back buildin 2 bay	7	100	0	0
117. Mr Ward landlord, Thomas Glendell, front 1 bay and half	$1\frac{1}{2}$	110	0	0
118. Mr Ward landlord, Joseph Drake, front 3, back building 2 bay	5			
119. Ocken landlord, Thomas Mariot, part of his house burnt 3 bay	3	40	0	0
120. Thomas Lane landlord, John Burton, front duble building 9 bay, the back building 7 bay	16	160	0	0
121. Mr Spencer landlord, Francis Odomes, front 2 bay, the back buildin 2 bay	4	82	0	0
122. Mis Martain landlord, Timothy Simkins, front 6 bay, the back building 17 bay	23	213	0	0
123. Charles Ems, front 2 bay and half, the back building 7 bay	$9\frac{1}{2}$	160	0	0
124. Mis Man, part of his[1] hous burnt	3	30	0	0
125. Tim. Simkins his hous, part of his hous burnt down	1	12	0	0
126. Bromig landlord, Francis Powers, front duble building 8 bay, the back buildin 21	29	270	0	0
127. Mr Blisset landlord, Gorg Flower, front 4 bay, back buildin 7 bay, Mis Prescot 1 bay	12	200	0	0
	$129\frac{1}{2}$	1712		

	Bay	Value		
128. Mr Gibbert landlord, Ben. Powers, front 7 bay, the back buildin 8 bay	15	200	0	0
129. Mr Gibbert landlord, front 3 bay, the back buildin 1 bay	4	90	0	0
130. William Smith, 1 bay	1	10	0	0
131. John Leeke, part of his hous burnt		3	0	0
132. Mis Weale landlord, Thomas Tan, the front [ ],[2] the back building 8 bay	8	80	0	0

[1] Sic.   [2] Space not filled in.

133. Widdow Farr, Corperation landlord, front and back building 3 bay	3	50	0	0
134. John Hix landlord, Robert Coole, the front 3 bay, the back building 2 bay, 1 bay of barning	6	120	0	0
135. John Hix, part of his house burnt		10	0	0
136. William Rooe, 1 bay of back buildin	1	8	0	0
137. Gorg Chinn landlord, Edward Deacon, front 2 bay	2	36	0	0
138. John Avens, front duble building 4 bay, the front[1] 2 bay	6	103	0	0
139. Mr Coolemore, 2 bay of buildin	2	30	0	0
140. Sir Henry Puckrin, 4 bay of back building	4	30	0	0
141. Mr Gibbert, hous in the New Street		110	0	0
142. Nathan Gilstop hous		30	0	0
143. Thomas Roberts, 2 bay of barning		20	0	0
144. Andrew Archer Esq.		20	0	0
The Coorthous		15	0	0
	52	965	0	0

The Number of Bays

$73\frac{1}{2}$
$155\frac{1}{2}$
150
177
186^{2}
119
$69\frac{1}{2}$
$88\frac{1}{2}$
$129\frac{1}{2}$
52
———
$1190\frac{1}{2}$

[1] Sic.
[2] Presumably the total of the eighth page, there given as '189'.

High Street

Mr Whadcock (1)   £100

Sept. the 5, '94. Lost by the Fyer to the value of one hundred pound in shop goods and household goods. Per Dev. Whadcock.

Thomas Dadley (2)   £236 15s. vide Church Streete £80

An Account of what I Thomas Dadley of the Borough of Warwick, butcher, have lost by the Fire which happened on the 5th day of September anno domini 1694.

Imprimis my dwelling house in High Street vallue	£150	
My houshold goods to the value of	20	
My house rented of Mrs Weale being partely the poores house at £3 6s. 9 per annum	66	15
My house in Church Street in the possession of John Hands, glover, vallue	80	
	———	
Totall losse	316	15
Tho: Dadley		

Thomas Watts (3)   £344 10s.

The Valuation of the Loss of Thomas Watts, apothecary, sustained by the late fire which happn'd in Warwick lately.

Imprimis in money, wearing cloths and house hold goods	94	10
Item my shop goods	50	
Item the value of the house I liv'd in	200	
	———	
	324	10

Mrs Martin att Mr Watts (3)   £25 10s.

The Valuation of the Loss of Mrs Mary Martin, widdowe, sustain'd by the late fire.

In pewter, bras, linnen, furniture, cloaths, money, etc.   £15 10s.
Books in folio, quarto and 12° to the value of at least   £10

                                                    Total   £25 10s.

Richard Kerby (4)   £185 1s.

An Account of what I Richard Kerby of the Borough of Warwick, butcher, lost by the late fire there.

My dwelling house and back buildings   £160
My houshold goodes and apparrell, linnen and woollen and
pewter   25   1

                                                    totall   185   1

Witnes my hand the 14th day of Sept. '94   Richard Kerbey

Mr Edward Norton's note (5)   £574

War. Bur. September the 5th 1694. Mr Edward Norton lost by the fier upon the day aforesaid

Imprimis. His house in the High Street at £15 per annum   £300
Goods in his house and shop   274

                                                                 574

Richard Grimes (6)   £180

Richard Grimes his Losse by the Fire on the 5th of Sept. anno domini 1694.

My dwellinge house, out houses, etc. in the High Street within the Borough of Warwick in the tenure of John Gibbs and George Tayler lett to them at nine pounds per annum   Vallue   ¨£180

Wittnes my hand the 14th day of Sept. 1694   Rich: Grimes

George Taylor (6)   £17 19s. 6d. Vide Mr Rd Grimes the house.

The Valuation of the Loss of George Taylor of Warwick, smith, sustained at the late fire in Warwick.

Imprimis windings and laths   1   12 10
Item my shop goods   3   0   0
Item fyles and working tooles   0   6   0

Item coales	2	10	0
Item an anvile block, a nest of drawers and shelves in the shop	0	12	0
Item 2 beds and 1 bolster and 2 pillowes	2	0	0
Item 3 bedsteads	1	4	0
Item a long table	0	18	0
Item barrells, tubbs, 2 pales and a coffer	1	0	0
Item palling woods, rakes and fork stales	0	17	6
Item one grindlestone	0	4	0
Item 2 coffers, court cubbord and a cradle	0	13	0
Item linnens	0	10	0
Item a large presse	0	16	0
Item a sett of curtaines	0	8	0
Item shelves, dressers and a bacon cratch in thehouse	0	11	0
Item chaires and stooles	0	6	8
Item a paire of stayes, flax and flaxen yarne	0	9	0
Glass bottles	0	1	6
	17	19	6

The house all burnt, the land of Mr Grimes, rent per annum   £4 4s. 0d.

Thomas More (6)   £47 10s.

Thomas Mooers loses by the fier.

In housold goods, bras, puter and beds and bedstids, in wilin and linin cloths and other goods	£40	0	0
In timber and fier wood	3	10	0
In tools and such meteryalls	4	0	0
	47	10	0

Susanna Smith (6)   10s.

Israell[1] Smith, the lose of then shellengs waren close.[2]

Martha Keen (6)   £3 2s.

The Valluation of the Goods of Martha Keen sustained by the late fire in Warwick.

---

[1] This change of Christian name is unexplained.
[2] Wearing clothes.

One bedstead, matt and coard, curtaines and valens, one
feather bolster, one coverlett, one blankett and one sheet £2 0 0
A paire of stayes, 3 pettycoates, two aprons, one brass
posnett and other small thinges 1 2 0

3 2 0

The house all burnt, being a border with Tho. Moore in the High Street.

John Gibbs (6)   £58 8s. 6d.

The Valluation of the loss of John Gibbs of Warwick, taylor, sustained att
the late fire in Warwick September the 5th 1694.

Imprimis my goods in the shop 9 15 6
Item all sorts of wearing apparrell, both linnens and
woollens, table linnens and other linnens 18 19 6
Item bookes 3 10 0
Item in bedding and all other houshold goods 24 8 6
Item in coales and hay 1 15 0

58 8 6

The house all burnt being the house of Mr Richard Grimes, rent per
annum 4 16 0

Mr Stokes (8)   £166 13s. 8d.

A Particular of the goods and chattells of John Stokes in the Swan Inne
besides the goods that were there of Mr Tarvers which were consumed and
lost by the dreadfull fire on Wensday the 5th of September 1694.

For wyne, beare and vessells £32 4 0
For fewell, hay and corne 20 0 0
For the furniture of a new roome 12 0 0
For linen 7 10 0
For brasse and pewter, forkes, knives, weights, scales and
irons and such things as will appeare by particulars 13 7 0
For sturgeon, anchoves, pickles and meate 3 5 0
For a chest of drawers, new bedsteads with other wooden
things as appears by particulars 6 17 8
For two piggs burnt 1 0 0
For feathers in the house 5 0 0

For money lost and wareing apparell	5	10	0
For money layd out on the house[1]	60	0	0
	166	13	8

John Pike (8)   £28 0 0

The valluation of the loss of John Pike of the Borough of Warwick, hornis maker, sustained att the late fire which happened in Warwick.

Imprimis five paire of new hornis, severall other shop goods, tooles, wearing apparrell and other materialls amounting in the wholl to   £28 0 0

Henry Falkener (8)   £4 6s. 4d.

The Valluation of the Loss of Mr Henry Faulkner, glover, sustained by the late fire which happened in Warwick.

Imprimis goods lost and burnt in his shop in the High Street near the Swan amounting to   £4 6s. 4d.

George Tongue (9)   £159 16s. 0d.

An account of the Loss sustained by George Teong, bookeseller, occasioned by the late dredfull fire at Warwick 7ber the 5th 1694.

Imprimis hiss household good, plate, beding, lining, brass and pewter, wooden vessels and all manner of aparell	79	0	0
Item his bookes and all sorts of working instruments and paper, wax, wafers, ink and quills with severall other good	80	16	0
	159	16	0

The house Mr Tarver landlord and the rent six pound ten shilling per annum.

Mrs Pywell (9)   £29 19 6

An account of the Loss sustained by Elizabeth Pywall by the late dredfull fire at Warwick September the 5th 1694.

Her money, gold and silver, aparell, linen and wollend amounting to   29 19 6

---

[1] Followed by 'more than' struck out.

Mr Vere (9)   £6

The loss of Mr Joseph Vere sustained by the late fire.

Hay, bridle, saddle, a coat and other things	£6	0	0

Jo: Vere

Samuel Brierly (10)   £19 0 0

Samuell Brierley, millener, in High Street in Warwick, lost by the fier, viz.

Lost in shop goods vallue	£13	10	0
Lost in house goods vallue	5	10	0
In all	19	0	0

Wittness my hand, Sam^ll Brierley.
September the 14th 1694

Thomas West (11)   £154 15 0

The Valluation of the Loss of Thomas West of the Borough of Warwick, chaundler, sustained at the late fire which happened in Warwick Sept. 5th 1694.

Imprimis in candles, tallow and shop goods	£109	7	0
Item in houshold goods	45	8	0
Sum totall	154	15	0

The house all burnt downe, the land of William Tarver, gent., rent per annum   £8 0 0

Ann Bolton (11)   £54

The loe[1] value of the lose of Ann Bolton amounts to	£54	0	0

Mr Thomas Stratford (12)   £238 3 0

The Valluation of the Loss of Mr Thomas Stratford sustained by the late fire which hapned in Warwick September the 5th 1694.

Imprimis his brass, beding, pewter and other househould goods, plate, linnen and all other utensils amounting	£78	3	0

---

[1] Possibly for 'whole'.

The two houses in my owne hands totally consumed, rent
per annum if they had been let at least   8   o   o[1]

Mary Taylor (12)   £2 10 0

The Valluation of the Loss of Mary Taylor, servant to Mr Stratford of Warwicke, sustained by the late fire in Warwick.

Imprimis her wearing apparrell both woollen & linnen amounting to
£2 10 0

Mr Crane and Sarah Bunter (13)   £400

Mr Richard Crane and Mrs Sarah Bunter's Loss by the fire in Warwick September the 5th 1694.

Imprimis the house call'd the Beare in the High Street in
Warwick   £400   o   o
                                                             Richard Crane
                                                             Sarah Bunter

Sarah Bunter (13)   £412 9 0

Sarah Bunter, widow, lost by fire the 5th day of Sept. '94:

In beds, beding and bedsteeds, hangins, linnings and
woollings, bras, puter, tables, cheairs, stools and forms and
brueing vessels to the valew of   £250   o   o
In wood and cole   30   o   o
In hay and oats and bens   7   o   o
In ale and beere   20   o   o
In wines   30   o   o
In hops   75   o   o
In straw   o   9   o
                                                             _____
                                                              412   9   o

                    Witness my hand,   Sarah Bunter
                    September the 13th 1694

John Howell, harper, (13)   £61 4 6

John Howell losse att the fier.
Seaven and twentie broad peeces of gold att £1 4s. a peece   £32   8   o[2]
Five guineas   5 10   o

[1] The annual rent is multiplied by 20 to give the value, here and elsewhere.
[2] Altered from £35 16 0.

Three Louidores	2	12	6
Weareing clothes	7	0	0
Lynen	0	15	0
Three hatts	0	10	0
Two harps	5	0	0
Fower dozen of plate buttons and silver lace	1	10	0
Sadle, pistolls and sword and bootes	2	10	0
Three perriwiggs	0	10	0
In money	2	0	0
For a chest and 2 boxes	0	10	0
For bookes	0	10	0
	61	5	6

Beverley Bedoes (13)   £30 0 0

Lost by the fier value   £30   0   0

Warwick Sept. 13th 1694. Witness my hand   Beverly Bedoes

William Kerby (13)   £8 0 0

Valluation of the Loss of William Kerby, servant to Mrs Bunter att the Bear in Warwicke sustained by the late fire which happened in Warwick.

Imprimis in money, wearing apparrell, one chest and two
boxes amounting in the wholl to   8   0   0

Mary Guttell[1] (13)   £1 10 0

Mary Tuttell lost by the fier, value   £1 10   0

Sept. the 13th 1694   Mary Tuttell

Samuell Willis (13)   £0 15 0

What goodes of Samuell Willes burne in the fiore in Warwick Sept. 5th 1694.

At Mrs Bunters loft one coalts skine bage and 24 pares of
trankes[2] with one pound of jarsy came to   £0 15   0

Samuel Willis

---

[1] This name appears to be a misreading by the writer of the endorsements.
[2] Altered from 'gloves'. Tranks are pieces cut out for making gloves but not yet sewn.

Sarah Hicks (14)   £398 0 0

An Accompt of what Mrs Sarah Hicks of the Borrough of Warwick lost by fire att the Dolphin in Warwick upon Wedensday the fifth of September anno domini 1694.

House rent £6 per annum	£100	0	0
more for her work-house	40	0	0
In household goods	160	0	0
In coale and wood	20	0	0
In hay, oats and straw	8	0	0
In the cellar, beer and vessels	30	0	0
In wearing apparell	20	0	0
In money, plate and swine	20	0	0
In toto	398	0	0

Witnes my hand,   Sarah Hickes

Thomas Hicks (14)   £24 10 4

The Valluation of the Loss of Thomas Hickes of the Borough of Warwick, chaundler, sustained by the late fire which happened in Warwick.

Imprimis in shop goods, other goods and utensills amounting in the wholl to   £24 10 4

The shop being part of my mother Hickes her house.

Mary Overton (15)   £382 8 5

The Valluation of the losse of Mary Overton of Warwick, widow, sustained by the late fire which happened in Warwick.

Imprimis my bedding, brass, pewter, wood, coales, hay, straw and other houshold goods, malt, barley and severall other materialls amounting in the wholl to   £162 8 5
The house totally burnt downe, my owne part in my owne occupation being worth   £8 0 0 per annum
Other part in the occupation of Mrs Hickes her rent per annum   3 0 0

Totall rent per annum   11 0 0
at 20 yeares purchase   220 0 0[1]

[1] This line added in the hand of the writer of the endorsements.

Richard Scudamore (15)   £16 19 0

An Account of Richard Skidmore.

Losses by fyer att Mrs Overtons hous being twelve quarters of malt amounting to   £16 19 0

Edward Venor (16)   £80 0 0

The Valuation of the Loss of Edward Venor of the Burrough of Warwick,
baker, sustained by the late fire Sept. the 5th 1694.

Imprimis wearing aparrell, money and other houshold
goods amounting in all to   £20 0 0
The rent of the house £7 10 0 per annum whereof
£3 0 0 per annum is consumed, the rest standing, the
whole belonging to Mr John Holioake of Morton Bagott
in the County Warr:

Thomas Russell (17)   £14

The Valluation of the Loss of Thomas Russell of Warwick, fellmonger, sustained at the late fire in Warr:

Imprimis my hay, straw, boards and timber in the barne
near where the fire broake out   £4 10 0
The barne all burnt, the land of Mr Corpson, rent per
annum   0 10 0

Joashey Parkes (18)   £50

The Valluation of the Loss of Joshua Perkes of Warwick, baker, sustained
att the late fire in Wawick.

Imprimis brush wood and other wood, coales and hay and
straw and other things   £8 16 8
Item a hogge   1   3 4
                                                             ----
                                                             10 0 0

The house my owne but not burnt, only two bayes of
stabling and barning and 3 bayes of old barning, a gate
house, a tyled pigsty and a house of office, some of the
outhouses for maulting much damaged, worth   £40 0 0

John Banbury (19)　　£86 13 0

The Valluation of the Loss of John Banbury of Worwicke, wever, jersey comer and flax dreser, sustained att the late fier which happened in Warwicke September the 5th 1694.

	£		
80 dosen of 8 peny flax at	£32	0	0
20 hundred of hurds	16	0	0
4 dosen of 4d. hurds	0	16	0
Flax in the ruffe	10	4	0
Two hoggs	3	10	0
Two loade of hay	1	16	0
9 dosen of sope	1	7	0
For a loft and 2 ware houses standing within my lanlords borne	4	0	0
For tobs, stale and bilits and pigsty, racke and mainger, bridels and sadel and panill and by spiners whose worke was burnt in all	3	0	0
	72	13	0

Besides other loses amongest my housold goods not reckned.

The dweling house standing, Mr Corpson landlord, rent at	4	0	0
The borning and hovill burnt being 3 bay	14	0	0
The totall loss sustained	86	13	0

George Harris (20)　　£73 3 0

What looste by the late fyore in Warwick Sept. 5th '94.

	£		
Burnt of my house to the value of	£50	0	0
Toe swine	3	0	0
In the stable haye, saddle and other things	0	14	0
In the swingall[1] hous brakes[2] and bords	1	0	0
In the hovill black fate[3] and dying tubes	1	10	0
Woode and polles	3	0	0
Flax in the rufe	2	10	0
Well rope and curve[4]	0	16	0

[1] To swingle: to beat flax, so a 'swingle-house': a house in which flax was beaten.
[2] Instruments for crushing flax.　　　　　　　　　　　　　　　　　　　　[3] A vat.
[4] Probably from 'corf', pl. 'corves': a basket, also a wooden tub or bucket, here presumably a well bucket.

Spune yarne, sheats and thride	10	3	0
Frute gother'd and upon the treayes	0	10	0

George Harris

Richard Sharp (21)   £147 6 0

Lost by me Richard Sharp in the late fire to the value of £97 6 0 by a modest computation, besides the loss of a shop-book.

Mrs Lucas's house which I dwellt in burnt, being 50s. rent per annum.

Mrs Lucus[1] her loss by the fire: £63 0 0

The Valluation of the Loss of Mrs Lucas of Warwick sustained by the late fire which happenned att Warwick.

Imprimis her wearing apparrell and other houshold good amounting to	£3	0	0
Item the dwelling house wherein Richard Sharp lived in the High Street, rent per annum £2 10s. upon a lease thô worth to be sold at least	60	0	0
Totall loss sustained	63	0	0

Richard Bromely (22)   £164 14 7

The Valluation of the Loss of Richard Bromley of the Borough of Warwick, shomaker, sustained att the late fire which happened in Warwicke.

Imprimis his crab mill and stone, verjuice, crabbs, hogges heads, pewter, bras, bedding, money, leather and implements of his trade, boards, timber and other houshold goods and utensills amounting in the wholl to	£84	14	7
The house totally consumed with the outhouses, the house being charitable land, rent per annum though worth a great deale more.	4	0	0

Margaret Clements (22)   £19 11 0

The Valluation of the Loss of Margarett Clemens of Warwick, spinster, sustained by the late fire att Warwick Sept. the 5th 1694.

---

[1] This unnumbered estimate found loose and inserted here. It is not clear where she lived.

Imprimis in money, two pieces of gold and three gold ringes	£9	0	0
Item pewter	1	0	0
Item brass	0	14	0
Item paire of sheets, 3 paire of pillow beers	2	10	0
Item 1 douzen of flaxen napkins, 4 table cloths and 8 towells	0	13	0
Item one bedstead, matt and board	0	10	0
Curtaines and valens	0	10	0
Item my owne wearing linnen, great and small	1	10	0
Item another box of small linnens	0	10	0
Item 6 chaires, one table, one joyn'd stoole	0	9	0
Item two spining wheeles	0	5	0
Item woollen, linnen and jersey yarne	1	5	0
Item 1 coffer, 1 trunk and 3 boxes	0	5	0
Item one barrell and pale	0	2	0
Item one paire of andirons, a spitt and frying pan	0	5	0
Item tinne ware and other odd things	0	3	0
	19	11	0

The house Mrs Ryders, renting one roome there.

Richard Eberall (22)   £16 19 3

A valluation of the loss of Richard Eborall sustained in the late fire wich hapened in the Burrough of Warwicke the 7th of September 1694.

Imprimis in beding, brase, pewter, linning, apparell and other housould goods	£16	2	9
In money	0	7	6
In all	16	9	3

Inmate to Richard Bromley in the High Street.

Sarah Ryder (23)   £187 3 10

An Account of wath I Sarah Rider have lost in the late fire appened in the Borough of Warwick the 5 day of Sept. 1694.

For beds, linnen, brasse, putre and all wath belong to househod goods the walu of	£77	3	10

Sarah Stanley (23)   £16 0 0

One feather bed, one feather bolster, six feather pillowes, two hillings, three pair of blankets, three bedsteads, two flock beds and bolsters, one chest, one grat cubbord, three coffers, one brass furnace, three brass potts, the iron work belonging to the furnace, one brass kettle, one skillet, nine pewter dishes, four pewter plates, four pewter porringers, one pewter candlestick, one pewter bason, one pewter salt, one pewter chamber pot, one pewter cup, one brass pot cover, one brasse skimmer and ladle, two looking glasses, three tables, four joynd stooles, ten chaires, two setts of curtaines and curtain rods, two window curtaines, nine pair of sheets, 2 dousen of towells and napkins, one trunk, four table clothes, one hogshead, three barrells, five tubs and covers, one skreene, one pair of andirons, five showells and tongues, a pair of bellowes, one steel malt mill, one trye,[1] one hair cloth, one strike, one peck and three buffet stooles to the value of £16

                                                                Sarah Stanley

Abraham Du Commune (23)   £41 18 5

An Account of wath I Abraham du Commun have last in the late fire appened in the Burough of Warwick the 5th day of Sept. 1694.

For beding, linnin, brasse, putre and all wath belong to
house hold good and for towls of my traide the walu of   £41 18 5

Humphrey Carter (24)   £73 9 0

The Valluation of the loss of Humphry Carter of the Borough of Warwick, taylor, sustained by the late fire which happened in Warwick Sept. the 5th 1694.

Imprimis in houshold goods as brasse, pewter, bedding,
wood and other materialls in the wholl amounting to   £23 9 0

The house Mr Fulk Weales all burnt downe, rent per
annum   £2 10 0

Thomas Dixon (25)   £107 12 1

The Valluation of the Loss of Thomas Dixon of the Borough of Warwick, smith, sustained att the late fire which happened in Warwick on the 5th of September anno domini 1694.

---

[1] A sieve or sifting screen.

Imprimis my wood and coale	£7	2	6
My working tooles	2	10	0
Lath and nailes	1	1	7
My coletrough	0	9	0
A nest of drawers and shelves in my warehouse	0	10	0
Stock locks, plate locks, horse lock, gate lockes and small joynts	1	2	0
Reaping hookes and edge tooles	0	16	0
Forkes and rakes	0	8	0
Screw plates, taps, a hand vice and other tooles	0	10	0
My brass and pewter lost	1	1	0
Barrells, tubs and pales	1	9	0
Three tables	0	17	0
One dresser	0	5	0
Formes, chaires and joynd stooles	0	9	0
Three bedsteads, 2 flock beds, one bolster and 3 feather pillowes	1	5	0
Curtaines and vallens	0	5	0
A trunck, a hatt and severall linnens	0	16	0
A hillen,[1] a blankett and a cloth both	1	2	0
Wearing apparrell for my selfe, wife and children	3	0	0
A chest and three coffers	0	12	0
Two wheeles	0	9	0
A cubbord and a dough trough, a meale seive and a search[2]	0	7	0
Spade trees, shovell trees and patten woods	0	8	0
Moneys lost, a looking glasse and other small things	0	18	0
	27	12	1
The house my owne all burnt downe with the back buildings, rent per annum	4	0	0

Dorothy Hopkins (26)   £240

The Valluation of the loss of Dorothy Hopkins, widow, sustained att the late fire which happened in Warwick.

Imprimis the White Lyon with all the outhouses and buildings being totally consumed by the said fire, the rent per annum being	£12	0	0

[1] A bed covering.
[2] A fine sieve for flour.

George Watts (26)   £322

The Valluation of the Loss of George Watts of the Borough of Warwick, inneholder and flaxman, sustained by a late fire which happened in Warwicke the 5th of September 1694.

Imprimis in houshold goods, beare, vessells, hey, straw and corne	£200	0	0
Item 21 load of watered flax	84	0	0
Item 190 stone of swingled[1] flax att 4s. per stone	38	0	0
	322	0	0

The White Lyon house, the house of Mrs Hopkins of Welsborn, rent per annum all burnt downe.	£12	0	0,

Richard Radford (26)   £3 10 0

An Account of what I Richard Radford of the Borough of Warwick lost by the fire which hapened there on the 5th day of September anno domini 1694.

Fower cow hides lodged at the White Lyon, vallue	£3	10	0

Wittnes my hand the 14th day of Sept. 1694   Richard Radford

Thomas Gibbs (27)   £357 18 0

High Street: Tho. Gibbs

Lost by a hous by laying out in repaires and conveniences in our trad	£50	0	0
By household goods, money and shopp goods with fewell and in mault and barly	157	18	0
By two trunks of good linen and plat of sistars Ann Gibbs	30	0	0
	237	18	0

Thomas Gibbs

[1] Beaten.

Jane Dale[1]

The loss of Jane Dale the wife of Phillip Dale, in a pees of serge and a pewter dish to the value of 16s. which ware left in the hands of my wife, which los I gave in soone after the fire.   Thomas Gibbs.

Mary Drury, servant (27)   12s.

The Value of the Loss of Mary Drury, servant to Thomas Gibbs, shoemaker, living in the High Street in the Burrough of Warwick as she sustained at the late dreadfull fire in the said Burrough on the 5th of September 1694, given upon oath before us theire Majestyes Justices of the Peace.

In linen and woollen clothes to the value of   £0 12   0

Mr Tomkys, High Street (28),

House	£2400	0	0
Goods	177	5	0
	2577	5	0

Dr Holden, Mrs Dolman and servants   17   7   0

September 26, 1694. Warwick Fire.

The goods I lost in the late sad accident of fire upon a reasonable computation we have valued to one hundred seaventy seaven pounds five shillings.

The loss in my house I have not skill to compute but can produce the accounts in the late building of it which amount to £2400 and upwards and what the loss ought to be reckoned in the said dreadful accident I refer to the master workmen of the town who knew the building of it and are herein imployed.

                              Isaac Tomkys

The loss of other persons belonging to my family:

My daughter Mrs Elizabeth Dolman	£8	10	0
Dr Henry Holden			
Servant maides Hannah Eires	6	0	0
Cook maid Liddia Perry	0	7	0
Servant man Jonathan Sturt	2	10	0

John Langton (29)   £36 4 6

The Value of the Lose of John Langton liveing in the Hystraet in the

[1] This unnumbered estimate found loose and inserted here.

Burough of Warwick as he sistaned att the late dreadfull fier in the said Buroar of Warwick bafore us theire magestrats Justises of the Pecse.

In beding, houshold goods, fuelle, corne and other things
to the value of   £37 4 6

   Wittnes my hand the 14 day of Sept. '94   John Langton

William Allen (30)   £5 5 0

The Valuation of the Loss of William Allen of the Borough of Warwick, shomaker, sustained by the late fire which happened in Warwick.

Imprimis his leather, shoes, working tooles and other
goods and utensills in his shopp amounting to   £5 5 0

The shop all burnt but was a part of William Eborall's shop.

William Ebrall (31)   £115

William Ebrall's Losse by the fire which happened of the 5th of Sept. 1694.

My bedding, brasse, pewter, linnen, wollen apparell,
houshold goods and shopp goods to the vallue of   £115 0 0
Togeather with the shopp booke.

John Welton (32)   £296 16 6

The Valuation of the Loss of Mr John Welton of Warwick sustained by the late fire which happened at Warwick on the 5th of September anno domini 1694.

Imprimis a part of my dwelling house in the tenure of Wil-
liam Eborall, rent per annum   £6 0 0
Item the other part of my house in the tenure of John
Langton, rent per annum   8 12 6
                                                                ─────────
                                                                14 12 6

Goods lost & burnt by the fire in the same houses left there.

Goods left in William Eboralls house   £1 1 6
Goods left in John Langtons house   1 5 0
Goods left at Mr Bartons, burnt   2 0 0
                                                                ─────────
                                                                4 6 6

Mrs Sandford, Mrs Norton, Mrs Bree (33)   £420

The valuation of goods, etc., lost in the house of Mrs Elizabeth Sandford, widow, gooldsmith, by the late fire.

High Streete

Imprimis her weareing apparell, money, plate, rings, beding, brass, pewter and other houshold goods to the vallue of	£270
Her daughter Norton and two daughters goods included.	
Her sister Sarah Bree in money & wareing apparell	£ 50
	£320

Susanna Wright (33)   goods £1 10 10

The Valluation of the Loss of Susannah Wright, servant to Mrs Sandford, sustained att the late fire which happened at Warwick.

Imprimis in clothes and weareing apparrell amounting in the wholl to	£1 10 10

Mrs Anne and Mr James Prescote (33)   £240
per Mrs Askells £140, Mr Rainsford £100.

The Valluacion of the losse sustained by Anne Prescott, widow, and James Prescott, gent., in the late dredfull fire which hapened att Warwicke on the fifth day of this instant September 1694.

Imprimis one house scituate in the High Pavement late in the occupacion of Elizabeth Askill, widow, of the yearly value of twelve pounds.
Item one other house scituate in the High Pavement aforesaid late in the occupacion of Elizabeth Sansford, widow, of the yearly value of five pounds.
Item one other house scituate in the Sheep Street and alsoe one barne in the New Street in the occupacion of Job Ransford or his assignes of the yearely value of five pounds.

Mrs Askell (34)   £280
An Account of Mrs Askells Losses by fyer.

Imprimis in druggs, tobaco and other shop goods	£150 0 0
In houshold goods, pewter, brass, bedding and linen	130 0 0
	280 0 0
The house rent per annum	£12 0 0

Francis Comander,[1] High Street, £2 0 0

Sept. the 5, '94.
The lose of Francis Commander, sarvant to Mrs Askell by the late fire which consumed almost all my linings and severall of my wolling cloths to the vally of forty shillings   £2 0 0

Witnes my hand Sep. the 5 day '94: Fransis Commander.

Elizabeth Roberts (34)   £70 0 0

The Valluation of the Loss of Elizabeth Roberts of the Borough of Warwick, widow, sustained att the late fire which happened at Warr. on the 5th of September 1694.

Imprimis her weareing apparrell and houshold goods, moneys, rings and other utensills amounting in the wholl to   £70 0 0

The house part of Mrs Askells in the High Street, her rent per annum for that part she lived in   £4 0 0

Thomas Maunder (35)   £277 8 0
                                                   5 0 0
                                          ——————
                                           282 8 0

The Valluation of the Loss of Thomas Mander of the Borough of Warwick, barber, sustained by the late fire which happened in Warwick.

Imprimis in houshould goods, shop goods, wood, coale, money lost and the lease of my house and other materialls amounting in the wholl to   £67 8 0

The house totally consumed, the house of Mr Richard Green of Abbington, the rent per annum being   £10 10 0

---

[1] This unnumbered estimate found loose and inserted here.

Mary Busbie (35)   goods 10s. 6d.

The Valluation of the Loss of Mary Busby, servant to Mr Thomas Maunder, sustained by the late fire which happenned in Warwick.

In weareing apparrell burnt by the said fire amounting in
the wholl to   £0   10   6

Mr James Yardley (35)   £28 9 0

The losse of James Yardley, lodger in the house of Mr Thomas Mandere, scituate in the High Streete, sustained by the late fier, my selfe being out of towne.

The bed, blanketts, chest of drawers with lynen and
weareing apparell with the rest of the furniture that was
in the chamber   £28   9   0

Witnesse my hand,   James Yardley

Mr Symons, High Streete, (35)   £20

An Estimate of the Loss Abraham Simonds, surgeon, sustained by the late fire, Warwick.

Per linnen and woollen cloths, some instruments, books
and medicines as plaisters, unguents, waters, species,
herbs, etc., to the value of twenty pounds   £20   0   0

George Barton (35)   £52 15 6

A Valuation of the Loss of George Barton then liveinge in the house where Counciller Smith lived, which hee sustained by the late fire which happen'd on the 5th of September in Warwick.

My household goods, fewell, hay and straw and my wives
wareing apparrell with other things that was then lost and
burnt   £52   15   6

Witness my hand
Geo: Barton

Mr Richard Greene (35), Mr Mander's landlord, High Streete
Houses £300
Standards £ 12

312

The Valuation of the Loss sustained by the late fire in Warwick by me Richard Greene of Abington in the County of Barks, owner of the house Thomas Mander lived in in Highstreete.

The house that he lived in, and that Mr Barton lived in, I value at	£300	0	0
In standards in the house (vixt.) 8 tables, 6 bedsteds, 5 court cupboards, glase case and chest, matts, cords and curtin rods, a large map, hangings, etc.	£12	0	0
	£312	0	0

Richard Greene

George Smith (36) High Streete, senior and junior.
House £100
Goods £ 44

£144

An Account of what I George Smith the elder and my sonne George Smith the younger of the Borough of Warwick, barbers, lost by the dreadfull fire which hapened in the said Borough on the 5th day of Sept. anno domini 1694.

My dwelling house, out houses, etc., which I rent of Thomas Archer, Esq., at £5 per annum.

Alsoe my houshold goods, fewell and hay which I then lost and was burnt I veryly beleive was worth, with my sonnes apparrell £44

Charles Harrison (37)   £109 19 6

15 Sept. '94. High Streete. Charles Harrison, sadler, liveing in the house of Thomas Archer, Esq., att £4 per annum, the severall losses in goods and wares in the abovesaid howse in the late fyre on the 5 instant hee suffered, the particulars whereof hee will be reddy to give and make appeare when thereto required.

	£		
Imprimis in howshold goods to the value of	£4	1	6
Wood, coales and boards	3	10	0
4 fyre bucketts	0	18	0
Wares in my shop	12	0	0
For impements and tooles	2	10	0
For goods of my customers	7	0	0
total	29	19	6

Mr Willson (38)   £430 0 0

Mr Edmund Wilsons losse by fire.

	£		
His dwelling house in the High Street to the value of	£350	0	0
His houshold goods of all sorts	80	0	0
Summe Total	430	0	0

Witness my hand the 11th day of September 1694,

Edmund Wilson.

Henry Rogers (38)   £145 0 0

September 5th '94.
In the house and shap of Mr Edmund Wilson in the High Street, burnt by the fire to the value of one hundred fourty and five pounds, of house and shop goods belonging to mee,

Henry Rogers.

Richard Hands (39)   £264 0 0

The Valluation of the Loss of Richard Hands of the Borough of Warwick, baker, sustained by the late fire which happened in Warwick.

	£		
Imprimis in wearing apparrell, houshold goods, wood, coales, oates, meale and other materialls amounting in the wholl to	£64	0	0
The house totally consumed the house of Mr William Cooke of London, the rent per annum	£10[1]	0	0

---

[1] Altered in another hand from '£12'.

Thomas Tipping (40)   £65

The Valuation of the Loss of Thomas Tipping of the Borough of Warwick, cutler, sustained by the late fire which happened in Warwick September the 5th 1694.

Imprimis in shop goods, wares, houshold good and other materialls amounting in the wholl to	£65	o	o
The house totally consumed the house of Mr Thomas[1] Cooke of London, rent per annum	£ 4	10	o

Mrs Dorothy Weale (41)

House, High Street	£400	Widow Ryder	£110
Goods there	150	Humphry Carter	50
	£550		

The Valluation of the Loss of Mrs Dorothy Weale of the Borough of Warwick, widow, sustained by the late fire which happened in Warwick.

Imprimis my dwelling house neare the Cross totally consumed, never sett for rent as I heard off, worth if it had been exposed to sale	£400	o	o
Item in shop goods and houshold goods in the said house lost and consumed by the fire	£150	o	o
Item my house wherein the widow Ryder lived in the High Street, rent per annum £5 10, worth after 20 yeares purchase	110	o	o
Item my house wherein Humphry Carter lived in the High Street totally consumed, rent per annum £2 10, worth	50	o	o
Totall loss sustained	710	o	o

Elizabeth Rands, (42) servant to Mary Overton, High Street, Loss £2

The Valluation of the Loss of Elizabeth Rands, servant to Mrs Overton in the High Street, sustained by the late fire which happened in Warwick.

Imprimis her wearing apparrell both woollens and linnens amounting to	£2	o	o

---

[1] *Sic*, probably an error for William.

Mary Stratford (43), grandaughter to Thomas Stratford, High Streete,
£1 17 6

The Valluation of the Loss of Mary Stratford, grandaughter of Mr Thomas Stratford, sustained att the late fire which happenned in Warwick.

Imprimis in wearing apparrell both woollens and linnens amounting in the wholl to £1 17 6

Mr Thomas Gibbs[1]

A true value of the losse of the goods of Mr Thomas Gibbs late Alderman at the dreadfull fire in Warwick Sept. 5th 1694.

Lost in the lease of his house, wherein he had about 14 years to come £45 0 0

Lost in goods of all sorts 55 10 0

Total 100 10 0

Thomas Gibbs, senior

Church Street

Robert Blisset (1)	Church Street	£420 0 0
	Jury Street	80 0 0
	Market Place	200 0 0
		700 0 0

The Valluation of the Loss of Robert Blissett sustained by the late fire which happened in Warwick the 5th September '94.

Imprimis the house I lived in that was my grandfather Smith's for his life and mine after, with the 2 shopps which were set for £20 per annum is £400

The house Mr Webb lived in at £4 per annum is £80

The Black Swan at £10 per annum £200

Lost in goods and fewell £20

Summ total £700 0 0

---

[1] This estimate was found in the High Street bundle but is not numbered.

Samuell Ainge (2)   £218 12 6

The Valuation of the Loss of Samuel Ainge of Warwicke sustained att the late fier in Warwick, Sept. the 5th 1694.

Imprimis goods in my shop	3	10	6
Item cloaths att my shop in marketplase	20	0	0
Item in the seler under the shope stockens and a press and wood and several sorts of goods	12	0	0
Item in the celer under the parlor one hogshead and barels and bruing vesels and drink	2	1	6
Item in the house severall goods, tables and chaires and stooles and glas botels	2	10	6
Item in the 4 chambers, bedsteads and tabls and beding and chaires and stools and curtains and valens and a chest full of gimp and silk bread[1] and laces and som other things	20	0	0
Item in cloaths, woolens and linines	3	10	0
Item in puter and brass and lead	1	10	0
Item wood and coales and hay	3	10	0
Item my house in the Church Street	150	0	0
	218	12	6

Susannah Gibbs (2)   £1 5 0

Sept. 5th 1694

Susance Gibbs lost by fier att Samuel Ainges house cloaths to the value of twenty five shilings.

Mary Goodalle (2)   20s.

Sept. the 5th 1694.

Mary Goodall lost by fier att Samuell Ainges house goods to the value of twenty two shilings.

Joseph Ainge (3)   £239 16 0

Sept. the 5 '94. The Valluation of the Loss of Joseph Ainge of Worwicke sustained att the late fier in Worwicke.

---

[1] Braid.

5400 of oak bordes	37	16	0
Warnut tree planke and borde	10	0	0
Oake quorters, rafters, bed poasts and stoole feete	10	0	0
Elven[1] borde and rafters, kill[2] lath	4	0	0
Ash borde and partree and planke	2	0	0
Elvenplanke and large paces	3	0	0
Ash planke	0	10	0
2 beds, blankets, pilloes, cortines and valens	3	10	0
3 bed steds	1	10	0
3 ovell tables	1	10	0
3 dresers, 2 with drores	2	10	0
1 chast drares and on table	1	10	0
One jack, handiales,[3] fire shelles[4] and tonges	3	0	0
Charers, stooles and one chast and 3 tables	1	0	0
Trunkes and boxes, trunkes, lockes and hinges	3	0	0
Close	1	10	0
Tooles	3	0	0
My dwelling house	150	0	0
	239	16	0

The Widow Ainge[5] (3)   £13 8 0

A true account of the Loss of Anne Ainge, widow, in the late fier in Warwick, Sept. 5th 1694.

3 tenements att the Butts sett for 3 pounds 6 shilins a yeare valied att sixty
pounds, for houshold goods and goods in my shop to the value of thirteen
pounds 8 shilings.

Katherine Bird (3)   £25

The lose of Katherin Bird sustain'd by the fire is 25 pounds.

Lane, barber, Mrs Tuckey's house (4)   £85 0 0

An Account of what I Hannah Tuckey of the Borough of Warwick, widow,
lost by the late fire on the 5th of Sept. 1694.

---

[1] Elm, in Warwickshire dialect.
[2] Kiln.   [3] Andirons.   [4] Shovels.
[5] There is another estimate of Anne Ainge, lacking the official endorsement, in which goods and
apparel are valued at £30.

My house in the Church Street in the possession of
Thomas Lane, barber, by lease at £4 5s. per annum   £85   0   0
My houshold goods burnt then, being standards,[1] to the
vallue of   £ 4   8   0
                                                                  ──────────
                                          summe   89   8   0

                        Witnes my hand, Hanah Tuckey.

Thomas Lane (4)   £32 5 0

An Account of whot I Thomas Lane of the Burough of Worwick, barber,
have lost by the last dreadfull fire.

My goods burned to the value of £32 5s. od and upward, the house of Mrs
Tuckey, widow, the rent £4 5 0 the year.

                                          Thomas Lane.

Mr Edward Heath (5)   House   £1300[2]
                              Goods   236
                                        ──────
                                        1436

An account of my loss in the late dreadfull fire which hapned at Warwick
Sept 5th 1694.

My house I was bad £400 for it about 4 yeares agon, since which it hath
cost me building and materialls of all sorts £900

Lost in wooll and serges, in severall sorts of house hold goods, and severall
other things, to the vallue of £236

                                          per Edward Heath

Mary Dickerson, widow, Busbies tenant, (5)   £5, vide Butts.

The valuacion of the losse sustained by Mary Dickerson, vid., att the dredfull fire which hapened att Warwick the fifth day of Sept. 1694.

In tables, chaires, stooles, coffers, linning, wareing apparell, bedsteds, coles
and wood for winter to the value of five pounds and upwards.

John Jarvis (6)   £488 4 0

Sep. the 6 day '94

---

[1] 'being standards' added in a different ink.   [2] Changed from £1200.

The loss of John Jarvis by the late fire: conshumed three
dwelling houses which did amount unto the some of   385   0   0

The loss of my goods by the same fire did amount unto
the some of   103   4   0

The hole some is   488   4   0

Witness my hand the 25 day of Sep. '94,   John Jarvis.

Samuell Cooke (6)   £3

Sep. the 6 day '94
The loss of Samuell Cook an aprentis to John Jarvis: the
loss of his best waringe cloathes with linings and his
books, the loss amounts too the some of three pounds by
a modest computasion, the some of   3   0   0

Elizabeth Farr (6)   £13

The loss that I sustained in furniture, linnins, brass, puter and other things
as neer as I can remember at the loest rate amounts to the vallue of 13
pounds

Eliz: Farre.

John Cole (7)   £20

John Cole of the Borough of Warwick, weaver, his losse by the fire on the
5th day of Sept. 1694.

My loomes, twisting mill, geaves, spooles, cloth, yarne,
shiftes, bedds and other houshold goodes and shopp
goodes to the value of   £20   0   0

Wittnes my hand the   John Cole
14th day of Sept. 1694   his marke

Anne Webbe (8)   £80   0   0

The valuation of Anne Webb of the Borough of Warwick, widow, sustained
by the late fire which happened in Warwick.

Imprimis her bedding, pewter, wood, coale and other
houshold good amounting to the value of   £20   0   0

The house totally burnt downe, the land of Mr John Jarvis
junior, rent per annum   £3   0   0

John Hands (9)   £113 0 0

The Account of the Loss that John Hands, glover in the Burough of Warwick, haith sustained by the fiar, which is as folloeth

	£		
In wood and coals, with beding and bedsteds	£4	0	0
A new greate chest, a greate trunk, and several coafers with goods in them, and several vesels full of drink, several brooing vesels, culoring, and other things which belonge unto my trade, as culoring stons and brishes[1]	2	10	0
A press, and counter, with all the shilves, several planks, and boards and poles, with trestles, and several forms and benches	3	0	0
A caster[2] hatt, a sadle, gerths and womties,[3] with a pilion and male pilions, crupers and bridles, also shoes and stockings	2	5	0
Tables, and tubs with charcoale, several cheers, and curtings, and curting rods, som dozens of glass botles	3	0	0
2 flaskits,[4] a washing stock, and hors, and several peices of usefull board, being fitt for shilves or other use	0	10	0
Some woolen cloaths, and some lineing	0	10	0
Goods belonging to my trade, 2 pair of buckskins and 10 pair of calfskins, and some dozens of sheeps leather	5	0	0
Several bundles of gloves of all sorts, and buskins	7	5	0
Goods damnified	0	10	0
the sume	33	0	0

The hous that I rented I paid full four pound a year to
Thomas Dadly, butcher.

September the 21, 1694.

Henry Smith (10)   £101

The Valluation of the Loss of Henry Smith of the Borough of Warwick,
butcher, sustained by the late fire which happened in Warwick.

---

[1] 'as culoring stons and brishes' inserted in a space.
[2] Castor or beaver.
[3] Womb-ties, girths.
[4] This word has several meanings; here probably oval tubs with handles, for washing clothes.

Imprimis in houshold goods, fewell and other utensills
amounting in the wholl to   £21   o   o

The house totally consumed, the house of Mr Fulk Weale,
rent per annum   £ 4   o   o

Mr Fulke Weale (10)   House in Church Street £ 80 o o
                               Market Place   110 o o
                                                         _____
                                                           190 o o

The Valluation of the Loss of Fulk Weale of the Borough of Warwick,
draper, sustained by the late fire which happened in Warwick.

Imprimis my house wherein Henry Smith lived in the
Church Street totally consumed, rent per annum £4 at 20
yeares purchase worth   80   o   o

Item part of my house wherein Thomas Smith lived in the
Market Place which was consumed by the late fire,
damage sustained   £110   o   o
                                                                         _____
                                 Totall loss consumed   190   o   o

Thomas Claridge (11)   £135 o o

September the 5th 1694. Thomas Claridge his loss by the
lat fire: his shop of goods and beding and bedstids and
other housold goods and fewell and other things to the
valew of thirty five pounds and upward   £35   o   o

His house rent is five pounds the yeare.

Mr Stephen Nicholes and Sanders Nicholes (12)   £87 6 2

The Loss of Mr Stephen Nicholes, chandler, sustained by the fire in Warr.
Sept. 5th '94.

Church Streete
The loss of household goods in my house, cheese, flax,
hurds and severall other things as by particulars appears
to the value   £87   6   2

                                 Stephen Nicholles.

Mary Carter (12)   £1 13 0

War. Bor. Sept. 5th 1694
Mary Carter, servant to Alixander Nicholles, lost in the
fyer the daye and year above said in mony and waring
cloathes to the value of   £1 13 0

                                        The mark
                                        of Mary Carter

Stephen and Allixander Nicholles not[e] (12)   £300 16 0

Warwich Borough. Sept. 5th 1694
Allixander Nicholles lost by the late fyer upon the daye
aforesaied goodes and wares out of his shope, sallors and
warehousin to the value of   £300 16 0

                                    Alexander Nicholles.

In[1] the worke house[2]	£ 5	13	0
In the barne		14 11	0
In the kiching[3]		35 18	0
In the 2 sallors[4]		39 3	0
Tallo in the sallors, work hows and garden 42[5]		105 0	0
In the shope goods came to[6]		42 10	0
In the leantoe over against the wo[rkhouse]		1 2	0
In the talloe house		0 12	0
In the dish house[7]		5 8	0
In the dark butory		4 12	6
In cheas that was lost		8 8	0
In the cocklaft[8]		2 11	0
In the spase chamber[9]		7 15	0

---

[1] This explanatory schedule is a separate piece of paper accompanying the signed estimate. There is also a draft in much greater detail, roughly written on absorbent paper and too illegible to publish as a text, but parts of it have been used to itemise some of the headings in the schedule in the footnotes following.

[2] 'mold 0 10 0, mold bord 0 5 0, sprayes 1 4 0, tallo tubes 1 0 0, tallo trof 1 0 0, presse 1 0 0, frame 0 4 0, windors 0 10 0'.

[3] 'Hony and wax 30 0 0, hony pres 0 10 0, ocker and whitting 0 18 0, stands, sives, callie sand and so forth 4 10 0'. Callis-sand: white scouring sand, originally from Calais.

[4] Including 'sope 11 0 0, candles 18 0 0'.

[5] Understand 'hundredweight'.

[6] 'Linseed oyle and other thinges.'

[7] 'Glas bottls came to quarts and pints and pottles.'

[8] Includes 'cotton 6 lb. 0 15 0'.

[9] 'Wheat 0 10 0, vessalles 0 4 0, red harringes 0 8 0, mostor seed 0 3 0, spone yarne 0 11 0, spolles 4 doz. 0 4 0, shilves to laye cheas 0 15 0, wick yarne 4 0 0, wet cloathes 1 0 0.' The name of the room is obscure.

In the chamber over the haull and shope[1]	18	16	11
Lost of hony in the churchyard	5	0	0
One wheale and flax	0	16	0
	297	16	5
Cloathe and a littil trunke	3	0	0
	300	16	0

William Horne, Church Street, (12)   £2
Warwick Borough. Sept. 5th 1694.
William Horne servant to Allixander Nicholles loste in
wollen cloathes and lininge with bootes and shoues the
daye and year above saied by the fyere to the full value of
fourty shillinges   £2   0   0
Wittnes my hand: William Horne.

Elizabath Morcot, widdow, note. (12)   £34   0   0
Warwick Borough. Sept. 5th 1694.
Elizabeth Morcott, widdo, lost in the late fyer of goodes
and monye to the value of   34   0   0
                                        Elizabeth Murcott.

Robert Taylor (13)   £85 5 0
The valluation of the loss of Robert Taylor, butcher, sustained by the late
fire in Warwick.
Imprimis in brass, pewter, bedding, hay, straw, ale, hogges
heads, brewing vessels, fewell, money and all manner of
houshold goods   £85   5   0
The house all burnt, the land of Mrs Palmer, rent per annum £10 4s., standards £1 6s., all   £11 10   0

Widow Palmer (13)   £26 in goods besides the house, all £230
A valuation of the house of Mrs Anne Palmer scituate in the Church Streete
in Warwicke lately in the possession of Robert Taylor, butcher, that was
burnt in the late fier there with severall standards belonging to the said house.
The losse of the house and standards, all   £230   0   0
                          Witness my hand: Ann Palmer

[1] Includes 'coffye 1 17 0, candle mold, peauter, 0 12 0'.

Thomas Catell (13)   £1 18 0

An acunt of the lose of Thomas Catell and Ann his dator lost by the fiuer in Worwick September the 5, 1694.

In waring aparial	£1	2	0
In money	0	8	0
his datores clothes	0	8	0
sum	£1	18	0

Thomas Catell

William Perkes (14)   £320

The Valluation of the Loss of William Perkes of the Borough of Warwick, malster and baker, sustained by the late fire which happened in Warwicke Sept. 5th anno domini 1694.

Imprimis his brass, pewter, bedding, linnens, woollens, all manner of houshold goods, wood, straw, corne, malt and other things amounting to in the wholl	£100	0	0
Item my dwelling house all burnt downe with the back buildings worth	£220	0	0
Totall loss sustained	320	0	0

Elizabeth Carr (15)   £298 0 0

The louse of Eliz. Carr in the leate fier in Warwick.

The louse of goods in the house	£148	0	0
The louse of hur house and stables and barnes	150	0	0
	298	0	0

The mark: E. of the sam Elizabeth Carr

John Eld (15)   £7 19 0

John Eld his lose by the fire: in close, mony and bookes and other thinges	£7	19	0

Joseph Hemmings (16)   £177 13 10

Sept. the 14th 1694. The Loss of Joseph Hemens by the late fire.

His hous being Corperation land, the rent being yearly	4	10	0
Loss in housall goods and molt and other things	84	4	10
1 quarter and 1 strike of molt of the goods of Jaramiah Goods of Baginton	1	11	6
1 quarter and 5 strike of molt of the goods of Mr Bell of Baginton	1	17	6

Mr John Dolphin (16)   £172 10 0

An account of the loss of John Dolphin, executor of Mr Edmond Aylesbury deseased,[1] by the fire.

A howse in the Church Street belonging to the Church held by lease from the Churchwardens, the lease twenty years to com and let by the said Edmond Aylesbury at seaven pounds per annum, standards belonging to the executor burnt to the vallue of six pounds.

In the said Edmond Aylesbury one[2] howse burnt belonging to me the exe-cutor, istills,[3] wormes,[4] hogsheds and tubs the vallew of eight pounds and ten shillings.
A tobacco engine and tobbaco press, weights and scales, a parcell of bords and other odd things five pounds and fifteen shillings.
Money melted and lost in the fire thirty two pounds and five shillings.

The vallew of the lease of 20 yers to com at 3 pounds a year the som of threscore pounds

The vallew of the said lease for 20 years to com with deduction of repairs and payments threescore pounds more

Sum tot. £172 10 0
per me J. Dolphin.

Sarah Mayow (16)   £134 10 0

Sept. the 14 1694.

The loss of Sarah Mayoh, sempstress, of housall goods and milon[5] goods and other things	£134 10 0

---

[1] Buried 14 Nov. 1693.
[2] i.e. 'own'.
[3] Stills.
[4] Coiled condensation tubes.
[5] i.e. 'millinery'.

Sarah Edwards (18)   House £52 0 0,[1] goods £30 0 0

The Value of the Loss as Sarah Edwards, widow, living over against the high parish church yard in a house of Mr Vicars as he leased out of Mr Oakens in the Burrough of Warwick as she sustained by the late dreadfull fire, made upon oath before us theire Majestyes justices of the peace.

For beds, bedsteds, bedcloths, linen and woollen, brass,
pewter and all maner of houshold goods and likewise
fewell and a pigg being in all to the value of   £30   0   0

Mrs Hannah Doolittle   £35 12 0

A valuation of the losse of Hannath Dolittle, tabler att the Widdow Edward's in the Church Streete, sustained by the late fier.

For household goods, lynen and weareing apparell   £35 12 0

Witnesse my hand: Hannah Doelittle

Mr John Biker (18)

In the Butts	house	£100	0	0
there	house	80	0	0
there	house	98	0	0
Church Street		82	10	0
Goods ditto		41	0	0
Improvements ditto		20	0	0
		421	10	0

An Account of what I John Biker, Rector of Burton super Dunsmore in the County of Warwick, lost by the fire which happen'd at Warwick on the 5th of September anno domini 1694.

A house near the Joyce-pool in the tenure of the Widow Manwhinnick lett at five pounds per annum and a goose.
Another adjoining to't in the tenure of William Matthews, combmaker, lett at four pounds per annum.
Another near to the aforesaid houses in the tenure of Job Rhodes, lett at four pounds eighteen shillings per annum.
A house of Mr Okens near St Marys Church for which I paid four pounds per annum and a goose.[2]
Houshold goods in the said house to the value of fourty pounds.

---

[1] Struck through.
[2] Followed by '2s. 6d., £2. 10 0' in the hand of the writer of the endorsements.

Laid out for the improvment of the said Mr Okens house twenty pounds.

Witnesse my hand: John Biker

Memorandum: The aforsaid houses of Whinnicks, Matthews and Rhodes's were valu'd by Mr Hugh Meades and Mr Christopher Ailsbury to my father at three hundred pounds in the deed of joynture made to my mother. Mrs Meades and my self have laid out since for the improvment of 'em fourty five pounds.

Sarah Glendall (18)   £2 4 4

The Valluation of the Loss of Sarah Glendall, servant to the widow Edwards, sustained by the late fire which happenned in Warwick.

Imprimis her wearing apparrell both woollens and linnens, a Bible and other things amounting to	£2	4	4

Sarah Bucknall (18)   £7 4 10

The Valluation of the Loss of Sarah Bucknall, widow, sustained at the late fire which happened in Warwick on the 5th of September anno domini 1694.

Ten quarter of oates burnt att the house of John Cakebread put out to him to make oatemeale of	£5	5	4
Item for a quarter of barley delivered there	1	0	0
Item for 11 baggs	0	16	6
Item 2 thrave of straw	0	3	0
	7	4	10

Mrs Alott (18)   £57 2 0

An Account of Mrs Allotts loss with the fire.

A wrought bed and bedsted and all things belonging to it	£10	0	0
A chest of drawers with lynen in it worth	4	0	0
Six chears and two stands worth	1	15	0
A hanging press with things in it worth	2	10	0
A mourning gowne and pettycoat worth	2	10	0
A new blackstuff pettycoat worth	0	8	0
An embroadered Holland peettycoat worth	1	0	0
A trunck full of dyaper, damask and Holland worth	15	0	0
Preserves, caudialls and other such like things worth	3	0	0

A trunke with course lynen in it worth	2	0	0
A pair of brass landiorns, tongs and snuffers worth	1	0	0
A cabinett and silver spoons worth	1	10	0
Two looking glasses and a still worth	2	0	0
A voider[1] and three wrought cussins worth	0	15	0
Bookes worth	3	0	0
A muff, two fans and a maske worth	1	0	0
The hangins of the roome worth	2	0	0
Seven large pewter dishes worth	2	10	0
A close stool and pan, a kettel, posnett, 6 plates	1	4	0
The whole sume	57	2	0

Hanah Aires (18)   £18 0 0, a tablear at the widow Edwards in the Church Street.

The loss sustained by me Hannah Aris is as followeth:

Imprimis a trunck with wearing clothes and other things to the value of	£10	0	0
Item linnen and jursey with other materialls to the value of	£ 8	0	0
in all	£18	0	0

Thomas Breedon (18)   £1 10 0

The Valluation of the Loss of Thomas Breedon sustained by the late fire which happened in Warwick.

Imprimis in two coates, one hatt, a paire of shoes, a shovell, a box and a cambrick apron which were in the custody of Mrs Allat amounting	£1	10	0

John Cakebread (19)   £48 9 6

The Valluation of the Loss of John Cakebread of the Borough of Warwick, malster, sustained by the late fire which happenned at Warwick on the 5th of September anno domini 1694.

Imprimis 20 strike of mault	£3	13	4
Greats, cutlings,[2] oatemeale, oates and all measures belonging to the same	25	0	0

---

[1] Probably a clothes-basket.   [2] Groats or coarse oatmeal.

Item 4 spinning wheeles	0	17	8
Item one feather bed, one flock bed, three bedsteads, curtaines and valens and chaires, 2 paire of sheets, 2 bolsters and two pillowes	10	0	0
Item one press	1	10	0
Item one long tubb and a dough kiver[1]	0	2	6
Item 3 pewter dishes, 2 plates	0	9	6
Item 2 great tubbs, one cowle[2] and pales	0	10	0
Item one load of hay	1	2	0
Item wood	2	0	0
Item two coffers and one box	0	4	6
Item two store piggs burnt	1	8	0
Item child bed linnen, flax and flaxen yarne	1	0	0
Item three tables and stooles	0	12	0
	48	9	6
The house Mr Okens land rented of Mr Bykar, rent per annum	2	8	0

Mr James Fish (20)   £208   0   0

Sept. 5th 1694. An Estimate of the Loss of James Fish at the late dreadfull fire in Warwick.

His house, etc.:
Imprimis one house or tenement standing in the Church Streete consisting of five bays in length and one in breadth and containing on the first floore a hall, parlour, kitchen, a coale and wood house with a cellar and brewhouse, as allsoe five lodging roomes above staires, the whole house newlie repair'd in every part, having 6 chimneys, two of them newlie erected, and in the backside a little stable with a leantooe for wood and hay valu'd at   £100   0   0

His books, instruments and goods:
Imprimis books of divinitie, law, physick, allsoe books mathematicall, geographicall, historicall, with schoole books, in all above 200 with some choice mathematicall instruments, allsoe some guineys, broad gold and gold rings, beding of all sorts, brass, pewter, tables, chaires, skreens, etc., brewing and washing vessells, barrells, hay,

---

[1] A shallow kneading tub.
[2] A tub with ears, for carrying on a cowl-staff.

wood, coales, boards and old wainscote, etc., all which as
shall appear by a particular and be attested upon oath, do
amount to the sum of   108   o   o

                              Totall of the loss   208   o   o

Note that his house was newly supply'd with water haveing two cocks at his kitchen and brew house, the leaden
pipes being above 30 yards long

Witness my hand this 27th day of September 1694:   James Fish

Sarah Asplin (21)   £13   o   o

Sarah Aspline her losse att the fire in money and goods the summ of thirteene poundes.

Edward Chesley (22)   £316 5 8

The Valluation of the Loss of Edward Chesley of Warwick, taylor, sustained
at the late fire.

Imprimis in houshold goods, wares, and other goods
burnt by the fire   £156   5   8

The house my owne all burnt downe, rent per annum   £8   o   o

Georg Chesley and John Twicross (22)   £26 18 10 and
                                                 6   o   o

The Valluation of the Loss of George Chesley of Warwick, taylor, sustained
by the late fire in Warwick.

In houshold goods, wareing apparrell and severall other
things   £26 18 10

The house my fathers all burnt

The Loss of John Twicross, servant to Edward Chesley:

Imprimis his wareing apparrell and all other necessaryes   £ 6   o   o

Mr William Edes (23)   House £180 o o
                              Goods   150 o o
                                    _____
                                    £330 o o

14 Sept. 1694

These are to certifie that the loss I susteined by the late fire on the 5th instant in my houshold goods, books, etc., does at a modest computation amount to the summe of one hundred and fifty pounds, as I can make appeare by particulars, and shall be ready to make oath thereof when required

William Edes

Anne Southern (23)   15s.

Anne Southern servant to Mr William Edes hath lost in wearing cloths to the value of fifteen shillings.

Anne Preston (23)   £148 13 6

Memorandum that this bill is but 48 13 6[1]

A valuation of the losse of Anne Preston, widdow, tabler att Mr Edes's, sustained by the late fier att Warwicke

Plate, pewter, linen and weareing apparell comes to   48 13 6

Witnes my hand: Anne Preston

Mrs Mary Murcott (24)   £517 12 0

Mrs Mary Murcotts loss by the fire in Warwick September the 5th 1694.

Imprimis my house in the Church Street over against St Maries Church	£300	0	0
In hangings, curtaines, valins, beding, bedsteed, linnen, woolen, in pewter, brass, brewing vessells, in beare in vessells, in wood, in cole and other necessaryes as will appeare by particulars	217	12	0
	517	12	0

Mr William Featherston and (25)	£240	0	0
Mr William Paston his son in law	60	0	0
	300	0	0

[1] The error arose through mistaking the lower arm of a bracket against the sum of money for a figure 1. Note that it was carried into the Book of Estimates in spite of this memorandum, but spotted in the Book of Reductions.

The Valuation of the Loss sustained by the late fire in Warwick by Mr Fetherston in part of Mrs Murcot's house against St Maries Church.

In houshold goods, moneys, plate and wood, cole and weareing apparrell	£240	o	o
In goods of his sonn's Mr Paston's and wareing clothes of his and wifes	60	o	o
	300	o	o

Wm. Fetherston   W. Paston

Mrs Elizabeth Lea in Church Street (26)   £20 o o

Eliz. Lee

Wood and coles	3	o	o
Household goods, brass and pewter, etc.	9	o	o
Wareing cloaths and lining	4	o	o
3 pare blanketts, 1 quilt, 1 rugg with curtins and furniture for beds	4	o	o
	20	o	o

Jury Street

Joshua Drake (1)   £65

The acount of the lose of Joshua Drake.

Fuell and howsall goodes	£5	o	o
My lanlords rent was, which Joshua Drake payed,	£3	o	o

Samuell Drake (1)   £2 10 o

Jurey Street
The acount of the lose of Samuell Drake at the fire in September the 5th 1694

In fuell, wood and cools as they ere justley wallewed come too	£1	10	o
The lose of bear and linin and woollins and other housowll goods justley reckned comes to	1	o	o
The sume is	2	10	o

Mr Warde, Jury Streete (1)   Houses £110

Old Mr Ward refus'd a hunderd and twenty pound for these houses, they were set for 5 pound ten shillings a yeare.

Thomas Glendall (2)   £53

The Valluation of the Loss of Thomas Glendall of the Borough of Warwick, shomaker, sustained by the late fire which happened in Warwick.

Imprimis in houshold goods, leather and working tooles amounting in the wholl to	£8	0	0
The house totally demolished, the land of Mr Ward of Barford, rent per annum	£2	5	0

Nicholas Paris (3)   £203 0 0

Mr Nicholas Paris loss by the late fire in Warwick September the 5th 1694.

Imprimis in timber for stocking guns	£20	0	0
In tooles lost in the shopp	17	0	0
In goods belonging to the shop	30	0	0
In fuell vizt. wood and cole	6	0	0
In goods in the house as will appeare by particulars	30	0	0
Item in my house being all burnt down	100	0	0
Totall	203	0	0

Nicholas Paris

Richard Goode (4)   £126 10 0

An account of the goods that Richard Goode received damage of by the late fire.

Paid yearley rent for my house	£4	10	0
and a dussn of cands[1] att	0	5	0
Received damige in my goods	31	10	0

Witness my hand: Richard Goode

---

[1] Presumably 'a dozen of candles'. The sum of money was misread as £5 to give the figure on the dorse.

Thomas Wall (5)   £185 0 0

The Valuation of the losse of Thomas Wall of the Burrough of Warwick sustaigned att the late fire which happened September 5th 1694.

Imprimis the house	£160	0	0
Household goods and shop good to the value of	25	0	0
	185	0	0

John Williams (6)   £11 14 4

The value of the loss that Mr John Williams sustained by the pulling down of parte of his house by the means of the late dreadfull fire which was in the Jury Streete in the Borough of Warwick, and the goods that Timothy Norbury loste, amounts to the sum of   £11 14   4

Mr George Webb (6)   £250 0 0
vide Jury Streete the house £80.

September 5th '94
Lost by the fire to the value of two hundred and fifty pound   £250

per Geo. Webb

Samuell Barber (7)   £10

The Value of the Loss as Samuell Barber, combmaker, in the Jury Street in the Burrough of Warwick sustained by the late dreadfull fire in the said Burrough, made upon oath before us theire Majestyes justices of the peace.

To the value of   £10   0   0

Richard Hands, joyner (9)   £5 14 0

The Account of Richard Hands, joyner, of the loses he haith sustained by the fier.

In goods lost to the value of	£0	13	4
In goods damnefied acording to the best of what I can remember in value	5	0	8

In witness here of I have set to my hand the 14th day of September 1694,   Richard Hands.

Mrs Anne Archer (9)   £2

Mrs Archer wooad[1] lost and damafied by the fire to the waley of to pound

by me, Ann Archer

Samuel Rainbow, Jurey Street, (10)   £5

The Value and Loss of Samuell Rainbow, shoemaker, living in the Jury Street in the Burrough of Warrwick as he sustained at the late dreadfull fire on the 5th of September 1694 by his goods being lost and broken and the house he lives in being broken, made upon oath before us theire Majestyes justices of the peace.

To the value of   £5   o   o

Sam. Rainbow

Joseph Bateson (11)   £8

With that tarable fier that hapned the 6th of September 1694:

Lost in some part of a hogget[2] of fine powder shuger to the valy of eight pound and upwards, by me   Jos. Battesson.

William Savidge (12)   House £5
                           Goods £2

The Value of the Loss of William Savidge, barber, in the Jury Street in War-wick as he sustained at the late dreadfull fire in the said Burrough of War-wick, by the loss of his goods in being broken, spoilt and lost, given upon oath before us theire Majestyes justices of the peace.

In loss of drink, lynen and houshold goods to the value of   £2   o   o

Nathan Gilstrop (13)   £7 16 4

The Value of the Loss of Nathan Gilstrup living at the end of the Jury Street in the Burrough of Warwick as he sustained by having his house pluckt down at the late dreadfull fire in the Burrough of Warwick, given upon oath before us theire Majestyes justices of the peace.

---

[1] The letters of this word are fairly clear. It may be intended for 'woad', 'wood', or perhaps in the con-text 'good'.
[2] A hogshead.

Burnt at Mr Heaths 4 quarters of mault	£5	12	0
In spoilt and lost goods to the value of	2	4	4
Damage and loss together	7	16	4

Castle Street

Robert Boyce Esq. (1)   £300

The loss susstained by the fire at Warwick the 5th Sept. '94 by Robert Boyce Esq., as followes:

A house neere to the High Cross that Mr Bradshaw lived in cost me some litle time since £300

Robert Boyse

Robert Boyse and Mr Bradshaw (1)   £51 11 0

Robert Boyce and John Bradshaw theire losses by the late fier one the fift of Sept. annoque domini 1694.

The rent of the house paid yearly was £13 per annum.

John Bradshaw his losse of goods in house and shop, etc.   £51 11 0

Thomas Marriot (2)   £60

Thomas Marriotts losse by fire

My dwelling house being parte burnt to the value of, bein the Corporacion house which I have by lease the repaires thereof will cost	£50	0	0
My houshold goodes and fuell	10	0	0

Wittnes my hand the 14th day of Sept. 1694:   Thomas Marrit.

Robert Ashbie (3)   £15

Sept. the 14 day 1694

The Loss of Robard Asbay by the late fire that happened in the Church of St Maryes in Warwick.

A chest of lininge and puter that was burnt	£12	0	0
and severall othar things that was burnt	3	0	0
The hole sume is	15	0	0

Witness my hand the 14 day of Sept. '94:   Robard Asby

Jonathan Smith (4)   £3 5 0

Jonathan Smith lost by the late fire as being broke and lost things to the value of	£3	5	0

Joan Cumberlidg, widow (5)   £4

The valuation of the losse of Joana Cumberledge, widow, in brasse kettles and pewter and some houshold goods to the value of	£4	0	0

William Jackson, Castle Street (6)   £1 5 0

The valuation of the losse of William Jackson of the Burrough of Warwick at the fire September 5th 1694.

Imprimis in houshold goods	£1	5	0

Sheep Street

John Atterbury (1)   £209 3 4

The Valluation of the Loss of John Atterbury of the Borough of Warwick, shomaker, sustained att the late fire in Warwick Sept. 5th 1694.

Imprimis laid out lately upon the improvment of my house	£49	5	0
Ten douzen of course napkins at 6s. per douzen	3	0	0
Four douzen of diaper and flaxen napkins	2	0	0
Four large table clothes	1	4	0
Eight course table clothes	0	16	0
Two douzen of towells	0	12	0
Ten flaxen pillow beers	0	13	4
Thirty six shifts	5	8	0
Nine shifts more	0	18	0
One crape gowne and pettycoate	0	15	0
One scarlett pettycoate with a gold lace	0	8	0
Three halfe cloth petty coates	0	12	0

One gowne and 2 under petticoates	0	5	0
My wives 2 hatts, scarffe and gloves	1	4	0
My foure coates, two pair of buckskin breeches and one paire of searge breeches	1	11	0
My 2 hatts	0	14	0
My 4 paire of stockens and 4 pair of linnens	0	8	0
My son John's wearing apparrell	3	7	0
My grandchild's wearing apparrell	2	2	2
My she apprentices apparrell	0	17	0
Two feather bedsteads, two bolster and 4 pillowes	8	10	0
In the roome next the leather chamber two bedsteads, 2 matts and coards	0	12	0
Five more bedsteads, matts and coards	1	15	0
One bedstead, matt and coard in the parlour	0	5	0
Six setts of curtaines, valens and curtaine rods	3	8	6
One great ovell table, one chest of drawers and one side table	3	0	0
One great chaire and great looking glass	0	18	0
One douzen of leather chaires, one class[1] cage and glasses	1	11	6
One grate, one pair of andirons with brass bosses and things on the chimney head	0	13	6
Three fire shovells and 3 paire of tonges	0	6	0
Two grates and 2 pair of andirons	0	16	0
In the Little Chamber			
Six chaires and one round table	1	3	0
One chest and one great cubbord	0	13	0
One chest of drawers and one joyn'd chaire	1	10	0
One coffer and one table	0	6	0
One chest, one trunk and one chest more	0	13	0
Hopps	1	10	0
In the cockloft, one great chest and a great trunk	0	13	0
One red cloake, carbine belt and buffe belt	1	3	0
One little coffer and feathers	0	10	0
Ten strike of malt	1	15	0
Three strike of wheate	0	13	6
Three bags of messelin[2]	1	7	0
25 paire of sheets	10	0	0
Five wooll beds	0	15	0
Five hillings and blanketts	2	14	0
One pair of stayes and 2 black hoods	0	15	0
Two wiskes and 2 holland cubbord clothes	0	12	0

---

[1] Probably a mistake for 'glass'.   [2] Maslin or mixed grain.

My brass and pewter and jack spitts and a gun	12	0	0
One great cubbord and a nest of drawers	0	7	0
7 joyne stooles and 4 chaires	0	10	0
One table, one dresser cubbord and one bacon cratch	0	10	0
Two tables, two chaires	0	9	0
One table and two chaires more	0	5	0
Four stooles and one great presse cubbord	1	11	0
Two silver spoones and a silver taster[1]	1	0	0
One dresser, one large box and bookes	1	0	0
Two tables, 4 chaires and one skreen	0	10	0
Two gross of bottles and 10 baggs	2	0	0
4 douzen of trenchers and wooden platters	0	5	0
Flaxen yarne, hempen yarne and wooll	0	8	0
My brewing vessels	2	16	0
Beare and hoggesheads	19	5	0
More beare and barrells, a chest and cheeses	1	2	4
Hay, coales and wood	9	15	0
My leather shoes, rossen and lasts	19	16	6
4 pales, 10 aprons, 4 paire of stockens and one paire of bodyes	0	18	0
Laid out lately upon Mr Edes his hovell to make a stable thereof and burnt	10	8	0
Totall loss sustained:	209	3	4

The house Mr Okens land given for charitable uses, rent per annum	2	0	0

and a peece of rosting beefe, but since improved by me worth 3 times that rent.

Thomas Scarlet (1)   £1 14   4

The Valluation of the Loss of Thomas Scarlett, servant to John Atterbury of Warwick, sustained at the late fire in Warwick.

Imprimis two coates, one paire of breeches	£1	4	0
Two neck clothes and a paire of shoes	0	4	4
One box, two hatts and 2 paire of stockens	0	6	0
Sum total:	1	14	4

---

[1] A small cup for tasting wine.

Richard Perry (1)   £1 4 0

The Valluation of the Loss of Richard Perry of the Borough of Warr', sho-maker, servant to John Atterbury att the Bird in Hand, sustained by the late fire in Warwick.

Imprimis his wearing apparrell both woollen and linnen, money and hatts and working tooles amounting in the wholl to	£1	4	0

Thomas Arpes (2)   £292 10 0

The Valluation of the Loss of Thomas Arpes sustained by the late fire in Warwick.

Imprimis in houshold goods, hay, straw, corne, wood, coale, ale, brewing vessells, etc.	£152	10	0
The house all burnt, the land of widow Hawkes of London, rent per annum	£ 7	0	0

Joseph Willis (3)   £58 13 0

The Valuation of the Loss of Joseph Willis of the Borough of Warwick, baker, sustained by the late fire which happened in Warwick.

Imprimis his wood, coales, hay, straw, bedding, brass, pewter, corne, meale, working tooles, utensils and other houshold goods amounting in the wholl to	£58	13	0
The house and back building totally consumed, the house of widow Ashwin, rent per annum	5	10	0
And standard goods	0	3	0

Elianor Ashwin, now Pierce (3)   £113 0 0

Account of the loss of Ellenour late the widow of Willyam Ashwin deceased but since married to Thomas Pierce of Harvington in the County of Worcester.

The joynture house in Sheepe Streete, Warwick, rent per annum	£5	10	0
Standard goods in the said house of the said Ellenour's, value	3	0	0

The tenant of the said house was Joseph Willes, baker, at the tyme of the fire.

Mary Low (3)   £0 19 0

The loss of a maid servant to Joseph Willis is   £0 19 0

John Pritchard and the Towne (4)   £537 17 0

The Valluation of the Loss of John Pritchett of Warwick sustained at the late fire which happened in Warwick Sept. 5th 1694.

Imprimis in bedding	£ 7	0	0
Curtaines, valens, coverletts and blanketts	6	0	0
One chest of drawers, one cabbinett, one table, 2 stands			
4[1] glasses of olive wood	5	0	0
Ringes, plate, silk, fine linnen and lace	12	0	0
One douzen of Turkey leather chaires	4	4	0
One workt chaire and 6 camlett covered chaires	2	6	0
8 red leather chaires	2	0	0
Ten chaires	0	10	0
Two chests with wearing apparrell	8	0	0
One trunk of table linnen and sheets	6	0	0
Six bedsteads	3	0	0
Brass and pewter	5	0	0
One chest of drawers, 10 tables, ten joyned stooles and 3 formes	7	0	0
One jack and leaden weights and 2 grates	1	10	0
2 hoggesheads, 3 barrells and brewing vessells	2	10	0
6 douzen of bottles	0	9	0
Wood and coale	4	0	0
One statute booke, 2 Bibles and severall other bookes	3	0	0
12 halfe quarter sackes	0	18	0
Four swords and 2 case of pistolls	3	10	0
One paire of bootes, one pair of inlaid spurrs and 2 new paire of shoes	1	0	0
One Hackney saddle	0	10	0
One cubbord and one table	1	0	0
Cheney[2] ware and provisions in house	1	10	0
	87	17	0

The house my owne all burnt, rent per annum	12	0	0
Besides another house next adjoyning also burnt, rent per annum	10	0	0

---

[1] Possibly 'stands for glasses', a phonetic mistake.
[2] 'china', an obsolete form.

Mariana Ducket (4)   £8

My loss by fire att Mr John Pritchetts	5	10	0
besids a box not my owne which was given mee in charge valu'd att	2	10	0

by mee Mariana Duckett.

Ann Eedes, widow, and Frances Edes (4)   £53

Anne Edes, widdpow, her losse by fire.

My bedding, linnen, houshold goods, shop goods and shop booke and apparrell to the vallue of	£50	7	0

Anne Edes

My daughter Frances Edes her losse

Her wearing apparrell, linnen, woollen, etc.	3	0	0
in all	53	7	0

Frances Edes

**The County Goale and House of Correction
and Mr Williams** (5)   Goods £191 17 7

John Williams, Keeper of theire Majestes Goale for the County of Warwick, his losses by the fire in Warwick September the 5th 1694.

In brass, pewter, brewing vessells, in bedsteeds, in tables, chaires, stooles, in linnen, woolen and all other necessaryes, etc., and in wood, cole and hay	£191	17	4
The County Goale	[		][1]
The House of Correction	96	0	0

Edward Birkback (5)   £18 0 0

An account of what Edward Birkbeck lost att the Goal in Warwick September 5th 1694 by the late fire.

Imprimis in feather beds, blanketts and other goods, etc., to the value of	£18	0	0

---

[1] Blank not filled in.

Robert Watts (7)   £330

The Valluation of the Losse of Robert Watts, senior, of the Borough of Warwick, chaundler, sustained by the late fire which happened in Warwick.

Imprimis in houshold goods, shop goods, tallow, wood, coale and other materialls amounting in the wholl to   £110 0 0

Item the house my owne which if sett would have brought at least per annum   11 0 0

Charls Watts (7)   £18

The Valluation of the Loss of Charles Watts of the Borough of Warwick, flaxdresser, sustained by the late fire which happened in Warwick.

Imprimis in weareing apparrell both woollen and linnen, flax and other materialls amounting to   £18 0 0

John Watts (7)   £152 0 0

The Valluation of the Loss of John Watts of the Borough of Warwick, chandler and flaxman, sustained by the late fire which happened in Warwick the 5th of September 1694.

Imprimis in flax and hemp, shop goods, boards, hey, sadles, bridles and other materialls amounting in the wholl to   £152 0 0

Item two messuages or tenements wherein Samuel Parsons lived, being the Crowne in the Sheepes Street and the house next adjoyning wherein John Burnill lived, the Crowne being a new house and the rent per annum of both being   14 17 6

Zachariah Sharp (8)   £143 10 0

The Ganrol Sadgol[1] of Goods which was totelly lost and distried by the fier which are as follows:

In housell goods, linings, willings, hamp, flex, yarne, ropry ware and working touls, fother,[2] fuill douth amount to £47 10 0
Which warr the goods of mine whos name is subscribed: Zachrieh Sharpe.

[1] 'general schedule'.   [2] 'fodder'.

Zachariah Sharp's servants (8)   16s.

Itam a ganorull sadgich[1] of the lose of the maid sarvont of Zacoriah Sharpe by the fier amounts to	o	12s. o
And like wise the lose of his aprentis amounts	o	4s. o
	o 16	o

Richard Harris (9)   £13 15 0

Richard Harris his losse [by] fire.

His bedding, brasse, pewter, houshold goodes and fewell
to the vallue of   sume: £13 15 0

Mrs Cawthorn (11)   £530

Houses

Church Street: Claridge 1	£5	o	o	per annum
[Sheep Street]: Martin Taylor 2	£7	o	o	” ”
Richard Harris 1	£3	10	o	” ”
Maning 1	£3	10	o	” ”
her owne 1	£5	o	o	” ”
2 at the Buts	£2	10	o	” ”

Totall 26 10 o

Mrs Cawthorne, widdow, her account of her houses and goods.

Houses to the value of	£530	o	o
Goods att	40	o	o
In all	570	o	o

Ann Newton (11)   £10

Ann Newton her account of her losse by fire.

Goods in brasse, pewter and other housolde goods at   £10 o o

Martin Taylor (12)   £178 0 0

The Valluation of the Loss of Martin Taylor of the Borough of Warwick,
baker, sustained by the late fire which happened in Warwick.

_____
[1] 'general schedule'.

Imprimis my hay, fuell, corne, meale, severall houshold goods and other utensills in the wholl amounting to	£38	o	o
The house totally consumed, the land of the widow Cauthorne, rent per annum	£ 7	o	o

Richard Hadley, senior (13)   £550

Richard Hadleys losse by the fire at Warwick on the 5th day of Sept. anno domini 1694.

Imprimis: My dwelling house, prisson house, back buildings and other out houses and stable to the vallue of	£400	o	o
Item: My bedding, linnen, brasse, pewter, houshold goods, brewing vessells and drinke in the cellar	£120	o	o
Item: My hay, wood, coles and timber in the backside to the vallue of	30	o	o
Totall Losse	550	o	o

Rich: Hadley

Richard Hadley, junior (13)   £6 5 2

The Value and Loss of Richard Hadley the younger, fellmonger and woollcomber, living with his father at the Green Dragon in the Sheep Street in the Burrough of Warwick, as he sustained at the late dreadfull fire in the said Burrough of Warwick, made upon oath before us theire Majestyes justices of the peace.

In wooll, coales and working tooles, weights and scales and other things to the value of	£6	5	2

Mary Overton (13)   £2

Mary Overton's losse by fire.

Her wearing apparrell and money	£2	o	o

Mary Overton

Katherine Drury (13)   £3 o o

An account of what Katherine Drury, servant to Serjeant Hadley, lost by the late fire which happened on the 5th day of Sept. anno domini 1694.

Her wearing apparrell, linnen and woollen and money to
the vallue of   £3   0   0

Katherine Drury K. her marke

John Butler (14)   £39 0 0

The Valluation of the Loss of John Butler of the Borough of Warwick, carpenter, sustained by the late fire which happened in Warwick.

Imprimis in houshold goods, shop goods, tooles, in timber
and other materials amounting in the wholl to   £39   0   0

The house totally consumed, the proper land of Mrs Wagstaffe but Mr Garrett of Henly has a long lease of it, the
rent per annum is   £4 10   0

William Gerrard (15)   £100 0 0

The valluation of Mr William Gerrard of Henley-in-Arden in the County of
Warwick sustained by the late fire which happened in Warwick the 5th of
September 1694.

Imprimis the damage sustained in the house which was
burnt downe wherein John Butler lived in the Sheep
Street in Warwick, haveing by improvement made upon
the said house doubled the rent and haveing a long lease
of about fourty yeares therein yet to come, amounting to   £45   0   0

Thomas Rush (15)   £86 12 8

The Value of the Loss of Thomas Rush, tailor, living in the Sheep Street in
the Burrough of Warwick in a house of fifty five shillings a year, as he did
sustain at the late dreadfull fire in the said Burrough of Warwick, given
upon oath before us theire Majestyes justices of the peace.

For vessells and drink, beding, household goods, clothes,
linen cloth, jersey yarn and fewell to the value of   £31   2   8

Marey Wagstaf (15) £55 and £55
Two houses

The loose of Marey Wagstaf for tow houeses in Sheep Stret burnt dowen
September the 5, 1694

Thomas Rushes houes rent   2 15 0
John Butler houes rent   2 15 0

Marey Wagstaf

Samuel Parsons (16)   £369 5 9[1]

The valuation of the losse of Samull Parsons at the Croun in Sheep Street in the Borrow of Warwick

In houshould goods, fewel and hay, hogsheds, alle, etc.   £71 15 9

The house all burnt down, John Wotsis land,[2] puranum   13   0 0

September 5th anno 1694

Mrs Lucas (16)   £3

Mris Lucas hath burnt by this fire in wearinge cloeaths, woolens and linnens and a couple of spinnen wheeles to the value of three pound which I can make upon oeath, in all   £3   0 0

Sarah Hill (16)   £12 0 0

The Value of the Loss as Sarah Hill, widow, living next to the Sign of the Crown in the Sheep Street in the Burr' of Warwick, as she sustained at the late dreadfull fire in the said Burrough of Warwick, given upon oath before us theire Majestyes justices of the peace.

For my late deceased husbands shopbook, my beding, clothes and houshold goods, to the value of   £12   0 0

Sarah Hill, Sheep Streete

Sir,

This is most humble to acquaint you that when I gave in my bill of the value of my losses as I sustained at the fire, I was in good hopes that I should have found or heard of some of my things again, but I cannot, soe that my loss is far greater than I expected by six pound more then I did set down. I would beseech your Worship for to consider me in the case.

Your servant,
Sarah Hill, widdow

---

[1] It is not clear how this figure is arrived at.
[2] 'John Watts his land.'

Goodwife Truelove (16)   £0 10 0

Gooddy Trulovess [loss] by the fire: one bedstid, to bed mats, one bed cord, to pound and a half of gersee and a cettell and sum of my linenn, the loss to the best of my knoledg comes to 10 shillins.

John Burnill (17)   £7 12 2

The Loss and Value of John Burnill, tailor, living in a house belonging to John Watts, flaxman, of £1 18s. a year rent next to the house of Mr Wise the lawyer, as he sustained by the late dreadfull fire, made upon oath before us theire Majestyes justices of the peace.

For beding, bedsteds, linen, woollen and other houshold goods and fewell, to the value of	7	12	2

Thomas Wyse (18)   £340 0 0
Bonds burnt q.[1]

The Valluation of the Loss of Mr Thomas Wyse sustained by the late fire which happened in Warwick Sept. 5th 1694.

In houshold goods as bedding, brass, pewter, wood and also wearing apparrell, bookes, papers and other materialls amounting in the wholl to	£100	0	0
Item in bonds burnt	83	10	0
The house my owne, not sett but worth to be sett above £12 per annum, and haveing been bid for it severall times about £200, I judge might have brought if I would have sold it	£240	0	0
Totall loss sustained	463	10	0

Job Rainsford (19)   £212 6 6

An account of the loss which Job Rainsford hath received by the late dreadfull fire which hapned in Warwick on the 5th of September 1694.

The whole loss which hee hath received is	£112	6	6

The house hee lived in together with a barn in New Streett hee paid £5 per annum rent to Mrs Anne Prescott, widow.

---

[1] For 'quaere'.

Mrs Nicholls (19)   £20

The valluacion[1] of the losse susteyned by Mary Nicholls, widdow, in the late dredfull fire which hapned att Warwicke on the fifth day of this instant September 1694.

In ready money, bedd, bedding, stooles, chaires, weareing apparell, coles and wood for winter to the vallew in all twenty six pounds[2]

Mary Yeardley[3] (19)   £5 6 6

Mary Yardleys loss att the fier.

Three blanketts, a paier of sheets and 2 pillows, curtaines and vallens, with a desk and what was in it	£1	10	0
One gown with five petticoats	2	0	0
Whood, tippett and great scarfe, with shooes and stockens and linen	1	1	0
4 pound of jerzey	0	6	6
2 barrells, candlestick and other household goods	0	5	0
[One] great rideing hood and stayes	0	4	0
	5	6	6

Stephen Allen (20)   servant to Capt. John Williams
the Turne key at the Goale: goods £8

The valuation of the losse of Stephen Allen of the Burrough of Warwick susteyned by the late fire September 5th 1694

Imprimus in money and goods   £8 0 0

Stephen Allen

The Shooe Makers Company's loss (21)   £14 10 0
Sheep Street

The Valluation of the Loss of the Shomakers Company within the Borough of Warwick sustained by the late fire which happened in Warwick

Imprimis their silver badge of armes, hearse cloth, bucketts and severall other things belonging to the company amounting to   £14 10 0

---

[1] The paper bears a 6d. blind legal stamp.
[2] Altered from 'twenty pounds'.
[3] Her estimate was sealed up as a letter and addressed: 'These to Mr James Yardley to be left at Samuell Burford's at the Singe of the Star in Warwick, to be gave him with speed.'

The Company of Sadlers, Chandlers et al. (22)
Lost to the vallue of £19. Sheep Streete.

The Valluation of the Loss of the Company of Sadlers, Chaundlers and others within the Borough of Warwick sustained by the late fire which happenned in Warwick.

Imprimis a hearse cloth, leather bucketts and severall other things belonging to the said company amounting in the wholl to   £19   0   0

Pibble Lane

Elisabeth Dyer (1)   £1   5   0

Sept. the 14 day '94

The Loss of Elise Dyar, widow, by the fire that happined in the alms houses of Mr Thomas Oken, the loss that I sustained was one pound five shillings   £1   5   0

Witness my hand the 14 day of Sept. '94
Eilse Dyar

Sarah Cooper (1)   £1   3   9

The Value and Loss of Sarah Cooper living in the Pibble Lane in the Burr' of Warwick as she sustained at the late dreadfull fire in the said Burrough of Warwick given upon oath before us theire Majesties justices of the peace.

In beding, bedcloths and wearing clothes and houshold goods to the value of   £1   3   9

Ann Dunn (2)   £1   1   3

The Value and Loss of Ann Dun, widow, living in the Pibble Lane in the Burrough of Warwick as she sustained at the late dreadfull fire in the said Burrough of Warwick, given upon oath before us theire Majestyes justices of the peace.

In beding, bedcloths and other houshold goods to the value of   £1   1   3

Mary Pestell (3)　　£3 3 0

The Value of the Loss as William Pestill lodging at his mother's Mary Pestill in the Pibble Lane in the Burrough of Warwick as he sustained by the late dreadfull fire in the said Burrough of Warwick, given upon oath before us theire Majestyes justices of the peace.

To the value of in cloths both linen and woollen　　　　　£3　3　0

Mary Bolton (4)　　£6 10 0

The Value and Loss of Mary Bolton, widow, living in the Pibble Lane in the Burrough of Warwick as she sustained at the late dreadfull fire in the said Burrough of Warwick, given upon oath before us theire Majestyes justices of the peace.

In bedsteds, beding, linen, woollen, brass, houshould goods and fewel to the value of　　　　　£6　10　0

Henry Butler (5)　　goods £93 16 6

The Valluation of the Loss of Henry Butler of the Borough of Warwick, carpenter, sustained by the late fire in Warwick.

Imprimis my brass, pewter, bedding, linnens and all other houshold goods together with my timber, boards and other materialls amounting to　　　　　£93　16　6

　　　　　　　　　　　　　　　Henry Butler

The house being all burnt being part of Mrs Atkins her house.

　　　　　　　　　　　　　　　John Sale.

Elizabeth Pain (5) servant,　　20s.

The Value and Loss of Elizabeth Pain as was servant to Henry Butler, carpenter and millwright, living in the Pibble Lane in the Burrough of Warr' as she sustained at the late dreadfull fire in the said Burrough of Warwick, given upon oath before us theire Majestyes justices of the peace.

In woolling and lynen clothes to the value of　　　　　£1　0　0

Sarah Atkins (6)　　goods　£45　4　6
　　　　　　　　　　　　house　200　0　0
　　　　　　　　　　　　　　　―――――――
　　　　　　　　　　　　　　　245　4　6

An Inventory of the Loase Sarah Atkins hath sustained by the late dreadfull fiar in Warwick.

In the sellor.

4 halfe hogsheds, one of them full beare		0	19	0
A parcell of tobbackoe		4	0	0
A parcell of suger	[			]¹
And in other odd things there		0	5	0

In the brewhouse.

A mash fatt and other brewing vessells to the vallew of	2	0	0
2 tunn coales and one load of clift wood	2	0	0

In the chambrs.

5 bedsteds and matts	2	0	0
1 fether bed and a bolster and six pillows, 1 large, with rugg and a counterpaine and curtains and 2 pair blanketts	5	12	0
2 pillyons and a pillion cloath	0	17	6
A large twigen cheire and a stoolpan	0	7	6
A large winscott chest full of lininge but what wee cannot justly tell but am sure to the vallew of	4	0	0
1 box with a silke gowne and severall parcells of silke and holland and sarge to the vallew	5	0	0
A large presse to hang cloase in and sum cloase in it and sume pewter and sume other odd things	1	0	0
5 tables and 2 winscott cheares and 6 joyn'd stooles and 8 stooles and chears	2	0	0

In the shopp.

And in suger and sume other odd things in the shopp to the vallew of	8	18	6
And counters and shilves and drawers	3	0	0
	41	19	6

Rent due at Mickelmasse from Henry Buttler £2, from Mrs Hiatt 15s., from Mrs Mary Yardley 10s., which money I dow nott expect	3	5	0
	45	4	6

Alice Hyatt, widow (6)   £7 18 6

The Valluation of the Loss of Alice Hyatt, widow, sustained at the late fire in Warwick.

¹ Blank not filled in.

Imprimis in bedding	£3	6	0
Item brass and pewter	1	9	6
Item chaires and tables	1	3	6
Item a box of bookes	0	5	0
Item a glass case and basketts	0	4	0
Item two chests with woollens and linnens therein	1	1	0
Item iron ware and earthen weare	0	9	6
	7	18	6

A lodger with Mrs Atkins

Widow Woodward[1] (7)   £23 7 0

An account of the loss sustained by the widow Woodward in the late fire wich hapened in the Burroug of Warwicke one 5 of 7ber 1694.

In beding, waring cloaths and houshold goods   £3 7 0

by me Amphilis Woodward

Hous rent £1 0 0 by the yeare, Mr Oaken's land.

Susanna Hancock (7)   £1 14 0

An account of the loss sustained by Susannah Hancoxe in the late fire which hapen'd in the Burrough of Warwick the 5th of 7ber 1694.

In beding, waring cloathes and houshold goods   £1 14 0

by me Susanah Hancox.

John Field (7)   £19

The Valluation of the Loss of John Feild, naylor, sustained by the late fire which happened in Warwick Sept. the 5th 1694.

Imprimis his nailes and other shop goods burnt and consumed in the said fire amounting to   £19 0 0

His shop totally consumed belonging to the dwelling
house of Widow Woodward in Peeble Lane.
His rent per annum   £1 0 0

---

[1] This estimate and the one following are written on the two halves of a sheet of paper previously used by another hand for pen trials, which include the first line of a letter 'Loving Sister, I desire you to send my. . . .'

John Foster (8)   £57

An account of loss sustained by John Foster in the late lementable fire that hapened in the Burrough of Warwicke one the 5th of September 1694 living att the uper end of the New Street, his yearly rent was £2 1 0, tenant to the widow Woodward, he hath lost to the value of £16 0 0.

J. Foster his marke

Mary Clements (9)

Goods	£40	18 2
Her owne house	200	0 0
	240	18 2

Vide Nich. Kaintons house

The Valluation of the Loss of Mary Clemens, widow, and Thomas Clemens of the Borough of Warwick, baker, sustained att the late fire which happened in Warr' Sept. the 5th 1694.

	£	s	d
Imprimis 4 load of wood	£1	4	0
Item 1 load of hay	0	16	0
Item 1 load of coales	1	0	0
Item a load of poles	0	12	0
Item some old timber	0	8	0
Item panniers and pack saddles	0	6	0
Item materialls in the bakhouse	2	11	0
Item two bread walletts and baggs	0	5	0
Item materialls in the shop	0	10	0
Item the kilne hair cloth and a try	0	15	0
Item a paire of scales and the brewing vessell	1	10	0
Item 2 hogges, a barrell, a halfe hoggeshead, a powdering tub and the settlesses[1]	2	0	0
Item 8 strike of meale and corne	1	10	0
Item 11 baggs 5 hundred and a halfe of hurds	4	12	0
Item severall goods in the buttery	0	15	0
Item goods in the parlour	0	18	0
Item goods in the hall	1	15	0
Item in the other parlour and the clossett	1	17	0
Item the goods in the roome over the hall	0	15	0
Item in the roome called the Talbott	0	14	0
Item the goods in the cross chamber	1	2	0
Item the woollens burnt	0	10	0
Item two wheels and a gold ring	0	10	0

[1] Settles: wooden stands for supporting casks.

	£	s	d
Item waring apparrell	1	0	0
Item 2 smoothing irons and provisions	0	5	6
Item a looking glass, a hair line and a chaffin dish and frying pan	0	5	0
Item 4 brushes	0	1	0
Item 3 hundred of boards	2	4	0
Item lead weights, shelves and other materialls	1	7	0
Item 1 feather bed and bolster	3	5	0
Item 3 paire and a halfe of sheets	1	8	0
Item 3 flock bolsters	0	8	0
Item one little pillow and a flagon	0	2	6
Item one green coverlett and 5 blancketts	0	18	6
Item one sett of yellow curtaines and valens, one sett of Kitterminster curtaines and valens, one sett of red curtaines and valens	1	6	8
In linnens	1	0	0
Item glass bottles, trenchers and other wooden ware	0	8	0
Item a saddle and bridle and 4 joynd stooles	0	9	0
Item other odd things	1	5	0
	40	18	2

	£	s	d
The house our owne, rent per annum	£10	0	0
The next house in the tenure of Nicholas Kington, rent per annum	2	4	0
Vallue of the houses	240	0	0[1]
Totall losse	£260	18	0[1]

Ann Mathews (10)   £62 5 0

The Valluation of the Loss of Anne Mathewes of Warwick, seamstresse sustained at the late fire

	£	s	d
In houshold goods of all sorts, wood, coales, cloths and other utensills	£12	5	0
The house all burnt, Mr Oken's land given for charitable uses, rent per annum	0	16	0

and a rump of beefe then worth £2 10 0 lately

[1] These totals are in another hand, not that of the endorsements.

Thomas Briscoe (10)   10s.

The Valluation of the Loss of Thomas Briscoe of the Borough of Warwick, sugarer,[1] sustained by the late fire.

Imprimis six elles of linnen cloth and a say apron burnt at the house of Anne Matthewes in the Peeble Lane amounting to   £0 10 0

James Rainbow (11)   £50

James Rainbow his lose.

Fore brandy, strong waters and tobako the whoule lose is fifty pound   £50 0 0

Swann Lane

John Averne (1)   £108 2 6

The Valluation of the Loss of John Averne of the Borough of Warwick, taylor, sustained by the late fire which happened in Warwick.

Imprimis his waring apparrell and other apparell and houshold goods amounting in the wholl to   £5 2 6

Item the house all burnt downe with the outhouses in the tenure of Richard Rawbone, Mr Roberts, Joseph Averne and my selfe.
Rent per annum   5 3 0

Joseph Averne (2)   £6 5 0

The valluation of the loss of Joseph Avarne of the Borough of Warwick, tayler, sufered by the late fire which hapned in Warwick.

Item his aparill and howsold goods and linings which amount in the wholle to   £6 5 0

Richard Rawbone (3)   £6

The Valluation of the Loss of Richard Rawbone of the Borough of Warwick, butcher, sustained by the late fire in Warwick.

Imprimis in houshold goods and other materialls consumed amounting in the wholl to   £6 0 0

[1] Presumably a miscopying of 'tugerer', a lath-splitter.

The house totally consumed, the house of John Averne,
rent per annum   £2   3   0

George Chinn (4)   £36

The Valluation of the Loss of George Chinne of the Borough of Warwick,
carpenter, sustained by the late fire which happened in Warwick.

Imprimis in damage sustained in the house wherein
Edward Deacon lived in the Swan Lane   £26 0   0

Edward Deacon (4)   £8

An account of the loss sustained by Edward Deacon of the Borough of
Warwick, shoomaker, in the late dreadfull fire which hapened one Wensday the 5th of this instant September 1694.

In linninge, brass and pewter, leather and shoos, lasts and
other tooles, stools and cheires, bedsteeds and bolsters
and iron ware to the value of six pounds   £8[1] 0   0

The rent of my house by the yeare is   1 16 0

Thomas Roberts (5)   £38 10 0

The loss of Thomas Roberts sustained by the late fire, 5 Sept. '94.

A barn at £1 10s. per annum, Mr Hicks.[2]
Wood in it   £3 10 0
Loss and damage in goods   5   0   0
                                                              _____
                                                                8 10   0

                                                    Tho: Roberts

The Markett Place

Charles Emes (1)   £190 19 0

The Valluation of the Loss of Charles Emes the younger of the Borough of
Warwick, feltmaker, sustained by the late fire in Warwick.

---

[1] Altered from '£6'.
[2] Altered from 'Mrs Townsends'.

Imprimis in houshold goods, shop goods, wooll for hatts, working tooles, hey, coales, wood and other utensills amounting to	£30	19	0
The house my owne, worth	160	0	0
Totall loss sustained	190	19	0

John King (2)   £133 15 0

The Valluation of the Loss of John King of the Borough of Warwick, sugarer,[1] sustained by the late fire which happened in Warwick.

Imprimis in houshold goods, tugar stuffe, turning stuffe, wood, turning tooles, hay, boards, seive, rimmes, new chaires and severall other materialls amounting to	£38	15	0
The house not totally consumed, the land of Mrs Man, rent per annum	£4	15	0

Francis Power (3)   £449

1694. An account of the losses that I Francis Power of the Borough of Warwick received by the late fier that happened upon the fith of September last past, in mault, corne, moneys and other goods was one hundred seventy and nine pounds and upwards, and the rent wich I paid for my house wich was then burnt was thirteene pound and ten shillings per annum.

George Flower (4)   £312 5 8

The Valluation of the Loss of George Flower of the Borough of Warwick, taylor and inneholder, sustained by the late fire which happened in Warwick.

Imprimis in houshold goods, shop goods, hoggesheads, beare, brewing vessell, hey, coales, wood and other utensills amounting in the wholl to	£112	5	8
The house totally consumed, the house of Mr Robert Blissett, rent per annum	£10	0	0

Jeremiah Good (4)   £5

The Valluation of the Loss of Jerom Good of Bagginton, baker, sustained att the late fire in Warwick.

---

[1] Almost certainly a mistake for 'tugerer', a lath-splitter.

Imprimis fifteen strike of wheat left at the house of
George Flowers in Warwick and measures   £3   0   0

Item twelve strike of mault burnt att the house of Joseph
Hemmings   2   2   0

                                                    Sum total   5   2   0

Benjamin Powers (5)   £247 16 6

The Valluation of the Loss of Bemiamin Powers of the Borough of Warwick, butcher, sustained by the late fire.

Imprimis my brass, pewter, ale, hoggesheads, brewing
vessells, linnens, hay, straw, wood, coales, houshold goods
and other utensills   £47 16 6

The house all burnt, the land of Mr Gibberd, rent per
annum   £10   0   0

Robert Coales (7)   £181 0 0

The valluattion of the los of Robert Coles of the Broh of Warwick, chandler, sustaned at the lat fier which happned in Warwick on the 5 of Sep-
tembr 1694.

Which los is   £61   0   0

The hous all burnet down, the rent was   6 10   0

John Hicks (8)   £18 0 0

The loss of John Hickes, smith, sustained att the late fire in Warwick.

Imprimis loss of houshold goods and utensills amounting
to   £3   0   0

The damage of my house by the fire thô not quite burnt
downe   15   0   0

                                                            18   0   0

The other house in the tenure of Robert Coale
totally consumed, rent per annum   £6 10 0

Job Burt (9)   £12

The valluation of the loss of Job Burt of the Borough of Warwick, flaxman, sustained by the late fire which happened in Warwick the 5th of September 1694.

Imprimis five quarter and more of flaxseed burnt, layd up at the house of Timothy Simpkin in Warwicke, being the best seed   £12 0 0

Thomas Smith (10)   £39 14 6
                        q.[1] the house.

The value of the lose of Thomas Smith liveing in the Market Place in the burough of Warwick as he sistaned att the late dradfull fyer in the sede buroue of Warwick, bafore us theire Majestis justises of the pecse.

In bading, housold goods, fuelle, heye, mony, buere, and other goods to the velue of   £39 14 6

Wittnes my hand the 14 dey of Sept. '94:   Thomas Smith.

Edward Wall (11)   £12

Edward Wall his los by the fire.

To the estimeshon of the carpenter and the mason: £12 0 0

Judeth Farr (12)   Houses £60   Market Place
                        Goods   60
                                ———
                                120

An accompt of what Judith Farr of the Borrough of Warwick, widow, lost by fire on Wedensday the 5th of September anno domini 1694.

In household goods   £30 0 0
In the cellar in beer and vessells   20 0 0
In coals and wood   10 0 0

Three bay of building belonging to her dwelling-house burnt down   £50[2] 0 0
More, a working-shop burnt   10 0 0

---

[1] For 'quaere'.
[2] Altered from '30'.

Goodman Flowers mayd   12s. 4d. Market Place

Goodman Flowers maide lost at the fire a ridine woode[1] and apparns and a shift and headcloths and a pare of pattins beside other things, the valie of them amounts unto   12s 4d

The Butts[2]

Edward Angrave (1)   £164 19 6

The valuation of the losses of Edward Angrave of the Borough of Warwicke sustained by the late fire which happened in Warwick.

Imprimis his bedding and other his houshold goods, hey, coales, fodder, loomes, working tooles and other materialls thereunto belonging, together with a hovell   £44 19 6

The house totally burnt downe, the land of Sir Henry Puckering, Barr., rent per annum   6 0 0

Widdow Harris, Saltisford (2)   House £80 0 0
                                       goods   24 0 4
                                              ─────────
                                               104 0 4

Anne Harris, widdow, her losse by the fire which happened on the 5th day of Sept. 1694.

Her bedding, linnen, pewter, brasse, brewing vessells, drink in the celler, hay, fewell and other houshold goods to the vallie of   £24 0 4

Anne Harris
At the Lamb

John Evitts (3)   £40

The Valluation of the Loss of John Evitts of the Borough of Warwick, flax-dresser, sustained by the late fire in Warwick

Imprimis flax in a barne, wood, timber, severall household goods, hey, coales and other utensills amounting to   £10 0 0

---

[1] 'riding hood'.
[2] Including houses in Joyce Pool and in the Saltisford.

The dwelling house not totally ruined but the barne and outhouse burnt downe, the damage sustained thereby amounting to at least   30   0   0

Totall loss sustained   40   0   0[1]

William Mathews (4)   goods £24 13 6
vide Mr Biker in Church Streete the house £80

The valluation of the lost of William Mathews of the Borrow of Warwicke substained at the late fier which hapened September the 5th 1694.

Item for houshold good and other materialls belonging to my trade   £24 13   6

Item the house all bornt down, the land of Mr John Bykers, rent   4   0   0

Manwhinnick, widdow (5)   goods £40
House vide Church Street £100

Widdow Manwhinick her losse by fire.

Her bedding, houshold goods, linnen, brewing vessells, drinke in the celler, hay and fewell to the value of   £40   0   0

Eliz: Manwhinick

Job Rhodes (6)   goods £34 0 0
House vide Church Streete £84

The valuation of the losse of Job Rodes of the Burrough of Warwick susteyned att the late fire which happened Sep. 5th 1694.

Imprimis for houshold goods, etc.   £34   0   0

Item the house all burnt down, the land of Mr John Biker, rent per annum   4 16[2] 0

---

[1] A draft, without endorsement or filing hole, accompanies this estimate. The total loss is the same, but is arrived at in the draft as follows:
'Imprimis one barne and stable totally consumed being full of flax drest and undrest, two load of timber being near it   £20   0   0
Item a little hey house and a coale house with the coales therein, a pigsty, a buttery joyning next to my house and part of the house and severall goods   20   0   0'
[2] Apparently altered from '10'.

Thomas Barthollemew, senior (7)   £25 9 0

The Value of the Loss as Thomas Bartholomew, pipemaker, living at the Joyce Pool in the Burrough of Warwick sustained by the late dreadfull fire in the said Burrough, given upon oath before us theire Majestyes justices of the peace.

My house, value	£19	10	0
In bedsteds, houshold goods and fewell to the value of	5	19	0
My whole loss	25	9	0

Wittnes my hand the 14th day of Sept. 1694,

Tho: Bartholomew senior T his marke

Thomas Barthollomew, junior (7)   £5 7 6

The Value of the Loss of Thomas Bartholomew the younger living at Joyce Pool in the Burrough of Warwick, as he sustained at the late dreadfull fire in the said Burr' of Warwick, made upon oath before us theire Majestyes justices of the peace.

In beding, houshold goods and fewell to the value of	£5	7	6

Wittnes my hand the 14th day of Sept. '94

Tho: Bartholomew junior B his marke

Edward Aston (8)   £25 10 0

September the 14 1694. The loss of Edward Aston by the late fire.

1 bay of dwelling hous with a leantwo and barne, the hous being my own, rent yearly	£1	4	0
In housal goods	1	10	0

John Miles (9)   £5

September the 14th 1694

The loses of John Miles by the late fire.

His hous upon rent att	£1	4	0
His goods both housall and others	5	0	0

Thomas Mayo, Jaespool (9)   £18

An acount of Thomas Mayo, flaxdresser, living at Jayes Poole his los by thay late dreadfull fire which happned in the borrough of Warwick one September the 5 1694.

In flax, in hurds, in hachell[1] and houseld goods	£8	14	0
The house of his one all burnt downe, the purchas	18	0	0

Thomas Mayo

Sarah Mayow (10)   £57

Sept. the 14 1694. The Loss of Sarah Maioh, widdow.

1 dwelling house being 1 bay and 1 bay of barning, the yearly rent being	£1	10	0
1 dwelling hous being a bake hous and 1 bay of barning, the purches being	20	0	0
Of housall good and 12 lood of fewell	7	0	0

Hannah Williams (11)   £34

Hannah Williams her loss by the late fire.

A house at the Jeas Pool, the rent one pound nine shillings per annum, burnt to the ground with goods and fuel to the value of five pounds and upwards.

Her husband being gone from her she has 5 children to maintain.

Jacob Dunkley (12)   £4

The Valluation of the Losse of Jacob Dunckley of the Borough of Warwick, joyner, sustained by the late fire which happened in Warwicke.

Imprimis clothes, bedsteads, corne, his working tooles and severall houshold goods amounting to	£4	0	0
The house totally consumed, the land of Thomas Griffin, smith, rent per annum	0	18	0

---

[1] Hatchel: a flax-comb.

Thomas Griffin (12)   £18

Thomas Griffin, blacksmith, his loss by the fire.

A house at Jaas Poole, the rent 18s. per annum, which Jacob Dunckley lived in burnt down to the ground.

Richard and Joan Hust (13)   £45 4 6

The Value of the Loss as Richard and Joan Hust, living at the Joyce Pool over against the Peacock in the Burrough of Warwick, sustained by the late dreadfull fire, made upon oath before us theire Majestyes justices of the peace.

For his house and backbuilding, houshold goods, cloths, wood, coales, corn and money to the value of   £45   4   6

William Francis (14)   £3 3 0
                             House q.[1] Mat. Busbie

The Value of the Loss of William Francis, living over against the Peacock by Joyce Pool in the Burrough of Warwick in a house of £1 3s. per annum, sustained by the late dreadfull fire in the said Burrough of Warwick, given upon oath before us theire Majestyes justices of the peace.

In houshold goods, linen and clothes and fewell to the value of £3   3   0

John Tatnal, mason (15)   £23 10 10

The valluation of the losse of John Tatnoll, mason, sustained att the late fire in Warwick.

Imprimus brass, pewter, bedding, houshold goods and severall working tooles and utensils   £3   10   0[2]

The house my owne, sett before I lived in it my selfe att
                                          £1   0   0 per annum

Joon Wyn (16)   goods 10s.
                      house John Sharley, vide—

An account of what Joane Wyn of the Borough of Warwick, widow, lost by fire on Wednesday the 5th of September anno domini 1694.

In beding and household goods   £0   10   0

---

[1] For 'quaere'.   [2] The pence figure can be misread as '10'.

Matthew Busby (17)   House £105 0 0
                            Goods   75 6 0
                                    ─────────
                                    180 6 0
                           vide William Francis house

September the 14, 1694. The loss of Mathew Busby by the late fire.

The dwelling house being Corporation land containing 8 bay and 1 bay of barning, the rent being yearly	£2 15 0
Layd out in repayrs and fiting up the hous for conveniant uces	50 0 0
For housall goods, fewill and hay	39 6 0
For hogsheads of ale and bottell'd ale	36 0 0
	─────────
For 1 dwelling hous of his owne in the tenuer of William Francis, the rent at 23s. per annum	1
	─────────

Abigaell Ryder (18)   £40 0 0
                       and   30 0 0

This is to satsfi you that I Abegall Rider have lost by the late fier here in Warwick to hoses, the rent of on was on pound twelf shill., the other 3 pounds and the lose of goods 8 pounds.

This was all I had to live upon for I am wors then a widow for my hosband is gone for a solder and I am laft alone with my child, so I hope you will be plesed to consider my pore condishon.

William Hadley (18)   £2 10 0

The Loss and Value of Will. Hadley, shoemaker, living next door to the Sign of the Peacock near the Joyce Pool, as he sustained at the late dreadfull fire in the Burrough of Warwick, made upon oath before us theire Majestyes justices of the peace.

For beding, bedsteds, wearing clothes and houshold goods and fewell to the value of	£2 10 0

---

[1] Totals struck out.

John Hadley (19)   £20

September the 14, 1694. The loss of Mr John Hadley.

2 bay of housing together with hogstys in the posesion of
Samuel Dunckley, the yearly rent   £1   o   o

William Haywood (20)   £19 10 0

An account of what William Haygood of the Borrough of Warwick lost by
fire on Wedensday the 5th of September anno domini 1694.

In household goods	£0	15	0
In wood and coale	0	5	0
In apparell	0	10	0
In all	1	10	0

Robert Watts (20)   £2 10 0

Robert Watts, schumaker.

For severall goods lost and broken att the fire to the
vallewe of   £2 10   o

Matthew Perry (21)   goods £61 o o
                           house 60 o o

The Value of the Loss of Matthew Perry, watercarryer, living at the Butts in
the Burrough of Warwick, as he sustained at the late dreadfull fire on the
5th of September 1694 in the said Burrough of Warwick, made upon oath
before us theire Majestyes justices of the peace.

In bedsteds, beding, wearing clothes, corn, houshold goods, wood, coales
and money and hay,

                    to the value of   £61   o   o

William Newbery (22)   goods £ 8 16 0
                             house 20   0 0
                                    ─────────
                                    28 16 0

The Valluation of the Loss of William Newbury sustained by the late fire in
Warwick.

	£	s	d
Imprimis the lease of my house being worth	£10	0	0
Item 3 load of wood	1	10	0
Item 3 bedsteads, matts and boards	1	10	0
Item 3 tables	1	6	8
Item 3 barrells	0	6	0
Item a new wascote	0	5	0
Item my daughters shifts	0	4	6
Item 2 cubbords	0	6	0
Item my children's wearing apparrell	0	4	0
Item one rugge	0	4	0
	15	16	2

The house all burnt, the rent thereof belonging to repaire
the high wayes, rent per annum   £1 0 0[1]
though now worth £1 per annum.

Elizabeth Glendall (23)   goods £ 6 3 0
house   20 0 0

26 3 6

The Value of the Loss as Elizabeth Glendole the wife of John Glendole
living next to the high parish pound as she sustained by the late dreadfull
fire, made upon oath before us theire Majestyes justices of the peace.

	£	s	d
Imprimis the house, stable, barn, slaughter house and other buildings	£20	0	0
For beds-cloths, bedsteds and other houshold goods to the value of	6	3	3
in all	26	3	3

Thomas Shatswell (24)   goods £ 5 0 0
house   25 0 0

30 0 0

Thomas Shatswells losse by the fire.

My house rented of Mr Bolton, worth 25s. per annum.

---

[1] Altered from '£0 7 0'.

My houshold goods, bedsteeds, bedding, brasse, pewter
and fewell   £5   0   0

    Witnes my hand the 14th day of Sept. 1694
                     Tho: Shatswell T his marke

Thomas Lynes (25)   goods   £ 6 8 8
                     house Mrs Ainge   26 0 0

The Value of the Loss of Thomas Loyns, pipemaker, living at the Butts in a
house of £1 6 0 a year in the Burrough of Warwick, as he sustained at the
late dreadfull fire, made upon oath before us theire Majestyes justices of the
peace.

For bed, bedcloths, houshold goods, fewell and cloths, tobacco, clay and
working tooles to the value of £6 8 10.

Edward Green, senior (26)   goods   £2 10 0
                        house Mrs Ainge   20   0 0
                                   ———————
                                 22 10 0

An Account of what I Edward Green of the Borough of Warwick, labourer,
lost by the late fire there.

My house being Mrs Ainge's which I pay 20s. per annum
rent   20s.

My houshold goods and fewell   £2 10   0

       Witnes my hand the 14th day of Sept. 1694
                    Edw. Green sen. X his marke

Edward Green, junior (27)   goods £4 2 8
                        house

Edward Greene, junior, losse by fire.

I Edward Green junior have lost 4 pounds 2 shillings 8 pence in flax that
was burned and consumed.

      Witnes my hand the 14th day of Sept. 1694
             Edward Green X his marke

William Mumford (28)   £6 10 0

The Value of the Loss as William Mumford, living at the Butts in the Burrough of Warwick in a house of twenty shillings a year rent, sustained by
the late dreadfull fire in the said Burr', made upon oath before us theire
Majestyes justices of the peace.

In bedsteds, beding, houshold goods and fewell to the value of £6 0 0

Nicholas Styles (29)   £31 8 0

Nicholas Styels hath lost by this fire at the Buttes in goodes and fewell to the value of 3 pound 8 shillings	£3 8	0
The rent of the house is one pound 8 shiling a yeer	1 8	0

Mary Woodcock (30)   £38 17 4

The Value of the Loss as Mary Woodcock, widow, living at the Butts in the
Burrough of Warwick sustained at the late dreadfull fire, made upon oath
before us theire Majestyes justices of the peace to the value of £2 17 4

Living in a house and barn at £1 16 0 a year.

William Cornwall (31)   £26 14 6

The Value of the Loss as Will. Cornwell living at the Butts in the Burrough
of Warwick sustained at the late dreadfull fire in the Burrough of Warr',
made upon oath before us theire Majestyes justices of the peace.

20s. per annum. The Loss of the house as I lived in		£14 0	0
For all my new building as I built		6 0	0
For beding, wearing clothes, houshold goods, wood, coales, hay, bacon to the value of		6 14	6
	My loss in all	26 14	6

John Hancox (32)   £15

The Value of the Loss of John Hancox the elder, living at the Butts in the
Burrough of Warwick, as he sustained at the late dreadfull fire in the said
Burrough, given upon oath before us theire Majestyes justices of the peace.

For the loss of his dwelling house	£5 0	0
For the loss of his new building	6 0	0

For the loss of his hay	3	0	0
For the loss of goods and cloths	1	0	0
his loss in all	15	0	0

George Francis (33)   £24 17 0

The valuation of the loss of George Frances of Warwick, swingler,[1] sustained at the late fire which happened in Warwick Sept. the 5th 1694.

Imprimis three bedsteads, one coffer, one cubbord and some linnens	£0	17	0
The house Mrs Cauthornes all burnt, rent per annum	1	4	0

John Hancock (34)   £24 18 0

John Hancok the yongor.

Lose by the fire in linens and wollines and goods [to the value] of to poundes	£2	0	0
And the rent of the house one	£1	4	0

Richard Hadley (35)   £19 15 0

The Value of the Loss of Richard Hadley, junior, flaxdresser, living at the Butts in a house of 18s. a year in the Burrough of Warwick, sustained by the dreadfull fire late in the said Burrough of Warwick, made upon oath before us theire Majestyes justices of the peace.

In beding, houshold goods, clothes and fewell to the value of	£1	15	0

Henry Styles (36)   £22 15 0

The valluation of Henry Styles of the Borough of Warwick, swingler, sustained at the late fire which happened in Warwick September the 5th anno domini 1694.

Imprimis 2 bedsteads, one bed, a coffer, a paire of sheets, one cubbord and some other linnens	£0	15	0
The house being widow Ryder all burnt, rent per annum	1	2	0

---

[1] Flax-beater.

Thomas Edwards (37)   tymber £26

These are to certifie that Thomas Edward of Hatton, junior, hath lost boards and other timber ammounting to the vallue of twenty six pounds and upwards, that was burnt in the dreadfull fire at Warwicke upon the 5th day of Sept. last, 1694, and is ready to testife the same upon oath. Witnes my hand,

Tho: Edwards

William Reeve (37)   barne £14 0 0

The valluation of the loss of William Reeve sustained by the late fire which happened at Warwick Sept. 5th 1694.

Imprimis two houses and one barne burnt downe standing neare Mr Colemores back gates, the rent per annum being	£2	14	0

Henry Wilson (38)   £33 0 0

The Losse of Henry Wilson of Warwicke sustained by the late fire in Warwick.

Imprimis one dwelling house and barne neare the Butts, rent per annum	£1	13	0
Vallue	33	0	0

Hen. Wilson

Edward Cornwall (38)   goods £3 7 6

The Valluation of the Loss of Edward Cornwell of the Borough of Warwick, weaver, sustained by the fire which happened in Warwick September the 5th 1694.

Imprimis one joyned bedstead, flock bed and bolster, a hilling and a paire of sheets, coard and matt	£1	10	2
One great coffer, one box, one trunke, one cubbord, one table, 2 chaires and four shifts	0	16	4
Item six napkins and hand towells	0	1	6
Item one linnen wheel and one woollen wheel	0	4	6
Item a box of child bed linnen	0	10	0

My weareing apparrell	o	4	o
Odde things	o	1	6
	3	7	6

The house Henry Wilsons, butcher, all burnt downe, rent
per annum   £1 5 o

New Streete[1]

Sarah Blythe (1)   £4 18 o

The Valluation of the Loss of Sarah Blith of the Borough of Warwick,
widow, sustained by the late fire in Warwick.

Imprimis jersey coffers, a table, chest, shillves[2] and other
goods burnt in my shop being part of Timothy Simpkins
his house, amounting in the wholl to   £1 10 o

Item in jersey and jersey yarne att my owne dwelling
house in the New Street amounting   3   8 o

                                    Totall losse sustained   4 18 o

Susanna Maule (2)   goods £5 15 o

An account of the loss sustained by Susanah Maule in the late fire wich
hapened in the Burrough of Warwicke the 5th of September 1694.

In beding, waring cloathes and houshold good   £5 10 o
In jarsey and flax   o   5 o

                                    by Susanah Maule

William Taft (3)   goods £4

An account of the loss sustained in the late lementable fire that hapened
the 5th of September 1694 in the Burrough of Warwicke by William Taft.

In houshold goods   £4 o o
                                    by me William Taft

The house damnified   £20[3] o o

---

[1] Including houses in the Market Place.
[2] 'chest, shillves' interlineated.   [3] Altered from '£15'.

The house[1] part burnt with the back buildings, the house
of William Roe, rent per annum   £4   5   0

William Roe (3)   £15 per house

The Valluation of the Loss of William Roe sustained by the late fire which
happened in Warwick.

Imprimis part of the dwelling house wherein William Taft
lives in the Newstreet together with all the barning and
out houses, damage sustained at least   £15   0   0

William Smith (4)   £23

The Valluation of the Loss of William Smith of the Borough of Warwick,
shomaker, sustained by the late fire in Warwick.

Imprimis his hay, coales, wood, leather, brewing vessell
and other goods amounting in the wholl to   £7   0   0

The losse of his barne and stable totally burnt downe, the
damage whereof amounting to, with part of the dwelling
house   £16   0   0
                                                                     _____
                                                                     23   0   0

Thomas Leeke (5)   £3

The Valluation of the Loss of Thomas Leeke of the Borough of Warwick,
taylor, sustained by the late fire which happened in Warwick.

Imprimis in houshold goods lost and damage sustained by
the tyles, etc., pulled off my house, in the wholl amounting
to   £3   0   0

John Burton (6)   £300 0 0

The Valluation of the Loss of John Burton of Warwick, inneholder, sustained by the late fire which happened in Warwick.

Imprimis my brass, pewter, ale, hoggesheads, linnens, bed-
ding, brewing vessell and household goods amounting to   £140 17   0

The house all burnt, the land of Thomas Lane, rent per
annum   £8   0   0

[1] This section inserted in a space by another hand.

Thomas Spencer (7)   £82

The Value of the Loss of Thomas Spencer, living at the Sign of the Bull at pillory in the Markett Place in the Burrough of Warwick, as he sustained by the late dreadfull fire in the said Burrough of Warwick, made upon oath before us theire Majestyes justices of the peace.

For a house as Frances Woodhams living in, the rent being four pound two shillings a year

The whole loss by computation is   £82   0   0

Francis Woodhams (7)   £87, viz. 82 and 5

I Francis Woodhams doe testifie upon oath what lossis i substain by the late dreadfull fire, the house that I lost was Thomas Spenser and the fewell that I had leaid in for winter and goods which was burned I value was five pound.

September the 14 1694.

Timothy Simpkins (8)   £121 15 6

The Value of the Loss as Timothy Simkins, living at the White Horse in the Market Place in the Burrough of Warwick, sustained at the late dreadfull fire in the said Burrough, given upon oath before us theire Majestyes justices of the peace.

For drink, hogheads, brewing vessells, mault, barley, hay, straw, coales, wood, houshold goods, tobacco, confectionary and backbuilding and stabling at a house of my own at the pillory, to the value of, in all   £121 15   6

My then dwelling house was ten pounds a year.

Elizabeth Martin (8)   £213 0 0

An Account of what I, Elizabeth Martin of the Borough of Warwick, widdow, lost by the late dreadfull fire there

My house knowne by the name of the White Horse in the Markett Place within the said Borough with the maulting house and other out houses thereunto belonging, late in the possession of on Timothy Simkins lett and sett to him by lease at tenn pounds per annum. Wittnes my hand the 12th day of September anno domini 1694.

Elizabeth Martin

And in goods burnt then and there to the vallue of   £13   0   0

Elizabeth Birt[1] (8)   £12 12 9

The loss sustained by Elizabeth[2] Burtt as followeth:

In holland and callicoes, in silk and flax and other things
burnt att John Jarvises to the vallue of   £12 12 9

Witness my hand——Elizabeth Burtt, Sept. the 14 day '94.

Mr Richard Gibbert (9)   House £110 0 0
                                goods   16 0 0
                                         ——————
                                        126 0 0
                    Vide Market Place house £200 and 90

An Account of what I Richard Gibberd of the Borough of Warwick lost by
the late fire there.

Imprimis my house in the Market Place known by the
name of the George Inne lett to Benjamin Powers at £10
per annum   £200 0 0
Item my house adjoyning late in the possession of Mrs
Goodalle at £4 10 0 per annum   90 0 0
Item my house in the New Street let to Mr Dodd at
£5 10s. 0d. per annum   110 0 0
Item in rough timber, sawed timber, lath and poles   16 0 0
                                                            ——————
                                    Totall losse   416 0 0
                                         Richard Gibberd

In divers places

The Towne Water Engin burnt, cost £40 (1)

The loss of a large ingeon for the exstinguishing of fire which was burnt in
the late fire in Warwick, the sum of fourty pounds.

Judeth Dunn in Richard Kerbies house in High Street £5 (2)

The Value of the Loss as Judith Dunn, widow, living at the house where
Richard Kirbey the butcher dwellt in the High Street in the Burrough of

---

[1] Also endorsed 'John Burtt' struck through, and 'Goody Burt'.
[2] Altered from 'John'.

Warwick as she sustained at the late dreadfull fire in the said Burrough of Warwick, given upon oath before us theire Majestyes justices of the peace.

To the value of in beding and clothes and houshold goods   £5   0   0

Mary Kempe of Worcester lost at the White Lyon in Warwick £4 goods
          (3) High Streete.

The Valluation of the Loss of Mary Kempe of the City of Worcester sustained by the late fire which happenned att Warwick

Imprimis in wearing apparrell, other goods and wares left
at the White Lyon in Warwick and there burnt and consumed amounting in the wholl to   £4   0   0

William Walton of Fernhill[1] lost at John Cakebreads in Church Street
          £2 6 0 (4)

The Valluation of the Loss of William Walton of Fernhill sustained by the late fire which happened att Warwick.

Imprimis in barley and baggs burnt and consumed att the
house of John Cakebread, maltster, in the Church Street
in Warwick amounting to   £2   6   0

Thomas Preist of Knowle lost at Robert Wattes in Sheepe Streete
          £3 16 0 (6)

The Valluation of the Loss of Thomas Preist of Knoll sustained by the late fire which happened in Warr.

Imprimis thirteen stone of week yarne[2] burnt and consumed in the said fire which was left at the dwelling-
house of Robert Watts in the Sheeps Street in Warwick
amounting to   £3   16   0

Elizabeth Gibbs servant to Mr Stoakes at the Swan in High Street £1 (7)

The Valluation of the Loss of Elizabeth Gibbes, servant to Mr Stokes at the Swan in Warwick, sustained by the late fire in Warwick

Imprimis her wearing apparrell both woollens and linnens
consumed by the fire amounting to   £1   0   0

---

[1] A farm at the northern end of Wedgnock Park.
[2] Wick-yarn.

THE BOOKE OF ESTIMATES OF THE LOSS BY FIRE

An Estimate of the Loss sustained in and by the late Fire which happened within the Towne of Warwick on Wednsday the fifth of this instant September 1694. as the same has beene given in by the respective Sufferers pursuant to an Order by the Mayor of the said Towne *et aliis* published to that purpose in manner following, viz.

Sufferers' Names	Theire Qualities, Trades and Professions	Landlords and Owners of each house	Loss in Houses			Loss in Goods, Money, etc.			Totall Loss in Houses, Goods, etc.		
			£	s.	d.	£	s.	d.	£	s.	d.
HIGH STREET											
Mr Devereux Whadcock	Mercer	Mr William Tarver	370	0	0	100	0	0	470	0	0
Thomas Dadley	Butcher	his owne	150	0	0	20	0	0	170	0	0 }
Idem		poore's land	66	15	0				66	15	0 }
Thomas Watts	Apothecary	his owne	200	0	0	144	10	0	344	10	0
Mrs Martin	Widow	idem				25	10	0	25	10	0
Richard Kerbie	Butcher	his owne	160	0	0	25	01	0	185	01	0
Mr Edward Norton	Watchmaker	his owne	300	0	0	274	0	0	574	0	0
George Taylor	Black smith	Mr Richard Grimes	180	0	0	17	19	6	197	19	6
Thomas Moore	Carpenter	Idem				47	10	0	47	10	0
Susanna Smith	Lodger						10	0		10	0
Martha Keene	Inmate					3	2	0	3	2	0
John Gibbs	Taylor	Idem				58	8	6	58	8	6
Mr Joseph Blissett	Mayor	his owne	500	0	0	100	0	0	600	0	0
Mr Stoakes	Inneholder	Mr William Tarver	1060	0	0	166	16	8	1226	16	8
John Pyke	Harness Maker	Idem landlord				28	0	0 }			
Henry Falkner	Glover	Idem				4	6	4 }	32	6	4
George Tonge	Book Seller	Ditto	440	0	0	159	16	0	599	16	0

Sufferers' Names	Theire Qualities, Trades and Professions	Landlords and Owners of each house	Loss in Houses	Loss in Goods, Money, etc.	Totall Loss in Houses, Goods, etc.
Mrs Elizabeth Pywell		Ditto		29 19 6	
Mr John Vere	Attorney	Ditto		6 0 0	
Samuell Brierly	Millener	Ditto		19 0 0	263 14 6
Thomas West	Tallow Chandler	Ditto		154 15 0	
Anne Bolton		Ditto		54 0 0	
Mr Thomas Stratford	Alderman	his owne	160 0 0	78 3 0	238 3 0
Mary Taylor	his servant			2 10 0	2 10 0
Sarah Bunter, widow	Inneholder	hers and Mr Crane's	400 0 0	412 9 0	812 9 6
John Howell	Harper and lodger there			61 4 6	
Beverly Bedoes	Ditto	Ditto		30 0 0	
William Kerbie	Ostler	Ditto		8 0 0	101 9 6
Mary Gattell[1]	Servant	Ditto		1 10 0	
Samuell Willis		Ditto		15 0	
Mrs Sara Hicks and family[2]	Inne holder	Edward Clopton Esq.	140 0 0	258 0 0	398 0 0
Thomas Hicks	Tallow chandler	Ditto		24 10 4	24 10 4
Mrs Mary Overton		her owne	220 0 0	162 8 5	382 8 5
Richard Scudamore				16 19 0	16 19 0
Edward Venner	Baker	Mr Holyoake	60 0 0	20 0 0	80 0 0
Thomas Russell	Felmonger	Mr Corpson	10 0 0	4 10 0	14 10 0
Joshua Perkes	Baker	his owne	40 0 0	10 0 0	50 0 0
John Banbury	Weaver	Mr Corpson	14 0 0	72 13 0	86 13 0
George Harris	Flax dresser	Quakers house	50 0 0	23 3 0	73 3 0
Richard Sharpe	Coller maker	Mrs Lucas	50 0 0	97 6 0	147 6 0
Richard Bromley	Shoemaker	Towne land	80 0 0	84 14 7	164 14 7
Margaret Clemens		Ditto		19 11 0	36 0 3
Richard Ebrall		Ditto		16 9 3	
Sara Ryder	Midwife	Mrs Doll Weales	110 0 0	77 3 10	187 3 10
Sara Stanley	her servant			16 0 0	16 0 0
Abraham Ducomin	Gunn Smith	Ditto landlady		41 18 5	41 18 5

Name	Occupation	Held of			
Humphery Carter	Taylor	Ditto	50 0 0	23 9 0	73 9 0
Thomas Dixon	Black Smith	his owne	80 0 0	27 12 1	107 12 1
George Watts	Inne holder	The Widow Hopkins	240 0 0	322 0 0	562 0 0
Richard Radford	Curryer	Ditto		3 10 0	3 10 0
Thomas Gibbs	Shoe maker	Town land	120 0 0	237 18 0	357 18 0
Mary Drury	his servant			12 0	12 0
Isaac Tomkes	Gent.	his owne	2400 0 0	177 5 0	2577 5 0
Mr Holden	Dr of Phissick	Ditto		8 10 0	8 10 0
Mrs Dolman	Widow				
Mrs Halford	Widow				
Hannah Eires and Lydia Perry	Servant maydes			6 7 0	
Jonathan Sturt	Servant man			2 10 0	8 17 0
John Langton	Baker	Alderman Welton		37 4 6	
William Allen	Shoe maker	Ditto		5 5 0	
William Ebrall	Sadler	Ditto		115 0 0	
John Welton	Alderman	his owne	292 10 0	4 6 6	454 6 0
Mrs Sandford & Mrs Norton[3]	Goldsmith	Mrs and Mr Prescott	100 0 0	270 0 0	
Mrs Sarah Bree	Lodger	Ditto		50 0 0	
Susanna Wright	Servant to Mrs Sandford			1 10 10	321 10 10
Mrs Askell	Apothecary	Mrs and Mr Prescott	240 0 0	250 0 0	590 0 0
Elizabeth Roberts	Ditto			70 0 0	
Thomas Maunder	Barber	Mr Richard Greene	215 0 0	67 8 0	282 8 0
Mary Busbie	Servant to Ditto			10 6	
Mr James Yardly	Attorney			28 9 0	48 19 6
Mr Abraham Simons	Surgeon			20 0 0	
Mr George Barton		Mr Richard Greene	97 0 0	52 15 6	149 15 6
George Smith sen. and jun.	Barbers	Mr Thomas Archer	100 0 0	44 0 0	144 0 0
Charles Harrison	Sadler	Ditto	80 0 0	29 19 6	109 19 6

[1] *Recte* Tuttell, see p. 151.
[2] 'and family' inserted in a space.
[3] 'and Mrs Norton' inserted in a space.

Sufferers' Names	Theire Qualities, Trades and Professions	Landlords and Owners of each house	Loss in Houses			Loss in Goods, Money, etc.			Totall Loss in Houses, Goods, etc.		
			£	s.	d.	£	s.	d.	£	s.	d.
Mr Edward¹ Wilson	Alderman	his owne	350	0	0	80	0	0	430	0	0
Henry Rogers	Apothecary	Ditto				145	0	0	145	0	0
Richard Hands	Baker	William Cooke	250	0	0	64	0	0	314	0	0
Thomas Tipping	Cuttler	Ditto	90	0	0	65	0	0	155	0	0
Mrs Dorothy Weale	Wollen Draper	her owne	400	0	0	150	0	0	550	0	0
Elizabeth Rand	Servant to Mary Overton					2	0	0			
Mary Stratford	Granddaughter to Mr Thomas Stradford					1	17	6	3	17	6
CHURCH STREET			£	s.	d.	£	s.	d.	£	s.	d.
Mr Robert Blissett	Wollen Draper	his owne	400	0	0	20	0	0	420	0	0
Samuell Ainge	Taylor	his owne	150	0	0	68	12	6	218	12	6
Susanna Gibbs	Servant					1	5	0	1	5	0
Mary Goodall	Servant to Ditto					1	0	0	1	0	0
Joseph Ainge	Joyner	his owne	150	0	0	89	16	0	239	16	0
Anne Ainge	Widow	Ditto				13	8	0	38	8	0
Katherine Bird		Ditto				25	0	0			
Thomas Leane	Barber	Mrs Tuckey's	85	0	0	32	5	0	117	5	0
Alderman Edward Heath	Gent.	his owne	1300	0	0	236	0	0	1536	0	0
The said Mr Heathe's	Servants: Richard Walford 20s., Elizabeth King 12s., Sarah Ward £1 10s.								3	0	2
John Jarvis	Barber	his owne	385	0	0	103	4	0	488	4	0
Samuell Cooke	his Servant	Ditto				3	0	0			
Elizabeth Farr	Widow	Ditto				13	0	0	36	0	0
John Cole	Weaver	Ditto				20	0	0			
Anne Webb	Widow	John Jarvis jun.	60			20	0	0	80	0	0
John Hands	Glover	Thomas Dadly	80			33	0	0	113	0	0

Name	Description	Property	£ s d	£ s d	£ s d
Henry Smith	Butcher	Mr Fulke Weale	80 0 0	21 0 0	101 0 0
Thomas Claridge	Shoe maker	Mrs Cawthorn	100 0 0	35 0 0	135 0 0
Mr Stephen Nicholes, Alderman					
Mary Carter	Chandler	Mr John Weale	300 0 0	87 6 2	387 6 2
Mr Alexander Nicholls	his Servant			1 13 0	1 13 0
William Horne[2]	Chandler	Mr Weale		300 16 0	300 16 0
Mrs Elizabeth Murcott	his Servant man	Ditto		2 0 0 ⎱ 34 0 0	} 36 0 0
Robert Taylor	Butcher	Mrs Palmer	230 0 0	85 5 0	315 5 0
Thomas Cattle	his Servant			1 18 0	1 18 0
William Perkes	Baker	his owne	220 0 0	100 0 0	320 0 0
Elizabeth Carr		her owne	150 0 0	148 0 0	298 0 0
John Eld	Labourer, Servant[3]	Ditto		7 19 0	7 19 0
Joseph Hemings	Maulster	Church house	90 0 0	87 13 10	177 13 10
Mr John Dolphin	Gent.	Ditto house	60 0 0	112 10 0	172 10 0
Sara Mayow	Millener	Ditto house		134 10 0	134 10 0
Sara Edwards	Widow	Towne land and } Mr John Biker	102 10 0	30 0 0	} 173 10 0
Mr John Biker	Gent.	Ditto		41 0 0	
Sara Glendall	Servant to Mrs Edwards	Ditto land		2 4 4	2 4 4
Sara Bucknall, widow	Oate meale maker	Ditto		7 4 10	7 4 10
Mrs Allott		Ditto		57 2 0	57 2 0
Hannah Ares		Ditto		18 0 0	18 0 0
Thomas Breedon				1 10 0	1 10 0
John Cakebread	Maulster	his owne		48 9 6	48 9 6
Mr James Fish	Parish Clarke	porch chamber	100 0 0	108 0 0	208 0 0
Sarah Asplin	Bell ringer			13 0 0	13 0 0
Edward Chesley[1]	Taylor	his owne }	160 0 0	156 5 8	316 5 8
George Chesley	Taylor	Ditto		26 18 10	} 32 18 10
John Twicross	Servant to Ditto			6 0 0	
Mr William Edes	Viccar St Maries	Viccarage	180 0 0	150 0 0	330 0 0
Anne Southern	his Servant			15 0	} 149 8 6
Mrs Anne Preston		Ditto		148 13 6	

---

[1] An error for 'Edmund'.   [2] This entry interlineated.   [3] 'servant' interlineated.

Sufferers' Names	Theire Qualities, Trades and Professions	Landlords and Owners of each house	Loss in Houses	Loss in Goods, Money, etc.	Totall Loss in Houses, Goods, etc.
Mrs Mary Murcott	Widow	her owne	300 0 0	217 12 0	517 12 0
Mr William Fetherston	Gent.	Ditto		240 0 0	300 0 0
William Paston	Gent.	Ditto		60 0 0	
Dorothy Welch		Widow Ainges		3 0 0	3 0 0
Mrs Elizabeth Lea	Widow	Church land		20 0 0	20 0 0
JURY STREETE					
Joshua Drake	Taylor	Mr Charles Warde	60 0 0	5 0 0	65 0 0
Samuell Drake	Taylor	Ditto		2 10 0	2 10 0
Thomas Glendall	Shoemaker	Ditto	50 0 0	8 0 0	58 0 0
Nicholas Parris	Gunn Smith	his owne	100 0 0	103 0 0	203 0 0
Richard Goode	Tallow Chandler	the Towne and Mr Wilson	95 0 0	31 10 0	126 10 0
Thomas Wall	Black Smith	his owne	160 0 0	25 0 0	185 0 0
John Williams and Tymothy Norbury				11 14 4	11 14 4
Mr George Webb	Mercer	Mr Robert Blissett	80 0 0	250 0 0	330 0 0
Samuell Barber	Comb Maker			10 0 0	10 0 0
Richard Hands	Joyner			5 14 0	7 14 0
Mrs Anne Archer				2 0 0	
Samuell Rainbow				5 0 0	5 0 0
Joseph Bateson	Confectioner			8 0 0	8 0 0
William Savage	Barber	Towne land	5 0 0	2 0 0	7 0 0
Nathaniell Gilstrop	Labourer	Mr Heath	30 0 0	7 16 4	37 16 4
Andrew Archer	Esq.	his owne	20 0 0		20 0 0
CASTLE STREETE					
Mr John Bradshaw	Apothecary	Robert Boyce, Esq.	300 0 0	51 11 0	351 11 0
Thomas Marriott	Shoe maker	Towne land	50 0 0	10 0 0	60 0 0

Name	Trade	Landlord / Property	£	s.	d.	£	s.	d.	£	s.	d.
Robert Ashbie	Taylor					15	0	0	}		
Jonathan Smith	Hatter					3	5	0	23	10	0
Joane Cumberlidge	Brazier					4	0	0	}		
William Jackson						1	5	0	15	0	0
The Mayor's Parlour		The Towne land	15								

SHEEPE STREETE

Name	Trade	Landlord / Property	£	s.	d.	£	s.	d.	£	s.	d.
John Atterbury	Shoe maker	Towne land	71	0	0	209	3	4	280	3	4 }
Thomas Scarlett	his Servant					1	14	4 }	2	18	4 }
Richard Perry	Ditto					1	4	0 }			
Thomas Arpes	Inne keeper	Mrs Hawkes	140	0	0	152	10	0	292	10	0
Joseph Willis	Baker	Widow Ashwins	113	0	0	58	13	0	171	13	0 }
Mary Lowe	Servant						19	0		19	0
John Pritchard	Yeoman	his lease and Towne land	450	0	0	87	17	0	537	17	0
Mariana Duckett		Ditto				8	0	0	8	0	0
Mrs Anne Edes	Apothecary	Ditto				50	0	0 }	53	0	0 }
Frances Edes	her Daughter	Ditto				3	0	0 }			
Capt. John Williams	Gent. and Goaler	The County's	700	0	0	191	17	4 }	891	17	4 }
Edward Birkebeck	Tapster in Ditto					18	0	0	18	0	0
The Sheire Hall			34	0	0				34	0	0
Robert Watts	Tallow chandler	The County's	220	0	0	110	0	0	330	0	0
Charles Watts	Flax dresser	his owne				18	0	0 }	170	0	0 }
John Watts	Chandler	Ditto				152	0	0 }			
Zachary Sharpe	Bridewell keeper	Ditto	96			47	10	0	143	10	0 }
His mayd and aprentice	Servants	The County's					16	0		16	0
Richard Harris	Towne Serjeant	Ditto	280			13	15	0	293	15	0
Anne Newton	Servant to Mrs Caw-thorne	Mrs Cawthorne				10	0	0	10	0	0
George Maning	Taylor	Ditto	140	0	0	38	0	0	178	0	0
Martin Taylor	Baker	Mrs Cawthorne				150	0	0	550	0	0 }
Richard Hadley senior	Inne holder	his owne	400	0	0	6	5	2			
Richard Hadley junior	a Skinner	Ditto				2	0	0 }	11	5	2 }
Mary Overton	Servant mayd	Ditto				3	0	0			
Katherine Drewry	Servant mayd	Ditto									

Sufferers' Names	Theire Qualities, Trades and Professions	Landlords and Owners of each house	Loss in Houses	Loss in Goods, Money, etc.	Totall Loss in Houses, Goods, etc.
John Buttler	Carpenter	Mr Jarrett and Mrs Wagstaffe	100 0 0	39 0 0	139 0 0
Thomas Rush	Taylor	Mrs Wagstaffe	55 0 0	31 2 8	86 2 8
Samuell Parsons	Inneholder	John Watts	297 10 0	71 15 9	369 5 9
Mrs Lucas		Ditto		3 0 0	
The Widow Hill		Ditto		12 0 0	
Goodwife Trulove		Ditto		10 0	23 2 2
John Burnhill	Taylor	Ditto		7 12 2	
Thomas Wise	Attorney	his owne	240 0 0	100 0 0	340 0 0
Job Rainsford	Attorney	Mrs and Mr Prescott	100 0 0	112 6 6	212 6 6
Mrs Mary Nicholles	Widow	Ditto		26 0 0	
Mary Yardley		Ditto		5 6 6	31 6 6
Stephen Allen	Servant to Capt. John Williams			8 0 0	8 0 0
The Shooe Makers Company				14 10 0	14 10 0
[ ] Hopkins[1]	Gent		102 0 0		102 0 0
The Company of Sadlers, Chandlers, etc.				19 0 0	19 0 0

			£ s. d.	£ s. d.	£ s. d.
PIBBLE LANE					
Elizabeth Dyer	poore	The Towne Almes Houses	60 0 0	1 5 0	
Sarah Cooper	Ditto	Ditto		1 3 9	
Anne Dunne	Ditto	Ditto		1 1 3	73 3
William[2] Pestle	Ditto	Ditto		3 3 0	
Mary Bolton	Ditto	Ditto		6 10 0	
Henry Butler	Carpenter	Mr Sales	200 0 0	93 16 6	293 16 6

Name	Occupation	Property	£	s.	d.	£	s.	d.	£	s.	d.
Elizabeth Paine	his Servant	Ditto				1	0	0			
Sara Atkins	Mercer	Ditto				45	4	6	54	3	0
Alice Hyett	Widow	Ditto				7	18	6			
Amphillis Woodward	Widow	Towne land	20	0	0	3	7	0	23	7	0
Susanna Hancock	Widow	Ditto				1	14	0	20	14	0
John Field	Naylor	Ditto				19	0	0			
John Foster	Coster Monger	Towne land	41	0	0	16	0	0	57	0	0
Mary Clemens	Baker	her owne	200	0	0	40	18	2	240	18	2
Anne Mathews	Semstress	Towne land				12	5	0	62	5	0
Thomas Briscoe	Tugeror[3]	Ditto					10	0		10	0
James Rainbow	Distiller	Mr Nicholas Rothwell	50	0	0	50	0	0	50	0	0

SWANN LANE

Name	Occupation	Property	£	s.	d.	£	s.	d.	£	s.	d.
John Averne	Taylor	his owne	103	0	0	5	2	6	108	2	6
Joseph Averne	Taylor	Ditto				6	5	0	12	5	0
Richard Rawbone	Butcher	Ditto				6	0	0			
Edward Deacon	Shoe maker	George Chinn	36	0	0	8	0	0	44	0	0
Thomas Roberts	Inne holder	his Barne	30	0	0	8	10	0	38	10	0

THE MARKET PLACE

Name	Occupation	Property	£	s.	d.	£	s.	d.	£	s.	d.
Charles Emms	Hatter	his owne	160	0	0	30	19	0	190	19	0
John King	Tugeror[3]	Mrs Mans	95	0	0	38	15	0	133	15	0
Francis Power	Butcher	Mr Bromage	270	0	0	179	0	0	449	0	0
George Flower	Taylor	Mr Robert Blissett	200	0	0	112	5	8	312	5	8
Jeremiah Goode	Baker	Ditto				5	0	0	5	0	0
Benjamin Powers	Inn holder	Mr Giberd	200	0	0	47	16	6	247	16	6
Robert Coale	Tallow Chandler	John Hicks	120	0	0	61	0	0	181	0	0
John Hicks	Black Smith	Ditto	15	0	0	3	0	0	18	0	0

[1] John Hopkins of Birmingham, undertaker of the Priory waterworks in March 1693/4 by agreement with Sir Henry Puckering, and constructor of the cistern or water-house in Sheep Street and pipes laid under the roads by licence from William Bolton, lord of the manor. [CR 26/1 (5)]. [2] Altered from 'Mary'. [3] Lath-splitter.

Sufferers' Names	Theire Qualities, Trades and Professions	Landlords and Owners of each house	Loss in Houses	Loss in Goods, Money, etc.	Totall Loss in Houses, Goods, etc.
Job Burt	Flax Dressor			12 0 0	12 0 0
Thomas Smith parte	Butcher	Mr Fulk Weale	110 0 0	39 14 6	149 14 6
Edward Wall	Husbandman	his owne parte burnt	12 0 0		12 0 0
Richard Gibert	Maulster	his owne	90 0 0		90 0 0
Judeth Farr	Innholder	Towne land	50 0 0	60 0 0	110 0 0
Goodman Flower's mayd				12 4	12 4
THE BUTTS[1]					
Edward Angrave	Weaver	Sir Henry Puckering	120 0 0	44 19 6	164 19 6
Widdow Harris	Inne Keeper	Sir Henry Puckering	80 0 0	24 0 4	104 0 4
John Evitts	Flax Dressor	his owne	30 0 0	10 0 0	40 0 0
William Mathews	Comb maker	Mr Biker	80 0 0	24 13 6	104 13 6
Widow Manwhinick	Innholder	Ditto landlord	100 0 0	40 0 0	140 0 0
Job Rhodes	Innholder	Ditto	84 0 0	34 0 0	118 0 0
Thomas Bartholemew	Pipe maker	his owne	19 10 0	5 19 0	25 9 0
Thomas Bartholemew jun.		Ditto		5 7 6	5 7 6
Edward Arton	Labourer	his owne	24 0 0	1 10 0	25 10 0
John Miles	Labourer	Thomas Mayow	18 0 0	5 0 0	23 0 0
Sarah Mayow	Baker	her owne	30 0 0	27 0 0	57 0 0
Hannah Williams		her owne	29 0 0	5 0 0	34 0 0
Jacob Dunckley	Joyner	Thomas Griffin	18 0 0	4 0 0	22 0 0
Richard Hurst	Labourer	his owne	23 0 0	22 4 6	45 4 6
William Francis	Flax dresser	Mathew Busbie	23 0 0	3 3 0	26 3 0
John Tatnall	Mason	his owne	20 0 0	3 10 10	23 10 10
John Sherley	Carpenter	his owne	30 0 0		30 0 0
Joane Winn	Widow	Ditto		10 0	10 0
Mathew Busbie	Innholder	Towne land	105 0 0	75 6 0	180 6 0

Name	Trade	Landlord / note									
Abigael Ryder		her owne	32	0	0	8	0	0	40	0	0
William Hadley	Shoe maker	Mrs Rider	60	0	0	2	10	0	62	10	0
John Hadley	Alderman	his owne	20	0	0				20	0	0 }
William Haygood	Heele maker	Mr Henry Heath	18	0	0	1	10	0	19	10	0 }
Robert Watts	Shoe maker	Ditto				2	10	0	2	10	0
Mathew Perry	Water carrier	Mr Ailworth	60	0	0	61	0	0	121	0	0
William Newberry	Shoe maker	for highwayes	20	0	0	8	16	2	28	16	2
Elizabeth Glendale		Sir Henry Puckering's land	20	0	0	6	3	3	26	3	3 }
The same[2]		Frekleton's barne	50	0	0				50	0	0 }
Thomas Shatswell	Labourer	Mr Bolton	25	0	0	5	0	0	30	8	0
Thomas Lynes	Pipe maker	Mrs Ainge	26	0	0	6	8	10	32	8	10
Edward Greene sen.[3]	Flaxman	Ditto				4	2	8	4	2	8
Edward Greene jun.	Labourer	Ditto	20	0	0	2	10	0	22	10	0
William Mumford	Shoe maker	Ditto	20	0	0	6	0	0	26	0	0
Nicholas Styles	Flax dresser	Mr Brookes	28	0	0	3	8	0	31	8	0
Mary Woodcock	Widow	Ditto	36	0	0	2	17	4	38	17	4
William Cornwall	Water carryer	Towne land	20	0	0	6	14	6	26	14	6
John Hancox sen.	Herdor	Ditto land	11	0	0	4	0	0	15	0	0
George Francis	Flax dresser	Mrs Cawthorn	24	0	0		17	0	24	17	0
John Hancox jun.	Labourer	Ditto	24	0	0		18	0	24	18	0
Richard Hadley	Labourer	William Reeves	18	0	0	1	15	0	19	15	0
Henry Styles	Flax dresser	Ditto	22	0	0		15	0	22	15	0
Thomas Edwards jun.	Tymber man	Ditto a barn	14	0	0	26	0	0	40	0	0
Edward Cornwall	Weaver	Henry Wilson	33	0	0	3	7	6	36	7	6

NEW STREETE[4]

Name	Trade	Landlord / note									
Sarah Bligh	Jersey comber					4	18	0 }	10	13	0
Susanna Maule	Spinster					5	15	0 }			
William Taft	Bodys maker	William Rowe	15	0	0	4	0	0	19	0	0

[1] Houses in Joyce Pool and the Saltisford are included.
[2] This entry interlineated.
[3] 'senior' and 'junior' appear to have been transposed, see p. 222.
[4] Houses in the Market Place and elsewhere are included.

Sufferers' Names	Theire Qualities, Trades and Professions	Landlords and Owners of each house	Loss in Houses	Loss in Goods, Money, etc.	Totall Loss in Houses, Goods, etc.
William Smith	Shoe maker	his owne	16 0 0	7 0 0	23 0 0
Thomas Leake	Taylor	his owne	3 0 0		3 0 0
John Burton	Inne holder	Thomas Leanes	160 0 0	140 17 0	300 17 0
Thomas Spencer & Francis Oadhams		Spencers	82 0 0	5 0 0	87 0 0
Timothy Simpkins	Maulster	Elizabeth Martin	213 0 0	121 15 6	324 15 6
Elizabeth Birt	Semstress	Ditto		12 12 9	12 12 9
Mr Richard Gibbert	Maulster	his owne	110 0 0	16 0 0	126 0 0
Sir Henry Puckering	Baronet	his owne	30 0 0		
William Colmer	Esq.	his owne	30 0 0		
Sir Thomas Wagstaffe	Knt.	the Colledge, his owne[1]			
IN DIVERS PLACES					
The Water Engin		The Townes		40 0 0	
Judeth Dunn	in Richard Kerbies house			5 0 0	
Mary Kemp of Worcester	at the White Lyon	George Watts		4 0 0	
William Walton of Fernhill	in Church Streete	John Cakebread		2 6 0	
Mary Dickerson	vide the Butts	q. Matthew Busbies		5 0 0	
Thomas Preist of Knowle	Sheep Streete	Robert Watts		3 16 0	
Elizabeth Gibbs, High Street	Servant to Mr Stoakes	the Swan		1 0 0	

[1] Remaining columns left blank.

The Names of the Streetes and Places	Totall Loss in Houses in each place			Totall Loss in Goods, etc. in each place			Totall Loss in Houses Goods, etc.		
	£	s.	d.	£	s.	d.	£	s.	d.
HIGH STREETE[1]	[9,865	5	0]	[5,343	2	9]	[15,208	7	9]
CHURCH STREETE	[4,683	0	0]	[3,194	16	6]	[7,877	16	6]
JURY STREETE	[600	0	0]	[504	4	8]	[1,104	4	8]
CASTLE STREETE	[365	0	0]	[95	1	0]	[460	1	0]
SHEEPE STREETE	[3,538	10	0]	[1,784	7	9]	[5,322	17	9]
PIBBLE LANE	[571	0	0]	[304	16	8]	[875	16	8]
SWANN LANE	[169	0	0]	[33	17	6]	[202	17	6]
THE MARKETT PLACE	[1,322	0	0]	[590	3	0]	[1,912	3	0]
THE BUTTS	[1,434	10	0]	[501	7	5]	[1,935	17	5]
NEW STREETE	[659	0	0]	[317	18	3]	[976	18	3]
The Collegiate Church of St Maries							25,000	0	0
[Grand total							£60,877	0	6]

[1] The totals in square brackets were not filled in, and have been supplied by the editor.

THE BOOK OF REDUCTIONS

Reduction of Losses in Houses and Goods

May 31 1695 and June 30 1695.
An Estimate of Losses in houses by the late fire in Warwick, taken by the persons underwritten desired by an order of the last Court to take account of the same.

Mr Bradshaw, house purchased for £300, formerly lett for £15 per annum, lett for £13, ground sold for £40, barn and garden rated at £40, deducted 80	220
Mrs Dorothy Weale, rent worth to be lett £12 per annum at 20 year purchase £240, deduct for ground £30	210
Mr Cooke, Richard Hands and J. Tipping tenants, rent £17 per annum at 20 years purchase £340, to bee deducted £60 for ground	280
Mr Wilson's house, rent £14 per annum at 20 years purchase £280, to bee deducted for ground 45	235
Mr Archer's house at £9 per annum, at 20 years purchase 180, to bee deducted for ground £60	120
Mr Green's house £11 per annum—20 years purchase 220, to bee deducted for the ground 50	170
Mr Prescot's houses £17 per annum, 20 years purchase 340, to bee deducted for ground 60	280
Mr Welton's houses, £17 per annum, at 20 years purchase £340, to bee deducted for ground 60	280
Mr Tomkys his house offered at £1300, to be deducted for ground and materials remaining £300	1000
Mr Gibbs Corporation house, one hundred pounds, to bee deducted for ground 20	80
Widdow Hopkyns rent £12 per annum 240, to be deducted for ground £60	180

Thomas Dixon rent £4 per annum, 20 years purchase 80, deducted for ground 10 — 70

Mrs Weale's houses, Carter and Ryder, rent seven pounds fifteen shillings, at 20 years purchase 155, deduct 30 — 125

Corporation house, Bromley £4 per annum, 20 years purchase 80 — 20[1]

Mrs Lucas rent £2 10s. per annum, 20 years purchase £50, deduct for ground 10 — 40

George Harris, rent £4 per annum, part demolished

Mr Corpson, John Banbury, 2 barns, rent 20s. per annum, £20 deduct £5 — 15

Mr Perks, barns etc at 30s. per annum, 20 years purchase £30 — 30

Mr Venner's house part demolished, loss £40 — 40

Mrs Overton rent £9 per annum, with the Dolphin parlour 20 years purchase £180, deduct for ground 30 — 150

Mrs Hick 2 bays in the garden a chattle 20s. a year — 20

Dolphin Inn £6 per annum, 20 years purchase 120, deduct for ground £30 — 90

....[2] Crane and Mrs Bunter rent £18 per annum 360, deduct for ground and barn 85[3] — 280

.... Stratford rent £6 at 20 years purchase 120, deduct for ground 15 — 105

[B]ell Inn at £24 per annum 480, deduct for ground 75 — 405

[Sw]an Inn fifty three pounds per annum one thousand & sixty pounds, deduct for ground £120[4] — 940[5]
Memorandum: to be deducted for ground 150 except Mr Tarver make it appear to the contrary by satisfieing the Commissioners that the articles are cancelled.

---

[1] A 'Q' is written in another hand against this figure.
[2] Edge of page missing, affecting this and subsequent entries.
[3] 'and barn' interlineated over a caret. '85' altered from '70'.
[4] Altered from '£50', which has itself been altered from '£120'.
[5] Altered from '910' which has itself been altered from '940'.

Mr Blissett 15 per annum £300, deduct for ground £40[1] 260

[... G]rimes rent £7 10s. 150, deduct for ground £40 110

[... N]orton £14 per annum 280, deduct for ground £40 240

[Ker]by £8[2] per annum 160,[3] deduct for ground 20 140

.... Watts house £11 per annum £220, deduct for ground 40 180

Thomas Dadley £6 per annum 120, deduct 15 105

Mrs Weale: poors rent 3. 7s. £67, deduct for ground £19 7s. 47 13

Mr Tarver 15 per annum 340, deduct for ground 40[4] 300[5]
Memorandum barn and garden within the rent.

Church Street

Thomas Dadley £4 per annum 80, ground 15 65

Mrs Weale £4 per annum 80, ground 15 65

Mr Clarridge £5 per annum 100, ground £25 75

Mr Nichols Mr Weale[6] £13 per annum 260, ground 50 210

Mrs Palmers £10 per annum 200, deduct for ground £30 170

William Perks 10 per annum 200, deduct for ground 25 175

Elizabeth Carr £7 per annum 140, deduct for ground 30 110

Church ground £10 per annum 200, deduct for ground 50 150

Okens[7] land £7 per annum 140, deduct for ground 30 110

Mr Fish £4 10s per annum £90, deduct ground 15 £75

Edward Cheslly rent £6 10s. per annum 135, ground 25 110

Mrs Murcott rent £12 per annum 240, ground 50 190

[1] This item has a cross drawn through the centre.
[2] Altered from '£7'.
[3] Altered from '140'.
[4] Altered from '35'.
[5] Altered from '305'.
[6] 'Mr Weale' interlineated over a caret.
[7] Altered from 'Bikers'.

Parsonage[1] house £10 per annum 200, ground 40   160

Okens land £7 per annum 140, ground 15   125

Pebble Lane

Okens Alms houses rent £4 per annum £80, ground £10   70

Oken: Widdow Mathews £2 10s per annum 50, ground £5   45

Okens land, Woodward £3 10s. peer annum 70, ground £10   60

Thomas Clements 2 houses rent £10 per annum 200, deduct for ground £30   170

New Street

James Sales, Atkins tenant, 8 rent 160, deduct for ground 20   140

John Hawks, Arps tenant, £7 per annum 140, ground 20   120

Mrs Ashwin, Joseph Willis rent £6 per annum £120, ground 20   100

John Pritchett & Mr Hands mortgage upon the house, principal £80 use £10,[2] rent £9 per annum 180, deduct for ground 30   150

Corporation house, Pritchet £8 per annum £160, ground £10   150

The Goale £35 per annum £700, for ground & materials[3] 120   580

Mr Watts house £8 per annum 160, ground deducted 30   130

The Water house loss £80   80

Matthew Busby, Okens land £5 per annum 100, ground £10   90

---

[1] This and the following two entries are joined by a bracket.
[2] 'Mr Hands ... £10' interlineated over a caret.
[3] '& materials' interlineated over a caret.

Widdow Rogers £4 per annum 70,[1] ground £10	60[2]
Mr Hadley, Dunkley 2 bay building £12,[3] ground 40s.	£10[4]
Edward Walls house part burnt £15	15
John Sharley 3 bay building 23s. per annum[5] 23, ground deducted £2	21
[John] Tatnall 20s. per annum 20, deduct ground	18
Matthew Busby 22s. per annum £22, deduct for ground £2	20
Richard Hurst 22s. per annum 22, ground £2	20
John Williams 23s. per annum 18,[6] ground deducted £2	16[7]
Thomas Griffin 18s. per annum 14,[8] for ground £1	13[9]
Mr Biker, Whinnick tenant, £5 per annum 100, for ground 15	85
Mr Biker, Matthews tenant, £4 per annum 80, for ground £10	70
Mr Biker, Rhodes tenant, £4 per annum 80, for ground 10	70
Thomas Bartholemew, rent 16s. £16, ground 1	15
Edward Aston 16s. rent £16, ground £1	15
Widdow Mayo 35s. per annum 35, ground £1 10s.	33 10s.
Thomas Mayo 12s. rent £12, ground 10s.	11 10
Thomas Shatswell 20s. £20, ground 40s.	18
Mr Ailworth £3 per annum 60, ground 42[10]	18[11]
John Hancox and Cornwall 22s. per annum, ground 40	20
Richard Hadley 18s. per annum 18, ground £1	£17

---

[1] Altered from '80'.   [2] Altered from '70'.
[3] Altered from '£16'.   [4] Altered from '£14'.
[5] '23s. per annum' interlineated over a caret.
[6] '18' written above '23' struck out.
[7] '16' altered from '21'.   [8] '14' altered from '18'.
[9] '13' altered from '17'.   [10] '42' altered from '35'.
[11] '18' altered from '25'.

George Francis 1 5[1] per annum £25,[2] ground £2 10[3]   22 10[4]

Mrs Cawthorn £1 5s.[5] per annum 25, ground 2 10   22 10

[. . . .] Reeve, Masters tenant, 12s. 12, ground £1   11

Henry Styles, Brook landlord 22s. per annum 22, ground £1   21

Brooks barn, Perry tenant with Woodcock, 44s. per annum old £30, ground £1   £29

Mrs Ainge 3 houses 3 bay 45s. per annum £35, ground £1   34

William Newberry, 18s. per annum 15   15

Henry Wilson 33s. per annum £27,[6] ground £2   25

Sir Henry Puckering 3 bay 25s. value £20, deducted ground £2   18

Sir H. Puckerings barn £2 10s. £42,[7] ground £2   40

	Yearly Rent	Value of houses	Ground	Whole Loss
Sir H. Puckering, Angrave tenant	£6 per annum	120	£20	100
Sir H. Puckering Widdow Harris tenant	4 per annum	80	15[8]	65[9]
John Evitts damag'd, in house and barn		10		
Mrs Cawthorn, 3 tenants	17 per annum	340	40	300
Serjeant Hadley his house	£23[10] per annum	460[11]	80	380[12]

---

[1] '1 5' altered from '18s.'.   [2] '25' altered from '18'.
[3] '2 10' altered from '£1'.   [4] '22 10' altered from '17'.
[5] '£1 5s.' altered from '15s.'.   [6] '£27' altered from '£33'.
[7] '£42' interlineated over a caret.   [8] '15' altered from '20'.
[9] '65' altered from '60'.   [10] '23' altered from '25'.
[11] '460' altered from '500'.   [12] '380' altered from '420'.

	Yearly Rent	Value of houses	Ground	Whole Loss
Mrs Wagstaffe, Jarrett[1] and Rush	6 15	135	20	115
John Watts, Parsons and Bonnell	150	300	50	250
Mr Wise	10	200	30	170
Mr Rainsford	£6	120	40	80
Mr Jarvis, Webb and Cole	14	280	40	240
Mr Heath		1000	100[2]	900
Mrs Tuckey	£4 per annum	80	20	60
Mrs Ainge	£14 per annum	280	40	240
Mr Blissett and Mr Webb	£26[3] per annum	520[4]	60	460[5]
John Wall	6[6]	120[7]	15[8]	95[9]
Corporation house, Goods	5	100	15	85
Nicholas Paris	5 10[10]	110	20	95
Mr Ward, Glendal and Drake	4	80	25	55

Castle Street

Okens land, Thomas Marriott, dammag'd		40		

New Street

Thomas Lane landlord, Burton tenant	8	160	30	130

[1] 'Jarrett' interlineated over 'Butler' struck out.
[2] '100' altered from '300'.   [3] '26' altered from '22'.
[4] '520' altered from '440'.   [5] '460' altered from '380'.
[6] '6' altered from '7'.   [7] '120' altered from '140'.
[8] '15' altered from '20'.   [9] '95' altered from '100'.
[10] '5 10' altered from '7 10'.

	Yearly Rent	Value of houses	Ground	Whole Loss
Spencer landlord, Odhams tenant	£4 5s.	70	£10	60
Mrs Martyn landlord, Simpkins tenant	£10	200	30	170
Charles Elms	£8	160	25	135
Mrs Mann	£4	80	20	60
Timothy Simpkins, damag'd		12		
Mr Bromwich, F. Powers tenant	£14	280	50	230
Mr Robert Blissett, Flower tenant	10	200	30	170
Mr Gibbard, Powers tenant Mr Gibbard, widdow Goodale Mr Gibbard, Dodd tenant	£9 3 7	180 60 140	50	330
William Smith, damag'd		15		15
Thomas Leake, dammaged		2		2
Mrs Weale, Smith tenant		50		50
Corporacion, Widdow Farr tenant, dammage		40		40
John Hicks, Robert Cole tenant Shopp to the house, dammage	5	100 10	15	85 10
Mr Roe, dammage		15		15
George Chinn, Deacon tenant	2	40	20	20
John Avern, R. Avern, Richard Rabonn	5 10	110	10	100
Mr Colmore at Butts, damage[1]		15		15
Sir H. Puckering		20		20
Mr Heath landlord, Nathan Guil-strop		30		30
Mr Roberts, dammage		20		20

[1] This line is on a tear, and the reading is doubtful.

	Yearly Rent	Value of houses	Ground	Whole Loss
Mr Archer, dammage		20		20
Court house, dammage		5		5

Aaron Rogers[1]	William Wilson	Commissioners present to
William Tarver	William Roe	assist: Mr Mayor,
Richard Lane		Mr John Newsham, Mr Thomas
J. Williams		Newsham, Mr Lingham,
Edward Norton		Mr Hands, Mr Davies
Thomas Roberts		

The Estimates of the losses of the several persons underwritten, were reduced by the persons whose names are subscribed, apointed and desired by the Commissioners to inspect the bills and reduce the said losses:[2]

Persons not Burnt

Richard Radford, currier	3	10	
Sarah Bucknell	7	4	10
Thomas Breden	1	10	
Timothy Norberry and Mr Williams	11	14	4
Samuell Barber	10		
Richard Hands, joyner	5	14	
Mrs Ann Archer	2		
Mr Samuell Rainbow	5		
Joseph Batson	8		
William Savage, barber	2		
Thomas Russell, barn	4	10	
Nathaniel Gilstrop	7	16	4
Robert Ashby, tayler	15		
Jonathan Smith, hatter	3	5	
Joan Cumberlidge, widow	4		
William Jackson	1	5	
Widow Hill	12		
Mrs Mary Nicholls, widow	26		
The Shoomakers Company			
The Company of Sadlers and Chandlers			
Sarah Cooper	1	3	9

[1] These 8 names are signatures.
[2] This heading begins a new page and the hand changes.

Ann Matthews, semstress	12	5
Thomas Briscoe	10	
James Rainbow		
Jeremiah Good, baker		
Robert Coale, chandler		
Robert Watts junior		
Edward Green[1]		
Sarah Blith	4	18
Matthew Perry	61	
Timothy Simpkins	121	15 6
Mary Kemp of Worcester		
Judith Dunn		
William Walton of Fernhill		

	Loss in Goods	To be deducted	The whole Loss
Mr Whatcoate	£100[2]	20[2]	
Thomas Dadley			
Mr Stoakes[3] at the Swan In	166 16 8		
John Pike, harness maker	28	8	20
George Tongue	159 16	59 16	100
Samuell Brierly	19	14	5
Thomas West			100
John Howell, harper			50
Beverley Bedoes[4] noe inhabitant			15
Richard Scudamore[4] of Hampton lost in barley sent in for malt			16 19
Richard Bromley, shoomaker			60
Sarah Rider	77		67
William Eborall, sadler	115		80
Mrs Sandford, goldsmith	270		200
Mrs Sarah Bree	50		35
Mrs Askell, apothecary	280		240
Mrs Elizabeth Roberts	70		50
Mr Mander			

[1] This entry struck out.
[2] These sums struck out.
[3] This whole entry struck out.
[4] 'Q' entered in the margin against each of these entries.

	Loss in Goods	To be deducted	The whole Loss
Mr Henry Rogers, apothecary	145		130
Thomas Tippin	65		55
Mrs Dorothy Weale	150		100

Q. Whether the goods charged in Mr Dolphin's bill of losses are the goods of the Widdow Carrs or his own

Mrs Sarah Mayo, semstress	134 10		80
Mr Fish	108		80

Memorandum that Ann Preston is charged in the book of estimates £148 13 6 and is but   48 13 6

Richard Good, chandler	31 10		20
John Bradshaw			40
Mr George Webb	250		180
John Atterbury	209 3 4		149[1]
John Prichard	87 17		80
Mrs Ann Eades[2]			50
Edward Birkbook, tapster to Mr Williams	18		16
Zachary Sharp	47 10		35
John Butler	39		35
John Field, nailer			
Mrs Nicholls, widow, querie what money found			
James Rainbow	50		30
Robert Coale	61		30
Edward Angrave	44 19 6		35
John Evitts	10		6
Job Rohds	34		30
Matthew Perry[3]	61		50
John Burton	140 17		100
Timothy Simpkins[3]	121	71	

Thomas Newsham[4]	Thomas Roberts
Joseph Blissett	Steven Comberladge
Stephen Nicholles	Thomas Lea
Edward Norton	Edward Reeve
J. Williams	Thomas Hickes
John Savage	William Roe

[1] Altered from '149 3 4'.   [2] This whole entry struck out.
[3] Matthew Perry appears twice, also Timothy Simpkins. [4] These names are signatures.

PETITIONS AND OTHER PAPERS (DATED)
LAID BEFORE THE COURT

Petition of J. Williams, gaoler

Sept. 20th '94.
Received of the Treasurers of the Charity given on account of the late fire five pounds towards the makeing some provision at the Shirehall for securing his fellon prissoners

5   0   0   per J: Williams

I humbly pray
To know if this five pounds above mentioned must be a part of twenty three pounds seventeen shillings of the divedent for my goods

J. Williams[1]

Petition of Stephen Nichols, tallow chandler

Warr' Borough. To the Rt. Honorable and others the Commissioners and Judges appointed by an Act of Parliament for the Rebuilding the Towne of Warwick and for determining differences touching houses burnt and demolished by reason of the late dreadfull fire there, July the 15th 1695

The Humble Peticion of Stephen Nichols of the Borough aforesaid, tallow chandler, Sheweth:
That your Peticioner was possessed of a messuage in the Church Street in the Borough aforesaid by lease from Thomas Stratford, gent., William Lee and John Farr, blacksmith, all of the Borough aforesaid, wherein your Peticioner had at the time of the late fire about nine hundred and fourty years to come at the yearly rent of eight pounds, haveing paid a fine of three and twenty pounds not many years before the said fire wherein the said messuage was totally burnt. That John Weale of this Borough, gent., claimes the inheritance of the said messuage at the time of the said fire, by vertue of the last will of his father Thomas Weale deceased, in which will his said father devises and bequeathes four pounds a year to his wife out of the said messuage for life, and the other £4 per annum to his son George Weale if he be liveing, and the revercions and remainders of the said messuage to him and his heirs for ever, and if he be dead, then he devises and bequeathes the premises to John Weale and his heirs for ever, and is unwilling to rebuild or

---

[1] This signature and the petition are in one hand, presumably that of Williams; the receipt and signature above are in another.

to discharge the Peticioner of the covenants on the part of the lessee to be performed, and the growing rent since the fire. That your Peticioner for the sake and in behalf of his son Alexander Nicholls who sustained a considerable loss by the late fire, and the better to enable him to redeem his loss and carry on his trade in the same place he formerly did, is willing to rebuild the said messuage, provided he may be discharged of the said covenants and the growing rent in the said lease contained, and have such an estate in the toft wheron the said messuage lately stood assured unto him or his son by decree of this Court, for such consideracion as shall be agreed upon by and between the Peticioner and the said John Weale.

Your Peticioner therefore humbly prayeth the summons of this Court to summon the said John Weale to appear in this Court of Judicature, to the end such order and decree may be made by this Court touching the premises as shall seem most just and reasonable. And your Peticioner shall ever pray, etc.

Petition of Richard Hands, maltster

Warr' Burr'. To the Rt. Honorable, and others the Commissioners and Judges appointed by an Act of Parliament for the Rebuilding the Town of Warwick and for determining differences touching houses burnt and demolished by reason of the late dreadfull fire there, July the 15 1695

The Humble Peticion of Richard Hands of the Borough aforesaid, maulster, sheweth:

That John Prichard of this Borough being seized of a messuage in the Church Street in the Borough aforesaid, did mortgage the same unto your Peticioner for the summ of four score pounds, the said messuage being totally burnt down by the said fire and there being due to your Peticioner in the principal and interest almost one hundred pounds.

Your Peticioner therefore humbly prayeth that he may have such proporcion allow'd him out of the Charity monies which shall be given to the said John Prichard, as this Court shall think most reasonable. And your Petitioner shall ever pray, etc.

Richard Hands

Petition of Thomas Mayo of Rugby

To the Rt Honorable and others the Commissioners sitting att the Mayor's Parlour on Munday the 16th day of Sept. 1695 by vertue of an Act of Parliament for rebuilding the Town of Warwick, etc.

The Humble Peticion of Thomas Mayo of Rughby in the County of Warwick, yeoman, Sheweth:

That Edward Mayo of this Borough of Warwick, carpenter, being seized of a messuage or tenement before the late fire scituate neere the Joyce Poole within the said Borough, and alsoe of one other messuage or tenement adjoyning to the messuage before mencioned, did on the 19th day of January 1691 for and in consideracion of the summ of £20 mortgage the said two messuages or tenements to William Lingham of this Borough, gent., for 1000 years att one pepper corn per annum to be paid to the said Edward Mayo with a provisoe that if he the said Edward Mayo should pay or cause to be paid the aforesaid summ of twenty pounds to the said Wm. Lingham on the 19th day of July then next following, then the said mortgage was to be void and of none effect or else to remaine in full force, and that the said Wm. Lingham did on the 18th day of January 1692 in consideracion of the above mencioned summ of twenty pounds assigne the said mortgage to your Peticioner for the numbers of years therein contained and to hold the same in such manner as he the said Wm Lingham might have done, the said 2 messuages being totally burnt down by the said fire, and that one Edward Aston lais claime to the ground whereon stood one of the said messuages in the said mortgage mencioned and expressed to be mortgaged and assigned over to your Peticioner and has[1] rebuilt on the same,[2] your Peticioner conceiveing noe interest the said Edward Aston can have in the same, humbly prays this Court would grant summons to warn the said Edward Aston to appear in this Court that thereby he may be compell'd to produce his title to the same and your Peticioner may have the same settled on him by Decree of this Court. And your Peticioner shall ever pray, etc.

Order regarding Nicholas Paris and Thomas Wall

Warr' Burg':[3] Die Mercurii scilicet decimo octavo die Septembris Anno
             Domini 1695
At this Court it is ordered that Mr Devereux Whadcock, Receiver or Treasurer of the Corporacion Revenews, doe receive of Nicholas Paris and Thomas Wall for the use of the said Corporacion the sume of twenty-five pounds being the consideracion moneys of a peice of burnt ground lyeing betweene the houses of the said Nicholas Paris and Thomas Wall and purchased lately by them of and from the Mayor, Aldermen and Burgesses of the Borough of Warwick aforesaid, and that Mr William Tarver be desired to obtaine from the Commissioners in the Act of Parliament for the Rebuilding of Warwick an order for the payment thereof out of the charitie

---

[1] 'have' in MS.
[2] 'and have rebuilt on the same' interlineated.
[3] This order is from the Borough Court, and is endorsed: 'Mr Mayor and Aldermen, order relateing to Thomas Wall and Nicholas Paris.'

moneys allotted to the said Nicholas Paris and Thomas Wall for and towards the rebuilding their houses

		Charles Hickes, Mayor
Aaron Rogers	Joseph Blissett	Ri: Lane
Wm Tarver	Stephen Nicholles	Tho: Young
Edward Heath	Rich: Hands	Henry Fawlkner

Petition of the Mayor, Aldermen and Burgesses

Warr' Burg.' To the Right Honorable and others the Commissioners sitting
att the Mayors Parlour on Munday the 23rd day of September 1695 by
vertue of an Act of Parliament for the Rebuilding the Town of Warwick,
etc.

The Peticion[1] of the Mayor, Aldermen and Burgesses of the Borough of
Warwick, Sheweth:
That the Mayor, Aldermen and Burgesses of this Borough are seized of the
toft whereon stood the house wherein lately dwelt Thomas Gibbs adjoyning to the house of Mr Tomkins scituate in the High Street, that Mr Tomkins hath made and putt out windows in the side wall next to and lookeing
into the said toft, that there were never any windows in the said wall where
they are now putt, which they conceive will be a great prejudice and injury
to the rebuilders of the said Corporacion house.
Your Peticioners therefore humbly pray the said Mr Tomkins may be summon'd to appear in this Court to answere the contents of this peticion, and
if it shall appear that he hath putt up lights where noe lights were before,
he may be compell'd by Order of this Court to stopp up the same. And your
Peticioners shall ever pray, etc.

Petition of William Holmes, brickmaker

To the Rt Honorable and others the Commissioners sitting att the Mayors
Parlour on Munday the 30th day of September 1695 by vertue of an Act of
Parliament for Rebuilding the Town of Warwick, etc.

The Humble Peticion of William Holms, brickmaker, Sheweth:
That your Peticioner is tenant to a certain peice of ground called Dorcans
Closes[2] adjoyning to the Pigwells, whereon he now maketh bricks and
tyles, and have noe way to bring the same in to this Borough, but through a
lane which is now very much out of repaire, and proves not onely prejudiciall to your Peticioner (by reason noe waggon or carts will come that way

---

[1] Preceded by 'Humble' struck through.
[2] These words were added later in a space left for them.

to bring the same) butt allsoe to those who are undertakers of buildings in the said Borough, who are forced to keep back their work for want of the same, your Peticioner haveing spoke with severall of the inhabitants who have right of common there, they are willing to grant a way soe long as the same continues common,[1] except John Prichard who is not willing thereto, tho' your Peticioner offers and is willing to allow reasonable sattisfaccion for the same.

Your Peticioner therefore humbly prays he may be allow'd to bring his said bricks and tiles through the said Pigwells by order of this Court, and your Peticioner shall ever pray, etc.

William Holmes

Petition of Judith Dunn, widow

War' Bor'. To the Rt Honourable and others the Commissioners sitting at the Mayors Parlour on Monday the 7th day of October 1695 by virtue of an Act of Parliament for rebuilding the Town of Warwick, etc.

The humble Petition of Judith Dunn, widow, against Thomas Dadley, Humbly Sheweth:
That your Peticioner having sold a messuage to Thomas Dadley of this Borough, butcher, excepting and reserving to her self one chamber in the said messuage, for her life, and that by agreement between the parties, before the late fire in which the said messuage was burnt down, your said Petitioner was [to] have twenty shillings per annum for her right to the said chamber, payable by 4 quarterly payments.
Your Peticioner therefore prays the summons of this Court, to summon the said Thomas Dadley to appear in this Court to answer the contents of this petition and that shee may receive and bee allowed what this Court shall thinke just and reasonable for her interest in the said messuage, and in proportion to her damage, and your Petitioner shall ever pray——.

Petition of Edward Heath

War' Bur'. To the Rt Honorable and others the Commissioners sitting at the Mayors Parlour on Monday the 7th day of October 1695 by virtue of an Act of Parliament for Rebuilding the Town of Warwick, etc.

The humble Petition of Edward Heath of the said Borough, gent., Humbly Sheweth:
That your Petitioner being seis'd of a certain tenement before the late fire, standing and beeing in the Jury Street adjoyning or very neer to St Peters, or the Eastgate Chappell, the said tenement, without the consent, and

---

[1] Part of the Pigwells Common may have been lammas land.

against the good will of your Petitioner, was untiled, and the timber frame cutt down by the order and directions of William Johnson, Dr of Physick, and assistance of Nicholas Paris,[1] and your Petitioner conceiving the said damage by defacing and pulling down the said tenement, occasioned by the pretence of stopping the progress of the said fire, which never came within the distance of 10 or 12 houses of the same, to bee within the cognisance of this Court,

Your Petitioner therefore humbly prays the summons of this Court, to summon the said William Johnson and Nicholas Paris[2] to appear in this Court of Judicature to answer the contents of this petition, and that this Court will award such satisfaction for the said damage (which your Petitioner will prove by the oaths of substantial and honest workemen, to bee neer the value of forty pounds) as shall bee most just and reasonable, and your Petitioner shall ever pray, etc.

Edward Heath

Petition of Thomas Watts, apothecary

To the Rt Honorable and others the Commissioners sitting att the Mayors Parlour on Munday the 11th day of October 1695

The Humble Peticion of Thomas Watts of this Borough, apothecary, Sheweth:

That your Peticioner being seized of a messuage scituate in the High Pavement within this Borough (burnt down by the late fire and since rebuilt againe), that Thomas Dadley being landlord of the house next adjoyning to your Peticioners hath placed a gutter on the same which will prove very prejudiciall to your Peticioner by throwing the raine (which in the time of wett weather will fall into the same) into your Peticioners backside, which will be a great prejudice to your Peticioner.

Your Peticioner therefore humbly prays a view of the same by this Court, and that Thomas Dadley may be by order of this Court compelled to prevent the same as this Court shall think fitt. And your Peticioner shall ever pray, etc.

Petition of Thomas Tippin, cutler

Warr' Burg' in Com' Warr'. To the Rt Honorable and others the Commissioners sitting at the Court of Record held at the Mayors Parlour on Munday the 14th day of October 1695 by vertue of an Act of Parliament for Rebuilding the Towne of Warwick, etc.

[1] 'and . . . Paris' interlineated over a caret.
[2] 'and Nicholas Paris' interlineated over a caret.

The humble Peticion of Thomas Tippin of the Borough aforesaid, cutler, Sheweth:

That William Cook of London, apothecary, is seized of an estate of inheritance of and in the toft of a messuage or tenement late scituate, standing and being on the south side of the street call'd the High Pavement in the Borough aforesaid, adjoyning on the west side thereof to one other messuage of him the said William Cook late in the possession of Richard Hands, baker, and on the east side to the late messuage of Mrs Dorothy Weale, widow. That your Peticioner was tenant in the said messuage burnt down by the late fire within this Borough att the time of the said fire, and haveing been at great charge in repaire of the same, your Peticioner will be a great sufferer unless relieved by this honorable Court. That the said William Cook is unwilling to rebuild the said house or discharge your Peticioner of the arrears of rent and the growing rent since the fire.

Your Peticioner therefore humbly prays that he may be discharged of the said arrears and growing rent, and that for a valuable consideracion such as [to] this Court shall seem reasonable, paid or secured to be paid to the said William Cook for the toft whereon stood the above mencioned messuage, he the said Peticioner may be admitted to rebuild the said messuage on the said toft and the same may be decreed to him and his heirs by this honorable Court. And your Peticioner shall ever pray, etc.

Petition of Richard Hands, baker

Warr' Burg' in Com' Warr'. To the Rt Honorable and others the Commissioners sitting att the Court of Record held at the Mayors Parlour on Munday the 14th day of October 1695 by vertue of an Act of Parliament for the Town of Warwick, etc.

The humble Peticion of Richard Hands of the Borough aforesaid, baker, Sheweth:

That William Cook of London, apothecary, is seized of an estate of inheritance of and in the toft of a messuage or tenement late scituate standing and being on the south side of the street called the High Pavement or High Street in the Borough aforesaid, adjoyning on the west side thereof to the late messuage of Mr Edmund Wilson, and on the east side to a late messuage in the possession of Thomas Tippin, cutler. That your Peticioner was tennant for term of years in the said messuage burnt down by the late fire within this Borough att the time of the said fire, and that haveing laid out considerable summs in repaireing and emproveing the said messuage and makeing it fitt for his trade, your Peticioner will be a great sufferer unless relieved by this honorable Court. That the said William Cook is unwilling to rebuild the said house and discharge and acquitt your Peticioner of the arrear of rent since the said fire and the growing rent.

Your Peticioner therefore humbly prays that he may be discharged of the said arrears of rent and growing rent since the said fire, and that for a valuable consideracion (such as to this Court shall seem reasonable) paid or secured to be paid to the said William Cooke for the toft whereon stood the above mencioned messuage, he the said Peticioner may be admitted to rebuild the said messuage on the said toft and the same may be decreed to him and his heirs by this honorable Court. And your Peticioner shall pray, etc.

Petition of William Savage of Tachbrook

Warr' Burg'. To the Rt Honorable and others the Commissioners sitting att the Mayor's Parlour on Munday the 11th day of November 1695,

The Humble Peticion of William Savage of Tachbrook, gent., Sheweth: That your Peticioner did buy of Mr Boyce of Welsborne, a certaine toft or parcell of burnt ground lying and being in the High Street within the said Borough whereon before the late fire stood a messuage late in the occupacion of John Bradshaw. That your Peticioner hath since the said fire built a house thereon. That Mr Fulk Weale being owner of the house next adjoyning in the High Street on the west side thereof hath putt up a gutter of lead over the back dore of your Peticioner's house, which in time of wett weather will throw the rain into the same, which will prove very prejudicially to your Peticioner. And alsoe your Peticioner humbly sheweth that he hath alsoe built a wall with brick and stone on the back part of his ground, which wall parts the backside of the said Mr Weale and the backside of your Peticioner. That Mr Weale laies claime to part of the said wall. Your Peticioner therefore humbly prays that a view of the said gutter may be had and reported to this Court by the jury this day impanelled and the dispute in controversie between your Peticioner and the said Mr Weale concerning the said gutter and the said wall may be by them determined, and your Peticioner shall ever pray, etc.

Petition of William Tarver

The Humble Petition of William Tarver of this Bor'
Humbly Sheweth
That your said Pettitioner haveing severall houses burnt downe in the late fire which paid a cheife rent to Wm Bolton Esq., Lord of the Manour, and are not as yett rebuilt, your Pettitioner humbly prayes to bee reliev'd by this Honorable Court from the payment of the same for such time as they shall

thinke meet and aportion the rent for the future, and your Pettitioner shall ever pray, etc.[1]

Wm. Tarver

Petition of John Parker, mason

Warr' Burg'. To the Rt Honorable and others the Commissioners sitting at the Mayors Parlour on Munday the 23rd day of December 1695
The humble Peticion of John Parker, mason, Sheweth:
That your Peticioner was about June last employed by Solomon Bray to work mason work and by agreement he was to allow your Peticioner and his son fifteen shillings by the week for every week as they should be by him employ'd. That he hath paid your Peticioner severall weeks wages att the same rate according to agreement, and that there remains now due to your Peticioner eight pounds three shillings and three pence according to the rate above said, which summ the said Solomon Bray refuses to pay to your Peticioner.
Therefore your Peticioner humbly prays that the said Solomon Bray may be sent for into Court to answer the same, and that your Peticioner may obtaine an order of Court where by hee may be compelled to pay the said summ, it being truly and justly due to him. And your Peticioner shall ever pray, etc.

Petition of Thomas Clemens, baker

Warr' Burg'. To the Rt Honorable and others the Commissioners sitting att the Mayors Parlour on Munday the 23rd day of December 1695
The peticion of Thomas Clemens, baker, Sheweth:
That your Peticioner hath lately sold a house (erected since the late fire) standing in the Newstreet within this Borough, to one James Bullymore for above the summ of one hundred pounds on condition hee may bee made a freeman of this borough.[2] That the said house will cost the purchaser before the same is finished nere fourty pounds more. That hee hath more ground to rebuild, which hee is not able to effect, unless hee sell part of what hee hath already built.[3]
Wherefore your Peticioner humbly prays the said James Bullymore may be admitted a freman of the said Borough and the purchaser also prays the same himself, to the end he may execute his trade within the said Borough without molestacion of any of the freemen now liveing in the same, and your Peticioner shall ever pray, etc.

[1] Endorsed: 'Nov. 11th 1695, Mr Tarver, chefe rent 16s. 8d.'
[2] 'on condition ... borough' interlineated in another hand.
[3] 'that hee ... built' inserted in a space in the same other hand.

Petition of William Cockbill of Barford, mercer

To the Rt Honorable and others the Commissioners or Judges appointed by an Act of Parliament for the Rebuilding the Town of Warwick, etc., sitting att the Mayors Parlour on Munday the 30th day of December 1695. The Humble Peticion of William Cockbill of Barford, mercer, Sheweth: That Mr Thomas Stratford of this Borough and Mary his daughter, being seized of a certaine messuage or tenement scituate in the High Pavement within the said Borough, did for the summ of fifty pounds paid to the said Thomas and Mary Stratford att two payments, on the 27th day of March 1693 mortgage the same with the appurtenances thereunto belonging unto your Peticioner for the term of five hundred years, with this provisoe, that if he the said Thomas or the said Mary Stratford should pay or cause to be paid unto your Peticioner the above mencioned summ of £50 as the same is therein appointed to be paid, that then the said mortgage deed to be void and of none effect, the said messuage being burnt down by the late dreadfull fire and the said mortgage not discharged.

Your Peticioner humbly prays he may have the benefitt of the toft of the said house and what other recompence out of the charity monyes this Court shall think fitt to allow for the future, and your Peticioner shall ever pray, etc.

Memorandum of an Agreement between Thomas Spenser and Thomas Lea

Memorandum February the 20th 1695[/6]. Then it was agreed by Thomas Spenser of the Borough of Warwick, yeoman, and Thomas Lea his son in law of the said Borough, flaxman, that as to the ground whereon a tenement lately stood consumed by the late great fire in Warwick in a certaine place or street there leading from the New Street towards the pillory, wherein Francis Woodhams did dwell att the time of the said fire, shall be rebuilt by them the said Thomas Spenser and Thomas Lea and that Thomas Lea shall have the rents, issues and profitts thereof during the naturall life of the said Thomas Spenser, the said Thomas Lea paying unto him yearly during his naturall life the summe of fourty shillings, and setling the same, by a decree from the Court appointed by a late Act of Parliament for the rebuilding of the said Towne of Warwick consumed by the said late fire for the payment of the same yearly annuity, on the said Thomas Lea and Sarah his now wife, daughter of the said Thomas Spenser, during the naturall life of them and the longer liver of them, and after their decease on the heires of the said Thomas Lea for ever. And it is hereby also agreed that the said Thomas Lea shall have all the Charity money that shall be due as to the loss and rebuilding the said house. Witnesse their hands the day and yeare first above written: the marke of Thomas Spenser.[1] Thomas Lea. Witnesse: Thomas Masters. Wm Roe.

Petition of William Holmes, brickmaker

Warr' Burg'. To the Rt Honorable and others the Commissioners or Judges appointed by an Act of Parliament for the Rebuilding the Towne of Warwick, etc., sitting att the Mayors Parlour on Munday the 23 day of March anno domini 1695/6
The humble Peticion of William Holmes, brick maker, Sheweth:
That your Peticioner hath lately bought a piece of ground in the Sheep-street on which before the late fire stood the house call'd the Black Raven, then in possession of Thomas Arps and adjoyning to the Pibble Lane, that your Peticioner hath clear'd the rubbish off the said ground, and being willing to begin to rebuild on the said ground,
Your Peticioner humbly prays the said ground may be sett out, and also the Pibble Lane thereto adjoyning that your Peticioner may begin to rebuild the same; And your Peticioner shall ever pray, etc.

Petition of William Holmes, carpenter, and Edward Reading, mason

To the Rt Honorable and others the Commissioners sitting att the Mayors Parlour on Munday the 13th of Aprill 1696
The humble Peticion of Wm Holmes, carpenter, and Edward Reading, mason, Sheweth:
That your Peticioners[2] were imploy'd in the rebuilding the house of Wm Perks, baker, and did article with him for the same, that your Peticioners have perform'd the same according to the said articles and have built an addition since to the said house, that the said Wm Perks refused to pay your Peticioner for their said work according to their demands, but did agree that it should be referr'd to 2 men the one to be chosen by your Peticioner and the other by the said Wm Perks. That the same was referr'd to two men by them chosen, that one of the referrees did value your Peticioners work att seven pounds 10s., the other att £5, both valued att less then your Peticioners work is worth, notwithstanding that, your Peticioner is willing to leave themselve to this Court, the said Wm Perks refuseing to pay your Peticioners any money.
    Your Peticioner humbly prays the said Wm Perks may be summon'd to appear and answere the same, And your Peticioners shall ever pray, etc.

---

[1] His mark is in the form of a capital T. 'Thomas Lea' is a signature.
[2] Altered from 'Peticioner'. There is some confusion between singular and plural in this petition.

Petition of some of the principal sufferers

Warwick. April 27th 1696

We, whose names are hereunto subscribed, some of the most principall sufferers by the late fire in Warwick, being desireous that all the clipt and course monies which are received upon the account of the Warwick brief, by the Receivers in London, and are now remaineing in their hands, should be disposed of to the best advantage, doe hereby humbly on the behalf of our selves and the rest of the sufferers, desire the Commicioners and Trustees of the said brief monies, that they will order the said Receivers, Sir Francis Child and Mr Richard Hoare, goldsmiths, to pay the same into his Majestys Receipt of Exchequer on the safest and most advantagious funds, or what other tearms they in their judgments shall think most fitt, whereby the said sufferers may be repaid the same againe, and not be loosers thereby.

Devereux Whadcock, Mayor	Nicholas Paris
William Tarver	Joseph Ainge
Edward Heath	John Jarvis
Joseph Blissett	John Smith
Robert Blissett	John Bradshaw
George Webb	Edward Norton
	Thomas Watts

Petition of Thomas Mayo of Rugby

To the Rt Honorable and others the Commissioners appointed by an Act of Parliament for the Rebuilding the Towne of Warwick, etc., sitting att the Mayors Parlour on Munday the 4th day of May 1696

The humble Peticion of Thomas Mayo of Rughby, yeoman, Sheweth:

That your Peticioner did on the 16th day of September last preferr his Peticion into this Court, thereby setting forth that your Peticioner had a mortgage upon two certaine tenements[1] standing before the late fire nere the Joysts Poole, and that one Edward Aston had built a house on the ground whereon one of the said tenements stood; but your Peticioner haveing better view'd the ground of the said 2 tenements that were mortgaged to your Peticioner and finding that the said Edward Aston hath not rebuilt on any part of the said ground, humbly prays the same may be decreed to him by this Court in consideracion of his said mortgage, whereby the said ground may be vested and settled in your Peticioner and his heirs freed from all incumbrances. And your Peticioner shall ever pray, etc.

---

[1] Preceded by 'messuages' struck out.

Petition of William Smith, shoemaker

To the Rt Honorable and others the Commissioners appointed by an Act of Parliament for the Rebuilding the Town of Warwick, etc., sitting at the Mayors Parlour on Munday the 4th day of May 1696

The humble Peticion of William Smith of the Borough of Warwick, shoemaker, Sheweth:

That your Peticioner was before and at the time of the late fire seized of a messuage or tenement scituate lying and being in the New Street within this Borough, which said messuage was burnt downe by the said fire; that your Peticioner hath since rebuilt the same; that one Richard Gibbard of this Borough hath arrested your Peticioner upon an accion of trespass, he pretending that your Peticioner hath made an encrochment upon building upon some part of his ground; that your Peticioner is ready to make it appear he has not made any encrochment upon his ground but hath built upon his own ground;[1] that your Peticioner being wrongfully arrested and conceiveing the same to be within the cognisance of this Court according to an Act of Parliament for Rebuilding the Towne of Warwick, etc.,

humbly prays the summons of this Court to summon the said Richard Gibbard to appear in this Court to answer the contents of this Peticion. And your Peticioner shall ever pray, etc.

Petition of William Holmes, brickmaker

War' Burg'. To the Rt Honorable and others the Commissioners appointed by an Act of Parliament for the Rebuilding the Town of Warwick, etc., sitting att the Mayors Parlour on Munday the 25th day of May 1696,

The humble Peticion of Wm Holmes, brickmaker, Sheweth:

That your Peticioner was on Munday the 11th day of November last ordered by this Court to leave four pounds in the hands of William Bolton, Esq., as a pledge for the indemnifying John Prichard for a way through the Pigwells from the Common; that your Peticioner did enjoy the said way whilst the same continued common, the said monys still remaineing in the hand of the said Wm Bolton.

Your Peticioner prays the said Pigwells may be view'd by such person or persons whom this Court shall think fitt to appoint to view the same, and the damage done to the same (if any) may be reported to this Court, that your Peticioner may have the benifitt of the residue of his money. Your Peticioner alsoe prays he may be allowed for his ground taken away from the Black Raven to enlarge the Sheepstreet, and alsoe that he may be admitted purchasor of a certaine peice of ground lying on the back side of

---

[1] 'own ground' interlineated above 'old foundacions' struck out.

the Black Raven ground, purchased by your Peticioner.[1] And your Peticioner shall ever pray, etc.

Petition of John Burton, innkeeper

To the Rt Honorable and others the Commissioners appointed by an Act of Parliament for the Rebuilding the Town of Warwick, etc., sitting att the Mayor's Parlour on Munday the 25th day of May 1696,

The humble Peticion of John Burton, inkeeper, Sheweth:

That your Peticioner was before the late fire in possession of a messuage or tenement scituate in the Markett Place nere the pillory, which said messuage was burnt down by the said fire; that the same did belong then unto Thomas Lean, your Peticioner's brother in law, as the ground of the same now doth, but if the said Thomas Lean should dye haveing noe issue, then the said ground would of right belong unto your Peticioner's wife and her sisters equally to be divided betwixt them; that the said Thomas Lean before the late fire went a soldier into Flanders and is not yett againe return'd; that your Peticioner hath rebuilt the said messuage and hath been at a great charge in rebuilding the same; that your Peticioner being willing to give a valuable consideracion for the ground whereon the said messuage now stands,

Humbly prays a price thereof may be sett by this Honorable Court, and that the said ground and the house now rebuilt thereupon, may be assured to your Peticioner and his heirs, and your Peticioner prays he may be allow'd for the ground taken away in the front to enlarge the street; your Peticioner alsoe humbly prays he may be allowed to build his gate house in the same place it formerly stood, and to hold the same with the same priviledge (paying the lord's rent) as he did before the said fire, And your Peticioner shall ever pray, etc.

Petition of William Lattimor and Edward Bloxwich

To the Rt Honorable and other the Commissioners appointed by an Act of Parliament for Rebuilding the Town of Warwick, etc., sitting att the Mayor's Parlour on Munday the 1st day of June 1696.

the Humble Peticion of William Lattimor and Edward Bloxwich against William Holmes, brickmaker, Sheweth:

That your Peticioners have articled with the said William Holmes for makeing 200,000 of tiles;[2] that the said William Holmes hath covenanted to pay your Peticioners 6s. per thousand for the same after burnt and the said number delivered to the said William Holmes, he the said William Holmes

---

[1] Followed by 'containing in length about' struck out.
[2] 'tiles' interlineated over 'bricks' struck out.

finding fuel for burning the same; that the said William Holmes was to pay to your Peticioners for their weekly subsistence soe much moneys as they should reasonably require for the said work; that your Peticioners are hinder'd from goeing on to perform their said agreement by reason the said William Holmes will not gett cole or fuel to burn the said tyles; that the said William Holmes will not pay your Peticioners their wages for their said work according to the said agreement, but refuses soe to doe.

Your Peticioners therefore humbly pray the said William Holmes may be summoned to appeare here and answer the same and be made to pay your Peticioners according to the said articles, that your Peticioners may thereby subsist, and that they may be disharged of the covenants therein contained. And your Peticioners shall ever pray, etc.

Petition of Elizabeth Martin, widow

Warr' Burg'. To the Rt Honorable and others the Commissioners or Judges appointed by an Act of Parliament for the Rebuilding the Towne of Warwick, etc., sitting att the Mayor's Parlour on Munday the 15th day of June 1696.
the humble Peticion of Elizabeth[1] Martin of this Borough, widow, Sheweth:
That your Peticioner was before the late fire seized for the term of her natural life of and in a certaine messuage scituate within this Borough, in a certaine place or lane leading from the pillory, unto a lane call'd the Pipple Lane, between a messuage then in the possession of Charles Emes on the one side thereof, and a messuage of John Burton, inkeeper, on the other side thereof, which said messuage was totally burnt downe by the said fire; that the loss of the said messuage was given in att £213, but was reduced (the value of the ground being taken off) to £170, for which your Peticioner hath received £21 5s., being 2s. 6d per lib. for the same out of the charity monys given for the relief of the sufferers by the said fire; that Richard Martin of London, your Peticioner's son, demands to know of your Peticioner, what she hath received for the loss of the said house, and your Peticioner doth veryly believe the said Richard Martin hath a design to sue her for all or part of the said charity monys, to vex and put her to a great charge. Your peticioner therefore submitting her self to this honorable Court,
Humbly prayeth the said Court will order the ground of the said messuage to be sold, or that the value of the said ground may be consider'd, and the interest of your Peticioner's life in the premises may be settled and determined by order of this Court, soe that the said Richard Martin may be bound to agree, and stand to such order and determinacion therein as the

---

[1] 'Elizabeth' inserted above 'Mary' struck out.

said Court shall think most meet, and that by such order your Peticioner may be sav'd harmless of and from all and all manner of pretences, claime and demand of him the said Richard Martin to the said charity moneys already received by your Peticioner, or any part thereof. And your Peticioner shall ever pray, etc.

[Endorsed] Mrs Martins peticion against her son Richard Martin att the Sign of the Bell in White Fryer Lane nere the Temple gate.[1]

Reports of Thatched and Timber Buildings[2]

An Account of all and every the buildings and outhouses parcell of or belonging to any house fronting the remaining parts of the Castle Street, the Jury Street, the High Street and the Markett Place, taken the 16th day of June 1696.[3]

Castle Street
Mr Oliver Fleetwood 2 large stables, a hovell and the pigstyes.
Thomas Clifton a leantoe and a barne.[4]
John Fowkes 2 barnes, a hovell and the pigstye.
William Fowkes sen. a barne.[4]
Richard Crooke a small hovell.
Edward Ley a leantoe.
Samuel Hurd a barne and pigstyes.
Thomas Abbotts a hovell.
Samuell Acocke a hovell.
Mrs Lane a stable.
Richard Wigley a malthouse, 2 stables and a hovell.
George Watts a barne and leantoe.
Mr White a stable.
Widow Chesley parte of a house, a barne and pigstyes.
Mrs Smith a hovell lately set up since the fire.
Mrs Paine part of a hovell.
Moses Holloway a pigsty. ⎫
Mr Horton a stable and pigstyes.[4] ⎬ These outhouses are at the upper end of Brittaine Lane and
Mr Chesley part of a hovell and pigstyes. ⎭ belong to their house in Castle Street

---

[1] In London.
[2] Note that some thatched buildings appear in both lists.
[3] Endorsed 'Order about thatch'd buildings, etc.'
[4] These entries are marked with a cross, the meaning of which is obscure.

Jury Street

Thomas Newsham Esq. a stable.[1]

Stephen Glendall 2 stables and a leantoe.

Richard Hands a little barne.

Mr Webb parte of a barne.[1]

Timothy Norbury a barn

Mr Charles Hickes a barne.

Samuell Barber a stable.[1]

High Street

Mrs Bunter a barne and a hutt.[1]

Richard Bromley a hutt.

George Harris a hovell.

Nicholas Morrell a stable.

Mr Combee 2 barnes.

William Roe parte of a stable.

William Lane a barne.[1]

Mr Fish a back building thatcht with broome lately.

William White a barne and pigstyes.

Widow Bucknall a barne and leantoe.

Thomas Slye a stable, a hovell and a pigstye.

Widow Farr a barne.

An Accompt of what buildings have been built since the fire with timber and pav'd up with brick.

In the **High Street** in the yards or backsides there

A barne in the tenure of Thomas Russell.

A barne in the tenure of George Harris.

A barne in the tenure of Mr Parquotts, currier.

Richard Hands, joyner, a barne.

Mr Chesley part of a stable.

Widow Dadley a bay of building built up before the Act came out; since, a pigsty and a house of office.

Jury Street

Thomas Wall a bay of building built up before the Act.

Church Street

Mr John Jarvis his buildings along the church yard, the greatest part built before the Act but some built since.

Mr Fish some back buildings, some built before the Act and some since.

---

[1] These entries are marked with a cross, the meaning of which is obscure.

Sheepes Street
Mr Watts some buildings but built up before the Act.
Mr Williams some back building built since the Act.

Markett Place
Timothy Simpkins a stable and a barne.
John Langton a stable.
Benjamin Powers his house built before the Act.
Henry Smith a slaughterhouse.
Widow Smith a barne built before the Act.

An account of all and every the Thatch Buildings within the Borough of Warwick taken the 16th day of June anno domini 1696[1]

West Street Ward
John Milward his house & barne.
Richard Walker a barne.
Mathew Ebb a hovell.
Richard Bromley a barne.
John Brookes a barne and stable.
John Geadon a hovell.
Edward Deacon parte of his house and a barne.
William Lucas two barnes.
Miles Redding two barnes and parte of a house.
Widow Reppingale a barne.
Thomas Griffin a barne.
Henry Winne a barne.
Widow Cowper a barne.
Widow Southam a barne.
Mr Faulkner a barne and leantoe.
William Warwick a barne.
Thomas Collins jun. a barne.
William Burch his house.
Henry Harper a barne.
Samuel Man his mill house and barne and tanhouse.
John Hadley a barne.
John Squires a barne.
Mr Savage a long barne and a hovell.

---

[1] Endorsed 'Robbinson's account of thatch'd houses'.

Mr Watson his tanhouse, a hovell and barne.
William Warner 2 barnes and a hovell.
Timothy Smith his tanhouses and barne.
Nicholas Faulkner a barne.
John Blason a barne.
Thomas Free a barne.
Widow Blackwell part of her house and a leantoe.
Richard Beards a leantoe.
William Lea a hovell.
John Edwards a barne.
Job Bench a hovell.
John Hawkes a barne.
John Jeacocks a hovell.
Job Burch a hovell.
Widow Walding a barne.
Thomas Chinne part of his house and a barne.
Richard Meades a pigstye.
Francis Dod a barne.
John Walding a barne.
Widow Trimnell a house.
John Gardner a house.
John Miles a house.
Widow Perkins a house.
Thomas Mason a house.
Mr Williams a barne in tenure Richard Walker.
Mr John Rogers a barne.
Thomas Hickes a barne and worke house.
William Allen his house.
Widow Coale a house.

Fryar Lane
Thomas Hyron a house.
Arthur Henley a house.
Richard Rawbone a house and barne.
Edward Newland a house.
John Lawrence a house—lately erected.
John Corser a house.
Edward Wilkins a house.
Abraham Curtis a house.
Henry Beesley a house.
William Shakeshaffe a house.
Thomas Roberts a barne.
David Griffin a brewhouse.

Widow Wilson a house.
Thomas Perry a house.
Widow Toms a house and barne.

Saunder his Rowe
John Dadley a house and barne.
Widow Clemens her house.
Joseph Rands his house.
Margarett Bromley her house.
Widow Sadler her house.
Thomas Smith his house.
Richard Lowe his house.
William Sabin his house.
William Coles his house.
Mr Smithes stables.
Richard Veale his house.
Samuel Hill his house.
Richard Yates his house.
Praise Tiddenham his house.
Widow Cornill her house.
John Raning and Richard Hixson a house.
Thomas Claridge his house.
William Huse his house.

Highstreet Ward
Thomas Russell 2 barnes, a dary house and a hovell.
John Glover his house.
Thomas Hickes 2 barnes in the back lane.[1]
George Harris a barne in the back lane.
Thomas Masters a barne there.
Richard Kerby a slaughter house.
Thomas Dadley a barne there.
The Corporacion barnes.
Robert Bromley part of his house and a barne.
John Phillips his house.
Widow Low and her sons a house.
Mrs Bunter a barne and a hutt.
Richard Bromley a hutt.
George Harris a hovell.
Nicholas Morrell a stable.
Mr Combee 2 barnes.
Mr Savage a barne.

[1] These entries are marked with a cross, the meaning of which is obscure.

Markett Place Ward

Thomas Rud a house.

John Dale a barne.

Mathew Heyward a hovell.

Peter Milward jun. a barne.

Peter Milward sen. a barne.

Job Burt a barne.

Thomas Wiseman a leantoe.

William Roe part of a stable.

William Lane a barne.

Widow Farre a barne.

William Evitts a barne.

Mr Fish a back building thatch with broom—new built.

John Wescott a barne.

George Coplin a leantoe.

Mr Henry Heath a barne.

Thomas Right a house.

John Crosse a barne.

Robert Farre a house.

Edward Bench a house.

Ralph Poulton a house.

William Bromfeild a house.

William White a barne and pigstye.

Thomas Slye a stable, barne and hovell and a pigstye.

Widow Bucknall a barne and leantoe.

Edward Wall 3 barnes.

John Green a house.

William Grey a barne.

Richard Hancox a hovell.

Thomas Smith a slaughter house.

Cocksparrow Hall

William Toms his house.

Thomas Eyres his house and barne.

Widow Archer her house.

William Ley sen. his house.

Elizabeth Bromley her house and barne.

William Squires his house.

Widow Wedge her house.

John Sharley his house.

John Miles his house.

Samuel Burford his tyle hovells.

Thomas Rogers a barne and hovell.

Saltisford Ward

James Bratherton his house and leantoe.
Richard Hurst his house.
Joseph Cakebread his house.
William Overton a house and a barne.
Edward Sheppard a house.
Thomas Prescott a barne.
John Smith a barne.
William Wilson a barne and leantoe.
William Smith his house.
Widow Varney her house.
Widow Baker her house.
Henry Sumners his house.
Thomas Cowper his house.
William Shakeshaffe his house.
Richard Ward his house.
Job Juckes a leantoe.
John King his house and barne.
Jacob Dunckley his house.
Richard Vickers his house and barne.
Clement Price his barne.
Clement Gibbins his house.
Robert Harris a barne.
Thomas Chaplin a hovell.
Martin Taylor a barne.
John Kerby a barne.
George Hands a barne and leantoe.
Nicholas Slyer his house.
John Ingoldsby his house.
Widow Woodcok her house and barne.
Trubshaw Swarback his house.
Francis Powers, Mr Hadlyes barnes.
Thomas Hands his barne and hovell.
Widow Dale her house.
Widow Sharley her house.
Thomas Lines his house.
Richard Hadley a worke house.
William Tranter his barnes and hovell.
Mr Colemore, Sir Henry Puckerings barne.
Thomas Brisco his house.
Widow West her barnes.
Samuel Clemens his leantoe.
Nicholas Rothwell 2 barnes and 2 leantoes in Saltisford.

John Manwhinick his barne and gate house.
Francis Powers barnes and stables also Mr Hadleys.
William Phillips[1] a leantoe.
Widow Butler a barne.
Nathaniel Cowper a leantoe.
Richard Harris part of a house.
Richard Mountford jun. a barne and leantoe.
Benjamin Michell a barne and leantoe.
Widow Barnes part of her house.
Thomas Hoggins his house.
Widow Bird her house and barne.
John Bidle his barne.
Widow Mills her barne.
Henry Mellowes part of his house and barne.
John Foster his barne.
Widow Whood her barne.
John Bromfield his house.
Widow Biddle her house.
Henry Styles his house.
Thomas Lea his house.
Mr Lingham a barne and a hovell.
Isabell Edes his[2] tenant part of a little house.
Job Roades a leantoe.
J. Meadowes a leantoe put up and thatcht since the fire.
Thomas Gazey a barne and leantoe.
Henry Garrett part of a house, a stable and pigstye.
Henry Clemens a hovell.
William Heacock a house.
Richard Hadley a house.
Robert Taylor a hovell.

Jury Street
Thomas Newsham, Esq., a stable.
Stephen Glendall two stables and a leantoe.[3]
Richard Hands a little barne.[3]
Mr Web parte of a barne.
Thomas Eedes a barne on the Backhills.
Timothy Norbury a barne.[3]
Mr Charles Hickes a barne.[3]

[1] 'William Phillips' interlineated above 'Stephen Bradley' struck out.
[2] Presumably Mr Lingham's.
[3] These entries are marked with a cross, the meaning of which is obscure.

Thomas Clifton a barne in Vineyard Lane.[1]
Samuel Barber a stable.[1]

Castle Street
Mr Fleetwood 2 large stables, a hovell and pigstyes.[1]
Thomas Clifton a leantoe at his house.[1]
John Fowkes 2 barnes, a hovell and pigstyes.
William Fowkes sen. a barne.[1]
Richard Crooke a small hovell.[1]
Edward Ley a leantoe.[1]
Samuel Hurd a barne and pigstyes.[1]
Thomas Abbotts a hovell.[1]
Samuell Acock a hovell.[1]
Mrs Lane a stable.
Richard Wigley a malthouse, 2 stables and a hovell.[1]
George Watts a barne and leantoe in Castle Street.
Mr White a stable.[1]
Widow Chesley part of a dwelling house and a barne and pigstyes.

Brittaine Lane
Mrs Smith a hovell and barne.
Mrs Paine parte of a hovell.
Moses Holloway a pigstye.
Mr Horton[2] a stable and pigstye.
Mr Chesley part of a hovell and pigstyes.
Mr Whadcock a barne.
Job Bench a house.
Widow West a house and pigsty.
George Taylor a house.
Richard Job a house.
Widow Cox a house.
Thomas Parsons a house.
Thomas Lucas a house.
Edward Scott a house.[3]
Thomas Hunt a house.[3]
Samuel Paris a barne.[3]
William Claridge a house and pigsty.
Richard Asplin a house and pigsty.
Francis Claridge a house.
Job Paddy a house.

[1] These entries are marked with a cross, the meaning of which is obscure.
[2] 'Horton' interlineated above 'Bradshaw'[?] struck out.
[3] These three are bracketed together and marked 'built since the fire' struck through.

Job Crooke a house and pigsty.
James Perkins a house.
Thomas Lea a flax barne.
Widow Hopkins a house.
Giles Elbridge a house.
David Phelps a hovell and 2 bay of barning.
Widow Perkes a house and leantoe.
Thomas Parsons jun. a house and leantoe.
Widow Bromley a house and barne.

ST NICHOLAS PARISH
Smiths Street
William Bolton, Esq., 2 barnes on the Backhills.
The house wherin Widow Moody lately lived 2 hovells.
Widow Moody a barne and hovell and leantoes.
John Hope a little barne and leanto.
Mr Young 2 barnes, part of a malting house and a stable.
Edward Warner about 4 bay of barning.
Benjamin Hope a barne.
Widow Smith a leantoe.
John Rose a hovell.
John Richardson a hovell.
Mathew Perry a barne lately set up.
Edward Keene about 4 bay of barning.
Thomas Savage a small hovell.
Mrs Tanton about 11 bay of barning.
Edward Owen a pigsty.
Thomas Perse a house.
George Watts a leantoe.
William Rawbone about 3 bay of barning.
Joseph Burford a hovell and a pigsty.
Anne Ordoway a little barne.
Edward Dingley a pigsty.
Joseph Kerby a barne, a leantoe and a hovell.
Richard Kerby a barne, leantoes and part of a house.
Widow Ashby a large hovell.
James Harris 4 bay of barning, a pigstye and house of office.
John Williams a small hovell.
John Atkins a small hovell.

Gaolard Lane
John Moore a leantoe.
Richard Toms a leantoe.

Mary Green a leantoe.
Widow Townsend a leantoe.
William Gazy a house.
Edward Jephcott a pigsty.
Widow Treen a leanto.
Widow Carter a house.
Widow Tomes a house.
Widow Battarum a house.
Widow Toms a house.
Widow Clift a house.
John Dadly a house.
Thomas Griffin a barne and pigsty.

St Nicholas Church Street
Anne Corbett a house.
Joseph Farman a house.
William Pestill a house.
Thomas Willinger a house.
Thomas Crabb a house and barne.
William Watnoll a house.
Thomas Lapworth a house.
Stephan Shotteswell a house.
Widow Busby a house.
Richard Wiggs a house and leantoe.
Edward Wiggs a little barne and a leantoe.
Mr Jemmatt a barne.
John Poulton a house.
Mary Wilding a house.
William Taylor a little barne, leantoe and pigsty.
Edward Wiggs jun. a leanto.
Mr Tarver 4 barnes and a cutt end.
Mr Smith, dyer, a callander house.

Cotten End
the Honorable Francis Grevill, Esq., about 11 bay of barning.
John Tue a house and barne.
Daniel Crosse a house.
Widow Taylor a house.
John Nicholls a house and leantoe.
Goodwife Hobley a house.
Widow Allen a house.
William Cornwell a house.
John Miles a house.

John Reading a great barne and leantoe.
Widow Wignall a barne.
Old Francis a house and barne.
John Hanks a house and leantoe.
John Lapworth a house and leantoe.
Abraham Bomage[1] a barne and stable.
William Mayo about 8 bay of barning.
Mr Fox about 5 bay of barning.
Mr Makepeace about 4 bay of barning.
John Masters a house.
Isaac Bromage a barne and cutt end.
Robert Bromwell malting roomes and a gate house and barn.
William Childs a house.
John Mayo a house and leanto.
Mr Griffin about 4 bay of barning and a hovell.
Abell Toms a house.
William Tue a leanto.
Joseph Harrison a house and leanto.
John Drayton a barne, part of a barne and a hovell and another great barne and leanto.
John Cater 2 barnes, 2 leantoes and part of the house.
Henry Marcer a house and a leanto.
Widow Creed a house.
Mrs Wagstaffe greatest part of the malting roomes, 4 barnes and stables.
Mrs Weale a house of office.
Thomas Free a house.
William Green a house and a leanto.
Edward Tue a house and leanto.
Thomas Bird a house and leanto.
Thomas Ballard a house, a leanto and pigsty.
Daniel Hill a little stable.
Widow Wiggs a little leanto.
Edward Dingley sen. a little leanto.
Mr Jemmat a little house in his tenure.
Widow Hitchcox a little house.
John Redding a house and a barne.
Widow Glover a house and a barne.
Widow Whiteaway 2 barnes and a hovell.
Thomas Williams a little barne and a leanto.
John Williams sen. a house and hovell.
Widow Willis two barnes.
John Muddiman a little stable and a leanto.

[1] Probably an error for 'Bromage'.

Edward Boddington 2 small leantoes.
John Welton a dyehouse and a leanto new erected.
Henry Edwards two little barnes.
William Nicholls a little leanto.
Robert Turner a little leanto.
Mrs Martin a leanto and a hovell.
Thomas Meades a house, a little barne.
Henry Townsend a house, a little barne.
Audry Kinson a house.
John Mushin a house, a hovell and leanto.
Mr Cart a house and barne.
John Glover about 7 bay of barning and hovelling.
Mrs Tuckey a barne.
John Burch 2 hovells.
John Davis a barne and leanto.

Bridgend
Oliver Cross a hovell
John Dawes a house, a leanto and a pigstye.
William Hampe a barne.
Charles Heath about 11 bay of barning and stabling.
Nathaniel Cross about 5 bay of barning and stabling.
George Perkins a barne and leantoe.
John Barnett sen. 2 hovells.
George Wharton a house, a stable and leanto.
Benjamin Court about 3 or 4 bay of hovelling.
Humphry Dowler 2 stables, a pigsty, a shop and a leanto.
Francis Hunt a house.
William Paine a house.
Roger Langdon a house and barne.
Edward Checkley a house and leanto.
Zachary Sharp a barne and pigsty.
Rice Tirrell a house, a barne and a cuttend.
Isaac Twicross about 14 bay of barning, stabling and hovelling.
Joseph Jeffkins a house.
Giles Clifton a house.
Saunders Furnice about 10 bay of barning and hovelling.
Mr Makepeace about 6 bay of hovelling and 5 bay of barning.
William Cattell about 5 bay of barning, a hovell and a leanto.
Stephen Pidgeon a house and a leanto.
Joseph Radford a house and about 5 bay of barning.
John Russell a house and about 4 bay of barning and 2 leantoes.
John Hall a house, a hovell and leanto.

Josiah Gardner a house.
Widow Furnice a house and barne and a leanto.
Thomas Canning a house and a leanto.
John Kerby a house.
John Jordan a house and barne.
James Perkins a little barne lately erected.
John Gibbes about 14 bay of barning, etc.
Francis Hobley a house and barne.
Joseph Dingley a house.
Nathaniel Nicholls a barne.
George Tompson about 4 bay of barning.
William Farman his house and about 7 bay of barning.
Mrs Glendall a house and about 3 bay of barning and a leanto.
Robert Watts a house and about 7 bay of barning and a leanto.
Samuel Rawlins a house and a hovell.
Nicholas Tibbitts a house and a hovell.
The great Tyth Barne.
John Cross part of his house about 6 bay of building.
William Reppingale a house and a hovell.
Francis Redding a barne.
William Kerby a barne.
Ralph Wignall a house, a barne and a leanto.
John Crosse a house and a leanto.
Widow Scott a house and barne.
John Barnett part of his house and about 4 bay of barning.
John Sharp a hovell, a barne and a leanto.
John Court about 3 bay of barning.
William Glover a hovell.
Thomas Shotteswell a hovell.

Petition of William Perks, baker

Warr' Burg'. To the Rt Honorable and others the Commissioners appointed by an Act of Parliament for the Rebuilding the Town of Warwick, etc., sitting att the Mayor's Parlour on Munday the 29th day of June 1696
The Peticion of William Perks of the Borough of Warwick, baker, Sheweth: That Joseph Martin, carpenter, entered into articles with your Peticioner to build a malt house and another building thereunto adjoyning about 40 foot in length and 14 foot wide. That your Peticioner was to give the said Joseph Martin the summ of one hundred pounds for the same and alsoe timber trees and other materialls then lying upon the ground worth about £40 more. That the said Martin hath taken the said timber from your Peticioners

ground and made use of it elsewhere, but promised to work up more substantial and sound timber in its stead. That the said Martin bought other timber, brought and layd it upon the ground of Mrs Cawthern in the Sheepstreet and fram'd the same for your Peticioner's use. That your Peticioner, finding the same to be fram'd and made ready for his use, paid the said Martin about threescore pounds in part of his bargaine. That the said Martin hath left your Peticioner's work and gone off. That Joseph Fenix, carpenter, went by night and took away the said timber soe fram'd out and pretends he hath bought the same of the said Martin. That your Peticioner is ready to prove that the said timber was fram'd for his use and for that he paid his money. That one Win hath alsoe taken away other timber from the ground of Mr Archer that was laid there for your Peticioner's use. That Charles Emes hath taken from your Peticioner's ground the pediments of 3 windows belonging to your Peticioner, he pretending he hath bought the same, and also lais claime to the windows. All which materialls aforesaid your Peticioner is ready to make appeare that the same were provided for his use. That your Peticioner hath paid to the said Joseph Martin much more money than his said work will amount unto.

Your Peticioner therefore humbly prays, if the same be within the jurisdiccion of this Court, that Joseph Fenix and Charles Emes may be summoned to appear in this Court and answer the contents of this Peticion, and be made to prove the payment for the said timber and his bargaine for the same with the said Joseph Martin. And your Peticioner shall ever pray, etc.

Petition of John Brown and Thomas Lewis, masons

Warr' Burg'. To the Rt Honorable and others the Commissioners appointed by an Act of Parliament for the Rebuilding the Town of Warwick, etc., sitting att the Mayor's Parlour on Munday the 6th day of July 1696.

The Peticion of John Brown and Thomas Lewis, masons, Sheweth:

That Joseph Martin did by articles of agreement undertake to build a mault house for William Perks, baker, in the Church Street. That your Peticioners did enter into articles with the said Joseph Martin to build all the brick and stone work contained in the said building, to be paid by the perch att the severall rates mencioned in the said articles, he the said Joseph Martin to find all materialls for building except lime, and that your Peticioners were to find. That your Peticioners according to the articles have worked upon the said building till the said work, with the charge of lime, amounted to almost the summ of thirty pounds. That your Peticioners have received toward the said work but £11 10s. That your Peticioners have alsoe worked for the said Joseph Martin att the house of John Atterberry, shooe maker, in the Church Street to the value of eight pounds more. That your

PLATE 1. High Street and Leycester Place from the Westgate, 1946. The fire started in an outbuilding behind the nearer timber-framed house.

PLATE 2.   The Archer family mansion in Jury Street before 1812, now part of the Lord Leycester Hotel. 'This house stopt the fury of the flames at the great fire.'

PLATE 3. Northgate House in 1951, at the northern limit of the fire, built by Sir Henry Puckering of the Priory on the site of the Lamb and four other houses.

PLATE 4.   23 High Street at the corner of Back Lane, in 1947. This large house was
rebuilt after the fire by Isaac Tomkiss.

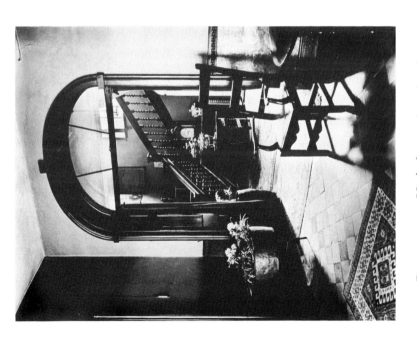

PLATE 5. 23 High Street, interior, in 1947, when the house was occupied by Lord and Lady Ilkeston. The staircase is typical of many in the post-fire houses.

PLATE 6.   The Aylesford Hotel on the corner of High Street and Castle
Street, *circa* 1918. The site was bought and rebuilt by William
Savage of Tachbrooke; the hotel bears the date 1696 on the
rainwater head.

The South East Prospect of St. Mary's Church in Warwick.

PLATE 7. The Church of St Mary *circa* 1740, showing the new balustrade with urns round both church and chancel, yew or fir trees in the churchyard, and cobbled paving in Church Street and the new square.

PLATE 8. Northgate Street in 1892, showing the unrestored Shire Hall, post-fire houses opposite, and St Mary's tower, built of Warwick sandstone on pillars of stone from Shrewley.

Peticioners doe conceive that the said William Perks hath not paid to the said Joseph Martin soe much money as will be an equivalent for the work done for the said William Perks.

Your Peticioner[1] therefore humbly prays the said work may be view'd by the Surveyors and a true estimate thereof by them be made and reported to this Court, and that this Court will make the said William Perks produce what moneys he hath paid to the said Joseph Martin. And if it appear that the said William Perks hath not paid to the said Joseph Martin soe much money as the said work will amount unto, your Peticioners may have the favour of this Court for the remainder of the said money due to the said Joseph Martin; and alsoe that the said John Atterberry may be order'd to prove that he has paid the said Joseph Martin for the work soe done to his house, and if the said money be not paid, that your Peticioner may have the benifit of the same toward his said work. And your Peticioner shall ever pray, etc.

Petition of Humphrey Hadley and Edward Abbotts of Lapworth

Warr' Burg'. To the Rt Honorable and others the Commissioners sitting att the Mayors Parlour on Munday the 6th day of July 1696.

The Peticion of Humphrey Hadley and Edward Abbotts of Lapworth in the County of Warr', Sheweth:

That your peticioners sold to Joseph Martin, an undertaker in this Borough, at the Parish of Lapworth in the County of Warr', timber to the value of £92 10s. That your peticioners have severall bonds for the said moneys of and from the said Joseph Martin payable att the severall times therein limitted. That the said money or any part thereof is not paid. That the said Joseph Martin hath taken the said timber from the said town of Lapworth and brought the greatest part thereof to this Borough and made use of the same. That Joseph Fenix, carpenter, out of pretence and with intent to defraud the said Joseph Martin his creditors hath taken away from some ground within this Borough timber to the value of £45 or thereabouts, he pretending he hath bought the same of the said Joseph Martin for the summ of £20. That the said Joseph Fenix owns the said timber to be worth £35 which your Peticioners are ready to make appear.

Your Peticioners therefore humbly prays, if the same be within the jurisdiccion of this Court, that your Peticioners may have the previledge of disposeing of that part of the timber which the said Joseph Martin hath not fetched away, and the benefitt thereof to their own use, and that the said Joseph Fenix may be summon'd to appear and answer this peticion and prove the payment of the money to the said Joseph Martin and his bargain for the same. And your Peticioners shall ever pray, etc.

[1] Sometimes singular and sometimes plural in this petition.

Petition of John Ladbrook of Cubbington

To the Rt Honorable and others the Commissioners appointed by an Act of Parliament for the Rebuilding the Town of Warwick, etc., sitting att the Mayors Parlour on Munday the 20th day of July 1696.

The humble Peticion of John Ladbrook of Cubbington, Sheweth:

That your Peticioner did on the 29th day of February last sell to Joseph Martin, workman within this Borough, 29 trees of oake for the considera-cion of the summ of fourty nine pounds, and other timber to the value of £5 5s.[1] more. That the said Joseph Martin sold to Joseph Fenix, carpenter, and John King part of the said trees for the summ of £20, for which summ your Peticioner hath a bond from the said Joseph Fenix and King and alsoe an agreement from the said Joseph Martin for the residue of the said money being £34. That the said Martin hath brought the said trees to this Borough and made use of the same att the house of John Watts in the Sheep Street and other buildings which the said Martin undertook.

Your Peticioner being inform'd that the said Watts hath not paid to Martin soe much money as will be an equivalent for the work done for him, humbly prays the said John Watts may be made to shew this agreement with the said Martin, and the said building and work done for the said Watts may be surveyed by the Surveyor and an estimate thereof made, and alsoe to pro-duce what he hath paid to the said Joseph Martin, and if any money appear to be due to the said Martin, that your Peticioner may have his proporcion thereof according to his said loss, and your Peticioner shall ever pray, etc.

Petition of the inhabitants of St Mary's parish

Warr' Burg'. To the Rt Honorable and others the Commissioners sitting att the Mayors Parlour on Munday the 20th day of July 1696 by vertue of an Act of Parliament for Rebuilding the Town of Warwick, etc.

The humble Peticion of divers of the inhabitants of St Mary's in the said Burrough, Sheweth:

That John Atterberry hath lately built a house upon some ground lately pur-chased by him of the executors of Elizabeth Carr deceased, lying in the Church Street on the west side thereof and adjoyning on the north side of the said building to the ground called the Church ground on which before the late fire stood a messuage or tenement then in possession of one[2] Hem-mings. That your Peticioners, conceiveing that the said John Atterberry hath made a considerable enrochment upon the said Church ground by building thereupon to the detriment of the said inhabitants, humbly prays a jury may be impanelled to sett out all the said Church ground and to view

---

[1] '5s.' interlineated over a caret.
[2] Altered from 'the widow'.

the building of the said John Atterberry, and according to their evidence to find whether he hath encroched upon the said ground or not, and that Nicholas Whitehead, Robert Ashby, Mr Stephen Nicholls, Joshua Perks and William Perks may be summon'd to appear to give evidence for your Peticioners touching the same, and your Peticioners shall every pray, etc.

Dev. Whadcock, Mayor	Tho. Newsham
Joseph Blissett	John Smith
Geo. Webb	Tho. Edes
Ri. Lane	

A Jury to view John Atterbury's house and their verdict

Warr' Burg'.[1] To Richard Hadley of the Bur' aforesaid, gent.

You are hereby comanded to cause to come before the Commissioners or Judges appointed by an Act of Parliament for the Rebuilding the Towne of Warwick, etc., att the next Court of Record to be held att the Mayor's Parlour on Munday the 27th day of this instant July by ten of the clock in the forenoon, twelve free and lawfull men of the said Borough to view and sett out the ground called the Church ground in the Church Street next adjoyning to the house lately built by John Atterbury on the south side thereof, and to view the building of the said Atterbury next adjoyning thereto, and upon their oaths according to their evidence, to find whether the said John Atterbury hath encroched upon the said Church ground by setting his walls and buildings upon any part thereof, and a true verdict thereof to make to this Court; and have you then and there the names of the jury and this precept, dated the 23rd day of July in the eighth year of the reigne of William the 3rd King of England, etc., annoque Domini 1696.

John Mitchener, Registr'

Warr' Burg'.   Nomina juratorum ad inquirendum et triandum differenciam inter inhabitantes de Burgo predicto, querentes, et Johannem Atterbury defendentem.

Aaron Rogers, gent.[2]	Ricardus Burnill[2]
Ricardus Hands, gent.[2]	Johannes Davis
Thomas Young, gent.[2]	Ricardus Kerby
Willelmus Mackepeace, gent.[2]	Ricardus Gibbard
Josephus Kerby	Johannes Atkins[2]
Thomas Griffin	Edwardus Barnacle[2]
Thomas Gibbs jun.[2]	Johannes Dreyton

---

[1] The following three documents are fastened together with a pin.
[2] These names are marked with a dash and the word 'jur'.'

Willelmus Nicholls[1]   Edwardus Owen[1]
Robertus Brommill[1]   Jacobus Fell[1]
Johannes Glover[1]   Francis Power
Johannes Catter[1]   Ricardus Fort[1]
Thomas Greenway[1]   Thomas Smith

July 27th 1696. The said Jurors upon view of the Church ground in the Church Street doe find that John Atterbury hath encroched and built upon the said Church ground in breadth twelve inches and in length 20 foot. That the wideness of the said Church ground from Mr Tarver's brick wall towards John Atterbury's house is 44 foot and one inch. That the wideness of the said ground by Mr Tarver's brick wall is 68 foot, and that the length of the said ground from Mr Tarver's wall between that and Mr Oken land to the Church Street is 156 foot, and the wideness of the same in the front to the street is 52 foot and 3 inches.

Petition of William Phillips

To the Rt Honorable and others the Commissioners appointed by an Act of Parliament for Rebuilding the Town of Warwick, etc., sitting att the Mayor's Parlour on Munday the 27th day of July 1696.
The Peticion of William Phillips, Sheweth:
That your Peticioner hath sold unto William Holmes bricks to the value of twenty six pounds. That the said William Holmes hath made use of the said brick upon the ground of Mr Prescott in the High Street which he pretendeth to have bought. That the said Holmes promised to pay your Peticioner the summ of twenty five pounds above 3 weeks since, but hath put him off from time to time and doth not produce money to pay for the said brick.
Your Peticioner therefore humbly prays the said Holmes may be summon'd to appear and answer the same, and be made to pay him for the said brick according to his agreement, and your Peticioner shall ever pray, etc.

Petition of Robert Boyce of Wellesbourne

To the Rt Honorable and others the Commissioners sitting att the Mayor's Parlour on Munday the 27th day of July 1696 by vertue of an Act of Parliament for Rebuilding the Town of Warwick.
The humble Peticion of Robert Boyce of Welsborne in the County of Warwick, gent., Sheweth:
That William Holmes, brickmaker, hath lately bought of Mr —— Edwards of Hampton on the Hill a certaine toft, peice or parcell of burnt ground late

---

[1] These names are marked with a dash and the word 'jur'.

the Widow Ashwin's lying in the Sheepstreet within this Borough adjoyning on the north side thereof to a messuage lately built by Joseph Willis, and on the south side thereof to the ground of the Black Raven, for the consideracion of the summ of fourty pounds. That the said William Holmes hath paid to the said Mr —— Edwards the summ of ten[1] pounds in part of the said purchase money and hath built a party wall on the said ground to the value of seven pounds more.

Your Peticioner therefore in behalf of the said William Holmes humbly prays the said Mr Edwards may be summon'd to appear the next Court, and by reason the said William Holmes is not able to build the said ground, he prays that the said William Holmes may be discharged of the said bargaine, and that the said Mr Edwards may repay the summ of ten pounds back againe and for the party wall that he hath built on the said ground. And your Peticioner shall ever pray, etc.

Robert Boyse

Petition of George Chinn, carpenter

To the Rt Honorable and others the Commissioners sitting att the Mayor's Parlour on Munday the 27th day of July 1696 by vertue of an Act of Parliament for Rebuilding the Town of Warwick, etc.
The humble Peticion of George Chinn, carpenter, Sheweth:

That your Peticioner did on the 13th day of Aprill last and 4th day of May last peticion to borrow the summ of £100 out of the Charity moneys given for the relief of sufferers by the late fire, upon which this Court did order the said summ should be lent to him, he giveing such security as in the said order mencioned. That your Peticioner haveing now great occasion for money to carry on his building in the High Street upon the ground lately purchased by him of one Mr Green, humbly prays that he may be allowed to have the said summ mencioned in the said order upon the security therein mencioned, and alsoe that he may have the one shilling and six pence in the pound for the loss given in for the house of the said Mr Green in the High Street before the late fire standing on the ground which your Peticioner hath now built upon to encourage him in rebuilding the same. And your Peticioner shall ever pray, etc.

George Chinn

Petition of Joseph Fenix, carpenter

Warr' Burg'. To the Rt Honorable and others the Commissioners appointed by an Act of Parliament for the Rebuilding the Towne of

---

[1] Altered from 'eight'.

Warwick, etc., sitting att the Mayor's Parlour on Munday the 27th day of July 1696.

The Peticion of Joseph Fenix, carpenter, Sheweth:

That your Peticioner did by oath of two wittnesses on Munday last make it appear that he had bought of Joseph Martin timber within this Borough for the summ of £20 lying upon the ground of Mrs Cawthern in the Sheep-street, and whereas this Court, being inform'd that the said timber was worth more than the said summ, did on Munday last order your Peticioner to goe with George Perkins and John Hope and shew them the said timber (and the said Perkins and Hope to estimate the same) which your Peti-cioner hath done in obedience to the said order, given them an account of what is lying upon the said ground and now in his hands, and alsoe as nere as he could what is made use of upon the house of John Watts in the Sheep-street, and alsoe three pieces of timber, part of your Peticioners bargaine, that William Perks, baker, hath since the said order made, taken from him in his absence, and fram'd and made use of the same in his building, notwithstand the said Perks sett forth in his peticion that the same was fram'd for his use before the said Martin went away.

Your Peticioner therefore humbly prays that whereas the said Watts hath taken away, and made use of greatest part of the timber, he the said John Watts may make satisfacion for the said timber soe used, and alsoe Perks for what he hath taken away, or else that this Court will take the resi-due thereof and make such order therein as he may have the money he paid to Martin repaid him back againe by the said John Watts, or otherwise as this Court shall think fitt, and your Peticioner shall ever pray etc.

Joseph Fenex

Petition of Thomas Mander, barber

Warr' Burg'. To the Rt Honorable and others the Commissioners appointed by an Act of Parliament for the Rebuilding the Town of War-wick, etc., sitting att the Mayor's Parlour on Munday the 24th of August 1696.

The humble Peticion of Thomas Mander of the Borough of Warwick, barber, Sheweth:

That Elizabeth Green wife of Richard Green of Abbingdon in the County of Berks. by the last will and testament of her mother Katherin Creed was seized of a messuage with th'appurtenances in the High Pavement in War-wick aforesaid for her life, from and after her decease to the use of Samuell Green son of the said Elizabeth Green and to the heirs of the body of the said Samuell, in default of such issue to the use of the second son of the said Elizabeth and the heirs of his body and soe successively in taile male, in default of such issue to the daughter and daughters, in default of such to her brother William Booth and the heirs of his body, for want of such to the right heire of the said Katherine for ever.

That your Peticioner was possessed by vertue of a lease of the said messuage, att and before the late fire, that neither the said Elizabeth Green or any of those in remainder are willing or able to rebuild the said messuage.

Your Peticioner therefore humbly prays that for a valuable consideracion such as to this Court shall seem reasonable, paid or secured to be paid to the said Elizabeth Green and Samuell Green her son, and others in remainder for the toft whereon stood the above mencion'd messuage, he the said Thomas Maunder may be admitted to rebuild a messuage on the toft, and that the same may be decreed to him and his heirs for ever by Decree of this honorable Court, and your Peticioner shall ever pray, etc.

Petition of Richard Green of Abingdon

Warr' Burr'. To the Rt Honorable and others the Commissioners appointed by an Act of Parliament for the Rebuilding the Town of Warwick, etc., sitting att the Mayor's Parlour on Munday the 24th day of August 1696

The humble Peticion of Richard Green of Abbingdon in the County of Berks., gent., Sheweth:
That Thomas Maunder of this Borough, barber, was before and att the time of the late fire within the said Borough lessee of a certaine messuage or tenement scituate in a street there call'd the High Pavement by vertue of a lease from Richard Creed of Abingdon aforesaid beareing date the 15th day of June anno Domini 1681 for the term of one and twenty years yeilding and paying yearly the rent of £10 and ten shillings att the two usual feasts in the year viz. att the feast of the Anunciacion of the blessed Virgin Mary and St Michael the Archangell. That att the time of the said fire there was allmost one half years rent due to your Peticioner from the said Thomas Mander, which the said Thomas Maunder hath upon severall demands made by your Peticioner refused to pay.

Your Peticioner therefore humbly prays the said Thomas Maunder may be summon'd to appeare and answer the same, and that he may be compell'd by Order of this Court to pay the rent due to the time of the said fire, and your Peticioner shall ever pray, etc.

Richard Greene

Petition of Alexander Nicholls

To the Rt Honorable and others the Commissioners appointed by an Act of Parliament for Rebuilding the Town of Warwick, etc., sitting at the Mayor's Parlour on Munday the 31st day of August 1696,[1] Sheweth:

[1] The usual sentence giving the petitioner's name has been accidentally omitted.

That your Peticioner hath lately purchased a peice of ground in the Church Street adjoyning to the house of William Perks, baker, on the north side thereof on which before the late fire stood a house in possession of Robert Taylor, butcher. That the said William Perks hath encroched upon your Peticioner by building his malt house on his said ground neer 3 foot in breadth and considerable in length, which building, after tyled and finished, will bring the water from his house into the middle of the Peticioner's well being in his backside. That your Peticioner is ready to prove by the tenants that lived in the house before the said fire that the eaves of the said Perks his building ran down into a gutter between the said well and the former wall of the said William Perks. That the said William Perks hath alsoe built the foundacion of his said mault house soe very slight that your Peticioner is very much afraid to build up to it for feare least the said wall should tumble down. That your Peticioner was very willing to have taken down the said wall and sett it up againe att his own charge but the said William Perks would not consent thereto.

Your Peticioner therefore humbly prays the said William Perks may be summon'd to answer the same, and that a jury may be impanelled to enquire upon their oaths what damage the said encrochment will be to your Peticioner, and that he may be awarded a reasonable satisfaccion for the same, and alsoe to view the said wall and to report the same to this Court, and your Peticioner shall ever pray, etc.

Alexander Nicholles

Petition of William Tranter and others

Warr' Burg'. To the Rt Honorable and others the Commissioners appointed by an Act of Parliament for the Rebuilding the Towne of Warwick, etc., sitting att the Mayor's Parlour on Munday the 7th day of September anno Domini 1696.

The humble Peticion of William Tranter, William Phillips, James Walker, John Pinley, John Hawkins, Oliver Fleetwood, Thomas White and Thomas Masters against William Holmes, carpenter, Sheweth:

That the said William Holmes hath lately bought of Mr James Prescott a certaine peice of ground lying and being in the High Street on which before the late fire stood a messuage in possession of Mrs Sandford[1] and hath begunn to rebuild thereon. That your Peticioners hath furnished the said Holmes with bricks, timber, stone and other materialls to carry on the said building, for which and for workmanship done in and about the same, the said Holmes is debtor to the Peticioners the summ of seventy one pound seventeen shillings and two pence. That upon severall demands thereof made, he refuses to pay the same, (except the Peticioners will make such

---

[1] 'Mrs Sandford' inserted later in a space left for the name.

abatements as he himself dose offer which will exceed more than six shillings in the pound) and all to defraud and cheat them. That the Peticioners are ready to prove the abovesaid summ of £71 17s. 2d to be truly and justly due to them and doe refuse to consent thereto.

Your Peticioners therefore humbly pray the said Court will summon the said William Holmes to appeare and answere why he deals soe unjustly with them, and be made to pay them the said summ due to them as aforesaid, and your Peticioners shall ever pray, etc.

Petition of William Tranter, brickmaker

Warr' Burg'. To the Rt Honorable and others the Commissioners appointed by an Act of Parliament for the Rebuilding the Towne of Warwick, etc., sitting at the Mayor's Parlour on Munday the 28th of September 1696.

The humble Peticion of William Tranter, brickmaker, Sheweth:
That one Joseph Martin did undertake to rebuild a house for Matthew Busby of this Borough. That the Peticioner hath laid in bricks to the value of [   ]¹ to be used toward the rebuilding the said house. That the said Martin is since runn away. That your Peticioner being inform'd that the estimate of the said Busby's building amounts to about £5 more then [he] hath paid to the said Martin. That the said Busby is very willing the Peticioner should have the overplus that remains unpaid toward the payment of his said brick.

Your Peticioner therefore humbly prays the said Matthew Busby may have the order of this Court to pay your Peticioner the said overplus or such proporcion thereof as this Court shall think fitt, and your Peticioner shall ever pray, etc.

Petition of George Taylor, blacksmith

To the Rt Honorable and others the Commissioners sitting at the Mayor's Parlour on Munday the 28th of September anno Domini 1696.

The humble Peticion of George Taylor of this Borough, blacksmith, Sheweth:
That your Peticioner sold unto John Hawkins of Henley, who undertook the timber work to be done in and about the house of Edward Norton of this Borough, gent., nailes and iron work to be used in and about the said house to the value of about four pounds. That the said goods were deliver'd to the said John Hawkins and to his man for the said use. That the said Hawkins hath severall times own'd the said debt to your Peticioner and hath promised to pay the same but now he refuses soe to doe. Your

¹ Space not filled in.

Peticioner being inform'd that the said Mr Norton hath not paid the said Hawkins in full for his said work, prays that Mr Norton may be summon'd to know whether hee hath any of the said monies remaining in his hands and that your Petitioner may bee paid his debt out of the same, and your Petitioner etc.

Petition of James Cook an infant

To the Rt Honorable and others the Commissioners appointed by an Act of Parliament for the Rebuilding the Town of Warwick, etc., sitting att the Mayor's Parlour on Munday the 28th of September 1696.

The humble Peticion of James Cook of the Borough of Warwick, infant, Sheweth:

That the said James Cook att the time of the late fire was and now is seized of a certaine messuage or tenement scituate in the Jury Street in possession of [   ].[1] That Joseph Blissett and John Smith gen' both of this Burrough are guardians to the Peticioner. That the said messuage was att the time of the said fire without the good will of the said guardians untiled by the order of William Johnson, doctor of physick, and that he hath been att the charge of about 3 pounds in repaireing the same. That the said guardians refuse to peticion and act in the behalf of the said Peticioner for and toward the repaireing him in the said damage occassion'd by untileing and defaceing the said tenement.

Wherefore the Peticioner humbly prays the summons of this Court to summon the said guardians or the said Doctor Johnson to appear in this Court of Judicature to answer the contents of this said Petition, and that this Court will award such satisfaccion for the said damage as shall be most just and reasonable, and your Peticioner shall ever pray, etc.

Petition of Job Rainsford

Warr' Burg'. To the Rt Honorable and others the Commissioners appointed by an Act of Parliament for the Rebuilding the Towne of Warwick, etc., sitting att the Mayor's Parlour on Munday the 5th day of October 1696

The humble Peticion of Mr Job Rainsford of the Borough aforesaid, Sheweth:

That your Peticioner did, since the late fire within this Borough, purchase of Mr James Prescott all that toft, peice or parcell of burnt ground scituate in the Sheepstreet, on which before the late fire stood a messuage in possession of the said Peticioner. That the peticioner hath since rebuilt a messuage on the said ground and in consideracion thereof, humbly prays he

---

[1] Space not filled in.

may be allow'd by the order of this Court one shilling and sixpence in the pound according to the loss of the said messuage burnt down by the said fire, as it is now reduced, as an encouragement for rebuilding the same, and your peticioner shall ever pray, etc.

Petition of Joseph Willis, baker

Warr' Burg'. To the Rt Honorable the Commissioners and others sitting att the Mayor's Parlour on Munday the 12th day of October 1696

The humble Peticion of Joseph Willis of this Borough, baker, Sheweth:

That your peticioner hath lately bought of Mr Alderman Hands the toft of a certain messuage before the late fire in possession of John Prichard, which toft was decreed to the said Mr Hands by decree beareing date the 4th day of May last. That your Peticioner hath since rebuilt a house on the said toft. That John Prichard threatens and tells the Peticioner he will have the said house now it is rebuilt. That the said Richard Hands refuses to deliver up the said writeings to your Peticioner. Your Peticioner therefore humbly prays the summons of this Court to summon the said John Prichard and Richard Hands to appeare in this Court and answer the same, and your Peticioner shall ever pray, etc.

Petition of John Sale of Moreton Morrell

To the Rt Honorable and others the Commissioners appointed by an Act of Parliament for the Rebuilding the Town of Warwick, etc., John Sale peticion and consent.[1]

I John Sale of Mourton Morrell, yeoman, doe hereby certify my consent that Samuell Roberts *alias* Burford shall have not only the ground whereon a certaine mesuage in a streete called Horsecheeping in the Borough of Warwicke lately stood, but alsoe all proffitts that shall acrew to him out of the Charity money as builder of the same againe or otherwise howsoever. Witness my hand this 24th day of Aprill 1697

The marke of John X Sale

Witnesse: Anmarrye[2] Sale.   The marke of Elizabeth X Sale.
            Anthony Power.   William Broockes.

Petition of Samuel Roberts, brickmaker

To the Rt Honorable and others the Commissioners appointed by an Act of Parliament for the Rebuilding the Town of Warwicke, etc., sitting att the Mayor's Parlour on Monday the 26th day of April anno Domini 1697.

---

[1] This preamble has been added in a space at the top of the document in another hand.
[2] 'Ann-Mary' in the parish register of St Mary's.

The Petition of Samuell Roberts, brickmaker, sheweth:
That your Petitioner hath lately built a mesuage or tenement att the corner of a streete called the Horse Cheepeing near adjoyneing to Peoble Lane upon the ground that did formerly belong to John Sale of Morton Morrell, and hath agreed with the said John Sale for the purchase of the said ground for the sume of £37. That your Petitioner being the builder of the said tenement may be allowed the building money due in such cases, and likewise have a decree out of this Honorable Court to assure his title to the premisses against the said John Sale and his heires.

This[1] is to assure you that I John Sale doe give my consent to dispose and parte with my right and titell of my land fully and wholy. Witness my hand X.

Petition of Oken's Feoffees

Warr' Burg'. To the Rt Honorable and others the Commissioners appointed by an Act of Parliament for the Rebuilding the Town of Warwick, etc., sitting att the Mayor's Parlour on Munday the 26th day of Aprill anno Domini 1697.
    The Peticion of the Feoffees of Thomas Oken, gent., Humbly Sheweth: That your Peticioners are feoffees in trust for the said Thomas Oken of a certaine toft or peice of burnt ground whereon before the late fire stood a messuage or tenement in the possession of [   ][2] lying and being in the Church Street adjoyning on the north side thereof to the howse of James Fish the elder, and on the south side thereof to the house [   ].[2] That your Peticioners are informed and have good reason to believe the said James Fish hath encroched with his back buildings upon the said toft or ground of the said Thomas Oken, and that he hath made many lights and windows in the said buildings lookeing into the court or backside of the said ground, more then were att the time of the late fire; and that he hath lately built upon the garden wall lately erected by order of the said feoffees about [   ][2] high without their consent and good likeing to the prejudice and anoyance[3] of the premises of the said Thomas Oken.
Your peticioners therefore humbly pray that a jury may be impanelled to enquire into the said encrochments and to sett forth the meets and bounds of the said ground betwixt the house of the said James Fish and the ground of the said Thomas Oken aforesaid, and alsoe into the number of new windows and lights made since the said fire and to give in their verdict of the same to this Court, and your Peticioner shall ever pray, etc.

[1] On a slip of paper enclosed in the preceding document.
[2] Space not filled in.
[3] Reading doubtful.

Petition of Thomas Mayo of Rugby

Warr' Burg'. To the Rt Honorable and others the Commissioners appointed by an Act of Parliament for the Rebuilding the Town of Warwick, etc., sitting att the Mayor's Parlour on Munday the 26th day of Aprill anno Domini 1697

The humble Peticion of Thomas Mayo of Rughby, yeoman, Sheweth:

That Edward Mayo of this Borough, carpenter, being seized of a messuage or tenement before the late fire scituate neer the Joyce Poole within the said Borough, and alsoe of one other messuage or tenement adjoyning to the before mencioned messuage, did on the 19th day of January 1691 for and in consideracion of the summ of twenty pounds mortgage the said two messuages or tenements to William Lingham of this Borough, gent., for 1000 years paying one pepper corn per annum to the said Edward Mayo, with a provisoe that if he the said Edward Mayo should pay or cause to be paid the aforesaid summ of £20 to the said William Lingham on the 19th day of July then next following, that then the said mortgage to be void or else to remaine in full force and vertue. That the said William Lingham did on the 18th day of January 1692 in consideracion of the above mencioned summ of twenty pounds assign the said mortgage over unto your Peticioner for the number of years therein contained and unexpired and to hold the same in such manner as he the said William Lingham might have done. That the said two messuages were totally burnt down by the said fire and your Peticioner being willing to undertake to rebuild the toft whereon the same before the late fire stood, humbly prays the said ground in consideracion of the aforesaid mortgage may be decreed to your Peticioner and his heirs by the decree of this Court, that thereby your Peticioner may be encouraged to rebuild the same, and your Peticioner shall ever pray, etc.

Petition of Moses Robinson and [   ]¹ Cook of Harbury, mason

Warr' Burg'. To the Rt Honorable and others the Commissioners appointed by an Act of Parliament for the Rebuilding the Town of Warwick, etc., sitting att the Mayor's Parlour on Munday the 26th day of Aprill 1697

The humble Peticion of Moses Robbinson and [   ]¹ Cook of Harbury, mason, Sheweth:

That whereas all the ground burnt by the late fire is fallen to the Commissioners, by reason of the proprietors and owners thereof have not built upon the said ground or lay'd any foundacions thereon within the two years limitted by the said Act, and whereas your peticioners are given to understand that the Commissioners doe give an allowance of 4s. in the pound for

---

¹ Space not filled in.

the losses sustained by the said fire for encouragement towards the rebuilding the same, your Peticioners therefore being desireous to undertake to
rebuild a certaine toft or peice of burnt ground called the Church ground
lying and being in the Church Street adjoyning on the south side of a house
lately built by the feoffees of Thomas Oken, do humbly propose they may
have a lease of the same for such a term of years as may encourage them
thereto, and be allowed such monies as shall be given towards the rebuilding the same ground, all which they submitt to the consideracion of this
Court, and humbly prays your resolucion in the same, and your Peticioners
shall ever pray, etc.

Digest of several petitions

Severall Peticions.[1] W. May the 31st 1697.

The Peticion of Nicholas Paris sheweth that whereas an Engine was destroyed by the late fire and hath been since by him repaired for the use of
the Town, the charges of which amounteth unto £5 10s. 0, the said
Engine being conceived to be a publick loss and not lyable to the charge of
the said Town, humbly prays the said repairacion may be allowed by this
Court, and the peticioner shall ever pray.

The Peticion[2] of William Savage of Tachbrook, gent., prays he may be
allowed 1s. 6d. in the pound for the loss of the house he purchased of Mr
Boyce.

The Peticion of Samuell Ainge prays he may have an allowance from
Thomas Lean for a building built by the said Lean upon the wall of the said
Ainge, he would have referr'd the damage to the Surveyors but Lean would
not agree thereto.

Thomas Lean prays he may be allowed 1s. 6d. per lib. for the loss of Mrs
Tuckeys house in Church Street as reduced to £60 being £4 10s.

George Chinn's Peticion prays that [   ][3] King may be sumon'd to
appear for refusing to pay for his party walls.

George Chinn and George Tayler prays they may be admitted purchasors
of a peice of ground in the Swan Lane late Mr Tarver's containeing 60 foot
in ground from the Red Lyon wall.

Richard Hancox prays he may be allowed 1s. 6d. per lib. for the loss of Mrs
Martin's house.

  [1] This paper of rough, abbreviated notes of petitions, some off which are crossed through, probably
relates to petitions to be made out for, or expected on this court day.
  [2] This whole item crossed out.
  [3] Space not filled in.

The humble Peticion[1] of Mr Richard Lane and Thomas Masters, prays they may have the allowance of one shilling and six pence in the pound as an encouragement for rebuilding the house in the Highstreet purchased of Mr James Prescott according the loss of the premises as reduced to £180.

The humble Peticion of Robert Cox of Southam, George Copland, Richard and John Williams of Warwick, carpenters, and William Grey, glazier, sheweth: That they have worked for John Burton[2] in and about the house lately built by him in the Markett Place, that there is due to them for materialls and work done about the said house about the summ of £33. The Peticioners heareing the said John Burton is about to mortgage the said house and thereby to defraud them, humbly prays the said Burton may be summon'd to answer the same and be made to pay your Peticioners for the said work, and your Peticioners shall ever pray, etc.

The humble Peticion of [   ][3] Ireland, carpenter, sheweth: that he hath worked for William Perks, baker, by articles made between them in and about his house in the Church Street. That there is due according to the articles to the said Ireland about the summ of two pounds and nine shillings which the said William Perks doth refuse to pay to the Peticioner. The Peticioner humbly prays the said Perks may be summoned to appear and be made to pay him for his said work done, and the Peticioner shall ever pray, etc.

The Peticion[1] of George Floor, inkeeper. George Floor humbly prays he may be allowed 1s. 6d. per lib. as an encouragement for rebuilding the ground he lately bought of Mr Robert Blissett lying in the Markett Place as reduced to £170, and the Peticioner shall ever pray, etc.

The Peticion[1] of John Atterbury, shoemaker. John Atterbury prays he may be allowed the one shilling and sixpence in the pound for the house he built in Church Street bought of the executors of Elizabeth Carr as reduced to £110, and your Peticioner shall ever pray, etc.

Petition of Edward Clopton of Bridgetown

Warr' Burg'. To the Rt Honorable and others the Commissioners sitting att the Mayor's Parlour on Munday the 22[4] day of August anno Domini 1697 appointed by an Act of Parliament for the Rebuilding the Town of Warwick, etc.

---

[1] This whole item crossed out.
[2] 'inkeeper' in a marginal heading.
[3] Space not filled in.
[4] Monday was the 23rd.

The humble Peticion of Edward Clopton of Bridgetowne in the parish of Old Stratford in the County of Warr', Esq., Sheweth:

That your Peticioner was before the late fire within this Borough seized in right of his wife Martha Clopton, daughter and heir of William Combe, Esq., and Ann Mary his wife, both deceased, to the use of him the said Edward Clopton and Martha his wife and the heirs of the said Martha, of and in one messuage or tenement, garden, orchard, stables, barns and backside with the appurtenances thereunto belonging, scituate lying and being in the said Borough in a certaine street there called the Highstreet called and known by the name or signe of the Dolphin, and was before the late fire in possession of William Bryan *alias* Stephens. That the said messuage or tenement and buildings thereunto belonging were totally burnt down by the said fire. That two whole years are passed since the said fire and the said ground whereon the said messuage stood remains yet unbuilt and the foundacions thereof not yet laid, in default whereof the disposall of the same is fall'n to the Commissioners or Judges appointed by the said Act. That your Peticioner haveing an interest as aforesaid in the said premises is willing to undertake to rebuild the said ground provided he may have the same assured to him and his heirs by decree of this Court. He therefore humbly prays that a jury may be impanell'd to assess and sett a price upon the ground whereon the said messuage with appurtenances before the late fire stood, and that this Court will award what summ he the peticioner shall pay (considering his interest in the premises) as a valuable consideracion for the premises soe as he may have the same decreed to him and his heirs, that thereby he may be encouraged to rebuild the said ground, and your Peticioner shall ever pray, etc.

Petition of Richard Hancox, glazier

Warr' Burg'. To the Rt Honorable and others the Commissioners sitting att the Mayor's Parlour on Munday the 23rd day of August 1697

The humble Peticion of Richard Hancox of this Borough, glazier, Sheweth:

That your Peticioner hath built 2 houses on a certaine peice of ground lying nere the Pillory on which before the late fire stood a messuage belonging to Mrs Martin, according to a decree of this Court beareing date the 12th day of September 1696, by which decree your Peticioner is ordered and decreed all the one shilling and 6d. in the pound[1] which shall be given towards the rebuilding of the said house. Your Peticioner therefore haveing rebuilt the same, humbly prays he may be allowed the said 1s. 6d. in the pound according to the said decree, and your Peticioner shall ever pray, etc.

[1] 'one shilling and 6d. in the pound' interlineated above 'charity moneys' struck out.

Petition of Thomas Dixon, blacksmith

Warr' Burg'. To the Rt Honorable and others the Commissioners sitting att the Mayor's Parlour on Munday the 23 day of August anno Domini 1697
   The humble Peticion of Thomas Dixon, blacksmith, Sheweth:
That your Peticioner was before the late fire seized of a messuage or tenement scituate in the High Street which said messuage or tenement was burnt down by the late fire. That Richard King, carpenter, did by articles of agreement undertake to rebuild on the ground whereon the said messuage stood, one other good and substantiall messuage or tenement containeing 19 foot and $\frac{1}{2}$ wide and 25 foot deep for the consideracion of £62 10s. od. That the said Richard King hath not performed all his bargaine according to the articles but nothwithstanding that your Peticioner and the said King hath reckon'd and there is due unto your Peticioner the summ of £1 8s. od. which summ the said King doth refuse to pay pretending he hath built more then the said articles doth express, which your Peticioner doth deny and is ready to make it appear to the contrary. That he hath nott made doors and windows according to agreement.[1] Your Petitioner therefore humbly prays the said King may be summon'd to appear and answer the same and be made to pay him the over plus. And your Peticioner shall ever pray, etc.

Petition of George Chinn

Warr' Burr'. To the Rt Honorable and others the Commissioners sitting att the Mayor's Parlour on Munday the 23rd day of August 1697
   The humble Peticion of George Chinn, Sheweth:
That your Peticioner built 2 houses in the High Street on the ground before the late fire in possession of Thomas Maunder. That Mr Mann of Killenworth employed one Richard King to build a house next to your Peticioners on ground purchased of Mr Archer. That the said King made use of your Peticioner's party wall and hath paid some part of the charge thereof but refuses to pay the whole charge thereof with interest for the same according to the Act of Parliament. Your Peticioner therefore humbly prays the said King may be summon'd to answer the same and be made to pay your Peticioner, and your Peticioner shall ever pray, etc.

Petition of Thomas Lean, barber

Warr' Burg'. To the Rt Honorable and others the Commissioners appointed by an Act of Parliament for the Rebuilding the Town of Warwick, etc., sitting att the Mayor's Parlour on Munday the 23rd day of August 1697.

---

[1] This sentence inserted in a space.

The humble Peticion of Thomas Lean, barber, Sheweth:
That your Peticioner lately purchased of and from Hannah Tuckey and
Samuel Tuckey for the consideracion of the summ of £25 the fee simple of
a certaine toft, peice or parcell of burnt ground whereon before the late fire
a messuage then in possession of the said Thomas Lean stood. That your
Peticioner haveing rebuilt the said toft, humbly prays he may be allowed
the consideracion of 1s. 6d. in the pound for the loss of the said house
burnt down in and by the said fire as the same is reduced to £60 as an
encouragement to him for rebuilding the same, and your Peticioner shall
ever pray, etc.

Petition of John Burton

Warr' Burg'. To the Rt Honorable and others the Commissioners sitting att
the Mayor's Parlour on Munday the 23rd day of August 1697
    The humble Peticion of John Burton, Sheweth:
That Thomas Lean, brother to your Peticioner's wife, was before and att
the time of the late fire seized of a messuage lying and being in the street
leading to the Pillory then in possession of your Peticioner. That the said
Thomas Lean before the said fire went a soldier into Flanders and is not
from thence yet return'd. That before his goeing away he made his will
wherein he gave (provided he never come againe) the said messuage and
garden thereto belonging to William Eborall, sadler, his youngest child[1]
whom he made executor, and did alsoe make the said William Eborall and
John Davis overseers of the said will. He alsoe leaves severall legacies to be
paid by his executor (viz.) £10 a peice to his 3 sisters and to each child of
the said William Eborall's £4. That the Peticioner was before and untill the
time of the late fire (in and by which the said house was burnt) tenant to
the said house. That the Peticioner not hearing of the said Thomas Lean,
undertook to rebuild a house on the burnt ground whereon the before
mencion'd messuage stood, and hath been att a great charge in rebuilding
the same, and must be utterly undone, except relieved by this Honorable
Court.
Your Peticioner therefore humbly prays the said ground on which he hath
rebuilt, or which doth belong to the same, may be assessed at the true value
it was worth presently after the said fire, and that the said mony soe
assessed to be disposed of by this Honorable Court to the severall partyes
interested in the same in such proporcion and after such manner as they in
their judgments shall think fitt and reasonable. And alsoe the Peticioner
humbly prays that he, paying for the said ground as this Court shall direct,
may have the same assured to him by Decree of this Court, and that
thereby the said Thomas Lean may be bound in case he comes againe to

[1] i.e. William Eborall's youngest child.

stand to such order and decree, and alsoe that William Eborall and John Davis may be summon'd to appear here next Court, and your Peticioner shall ever pray, etc.

Petition of William Hunt for Mr Cook of London, apothecary

Warr' Burg'. To the Rt Honorable and others the Commissioners sitting att the Mayor's Parlour on Munday the 23rd day of August 1697

The Humble Peticion of Mr William Hunt for and in behalf of Mr Cook of London, apothecary, Sheweth:

That the said Mr Cook was, att and before the late fire, seized of 2 certaine messuages or tenements then in possession of Thomas Tippin, cutler, and Richard Hands, baker. That the said 2 messuages were burnt down by the said fire, and the said Mr Cook hath by writeing under his hand and seale, assured and conveyed all his right and title to the same unto Thomas Dadley, butcher, deceased, and Edward Chesley, taylor, to hold the same to them and their heirs for ever, reserveing to himself all the monies which shall be given toewards the loss of the said 2 houses, the said 2 houses being rebuilt. Your Peticioner humbly prays he the said Mr Cook may be allowed the 1s. 6d. in the pound given towards the rebuilding of the same, and your Peticioner shall ever pray, etc.

Petition of Thomas Masters, carpenter

Warr' Burg'. To the Right Honorable and other the Commissioners sitting att the Mayor's Parlour on Munday the [   ][1] day of August anno Domini 1697 by vertue of an Act of Parliament for the rebuilding the town of Warwick, etc.,

The Humble Petition of Thomas Masters of the Borough aforesaid, carpenter, Sheweth:

That whereas there is a certaine toft or peice of ground lying in the High Street whereon before the late fire stood a messuage commonly called the White Lyon Inn now unbuilt, and the proprietors and owners thereof have not within the space of 2 years limitted by the said Act laid the foundacions thereof in order to rebuild the same. That the said ground is vested in one Dorothy Hopkins now of Charlecoate for the term of her life and after her decease to Mary Neale wife of James Neale of the said Borough, shoemaker, and to Rebekah the wife of John Sumner of Charlecoate aforesaid, yeoman. That by reason the said ground is yett unbuilt and the foundacion thereof not laid within the said 2 years, the peticioner conceives the disposall of the same to be in this Honorable Court. That your Peticioner is willing to undertake to rebuild one ½ of the said ground whereon the said

[1] Space not filled in.

White Lyon inn stood and hath treated with the said Dorothy Hopkins, James Neale and Mary his wife and John Sumner and Rebekah his wife for the same, and they and every of them have consented and agreed that for the consideracion of the summ of £30 of lawfull money of England, he your Peticioner shall have all that one moiety or half part of the said ground with one half of all bricks, stones and materialls lying on the same, viz. all that one moiety or half part of the said ground lying and being and next adjoyning to the house of Thomas Dixon on the west side thereof equally to be divided, and alsoe to have one half of all commons and common of pasture, gardens, backsides and appurtenances thereto belonging, to him and his heirs for ever, as by articles of agreement under their hands and seales beareing date the 20th of October last doth and may appear. Your Peticioner therefore humbly prays that for the consideracion aforesaid he may have the said ground assured to him and his heirs by decree of this Court, soe that he may be encouraged to goe on and rebuild the same, and your Peticioner shall ever pray, etc.[1]

A Jury to value ground encroached by John Atterbury dec.

Warr' Burg'.[2] To Richard Hadley of the Borough aforesaid, gen.

By vertue of an order of the Court of Record held att the Mayor's Parlour on Munday the 31st day of May last by vertue of an Act of Parliament for the Rebuilding of the Town of Warwick, etc., you are hereby required to cause to come before the Commissioners or Judges appointed by the said Act the next Court of Record to be held att the Mayor's Parlour on Munday the 6th day of this instant September by ten of the clock in the forenoon, twelve free and lawfull men of the said Borough to assess and sett a price upon a certaine peice of ground taken out of the Church ground in the Church Street lying next and adjoyning to the wall of Mr William Tarver and now in the possession of [   ][3] the wife of John Atterbury lately deceased,[4] and alsoe to sett a price upon the 12 inches of ground in breadth and twenty foot in length which was found by a jury on the 27th day of July 1696 to be built upon and encroched out of the said ground by the said John Atterberry, and a true verdict thereof shall make to this Court according to the best of their judgements, and have you then and there the names of the jury and this precept. Dated the 1st day of September in the ninth year of his now Majesty's reign annoque Domini 1697

John Mitchener, Reg'.

[1] Endorsed 'A Peticion by one who would buy ground and build of Commissioners.'
[2] This and the next document are fastened together by a pin.
[3] Space not filled in.
[4] John Atterbury was buried 6 Aug. 1697.

Warr' Burg'. Nomina juratorum inter inhabitantes de Burgo predicto et Johannes [*sic*] Atterbury dec.[1]

Aaron Rogers, gen.
Devereux Whadcock, gen.
Josephus Blissett, gen.[2]
Ricardus Grimes, gen.
Ricardus Lane, gen.
Thomas Young, gen.[3]
Johannes Rogers, gen.
Willelmus Makepeace, gen.[2]
Johannes Davis[3]
Edwardus Barnacle
Thomas Lea[3]
Edwardus Owen[2]
Thomas Griffin, gen.

Willelmus Nicholls
Ricardus Burnill[2]
Richard[4] Fort[2]
Josephus Kerby[2]
Thomas Greenway[3]
Johannes Cater
Johannes Atkins[3]
Thomas Gibbs jun.
Johannes Glover[3]
Robertus Bromill[3]
Johannes Dreydon[3]
Timotheus Smith[3]

[Endorsed] The said jurors doe find the ground belonging to the back part of the Church ground in the Church Street and now in possession of the widow Atterberry to be worth £5 and the 12 inches of ground in breadth and twenty foot of ground in length to be worth two shillings and six pence.

Precept to summon Churchwardens concerning the Church ground

Warr' Burg'. To Richard Hadley of the Borough aforesaid, gent.

By vertue of an order of Court held att the Mayor's Parlour on Munday the 23rd day of August last, you are hereby required to summon the church wardens of the parish of Saint Mary in this Borough, to appear in this Court on Munday next being the 6th day of this instant September then and there to shew cause why the Commissioners may not sell the ground call'd the Church ground in the Church Street to such person or persons who will undertake to rebuild the same, and hereof faile not. Dated the 1st day of September 1697.

John Mitchener, Reg'.

Precept to summon John Davis, baker, and William Eborall, saddler

Warr' Burg'. To Richard Hadley of the Borough aforesaid, gen'.

By vertue of an order of the Court of Record held at the Mayor's Parlour on Munday the [   ][5] day of [   ][5] by the Commissioners or Judges

---

[1] 'dec.' added below the name.
[2] These names are marked with a dot.
[3] These names are marked with a dot and the word 'jur'.'.
[4] Written above 'Johannes' struck out.
[5] Space not filled in.

appointed by an Act of Parliament for the Rebuilding the Towne of Warwick, etc., and upon reading the Peticion of John Burton, inkeeper, for relief and order to be had and made touching the matters therein mencioned, exhibited into the said Court and there remaineing, You are hereby required to summon John Davis of this Borough, baker, and William Eborall, sadler, to appear att the next Court of Record to be held att the Mayor's Parlour within this Borough on Munday the 6th day of this instant, to the end that matters in differences contained in the said Peticion may be there heard and determined by the Commissioners or Judges according to the Act aforesaid, and hereof you are not to faile. Dated the 1st day of September in the 9th year of his Majesty's reign annoque Domini 1697.

John Mitchener Reg'.

Precept to summon Richard King, carpenter

Warwick Burg'. To Richard Hadley of the Borough aforesaid gen'.

By vertue of an order of the Court of Record held at the Mayor's Parlour on Munday the [   ]¹ day of [   ]¹ by the Commissioners or Judges appointed by an Act of Parliament for the Rebuilding the Towne of Warwick, etc., and upon reading the Peticions of Thomas Dixon, blacksmith, and George Chinn, carpenter, for relief and order to be had and made touching the matters therein mencioned exhibited into the said Court and therein remaineing, You are hereby required to summon Richard King, carpenter, to appeare at the next Court of Record to be held att the Mayor's Parlour within the said Borough on Munday the 6th day of this instant September to the end that the matters in difference contained in the said Peticions may be there heard and determined by the Commissioners or Judges according to the Act aforesaid. Dated the 1st day of September in the 9th year of his now Majesty's reign, annoque Domini 1697

John Mitchener, Regist'.

Petition of Thomas Mayo of Rugby

Warr' Burg'. To the Rt Honorable and others the Commissioners sitting at the Mayor's Parlour on Munday the 6th day of September 1697.

The Humble Peticion of Thomas Mayo of Rughby in the County of Warwick, yeoman, Sheweth:
That Edward Mayo of the said Borough, carpenter, being seized of a messuage or tenement before the late fire, scituate neer the Joyce Poole in the said Borough, and alsoe of one other messuage or tenement next adjoyning to that before mencioned, did on the 19th day of January 1691, for and in consideracion of the summ of £20, mortgage the same to William Lingham

---

¹ Space not filled in.

of this Borough, gent., for 1000 years att one pepper corn per annum to be paid to the said Edward Mayo, with provisoe that if he the said Edward Mayo should pay or cause to be paid the aforesaid summ of twenty pounds to the said Mr Lingham, on the 19th day of July then next following, that then the said mortgage to be void and of none effect, or else to remaine in full force. That the said William Lingham did on the 18th day of January 1692 in consideracion of the above mencion'd summ of £20, assigne the said mortgage over unto your Peticioner for the number of years therein contained, and to hold the same in such manner as he the said Mr Lingham might have done. That the said messuages were burnt down by the said fire, and the ground thereof remaines yet unbuilt, by reason whereof the same is now fall'n into the hands of this Honorable Court, to dispose and sell the same to such person or persons who will undertake to rebuild the said ground. That the Peticioner being willing to undertake to rebuild the said ground, humbly prays that in consideracion of his said mortgage he may have the same assured to him and his heirs by decree of this Court, and your Peticioner shall ever pray, etc.

Petition of Thomas Masters, carpenter, and William Smith, mason

Warr' Burg'. To the Rt Honorable and others the Commissioners sitting att the Mayor's Parlour on Munday the 6th day of September 1697

The Humble Peticion of Thomas Masters, carpenter, and William Smith, mason, Sheweth:

That your Peticioners did by articles of agreement made between Mr Fulk Weale, draper, and your Peticioners undertake to build for him the said Mr Weale on his toft of burnt ground next adjoyning on the east side to the corner ground of the High Street on the south side of the said street, and on the west side to the ground of Mr Cook since purchased and built upon by Thomas Dadley, butcher, deceased,[1] one good and substantiall messuage according to the draught then agreed on by the said Mr Weale. That your Peticioners built the party wall of 9 inches thick upon the said ground soe purchased by the said Thomas Dadley, finding all materialls and workmanship used in and about the same. That the said Thomas Dadley made use of and built upon the said party wall. That your Peticioners have made demand according to the Act of Parliament of the widow Dadley for the charges of the same, but she utterly refuses to pay them, pretending that she is forbid by the said Mr Weale. That your Peticioners have built and done considerable more work for the said Mr Weale in and about his house, by his order and direccion, more than is contained and expressed in the said articles. That they have severall times demanded of the said Mr Weale their money for such their extraordinary work, but he doth utterly

---

[1] Buried 12 Nov. 1696.

refuse to pay them or to come to any account with them for the same. Your Peticioner therefore humbly prays that the said widow Dadley may be summon'd to appear and compelled by order of this Court to pay for the said party walls, and that the said Mr Weale may be also summon'd to appear to answer the contents of this Peticion and be brought to account, and made to pay what shall appeare to be due to your Peticioners on the ballance of the said account, and your Peticioners shall ever pray, etc.

Petition of George Tippin, cutler

Warr' Burg'. To the Rt Honorable and others the Commissioners or Judges appointed by an Act of Parliament for the Rebuilding the Town of Warwick, etc., sitting att the Mayor's Parlour on Munday the 6th day of September anno Domini 1697

The Humble Peticion of George Tippin, cutler, Sheweth:
That after the late fire in this Borough, one Alfick, refiner, was employed to wash and refine the lead and bell metall lying amongst the rubbish of the Church of Saint Maryes. That after the said Alfick had done and was gone, and the rubbish of the tower removed, your Peticioner undertook to wash and refine the lead and bell metall which he could find lying amongst the said rubbish, and was to be allowed the price of one half of such lead and bell metall that he should soe find and refine (viz.) for the said lead att the rate of £10 per tunn, and for the bell metall att the rate of 8d. per lib. being the same rates as the said Elfick had.

That your Peticioner wash'd and refin'd out of the said rubbish of the church 69 piggs of lead weighing	77c.	3qrs	10li
And out of the rubbish of the chancell and vestry 12 piggs weighing	12	0	0
That the whole weight of the said lead was	89	3	10

And that he found out and refin'd 1c. 1qr 3li
of bell metall which att 8d. per lib. is £4 15s. 4d.

The half of which is due to your Peticioner being	£2	7s.	8d.
That one half of the said 89c. 3qr 10li of lead is two tun 4c. 3qrs 19li att £10 per tunn is	22	9	0
The summ due to your Peticioner is	24	16	8

That he had £20 of Mr Whadcock then Mayor at first
when he went about the said work to pay workmen

and buy charcoale to refine the same	20	0	0
Soe there remains due to him	4	16	8

That he applyed himself to Mr Whadcock for the said £4 16 8 but he told your Peticioner he must peticion this Court to know by whom the same must be paid. Your Peticioner therefore humbly prays, he haveing occasion for the said money, to know by whom he must be paid the same, and your Peticioner shall ever pray, etc.

Petition of Edward Kitchin of Alveston and Thomas Whitacre of Wellesbourne

Warr' Burg'. To the Rt Honorable and others the Commissioners sitting att the Mayor's Parlour on Munday the 6th day of September 1697

The humble Peticion of Edward Kitching of Alveston and Thomas Whitacre of Welsborn, Sheweth:

That John Avern of this Borough, tayler, bought of your Peticioners one thousand foot of elm boards for £4 17s. 6d. That the said Avern brought the same and used them in and about his 2 houses in the Swan Lane. That one of the said houses is now in the possession of Joseph Avern, son of the said John, and the other in the possession of Barnaby Ashby. That the said John Avern never paid your peticioners for the said boards and is now gone off, as your Peticioners veryly believe, on purpose to defraud his creditors. Your Peticioners therefore pray that this Court will take the same into their consideracions and make some order therein that they may have their said money, either by the rent of the said house or by some other means, and your peticioner shall ever pray, etc.

signum
Edward X Kitchin

Petition of Thomas Lea, innkeeper

Warr' Burg'. To the Rt Honorable and others the Commissioners sitting att the Mayor's Parlour on Munday the 11 day of October anno Domini 1697.

The humble Peticion of Thomas Lea of this Borough, inkeeper, Sheweth:

That your Peticioner hath since the late fire in this Burr' built a house in the Markett Place neere the pillory. That he alsoe built att his own charge the partyes walls of the said house and left sufficient toothing for the joyning the next house that should be built to the same. That one James Wilson a Scotchman hath made use of the said party wall by building thereupon and refuses to pay your peticioner for the same, the charge of which come to £7 8s. 5d., of which he the Peticioner hath received £4 but the said Wilson doth refuse to pay the residue thereof being £3 8 5. Your Peticioner therefore humbly prays the said Wilson may be summon'd to answer the said Peticion and be made to pay the same, and he alsoe prays he may be allowed for 160 foot of ground taken away from him to enlarge the street, and your Peticioner shall ever pray.

Petition of George Chinn, carpenter

Warr' Burg'. To the Rt Honorable and others the Commissioners sitting att the Mayor's Parlour on Munday the 11 day of October anno Domini 1697

The humble Peticion of George Chinn of the Burr' of Warr', carpenter, Sheweth:

That your Peticioner since the late fire built two houses in the High Street upon the ground whereon before the late fire stood a messuage in possession of Thomas Maunder, leaveing sufficient party walls for the next builder of the ground adjoyning on the west side thereof. That Mr Richard Lane and Thomas Masters bought the said ground and have built upon the same and made use of your Peticioners said party walls. That your Peticioner sold the 2 houses to Mr Mann of Killenworth and the said Mr Mann sold one of the same to Thomas Abbotts, shoemaker. That the said Thomas Abbotts built an additionall building backward and made use of some part of the said wall valued by the Surveyor att £1 10s. 4d. which said summ the said Mr Lane, Thomas Masters and Thomas Abbotts and every of them refuses to pay. Your Peticioner therefore humbly prays the summons of this Court to summon the said partyes to appear in this Court, and they or one of them may be ordered to pay for the same, and your Peticioner shall ever pray.

Your Peticioner further prays that he may borrow the sum of £40[1] out of the Charity monies, he giveing security of his houses in the Swan Lane by mortgage or. . . .[2]

Petition of Mr Aileworth of Wellesbourn

Warr' Burg'. To the Rt Honorable and others the Commissioners sitting att the Mayor's Parlour on Munday the 11th day of October anno Domini 1697

The humble Peticion of Mr Aileworth of Welsborne, gent., Sheweth:

That your Peticioner was before the late fire seized of a messuage or tenement scituate lying and being in a place call'd the Butts. That the same was burnt down by the said fire. That your Peticioner hath rebuilt on the toft whereon the same did stand one other good and substantiall messuage or tenement. Your Peticioner therefore humbly prays he may be allowed 1s. 6d. in the pound for the loss of the said messuage soe burnt down as the same is reduced to £18, and your peticioner shall ever pray, etc.

---

[1] Followed by 'or £50' struck out.
[2] This sentence is left unfinished.

Memorandum of an agreement between Thomas Lane, saddler, and John Burton, silkweaver

Memorandum, the seaventeenth day of February anno Domini 1697[/8] it was then fully agreed upon between Thomas Lane late of the Borough of Warwick, sadler, and John Burton of the said Borough of Warwicke, silkweaver, that whereas there is a parcell of ground lying neare the Markett Place within the said Borough of Warwick and now in the tenure or occupacion of the said John Burton and on part whereof the said John Burton hath lately built a new house and whereon lately stood a messuage or tenement before the late dreadfull fire in Warwick called the King's Arms Inne and being the proper land of the said Thomas Lane, that the Commissioners appointed by the late Act of Parliament intituled an Act for the Rebuilding of the Towne of Warwicke consumed by the late dreadfull fire do take cognizance of the same and do if they think the same proper grant a decree of all the said ground to the said John Burton his heires and assignes for ever, with a privisoe therein neverthelesse that the said John Burton and his heires do and shall within one month next after such decree made, well and truly pay or cause to be paid unto the said Thomas Lane his executors, administrators and assignes the summe of fourty pounds of lawfull money of England, and also all such charitable money received by him the said John Burton by order of the said Comissioners for the losse of the said house, and also the benefitt of all other charitable money that shall hereafter be paid upon the same account. To which agreement the said Thomas Lane and John Burton have hereunto sett their hands and seales the day and yeare first above written.

Sealed and subscribed	Thomas Lane [seal]
in the presence of	
Thomas Roberts	The marke of
William Roe	John X Burton [seal]

Petition of the Mayor and Aldermen

Warr' Burg'. To the Rt Honorable and others the Commissioners sitting att the Mayor's Parlour on Munday the [   ][1] day of [   ][1] anno Domini 1697,

The humble Peticion of the Mayor and Aldermen of the said Borough: That your Peticioners have lately sold unto John Williams of the Borough aforesaid, carpenter, a certain peice or parcell of burnt ground whereon before the late fire stood a messuage or tenement on the south side of the High Pavement then in possession of Mr Gibbs adjoyning on the east side

---

[1] Spaces not filled in, exact dates uncertain.

to Mr Tomkys, on the west to the ground whereon before the said fire the White Lyon Inn stood. That the said John Williams is by agreement to pay for the said ground to your Peticioners the summ of £25. That two whole years were passed since the said fire and the foundacions of the said ground not then laid, in default whereof your Peticioners conceive they cannot make the said John Williams a sure title to the said ground. That the said Mr Tomkys hath made a window in that part of his house looking into the said ground which if not stopped up will prove very prejudiciall to the builder of the same. Your Peticioner therefore humbly prays that the said Mr Tomkys may be summon'd to appear in Court or that a jury may be impanelled to determine the same, and that the said ground for the consideracion aforesaid may be decreed to the said John Williams, and your Peticioner etc.

Petition of Oken's Feoffees

Warr' Burg'. To the Rt Honorable and others the Commissioners sitting att the Mayor's Parlour on Munday the [   ]¹ day of [   ]¹ anno 1697

The Humble Peticion of the Feoffees of Thomas Oken, gent., deceased,² Sheweth:
That whereas severall of the houses of the said Thomas Oken's were burnt down by the late fire, and your Peticioners being obliged to rebuild the same, and whereas the rents of the said Thomas Oken's being much lessened by the said fire, that there hath been already the summ of one hundred pounds borrowed toward rebuilding the same out of the Charity moneys, your Peticioners therefore humbly prays they may be lent the summ of £150 more out of the Charity moneys to make the said summ of £250 for the repayment of which they are willing to mortgage the new house in the Church Street now in the possession of Mr Thomas Newsham.

[Endorsed in another hand] A Peticion to the Commissioners from the Mayor and Alderman for an allowance for the fronte ground in the Sheep Street taken away from the parsonage house and for Mr Oken's house next adjoyning. Alsoe for some rubbish stone neare the parsonage house to make a house of office for Mr Edes, minister.

Petition of Dorothy Hopkins of Charlecote, widow, and others

Warr' Burg'. To the Rt Honorable and others the Commissioners sitting att the Mayor's Parlour on Munday the[   ]³ day of [   ]³ 1697

¹ Spaces not filled in, exact dates uncertain.
² The rest of the page is blank. The text of the petition is written on a small piece of paper folded within it.   ³ Space not filled in.

The humble Peticion of Dorothy Hopkins of Charlecoate, widow, James Neale of the Burrough aforesaid, shooemaker, and Mary his wife, and John Sumner of Charlecoate aforesaid, yeoman, and Rebekah his wife, Sheweth: That your Peticioner Dorothy Hopkins was before the late fire seized of a certaine messuage or tenement scituate on the south side of the Highstreet in the said Burrough called or known by the name of the White Lyon Inn then in possession of George Watts adjoyning on the east side thereof to the house belonging to the Corporacion then in possession of Thomas Gibbs, and on the west side thereof to a messuage or tenement then in possession of Thomas Dixon, for the term of her naturall life, the remainder to Mary Neale, wife of the said James Neale, and Rebekah Sumner, wife of the said John Sumner, daughters of the said Dorothy Hopkins by John Walford her first husband. That the said messuage was totally burnt down by the said fire. That neither of the peticioners are able to rebuild the same. That 2 whole years are passed since the said fire and the foundacions of the said ground not yett laid, in default whereof your Peticioners conceive the disposall of the same to be in the Commissioners or Judges appointed by the said Act. That your Peticioners have contracted and agreed with Thomas Masters, carpenter, for one moiety or half part of the said ground (viz.) that half part next adjoyning to the house and ground of Thomas Dixon with one half of all commons and common of pasture to the same belonging, and alsoe one half of all brick, stone and other materialls for building lying on the said ground, for the consideracion of the summ of £30 to be paid to the said James Neale and Mary his wife. Your Peticioners therefore humbly prays that the said Thomas Masters may be summon'd to appear and that the said agreement may be confirmed by decree of this Court, and your Peticioners shall ever pray, etc.

Petition of Oken's Feoffees

Warr' Burg'. To the Rt Honorable and others the Commissioners for Rebuilding the Town of Warwick, etc., sitting att the Mayor's Parlour on Tuesday the 9th day of August 1698

The Petition of the Feoffees of Thomas Oken deceased, Sheweth:
That Matthew Busbie was before the late fire tenant to your Peticioners in a house lying in a back street within this Borough cald by the name of the Peacock. That the said house was burnt down by the late fire, and remaines yett unbuilt. Your Peticioners therefore humbly pray that a jury may be impanelled and sworn att the next Court to view and sett out the ground whereon before the late fire the said house stood, and alsoe that witnesses may be summon'd to give evidence to the said jury relateing to the meets and bounds of the said ground, and your Peticioner shall ever pray, etc.

Letter of William Challoner

Sir, pray yow lett me begg the favour of yow to gett John Burton's decree drawne upp, for I cannot gett one penny of my money for want of it, and he tells me his money is and hath beene longe since ready if that were done. Pray yow lett me entreate your speedy kindnes herein, which will much oblige, Sir,

Stratford   Your very humble servant,
14 Jan. 1698[/9]   Wm. Challoner
              It was made the beginning of August last.

[Endorsed] These for Thomas Newsham, Esq. att his house in Warwicke.

Petition of George Chinn, carpenter, and George Taylor, blacksmith

Warr' Burg'. To the Rt Honorable and others the Commissioners sitting att the Court of Record held att the Mayor's Parlour on Munday the 16th day of January 1698/9.

    The Humble Peticion of George Chinn, carpenter, and George Tayler, blacksmith, Sheweth:
That your Peticioners hath lately built two houses in the Swan Lane on part of the ground call'd the Bell ground, purchased by your Peticioners of William Tarver, gen., being about one half of the said ground call'd the Bell ground. Your Peticioners therefore humbly pray that they may be allow'd one shilling and six pence in the pound for such part of the loss of the said Bell ground given in by the late fire as this Court shall think fitt, and your Peticioners shall ever pray, etc.

Petition of George Chesley, tailor

Warr' Burg'. To the Rt Honorable and others the Commissioners sitting att the Court of Record held by vertue of an Act of Parliament for Rebuilding the Town of Warwick, etc., at the Mayor's Parlour on Munday the 16th day of January 1698/9,

    The Humble Peticion of Georg Chesley of the Borough of Warwick, tayler, Sheweth:
That Edward Chesley, your Peticioner's father lately deceased,[1] did sometime before his death erect and build all that one messuage or tenement scituate lying and being on the south side of the Highstreet adjoyning on the west side thereof to the house built by Edmund Wilson, gent., and on the east side thereof to a house now in possession of Francis Bickley. That the said Edward Chesley did alsoe build a garden wall lying between the

---

[1] Buried 11 July 1698.

garden ground of the said Mr Wilsons house and the garden ground of your Peticioner soe farr as this Peticioner conceived his right was to build the same. That the mound att the bottom of your Peticioners garden lyes still open, to the great prejudice of your Peticioner. That your Peticioner conceives the right of the said mound to be in the said Edmund Wilson. Your Peticioner therefore humbly prays the said Edmund Wilson may be summon'd to appear in this Court and that he may be ordered to make up the said mound within such time as this Court shall think fitt, or that a jury may be impanelled to determine, and your Peticioner shall ever pray, etc.

Petition of inhabitants of Jury Street

Warr' Burg'. To the Rt Honorable and others the Commissioners or Judges appointed by an Act of Parliament for the Rebuilding of the Town of Warwick, etc., sitting att the Mayor's Parlour on Wednesday the 2nd day of August 1699,

The Humble Peticion of severall inhabitants of the Jury Street within the said Borough in behalf of themselves and the rest of the inhabitants there, Sheweth:

That severall of the owners and proprietors of houses fronting the Jury Street and Castle Street within this Borough have neglected to unthatch severall of the outhouses and buildings, parcell of and belonging to such their houses fronting the said streets, and to slate or tyle the same according to an Act of Parliament for Rebuilding the said Town; by reason whereof your Peticioners conceive themselves to live in great danger, in case a fire should againe happen within this Borough, if not timely prevented. Your Peticioners therefore humbly pray that this Court will take the same into consideracion, and make such order therein as may bind and compell the owners of such buildings to tyle the same according to the said Act within such time as this Court shall direct. And your Peticioners shall ever pray, etc.

Wm. Tarver	Geo. Webb	Tho. Edes
A. Prescott	Geo Tipping	John Hands
Roger Smith	Tim. Norbury	Ed. Tippin
Brook Chernocke	Ebenezer Clyton	John Bullock
Ann Comerford	Sam. Barber	Joseph Horton
John Smith	John Kent	

Petition of Richard Hands, joiner

Warr' Burg'. To the Rt Honorable and others the Commissioners appointed by an Act of Parliament for Rebuilding of the Town of Warwick sitting att the Mayor's Parlour on Thursday the 25th day of January 1699[/1700],

The Humble Peticion of Richard Hands of the said Borough, joyner, Sheweth:

That your Peticioner is willing to become purchaser of a certaine toft or peice of burnt ground lying on the north side of the High Street within the said Borough called the Bell ground adjoyning on the west part to the new house built by Samuell Acock, in case he may be allow'd to build on the said ground forty foot in building up the Swan Lane and then to make a brick wall from the said building up to the house built by George Tayler in said Swan Lane. Your Peticioner therefore humbly prays he may be admitted to build in manner aforesaid on the said ground up the said lane and to make a wall as aforesaid, and your Peticioner shall ever pray, etc.

Petition of William Edes, Vicar of St Mary's

Warr' Burg'. To the Rt Honorable and others the Commissioners appointed by an Act of Parliament for Rebuilding of the Town of Warwicke sitting att the Mayor's Parlour on Thursday the 25th day of January 1699[/1700]

The Humble Peticion of William Edes, Vicar of St Maryes Parish within the said Borough, Sheweth:

That your Peticioner out of his sallery as Vicar of St Mary's parish aforesaid setts off with the Corporacion of the said Borough the summ of three pounds, which summ he allows in lieu of the proffitt to be made by the church yard of St Mary's Church. That since the takeing up of the old foundacions of the said church and removeing the rubbish of the same and by digging severall quarrys to gett stone out of the said church yard, your Peticioner hath been att a considerable damage in looseing the benefitt which he could have made thereby yearly since the late fire within this Borough and as the proffitts of the same was to him yearly before the said fire. Your Peticioner therefore humbly prays that whereas he was a great sufferer by the said fire, and in consideracion of the considerable allowance made by him to the Corporacion out of his said sallery for the said church yard and the considerable damage he hath sustained by reason aforesaid, this Court will take the same into consideracion and make such allowance to him for the same as they in their judgments shall think meet, and your Peticioner shall ever pray, etc.

Petition of Thomas Lea and others

Warr' Burg'. To the Rt Honorable and others the Commissioners appointed by an Act of Parliament for Rebuilding the Town of Warwick sitting att the Court of Record held the 17th day of June 1700,

The Humble Peticion of Thomas Lea, John Burton, James Wilson and Richard Hancox, Sheweth:

That your Peticioners being owners of ground scituate lying and being in the street leading to the Pillory, have had great numbers of feet of ground taken away from them by this Court to enlarge the said street, by which they were reduced into a very narrow compass to rebuild their houses there which proves very prejudiciall to them, your Peticioners therefore humbly pray that this Court will take the same into consideracion and allow them more by the foot then is already allow'd them by order of Court of the 16th day of January last, that Court haveing order'd but 5d. per foot, and your Peticioners shall ever pray.

Petition of John Hollyoake

To the Rt Honorable and others the Commissioners sitting att the Mayor's Parlour on Munday the 12th day of May 1701 by vertue of an Act of Parliament for Rebuilding the Town of Warwick, etc.,

The Humble Peticion of John Hollyoake of the Borough aforesaid, gent., Sheweth:

That your Peticioner did since the late fire which happen'd within the said Borough rebuild a certain messuage or tenement in the Highstreet now in the possession of Edward Venor, baker, next adjoyning on the east thereof to the ground (now unbuilt upon) [on] which before the said late fire stood a certaine messuage or tenement belonging unto and in the possession of Mary Overton, that the mounds lying between your peticioners ground and the said ground now unbuilt upon did belong unto the said Mary Overton and she to putt up and repaire the same, and alsoe that the mounds lying between your peticioners ground belonging to his now dwelling house and the ground before the late fire belonging to the two inns call'd the Dolphin Inn and the Bear Inn doth now belong unto John Pinley, mason, and George Chinn, carpenter, late purchasers of the said ground. That neither the said Mary Overton now the wife of [   ]¹ Jeacocks of Lightorn (or any one for her), John Pinley and George Chinn hath taken any care to make up their said severall mounds to the prejudice of your Peticioner but doth refuse or att least neglect soe to doe. Your Peticioner therefore humbly prays that the said partyes may be summon'd to appear in this Court to answer such their neglect and that he may be speedily reliev'd in the premisses by this Court, and your Peticioner shall ever pray, etc.

---

¹ Space not filled in.

Petition of Matthew Busby, Edward Deacon and Joseph Avern

Warr' Burg'. To the Rt Honorable and others the Commissioners apponted by an Act of Parliament for the Rebuilding of the Town of Warwick, etc.,[1]

The Humble Peticion of Matthew Busby, Edward Deacon and Joseph Avern, all of the said Burrough, Sheweth:

That your Peticioners are seized of three certaine messuages or tenements scituate lying and being in the Swan Lane in the said Borough. That the watercourses running from their said messuages did before the late fire goe through the ground before the said fire belonging to the Swan Inn into the ground of Mr Joseph Blissett. That the said watercourse is now stopt up by reason of the rubbish now lying on the said Swann ground to the great damage of your Peticioners. That Thomas Masters being now the owner of the said ground, your Peticioners humbly pray that the said Masters may be summon'd to appeare and that your Peticioners may be relieved therein as to this Court shall seem meet, and your Peticioners shall ever pray, etc.

Petition of Francis Smart

Warr' Burg'. To the Rt Honorable and others the Commissioners appointed by an Act of Parliament for the Rebuilding of the Town of Warr' etc.,[2]

The Humble Peticion of Francis Smart, Sheweth:

That your Peticioner is seized of a certaine messuage or tenement scituate in the Church Street in the said Borough now in the possession of [   ][3] Mayo, millener. That Mr[4] Nicholas Wrothwell haveing bought of Mr William Tarver a certaine garden call'd the Swann garden lying att the west side of the garden belonging to your Peticioner's house, hath built up on part of the said Swan garden a certaine building for a stable with roomes over the same, and hath put up in the said building a window or light looking into your Peticioner's garden which is like to be a damage to him, his tenants abovesaid haveing very much complained thereof. Your Peticioner therefore humbly prays that the said Mr Wrothwell may be summon'd to appear in this Court, and there being noe building on the said garden ground before the late fire, may be obliged to stopp up the said light, and your Peticioner shall ever pray.

Jury upon this March the 31st 170[4?][5]

---

[1] Endorsed: 'Matt. Busby etc. peticion July 2nd 1702.'
[2] Endorsed: 'Francis Smart peticion July 2nd 1702.'
[3] Space not filled in.
[4] 'Mr' inserted in a space by another hand.
[5] Added in the margin by another hand. '170[4?]' altered from '170[3?]'.

Petition of Thomas Clements, baker

Warr' Burg'. To the Rt Honorable and others the Commissioners appointed by an Act of Parliament for the Rebuilding of the Town of Warwick, etc.,[1]

The Humble Peticion of Thomas Clements of the said Borough, baker, Sheweth:

That Richard Hands, joyner, hath by consent of your Peticioner built on a certaine piece or parcell of ground which before the late fire did belong to your Peticioners dwelling house and now is lying into the square against the west end of the Church of St Mary. That the said peice of ground as the same was measured by Mr James Fish did amount unto six hundred and twenty foot. That the said Richard Hands and your Peticioner did agree to leave the price of the said ground to this Court, and they to order what summ your Peticioner should receive for the same. Your Peticioner therefore humbly prays that this Court will take the same into their consideracion, and allow him such summ for the said ground as they in their judgments shall think most reasonable and shall deserve for the same, and your Peticioner shall ever pray, etc.

Petition of William Jeacock of Lighthorne

Warr' Burr'. To the Rt Honorable and others the Commissioners for Rebuilding the Towne of Warwick, etc., the 12th day of July 1703,

The Humble Peticion of William Jeacock of Lightorne in the County of Warwick, Sheweth:

That your Peticioner did by the direccion of Mr William Tarver bring and lay downe a considerable quantity of lime to be used in and about the rebuilding of the house of the said William Tarver now in possession of Mr Whadcock. That the said William Tarver paid your Peticioner for part of the said lime and there is now remaineing due the summ of three pounds, which your Peticioner hath demanded of the said Mr Tarver but he refuseth to pay the same, telling your Peticioner that he must look after his money of one Mr Bray who was the builder of the said house. That the said Mr Tarver never att any time told this Peticioner that he must receive mony for the said lime of the said Bray, but did severall times desire him not to lett the workmen want lime for his house. Your Peticioner therefore humbly prays that this Court will take the same into consideracion and that he may have relief therein, and your Peticioner shall ever pray, etc.

---

[1] Endorsed 'Thomas Clements peticion July 2nd 1702.'

Petition of John Phillipps, carpenter

Warr'. To the Rt. Honorable and other the Commissioners and Trustees sitting att the Court of Record within this Borough held the 30th day of March 1704

The Humble Peticion of John Phillipps, carpenter, Sheweth:

That your Peticioner was elected by this Court one of the Surveyors to sett out the severall streets and to doe other matters that this Court should direct and appoint and in order thereto was sworn on the 22nd day of July 1695. That your peticioner did assist in the setting out of the streets, altering the foundacions and other matters by the direccion and appointment of this Court and never was yett allow'd anything for the same. Your peticioner therefore humbly prays that he may have some allowance for his attendance upon the said Court and assisting as aforesaid, and your Peticioner shall ever pray, etc.

Petition of Matthew Busby, innkeeper

To the Rt. Honorable and other the Commissioners for Rebuilding the Towne of Warwick sitting att the Mayors Parlour the 30th day of March 1704

The Humble Peticion of Matthew Busby of the said Borough, inkeeper, Sheweth:

That your Peticioner is seized of a certaine messuage or tenement scituate lying and being within the Swann Lane in the said Borough. That the watercourse running from his said messuage did before the late fire go through the ground then belonging to the Swann Inn and from thence into the ground of Mr Joseph Blissett. That the said watercourse is now stopt up by reason of the rubbish now lying on the said Swann ground to the great damage of your Peticioner. Your Peticioner therefore humbly prays that the owners of the ground through which the said watercourse did formerly runn may be summon'd to appear att this Court, and that your Peticioner may be relieved therein as [to] this Court shall seem most necessary, and your Peticioner shall ever pray, etc.

Petition of Timothy Roberts, draper, and Thomas Wall, smith

Warr' Burg'. To the Rt. Honorable and other the Commissioners or Judges appointed by an Act of Parliament for the Rebuilding of the Town of Warwick, etc., sitting att the Mayors Parlour on Thursday the 21st day of September 1704,

The Humble Peticion of Timothy Roberts of the said Borough, draper, and Thomas Wall of the same, smith, Sheweth:

That your Peticioners are the owners of two certaine messuages or tenements lying within the said Borough in a certaine street there call'd the Highstreet built since the late fire which happen'd in the said Borough on the toft or burnt ground purchased of Mr Welton deceased. That there is a chief rent of twenty shillings issueing and payable yearly out of the said messuages which is a great incumbrance upon the same. Your Peticioners therefore humbly pray that the said chief rent may be abated to the summ of ten shillings yearly, and your Peticioners shall ever pray, etc.

Petition of Thomas Roberts, innkeeper

Warr' Burg'. To the Rt. Honorable and other the Commissioners or Judges appointed by an Act of Parliament for the Rebuilding the Town of Warwick, etc., sitting att the Court of Record held at the Mayor's Parlour on Thursday the 21st day of September 1704,
The Humble Peticion of Thomas Roberts of the said Borough, inkeeper, Sheweth:
That your Peticioner is tenant of a certaine messuage or tenement within the said Borough call'd and known by the name of the Red Lyon Inn. That this Court did formerly take a quantity of ground from the ground belonging to the said inn to enlarge the Swan Lane, and did order a wall to be built next the said Lane to mound out the ground soe taken away. Now your Peticioner humbly prayeth that this Court will order that part of the said lane against the said wall to be pitch'd with pibbles, the same being now a very bad way and that your Peticioner may not be putt to any charge towards doeing the same, he haveing but a very short term of years to come in the premisses aforesaid, and your Peticioner shall ever pray, etc.

Petition of Edward Norton

Warr' Burg'. To the Rt. Honorable and other the Commissioners or Judges appointed by an Act of Parliament for the Rebuilding of the Towne of Warr', etc., sitting att the Court of Record held att the Mayor's Parlour on Thursday the 21st of September 1704,
The Humble Peticion of Edward Norton of this Borough, gent., Sheweth:
That your Peticioner hath since the late fire rebuilt a messuage or tenement on the north side of the Highstreet adjoyning to the house now in the possession of Thomas Maunder. That there is a rent issueing and payable to the Lady of the manner for the said messuage the summ of six and twenty shillings yearly, which is a very great charge and incumbrance upon the same. Your Peticioner therefore humbly prayeth that this Court will in consideration of the great charge and expence he hath been att in building since the said fire, abate the said chief rent unto five shillings per annum, or

to such other summ as you in your judgements shall think most meet, and your Peticioner shall ever pray, etc.

[Endorsed] Mr Edward Norton's Peticion referr'd to the next court.

Petition of George Watts, innholder, and John Watts, chandler

Warr' Burg'. To the Rt Honorable and other the Commissioners or Judges appointed by an Act of Parliament for the Rebuilding of the Town of Warwick, etc., sitting att the Court of Record held att the Mayor's Parlour on Thursday the 21st day of September 1704,

The Humble Peticion of George Watts of this Borough, inholder, and John Watts of the same Borough, chandler, Sheweth:

That your Peticioners being the owners of two certaine messuages or tenements scituate on the east side of the Sheepstreet in the said Borough, the one in the possession of Henry Smith, butcher, and the other of your Peticioner George Watts, did on the second day of July 1702 peticion this Court to be reliev'd as to the watercourses running from the back part of their said houses.

That nothing was done in that matter untill the Court held the 8th day of Aprill 1703 att which time a jury was impanell'd and sworne to inquire into the same, and upon their verdict did find that there was noe water course running into the ground of Richard Hadley from the ground of your Peticioners said houses but what was through a certaine mound of pales which is now a stone wall, upon which the said Court did order the same to be soe decreed. That the said back part of the said ground being very low from the said street, your Peticioners are likely to be very much prejudiced in their houses if noe watercourse can be had from the same. Your Peticioners therefore humbly pray that before any decree be pass'd against them, a view thereof may be had by this Court and that they may be reliev'd in the premisses as you in your grave judgements shall think fitt, and your Peticioners shall ever pray, etc.

Petition of Samuel Acock, painter

Warr' Burg'. To the Rt Honorable and others the Commissioners or Judges appointed by an Act of Parliament for Rebuilding the Town of Warwick, etc., att the Court of Record held att the Mayors Parlour on Thursday the 21st day of September 1704,

The Humble Peticion of Samuell Acock of this Borough, painter, Sheweth:

That George Chinn being the owner of the messuage or tenement in the Highstreet within the said Borough call'd by the name of the Elephant and

Castle Inn hath putt up spouts under the eves of the back part of the said house which throws the wett upon the house now in the possession of your Peticioner to his very much prejudice and damage, and alsoe that he the said George Chinn hath undermin'd the garden wall of the said house by digging a quarry on the ground formerly the Bear ground, which will cause the said wall to fall if not timely prevented. Your Peticioner therefore humbly prayeth that this Court will order the said spout and wall to be viewed by the Surveyors and a report thereof made to this Court and that the Peticioner may be reliev'd in the premises, and your Peticioner shall ever pray, etc.

Petition of Thomas Clements, baker

Warr' Burg'. To the Rt Honorable and others the Commissioners or Judges appointed by an Act of Parliament for the Rebuilding the Town of Warwick and for determining differences touching houses burnt and demolished by reason of the late dreadfull fire there, sitting att the Mayor's Parlour the 8th day of November 1704,

The Humble Peticion of Thomas Clements of the Borough of Warwick, baker, Sheweth:

That William Clements your Peticioner's late father by his last will and testament bearing date the 20th day of May in the year of our Lord 1691 did give and bequeath unto Mary Clements your Peticioner's mother three cottages lying in Saltisford within the said Borough for and dureing her natural life and after her decease to goe unto his sons Samuell Clements and Abraham Clements and his grandchild John Clements and their heirs in such manner as is therein mencioned.

That the said William did likewise give unto the said Mary the house he then lived in being within the Markett Place Ward within the said Borough for and dureing her natural life and after her decease to your Peticioner Thomas Clements and his heirs for ever, and did likewise give unto your Peticioner after the decease of his said mother severall goods then lying and being in his said dwelling house together with all and singular his utensills and implements belonging to the trade of a baker, he your Peticioner paying unto Samuell Short the testator's son in law att the end of two years after his and his said wife's decease the summ of £20, and to his son in law William Silk after the expiracion and end of 4 years after his and his said wife's decease £20 more, and all the rest of his goods, chattells and personall estate he bequeathed unto his said wife Mary Clements whom he made executrix of his said last will.

That the said house in the Markett Place together with the greatest part of the goods were burnt and consumed in and by the late dreadfull fire which happen'd within the said Borough. The said house and goods being burnt and the said Mary not dying untill about 8 years[1] after the said fire, your Peticioner did not nor could enjoy any of the premisses bequeathed to him as aforesaid, notwithstanding which the said Samuell Short and William Silk threatens to sue your Peticioner for the £20 a peice to them bequeathed as aforesaid.[2] Your Peticioner haveing never possess'd the said goods conceiveth that he hath noe right to pay the said legacyes of £40[3] a peice unto the said Samuell Short and William Silk and[4] therefore humbly prays that this Court will take cognizance thereof and make such order and decree therein soe as he may be discharged of the said legacyes, and your Peticioner shall ever pray.

[Footnote] William Silk and his wife are both dead, the legacy if to be paid not due untill almost two years hence. Samuell Short hath given a release.

Petitions and other papers (undated) laid before the court

Petition of Mary Lock[?], widow

To the Right Honorable and the Right Worshipfull the Commissioners appointed by an Act of Parliament intituled an Act for the Rebuilding of the Borough of Warr' consumed by the late fire there,
   The humble peticion of Mary Louke,[5] widow, humbly sheweth:
That whereas your peticioner haveing severall goods which were burnt and consumed at the house of Richard Bromley liveing in the High Street in Warwick by the late fire amounting to fourty shillings or thereabouts, a bill of which was delivered unto the late Mayor of Warwick Mr Blissett, which bill your petitioner supposes is lost and she never hearing anything of it, nor hath received any thing of the Charity as other sufferers have, humbly desires that the premisses may be considered by you and that she may have a proportionable share of the said Charity as others have had or are like to have, for which great favour your petitioner shall be most thankfull and dayly pray for your Honours and Worships etc.

Petition of Robert Cole, tallow chandler

To the Rt Honorable, Rt Worshipfull and Worshipfull the Commissioners appointed by Act of Parliament for rebuilding of Warwicke and determine-ing differences concerning the same,

---

[1] Mary Clemens, widow, buried 5 June, 1702.
[2] 'notwithstanding ... aforesaid' underlined, possibly as cancellation.
[3] Altered from '£20'.
[4] 'a peice ... and' underlined, possibly as cancellation.
[5] The petition is endorsed 'Mary Lock, widow'.

The humble Peticion of Robert Cole of Warwick aforesaid, tallow chandler, Sheweth:

That your Peticioner is lessee to one John Hickes of a messuage lying in the Markett Place in Warwicke aforesaid, the greatest part whereof was lately burnt and part whereof is now rebuilt, and that your Peticioner hath 5 yeares and better to come in his lease and hath paid a fine att his entry of £23 besides £2 per annum reserved by the said lease to this present tyme, and hath given £8 towards rebuilding that part that is now new built which part cost £35 building, and that your Peticioner hath proferred to allow unto him 1s. for every pound that he hath laid out in the said building besides the said yearly rent of £2, but now the said John Hickes, takeing the advantage of your Peticioner, proposes unreasonable rent for the same and denyes your Peticioner the benefitt of his lease. Your Peticioner therefore humbly prayes that he may be releieved in such sort as to your grave wisdomes shall seeme most meete, and your Peticioner as in duty bound shall ever pray, etc.

Petition of Richard Kerby, butcher, and Jane his wife

To the Right Honorable and others the Commissioners and Judges appointed by an Act of Parliament for Rebuilding the Town of Warwick and for determineing differences touching houses burnt and demolished by reason of the late dreadfull fire there,

The Humble Peticion of Richard Kerby of this Borough, butcher, and Jane his wife,[1] Sheweth:

That Jane Kerby wife of your Peticioner was before the late fire seized of a messuage or tenement scituate in the High Pavement in the Borough aforesaid by vertue of the last will of Samuell Medly her late husband deceased, in which will he did bequeath severall legacies to be paid out of the said messuage at the death of the said Jane Kerby, as by the said will, relacion being thereunto had, will more fully appear, and whereas the said messuage was totally burnt down by the late fire and your Peticioner haveing greate occasion for mony, hath sold the peice of burnt ground whereon the said messuage did stand unto Mr Edward Norton of this Borough for the summ of one pound and three shillings in hand paid and the summ of twenty pounds to be paid to your Peticioner and the said Jane Kerby by the said Edward Norton after the said peice of ground shall be assured to him, as by articles of agreement bearing date the 3rd day of February annoque Domini 1694 made between your Peticioner and the said Jane Kerby of the one part, and the said Edward Norton of the other part, will more fully appeare. Your Peticioner therefore humbly prays this Court to assure and

---

[1] 'and Jane his wife' inserted in a space in another hand.

confirm the same to the said Edward Norton and his heirs for ever by Decree of this Court, whereby your Peticioner may receive the summ of twenty pounds according to the said articles, and your peticioner shall ever pray, etc.

Richard Kerby

Petition of James Fish for William Cooke

To the Right Honorable etc. the Commissioners for the rebuilding of the town of Warwick, the humble Petition of James Fish for and upon the account of Mr William Cooke, a sufferer by the late dreadfull fire, humbly sheweth:
That whereas the said William Cooke did sell severall parcells of burnt ground lying in the High Street in this Borr' of Warwick, reserving to himself all manner of charitie money that either was come in before the selling of the said parcells of ground or should hereafter come in to the use and reliefe of the said sufferers, your Peticioner does on the behalf of the said William Cooke most humbly pray that all such moneys as are due to the said William Cooke may be order'd to be paid into the hands of Mr William Hunt of Stratford upon Avon his lawfull attorney, and your Petitioner shall as in duty bound ever pray, etc.

[Endorsed] Mr William Cooke for £8 1 0

Petition of Thomas Hickes and Thomas Roberts

To the Right Honorable and the Right Worshipfull the Commissioners or Judges appointed by a late Act of Parliament intituled an Act of Parliament for the Rebuilding of the Borough of Warwick consumed by the late dreadfull fire,
    The humble peticion of Thomas Hickes and Thomas Roberts of the said Borough of Warwick humbly sheweth:
That whereas one of your petitioners being interested in the Red Lyon Inne in Warwick after the death of Mrs Townsend, an aged infirme woman, and the other by a lease thereof for some yeares yet to come, and understanding that it is your pleasures that the Swan Lane shall be stopped up and a new street made through almost the midle of the said Inne, whereby the said Inne will be made very incommodious one part of it lying on the one side of the street to be made and the other part on the other side, which will be very incommodious and almost unusefull, and bring the rent of the said Inne which is now near twenty pounds per annum not to halfe the value, and will also prove very incommodious to all the neighbourhood who have houses in the upper part of the said Swan Lane. Humbly therefore praying

your Honours and Worships seriously to weigh the bad consequences which will not only attend your petitioners by such a new street made but also the neighbourhood there; hoping upon your grave consideracion a better expedient may be found out which may be lesse prejudiciall to your petitioners and others, for which noble bounty your petitioners shall be most thankfull and dayly pray for your Honours and Worships.

Thomas Hickes
Tho: Roberts

Petition of John Avern, George Chinn, Joseph Avern and Timothy Hill

To the Right Honorable and the Right Worshipfull the Commissioners or Judges appointed by a late Act of Parliament intituled an Act for the rebuilding of the Borough of Warwick lately consumed by a late dreadfull fire,

The humble peticion of John Averne, George Chinne, Joseph Averne and Timothy Hill of the Swan Lane within the said Borough, humbly sheweth:

That whereas your petitioners being informed that you are about to stop up the passage of the said Swan Lane and to make it uselesse as to the lower end thereof, your petitioners being tradesmen and haveing their all lying there, humbly conceive that if the same be done your petitioners and their familyes must inevitably be ruined as also others of the neighbourhood for want of a trade; nothing of trade can be proposed in such a corner and the houses and ground by some of them lately purchased will not answer halfe the purchase, and are the more surprized by reason that they have laid out money in materialls to rebuild what was consumed there, and had before this rebuilt up part of the same had the ground been sett out as was humbly desired a month or six weekes since, but if this goes on your petitioners and their familyes will be utterly ruined and undone. Humbly therefore beseeching your Honours and Worshipps seriously to take the premisses into your grave consideracion, hoping you may finde out some better expedient that so many familyes may not be totally ruined, and your petitioners shall be most thankfull to your noble bounty and as in all duty bound dayly pray for your Honours and Worships.

John Avarne	Richard Clemens
George Chinne	Edward Scambler
Joseph Avarne	William Greenway
Timothy Hill	

Petition of John Hicks, smith

...[1] and Right ... Parliament for the rebuilding of the ... [War]wick ...
[Pet]icion of John Hickes of the said ..., Humbly Sheweth:
That whereas Charles Emes of the said Borough before the late dreadfull
fire by the right of his second wife deceased was interrested in a messuage
or tenement in the Borough aforesaid in the Market Place Ward there for
the terme of his life only,[2] part of which house was consumed by the said
fire and other part pulled downe to put a stop to the fire, the which timber
tyle brick and other materialls there left the said Charles Emes has taken to
his use and has declared he doth not designe to rebuild and has given in his
bill of the valuation of the loss of the said house as thô the same had been
his and his heires for ever, when after his decase the said house would have
come and descended as the ground doth[3] to your peticioner and his heires
for ever, and the said Charles Emes expects to have his proportion of the
charitable money as if the same had been his estate to him and his heires
for ever. Humbly therefore praying your Lordships and Worships to take
the case of your petitioner into your grave consideration and to order matters relating to the premisses as you shall think most meet in your wise consideration, for which noble bounty your petitioner shall be most thankfull
and dayly pray etc.
[Endorsed] The Peticion of John Hicks, smith, v. Emes.

Petition of Mary Wagstaff, widow

Warr' Borough. To the Rt Honorable and others the Commissioners and
Judges appointed by an Act of Parliament for the Rebuilding the Towne of
Warwick and for determining differences touching houses burnt or demolished by reason of the late dreadfull fire there,
   The Humble Peticion of Mary Wagstaff, widow, of the Borough aforesaid, Sheweth:
That Mary Wagstaff of this Borough, widow, and Elias Webb of Sherborne
in this county, gent., being one or both of them seized of an estate in fee in
two messuages lying in the Sheep[4] Street in this Borough, did demise the
same for the term of fourty one years commencing from the one and twentieth day of December, 1691, to one William Gerrard of Worcester, gent., at
the yearly rent of five and fifty shillings with covenants for the tenant to
repaire, maintaine and support the premisses dureing the said term, and
soe repaired, amended, maintained and supported at the end or other

---

[1] This petition is damaged and partly missing at the top.
[2] 'only' interlineated over a caret in another hand.
[3] 'as the ground doth' interlineated over a caret in another hand.
[4] 'Sheep' interlineated over a caret above 'Church' struck out.

sooner determinacion thereof, leave and yeild up the same to the lessors; that the said two messuages were totally burnt down by the late fire in this Borough; that the said William Gerrard hath not cleared the rent due before the said fire, nor paid the growing rent since; that the under tenants weekly make advantage of the ground lying before the front of the said two late messuages by sheeppens, and refuse to make any allowance or pay rent therefore; that the said William Gerrard forbids and discharges the lessors to remove the rubbish, or doe other matters in order to rebuild the same; that the lessors, both or one of them, provided the said William Gerrard will pay the arrears of rent due before the said fire and account for the proffits made since the same by the said sheeppens and deliver and surrender up his lease, is willing to rebuild the said messuages. Your Peticioner therefore humbly prayeth the summons of this Court, to summon the said William Gerard to appear in this Court of Judicature to answer the contents of this Peticion (i.e.) that he may either pay his arrears of rent and alsoe the growing rent, and be obliged to rebuild the said messuage, or that he may deliver up his lease to be cancell'd, that soe your Peticioner may be encouraged with safety to rebuild the same, and your Peticioner shall ever pray.

Mary Wagstaf.[1]

Petition of Mary Man, widow

To the Right Honorable, Right Wourshipfull and all the worthy Commissioners for the rebuilding of the Borough of Warwick, the Petition of Mary Man, relict of Thomas Man late of the same Borough, and William Man her only child, humbly shewith:

That at the time of the said fier in Warwick she was in full and perfect possession of one house, scituated near the pillory, which was in part burnt and in part pulled downe. It is her intention to rebuild the said house, being the whole estate she hath in the world, for herselfe and son, and hath accordingly given in her name, as a builder. But, before she begins, she desires the said Commissioners to settle the right to the same in herselfe and son, because, at the first purchase thereof, the remainder was settled upon Thomas Man and Robert Man, sons of the aforesaid Thomas by Alise Fox, after the death of Mary Man, William Man and Edward Man, thô purchased wholly with the portion of the said Mary, and also because John Hicks, brother to the seller of the said house, lays a claim to the same, by vertue of his father's will after his brother's death, your Petitioner humbly desiers, that writings on all sides may be produced and considered, and the right settled, according to justice, on the rebuilder.

---

[1] There is another, rougher copy of this petition, unsigned, in which the messuages are said to lie in Church Street, endorsed 'Mr Nichols petition' and 'Mary Wagstaff, widow'.

Petition of Mary Man, widow

To the Rt Honorable and others the Commissioners appointed by an Act of Parliament for the Rebuilding the Towne of Warwick and for determineing differences touching houses burnt and demolished by reason of the late dreadfull fire there,

The Humble Peticion of Mary Mann of this Borough, widow, Sheweth: That your Peticioner Mary Mann was att the time of the late fire possessed of a messuage scituate neer the Pillory within this Borough, which messuage was part burnt and part pulled down to stopp the progress of [the] late fire, and conceives the sole title of the toft whereon the said messuage lately stood to be in your Peticioner and William Mann her son by Thomas Mann her late husband deceased, and that your Peticioner and her sonn William have power in themselves to make a full bargaine and sale of the same when the said William shall attaine the age of twenty one years, without the consent of Thomas Mann and Robert Mann, sons of the aforesaid Thomas by Alice Fox, theire interest being very small in the premisses, and there being ordered fourty shillings to be paid to John Hick, your Peticioner is willing to pay the same, and humbly prays this Court would moderate the summ to be given to the said Thomas and Robert Mann, that your Peticioner may be encouraged to rebuild the said messuage soe demolished, and your Peticioner shall ever pray, etc.

Petition of William Perkes

To the Right Honorable and the Right Worshipfull the Commissioners appointed by a late Act of Parliament intituled an Act for the rebuilding of Warwick consumed by the late dreadfull fire there,

The humble peticion of William Perkes of the said Borough of Warwick, Humbly Sheweth:
That whereas your petitioner being about the rebuilding of his late house consumed by the late fire, and whereas there is a party wall between the said house and another house which now belongs to one John Eld, executor of one Elizabeth Carr deceased, which is in contest betweene your petitioner and the said John Eld whereby his worke is retarded, humbly praying your Honours and Worships that a jury may be impanelled to enquire into the premisses, and that the same may be by them adjusted with as much convenient speed as may be, that your petitioner may go forward with his building, for which great favour your petitioner shall be most thankfull and dayly pray, etc.

Petition of John Ashwin of Bretforton

To the Right Honorable and the Right Worshipfull the Commissioners appointed by a late Act of Parliament intituled an Act for rebuilding of Warwick, etc.,

The humble peticion of John Ashwin of Bradforton in the County of Worcester, Humbly Sheweth:

That whereas your petitioner is interrested in a messuage or tenement in Sheepes Street after the death of Elianor Peirce wife of Thomas Peirce sen. of Harvington in the said County of Worcester, late Elianor Ashwin, who has the same for her life only, and has put in her bill of the estimate of her losse as though the said house had been really her owne estate for ever, and whereas she utterly refuses to rebuild the same and your petitioner being willing to build if he might have her right therein for her life at a reasonable price, humbly therefore praying your Honours and Worships to take the premisses into your grave consideracions, and that she may not have all the Charity money that may be the proporcion for the said house, seeing your petitioner has the revercion and that if it may be, your petitioner may have the ground to build on at a reasonable rate for which noble favour your petitioner shall be most thankfull, etc.

Petition of Elizabeth Cawthorn, widow, and Richard Cawthorn, clerk

To the Right Honorable, Honorable, Right Worshipfull and all other Commissioners for the rebuilding of Warwick: the humble petition of Elisabeth Cawthorn, widow, and Richard Cawthorn, clerk, doth hereby suggest

That your petitioners lost six houses by the late dreadfull fire, being all that they were possessed of within this Borough. That they do intend, with all convenient speed, to erect that house which they had in the Church Street, inhabited at the time of the fire by Thomas Claridge jun., and do therefore pray these three things:

1. That, whereas the limits of their ground, on that side where it toucheth the ground of Mr Fulk Weale, is uncertain, a jury may be appointed to set it forth.

2. That, whereas about 270 feet of ground are taken from your petitioners, in order to the making of the street straight, a like proportion of ground may be appointed out of the same parcel, which makes Mr Weale repairations.

3. That they may be allowed 2s. 6d. per lib. for those houses, which they do not build, and for their goods lost, as also 4s. per lib. for this house, which they now design to build. If you shall be pleased to grant these requests, they will build immediately, and for ever pray, etc.

Petition of Richard Gibbard, maltster

To the Right Honorable and others the Commissioners appointed by an Act of Parliament for the Rebuilding the Town of Warwick and for Determining Differences touching houses burnt and demolish'd by reason of the late dreadfull fire there,

The Humble Peticion of Richard Gibbard of this Borough, maulster,[1] Sheweth:

That your Peticioner before the late fire was seized of a messuage or tenement against the Boothall in the Markett Place called the George Inn, which said messuage was totally burnt downe by the said fire, and your Peticioner hath since rebuilt the same, and there lying a gutter before the late fire between your Peticioner and the Signe of the Blew Bell, the house of Mrs Dorothy Weale, which gutter was alwaies repaired by the said Mrs Weale, and taken away and preserved by her att the time of the late fire, and shee now utterly refuseing att the request of [your] Peticioner to put up the said gutter as formerly it was, except your Peticioner will bear half charges for doeing the same, which your Peticioner is unwilling to doe, and is ready to prove that the said gutter was att first putt up and hath alwayes since been repaired by the said Mrs Weale. Your Peticioner being very much damnified thereby, humbly prays this Court to summon the said Mrs Weale to appeare and be compell'd to putt up the same, and your Peticioner shall ever pray, etc.

Petition of Richard Gibbard, maltster

Warr' Borough. To the Rt Honorable and others the Commissioners appointed by an Act of Parliament for the Rebuilding the Town of Warwick and for determineing differences touching houses burnt and demolished by reason of the late dreadfull fire,

The Humble Peticion of Richard Gibbard of this Borough, maulster, Sheweth:

That your Peticioner did on Munday the 26th day of August[2] last preferr his Peticion into this Court setting forth a gutter of lead to be in dispute between your Peticioner and Mrs Dorothy Weale, and desireing to know in whom the right of the said gutter did belong, whether in your Peticioner or the said Mrs Weale, a jury was impanell'd to try the same, and the said jury did find the right of the said gutter to bein the said Mrs Weale and for her to repaire the same, which she hath not done nor made any preparacion to doe or putt up the said gutter, whereby your Peticioner hath been since much damnified by the wett weather. Your Peticioner therefore humbly

---

[1] 'maulster' written after 'inkeeper' struck out.
[2] The 26th August fell on a Monday in 1695.

prays the said Mrs Weale may be forthwith compell'd or a time limitted to putt up the same, and your Peticioner shall ever pray, etc.

Petition of Timothy Norbury, baker

Warr': To the Right Honorable and others the Comicioners appointed by an Act of Parliament for the Rebuilding the Town of Warwick, etc.,

The Humble Peticion of Timothy Norberry of this Borough, baker, Sheweth:

That your Peticioner before the late fire was, and now is, tenant to John Williams of this Borough, gent., of a messuage or tenement lying and being in the Jury Street within the said Borough, which said messuage was untiled and the roofe took down by order of Mr Joseph Blissett, then Mayor of this Borough, in order to stopp the progress of the late fire, and that your Peticioner did att the request of the said Mr Williams repaire the said house upon his promise to allow for the same, and now the said John Williams demands of your peticioner the whole rent and refuses to allow anything towards the reparacion done as aforesaid, althô he hath putt his loss in as his own.[1] Your Peticioner therefore humbly prays this Court would grant summons to warn the said John Williams to answer the same and be compelled to allow the reparacion done as aforesaid, and your Peticioner shall ever pray etc.

Timothy Norbury

Petition of William Bolton, lord of the manor

To the Right Honorable and Honorable the Commissioners appointed by an Act of Parliament intituled An Act for the Rebuilding the Towne of Warwick and for determining differences touching houses burnt or demolished by reason of the late dreadfull fire there,

The humble peticion of William Bolton, Esq., Lord of the Mannor of Warwick, sheweth:

That 5° *Jacobi primi* [1607–8] a messuage or tenement in the High Pavement in Warwicke aforesaid was granted by copy of court roll of the said Mannor to one John Weale for the terme of 99 yeares under the yearely rent of 6s. 8d. as by a booke of proceedings att a court of survey held for the said Mannor appeares, which also setts forth the content of the said messuage, and a former survey *tempore Elizabethe* setts forth the butts and bounds thereof. That Fulke Weale, draper, was in possession of the said messuage att the tyme of the said late dreadfull fire in which the said messuage was burnt. That the said Fulke Weale is now building a dwelling

---

[1] 'althô ... own' inserted in a space.

house upon the ground where the said messuage stood and other ground which hath by this Honorable Court been allowed to the said Fulke Weale. That by reason of such addicionall ground and other alteracions there made by vertue of the orders or decrees of this Honorable Court, it wilbe very difficult hereafter to know the just bounds of the land whereon the said copy hold messuage stood, whereby your peticioner wilbe in danger to loose both the rent and the revercion thereof unles releived by a decree of this Honorable Court. Therefore your peticioner humbly prayes your Honours will sett forth the said copy hold lands by your Honours decree by meets and bounds for the preservacion of your peticioners interest therein, and that in order thereunto a jury may be impannelled and sworn to inquire of the premisses, and your peticioner shall ever pray, etc.

Plea of Fulk Weale, draper

The Plea and Answer of Fulk Weale, draper, to the Peticion of William Bolton, Esq.

The Respondent (saving to himself all advantages which may be taken of the many insufficiencys of the said Petition and taking it by protestation that the messuage or tenement in the Petition mention'd was not copy hold or chargeable with the payment of any rents to the lords of the mannor of Warwick) by way of plea he farther saith that long before the said dreadfull fire, the Petitioner did exhibit his bill in the Court of Exchequer at Westminster against the Respondent and Dorothy his mother and others and did by the said bill among other things particularly charge upon the Respondent and his said mother that the said messuage or tenement in the said Petition mention'd was antiently demis'd by copy of court roll for a long terme of yeares under such rents as in the Petition is set forth, but that by reason of greate alterations made in the buildings the same could not be known by the descriptions thereof in the said copy hold lease or any survey antiently made thereof, and therefore he pray'd a discovery of the truth by the answers of the respondent and his mother, to which bill the respondent and his mother upon oath answered that noe houses which they or either of them claim'd title to within the Borough of Warwick were copyhold or granted to any person or persons under which they or either of them claime title for any particular estate for lives or yeares, for that all theire deeds and writings did describe and take notice of the same as freehold and inheritance. To which answer the Petitioner excepted, and his exceptions were overrul'd and the said answer adjudg'd sufficient, and thereupon the Petitioner did not think fit any farther to prosecute his said bill, but suffered the same to be dismist with costs as by the said bill, answer and other proceedings thereupon of record in the said Court of Exchequer may appear; and forasmuch as the matter of the dispute complain'd of in the said petition did not arise between the Petitioner and this Respondent by reason of the late dreadfull fire, forasmuch as the quantity of ground added to or taken from this Respondent remains of record in this Honorable Court, and cannot be more ascertain'd by the verdict of any jury, therefore this Respondent humbly craves the judgement of this Honorable Court, whether they can or will take cognizance of the said Petition.

Exceptions of William Bolton, lord of the manor

Excepcions taken by William Bolton, Esq., Lord of the Manor of Warwick, Peticioner, to the plea and answer of Fulk Weale, draper, Respondent.

Whereas the said plea and answer appeares by the conclusion thereof to be pleaded and intended to oust the jurisdiccion of this Court, and the Respondent having so applyed it, no other use can or ought to be made thereof, so that in case it be not sufficient for that purpose, then the Peticioner ought without further proces to have the fruit of his Peticion and what he seeks for thereby to be adjudged to him. Now to manifest the insufficiency of the said plea and answer to oust the jurisdiccion of this Court in this case, the said Peticioner doth except thereunto:

[His numbered exceptions fill five foolscap sheets, but can be summarised as follows:

1. No plea concerning the jurisdiction of any court can be admitted, unless the party makes oath of the truth of the matters contained in it, which the respondent has not done.

2. The respondent has put in a plea challenging the jurisdiction of the court, and also an answer to the matters charged against him in the court, which is an acknowledgment of its jurisdiction, so overruling his own plea.

3. The respondent relies on records in the Exchequer, which this court cannot see. He should instead have submitted an exemplification of them, to avoid delay in this court, where the proceedings are to be summary.

4. The point now in question, which is the bounds of the petitioner's lands, was never raised in the Exchequer suit, but only whether the respondent and his mother knew any of their lands to be copyhold.

5. The dismissal of the case in the Exchequer, before evidence had been heard, is no bar to the present petition. The copyhold lease to John Weale, now said to be dated 15 James I [1617–18], might have been suppressed by the respondent's ancestors, and so be forfeit. The respondent's answer in the Exchequer, that he knows nothing of it, is no bar to the petitioner's now proving the lease from his surveys. The petitioner's title to a copyhold messuage is changed, by the respondent's new building on the site, into part of a messuage. Although the bounds may now be difficult for a jury to ascertain, the court is directed by the Act to inquire into disputes over bounds and extents, by a jury or otherwise, and to determine them.]

And therefore and for all the reasons aforesaid and for the reasons set forth in the said peticion, the Peticioner doth pray as in his said peticion he hath already prayed, and that notwithstanding the Respondent's said pretended plea and answer or anything therein contained, this Court will proceed to set forth the said copyhold premises by a decree by meets and bounds, and that in order thereunto a jury may be impanelled and sworn to inquire thereof.

Petition of William Bolton, lord of the manor

To the Right Honorable and Honorable the Commissioners appointed by Act of Parliament intituled an Act for the Rebuilding the Towne of Warwick and for determining differences touching houses burnt or demolished by reason of the late dreadfull fire there,

The humble peticion of William Bolton, Esq., Lord of the Mannor of Warwicke, Sheweth:

That your peticioner did lately prefer his humble peticion to this Honorable Court to have the bounds of a certaine ground ascertained, therein claimed by your peticioner to be copy hold, where a messuage formerly stood which was in the occupacion of Fulke Weale, draper, att the tyme of the said fire, whoe is building a dwelling house upon the said copy hold ground and other ground thereto adjoyneing. To which peticion the said Fulke Weale put in a plea and answere claimeing the said ground to be his freehold. That upon heareing the cause this Court was pleased to order a jury to view and sett out the dimencions, meets and bounds on all parts of the said ground claimed by your peticioner as copy hold, without inquireing whether the same be freehold or copy hold. That in drawing up the said order there are some materiall mistakes.

1. In that the order as drawne is betweene your peticioner and Mrs Dorothy Weale whoe was noe party to the controversy, whereas it should have bine between your peticioner and the said Fulk Weale.
2. In that the order as drawne doth allow the ground in question to be Mrs Weale's, whereas this Court intended not to meddle with any persons tytle in this case, but onely to bound the ground claimed.
3. In that all the ground of the messuage wherein the said Mrs Weale lived with her son the said Fulke Weale before the fire is not claimed by your peticioner but onely soe much as the surveyes of the said Mannor doe in that behalfe specify, the bounds whereof being made doubtfull by reason of the fire and new building, therefore your peticioner prayes the ascertaineing those bounds in order to which an inquiry by a jury was directed, thoe the order for the same be mistaken as aforesaid.

Your peticioner prayes a rectificacion of the said order accordingly and that a jury may inquire of the dimensions, meets and bounds of the said ground by him claimed to be copyhold, without inquireing whether the same be copyhold or freehold or ascertaineing to whome the same doth belonge, and your peticioner shall dayly pray, etc.

Petition of Fulk Weale, draper

The Humble Peticion of Mr Fulk Weale, draper, Sheweth:

That your Peticioner was before the late fire seized of a messuage or tenement in the High Pavement which said messuage was burnt down by the said fire. That your Peticioner hath since rebuilt the same. That Mr Savage hath built a house on the east side of your Peticioners and hath caused a trench to be dugg in his backside soe neer your Peticioner's foundacion that hath made a very grate breach and settlement in your Peticioners building, insoemuch that your Peticioner is afraid to sitt in that part of the said house, and alsoe that the said Mr Savage hath sunk his vault soe much deeper then before, which brings the water out of the same into your Peticioners well, which is a great prejudice to him. Your Peticioner therefore humbly prays his said house may be viewed by the Surveyors and the same be reported to this Court, that thereby your Peticioner may be awarded such reasonable satisfaccion for the damage soe done as aforesaid as this Court shall think meet.

Petition of Elias Webb *alias* Morrell

To ...[1]

The Humble Peticion of Elias Webb *alias* Morrell[2] on the behalf of himself and Thomas Webb *alias* Morell being an infant above the age of seven years and under the age of eight yeares and being the only child of the said Elias Webb *alias* Morrell by Mary his late wife, now deceased, who was the daughter of William Wagstaffe also deceased and of Mary Wagstaffe now widow and formerly the wife of the said William Wagstaffe, Sheweth:
That by vertue of a setlement made before and in consideracion of the marriage between your Peticioner and the said Mary his late wife, the said Mary Wagstaffe, widow, was at the time of the late dreadfull fire in Warwick seized of and in all those two mesuages with th'appurtenances situate and being within the parish of St Mary in Warwick aforesaid in or near a certain street there called the Sheep-Street otherwise North-gate Street, between a certain mesuage there called the Green Dragon and a certain other mesuage there called the Crown, for the term of her natural life with remainder to your Peticioner for and during the term of his natural life if the said Thomas his son shall so long live, with remainder to Samuel

---

[1] A space left for the formal address was never filled in.
[2] This 'alias' cannot be explained.

Jemmat, clerk, and Edward Townsend, gentleman, and their heirs to support the contingent uses in the said setlement, with remainder to your Peticioner's first son by the said Mary his wife in tail (which was and is the said Thomas Webb *alias* Morrell) with remainder to Josuan the wife of Joseph Fox, one other of the daughters of the said William Wagstaffe, in tail, and with the next and last remainder to the right heirs of the said William Wagstaffe, which said two first mencioned mesuages were burnt down in the said fire, and the said Mary Wagstaffe is now seized of the ground whereon the same stood and of the ground with th'appurtenances which did belong to them, of such estate as aforesaid and with such remainders as aforesaid.

That your Peticioner is willing to rebuild the same two mesuages in case the same with the ground and th'appurtenances thereto belonging may be setled on your Peticioner for his life with remainder to his said son Thomas in tail, and with the next and last remainder to the right heirs of your Peticioner, which the said Mary Wagstaffe, widow, Samuel Jemmat, Edward Townsend, Joseph Fox and Josuan his wife do refuse to consent unto, neither will they give your Peticioner and his son any reasonable consideracion for their said interest in the premises, and rebuild the said houses themselves. Therefore your Peticioner humbly prays that this Honorable Court will make such order and decree either to incourage your Peticioner to rebuild the said houses, or for a recompense to be made to him and his said son for their interest therein as shall be just and reasonable. And your Peticioner shall ever pray, etc.

Petition of John Woods of Claverdon

To the Rt Honorable and others the Commissioners appointed by an Act for Rebuilding of Warwick, etc., the humble Petition of John[1] Woods of Claverdon in the County of Warwick, humbly Sheweth:

That whereas Mary Mann, widow, of this Borough was seis'd of a mesuage within this Borough, standing at the time of the late fire in the Markett Place, and in the possession of John King, and by a decree of this Court the estates of remainder were barr'd and the inheritance settled and vested in her the said Mary Mann, and shee the said Mary Mann ordered and decreed to rebuild the said messuage demolished by the said fire, and whereas shee her self is unable to rebuild the same, but hath contracted with your Petitioner for the summ of £40 to rebuild it according to the said decree and Act of Parliament for Rebuilding the Town of Warwick, now your Petitioner having contracted for the said toft and to rebuild the said messuage in manner and form aforesaid, humbly prays that the said toft with the appurtenances may bee decreed to your Petitioner on a condition that hee rebuild the same and that the said Mary Mann may have the

---

[1] 'John' interlineated above 'Richard' struck out. The paper is endorsed 'The Petition of Richard Woods'.

present 1s. 6d. per pound given for encouragement of building, hee the said Petitioner having made his agreement and contract with the said Mary Mann for the said toft at an under rate proportionably, and your Petitioner shall ever pray.

Petition of William Smith, shoemaker

To the Right Honorable and the Right Worshipfull the Judges or Commissioners appointed by a late Act of Parliament intituled an Act for the Rebuilding of the Towne of Warwick lately consumed by the late dreadfull fire,
   The Humble Peticion of William Smith of the said Borough of Warwick, shomaker, Humbly sheweth:
That whereas Richard Gibberd of the said Borough haveing had severall buildings consumed by the late fire, and upon the same ground or neare thereunto he hath lately caused to be made a quarry to gett stone thereout very near to your petitioners dwelling house, garden and outhouses, and hath brought the same so near to your petitioners ground that part of his garden is coped into the said quarry, and has so undermined the said quarry that your petitioner is in great dread that the same quarry may much endanger his dwelling house and ruine the same unlesse prevented by your order. Humbly praying your Honours and Worships to be pleased to take cognizance of the same by your view or by your substitutes, and that your petitioner may be made sufficient satisfaction for the wrong sustained as shall most justly appeare before you upon such view, for which noble favour your petitioner shall be most thankfull and dayly pray for your Honours and Worships, etc.

Petition of Andrew Parker, carpenter

Warr' Burg'. To the Rt Honorable and others the Commissioners or Judges appointed by an Act of Parliament for the Rebuilding the Town of Warwick, etc., att the Mayors Parlour on Munday the [   ]¹ day of [   ]¹ anno Domini 169[ ],¹
   The Humble Peticion of Andrew Parker, carpenter, Sheweth:
That your Peticioner was employed by William Holmes to work in the house of William Perks, baker, in laying the floors of the said house, and the said Holmes being arrested and restrained from his liberty, your Peticioner refused to work any longer there, not knowing by whom he should be paid. That the said William Perks came to your Peticioner and desired him to continue his work till it should amount to the summ of twenty shillings, and

¹ Blanks not filled in.

he would pay him, which accordingly your Peticioner did till it came to 20s. and upwards, but the said Perks refuses to pay your Peticioner according to his promise. Your Peticioner therefore (being ready to prove that he was employ'd by the said Perks, and that he did promise to pay as abovesaid) humbly prays the summons of this Court to summon the said William Perks to answer this peticion and that he may be, by order of this Court, compell'd to pay your peticioner for his said work, and your Peticioner shall ever pray, etc.

Petition of John Canning and Henry Coale, sawyers

To the Right Honorable and the Right Worshipfull the Judges or Commissioners appointed by a late Act of Parliament entituled an Act for the Rebuilding the Towne of Warwick consumed by the late dreadfull fire,

The humble peticion of John Canning and Henry Coale of the Borough of Warwick, sawyers, Humbly sheweth:
That whereas your petitioners being imployed in sawing for one Joseph Martin an undertaker in severall of the new buildings and had sawed up worke for him which came to thirty shillings, but the said Martin being runne away from Warwick not only in your petitioners' debt (who are very poore men and haveing great familyes of small children to maintaine) but also in severall other peoples debt and contriving (as is verily beleived) with one Mr Phenix, another undertaker, to cheate every one he had to deale with, made a pretended bill of sale to the said Mr Phenix of all his timber and boards that he had and that was ready framed for severall of the builders, which the said Mr Phenix or by his order was removed from off severall of the builders ground in the night time unaware to any of the people concerned with the said Martin. And your petitioners verily beleiveing this bill of sale was made really to cheate the persons concerned with Martin, and therefore humbly pray that your Honours and Worships will be pleased to take cognizance of the premisses and redresse such ill practices, if it may stand with your good pleasure, for which noble favour your petitioners shall be most thankfull to your noble bounty and dayly pray, etc.

John Caning
Henery Cole

Petition of George Chinn, carpenter

To the Right Honorable and the Right Worshipfull the Commissioners appointed by a late Act of Parliament intituled an Act for the rebuilding of the Borough of Warwick lately consumed by the late dreadfull fire,

The humble peticion of George Chinne, Humbly sheweth:
That whereas your petitioner being desirous to rebuild his house in Swan

Lane in Warwick next to the King and Queens Head there and not knowing your pleasures as to the setting out of the foundations there, humbly
desires that you will as speedily as may be sett out the same, that he may go
on and not loose this summer, or be forced to remove his foundation if he
should begin according as it is sett out, not knowing whether you are fully
agreed upon the same, for which great favour your petitioner shall be most
thankfull, etc.

George Chinne

Petition of George Chinn, carpenter

To the Right Honorable and the Right Worshipfull the Commissioners
appointed by a late Act of Parliament intituled an Act for Rebuilding of
Warwick,
   The Humble peticion of George Chinne, carpenter, Humbly sheweth:
That whereas your petitioner haveing had a house in Swan Lane next to
the King and Queen there, part whereof was burnt and other part pulled
downe to put a stop to the late fire, and being desirous this summer to
rebuild the same, humbly desires that the ground may be sett out with as
much convenient speed as may be, that the same may be rebuilt before the
summer is over, and the rather because he has contracted with workmen
for the rebuilding the same in a short time, and alsoe prayes that he may
have the like encouragement as other builders are designed to have, for
which great favour your petitioner shall think himselfe highly obleiged to
your noble bounty and dayly pray for your Honours and Worships, etc.

George Chinne

Petition of George Chinn, carpenter

To the Right Honorable and the Right Worshipfull the Commissioners
appointed by a late Act of Parliament intituled an Act for the Rebuilding of
the Borough of Warwick consumed by a late dreadfull fire,
   The humble peticion of George Chinne, Humbly sheweth:
That whereas your petitioner being desirous to rebuild his house in Swan
Lane consumed by the late fire and haveing materialls in readinesse, and
which house might have been up before this if your Honours and Worships
had agreed where he should build, and to that end he did petition you this
day was eleven weekes and also since, and has waited with a great deale of
patience to hear your result, but finds nothing done to his great damage
and hindrance, and now being going on with the front, humbly desires your
grave judgement what he must doe and that he be not further retarded in
his buildings, for which noble favour your petitioner shall be most thankfull
to your bounty and dayly pray, etc.

Agreement between Samuel Burford and John Burton

[Plan of Samuel Burfoote's and John Burton's ground in Pebble Lane and the new street—see opposite page]

Petition of Joseph Willis, baker

Warr' Burg'. To the Rt Honorable and others the Commissioners sitting at the Mayors Parlour on Munday the [   ]¹ day of [   ]¹ by vertue of an Act of Parliament for the Rebuilding the Town of Warwick, etc.,

The Humble Peticion of Edward² Willis of the Borough of Warwick, baker, Sheweth:

That your Peticioner hath lately bargained with Mr Richard Hands of this Borough, maulster, for a certain toft or parcell of ground lying in the Sheep-street on which before the late fire stood the house of Mr John Prichard.³ That your Peticioner haveing cleared the rubbish off the said ground would begin to rebuild the same if that side of the street was sett out. Your Peti-cioner therefore humbly prays that the said ground may be sett out that your Peticioner may begin to rebuild and your Peticioner shall ever pray etc.

Charges of Moses Robinson

The Charges⁴ of Moses Robinson in obeying the severall commands laid upon him by the Honorable Commissioners

Imprimis for horse hire and his charges in going to gett the hands and seales of severall of the Commissioners about Sir John Burgoyns money
two days.⁵

Item for horse hire and charges in going to severall Commissioners with the Booke to get their hands thereto to confirme Cookes title to another part of the Church land being so commanded by the Commissioners, Mr Mitchenar being then sick   two days.⁵

Item for going out into the country to gett teames to carry rubbish to fill up Mr Bolton's quarry and the hollow leading from Mr Colmores stable to Jury Street and looking after the workmen and teames to see they did their duty . . .

Item in getting teames and workmen to carry away the rubbish lying in the square to Serjeant Hadlyes quarry and looking after the teames and work-men . . .

¹ Blanks not filled in.
² 'Edward' written in a space in another hand, probably a mistake for Joseph.
³ Followed by 'for the summ of' struck out.
⁴ The sums of money have not been filled in.
⁵ 'two days' added in another hand.

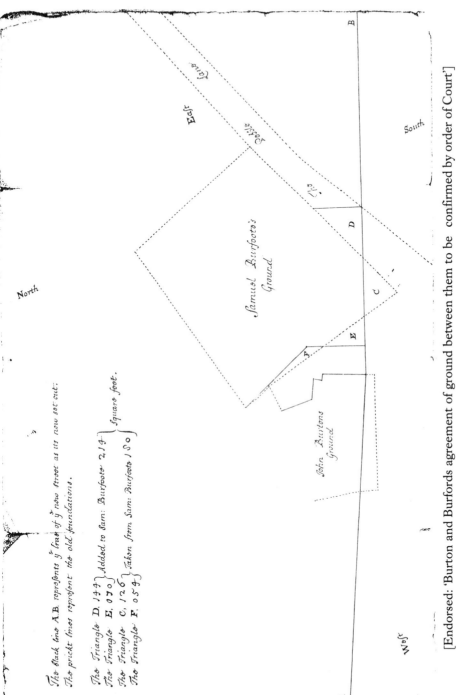

North

East

West

South

A

B

C

D

E

F

1/3

1/3

Double

Double

Samuel Burfootes Ground

John Burtons Ground

The black line A.B. represents ye line of ye new street as its now set out.

The prickt lines represent the old foundations.

The Triangle D. 144 } Added to Sam: Burfoote 214 } Square foot.
The Triangle E. 070 }
The Triangle C. 126 } Taken from Sam: Burfoote 180 }
The Triangle F. 054 }

Item for his paines from time to time in looking after the lead and iron worke and see the same weighed and taking an account thereof which was used about building the steeple from Mr Lanes, Mr Paris and Mr Marshalls . . .

Notes of evidence concerning Thomas Lean's family

Paper relateing to Alice Mattson, William Eborall and John Burton, etc.[1]

Alice Lane now Matson: Claimes part of Burtons house as heir att law to her mother, the same being joyntur'd to her said mother by Edward Lane, elder brother to Thomas Lean sen.; severall suits at law were commenced by her said mother, she produces a coppy of report of a Master in Chancery.

Eborall: That since suits in Chancery were commenced Thomas Lean obtained a decree about *anno* 1692 for a term of the premises for 99 *annis.* That Mr Challenor who was attorney for the said Lean told him nothing was done in it since Thomas Lean sen. dyed. That he does believe the said Alice Mattson hath a right after 99 years are expired.

John Fosters wife: Sais she being servant to Thomas Lean sen. heard the grandmother of the said Alice Mattson say that if the said Alice had her right 'towld[2] be hers after her mothers death.

Katherine Silvester: That she lived with Thomas Lean and his wife, the said Alice came upon a visitt to Warwick and desired to see the writeing that she might know what right she had in the premises, one Mr Palmer told her that she needs noe writeings for that she had a good tytle after her mothers death the wife of Edward Lane; this was about 30 years agoe, her grandmother dyed about 17 years agoe, her mother about a year agoe.

Amphillis Woodward: That she went to London for to see her sister, that the mother of Alice came to see her and told her that she had received a letter from Warwick writte as tho' it came from her husband to send him down the deeds to Warwick (which she did) for that they might save his life.

Thomas Clemens: That he heard Thomas Lean sen. say that if his cousin Alice had the house she must pay him £20 else he would pull down the back stable.

Thomas Lean jun. when he went into Flanders made Eborall and John Davis a letter of attorney to act for him in his absence, and made a will that if he never came againe Eborall son should be executor, he leaves severall legacies to be paid (viz.) £10 a peice to his 3 sisters and £4 a peice to Eborall's children.

By a mortgage made in '48 Thomas Leane holds the house for 99 years.

[1] Endorsement.   [2] 'it would'.

John Lane father of Edmund Lane indebted to Edward Berlbane.
Edmund had John, Richard and Alice; Richard and John dyed leaving Alice.
Frances the widow of John deceased about 18 years.

Petition of Edward Clopton of Bridgetown

Warwick Borough in the County of Warwick. To the Rt Honorable Foulke
Lord Brooke and others the Commissioners and Judges appointed by an
Act of Parliament for the Rebuilding the Towne of Warwick and for determineing the differences touching houses burnt and demolished by reason
of the late dreadfull fire there,
   The humble Peticion of Edward Clopton of Bridgetowne in the parish of
Old Stratford in the County of Warwick, Esq., Sheweth:
That your Peticioner was seized in right of his wife Martha Clopton, daughter and heire of William Combe, Esq., and Anne Mary his wife both
deceased, to the use of him the said Edward Clopton and Martha his wife
and the heires of the said Martha, of and in one messuage or tenement,
garden, orchard, stables, barnes and backside with the appurtenances thereunto belonging scituate lying and being in the Burrough of Warwick aforesaid in a certaine street or place there commonly called or knowne by the
name of the High Street, which said messuage or tenement was commonly
called or knowne by the name or signe of the Dolphin and was late in the
tenure or occupacion of one[1] William Bryan *alias* Stephens. That the said
messuage or tenement and buildings thereunto belonging were totally
burnt downe and consumed by the late fire in the Borough aforesaid, and
forasmuchas the said Edward Clopton is willing to rebuild the same provided that he may have the order and decree[2] of this Court for doeing of
the same and for the settling of the said ground whereon the said messuage
stood, and the said messuage or tenement with the appurtenances so to be
rebuilt as aforesaid, upon him and his heires and assignees for ever and to
or for no other use, intent or purpose whatsoever.
Wherefore your peticioner humbly prayeth the summons of this Court for
the appearance of the said Martha Clopton in this Court of Judicature, to
the end such order and decree may be made by this Court touching the
premisses as shall seem most just and reasonable, and your Peticioner shall
ever pray, etc.

Petition of Samuel Ainge and Thomas Lean

Warr' Borrough. To the Rt Honorable and others the Commissioners
appointed by an Act of Parliament for the Rebuilding the Town of Warwick, etc.,

[1] 'one' interlineated over 'Mr' struck out.
[2] 'and decree' interlineated over a caret.

The Humble Peticion of Samuell Ainge and Thomas Leane both of this Borough, Sheweth:

That your Peticioners being seized of two peices or parcells of ground whereon before the late fire stood 2 messuages scituate in the Church Street within this Borough, have made an exchainge for some part of the same to make the buildings more usefull to your Peticioners then before, and your Peticioners haveing delivered in a draught of the said ground as the same is now sett out by the Surveyors and agreed on by your Peticioners, humbly prays this Court will confirm the same by Decree of this Court that your peticioners may have sure title to each parcell of ground so exchainged, and your Peticioners shall ever pray, etc.

Petition of Thomas Dixon, blacksmith

Warr' Borough. To the Rt Honorable and others the Commissioners and Judges appointed by an Act of Parliament for the Rebuilding the Town of Warwick and for determineing differences touching houses burnt and demolished by reason of the late dreadfull fire there,

The Humble Peticion of John[1] Dickson of this Borough, blacksmith, Sheweth:

That your Peticioner before the late fire was seized of a messuage or tenement lying on the south side of the High Street adjoyning to the White Lyon Inn, and that the said house was totally burnt down by the said fire. That your Peticioner is willing to rebuild the said messuage provided he may have the whole ground whereon the said messuage stood, but soe it happens that upon viewing the foundacions of the said messuage and the foundacions of the White Lyon Inn next adjoyning to it, he conceivs and is ready to prove the cellers of the said inn are digged under and doe undermine your Peticioners foundacions, whereby your Peticioner cannot lay the foundacions of his intended house, unless he goes to the bottom of the said cellars for the same, which will put him to an extraordinary charge and expence. Your Peticioner therefore humbly prays the foundacions and bounds of his said messuage may be viewed and the same be settled, as to this Court shall seem most just and equell, that soe he may proceed with safety and security to rebuild his said messuage, and your Peticioner shall ever pray, etc.

Thomas Dixon

---

[1] An error for 'Thomas'.

Petition of Thomas Dixon, blacksmith

Warr' Borrough. To the Rt Honorable and others the Commissioners appointed by an Act' of Parliament for the Rebuilding the Town of Warwick, etc.,

The Humble Peticion of Thomas Dixon of this Borough, blacksmith, Sheweth:

That your Peticioner was before the late fire seized of a messuage or tenement lying on the south side of the High Street adjoyning to the White Lyon Inn, which messuage was burnt down by the said fire, and your peticioner have raised his foundacion and laid his first floor in order to rebuild the same, and the charities[1] allowed your Peticioner in the distribucion of 4s. in the pound as a builder being very small, the summ which your Peticioner had received before being deducted out of it, which summ if your Peticioner had not had would not have been able to have carried on his trade, thinks it very hard. Your Peticioner therfore humbly prays an allowance for the ground taken away to enlarge the High Street and what other encouragement this Court shall think fitt whereby he may rebuild the same, and your Peticioner shall ever pray, etc.

Thomas Dixon

Petition of Moses Robinson

To the Right Honorable and Right Worshipfull the Commissioners appointed by a late Act of Parliament for the rebuilding the Towne of Warwick consumed by the late dreadfull fire there,

The humble peticion of Moses Robinson, Humbly sheweth:

That your petitioner did sometime since agree with your Honours and Worships for the rebuilding of a house on part of the land belonging to St Maryes Church in Warwick, and by which agreement your petitioner was to have a lease of the same for sixty yeares at the yearly rent of five pounds, and whereas your petitioner has laid out a considerable summe of money in building back buildings and other things more then was allowed for the building up a tenement upon the said land, and whereas your petitioner has not any assureance granted him for his enjoying the same according to his agreement, your petitioner humbly beggs that your Honours and Worships will be pleased to take the premisses into your wise and grave consideracion, and to be pleased to order that he may have some assurance granted him that he may enjoy the said tenement according to his former agreement, for which noble bounty your petitioner shall be most thankfull and shall daily pray for your Honours and Worships, etc.

---

[1] 'charities' interlineated over 'monies' struck out.

Petition of Joseph Ainge and other joiners

The humble Peticion of Joseph Ainge, Richard Hands, Nicholas Kineton, Thomas Masters[1] and others, joyners and inhabitants within the Burrough of Warwick, Sheweth:

Whereas by the said Act page 13[2] it is enacted that all carpenters, bricklayers, joyners, etc., and other artificers, workmen and labourers fitt to be employ'd in the said buildings although not freemen of the said Burrough dureing the space of seven years and untill the said buildings are finished, shall and may work and be employed in the said buildings as well as freemen of the said Borough of the same trades and professions, Now this Peticion humbly sheweth that John Ellis, William Edgerton and Matthew Ebb, Richard King, joyners, and severall others who are not any wise employ'd in and about the said building have not only taken houses and rooms within this Borough in order to work about buildings according to the Act, but have used and exercised the said trade of a joyner in such houses and rooms and have exposed the goods soe work'd up to sale within this Borough as if they had been freemen of the said Burrough, which is a great detriment to your peticioners who are freemen of the said Burrough, and that many of them not only work in new buildings but doe alsoe undertake for severall inhabitants of this Borough to pull down and repaire buildings which never were burnt or any wayes damnified by the said fire. That neither the said workmen befor the said fire had any liberty to work within this Burrough or use or exercise their trades within the same, and your Peticioners doe conceive that by the said Act they cannot work or exercise their trades otherwise then in rebuilding and finishing houses burnt down by the said fire. Your Peticioners therefore humbly prays they will take the same into consideracion and make such order and decree soe as to barr the said workmen from useing and exerciseing the trade of a joyner or undertake buildings within this Borough according to the Act as they in their judgements shall seem reasonable, and your Peticioners will ever pray.

Joseph Ainge	Richard Williams
Richard Hands	Thomas Masters
Nich. Kington	

Petition of Sarah Mayo

To the Worshipfull Commissioners constituted and appointed concerning the late great and dreadfull fire in Warwick.

The most humble petition of Sarah Mayo, inhabiter at the Joyce Pool in the said Burrough of Warwick, most humble craves your serious considera-

---

[1] 'Thomas Masters' interlineated over a caret.
[2] See p. 129.

tions on these following matters. Whereas the said Sarah Mayo is the wife of one Edward Mayo, flaxdresser, but he being some years absent whether he be living or dead she knows not, but before he went away he sold a parcell of building and ground to his brother Thomas Mayo, but the said Thomas Mayo went to London and there marryed, but he being killed by an accident left no issue nor his wife not with child, soe that the said premises fell to the said Edward Mayo again and to his issues. Now the said building being consumed at the fire your humble petitioner craves your approbations and good will, she being left with three children to take care for, that if there be any right, title, clayme or interest in the said premises belonging to her children on the said account, that she may have an order granted her by you, and she will use her utmost endeavor with her freinds for to build a little house on the said ground for her and her children to live in.

Petition of Sarah Mayo

To the Rt Honorable Ld Brooke and to the Rt Worshipfull Commissioners who are appointed to doe Justice and Equity concerning the late great and dreadfull fire as happened in Warwick

Most worthy Gentlemen, your humble petitioner Sara Mayo hath made bold to present you with a writing for to put you in mind of a former petition as she presented to your serious considerations being the wife of one Edward Mayo formerly an inhabiter at Joyce Pool in this said Burrough. Whereas the said Edward Mayo did sell unto his brother Thomas Mayo part of a house and ground scituate at the said Joyce Pool, and then and after he did mortgage the remainder unto his uncle Thomas Mayo of Rugbey. The said Edward Mayo went away and left his wife and three children to shift for themselves, and afterwards his brother Thomas Mayo allso went to London and was there marryed, but by an accident was killed and left noe issue nor his wife with child. Now this said Thomas Mayo, uncle to the said Edward, hath the grand writings of the whole and layes claime to it, though part of it was sold by Edward Mayo to his brother Thomas Mayo before any mortgage was set by Edward Mayo to his uncle Thomas Mayo. Soe I most humble desire that if it be any of my right in this case for to have the said ground as was sold by Edward Mayo to his brother Thomas Mayo deceased, for to have leave and liberty from your Worshipfull Court to have the said land, and I will use my utmost endeavor with the assistance of my good freinds to build me a habitation for mee and my three children for to live in, for if the said Thomas Mayo, uncle to my husband Edward Mayo, fraudently have the ground I shall be disinhabited and allsoe undone in my calling as I now exercise for the releife of me and my three children.

Petition of William Pestill, shoemaker

To the Worshipfull Commissioners appointed for the late great and dreadfull fire as did happen in Warwick,
The most humble petition of William Pestill, shoemaker, who at the said fire did live in the Pibble Lane at the house as his mother did dwell in, and did sustain the loss of three pounds three shillings by the said fire. He having put in two bills allready and hath not been considered for the loss as he did sustain at the said great calamity, he doth most humble beseech that he may have some recompence according to his loss as other poor sufferers had for theire losses.

Petition of Anne Palmer, widow

To the right Honorable and Honorable the Commissioners for the rebuilding the Town of Warwick and for determining differences touching houses burnt or demolished by reason of the late dreadfull fire there,
    The humble peticion of Anne Palmer, widow, Sheweth:
That whereas your petitioners house in the Church Street in Warwick was consumed by the late dreadfull fire there, and since by your order the streets was enlarged and part of her front ground taken away, which by the computacion of the Surveyors was five hundred and seaventeen foote, and understanding that it was your order that such ground as was taken away from any of the sufferers and laide to the streete, they should be paid for the same out of the charity mony, your peticioner hath not received one penny for her ground though she hath made severall journeys about it and then they will pay her but thirteen pounds ten shillings, although her ground comes to nineteen pounds seaven shillings and nine pence, and that she must take in small clipt mony with a great deal of unpassable naughty brasse mony amongst it and guineas at thirty shillings apeece, which your peticioner looks upon to be very hard measure. Humbly therefore prays your Honours to take the premises into your grave consideracions, and to be pleased to order that she may have such mony as is payable and at the rate it nowe goes, for if she must take it otherwise she will not recieve much above halfe as others have received, for which noble favour your peticioner shall be most thankfull and dayly pray for your Honours, etc.

Petition of James Fish senior

To the Right Honorable, etc., the Commissioners for the rebuilding the Town of Warwick, the humble petition of James Fish senior, one of the sufferers by the late dreadfull fire, humbly sheweth:
    That whereas there is a party wall rais'd by your Petitioner adjoyning to

the house of Edward Chesley in the Church Streete in this Borrough of Warwick, your petitioner being the first builder, which party wall has been measur'd by the Surveyours appointed for that purpose and is found by them to containe 138 foote which at the rate of £4 18sh. per rod comes to £2 9sh. 8d½ as will appear by a note under the hands of the said Surveyours. And whereas the said Edward Chesley being often ask'd for the said sum by your Petitioner, has refus'd to pay the same to him or to his order, your Petitioner therefore does most humbly request that he may (by your Honour's order) receive the said sum of £2 9s. 8d½ with intrest[1] out of what moneys the said Edward Chesley is to receive for ground taken away from his house, and your Petitioner shall as in duty bound ever pray, etc.

Petition of Thomas Wise

To the Rt Honorable and others the Commissioners appointed by an Act of Parliament for the rebuilding the Town of Warwick, etc.,

The Humble Peticion of Thomas Wise of this Borough, gent., Sheweth: That your Peticioner being about to rebuild his house in the Sheepstreet, burnt downe by the late fire, and haveing employed workmen to cleare the rubbish of some part of the same in order to lay his foundacion, is forbidden and discharged to goe on with the same by Mr Job Rainsford next adjoyning to your Peticioner. Your Peticioner therefore humbly prays the said Job Rainsford may be summon'd to answer the same, and your Peticioner shall ever pray, etc.

John Burton's agreement with Mr Eborall, etc.[2]

Thomas Lean, owner of a house in the street leading to the Pillory called the Kings Armes in possession of John Burton, went before the late fire in Warwick into Flanders—before his goeing away made his will wherein he makes William Eborall his younger son[3] executor and William Eborall and John Davis overseers of the said will—he gives severall legacies to be paid by his executor viz. £10 a peice to his 3 sisters and to each child of the said Eboralls £4. That the said house was burnt down by the late fire, and John Burton brother in law to the said Thomas Lean built up a house on part of the ground whereon before the late fire the said Kings Armes stood. Thomas Lean upon his return from Flanders made an agreement with John Burton,[4] that the Court should decree the inheritance of the ground to

---

[1] Followed by 'as by Act of Parliament ordered' struck out.
[2] Endorsement.
[3] i.e. William Eborall's younger son John Eborall.
[4] The handwriting of this document changes at this point.

John Burton, the said John Burton paying to the executor £40 viz. (J. Eborall) and all such charitable mony as has bin received by John Burton, or
shall arise hereafter on the charity. John Burton agrees to pay the £40 to
the executor within a month after the decree. John Burton to bee allowed
for the loss of his goods 2s. 6d. per pound. John Eborall to bee allowed the
charity for the house and ground, and John Burton to refund all the charity
mony hee hath received over and above what the loss of his goods comes
to. The £4 10s. 0 paid to the reversioner by John Burton to bee deducted
out of the £40 given by T. Lane to the executor. John Eborall the executor
to pay Mr Challoner for law bills upon bond £20. William Eborall to pay
the bond of £10 which John Burton was bound for with the father of
Thomas Lane formerly owner of the house to Mrs Dowley, now Fisher.
John Burton to pay the creditors for the materialls and building of his
house, such as hee contracted with them for.[1]

	£	s.	d.
John Burton to pay the charity money he received for the loss of the house being 4s. per li. for 130	26	0	0
John Burton to pay by the agreement over and above the charity money aforesaid	40	0	0
	66	0	0

	£	s.	d.		£	s.	d.
John Burton hath paid to Mr Challenor	20	0	0				
paid by him more to Mr Fisher by Makepeace	13	0	0		47	10	0
paid to Mr Eborall by John Burton	10	0	0				
paid to Mrs Matteson	4	10	0				

	£	s.	d.
John Burton remains debtor to pay to Mr Eborall according to the agreement and the decree	18	10	0

Petition and letter of Fulk Weale, draper

To the Honorable the Commissioners for determining differences arising
by the late dreadfull fire in Warwick,

The Humble Petition of Fulk Weale, draper, sheweth that your Petitioner haveing sustain'd by the said dreadfull fire a loss in houses and goods
amounting according to the most modest computation to the sum of eight
hundred and fifty pounds, did accordingly give in his said loss in hopes of
receiving his proportion of the charity money according to the said true
account of his loss, but soe it is that certain persons appointed by the said
Honorable the Commissioners to consider of and give theire opinion of the
losses of the particular sufferers by the said fire who were not upon oath,
either through misrepresentations by other persons or prejudices of theire

---

[1] The handwriting changes back to the first writer.

own, did sink your Orator's loss to the sum of five hundred and fifty pounds, according to which proportion only your Petitioner hath received of the said charity money, though others received to the full of theire losses, and though your Pctitioner's loss was as aforesaid as he is able to make out by undoubted testimony of witnesses, by which misrepresentation of his said loss, and also by the dammage he sustain'd by the narrow moneys (not haveing it although desir'd as early as others) borrowed by him out of the said charity money, your Petitioner hath received a very greate prejudice which he humbly represents to your Honours consideration, hopeing you will be pleas'd to give him such relief in and touching the premises as to your Honours great wisdome and charity shall seem reasonable, and your Petitioner shall ever pray, etc.

Good Sir,[1]
I desire the favour of you to deliver this inclosed Petition for me with the reasons of my not appearing abroad, and lik-wise to communicate this letter to the Honorable Commissioners.
1st. That I will take my oath that my loss was greater than Mr Tomkisses or Mr Heaths, or otherwise desire it may be left to the masons and carpenters that knew the houses before the dreadfull fire.
2d. Mr Norton (being one of the sufferers Judges) hath kept up the loss of his goods to £274 and have reduc'd mine to £100 who lost as much more in value than he in goods.
3dly. There is put down £400 for our late dwelling house when I order'd but £350.
4thly. I desire that if the Honorable Court will not take it into consideration to day, that I may be admitted to speake for my selfe the next Court day.
5thly. If I had had the moneys as early as Mr Tomkis and others I had sustain'd noe loss, but I might not, though desired, and therefore hope it will be consider'd.
6thly. I have received nothing for my ground taken away before my dwelling house.

Your humble Servant,
Fulk Weale.

Petition of the Mayor and Aldermen

Warwick Borough. To the Right Honorable and others the Commissioners and Judges appointed by Act of Parliament for the rebuilding of the Towne of Warwick and for determining differences touching houses burnt and demolished by reason of the late dreadfull fire there,

---

[1] This letter is pinned to the foregoing petition; there is no address.

The Peticion of the Mayor and Aldermen of the said Borough and others the Inhabitants of the High Street and places there adjacent, Sheweth:
That your said Peticioners understanding that this Court designes to enlarge the Swan Lane, and that by soe considerable a defalcacion from the ground of Mr William Tarver on which the Swan Inne formerly stood, as will render his rebuilding a sufficient house of publick recepcion there morally impossible, and the want of such an Inne or Taverne in that place will certainly transfere the usuall trade of the Towne to some other parte of it, to the unspeakable detriment of your Peticioners and their successors. Therefore your Peticioners doe humbly pray that some other meanes may be found out for the enlargment of the said lane, and the toft left to the discretion of the said Mr Tarver who designes to build a convenient house thereon.

Charles Hickes, Mayor

Rob. Ashby	Thom. Clifton	Joseph Blissett
Oliver Heselwood	Timothy Norbury	Dev. Whadcock
William Perkes[?]	Thomas Masters	Stephen Nicholles
Job Faulkner	Thomas Wall	Geo. Webb
Jo. Horton	John Hands	Richard Grimes
Thomas Abbott	Richard Hands	Richard Goode
Wm. Eborall	John Bird	Tho. Edes
Geo. Smith	William Fowkes	Sam. Barber
George Chesley	Ri. Lane	John Bullocke
Edward Chesley	John Jarvis	Stephen Comberladg
Richard Crooke	Edward Tipping	John Bacon
John Fowks		

Petition of John and George Watts

Warr' Burg'. To the Rt Honorable and others the Commissioners appointed by an Act of Parliament for the Rebuilding of the Town of Warwick, etc.,

The Humble Peticion of John Watts and Georg Watts[1] Sheweth:
That your Peticioners being the owners of two certaine messuages lying and being in the Sheep Street in the said Borough, the one in the possession of the said George Watts and the other in the possession of Henry Smith, butcher. That the watercourse before the late fire did runn from the messuages then standing on the said ground into the back ground belonging to Richard Hadley. There being a wall built and the watercourse thereby stopt to the great prejudice of your Peticioners. Your Peticioners therefore humbly pray that the said Richard Hadley may be

---

[1] Followed by 'and Elias Webb' struck out.

summon'd to answer the same and that they may be relieved therein, and your Peticioners shall ever pray, etc.

Petition of Oken's Feoffees

Warr' Burg'. To the Right Honorable and others the Commissioners appointed by Act of Parliament for the Rebuilding the Towne of Warwick, etc.,

The Humble Peticion of the Feoffees of Mr Thomas Oken, deceased, Sheweth:

That the said Thomas Oken was seized of a peice of building called a kitchen scituate on the south side of the High Pavement let with a messuage at and before the late fire in the possession of Mrs Dorothy Weale, widow, or Fulke Weale her sonne, [and] did devise the same to charitable uses. That by the said fire the said kitchen was burnt downe and by meanes thereof the foundacions, demencions and scituacion thereof are become uncertaine. Wherefore the said Peticioners doe humbly pray that a jury may be impannelled to inquire into and set forth the foundacions and ground whereon the said kitchen stood before the said fire, that soe the same may be ascertained and the said Feoffees may be the better enabled to apply the rents and proffitts ariseing thereby to the uses they were first designed, and your peticioners shall ever pray, etc.

Joseph Blissett	Aar. Rogers
Geo. Webb	Wm. Tarver
Rich. Hands	Charles Hickes

Petition of John King, tugerer

To the Right Honorable and the Right Worshipfull the Commissioners upon the Act of Parliament for the Rebuilding of the Borough of Warwicke,

The humble peticion of John King, sugarer,[1] an inhabitant within the said Borough, Humbly Sheweth:

That whereas your petitioner being tennant to a house of Mrs Man, widow, near the Pillory in Warwick before the fire, which house a great part was consumed by the late fire but part of the front was only pulled downe to put a stop to the fire, and for want of a place to drive a trade in, your petitioner was forced to take the same att £3 per annum being only a shop and one other ground roome but no rooffe to them, and for want of takeing care by the landlady, before midsummer last the chimney and the floores overhead fell downe and had like to have killed your petitioner and his family, and spoyled and broke a great quantity of his goods and wares, and his landlady

---

[1] Almost certainly an error for 'tugerer', a lath-splitter.

demands the quarters rent being nothing more behinde and it not being due when the fall was, and she refuses to build or take any care to repair the same, and your petitioner cannot get a place to be in, desires your assistance as to the rent then due at the fall and what he must do for a place to be in, for which great favour your petitioner shall be most thankfull and dayly pray for your Honours and Worships, etc.

Letter of Abraham du Commun, gunsmith

My Lord,[1]
I being informed that your Lordship and the rest of the Commissioner would meet this day concerning the late great fire in this town of Warwick, so I have made bold to wright to your Lordship. I hope your Lordship and the rest of the Commissioner will pardon me my boldnesse. I was set up of my trade newly before the said fire and bought my freedom, so I had lead out all what I had got in my trawels to put my self in a way to live in the world, and it plaised God to afflict us in that great fire, I being of the first houses that was burnt I could save nothing. I am affraid there hath bin some misse information against me, having had so litle of the mony that was given to the soffrer, I do not question but the Comissioner did give suficiently to them that were totaly burnt to go on with their trade. Indeed I thinck it is wery smale thing for me to have but seven pounds to buy houshold goods again and tools and stuff to worck and to be clothed again as Christians, having last all what I had and more then my owne that som people hath made me paye again sence the fire, if I had had no credit to buy goods in trust I could not go on with seven nor meny seven pounds, but by the good will and civility of the people in this contrey I bought goods in trust, now with all justicy I must paye them for their goods, and times being wery hard with me having had great sicknesse in my family sence the said fire, without question but your Lordship is well informed of it, being your Lordship's chaplin was doctor in my family, I desire your Lordship and the rest of the honnorable Commissioner to consider me being in great want of mony to pay my deptes for mentioned, or els I shall com to truble, so I rest your Lordships most humble servant,

Abraham du Commun, gunsmith.

Petition of Sarah Bucknall, widow

To the honorable and worshipfull Commissioners and Judges of the Court of Record for the rebuilding the Towne of Warwicke, etc.,

[1] Endorsed 'For the Reight Honorable Foulck Lord Brook in Warwick'. The writer's English is imperfect.

The humble Peticion of Sarah Bucknall of the Burrough of Warwicke in the County of Warwicke, widow, Sheweth:
That your Peticioner upon the request of John Burton of the Borrough of Warwicke aforesaid, silkeweaver, furnished him with drinke to the value of £1 6s. 8d. which if your Peticioner had not done his workemen would have left his building, and your Peticioner is informed, as the said John Burton is gone aside, your Honors and Worships have power to dispose of his house and other effects for the payment of his just debts. Your Peticioner therefore humbly prayes your Honors and Worships to take her condicion into your serious consideracions, and to releive your Peticioner as to your grave judgments shall seeme most meete, and your Peticioner as in duty bound shall ever pray, etc.

Petition of John Cakebread

To the Right Honorable and Honorable the Commissioners for the rebuilding of Warr'.
    The humble Petition of John Cakebread, one of the sufferers by the late dreadfull fire, humbly sheweth:
That whereas your Petitioner did deliver in an account of his loss by the said fire of all such goods as then came to his mind, but thro' hast omitted many things of his own as well as severall parcells of goods, viz. barley and mault, of other persons for which your Petitioner has since paid as will be attested upon oath by the owners of the said goods, your Petitioner does most humbly beg your Honours favour, that hee may have such further allowance of the Charitie money as shall seeme meet to your Honours wisdome and discretion, and your Petitioner as in duty bound shall ever pray, etc.

An Account of such goods of John Cakebread's which were destroy'd by the late dreadfull fire in Warwicke and were not entred in his [former][1] account of his loss, viz.

Two hair cloths	0	16	0
One mault mill	0	12	0
Wearing cloths	2	0	0
Paid to John Atterbury for mault burn'd	8	11	0
Paid to Mrs Bree for barley burn'd	1	12	0
To Francis Atterbury paid for seven strike of mault	0	18	6
Totall	14	9	6

[1] This word is obscured by a blot.

Petition of William Newberry

To the Right Honorable my Lord Brooke,

The humble peticion of William Newberry of the Borough of Warwick, Humbly sheweth:

That your poore petitioner, haveing three small children to maintaine and haveing no house to live in, being burnt out by the late dreadfull fire, and being willing to have a place to live in has endeavoured to rebuild him a small house, but he finds it will be a greater charge then he expected or his purse and freinds able to compleat, and so must of necessity be enforced to desist unlesse he have some assistance. Humbly therefore begging your Lordships gracious favour, that he may have something allowed him at present to goe on with his building what it shall seeme most meet in your Lordships and the other Commissioners wise consideracion, for which noble favour your petitioner shall be continually bound to pray for your Lordship and your most noble family.

Petition of Charles Emms, feltmaker

Warr' Bor'. To the Rt Honorable, Honorable and others the Commissioners of the Court of Record for Rebuilding the Town of Warwick, etc., the Humble Petition of Charles Emms of the said Borough, feltmaker, against John Hicks of the same, blacksmith, Humbly Sheweth:

That your Petitioner before and at the late fire in this Borough was seis'd in right of his wife of a messuage in the Markett Place neer the Pillory, the messuage of Mrs Martin on the one end, and the messuage of Mrs Man on the other end thereof. That the said messuage, all except the shopp part thereof, was consum'd by the said fire. That your Petitioner's wife, whilst sole, purchas'd the said messuage for eight score[1] pound. That after the intermarriage your petitioner laid out considerable sums in repairing and building the same, and in suits of law in clearing the title thereof, and improved it thereby to the value of £8 per annum; that hee is willing to rebuild the same, if hee may have the encouragement of a builder, and the toft whereon it stood may bee assured to him by Decree of this Court. Wherefore your Petitioner prays that after allowing what summs of mony this Court shall thinke fitt to the reversioner for his interest and estate therein, the inheritance of the toft may bee decreed to him and that hee may have the advantage and the benefitt giv'n for the encouragement of rebuilders, and hee shall ever pray, etc.

---

[1] 'eight score' interlineated above '80' struck out.

Petition of Margaret West, widow

To the Right Worshipfull his Majestyes Justices of the Peace for the County of Warwick.

The humble peticion of Margarett West of the Borough of Warwick, widow, Humbly Sheweth:

That whereas your poore petitioner being utterly ruined by a sudden and unexpected fire which happened in the outhouses belonging to your petitioners house[1] in Warwick on the eighth day of May last past about one of the clock in the morning of the said day (none knowing how it happened) which in a short space burnt downe and consumed nine bayes of building belonging to the said house, fifty quarter of malt and barley of her owne, the mault garners, besides houshold goods and other materialls amounting in the wholl to three hundred ninety and eight pounds and upwards, upon a strick enquiry and accompt taken and made by honest and substantiall neighbours, besides a great quantity of malt belonging to other people, whereby your poore petitioner and her family are utterly ruined and undone, and the rather att this juncture since the better part of the Towne of Warwick being consumed by the late dreadfull fire that they cannot assist your petitioner with their charity, neither can your petitioner have any benefitt of the late charity, haveing made her application to the Commissioners who cannot allow her to participate thereof, and so must sinke under the pressure of her losses unlesse your Worships please to take her most deplorable condition into your gracious compassion, and to be pleased to grant her your gracious order, that she may have the liberty to aske the charity of well disposed Christian freinds within this county, for which noble bounty your petitioner shall be most thankfull, and as in all duty bound dayly pray for your Worships, etc.

Petition of Alexander Nicholls

To the Right Honorable and Right Worshipfull the Commissioners or Judges appointed by a late Act of Parliament intituled an Act for the Rebuilding the Towne of Warwick consumed by the late dreadfull fire,

The humble peticion of Alexander Nicholls[2] of the said Towne of Warwick, Humbly sheweth:

That whereas your petitioner haveing bought the ground late Mrs Palmer's lying in St Maryes Church Street in Warwick, has built and finished a house upon the said ground, and understanding that other builders have received eighteen pence in the pound according to a former valuation of the houses standing and being upon such ground rebuilt againe, your petitioner

---

[1] Widow West had a thatched house in Brittaine Lane in 1696.
[2] Endorsed 'Mr Stephen Nicholls'.

humbly desires that he may have the same kindnesse shewed to him as hath been to others, and humbly desiring your order that he may receive eighteene pence in the pound, for which great favour your petitioner shall be most thankfull and dayly pray [for] your Honours and Worships, etc.

Petition of Thomas Griffin and his daughter

To the Right Honorable and Worshipfull Commissioners for the rebuilding of Warwick, the humble petition of Thomas Griffin and his daughter Hannah Olds, who is somtimes called Hannah Williams (their interest being all the same) humbly sheweth:
That your Petitioners had two houses burnt in the late dreadfull fire and they have made very hard shifts, by borrowing of money and by pawning their own and friends credit, to rebuild and finish the said houses, the value whereof was delivered to your Honours in the first estimate, and do therefore humbly pray the benefit of your order for their receiving four shillings in the pound as other sufferers have done, and your Petitioners shall ever pray.

Petition of William Pestill, shoemaker

To the Rt Worshipfull Commissioners constituted and appointed for the Redresses of the poor Sufferers at the late dreadfull fire as hapened in Warwick,
     The most humble petition of William Pestill, shomaker, who lay at his mother's house in the Pibble Lane in Warwick when the said late dreadfull fire did happen in Warwick, whereas he had the loss of three pounds three shillings in clothes and money, and he did formerly give in a bill but by some meanes it did miscarry, soe he doth most humble crave, being a poor man, for to have some consideration towards his loss.

Petition of Benjamin Woodhams

To the Rt Worshipfull Commissioners constituted and appointed for the Redresses of the poor Sufferers at the late dreadfull fire as hapened in Warwick,
     The most humble petition of Benjamin Woodhams, servant to John Atterbury, shoemaker, in the Sheepstreet in Warwick, who haveing suffered loss in clothes and working tooles to the value of thirty shillings at the said fire, and hath had noe consideration towards his loss, he doth most humble crave that he may have some consideration for his loss as well as other poor Sufferers.

Petition of Thomas West

To the Right Honorable and the Right Worshipfull the Commissioners appointed by a late Act of Parliament intituled an Act for the Rebuilding of Warwick consumed by a late dreadfull fire,

The humble peticion of Thomas West, Humbly sheweth:

That whereas your petitioner being a sufferer by the late fire, did put in his bill being £154 and upwards, haveing lost almost his all, but by what meanes he knowes not was struck of £54, though your petitioner is ready to make oath that his losse was a great deale more then he put into his bill, and he has spoke with severall of the jurors who were upon the adjusting the severall bills of the sufferers, who know nothing of its being cutt off, and your petitioner thinks he has very hard measure, and humbly desires that the premisses may be further enquired into and he not loose his proportion of the Charity as other sufferers are like to enjoy, for which noble bounty your petitioner shall be most thankfull and dayly pray for your Honours and Worships.

Petition of George Francis, flaxdresser

To the Rt Honorable and Worshipfull Commissioners now sitting in Commission concerning the late desolation as did happen in this said Burrough of Warwick,

The most humble petition of George Francis, flaxdresser, late an inhabiter at the Butts in this said Burrough, whereas at the late desolation he did suffer great damage to his great ruine and loss and hath had noe satisfaction, doth most humble crave your serious consideration, that your Worships would be pleased for to allow him somewhat out of the charitable gifts of good Christian people towards his said loss, and he will be in duty obliged to pray for each one of your healths and welldoeing.

Notes of various petitions and persons to be summoned

[1]Matthew Busby, Edward Deacon and Joseph Avern: Peticions to have the watercourse from their severall houses in the Swann Lane to goe throw the Swann ground as formerly.

John Watts and George Watts: Peticions to have the watercourse leading from their severall houses in the Sheepstreet to goe as formerly into the back ground of Serjeant Hadley.

---

[1] This paper is endorsed 'about Peticions, etc.' and appears to be a partial agenda for the court held 2 July 1702, and note of orders made at that court.

Francis Smart: Peticions to have the window made in the stable of Mr Wrothwell looking into his ground stopp'd up.

Thomas Clements: Peticions to be paid for the ground which Richard Hands has built upon amounting in the whole to six hundred 20 ft.

Richard Hands: Peticions to have the price of the ground in the Square sett.

The whole measure of Richard Hands his ground	4856 0 0
of which is Thomas Clements his ground	620 0 0
	4236 0 0

Richard Hands about settleing the chief rent upon the Bell ground.

Elias Webb peticions against Serjeant Hadley about a water course.

To summon: Mr Hollyoak, John Pinley, Richard Hands, Thomas Clements, Serjeant Hadley, Madam Beaufoy.

Petition of Mary Clemens, widow, and Thomas Clemens

To the Right Honorable and the Right Worshipfull the Commissioners appointed by a late Act of Parliament intituled an Act for the Rebuilding of Warwick, etc.

The humble peticion of Mary Clemens, widow, and Thomas Clemens of the Borough of Warwicke, Humbly sheweth:

That whereas your petitioners haveing been great sufferers by the late fire and haveing had two houses totally burnt downe by the said fire, and haveing since the fire rebuilt two tenements againe which within a weeke will be compleated, and haveing some moneyes due to the workmen which they must pay them and which they have not at present, and hopeing they might have been encouraged out of the charitable money which at present they extreamly want, hoping and humbly desiring therefore that your Honours and Worships will take the condition of your petitioners into your wise consideration, and to be pleased to order them some money out of the charitable money for their present occasions what it shall seeme most meet in your grave consideration, for which noble favour your petitioners shall be most thankfull and dayly pray, etc.

Petition of Richard Scudismore

To the Right Honorable and the Right Worshipfull the Commissioners appointed by a late Act of Parliament intituled an Act for the Rebuilding the Borough of Warwick,

The humble peticion of Richard Scudismore, Humbly sheweth:

That whereas your petitioner haveing sustained loss by the late dreadfull fire and did put in an estimate thereof att the first as other sufferers did, and not haveing had any thing of the charity money as severall others have, thinks himselfe forgott, and humbly prayes that he may have his proportion of the charity as other sufferers, for which noble favour your petitioner shall be most thankfull and as in all duty bound dayly pray for your Honours and Worships, etc.

Petition of John and Catherine Hancox

To the Rt Worshipfull Commissioners now sitting in Commission in the Burrough of Warwick concerning the late and dreadfull desolation which happened by fire,

   The humble petition of John and Catherine Hancox, late inhabiters at the Butts in the said Burrough of Warwick, whereas they have with that as was theire own, and allsoe with the charitable money of good Christian people as was bestowed on them, they have rebuilded theire house soe far as possible they could, but they haveing sold all as they had and cannot make noe further shift whereby for to finish there house, doe most humble beseech your serious considerations and assistance to support them in the finishing of the same, that they may have a house to shelter them in and not to perish, and in conscience they will be obliged to pray for each one of your healths and happiness in this world and joy eternall in the world to come.

Letter of J. Holyoak

Mris Overtons waull is 21 pearch and 2 foote which
at 3s 6d. the pearch comes to   3 13 6
The party waull of Mr Vennors howse betwixt Mr
Overton and me is one rod and quarter and 3 pearch
which comes to about   7 10 0
Besides the intrest ever since the fieor after six per cent
Mr Michnor, this is all I desieor to know, how I shall be reimburst this money and intrest, and when you see a convenient oportunity pray send for me to the Court

                                                            J. Holyoak[1]

order'd

---

[1] Endorsed 'Mr Holyoak's letter of business to be done'.

Note of money due to the Corporation

Corporation Houses burnt.[1] The Value of the Houses and ground whereon they stood, with the Allowance to each of them out of the Charitie Monies

2s. 6d. per pound	Houses.	Ground.	Deduct.	Allowance		
Mr Gibbs house in High-street	£100	£20	£ 80	£ 10		
Bromley in High Street	80	20	60	7	10s.	
Pritchett in Sheepstreet	160	10	150	18	15	
Good	100	15	85	10	12	6d.
Court house dammage	5				12	6
Parsonage house 4s. per pound	200	40	160	20	0	0
Corporacion ground sold to Paris, etc.				25	0	0
Parsonage ground to bee sold				50	0	0
Timber sold at Radford				12	0	0
Timber sold in St Nicholas Parish				7	0	0
				171	10	0
To be paid by the Commissioners at present				117	10	0

Note of William Tarver's losses

Mr Tarvers Loss by the Fire of Warwick[2]

The Ground

£ 75 0 0	The houses on the Bell ground	£480	0 0
120 0 0	The Swan	1060	0 0
40 0 0	Mr Whadcocks house[3]	340	0 0
235 0 0	Loss in goods	295	0 0
		2175	0 0
	Abate for ground	235	0 0
		1940	0 0

[1] This appears to be a calculation of money due to the Corporation from several sources. The total should be £161 10s.

[2] This is the more concise of two similar calculations.

[3] Also referred to as 'the house at Cross'.

£1940 at 2s. 6d. per li. is	242	10	0
18d. per li. for Mr Whadcocks house	22	10	0
18d. per li. for a house adjoyneing[1]	4	17	6
	269	17	6
of which summe received	145	12	6
	124	5	0

Measurements of ground exchanged by George Chinn

Account of ground exchanged by Chinn, etc.[2]

The ground that Gorg Chine purchesed of Homes that did belong to the ground on wich the new Inne is builded is 67 foot in length and 5 foote in breath.

The grownd belonging to bouth houses purches of Gorg Chin is thirty three foot and a halfe in breadth, that is sixteen foot and nine inches to each house and the ground is on hundred twenty and five foot in length and the length is the same to bouth houses.

The ground purchesed by Mr Lane and Mr Masters of Gorg Chin is 58 foot by 50 foot which is 2900 foot.

The demencion of the ground betwen Mr Man and Mr Lane and Mr Masters. The ground taken from Mr Lane to the ground now in the teniour of Thomas Abbott is 5 foot wide by 40 foot long which is 200 foot. The ground purchesed of Mr Man by Mr Lane and Mr Masters is 45 foot long by 15 foot 2 inches wide which is 680 foot.

Note of Isaac Mayo's sale to Edward Aston

Mayos writing[3]

Isaac Mayo to Edward Aston for £3 in consideracion of his marriage with his daughter sells all that 3rd part of a messuage which was lately purchas'd of Robert Bromley formerly the land of William Hadley, which 3rd part is the middle part of the said messuage and late in the tenure of William Hadley between the other 2 parts of the said messuage, one of which lyeth on the west part and is the land in the tenure of the said Isaac Mayo or one of

---

[1] Also referred to as 'Dadleys house in Church Street'.
[2] Endorsement. The following four rough notes are on small scraps of paper.
[3] Endorsement. This is another tiny scrap of paper.

them, and another on the east part in the tenure of Thomas Bartlemew, containe 10 foot in front.

Surveyors' estimate of work needed for widow Bucknall

An Estemat of the Charg of the widdow Bucknall back building to make itt fitt for tyleing in purseuance to a late Act of Parlement for the Rebuilding the town of Warwick, taken by William Smith and Samuel Dunckley.
The Charg of which for timber, lath, lime and tyles comes to thirty two pound and 4 shillings: 32 4 0.

Will. Smith   Sam. Dunckley.

Petition to Parliament of the Mayor, Aldermen and Burgesses

To the Right Honorable the Knights, Citizens and Burgesses in Parliament Assembled,

The Humble Peticion of the Mayor, Aldermen and Burgesses[1] of the Towne of Warwick in behalf of themselves and others the Inhabitants, Sufferers by the late dreadfull fire there,[2] Humbly Sheweth:

That whereas in one Act of Parliament made *anno septimo & octavo Gulielmi Regis* entituled an Act for granting to his Majesty severall Rates and Dutyes upon Houses for makeing good the Deficiences of the Clipped Money, there was a Provisoe *in haec verba*, Provided alwayes that such houses as have ben or shall be built within the Towne of Warwick since the late dreadfull fire there on the 4th day of September 1694 shall not be charged with any the Dutyes mencion'd in this Act, any thing in this Act to the contrary notwithstanding. Which said Act was continued by two other Acts to the first day of August 1710, and whereas your Peticioners are informed by the printed votes of this Honorable House a bill is order'd to be brought in for the farther continuacion of the said Acts, your Peticioners humbly hope and pray that in consideracion of the said dreadfull calamity and insupportable losses thereby sustained, whereby the inhabitants are soe much impoverished that severall parcells of burnt ground remaine still unbuilt, and the generality of the houses rebuilt repay not half interest of the monies expended in rebuilding the same, to the great discouragement of the builders and disabling those that have already built from carrying on their respective trades, this Honorable House will extend their favour and compassion in continueing the said Provisoe and exemption to such longer time for the help and benefitt of the said sufferers as to their wisdoms shall seem meet and expedient, and your Peticioners shall ever pray, etc.

---

[1] Followed by 'and Inhabitants' struck out.
[2] 'in behalf . . . there' inserted in a space.

SIR WILLIAM WILSON'S LETTER

Sir William Wilsons letter and the Value of his Work[1]

This for Wm. Colemore Esq. at Warwick.

Sir,   Sutton Corfield Feb. 13 1705[/6]
In answer to some of yours, I doe aver, and will sware before the eternall
God that tho' you did not verbaly make a bargan for the carveing at Warwick Church with me, you was by, when I said that the £100 set down for
survaing was too little, except I either lived there or had some worke about
the Church, upon which my Lord Brooke said that wee, meaning the Commissioners, will allow £100 for carving, there was not one of you said a
word against this promis which was made upon honour, and you know,
that upon this I did the worke, and that it was all done before the new touer
was thaught of, soe that my Lord Brooke is in a great mistake as to the
time, and as for what I said about stattues, it was an addisionall charg which
Sir H. Puckering was not willing to; soe it was concluded as my Lord says,
that they would not exceed the £100, this is truth if there be any in earth.
And as for the tops of the pillers, I did order stone to be added soe that they
should a bin done well, but you without my knowleg set them to a plasterer;
soe that it is not my fault if they are not as they shood be, nor for the charge
am I in fault. Had I bin worthy to know your minds I would a saved you the
charge of the piller heads and the mending of the monument in your chan-
cill, if I had known that such stuff would a pleas'd. I thank you for [staing?][2]
for me about the finishing of the carving, and am amaz'd at what some of
the Commissioners would a done on my account about what was to be
done, as for what had bin done I was not paid soe much as wood pay my
quarters while my worke men did it, and for the last worke they would not
pay any peny, soe that there is above £5 for diet still owing to the master of
the 3 Tunns; these things are hard and soe is your thoughts about the carving. I hope you doe not take me to be such a foole to doe worke without
order, nor such a knave to say I had orders and had non, for you own that
you have heard there was a bargan tho' you did not make it, and you know
you might a stopt it at the same time you enquired what my man had for a
windoe. Now since you know al this and my Lord owns the bargan was,
thoe he has mistooke the time, yet in truth you may set this in a clear light,
and doe noe man rung but me a great deall of right. Now what I have done
you know and the reasons why I did it, and why noe more was done. When

---

[1] Endorsement.
[2] 'Sta. . .'. There is a hole in the paper. The word may be 'staing', i.e., 'staying'.

you pleas to be soe kind to represent this matter wholly to my Lord he must own that my demands are reasonable, and soe must all honest men. I sent you word that I would bate £30 of the £100, and I have nothing but complaints back. If you had said what you wood give me it wood a look't· better than it does, and if it had bin anything like reason, I would a bin content, and will, rather than be at the trouble to bring this matter before any strangers. I observe you have noe mind to stand to my Lords promis, nor he to cal to mind when he made it, and this is to save money, which you will if I set a value of the worke, which if there had bin noe bargan I would set down for each particuler as follows

For 4 north windows and 4 south, 24s. a window	£9 12 0
2 in the west end of the Church	0 16 0
3 in the 1st story of the tower	1 4 0
4 in the 2nd story of the tower	3 4 0
4 in the 3rd story of the tower, thes are biger than the other	4 16 0
For 42 bottoms of the neiches in the tower at 5s. each	10 10 0
For 20 urnes standing on the principalls betwixt the rail and balister	20 0 0
For carving the old tower which was all spoyled, it not being big enough for the new one, I know not what, but it was all done soe that I charg it, thoe too little, at	2 0 0

Sir, I hope this charg will be thaught reasonable, but if [it] be not I will leave the prices to be set by an unprejudicst worke man, and to shew that I will doe fair, I will send a draft of each particular and its demention and will stand to what is soe awarded to your most faithfull servant.

Will. Wilson

DRAFT DECREES OF THE COURT

Decree for Stephen Nicholls, tallow-chandler

Warr' Borough.[1] At the Court of Record held before the Commissioners or Judges appointed by an Act of Parliament for the rebuilding the Town of Warwick and for determining differences touching houses burnt and demolished by reason of the late dreadfull fire there, at the Mayors Parlour on Monday the twenty sixth day of August 1695.

Stephen Nicholls of the Borough aforesaid, tallow-chandler, petitioner against John Weale of the same Borough, gent.

Whereas the said Stephen Nicholls hath exhibited his Petition[2] into this Court, thereby setting forth in effect, that [recital of the petition]. Whereupon summons were granted and issued accordingly and the afforesaid John Weale appeared personally here in Court this day, and upon reading the said recited petition and hearing what could be alleadged on either side, it appearing to this Court that Thomas Weale, father of the said John Weale, was seized of the premises in fee, and by his last will in writing bearing date the fourteenth day of January in the thirtieth year of the late King Charles the second [1678/9] did devise and bequeath unto Jane his wife four pound per annum for her life to be paid her half yearly out of the said messuage, and the other four pounds per annum out of the said messuage to his son George Weale, if he were then liveing, and the revertion and remainders of the said messuage with the appurtenances after his wifes decease to his son George Weale and to his heirs and assigns for ever, and if his said son George Weale were then dead, he gave and bequeathed the premises to his said son John Weale the defendant and his heirs for ever. And it appearing to this Court that the said George Weale went beyond the seas in the life time of his father, and before his fathers death was credibly reported to be dead, and that the said messuage was devised to him but conditionally if he were living, and that he hath never been seen or heard of for about twenty one years last past and therefore most strongly to be presumed he is long since dead. And it likewise appearing to this Court, that Jane the relict of the said Thomas Weale, now living, had a rent of four pounds per annum for her life payable out of the said messuage which hath been constantly paid her by the said Stephen Nicholls the petitioner as the same grew due and payable. And that John Weale the defendant for sixteen years last past hath been the reputed proprietor of the said messuage, and acknowledged so to be by the petitioner who hath yearly paid him the rent

[1] This decree exists as a rough draft, and also as an attested copy made on 8th August 1764 from the signed original, now lost.

[2] See p. 255.

growing due and payable for the same. And it further appearing to this Court, that by agreement had and made between the petitioner and the said John Weale, he the said petitioner is to pay the sum of ninety and five pounds to the said John Weale the defendant, for the fee simple of the premises together with the benefit that shall acrue to the rebuilder out of the charity moneys and all other charitys that shall be applied to the sufferers by the loss of the said messuage burnt down by the late fire, and that the said John Weale own'd the said agreement and consented that the same be decreed accordingly. Therefore for a final determination of all differences betwixt the petitioner and the defendant and confirmation of the agreement made between them touching the premises, this Court doth order and decree that the said petitioner Stephen Nicholls on or before the twenty ninth day of this instant August well and truly pay or cause to be paid unto the said John Weale ... the sum of ninety five pounds ... and to the said Jane Weale the sum of eight pounds ... on or before the 25th day of March next ensuing for her interest therein, and in consideration thereof this Court doth Order and Decree the inheritance of the ground ... and the materials for building remaining thereupon unto the petitioner Stephen Nicholls ... for ever; and this Court doth further order and decree that the said Stephen Nicholls ... with all convenient speed shall erect and build upon the aforesaid toft one or more good and substantiall tenement or tenements according to the rules and directions of the said Act, and orders of this Court for building. ... [The petitioner is discharged of all rent since the fire under the lease, which is to be delivered up and cancelled, and John Weale is to hand over all deeds and evidences relating to the premises].

		Brooke
Charles Hickes, Mayor	Wm. Bolton	F. Grevill
	Tho. Wagstaff	H. Puckering
	John Newsham	Wm. Colmore

Decree for William Tarver

At the Court of Record held before the Commissioners or Judges appointed by an Act of Parliament, etc.

... Whereas the said Court haveing view'd the corner burnt ground of Mr William Tarver nere the Cross on which before the said late fire stood a messuage or tenement in the possession of Devereux Whadcock, mercer, did on the 22nd day of May 1695 think fitt and adjudge necessary that thirty four foot of ground in length and ten foot in breadth att the one end and eight foot six inches att the other end, containeing in the whole three hundred and fourteen foot six inches, be taken from the aforesaid burnt ground lying and being in the Church Street for and towards the enlargement of the said street, and that the whole plott or parcell of burnt ground called the Poors Ground on which before the late fire stood a messuage or tenement in the High Street belonging to John Weale, gent., then in the possession of Thomas Dadley, butcher, being in length 30 foot and in breadth att the end toward the front 11 ft 6 inches and att the other end 10 ft, containeing in measure three hundred eighty seven foot, be laid to and added to the aforesaid ground of the said Mr Tarver as an equivalent to the ground of the said William Tarver in lieu and full recompence of his ground abovesaid soe taken away to enlarge the said Church Street. And whereas it appear'd to this Court that the said ground called the Poors Ground was the ground of the said John Weale and the tenement which before the late fire stood thereon the house of the said John Weale lett att the yearly rent of three pounds seven shillings, and that the rent or summ of £2 12s. was paid yearly out of the said premisses to and for the use of the poor of the parish of St Maryes and of the parish of St Nicholas within the said Borough of Warwick by equall portions, and whereas this Court did order the summ of nineteen pounds seven shillings to be paid for the whole ground call'd the Poors Ground aforesaid, and that the said John Weale should have and be paid the summ of £4 13s. 4d. out of the said summ of £19 7s. in full recompence and satisfaccion for his interest in the premises, and that the summ of £14 3s. 8d. the residue and remainder thereof should be equally divided, and one half thereof paid into the hands of the churchwardens of the parish of St Marys aforesaid and the other half into the hands of the churchwardens of St Nicholas parish aforesaid, to be by them apply'd to and for the use of the poor of the said parishes in such manner as the same was apply'd before the said fire. And whereas the said John Weale hath had and received of the Commissioners for Rebuilding the Town of Warwick the aforesaid summ of four pound thirteen shillings and four pence, he the said John Weale did in consideration thereof and of the aforesaid summ of £14 13s. 8d. to be paid as aforesaid, consent and agree that the aforesaid plot or parcell of ground call'd the Poors Ground ... should be decreed to the said William Tarver ... whereupon this Court pronounced the same decreed accordingly. And it appeareing to this Court that the said William Tarver hath rebuilt all the ... Poors Ground aforesaid being part of the corner house of the said William Tarver now in the possession of the aforesaid Devereux Whadcock, Now therefore for a finall determinacion of all differences ... This Court ... doth Order and Decree ... the inheritance of all and singular the said ground called the Poors Ground [and] the buildings thereon erected ... unto the said William Tarver, his heirs and assigns for ever. ...

Decree for Nicholas Paris, gunsmith, and Thomas Wall, blacksmith

At the Court of Record held before the Commissioners or Judges appointed by an Act of Parliament for Rebuilding the Town of Warwick and for determineing differences touching houses burnt and demolish'd by reason of the late dreadfull [fire] there, att the Mayors Parlour on ——.

Whereas the Mayor, Aldermen and Burgesses of the Borough of Warwick in the County of Warwick were before the late fire which happen'd within the said Borough on Wednesday the 5th day of September in the year of our Lord one thousand six hundred ninety four seized of a certaine messuage or tenement scituate lying and being within the said Borough in a certaine street there called the Jury Street then in the possession of Richard Good, tallow chandler, and whereas the said messuage or tenement was totally burnt down and consumed by the said late fire, and it appeareing to this Court that the said Mayor, Aldermen and Burgesses were so seized and that an agreement was had and made between the said Mayor, Aldermen and Burgesses and Nicholas Paris of the said Borough, gunnsmith, and Thomas Wall of the same Borough, blacksmith, by which agreement they the said Mayor, Aldermen and Burgesses did for the consideracion of the summ of five and twenty pounds of good and lawfull money of England to them in hand paid, that is to say the summ of twelve pounds and ten shillings by the said Nicholas Paris, and the summ of twelve pounds and ten shillings by the said Thomas Wall, the receipt whereof they did acknowledge, consent and agree that the back part of the toft and peice of burnt ground on which before the said fire the said messuage or tenement stood, should be assured unto the said Nicholas Paris and Thomas Wall and their heirs and assigns for ever by decree of this Court as the said ground was then sett out and divided and since built upon by the said Nicholas Paris and Thomas Wall, reserveing to themselves the benefitt of the forepart of the said ground laid into the street by order of this Court for enlarging the same, which said agreement and consent is mencioned in a former order of this Court of the first day of July in the year of our Lord 1695, whereupon this Court pronounced the same decreed accordingly, and whereas the said Nicholas Paris hath since the agreement made, rebuilt one moiety or half part of the toft aforesaid viz. the east part thereof being part of his now dwelling house, and the said Thomas Wall hath likewise rebuilt the other moiety or half part viz. the west part thereof, being the messuage or tenement now in the possession of George Smith, barber, Now therefore for a finall determinacion of all differences which shall or may hereafter happen to arise by and between the said Mayor, Aldermen and Burgesses . . . and the said Nicholas Paris and Thomas Wall . . . This Court in pursuance of the powers and authorityes given them by the said Act, doth Order and Decree as followeth, that is to say [that the two halves of the piece of burnt ground, with the buildings now erected on them, and half each of the common rights, etc., belonging to it, shall be assured to Nicholas Paris and Thomas Wall respectively, in consideration of £12 10s. apiece paid to the Mayor, Aldermen and Burgesses.]¹

Decree for Mary Mann, widow

Warr' Borrough. At the Court of Record held before the Commissioners or Judges appointed by an Act of Parliament for the Rebuilding the Towne of Warwick and for determineing differences touching houses burnt and demolished by reason of the late dreadfull fire there, att the Mayors Parlour on Munday the 26th day of August 1695

Mary Mann, widow, Peticioner against William Mann her son, Thomas and Robert Mann and John Hicks, defendants.

Whereas the said Mary Mann, widow and relict of Thomas Mann late of this Borough, hath exhibited her Peticion into this Court of Judicature thereby setting forth in effect, that she the said Peticioner Mary before and at the time of the late dreadfull fire within this Borough, was seized of an estate for life in a messuage with the appurtenances standing and being in the Markett Place in the Borough aforesaid then or late in the tenure and occupacion of John King which said messuage with the outhouses, barns, stables, gardens, commons, etc. thereunto belonging were the inheritance of Thomas Mann, deceased husband of the said Peticioner, and were in consideracion of a marriage then had and solemnized with and for a joynture to the said Peticioner Mary, by indenture beareing date the first day of September in the third yeare of the reigne of the late King James the second [1687], settled on the said Peticioner Mary, for life, after her decease, on the heirs of the said Thomas on the body of the said Mary lawfully begotten, and for default of such issue on the right heirs of the said Thomas for ever. That the said messuage was in part burnt down and in part pull'd down, to stopp the progress of the said late dreadfull fire. That John Hicks one of the defendants and brother of Thomas Hicks who bargained and sold the messuage to Humphrey Yardley, and of which a recovery was suffered to the use of the said Thomas Mann and his heirs, layes claime to the said messuage by vertue of the last will and testament of his father John Hicks. That her son William Mann is not able or willing to rebuild the said messuage, nor either Thomas or Robert Mann, two other of the defendants, sons of her late husband Thomas Mann by Alice his former wife, but they and each of them refuse soe to doe. Wherefore the Peticioner humbly pray'd this Court would grant summons to warn the said

¹ There is a separate undated draft decree to Nicholas Paris for his half of the ground, in almost identical terms.

William Mann, Thomas and Robert Mann and John Hicks to appear in this
Court, to the intent, the said house may be rebuilt, or they may receive a
reasonable satisfaccion for theire interests and pretences thereunto, and be
concluded by Decree of this Court, and the inheritance of the premises may
be vested and settled in the Peticioner and her heirs, which unless this
Court be pleased to grant and allow, the Peticioner considering the great
expence of rebuilding the said messuage, thinks not her interest therein
sufficient to induce her to undertake the same. Whereupon summons were
granted and issued accordingly, and Thomas Fox grandfather by the
mother side of the said Thomas and Robert Mann in behalf of the said
minors ... and the said John Hicks appeared in this Court, and ... it
appeareing to this Court that the Peticioner Mary Mann had an estate for
life in the premises ... and that by agreement ... between the Peticioner
and the said John Hicks, the said Peticioner was to pay to the said John
Hicks fourty shillings in full satisfaccion of all demands ... And it lastly
appeareing to this Court that the toft whereon the said messuage stood
and the materialls of building thereon are but of a small value, and that the
said William Mann ... is not willing or in a capacity to rebuild the same,
Therefore for a final determinacion of all differences ... this Court doth
Order and Decree that the said Peticioner paying ... the said summ of
fourty shillings to the said John Hicks ... and paying ... or lawfully tendring
the summ of one pound and ten shillings to the said Thomas Fox of this
Borough, viz. twenty shillings to him in trust for the said Thomas Mann
and ten shillings to him in trust for the said Robert Mann for their respective interests ... and the summ of five pounds to T— Griffin of the parish
of St Nicholas within this Borough, gent., in trust for the said William Mann
... the inheritance of the premises be vested and settled in the Peticioner
Mary Mann and her heirs ... [and] that the said Peticioner ... shall with all
convenient speed erect and build upon the toft of ground ... one other
good and substantiall messuage or tenement according to the rules of the
Act and orders of this Court touching building. And lastly this Court doth
Order and Decree that the said Peticioner ... shall ... have, hold and enjoy
the said toft ... as alsoe all the walls and buildings thereupon ruined and
damnified by the said fire ... and the messuage and buildings thereupon to
be erected and rebuilt. ...[1]

Decree for Edward Heath

Edward Heath of the Borough of Warwick, Petitioner, against William
Johnson of the same Borough, Dr of Physick, Defendant.
  Whereas the said Edward Heath hath exhibited his Petition bearing date

[1] Endorsed: 'Memorandum that the Peticioner Mrs Mann be ordered and decreed to pay one penny
halfpenny for a cheif rent due to the Lord of the Mannor.'

the 7th day of October last into this Court of Judicature thereby setting forth in effect, that hee the said Petitioner being seis'd of a certain messuage or tenement before the late dreadfull fire standing and beeing in the Jury Street within the Borough aforesaid adjoyning or very neer to St Peters or the Eastgate Chappell then or late in the possession of Nathaniel Guilstrop. The said tenement, without the consent and against the good will of the Petitioner, was untiled and the timber frame thereof cutt down on pretence of stopping the progress of the said fire by the order and direction of the said William Johnson with the assistance of Nicholas Paris of the said Borough, gunsmith; that the Petitioner conceiving the[1] subject matter of his petition to be within the cognisance of this Court and that the damage sustain'd thereby was to the value of £40, did therefore humbly pray the summons of this Court to summon the said Defendant to answer the contents of the said Petition and that might be awarded and made such satisfaction to the Petitioner for the said damage hee sustain'd thereby, as should bee prov'd by good evidence and seem most just and reasonable to this Court.

Whereupon summons were granted and issued accordingly and the said William Johnson appear'd in Court, and a jury duly summon'd beeing impannell'd by order of this Court of free and lawfull men of this Borough to try and resolve upon their oaths the question of the fact in dispute between the said parties, according to the direction of the aforesaid Act of Parliament, and the said jury viz. A: B: C: D: E appearing and beeing sworn after a full hearing of the evidence in Court on both sides did by their oaths find the said tenement of the said Edward Heath late in the possession of the said Nathaniel Gilstrop to bee pull'd down at the time of the said late fire by the order of the said Dr William Johnson, and that the damage thereby done to the said tenement amounted to the value of twenty pounds of lawfull English mony.

Wherefore this Court having duly weighed and considered the evidence and verdict above said and what could bee alledged on all sides, and it appearing by the said inquisition and allegations, that the said tenement was pull'd down by the order and directions of the said William Johnson, doe order, adjudg and decree that the said William Johnson shall in consideration of the damage above mention'd, before the Feast of the Purification of the blessed Virgin commonly call'd Candlemass day next ensuing the date hereof, pay or cause to bee paid to the said Petitioner Edward Heath, the sum of twenty pounds of lawfull mony of England. And this Court doth further order, adjudg and decree . . . [that the Petitioner release

---

[1] Followed by 'damage and wrong done to him by defacing and pulling down the said tenement to be within the cognisance of this Court (forasmuch as the said fire never came within the distance of sevrall houses of the same)' struck out.

and quitclaim all actions and demands arising from the pulling down of the house].[1]

Decree for Mrs Dorothy Weale, widow

Warr' Borough. At the Court of Record held before the Commicioners or Judges appointed by an Act of Parliament for the Rebuilding the Town of Warwick and for determineing differences touching houses burnt and demolished by reason of the late dreadfull fire there, att the Mayors Parlour on Munday the [   ][2] day of October *anno Domini* 1695.

Whereas William[3] Cook of the Citty of London, apothecary, is seized of an estate of inheritance in a certaine toft or parcell of burnt ground lying, scituate and being on the south side of a street call'd the High Pavement or Highstreet in the Borough aforesaid whereon att and before the late dreadfull fire which happen'd within the said Borough on the fifth day of September in the year 1694 stood two messuages[4] being the houses and lands of the said William Cook then or late in the tenure and occupacion of Richard Hands, baker, and Thomas Tiping, cutler,[5] and adjoyning on the east side thereof to the messuage of Dorothy Weale, widow, or Fulk Weale, woollen draper, her son, or one of them, on the west side thereof to the messuage or tenement of Edward Wilson, apothecary, containeing in the whole [   ][2] superficiall feet more or less, which said messuages together with the messuages on the east and west side thereof were wholly consumed by the said fire, and whereas this Court mindeing and haveing an especiall regard to the more convenient and regular rebuilding the said street, pursuant to the powers and authorityes given by the said Act for regulateing foundacions as they shall think most convenient for the buildings and least prejudiciall to the streets of the said Borough, did in order thereunto think fitt by order of this Court beareing date the sixth day of May last, to take away from the said toft of the said Mrs Weale one hundred thirty eight foot whereof eighty four feet were to be laid into the High Pavement, for enlargeing and makeing more convenient the same, and fifty four feet to be laid to and make good the toft or ground of Mr Savage in lieu of and for a recompence

[1] This draft decree is endorsed with the following unrelated note: 'John Woods of Clardon purchases of the Widdow Mann a toft in the Markett Place, Timothy Simkins on one side and Charles Emms on the other, for £40, the widdow to have the 1s. 6d. per pound Charity mony. John Woods purchases of Charles Emms a piece of burnt ground containing 64 [ft] in deepth, in breadth in the fore part 2 foot four inches and att the back part 6 foot and 2 inches, the ground of John Wood bought of Mrs Mann on the north side and Charles Emes on the south side, the ground of Mrs Martin on the east and back part thereof.'
[2] Blank not filled in.
[3] 'William' interlineated above 'Richard' struck out, and so throughout.
[4] Altered from 'one messuage'.
[5] Marginal notes: 'Memorandum a quitt rent to Sir H. Puckering out of Tippings or Hands house and alsoe to Mr Bolton.' 'Sir H. Puckerings quitt rent 3s. out of R. Hands house.'

to the said Mr Savage for the like quantity taken from his ground to enlarge the said street, and by another order beareing date with the last recited order did alsoe think fitt to take away from the said toft of the said Mr Cook one hundred sixty and one[1] feet and to add and lay the same to the above mencioned toft of the said Mrs Weale as an equivalent and a recompence to the said Mrs Weale as abovesaid and in consideracion of the said one hundred sixty and one feet soe taken away from the said Mr Cook, did order the summ of eight pounds and one shilling[2] to be given and paid to the said Mr Cook being after the rate of one shilling per foot, in full payment and satisfaccion for the same, which said summ of eight pounds and one shilling the said Mr Cook did by James Fish of the Borough aforesaid, surveyor, his atturney lawfully empowered thereunto,[3] agree to and accept as a valuable consideracion and in full satisfaccion of the said ground soe taken away and the receipt thereof did acknowledge, Therefore for the better and more effectuall conveying and assureing the said one hundred sixty and one feet of ground to the said Mrs Weale and for a final determinacion of all differences ... This Court doth Order and Decree ... the aforesaid one hundred sixty and one foot of ground and the building thereon erected and to be erected, to the aforesaid Mrs Dorothy Weale and her heirs. ...

Decree for Thomas Tippin, cutler

Warr' Borough. At the Court of Record held before the Commissioners or Judges appointed by an Act of Parliament for the Rebuilding the Town of Warwick and for determineing differences touching houses burnt and demolished by reason of the late dreadfull fire there, att the Mayors Parlour on Munday the [   ][4] day of October *anno Domini* 1695

Thomas Tippin of the Borough of Warwick, cutler, Peticioner against William Cook of London, apothecary.

Whereas the said Thomas Tippin hath exhibited his Peticion into this Court of Judicature thereby setting forth in effect that he the said Peticioner being possessed of a messuage with the appurtenances on the south side of the High Pavement standing and being betwixt the messuage late in the possession of Mrs Dorothy Weale, widow, on the east side thereof and the messuage late in the possession of Richard Hands, baker, on the west side thereof att the yearly rent of four pound ten shillings, and had laid out considerable sums upon the said house, that the said messuage was totally burnt down by the said fire, and that the said William Cook is unwilling to

---

[1] Altered from 'one hundred fifty and seven', and so throughout, correcting a mathematical error in the Order Book.

[2] Altered from 'seven pounds seventeen shillings', and so throughout.

[3] 'by James Fish ... thereunto' interlineated over a caret.

[4] Blank not filled in.

rebuild the said messuage or discharge the Peticioner of the arrears of rent incurred, and growing rent since the said fire, that the Petitioner is desirous to rebuild the said messuage if he may be encouraged thereunto by the Decree of this Court, wherefore the Peticioner humbly pray'd this Court would grant summons to warn the said William Cooke to appeare in this Court to answer the contents of the said Peticion, whereupon summons were granted and issued accordingly and James Fish of the Borough afore-said, surveyor, being thereunto lawfully empowered and authorized appear'd for and in behalf of the said William Cook, and upon reading the said recited peticion and heareing what could be alleaged on either side, it appeareing to this Court that by agreement since the fire between the Peti-cioner and the said James Fish, he the said Peticioner was to pay the summ of fifty nine pounds[1] for the fee simple of the said toft and other the premises, and the said James Fish for and in behalf of the said William Cook own'd the said agreement and consented that the same be decreed accordingly, wherefore . . . this Court doth Order and Decree that the said Thomas Tipping[2] shall pay or cause to be paid with all convenient speed unto the said James Fish to and for the use of the said William Cook the summ of [   ][3] and that in consideracion thereof this Court doth Order and Decree that the said Peticioner be discharged and acquitted of all arrears of rent and growing rents since the said fire . . . and farther this Court doth Order and Decree that the said Peticioner doe erect or cause to be erected on the said toft one other good and substantiall messuage according to the rules laid downe in the said Act for building, and orders of this Court. And lastly this Court doth Order and Decree that the said Thomas Tippin . . . shall have, hold and enjoy the aforesaid toft and ground whereon formerly stood the said messuage as alsoe the walls and ruins and the messuage and buildings to be erected and rebuilt in pursuance of this Decree. . . .

Decree for Richard Hands, baker

Warr' Borough.[4] At the Court of Record held . . . on Munday the [   ][3] day of October *anno Domini* 1695.

Richard Hands of the Borough of Warwick, baker, Peticioner against William Cook of London, apothecary.

Whereas the said Richard Hands hath exhibited his Peticion . . . that he the said Peticioner being possessed of a messuage with appurtenances on the south side of the High Pavement standing and being betwixt the

---

[1] 'fifty nine pounds' struck out.
[2] Altered from 'William Tipping', interlineated above 'Richard Hands' struck out.
[3] Blank not filled in.
[4] This decree uses the same clauses and wording, and is by the same hand as the preceding decree for Thomas Tipping.

messuage late in the possession of Thomas Tippin on the east side thereof, and the messuage of Mr Edmund Wilson on the west side thereof at the yearly rent of ten pounds . . . [that the house was burnt down, and it appearing to the Court that agreement has been reached between Richard Hands and William Cook's attorney James Fish, for the purchase of the site for £59 10s. and to be discharged of arrears of rent, the Court decreed the site with the walls and ruins to Richard Hands, and the new house to be built upon it.]

Decree for John Atterbury

Petition of John Eld of Killingworth and Thomas Carr of Barkswell versus John Atterbury.

Decree.[1] Whereas the said John Atterbury hath exhibited, etc. That Elizabeth Carr as hee is informed was seised of an estate of inheritance of and in a toft or piece of burnt ground whereon, etc.[2] That since the said fire the said Elizabeth, by her last will and testament in writing, did devise the said toft to the said John Eld and Thomas Carr and their heirs and soon after dyed. That the said defendants beeing soe seis'd of the said toft did contract and agree with the Petitioner John Atterbury that hee the said John Atterbury paying the summ of thirty six pounds should have the said toft, etc., assured and convey'd to him and his heirs freed from all incumbrances. That hee hath cause to suspect and fear the said defendants cannot make him a good and sufficient title in law to the premisses, for that the said John Eld, etc., neglect and refuse to doe and perform what on their parts by the said agreement ought to bee done and performed. Wherefore the Petitioner pray'd the aid of this Court, to enforce and compell the performance and execution of the said agreement. Whereupon summons, etc. And the said John Eld and T. Carr appear'd personally in Court and upon hearing what could bee alledged on both sides, it appearing to this Court, that Christopher Ailsbury late of this Borough was seis'd in his demesne as of fee, of and in the above mention'd messuage, since burnt down by the said fire, that beeing soe seis'd did by his last will and testament in writing give and devise the same with the appurtenances to Elizabeth Carr late of this Borough and her heirs. That the said E. Carr was seis'd of the said messuage by virtue of the said last will and testament of the said Christopher Ailsbury but that soon after the said messuage, outhouses, etc., were consumed and demolished by the said late fire within this Borough. That the said Elizabeth Carr being then seis'd of the toft and burnt ground whereon the said messuage formerly stood with the appurtenances, did make her last will and testament in writing and therein did give and devise the said

[1] This is a very rough and much altered draft, in the nature of notes for a decree.
[2] See p. 49.

toft and burnt ground to the defendants John Eld and Thomas Carr and
their heirs, chargeable nevertheless with the payment of £5 to the poor of
the Parish of St Maries, Warwick, and one other £5 to the poor of the
Parish of St Nicholas, Warwick, to bee distributed by the churchwardens of
the respective parishes as by the said will, relation being thereunto had
doth and may more fully appear. And it further appearing to this Court that
by agreement had and made, etc. And lastly that a rent for the Lord of the
Mannor.[1] Wherefore the Court decreed the same accordingly. Therefore
for a final determinacion of all differences this Court doth Order and
Decree, etc. That the said John Atterbury pay, etc., and that in consideration of the said summ the inheritance bee vested *vide* some other decree.
And this Court doth further Order the payment of the rent if any and that
hee rebuild according to Act of Parliament, *vide* decrees. And lastly that
hee paying, etc., enjoy the said toft.

Decree for Charles Emes, feltmaker

Warwick Borough. At the Court of Record held before the Commissioners
or Judges appointed by an Act of Parliament for the Rebuilding the Towne
of Warwick and for determineing differences touching houses burnt and
demolished by reason of the late dreadfull fire there, att the Mayors Parlour
on Monday the [   ]² day of [   ]² *anno Domini* 169[ ]².
    Charles Emes of the Borough of Warwick, feltmaker, against John Hick
of the same Borough, defendant.
Whereas the said Charles Emes hath exhibited his Peticion into this Court
of Judicature thereby setting forth in effect that the said Peticioner before
and att the time of the late dreadfull fire within this Borough, was seized of
an estate for life of a messuage with the appurtenances standing and being
in the Markett Place in the said Borough neer the Pillory, haveing on the
[   ]² end thereof the messuage of Mrs Martin and on the [   ]² end
thereof the messuage of Mrs Mary Mann, widow, that the said messuage
(except the shopp part thereof) was wholly demolished by the said fire,
that the Peticioners wife whilst sole, and before her intermarriage with
him the Peticioner, purchased the said messuage with the appurtenances of
and from [   ]² for the consideration of the summ of one hundred and
[   ]² of lawfull money of England, and after her said intermarriage the
Peticioner and his wife laid out and expended considerable summs in
repaireing and additional building to the same, and suits of law and clearing
her title thereunto. That the Peticioner provided he may have the encouragement given to rebuilders of houses burnt downe by the said fire,
and the inheritance of the toft whereon stood the said messuage and other

---

[1] 'Q' in the margin against this.
[2] Blanks not filled in.

ground thereunto belonging att the time of the said fire, assured to him and his heirs by the Decree of this Court, is willing and will undertake to rebuild the said messuage. Wherefore the Peticioner humbly pray'd this Court would grant summons to warn the said John Hicks to appeare in this Court, that he may receive a reasonable satisfaccion for his interest.... [The defendant appeared, and the Court, taking notice of an agreement between them, under which the petitioner was to pay to the defendant £15 for his interest in the toft, and allow him a half part of the charity money allotted for the loss of the house, decreed accordingly, saveing to the Lord of the Manor fealty, suit of court and an unspecified yearly rent as usually performed and paid for the house before the fire] And this Court doth farther Order and Decree that the said Peticioner ... shall with all convenient speed erect and build upon the toft of ground whereon the said messuage stood ... one other good and substantiall messuage or tenement according to the rules of the Act abovesaid and Orders of this Court touching building ... [and the petitioner shall have peaceable enjoyment of the said toft] whereon formerly stood the said messuage, as alsoe all the walls and buildings thereupon ruin'd and damnified by the said fire ... and the messuage and buildings thereupon to be erected and rebuilt. ...

Decree for John Woods of Claverdon

At the Court of Record held before the Commissioners or Judges appointed by an Act of Parliament for the Rebuilding the Towne of Warwick and for determineing differences touching houses burnt and demolished by reason of the late dreadfull fire there, att the Mayor's Parlour on Munday the [   ][1] day of [   ][1] *anno Domini* 169[ ][1]
Whereas[2] the said Mary Mann of the Borough aforesaid, spinster,[3] widow and relict of Thomas Mann late of the same Borough, deceased, hath exhibited her Peticion[4] into this Court of Judicature thereby setting forth in effect that the said Peticioner Mary before and at the late dreadfull fire within this Borough was seiz'd of an estate for life in a messuage standing and being in the Market Place in the Borough aforesaid then or late in the tenure and occupacion of John King, haveing on the north side thereof a messuage then in possession of Timothy Simpkins and on the south side thereof a messuage then in possession of Timothy Simpkins,[5] which said messuage was in part burnt down by the said fire, and in part pull'd downe to prevent the progress of the same. That neither her son William Mann, or Robert or Thomas Mann, sons of her late husband Thomas Mann by his

[1] Blanks not filled in.
[2] This decree exists as a rough draft and also a relatively fair copy.
[3] Possibly her trade; it appears in both texts.
[4] A fresh petition, mentioned in the Order Book under 27 Jan. 1695/6.
[5] This name has been inserted by another hand in a space left for it.

former wife Alice, being able to rebuild the said messuage, she the said Peticioner obtained the Decree of this Honorable Court for the consideracions in
the said Decree mencioned, to barr the revercions and remainders and all
estate right title interest or demand of any person whatsoever in and to the
toft whereon before and at the said fire the said messuage stood and all and
singular other the premises with the appurtenances thereunto belonging, by
which above recited Decree shee the Peticioner her heirs or assigns were
ordered, adjudged and decreed to erect and build on the said toft one other
good and substantial messuage according to the rules of the said Act of Parliament for Rebuilding the Towne of Warwick, and whereas according to the
said Peticion it appears to this Court that neither the said Peticioner or her
heirs are in a capacity to rebuild the said messuage and being become utterly
unable to perform the same, are thereby become lyable to the penaltyes that
may or shall be inflicted by vertue of the said Act on persons who shall dis-
obey or doe not performe the Orders and Decrees of this Court. Wherefore
the Peticioner pray'd, that she and her heirs might be indemnified and sav'd
harmless from the said Decree, and the penaltie she might thereby incurr by
nonperformance of the contents thereof, she the Peticioner haveing agreed
and contracted with John Woods of the parish of Claverdon in the County
aforesaid for the consideracion of the summ of fourty pounds and one shilling
and six pence in the pound according to the estimate of the loss given for the
said messuage soe burnt downe as aforesaid being the monies given by the
Trustees or Commissioners for the disposall of the monies ariseing by the
brief for the said fire as the encouragement to and for rebuilders of the houses
burnt downe by the said fire, to convey the inheritance of the said toft . . . to
the said John Wood [discharged of all incumbrances except fealty, suit of
court and yearly rent due to the lord of the manor]. Whereupon this Court . . .
being satisfied of the inability of the Peticioner to rebuild the said messuage
. . . and withall haveing an especiall regard to the Publick Weale of the said
Borough which very much depends on the speedy rebuilding the same, doth
think fitt to Order and Decree that the said John Woods [if he rebuild the
house, shall have peaceable possession of the toft and new house, and the
petitioner shall be discharged from any penalties to which she might be liable
for nonperformance of the former decree].

Decree for William Cockbill *alias* Deason of Barford

At the Court of Record held before the Commissioners or Judges
appointed by an Act of Parliament for the Rebuilding the Town of Warwick
and for determineing differences touching houses burnt and demolished by
reason of the late dreadfull fire there, att the Mayor's Parlour on Munday
the [   ]¹ day of [   ]¹ *anno Domini* 1695/6.

¹ Blanks not filled in.

William Cockbill *alias* Deason of Barford, Peticioner against Thomas Stratford and Mary his daughter of the Borough aforesaid.

Whereas the said William Cockbill *alias* Deason hath exhibited his Peticion[1] into this Court of Judicature thereby setting forth in effect that the said defendants or one of them being seized of an estate of inheritance of and in a certain messuage scituate lying and being in a street called the High Street or High Pavement in the Borough of Warwick and heretofore being two tenements then in the occupacion of the said Thomas Stratford and adjoyning on the east[2] side thereof to another messuage late of the said Thomas Stratford, and to a messuage on the west side thereof heretofore used as the Common Goale of the said County of Warwick, together with the barns, stables, outhouses, [etc., mortgaged the premises to William Cockbill by a deed dated 27 March 1693 for £35, later increased to £50 by an endorsement, to be repaid by two annual instalments. No money was paid by the end of the first year, and house was burnt down by the fire before the date appointed for the last payment.] That the said Thomas Stratford and Mary his daughter and either of them are by reason of the said loss by fire, utterly disabled to redeem the said premises soe mortgaged, and are become incapable to rebuild the said messuage, att least refuse soe to doe, wherefore the Peticioner humbly pray'd this Court would grant summons ... whereupon summons were granted and issued accordingly, and the said Mary Stratford appeared in Court, but Thomas her father the other defendant by reason of his great age and infirmities, could not. ... It appeareing to this Court that ... the said toft and premises were of much less value than the monies lent thereupon, and that by agreement had and made by and between the said defendants and the Peticioner, in consideracion the said Peticioner would discharge the defendants of all the provisoes, covenants and agreements in the said indenture of demise mencioned, and accept and take the said toft or burnt ground with the appurtenances in lieu and full satisfaccion of the said principall money and interest and all demands for and concerning the same, the inheritance of the said toft and other the premises ... were to be vested in the Peticioner and his heirs, and the said Peticioner and defendants own'd the said agreement and consented that the same be decreed by this Court, wherefore this Court pronounced the same decreed accordingly [reserving a rent of 3d. to the lord of the manor]. ... And this Court doth farther Order and Decree that the said Peticioner ... shall and will with all convenient speed erect and build ... upon the toft or burnt ground ... one other good and substantiall messuage or tenement according to the rules of the Act abovesaid and Orders of this Court touching building. ...

[1] See p. 264.
[2] 'east' altered from 'west'.

Decree for Richard Hands, maltster

Richard Hands, maulster, against John Pritchard, etc.

Whereas the said Richard Hands hath exhibited, etc., that hee the said John Pritchard being seiz'd of a messuage on the west side of a street call'd the Sheep[1] Street, *alias* Northgate Street, in the Borough aforesaid, having a messuage on the north side thereof then or late in the occupacion of A B, and a messuage then or late in the occupacion of C D on the south side thereof, did mortgage the said messuage to the said Richard Hands the Petitioner for the summ of four score pounds of lawfull mony of England, that the said messuage was burnt down, etc., and that there was due at the time of the said fire, for the said principal mony and lawfull interest due thereupon, neer the summ of one hundred pounds, wherefore the Petitioner pray'd in consideracion the said messuage which was his security for the said principal mony and interest, was burnt down and thereby hee the Petitioner likely to become a great looser, that hee might have such proportion of the charitie monies as should have fall'n and accrued to the defendant for and in respect of his losses sustain'd in the said messuage, awarded and giv'n to him by the said Commissioners towards repairing of the losses of his monies, as to them should thinke most just and reasonable. Whereupon the said Court granted summons to warn the said defendant to appear ... and it appearing to this Court ... that the defendant was and is unable to redeem the said mortgage and pay off the said principal mony and interest, and farther that hee is not able to rebuild the said messuage or any part thereof, and that by agreement had and made between the Petitioner and Defendant, on condition the defendant for himself and his heirs would remise, release and for ever quittclaime to the said Petitioner and his heirs all his right, title and interest and demand whatsoever in the toft whereon the said messuage stood ... hee the Petitioner was to cancell the said mortgage and deliver up the same soe cancelled to the defendant ... and by the said agreement the Petitioner was in consideration of the small value of the toft, to have the benefitt of such charitie monies as should bee allotted. ... Whereupon this Court ordered, etc. ...

Decree for John[2] Hancox, glazier

Decree to John Hancox of Mrs Martyns ground.

Whereas Elizabeth Martyn of this Borough, widow, did exhibit, etc.,[3] that shee the said Petitioner at and before the late fire which hapen'd within this Borough was seis'd for the term of her natural life of and in a certain messuage or tenement scituate, etc. (as in the Petition), that Richard

---

[1] Interlineated above 'Church' struck out.

[2] Contemporary mistake for 'Richard', and so throughout this petition, but corrected in an endorsement.   [3] See petition p. 269.

Martyn of the Citty of London, silkweaver, son of the said Elizabeth, was seis'd of the reversion of the same, that the said messuage was totally burnt, etc., that the value thercof amounted to £170, for which loss of £170, the Petitioner received out of the charitie monies giv'n for the relief of the sufferers by the said fire, the summ of £21 5s. after the rate of 2s. 6d. per pound. That the Petitioner having reason to beleive the said reversioner intended to sue and molest her for all or part of the said £21 5s. shee had soe receiv'd, submitted her self therein to the directions and orders of this Court, and humbly pray'd that this Court would consider the value of her intrest in the premisses and so award her such proportion of the said £170 as they should think most just and reasonable and did further pray the said toft whereon the said messuage stood and all other the premisses might be sold, and that the consideration or purchase money might be divided betwixt the tenant for life and the reversioner in fee, according to the value of theire respective interests therein. Whereupon summons, etc.

And the said Richard by his wife Mary did exhibit his cross petition into this Court, setting forth his reversion in fee in the premisses, and praying that hee might have his share in the said charitie monies proportionable to his interest therein, and that his mother might be summon'd to appear and refund and pay back such part of the 21 5s. which shee had received, as to the discretion and judgment of this Court should seem reasonable, equall and just according to the respective interests of the tenant for life and reversioner in fee therein. And further, the said Richard Martin did by writing under his hand and seale constitute and appoint Edward Atkins of the Borough of Warwick, mercer, and his said wife Mary, his true and lawfull atturneys ... to sell to or contract and agree with any person or persons for the sale of the said toft. ... And ... it appearing to this Court ... that the said Elizabeth Martin had received the aforementioned 21 5, being the whole summ allotted for the loss of the said messuage burnt down at the rate of 2 6 per pound: and that by agreement had and made between the said Elizabeth Martin, the said Edward Atkins and Mary Martin for and in behalf of the said Richard Martin, shee the said Elizabeth in consideracion of the reversionary estate and interest in the premisses was to refund and pay back 2/3rd parts of the said £21 5s. to the said Richard Martin or his said atturney, provided the said Elizabeth might deduct and discount £10 out of the said £21 5, being a debt upon bond, from the said Richard to the said Elizabeth, which bond was produced in Court ... and according to the said agreement, the said bond was cancell'd in Court. Whereupon the Court decreed the same accordingly, and it further appearing to this Court, that by agreement had and made by and between the said Petitioner and the said atturnies of Richard Martin and John Hancox of the Borough aforesaid, glazier, that hee the said John Hancox, for and in consideracion of the summ of £45 of lawfull English money paid or secured to bee paid to the said Elizabeth Martin and Richard Martin or his said atturnies, should have a perfect and absolute estate in fee simple convey'd to him and his heirs of the said toft and other the premisses and the benefitt of the 1s 6d. per pound giv'n and allow'd to rebuilders ... the Court pronounced the same decreed accordingly. Q. if rent out of it to Mr Bolton.

... And this Court doth further Order and Decree, that the said John Hancox doe pay ... the summ of £45 ... the said summ to bee divided betwixt the said Petitioner and the said Richard Martin in the proportion herein after expressed, that is to say 2/3rds of the said sum to the said Richard or his wife Mary for and in consideracion of his interest in the premisses and one 3rd to the said Elizabeth for and in consideracion of her interest in the same. ... This Court ... more over doth order and decree all the charitie monies that shall arise or bee allotted to the sufferers by the said fire, over and above the first one shilling and shilling and 6d. which by consent of all the parties to the agreement abovesaid shall be allowed and paid to the said John Hancox, to the said Elizabeth Martin and Richard Martin ... in the same proportions, as the above said £21 5 and the £45 have been divided and shared. ... [And] this Court doth Order and Decree that the said John Hancox doe pay ... the said summ of £45, and that hee paying the said summ and giving security, such as this Court shall judg sufficient and good, to rebuild the said messuage soe burnt down, shall enjoy (as in other Decrees). ...

Decrees for Thomas Lean, barber, and [William] Savage of Bishops Tachbrook

Decrees : Hannah and Samuell Tuckey to Thomas Lean, barber
          : To Mr Savage of a peice of Mrs Weale ground[1]

Hannah Tuckey and Samuel Tuckey v. [   ]
Whereas the said Hannah Tuckey and Samuel Tuckey her son a minor did exhibit, etc. That shee the Petitioner H. Tuckey was at the time of the late dread[ful fire] etc. seis'd of an estate for life in a messuage or tenement scituate in etc. of which said messuage Thomas Leane was at and before the said fire tenant in possession. That hee the other Petitioner at the time aforesaid was seis'd of the reversion and inheritance of the said inheritance. That neither of the Petitioners being able to rebuild the said messuage within the time limited by the Act of Parliament for rebuilding the Town of Warwick, did contract with the said Thomas Leane for the summ of twenty five pounds to convey and pass away their respective rights and titles to the said Thomas Leane, but that by reason of the minority of the Petitioner Samuel Tuckey they conceived they could not make a good grant of the

---

[1] These two draft decrees are on the same sheet of paper.

same and make such conveyance and assurance as the law requireth to vest
the inheritance of the premisses in the purchaser T. Leane and his heirs.
Wherefore the Petitioners, etc. And the said Petitioners for the reasons
abovesaid did humbly pray the said attorney might be admitted, and that
the said guardian might be admitted by this Court, for the ends and purposes above mentioned.

Whereupon this Court having duly weigh'd and considered the allegations
and reasons in the said Petition sett forth, as alsoe the legality of the said
letters of attorney and the prayer of the Petitioner Samuel Tuckey that the
said Joseph Blissett might bee admitted his speciall guardian for the ends
above mention'd did allow and approve of the same, and doe hereby allow
and approve the said Joseph Blissett to be true and lawfull attorney of the
said Hanna Tuckey.... And it appearing to this Court that by agreement
since the said fire between the said Joseph Blissett (for and in behalf of the
Petitioners) and the said Thomas Leane ... and the said Joseph Blissett and
Thomas Leane own'd the said agreement and consented that the same be
decreed by this Court, wherefore this Court pronounced, etc....

Mr Savage v. Mrs Dorothy Weale[1]
Whereas by virtue of an Act of Parliament entituled an Act for the Rebuilding the Town of Warwick, and for determining differences, etc., the Commissioners or Judges therein nominated and appointed, or any 5 or more of
them are by authority of the same constituted a Court of Record ... the
said Commissioners are empowered to regulate and alter inconvenient and
irregular foundations as by them shall bee thought most usefull and convenient for the said houses and buildings to bee new erected and least in-
jurious to the streets or lanes. And whereas the said Court having view'd
the south west corner of the High Street near the High Cross, beeing the
toft or burnt ground of John[2] Savage of Tachbrooke Episcopi, gentleman,
doe thinke fitt and adjudge necessary that 14 foot in length and 3 foot and 9
inches in depth containing in measure 54 foot bee taken from the burnt
ground of the said Mr John[2] Savage, where on at and before the said fire
stood the messuage then or late in the tenure and occupation of John Bradshaw, apothecary, for and toward the enlargement of the said High Street;
and that 4 foot and $\frac{1}{2}$ in length and 12 foot deep bee taken from the ground
of Mrs Dorothy Weale next adjoyning on the west side to the ground
abovesaid of the said Mr Savage, the same to bee laid and added as an
equivalent to the ground of the said Mr Savage in lieu and recompence of
his ground abovesaid soe taken away to enlarge the said High Street. And it

[1] A copy of this decree is with the deeds of the property (CR 1908/175/3) and is dated 12 October
1696; in it Mr Savage's first name was left blank and later filled in 'William'.
[2] An error for 'William'. The toft was conveyed by Robert Boyce of Wellesbourne Mountford to William Savage the younger of Bishops Tachbrooke on 9 Nov. 1694 (CR 1908/175/1).

appearing to this Court, that by agreement had and made between the said
Mr Savage and Mrs Weale, the said Mrs Weale in consideracion of 4 feet and
9 inches in length and thirty four feet deep containing in the whole 157 taken
by the said Commissioners or Judges from the ground of Mr Cooke next
adjoyning to her ground on the west side thereof, and laid to the ground of
the said Mrs Weale as an equivalent for her ground taken away and laid to
that of Mr Savage (for which 157 foot of the said Mr Cooke soe taken away
hee the said Mr Cooke hath had a full recompense and satisfaction made him
by this Court) shee the said Mrs Weale for herself, her heirs and assigns hath
acknowledg'd her self fully contented and satisfied and hath owned the said
agreement, and consented that shee and her heirs for ever bee barr'd of all
estate, right, title, interest and demand whatsoever to and in the four foot and
a half in length and 12 foot deep of the ground of her the said Mrs Dorothy
Weale, and laid to the ground of the said Mr John[1] Savage, with the appurtenances, by Decree of this [Court]. Wherefore the Court decreed the same
accordingly.... And this Court doth further Order and Decree that the said
14 foot of ground in length, and 3 foot and 9 inches in depth, beeing the
proper ground and inheritance of the said Mr John[1] Savage, before the taking
away the same and laying it to the High Street, as abovesaid, for the enlargement of the same, shall ever hereafter remain to, and be actually vested in the
person and persons who are or shall bee owners of the soil and ground of the
common streets and highways within the said Borough....

Decree for Thomas Maunder[?]

Thomas Maunder v. Elizabeth Green, Richard Green and Samuel Green.[2]
Whereas the said etc. hath exhibited etc. that hee the said petitioner beeing
possess'd, at the yearly rent of etc. by virtue of a lease bearing date the
[   ][3] wherein at the time of the said fire were [   ][3] years to come
and unexpired, and that during the time of his beeing possess'd thereof had
laid out considerable summs in repairs and additional building thereunto.
That the said messuage was totally burnt down etc. and that the said
Elizabeth Green etc. are unwilling to rebuild etc. or discharge the petitioner of the growing rents since the said fire. Wherefore the Petitioner etc.
Whereupon summons were granted etc. and the said Richard Green etc.
appear'd in Court and upon reading etc. and hearing what could be
alledged on all sides it appeared to this Court that by agreement etc. hee
the said petitioner was to pay etc. and the said Richard Green etc. own'd
the said agreement. Wherefore the Court pronounced etc. And it appearing to this Court that a rent is issuing etc. Therefore for a final etc. This

[1] See p. 387 n. 2.
[2] Endorsed 'Chinn's Decree for Green's Ground'.
[3] Blank not filled in.

Court doth Order and Decree the inheritance etc. saving to the Lord of the Mannor fealty etc.

And forasmuch as 2 whole years are pass'd and expired since the said fire, and the said messuage soe burnt down is not rebuilt, in default whereof, this Court is empowred by the said Act by their Order and Decree to dispose of and assign all the estate and interest of the said owners of the said houses soe to be rebuilt, and of the ground and soyle thereof and of all yards, backsides, gardens, orchards and other appurtenances thereto belonging to such person or persons who will give security to rebuild the same within such time as the Court shall direct and appoint, and to award what money or other satisfaction the person who undertakes to be the rebuilder, shall give the proprietor making default as aforesaid. Now this Court doth award the said summ of [   ][1] to the said S. Green etc. as a valuable consideration and in full recompense and satisfaction of the premisses soe purchased. . . .

Decree for George Chinn

Warr' Burr'. At the Court of Record held before the Commissioners or Judges appointed by an Act of Parliament for the Rebuilding of the Town of Warwick, etc., the 27th day of [   ].[1]

Whereas Richard Crane, citizen and upholster of London, John Bunter of the Borough of Warwick aforesaid, innholder, and Sarah Bunter of the said Borough, widow, were before the late fire which happen'd within the said Borough on Wednesday the 5th day of September in the year of our Lord 1694, seized of a certaine messuage or tenement scituate and being on the north side of a certaine street there call'd the High Street or High Pavement commonly call'd and known by the name of the Bear Inn with barns stables and other buildings to the said inn belonging, and whereas the said messuage or tenement and all buildings thereto belonging (except one barn adjoyning to a certaine lane or place there call'd the Cow Lane) were totally burnt downe by the said fire, and it appeareing to this Court that the said Richard Crane, John Bunter and Sarah Bunter or any of them did not within the two years limitted by the Act of Parliament aforesaid for Rebuilding the said Towne beginn to build on the burnt ground whereon before the said fire the said messuage or tenement and buildings stood, or lay the foundacions thereof in order to rebuild the same, And it farther appeareing to this Court that the said Richard Crane, John Bunter and Sarah Bunter have by their indenture of feoffment under their hands and seales bearing date the 25th day of this instant September for the consideracion of the summ of threescore and eighteen pounds of good and

[1] Blank not filled in.

lawfull money of England to them paid and in the said indenture acknowledged to be by them received, given, granted, bargain'd, sold, enfeoff'd and
confirm'd unto the said George Chinn all that the said toft, peice or parcell
of burnt ground whereon before the said late fire the said messuage or
tenement and buildings call'd the Bear Inn stood, scituate, lying and being
on the north side of the Highstreet or High Pavement adjoyning to the
house and ground now in the possession of Samuell Acock, painter, on the
east side thereof and on the west side thereof to a new erected messuage or
tenement lately built by John Pinley, mason, on the burnt ground call'd the
Dolphin ground, and alsoe all that barn standing on the said ground and
which did belong to the said Bear Inn, haveing the street or lane call'd the
Cow Lane on the north side thereof and alsoe the house of office standing
on the said Bear ground, together with all commons, easements, proffitts,
commodities, emoluments, hereditaments and appurtenances to the said
burnt ground belonging. . . . And it alsoe appeareing to this Court that the
said George Chinn hath erected and built on the said burnt ground two
messuages or tenements, Therefore for a finall determinacion . . . this Court
. . . doth Order and Decree to the said George Chinn . . . the inheritance of
all and singular the aforesaid toft . . . and also all those two messuages or
tenements on the said burnt ground lately rebuilt by the said George
Chinn. . . .

Decree for William Colemore, Esq.

Warr' Burg'.[1] At the Court of Record held before the Commissioners or
Judges appointed by an Act of Parliament for the Rebuilding the Town of
Warwick and for determineing differences touching houses burnt and
demolished by reason of the late dreadfull fire there, att the Mayors Parlour
on Munday the [   ][2] day of [   ][2] *anno Domini* 1696.
William Reeves Peticion.
Whereas the said William Reeves hath exhibited his Peticion into this
Court thereby setting forth in effect that he the said Peticioner before and
att the late fire which happened within this Borough on Wednesday the
fifth day of September *anno Domini* 1694 was seized of an estate of inheritance of and in two certaine cottages[3] and [a] barn with the orchards and
gardens thereunto belonging or always reputed and taken so to be, that the
said cottage[s] and barn were wholly consumed by the said fire and that he
the Peticioner was not or is able to rebuild the same, and that by reason of
the limitacions contained and expressed in one pair of indentures beareing
date the first day of May in the fifteenth year of the reigne of the late King

---

[1] There are two drafts of this decree, one of which incorporates changes made in the other.
[2] Blank not filled in.
[3] Altered in the earlier draft from 'a certaine cottage'.

Charles the second [1663] under which he holds his title to the said cottage[s] and enjoyed [them] till the same were burnt downe by the late fire, he cannot alien transfer and convey the said toft whereon the said cottages stood as abovesaid and other the premisses with th'appurtenances to some person or persons who is or are capable to rebuild the same according to the Act for Rebuilding Houses destroyed by the said fire, unless therein aided by the Decree of this Court, and farthermore that he the Peticioner not haveing laid the foundacions of the said cottage[s] and premisses within the space of two years next ensueing the said fire, in default thereof the disposall of the said toft or burnt ground is fall'n to the Commissioners or Judges appointed by the said Act, wherefore he pray'd the aid of this Court and that the inheritance of the said toft and other the premisses might be conveyed to William Colemore Esq. pursuant to the powers and authorityes given by the said Act, and according to a contract and agreement between them made whereby for the consideracion of the summ of eight pounds of lawfull money of England to the said Peticioner by the said William Colemore paid or secured to be paid the inheritance of the said toft and other the premises were to be vested and settled in the said William Colemore and his heirs and that summons might be granted to warn the said William Colemore to appear in this Court ... whereupon summons were granted ... and alsoe it appeareing that the said William Reeve had a tytle to the premisses, but that the same was an estate taile and the remainders could not be barr'd without the aid of this Court ... wherefore this Court pronounced the same Decreed accordingly. . . .

Decree for Samuel Roberts *alias* Burford, brickmaker

Att the Court of Record held, etc.

Whereas Samuell Roberts *alias* Burford of the parish of St Mary in the Borough aforesaid, brickmaker, did on the 26th day of Aprill in the year of our Lord 1697 exhibit his peticion[1] into this Court of Judicature thereby setting forth in effect that he the said Samuell Roberts *alias* Burford had then lately agreed with John Sale of Moorton Morrell in the County of Warwick, yeoman, to purchase of him the said John Sale for the consideracion of the summ of thirty seven pounds, all that toft, peice or parcell of burnt ground lying and being att the corner of a certaine street in the said Borough called the Horse Cheeping and adjoyning to a lane called the Pibble Lane on which before the late fire which happened within the said Borough stood a messuage or tenement then in the possession of Henry Butler, carpenter, and Sarah Atkins, widow. That the said John Sale being the owner and proprietor of the said toft or burnt ground whereon the said

---

[1] See p. 295.

messuage before the said late fire stood, had not laid the foundacions of the said burnt ground within two whole years after the said fire in order to rebuild the same, by reason whereof the said Peticioner did conceive that the said John Sale could not make a good and sufficient tytle in law of the said ground to him and his heirs without the aid of this Court, wherefore the Peticioner humbly pray'd that the inheritance of the said ground whereon the said messuage and buildings stood, with all commons to the same belonging and all and singular the premisses with th'appurtenances and every part thereof might for the aforesaid summ of £37 be decreed to him and his heirs for ever pursuant to the agreement between him the said John Sale and the Peticioner thereof had and made, and alsoe pray'd that summons might be granted to warn the said John Sale to appear in this Court that the said agreement might be confirmed, whereupon summons were granted.... Wherefore this Court pronounced the same Decreed accordingly. And it further appeareing to this Court that the said Samuell Roberts *alias* Burford hath since the said agreement made, erected and built one messuage or tenement and other outhouses and buildings on the ground herein before mencioned and expressed. Therefore for a finall determinacion ... This Court ... doth Order and Decree for the consideracion aforesaid to the said Samuell Roberts *alias* Burford the inheritance of all and singular the aforesaid toft, piece or parcell of burnt ground whereon before the said fire the said messuage or tenement and buildings stood, and alsoe all that new messuage or tenement, outhouses and other buildings on the said burnt ground herein before mencioned to be erected and rebuilt by the said Samuell Roberts *alias* Burford scituate lying and being in a certaine street leading to the Pillory[1] and adjoyning to the ground of John Burton, innkeeper on the north side thereof, and the new house built by and in the possession of John Foster, fruiterer, on the south side thereof, together with all easments, commons, proffitss, comodities. . . .

Decree for George Chinn, carpenter

Whereas[2] William Tarver of the Borough aforesaid, gent., hath exhibited his Peticion into this Court of Judicature thereby setting forth in effect that he the said William Tarver was before the late fire seized of all those two messuage[s] or tenements, buildings, gardens and backsides thereunto belonging before the late fire in possession of one [   ][3] Drake[?],[4] tayler, and of one Edward Owen scituate lying and being on the west side of the Swan Lane in the said Borough adjoyning on the north side thereof to the

---

[1] The street leading to the Pillory was a new street; this is probably the reason for the change in description of the property.

[2] This draft decree is written on the back of an unused printed warrant to the Land Tax assessors dated 9 Feb. 1696[/7].

[3] Blank not filled in.   [4] Reading doubtful.

garden wall belonging to the Red Lyon Inn then in possession of Thomas Roberts, inkeeper, and on the south side thereof to the back buildings belonging to the said William Tarver then in possession of George Tongue, bookseller. That the said two messuages were formerly and untill the late fire part of and belonging to the inn called the Bell Inn. That all and every of the said buildings were totally burnt down by the said fire. That the said Peticioner, being the owner and proprietor of the ground whereon the said buildings before the said fire stood, had agreed to sell unto George Chinn of the Borough aforesaid, carpenter, for the consideracion of the summ of £23 12s. all that one part, peice or parcell of the ground aforesaid adjoyning on the north side thereof to the said garden wall containeing in breadth in the front from the said wall 30 feet and in breadth in the back part thereof 24 feet, and in length 122 feet and a half, be the same more or less, adjoyning on the back part thereof to the ground call'd the Bare ground. That the Peticioner haveing not laid or caused to be laid the foundacions of the said ground within the time limitted by the Act of Parliament for laying the same in order to rebuild the same, but that 2 whole years were lapsed since the said fire and the said ground not built upon by reason whereof he conceiveth that he cannot of himself make any good assurance or title of the premisses to the said George Chinn but that the said ground soe unbuilt upon is fal'n to the Commissioners or Judges appointed by the said Act to dispose of the same. Wherefore the peticioner humbly pray'd the aid of this Court, and that the inheritance of the said ground . . . might . . . be Decreed to the said George Chinn and his heirs pursuant to the said agreement, together with all commons now belonging to the said ground or which have been heretofore used and enjoyed with the same or any part thereof, and alsoe pray'd that summons might be granted to warn the said George Chinn . . . and the said George Chinn appeared in Court. . . . It appeareing to this Court that . . . the said ground and premisses with appurtenances were to be assured and confirmed unto the said George Chinn[1] and his heirs by the Decree of this Court freed and discharged of and from all . . . incumbrances whatsoever saveing and excepted out of the premisses to William Bolton Esq. Lord of the Mannor of Warwick his heirs and assigns the yearly rent of summ of three half pence, wherefore this Court pronounced the same Decreed accordingly. . . . And this Court doth Order and Decree that the said George Chinn shall and will erect and build or cause to be erected and built upon the aforesaid peice or parcell of ground one other good and substantiall messuage or tenement and shall in all things finish the same according to the rules and direccions of the aforesaid Act of Parliament and orders of this Court touching building. . . .

---

[1] 'Tayler' interlineated above 'Chinn' not struck out, and so in two other places in this document.

Decree for Thomas Masters, carpenter

Dorothy Hopkins, widow, James Neale and Mary his wife and John Sumner and Rebekah his wife, peticioners; Thomas Masters, defendant.[1]

Whereas the said Dorothy Hopkins of Charlecoate in the County of Warwick, widow, James Neale of the Burr' of Warwick, shoomaker, and Mary his wife, and John Sumner of Charlecoate aforesaid, yeoman, and Mary[2] his wife, have exhibited their Peticion[3] into this Court, thereby setting forth in effect that she the said Dorothy Hopkins was before the late fire seized of a certaine messuage or tenement scituate on the south side of the Highstreet called and known by the name of the White Lyon Inn then in possession of George Watts adjoyning on the east side thereof to the house belonging to the Corporacion then in possession of Thomas Gibbs, and on the west side thereof to a messuage or tenement then in possession of Thomas Dixon, for the term of her naturall life, the remainder to the right heirs of Mary Neale wife of the said James Neale and Rebekah wife of the said John Sumner, daughters of the said Dorothy Hopkins by John Walford her first husband, that the said messuage was totally burnt down by the said fire, that neither of the Peticioners were able to rebuild the said messuage, and that two whole years were passed since the said fire and the foundacions thereof not yet laid in order to rebuild the same, in default whereof the disposall of the said toft or burnt ground whereon the said messuage stood is fal'n to the Commissioners or Judges appointed by the said Act. Therefore the Peticioners humbly pray'd the Ayd of this Court, and that the said toft might be equally divided into 2 parts, and that the inheritance of one moiety or half part thereof, that is to say all that moiety or one half part of the said ground next adjoyning to the house and ground of Thomas Dixon, blacksmith, and one half of all commons and common of pasture to the said White Lyon Inn belonging, and alsoe one half of all bricks and stones and other materialls lying upon the said ground might be conveyed to Thomas Masters of the Borough aforesaid, carpenter, pursuant to the powers and authorityes given by the said Act and according to a contract and agreement between them made, whereby for the consideracion of the summ of thirty pounds of lawfull money of England to the said James Neale and Mary his wife by the said Thomas Masters in hand paid. . . . Wherefore this Court pronounced the same Decreed accordingly. . . . And this Court doth Order and Decree that the said Thomas Masters shall and will erect and build . . . upon the said moiety or half part of the said ground one good and substantiall messuage or tenement according to the rules and direccions of the aforesaid

---

[1] Endorsed: 'Decree of part of the White Lyon ground to Thomas Masters, August 30th 1697'. This draft decree is written on the back of an unused printed warrant to the Land Tax assessors, dated 9 Feb. 1696[/7]. Another draft decree to Thomas Masters in similar terms, but reciting his own petition (see p. 303) is endorsed 'A Copy of Decree not made use on August the 30th 1697'.

[2] An error for 'Rebecca'.   [3] See p. 312.

Act of Parliament and orders of this Court touching building and shall in all things finish the same on this side and before the [ ]¹ day of [ ]¹ next ensueing the date hereof. And lastly this Court do Order and Decree . . . the inheritance of the said ground . . . to the said Thomas Masters freed from all . . . incumbrances saveing to the said Lord of the Mannor of Warwick . . . fealty, suit of Court and the yearly rent of 2¼d. being one moiety of the rent payable. . . .

Decree for William Colmore, Esq.

Mr Colmores Decree
Whereas the said William Colmore hath exhibited his Petition, etc., that the said Petitioner at and before the late fire was seis'd of a barn and coach house with ground lying to it containing in the whole 152 [foot] in length and twenty foot in bredth, scituate lying and being within the Borough of Warwick under the wall of a certain house call'd the Deanry on the east side of the said house extending it self from the Colledg gate to a certain barn call'd Brooks his Barn on the north side thereof and near the Butts call'd St Maries Butts, that the said barn or coach house of the Petitioner was damnified and defaced² by the late fire, that William Bolton, Esq., Lord of the Mannor of Warwick claimes the said toft and other the premisses containing as abovesaid 152 feet in length and 20 in bredth to be copyhold for term of years and held of the said Lord of the Mannor by copy of court roll. That the Petitioner is well assur'd that the premises were long since enfranchis'd and pray'd that the said William Bolton might be warn'd to appear in this Court, to answer the same, and also pray'd the aid of this Court to hear and determine the differences and demands aforesaid, or which might or should hereafter arise touching the estate or right in and to the premises, and that the inheritance of the said toft containing 152 feet in length and 20 in breadth might be convey'd to the Petitioner. Whereupon summons, etc.

It appearing to this Court, that the said toft and other premisses were formerly holden by copy of court roll but that the same was long since enfranchis'd. . . . And it farther appearing to this Court that by agreement had and made by and between the Petitioner and the said William Bolton, hee the Petitioner paying the yearly rent of 12d. per annum to the said William Bolton, was to have the inheritance of the said 152 feet of ground in length and 20 in breadth, and more over 50 superficial feet of wast ground adjoyning on the [ ]¹ side thereof to the said toft, and the said Petitioner and the said William Bolton own'd the said agreement and consented that the same be decreed by this Court, wherefore this Court decreed, etc. . . .

¹ Blanks not filled in. .
² 'damnified and defaced' interlineated above 'burnt down' struck out.

Decree for Edward Clopton of Bridgetown, Esq.

Whereas[1] the said Edward Clopton of Bridge Town in the parish of Old Stratford in the County of Warwick, Esq., hath exhibited his Peticion into this Court of Judicature thereby setting forth in effect that he the said Edward Clopton was before the late fire seized in right of his wife Martha Clopton, daughter and heir of William Comb, Esq., and Ann Mary his wife, both deceased, to the use of him the said Edward Clopton and his said wife Martha and the heirs of the said Martha of and in one messuage or tenement, garden, orchard, stables, barns and backsides with the appurtenances thereto belonging scituate lying and being on the north side of the High-street in the said Borough called and known by the name of the Dolphin Inn and before the said fire in possession of one William Bryan *alias* Stephens. That the said messuage or tenement and buildings thereunto belonging were totally burnt down by the said fire; that he the said Edward Clopton was willing to rebuild the same provided he might have the Decree of this Court to settle the ground whereon the said messuage or tenement and buildings thereunto belonging stood to him, his heirs and assignes for ever, for which purpose hee the Peticioner humbly prayed the summons of this Court to summon the said Martha Clopton his wife to appear in this Court to the end the severall and respective interests of the said Peticioner and Martha his wife might bee valued and settled by this Court, to the satisfaction of both parties. That 2 whole years were lapsed since the said fire and the foundacions thereof not yet laid in order to rebuild the same, in default whereof hee the peticioner conceived the disposall of the burnt ground whereon before the said fire the said messuage or tenement and building stood is fal'n to the Commissioners or Judges appointed by the said Act. Therefore the Peticioner humbly pray'd, in case hee and the said Martha could not agree on the value of their respective interests, that a jury might be impanelled to view and sett a value and price upon the said ground, and that this Court would award and decree what summ he the said peticioner should pay as a valuable consideracion for the said premises to the person or persons interested therein soe as he might have the same decreed to him and his heirs for ever. Whereupon the said Martha was summon'd to appear in this Court, but shee the said Martha making default, a jury was summon'd and sworn accordingly, and upon view and examinacion thereof had and made the said jurors by their verdict did find the said ground to containe 7020 feet and did award the summ of £36 to be a valuable consideration and resonable satisfaccion for the same. And it appearing to the said jury that the said Edward Clopton and Martha his wife were the owners of the said ground before, at and since the said fire

---

[1] This draft decree is written on the back of an unused printed warrant to the Land Tax assessors dated 9 Feb. 1696.

till in default of rebuilding the same fell to the disposal of the said Commissioners by vertue of the said Act, and that the said Edward Clopton was willing to purchase his said wife's interest in the premises and to rebuild the same, in consideracion of which and of his the said Petitioners interest therein the said jurors did assess the sum of nine pounds as a full recompense and satisfaction to the said Martha.... Whereupon the Petitioner humbly pray'd that, he paying into Court the said summ of nine pounds to bee disposed of as shee the said Martha or her assigns shall direct,[1] the said ground and premises ... might be Decreed to him and his heirs for ever by Decree of this Court. Wherefore this Court pronounced the same Decreed accordingly.... And this Court doth farther Order and Decree that the said Edward Clopton shall and will erect and build ... upon the said burnt ground one good and substantiall messuage or tenement according to the rules and direccions of the aforesaid Act of Parliament and orders of this Court touching building, and shall in all things finish the same on this side and before the first day of November which shall be in the year of our Lord one thousand six hundred ninety and nine. [Saving to William Bolton, Esq., Lord of the Manor of Warwick, the yearly rent of 8d. at Michaelmas]....

Decree for Thomas Mayo of Rugby

Whereas[2] Thomas Mayo of Rugby hath exhibited his Peticion[3] into this Court of Judicature ... upon reading of which recited Peticion and due enquiry and examinacion thereof by this Court had and made touching and concerning the premisses, and upon reading the said recited indenture in the said Petition sett forth, it appeared to this Court that the said Edward Mayo being seized of an estate of inheritance of and in all the said 2 messuages or tenements and premises above mencioned did make the above recited demise of the same to the said William Lingham for the consideracion in the above said indenture mencioned and expressed, and that the said William Lingham did, for the consideracion of the summ of £20 to him in hand paid by the said Thomas Mayo the Peticioner by an indorsement on the back side of the said indenture, grant assign and sett over to the said Thomas Mayo ... all and singular the messuages or tenements and premises in the same indenture mencioned and expressed.... It alsoe appeared to this Court that the ground whereon before [the said fire] the said two messuages or tenements [stood] ... is the ground now lying and being in a certaine street or place called the Joyce Pool adjoyning on the

---

[1] 'into Court ... direct' interlineated over 'his said wife Martha' and 'the assigns of his said wife Martha' both struck out. A note in the lower margin reads '(*Quaere* to whom to be paid: wife the same person)'.

[2] This draft decree is written on the backs of three printed sheets, each containing eight receipt forms, to be cut up and used by the sub-collectors of the Land Tax.

[3] See p. 297.

east side to the house now in possession of [   ],[1] on the west side to
the new house built by Edward Aston containeing in the front to the said
street [   ][1] feet and in length to the utmost extent of the ground backward [   ][1] feet be the same more or less, and that the same is yett unbuilt
and the foundacions thereof not yett laid. Therefore for a finall determinacion of all differences . . . this Court doth Order and Decree the inheritance
of all and singular the premisses to the said Thomas Mayo and his heirs
freed acquitted and absolutely discharged of and from all payments,
claimes, tytles, dowers and demands of any person or persons whatsoever
. . . and this Court doth farther Order and Decree that the said Thomas
Mayo . . . shall and will with all convenient speed erect and build . . . upon
the ground whereon before the late fire the said 2 messuages stood, one
other good and substantiall messuage or tenement according to the rules of
the Act abovesaid and orders of this Court touching building, and shall in
all things finish the same on this side and before [   ]. . . .[1]

Decree for Samuel Roberts *alias* Burford, brickmaker

Warr' Burg'. At the Court of Record held, etc.
Whereas John Ashwin of Bretfordton in the County of Worcester, yeoman,
being seized of a certaine toft, peice or parcell of burnt ground lying and
being in a certaine street with in the Borough of Warwick aforesaid call'd
the Sheep Street on which before and att the time of the late fire . . . stood a
certaine messuage or tenement then in the possession of [   ],[1] did on
the 25th day of October in the year 1697 exhibit his peticion into this Court
of Judicature thereby setting forth that he the said John Ashwin had sold
unto Samuell Roberts *alias* Burford of the said Borough, brickmaker, for
the consideracion of the summ of thirty pounds the inheritance of all that
the aforesaid toft, peice or parcell of burnt ground and alsoe all the charity
monies that should be given for or towards the encouragement of rebuilding the same. That he the said Peticioner haveing not then laid the foundacions of the said ground within the 2 years limitted by the aforesaid Act in
order to rebuild the same, conceived that he could not of himself make a
good and sufficient tytle in law of the premisses unto the said Samuell
Roberts *alias* Burford without the aid of this Court, he the Peticioner therefore humbly pray'd that the said toft or burnt ground aforesaid might be
decreed unto the said Samuell Roberts *alias* Burford and to his heirs for
ever by the Decree of this Court, and also pray'd that the said Samuell
Roberts *alias* Burford might be warn'd to appear in this Court to confirm
the said agreement. Whereupon summons were issued accordingly and the
said John Ashwin and the said Samuell Roberts *alias* Burford appeared in

---

[1] Blanks not filled in.

Court. . . . Wherefore this Court pronounced the same decreed accordingly . . . [and] this Court . . . doth Order and Decree . . . the inheritance of all and singular the aforesaid toft, peice or parcell of burnt ground scituate lying and being in the Sheep Street aforesaid adjoyning on the north side thereof to a new house lately built by John Pritchett, and on the south side thereof to a house now in the possession of [ ]¹ Rawbone call'd or known by the name of the Black Boy. . . . And this Court doth further Order and Decree that the said Samuell Roberts *alias* Burford . . . shall and will erect and build or cause to be erected and built upon the said ground one other good and substantiall messuage or tenement according to the rules of the abovesaid Act and orders of this Court touching building, and shall in all things finish the same on this side and before the first day of [ ]. . . .¹

Decree for John Williams, carpenter

A Coppy² of the Decree from the Corporacion to John Williams, January the 16th 1698/9

Warr' Burg'. At the Court of Record held before the Commicioners or Judges appointed by an Act of Parliament for the Rebuilding of the Town of Warwick . . . at the Mayors Parlour on Munday the sixteenth day of January anno Domini 1698/9.
The Mayor, Aldermen and Burgesses of the Borough of Warwick to John Williams of the Borough of Warwick, carpenter.

Whereas the Mayor, Aldermen and Burgesses of the Borough of Warwick have exhibited his Peticion into this Court of Judicature thereby setting forth in effect that they the said Peticioners were before and att the time of the late fire seized of a certaine messuage or tenement scituate on the south side of the Highstreet in the said Borough then in possession of Thomas Gibbs, shooemaker, adjoyning on the east side to the house of Isaac Tomkis, gent., and on the west side to a certaine inn commonly called and known by the name of the White Lyon Inn then in possession of George Watts, that the said messuage or tenement and buildings thereunto belonging were totally burnt down by the said fire, that the peticioners being the owners and proprietors of the burnt ground whereon before the said fire the messuage or tenement and buildings stood, had agreed to sell unto John Williams of the Borough aforesaid, carpenter, for the consideracion of the summ of twenty five pounds of lawfull money of England, all that toft, peice or parcell of burnt ground whereon before the said fire the said messuage and buildings stood with the garden and backsides thereunto belonging, that two whole years were passed since the said fire and

---

¹ Blanks not filled in.
² This is not a draft but a copy of the completed decree, including the signatures.

the foundacions of the said ground not then laid in order to rebuild the same within the time limited by the said Act for laying the same, by reason whereof they conceive that they cannot of themselves make any good assurance or tytle of the premisses to the said John Williams, but that the said ground soe unbuilt upon is faln to the Commicioners or Judges appointed by the said Act to dispose of the same, wherefore the Peticioners humbly pray'd the aid of this Court and that the inheritance of the said ground whereon the said messuage and buildings stood with all commons to the same belonging and all and singular the premisses with th'appurtenances and every part thereof might for the consideracion aforesaid be decreed to the said John Williams and his heirs pursuant to the said agreement, and alsoe pray'd that summons might be granted to warn the said John Williams to appear in Court that the said agreement might be confirmed, whereupon summons were granted and issued accordingly and the said John Williams appeared in Court ... wherefore this Court pronounced the same decreed accordingly, and it farther appeareing to this Court that the said John Williams hath lately erected and built one messuage or tenement and other outhouses and buildings on the ground hereinbefore mencioned and expressed ... this Court ... doth Order and Decree for the consideracion above mencioned the inheritance of all and singular the aforesaid premisses with th'appurtenances to the said John Williams and his heirs ... freed and discharged of and from all and all manner of incumbrances whatsoever.... In witness whereof the Commicioners or Judges appointed by the Act aforesaid have hereunto sett their hands the day and year above named. Sign'd

Ri. Lane, Mayor	H. Puckering	Wm. Colmore
Tho: Newsham	Wm. Peyto	Tho: Peers
		Wm. Bolton

Decree for John Burton

Decree for John Burton:
Whereas John Burton, etc., setting forth in effect, that hee the Petitioner at and before the late fire was tenant in possession of a certain messuage scituate, etc., of which said messuage one Thomas Lane of —— was seiz'd of an estate in fee taile, that the said Thomas Lane at and after the time of the said fire beeing a souldier in the English Army in Flanders, and hee the Petitioner having intermarried with A one of the sisters of the said Thomas Lane, did adventure at his own costs and charges to erect a messuage on the ground, being of small value,[1] whereon before the said fire the above mentioned messuage stood; that the said Thomas Lane before his going

---

[1] 'being of small value' interlineated over a caret.

beyond the seas made his last will and testament wherein hee appointed and made —— Eborall, son of William Eborall, who had married one other of his the testator's sisters, executor, and after his return from beyond the seas, which was in the year 1697, by agreement under hand and seale made, between him the said Thomas Lane and the Peticioner it was agreed that the Commissioners appointed by the Act of Parliament for rebuilding the Town of Warwick should take cognizance of the matters in controversie between them touching the said burnt ground and the new messuage on part thereof erected by the Petitioner and should if they thought fitt by vertue of the powers and authorities given them by the said Act, decree the inheritance of the said burnt ground to the said John Burton, with a provisoe nevertheless that the said John Burton his heirs or assigns, should within one month next after such decree, pay or cause to be paid to the said Thomas Lane his executors, administrators or assigns the summ of £40 and all such charitie moneys as hee the said John Burton had already received on account of the loss of the said messuage soe burnt, with the benefitt of all charitie money which should hereafter accrue and arise on account of the loss of the said house by being burnt, the Petitioner therefore humbly pray'd the said agreement might be confirmed by the Decree of this Court, and the inheritance of the burnt ground and building thereon erected bee vested in the Petitioner.

Upon hearing which petition read and hearing what could be alleaged on all sides, and perusing and being fully satisfied of the reality of the said agreement produced in Court, and that the same was legally executed by the within mentioned parties and that the said Thomas Lane was the owner and proprietor of the said burnt ground, and that the said John Burton had at his own proper costs and charges erected thereon a new messuage, and that since the said agreement executed as abovesaid, the said Thomas Lane is dead; and the said John Burton and the said William Eboral father of —— Eborall executor of the will abovemention'd own'd the said agreement and consented that the said agreement should be confirm'd and ratified by the Decree of this Court, and it farther appearing to this Court that the reversion of the premises was in one —— of London, spinster, and that there are sevrall debts contracted by the said John Burton for worke and materials in building the said new erected messuage and otherwise yet unpaid, Therefore for a final determination of all differences ... this Court ... doth Order and Decree the inheritance, for the above mentioned consideracion of £40 and refunding or repaying all such charitie monies as hee hath hitherto received by order of the Trustees ... on account of the loss sustain'd by the said Thomas Lane in the said messuage, outhouses, etc., being burnt in the said late fire and all such monies as shall hereafter arise and be ordered by the said Trustees upon any dividend to bee made amongst the said sufferers, on account of the said messuage, etc., soe burnt down, and paying to Samuell Jemmat, clerke, Vicar of St Nicholas, Warwick, the summ of —— beeing monies lent by him the said Samuell Jemmat to the said John Burton to supply his necessities, and likewise discharging all such debts contracted for worke and materialls in and about building the said new erected messuage as shall appear to this Court to bee just and true debts, . . . of the said new erected messuage and burnt ground . . . to the said John Burton and his heirs.

And this Court doth further order and decree that the said John Burton shall have all the charitie monies that have arisen or shall arise and bee ordered on account of the loss sustain'd in the loss of the goods of the said John Burton then tenant in possession of the said messuage burnt in the said late fire, and that it shall and may be lawfull to and for him the said John Burton to deduct and retain in his hands out of the above mention'd £40, the sum of £4 10s. by him paid to the said —— reversioner for her interest in the premises. And this Court doth further order and decree, that the summ of £20[1] shall bee paid by the executor William Eborall to William Challoner, attorney at law, for his bill of charges in a suit of law about the title of the said messuage, and allsoe the summ of 10s. for which the said John Burton became and stands bound with —— the father of the said Thomas Lane to Mrs Dowley, now Fisher, in a bond of £20 beeing the proper debt of the father of the said Thomas Lane, which said severall summs this Court doth order and decree to be paid out of the said £40, and such monies as have or shall become due to the said executor, out of the above mentioned charitie monies. . . .

Q. whether any rent to Lord of Mannor.

Decree for John Pritchett

Warr' Borough. At the Court of Record held, etc., the [   ][2] day of [   ][2] 1699.

Whereas the Mayor, Aldermen and Burgesses of the Borough of Warwick in the County of Warwick did by indenture beareing date the 20th day of January in the year of our Lord 1681[/2] for the consideracions of the rents, covenants, provisoes and agreements therein mencioned, did demise, grant, sett and to farm lett unto John Pritchett of the said Borough, gent., all that one little house or tenement conteineing one bay of building or thereabouts with the backside thereunto belonging conteineing in breadth fronting the street twenty foot and in breadth backwards two and twenty foot and in length threescore and sixteen foot of ground scituate and being in the parish of St Mary in the Borough of Warwick aforesaid in a certaine

---

[1] 'summ of £20' struck out and 'said John Burton' interlineated, but this alteration was not followed through, and the sense requires its reinstatement.
[2] Blanks not filled in.

street there called the Sheepstreet and adjoyning unto the Shire Hall there, to have and to hold the same unto the said John Pritchett his executors, administrators and assignes from the feast of St Michael the Archangel then last past for and dureing the full end and term of one and fifty years from thence next ensuing. And whereas the said little house or tenement and buildings thereunto belonging were totally burnt down in and by the late dreadfull fire . . . , and whereas it appeareing to this Court the foundacions of the toft or peice of burnt ground whereon before the late fire the said little house and buildings stood were not laid within the space of two year after the said fire being the time limitted by the said Act of Parliament for laying the same in order to rebuild on the said ground but doth remaine still unlaid, by reason whereof the said ground soe unbuilt upon is faln to the Commissioners or Judges appointed by the said Act to dispose of the same, and whereas the Mayor, Aldermen and Burgesses of the said Borough have agreed with the said John Pritchett that he paying the summ of twenty pounds shall and may have the inheritance of all and singular the said toft and premisses decreed to him and his heirs by the decree of this Court. Now therefore for a finall determinacion of all differences . . . This Court . . . doth Order and Decree for the consideracions above mencion'd the inheritance of all and singular the aforesaid toft whereon before the said fire the said little house or tenement stood . . . unto the said John Pritchett and his heirs, and this Court doth farther Order and Decree that the said John Pritchett his heirs and assigns or some or one of them shall and will erect and build . . . upon the said toft one other good and substantiall messuage or tenement according to the rules of the Act abovesaid and orders of this Court touching building and shall in all things finish the same on this side and before the [   ]¹ day of [   ]¹ next ensueing. . . .

Decree for Richard King

Warr' Burr'. Att the Court of Record held etc.
Whereas Ann Lucas late of the Borough aforesaid widow, lately deceased, was before and att the late dreadfull fire seized for the term of her naturall life of a certaine messuage or tenement then in the possession of Richard Sharpe, collermaker, scituate, lying and being on the south side of the Highstreet or Pavement between a messuage or tenement on the west side thereof in the possession of George Harris, flaxdresser, and a messuage or tenement on the east side thereof in the possession of Richard Bromley, shooemaker, which said messuage or tenement was totally burnt down in and by the said late dreadfull fire which happen'd within the said Borough on Wednesday the 5th day of September in the year of our Lord 1694, and

¹ Blanks not filled in.

THE GREAT FIRE OF WARWICK

whereas by the death of the said Ann Lucas the estate, right, tytle and interest of the toft whereon before the said late fire the said messuage stood is come to Charles Lucas of the parish of St James in the County of Middlesex, gent., son of the said Ann Lucas, deceased, whereby the said Charles Lucas being after his said mother's death seized of an absolute and indefeasible estate of fee simple in the said toft, peice or parcell of burnt ground on which before the late fire the said messuage stood, did by articles of agreement beareing date the 9th day of September 1700 made between him the said Charles Lucas of the one part and Richard King of the etc. of the other part, sell the said ground unto the said Richard King for the consideracion of the summ of six pounds of lawfull money of England . . . and alsoe did consent and agree to and with the said Richard King, that the said articles of agreement between them soe had and made should be ratified and confirmed by the Decree of this Court, and it appeareing to this Court that the owners and proprietors aforesaid had not begunn to build on the aforesaid burnt ground within the space of two years limitted by the said Act and that the foundacions thereof att the time of makeing the said agreement were not laid in order to build on the same and that the said ground is yett still unbuilt upon, Therefore for a finall determinacion of all differences . . . this Court . . . doth Order and Decree to the said Richard King, for the consideracion of the aforesaid summ of six pounds in hand by him already paid to the said [Charles] Lucas, the inheritance of all and singular the aforesaid toft, peice or parcell of burnt ground together with all profitts, commons, advantages and appurtenances whatsoever to the said burnt ground or any part thereof belonging . . . and this Court doth further Order and Decree that the said Richard King his heirs and assigns or some of them shall and will erect and build or cause to be erected and built upon the burnt ground aforesaid one other good and substantiall messuage or tenement according to the rules of the Act abovesaid and orders of this Court touching building, and shall in all things finish the same on this side and before the [   ]¹ day of [   ]¹ next ensuing the date hereof. . . .

Decree for Thomas Masters

Warr' Borough.² At the Court of Record held, etc.
Whereas William Tarver of the Borough of Warwick aforesaid, gent., was before and att the time of the late fire which happen'd within the said Borough on Wednesday the 5th day of September in the year of our Lord 1694 seized of a certaine messuage or tenement scituate and being on the

---

¹ Blanks not filled in.
² A fair copy of this decree, found in a Warwick solicitor's collection (CR 1618/WA12/40) is dated 21 August 1701 and includes copies of the signatures of John Clopton, Geo. Lucy, Wm. Palmer, Tho. Peers, Tho. Newsham and Thos Young, Mayor, at the foot.

north side of a certaine street there call'd the High Street or High Pavement commonly call'd and known by the name of the Swann Inn with
barns, stables and other buildings to the said Inn belonging, and whereas
the said messuage or tenement and all buildings thereto belonging were
totally burnt by the said fire, and it appeareing to this Court that the said
William Tarver did not within the two years limitted by the Act of Parliament for rebuilding the said Town begin to build on the burnt ground
whereon before the said fire the said messuage or tenement and buildings
stood nor hath yett laid the foundacions of the said ground or any part
thereof in order to rebuild the same, and it farther appearing unto this
Court that the said William Tarver hath by indenture under his hand and
seale beareing date the 10th day of September 1700 for the consideracion
of the summ of £60 of lawfull money of England to the said William Tarver
paid and thereby acknowledged to be by him received, granted enfeoffed
and confirmed unto the said Thomas Masters all that the aforesaid toft,
peice or parcell of burnt ground whereon before the said late fire the aforesaid messuage or tenement and buildings call'd the Swan Inn stood containeing 69 feet in front or thereabouts, seventy three foot in breadth
backward next the Swan Garden or thereabouts, and 215 foot in length or
thereabouts, together with all commons, wayes and passages to the same
belonging or in any wise appertaineing and the revercion and revercions,
remainder and remainders thereof. . . . Therefore for a finall determinacion
of all differences . . . this Court . . . doth Order and Decree to the said
Thomas Masters for the consideracion of the aforesaid summ of sixty
pounds in hand by him already paid to the said William Tarver as aforesaid,
the inheritance of all and singular the aforesaid toft, peice or parcell of
burnt ground call'd the Swan Ground haveing the new house and garden
belonging to and now in the possession of Joseph Blissett, gent., on the east
side thereof, the High Street or High Pavement on the south side thereof,
the lane call'd the Swan Lane on the west side thereof and the new house
built by one John Avern and the garden call'd the Swan Garden on the
north side thereof, together with all commons, wayes and passages to the
same belonging . . . and this Court doth further Order and Decree that the
said Thomas Masters, his heirs and assigns or some of them shall and will
erect and build or cause to be erected and built upon the burnt ground
aforesaid one or more messuage or tenements[1] according to the rules of the
Act abovesaid and orders of this Court touching building,[2] and shall in all
things finish the same on this side and before the 1st day of November
which shall be in the year of our Lord 1702. . . .[3]

---

[1] CR 1618/WA12/40 has 'two or more messuages or tenements'.
[2] Inserted in the margin 'q: whether one or two—and time for building'.
[3] CR 1618/WA12/40 omits this clause and date.

Decree for John Mitchener

Att the Court of Record held before the Commissioners or Judges appointed by an Act of Parliament for the Rebuilding the Town of Warwick, etc., at the Mayor's Parlour the 8th day of November 1704.

Whereas Fulk Weale of this Borough the reputed owner or proprietor of a certaine toft of peice of burnt ground now unbuilt upon on the south side of the Highstreet, William Jeacocks and Mary his wife the reputed owners and proprietors of a certaine toft or peice of burnt ground now unbuilt upon on the north side of the said Highstreet, and Francis Smith[1] the reputed owner and proprietor of a certaine toft or peice of burnt ground att the upper end of the Sheepstreet, have neglected to rebuild the said tofts notwithstanding severall orders have been made by this Court for the rebuilding the same, and in and by one order of Court of the 21st day of September last past, it was agreed and resolved that if the said proprietors did not effectually proceed to rebuild their said severall parcells of ground before the 21st day of October next following according to the said Act and orders of this Court touching building, that then this Court would immediately after the said day proceed to sell the said ground to any such person as would bid the summ of five shillings or more for each parcell of the said ground, and that such person or persons who shall become purchaser or purchasers thereof should for their further encouragement be allowed the 1st. 6d. in the pound according to the losses sustained in the houses burnt downe by the said fire towards rebuilding the same, and whereas notwithstanding the said last recited order the said Fulk Weale, William Jeacocks and Mary his wife, and the said Francis Smith have not either of them begun to build on their respective parcells of ground aforesaid or taken any effectuall care in order to rebuild the same pursuant to the said order. And whereas[2] John M. of this Borough, gent., hath in Court offered and tendered the summ of 15s. for the said 3 tofts or parcells of burnt ground unbuilt (i.e.) 5s. for the toft of the said Fulke Weale, 5s. for the toft of William Jeacocks and Mary his wife, and 5s. for the toft of [   ][3] Cawthorn or Francis Smith, and alsoe offered to this Court T.N.[4] of this Borough for his security that hee will rebuild or cause to be rebuilt the said 3 tofts within the space of 4 years

Now this Court by vertue of the powers and authoritie, given by the said Act, to dispose of and assign all the estate and interest of the said owners and proprietors of the said houses soe to be rebuilt and of the ground and soile thereof and of all yards, backsides, gardens, orchards and other appur-

---

[1] 'Cawthorn' interlineated above 'Smith'.
[2] From this point this draft decree is continued in another hand, with many alterations and abbreviations.
[3] Blank not filled in.
[4] Thomas Newsham.

tenances thereto belonging to such person or persons who will undertake
to rebuild the same within such time as the said Court shall direct and
appoint, doth award the summ of 5s. to the said Fulke Weale for his said
toft of ground, the summ of 5s. to the said William Jeacocks and Mary his
wife for his and her toft of ground, and 5s. to Richard Cawthorn or Francis
Smith for his or their toft of ground, and for a final determinacion of all differences which shall or may hereafter happen to arise between the said
John Mitchener and the said Fulke Weale, Wm. Jeacocks and Mary his wife,
or the said Richard Cawthorn or Francis Smith, this Court doth order and
decree, for the consideracions above mentioned, the inheritance of all and
singular the aforesaid toft, piece or parcell of burnt ground of the said Fulke
Weale, together with all commons, proffits, commodities and appurtenances to the said toft or parcell of burnt ground belonging to the said John
Mitchener and his heirs freed, acquitted and absolutely discharged of and
from all payments, claimes, titles, dowers, charges, incumbrances and demands whatsoever . . . [followed by similar clauses relating to the other two
tofts, excepting only a chief rent of 2s. yearly charged on the toft of Wm.
and Mary Jeacocks]. . . .

And lastly this Court having accepted and taken the security of the said
Th. N. for the rebuilding the said tofts, doth order and decree that the said
J.M. his heirs and assigns shall and may for the consideracions above mentioned peaceably and quietly have, hold and enjoy the said 3 tofts and all
and singular the premises hereby decreed. . . .

COLLECTION ON THE BRIEF IN COTHERIDGE, WORCS.

Collected upon the Brief for Warwick in the Parish of Cotheridge[1] in the County and Diocese of Worcester, March the 25, 26, anno 1695 as followeth

	£	s.	d.		£	s.	d.
Sir Rowland Berkeley	10	0	0	Alice Palmer	0	0	6
Sir Thomas Street	5	0	0	Anne Palmer	0	0	6
The Lady Street	2	0	0	Robert Brandfield	0	2	6
Mrs Dorothy Berkeley	0	10	0	Thomas Best	0	0	4
Mrs Penelope Greene	0	5	0	John Spicer	0	1	0
Mrs Rebecca Greene	0	2	6	Richard Long	0	1	0
Mrs Cicely Perin	1	0	0	Mary Gunter	0	0	6
Charles Davies	0	2	0	Anne Leister	0	0	6
Mary Burton	0	0	6	Widow Cooke	0	0	6
Mary Noxon	0	0	6	Anne Cooke	0	1	0
Symons Hawkins	0	2	6	Martha Higgs	0	1	0
Dorothy Turner, widow	0	1	0	James Heming	0	0	6
John Clifton	0	0	6	Thomas Edwards	0	0	6
William Dyer	0	0	2	James Lander	0	0	6
John Munn	0	0	2	John Lander	0	0	6
William Batchelour	0	0	6	Elizabeth Griffiths	0	1	0
Widow Woormington	0	0	6	Frances Lyes	0	0	6
William Woormington	0	1	6	Widowe Hundley	0	0	6
Margeret Turner	0	0	6	William Hundley	0	1	0
Mary Downes	0	0	6	Thomas Watkins	0	2	0
Miles Tayler	0	0	6	Henry Edwards	0	1	6
William Withey senior	0	1	0	Francis Yarnway	0	1	0
Joseph Evans	0	1	0	Edward Cooke	0	0	6
Daniel Clifton	0	0	6	William Wythye junior	0	2	6
Edward Evans	0	0	8	Robert Johnson	0	2	0
Richard Clifton	0	0	3	John Gardiner	0	0	6
James Awkett	0	0	6	Thomas Cooke	0	0	6
Anne Awkett	0	0	6	Thomas Clewer	0	0	6
Thomas Need senior	0	0	3	Joseph Noxon	0	0	6
Thomas Need junior	0	0	3	Phillip Thomas	0	0	6
John Berwick	0	0	3				

[1] A village 3¾ miles west of Worcester, with 228 inhabitants in 1841. Sir Rowland Berkeley founded an apprenticing charity there in 1694.

£   s.   d.

	£	s.	d.
Henry Brandfield	0	2	0
Robert Jones	0	10	0

In all   21 12   7

Subscribed this collection in the Parish Church of Cotheridge March the 31st 1695, by us

Robert Jones, Curat.   John Walker, Thomas Day, Church-Wardens

Received of the minister and church wardens of Cotheridg in the County and Archdeaconry of Worcester twenty one pounds twelve shillings and seaven pence being collected for the relief of the poor sufferers by fire in Warwick; 20 Apr: 1695, by mee Hen. Hodges, Reg.

AN ACCOUNT FOR LETTERS PATENT AND THE ACT

An Account[1] of the Moneys disbursed (by Order) by Mr Newsham for the obtaining their Majesties Letters Patents for the late fire in Warwick, and discharging the fees, due in House of Lords and Commons, for the Act of Parliament for the same Town.

		£	s.	d.
[1694/5]				
Imprimis paid Lord Keepers secretary, fees for warrant for briefe		33	2	6
Jan. 7th	—Paid Mr Fall, Clerke of the Briefs, his bill[2]	46	0	0
	Paid Lord Keepers secretaries clerke for the warrant	0	10	0
	Paid the first advertisement put in the Gazett	0	10	0
	Paid writeing 54 letters to all Archdeacons of England	0	9	0
Feb. 26th	—Paid the stacioners bill for paper, packthread, etc.	0	7	0
	Paid[3] for parchment for Address	0	1	0
	Paid engrossing it	0	2	6
	Paid for the 2nd advertisement put in the Gazett	0	10	0
	Paid carriage of the draught of Town and Church to Sir Chris: Wren and Dr Barebone	0	1	0
	Paid the fees of the Warwick Bill passing H. of Lords	36	10	0
	Paid per hands of Mr Colemore H. of Common fees	18	10	0
	Paid more fees to the House of Commons	9	6	8
	Paid for a coppy of the Bill	0	13	0
March 6th	—Paid for printing 250 Acts of Parliament for Warwick	5	0	0
May 2nd	—Paid Mr Fall, engrossing duplicate of brief, stamping, being £2	3	0	0

[1] The title was first written 'Moneys laid out (by Order) for the Town of Warwick', then extended by another hand.
[2] See below, p. 411.
[3] This item and the next are struck out, but not the sums of money.

Paid Mr Middletons bill, sending out briefs, etc.	1	4	6
Paid stamp for Mr Ayres agreement	0	0	7
Paid printing 1000 Warwick briefs	2	0	0
Paid printing 12600 bishops letters	9	0	0
Paid printing 12000 acquittances	2	10	0
Paid box bringing down Acts of Parliament, Patent, etc.	0	2	6
Paid more sending briefs per carrier, paper, etc.	0	14	6
Paid Mr Goodwyne printing 1000 bishops letters more by Mr Colemors directions	1	4	0
Paid given Sir Christopher Wren's gentleman by Lord Brooks order	3	15	0
	175	3	9
Paid[1] for a vellum book, to record the Decrees of the Court in	1	8	0
	176	11	9
Taken out as struck through as above		3	6
	176	8	3

[Mr Fall's Bill]

Warwick Breife, Dec. 1694

	£	s.	d.
For the peticion and drawing the breife	1	5	0
For a vellum skin and silke string	0	7	6
For stamping the patent	2	0	0
For preparing the patent for the Great Seale with Hanaper and Docquet fees and the Clerke of the Breifs fees for 52 Countyes	19	6	8
For 27 reame of paper and printing 12000 coppies on a large broad side	24	0	0
	46	19	2

For my paines in severall attendances about the draught, etc.

7th January 1694
Received then of William Collmar Esq. the summe of forty six
pounds in full of this bill   £46
                                                    Wm. Fall.

---

[1] This item and the next are added in the same hand as the alterations to the title.

WILLIAM TARVER'S OCCASIONAL PAYMENTS

Mr Tarver's Bill of Disbursments [1694-5]

Moneys paid on Several Occasions

	£	s.	d.
To William Cole, John Mills, Richard Toms and Henry Toms 12d. apeece for watching	0	4	0
To yong Mr Challoner for drawing the Sessians Certificate	0	5	0
Paid for horse to Worcester and Lichfeild and messengers expence	0	16	0
To 4 master carpenters and 4 master masons being abroad 5 days to give an estimate of the building, in which time they expended 40s., and 6s. 8d. each is in all	4	13	4
To Sam Dunckly to pay 30 men as put out the fire at Hall[1] and theire expence, all	2	6	0
To Mr Robinson to Cambridge, etc.	1	10	0
To Richard Harris for goeing to Sir Richard Nudigate's for his hand to Sessians Certificate	0	4	0
To William White for goeing to Lord Northampton	0	8	0
To Matthew Perry, John Gibbs, Mrs Atkins and Sam Aing for present releife after the fire 10s. each by Mr Blissett, mayor	2	0	0
To severall person for watching after the fire	0	11	6
To James Fish for 4 men that put the fire out at Chappell[2]	0	4	0
Paid a messenger from Coventry to Darby with letters	0	6	0
Paid for post letters from severall places and money expended on persons as brought in money	0	9	6
To Richard Wigh for diner, beare and horse meate for Darby men	0	8	0
To Moses Robinson for goeing to Parshaw, horse hire and expense	0	8	0
To Mr Savage for expence at Tanton	0	16	8
To Mr Lane his charges in Barlishway Hundred and Kington	1	13	7
Mr Hands and Mr Roberts in Hemlingford Hundred	5	9	0
Henry Harper in Knightlow Hundred	1	6	11
Mr Nicholes in Kingdon Hundred	1	2	6
	25	12	0

[1] Presumably the Shire Hall.   [2] Presumably the Beauchamp Chapel in St Mary's Church.

To Mr Bray for takeing downe the steeple and in part for removeing the rubidge   23 10 0

To John Burton per order Comitioners, as money given to take downe part of his house haveing incroached into the streete[1]   5 0 0

More paid for letters and expended on persons as brought in money   0 6 0

    28 16 0

other side   25 12 0

    54 8 0

May 7th '95. To the Towne Clerk of Northampton   3 15 0

To Mr Webb for 5 guineyes he paid in London, to Mr Midleton for manageing the breife[2]   7 0 0

To Mr George Tongue for a booke   0 5 6

A note of charges, letters and messengers, etc.   0 7 0

To Mr Eedes for a booke   0 6 0

To him for pipes to the parlor   0 4 0

To Mr Webb for paper   0 4 7

    66 4 1

To John Smith Esq.[3] for his paines in drawing the Act of Parliament for Building the Towne of Warwick   5 guineys   7 10 0

To Thomas Newsham Esq. for his paines and charges in attending in London in passing the Act and the breifes and many other attendances in the business of Warwick   30 0 0

To John Mitchell[4] clearke to Mr Newsham for his great paines in writeing letters and other service doon in the business of Warwick, etc.   5 0 0

    108 14 1

Received the abovesaid £30 for the use of my master Thomas Newsham Esq., and £5 for my selfe in all I say received   £35
per me John Mitchener

---

[1] 'as money ... streete' added later in a space.

[2] 'to ... breife' added later in a space.

[3] Altered from 'Mr John Smith'. A reference in 1711 to this payment names the recipient 'Baron Smith', the barrister John Smith who became a baron of the Exchequer in 1702, sat once as a fire commissioner at Warwick on 21 Sept. 1704, and founded a Warwick apprenticing charity by a deed dated 1 Nov. 1704. He became chief baron of the Exchequer in 1708.

[4] An error for 'Mitchener'.

July the 8th 1695
This bill amounting to one hundred and eight pounds four-
teene shillings and one penny being examined by us doe
allow and approve the same   £108 14   1

Brooke   Geo. Lucy   Wm. Bolton
H. Puckering   Andr. Archer   Tho. Fetherston
Tho. Wagstaffe   Wm. Colmore

DISTRIBUTIONS TO SUFFERERS

Distributions[1] 1, 2, 3, 4, 5, 6, 7.

Sept. 10 [1694]	£	s.	d.		£	s.	d.
Thomas Watts	10	—	—	John Cole	3	—	—
George Tayler	8	—	—	Benjamin Bower	4	—	—
Charles Harrison	5	—	—	Josiah Drake	3	—	—
George Watts	5	—	—	Woodhams	1	10	—
Thomas Marriot	5	—	—	Richard Hadley	3	—	—
Thomas Dixon	5	—	—	Frances Power	5	—	—
George Barton	10	—	—	Richard Harris	3	—	—
Henry Rogers	2	10	—	Ann Harris	3	—	—
William Eborall	10	—	—				
Thomas Tipping	5	—	—		227	10	—
Richard Hand	10	—	—	George Flower	3	—	—
William Allen	1	—	—	Richard Good	5	—	—
Humphry Carter	5	—	—	William Perks	5	—	—
Richard Bromley	2	10	—	William Mathews	4	—	—
Samuel Ainge	5	—	—	Job Rhodes	4	—	—
John Jarvis sen.	3	—	—	Robert Harris	1	—	—
Thomas Wall	5	—	—	John Evitts	—	10	—
Joseph Ainge	6	—	—	Sarah Mayo	2	—	—
Thomas Mander	10	—	—	Charles Emes	5	—	—
Nicholas Paris	10	—	—	John Watts	5	—	—
Thomas West	10	—	—	Robert Coles	5	—	—
Elizabeth Askell	2	10	—	Robert Watts	5	—	—
Thomas Stratford	10	—	—	Thomas Rush	2	—	—
John Stoakes	10	—	—	John Forrester	1	—	—
John Bunter	10	—	—	Robert Tailer	4	—	—
John Hands	5	—	—	John Hicks	6	—	—
Thomas Glendall	2	—	—	Thomas Claridge jun.	5	—	—
Sarah Hicks	10	—	—	John Atterbury	5	—	—
Henry Smyth	3	—	—	Elizabeth Whinnick	3	—	—
Ann Bolton	2	—	—	Edward Angrave	5	—	—
Richard Sharp	7	10	—	John Burnill	2	—	—
John Langton	5	—	—	Thomas Clemens	5	—	—
Samuel Brierly	2	—	—	Ann Matthews	1	—	—

[1] Also entitled on the dorse 'Distribucions as per Booke'.

	£	s.	d.
Joan¹ Hurst	1	—	—
Richard Kerby	5	—	—
Stephen Bradley	1	—	—
Timothy Simkins	3	—	—
William Wilson, Martin Taylor²	5	—	—
John Burton	5	—	—
John Sherley	3	—	—
Thomas Bartholomew	1	—	—
Thomas Bartholomew jun.	1	—	—
Matthew Busbey	5	—	—
William Francis	1	—	—
Richard Hadley	1	10	—
William Nuberry	1	10	—
Thomas Smyth	3	—	—
George Francis	1	—	—
Henry Butler	4	—	—
Nicholas Styles	1	10	—
Nurse Glendall	—	10	—
Mary Woodcock	1	—	—
	356	—	—
To Sarah Mayo, widow	4	—	—
To Thomas Gibbs		7	10
To John Butler	4	—	—
To John Averne	1	—	—
To Joseph Averne	3	—	—
To Edward Deacon	1	—	—
To John Miles	2	—	—
To William Williams	1	—	—
To John Cakebread	3	—	—
To Sarah Atkins	4	—	—
To Matthew Perry	3	—	—
To Edward Green	1	—	—
To John Tatnall	1	—	—
To Henry Styles	1	—	—
To Hanna Williams	1	10	—
To Thomas Leeke	1	—	—
To Mary Dikens	—	10	—

	£	s.	d.
To John Leeke	1	—	—
To Martha Keen	1	—	—
To John Hancock	1	—	—
To Jacob Dunkley	1	—	—
To William Muntford	1	—	—
To George Manning	1	—	—
To William Heygood	1	—	—
To Joan Winn	—	10	—
To Alice Hyate	1	—	—
To Sarah Ryder³	—	10	—
To William Hadley	1	10	—
To Nathan Gilstrop	1	—	—
To Judith Kington	2	—	—
To John Gibbs	10	—	—
To Mary Wills	7	—	—
To Abigale Rogers	1	10	—
To Abigale Woodward	2	—	—
To Widow Edwards	2	—	—
To Zachariah Sharp	4	—	—
To Katherine Bird	1	10	—
To George Harris	4	—	—
To Abraham Ducommun	5	—	—
To William Cornhill	2	—	—
To Mary Taft	2	—	—
	450	00	00
Ann Newton	1	—	—
Alixander Nicholls	5	—	—
Richard Hadley, Pritchett⁴	4	—	—
Mr Welton	3	—	—
Richard Rawbone	3	—	—
Thomas Lynes	2	—	—
Thomas Shatswell	1	—	—
William Savage	2	10	—
7 Alms women	3	10	—
Thomas Wise	7	—	—
Thomas Moore	10	—	—
Joseph Hemmings	3	—	—

¹ 'Richard' written above.   ² 'Martin Taylor' added in another hand.
³ This name is doubtful.   ⁴ 'Pritchett' added in another hand.

	£	s.	d.		£	s.	d.
John Banbury	6	—	—	Elizabeth Murcott	2	—	—
George Tong	10	—	—	John Falkner	2	10	—
Sarah[1] Parsons	5	—	—	Ann Archer	—	10	—
Edward Aston	1	10	—	Widdow Sanford[3]	1	10	—
Widow Trulove	1	—	—	Sarah Harris[3]	—	10	—
Mrs Edes, widdow	4	—	—				
John Burton	0[2]	—	—		56	10	—
Mrs Cauthern	1	—	—		2		
	523	10	—		54	10	—

The 2nd Distribucion made the 17th September 1694				**The 3rd Distribucion ordered the 15th of October 1694**			
Elizabeth Martin	2	—	—	Mary Martin	2	—	—
John Pike	1	—	—	John Pike	1	10	—
Mary Yardley	—	10	—	Elisabeth Pywell	1	10	—
Edward Cheseley	2	—	—	Richard Bromley	2	—	—
Thomas Arps	2	—	—	Elizabeth Sandford	8	—	—
Bridget King	1	—	—	Abraham Simmonds	1	10	—
Edward Cornwell	—	10	—	Henry Rogers	4	10	—
John Hancox jun.	—	10	—	Thomas Tippin	2	10	—
Ann Ainge, widow	2	—	—	Samuel Ainge	5	—	—
Sarah Blith	1	—	—	Joseph Ainge	4	—	—
Thomas Lane	1	10	—	John Jarvis jun.	7	—	—
Lettice Francis, widow	—	10	—	Alexander Nicholls	5	—	—
John Williams	5	—	—	William Perks	5	—	—
Sarah Rider	3	—	—	John Cakebread	2	—	—
Elizabeth Askell	2	10	—	Edward Cheseley	6	—	—
Judith Farr	2	—	—	Thomas Arps	6	—	—
Henry Wilson	1	—	—	Ann Eades, widow	1	—	—
John Jarvis, jun.	3	—	—	John Atterbury	4	—	—
Mr Simmonds	1	10	—	John Pritchet	6	—	—
Richard Eborall	1	—	—	Elizabeth Cauthorne	4	—	—
James Fish	3	—	—	Richard Hadley	7	—	—
Mr Eades	10	—	—	Henry Butler	4	—	—
Samuell Drake	1	—	—	Mary Clemens	4	—	—
Judith Dunn	1	—	—	Judith Farr	2	—	—
Sarah Asplin	1	—	—	Widdow Mayo	5	—	—

[1] 'Samuel' written above.
[2] Altered from '5'. This name is marked with a cross.
[3] These names are marked with a cross.

	£	s.	d.		£	s.	d.
Abigall Rogers	1	10	—	George Chesley	1	10	—
Matthew Perry	1	10	—	Edward Chesley	2	—	—
Thomas Edwards jun.	1	10	—	Hannah Williams	—	10	—
Timothy Simpkins	2	—	—	William Smyth	1	—	—
John King	1	—	—	John Bambry	2	—	—
Thomas Lines	1	—	—	Thomas Dadley	10	—	—
John Welton	3	—	—	Robert Watts	5	—	—
Margarett Clemens	1	—	—	John Watts	5	—	—
Robert Watts	5	—	—	Joane Cumberlidge	2	—	—
John Watts	5	—	—	Ann Mathews	1	—	—
George Watts	5	—	—	Thomas Griffin	1	—	—
Sarah Rider	1	—	—	Mr Brooks	3	—	—
Thomas Satchell	1	—	—	John Jarvis jun.	5	—	—
Mr Eades	5	—	—				
	135	—	—	The Summ of 4th Order	69	—	—
Mrs Askell	5	—	—				
Mr Bradshaw	2	10	—				
Thomas Gibbs	2	10	—	**The 5th Distribucion ordered**			
John Burmill	1	—	—	**the 19th of November 1694**			
William Francis	—	10	—	George Watts	5	—	—
				Elizabeth Lea	1	—	—
				John Tatnall	1	—	—
The 3rd Distribution is	146	10	—	Elizabeth Glendall	—	10	—
				Mary Yardley	1	—	—
				Sarah Edwards	1	—	—
The 4th Distribucion made				Katherine Bird	—	10	—
the 5th of November 1694				Thomas Wise	8	—	—
Widdow Ainge	2	—	—	James Fish	7	—	—
Thomas Dixon	3	—	—	Thomas Arps	6	—	—
John Burton	3	—	—	Edward Chesley	5	—	—
Richard Hurst	1	—	—	Elizabeth Farr	1	—	—
Edward Wall	1	—	—	George Flower	2	—	—
William Jackson	—	10	—	Robert Ashby	1	—	—
Francis Woodham	1	—	—	Samuel Ainge	1	—	—
Thomas Wall	4	—	—	Joseph Ainge	2	—	—
Joseph Hemmings	1	—	—	Mrs Cauthorne	5	—	—
Francis Power	4	—	—	Sarah Bucknell	—	10	—
John Averne	2	—	—	John Feild	1	—	—
Thomas Watts	5	—	—	Job Rodes	2	—	—
Charles Watts	1	—	—	William Perks	5	—	—
Sarah Hill	1	—	—	Mrs Askell	4	—	—

	£	s.	d.		£	s.	d.
John Hancox, sen.	1	—	—	Sarah Rider	2	—	—
John Atterberry	1	—	—	Nicholas Styles	—	10	—
John Averne	2	—	—	Thomas Bartholomew	1	—	—
Mr Bromidge	13	—	—	Mary Woodcock,			
Widdow Clemens and				widdow	—	10	—
son	3	—	—	Edward Aston	1	—	—
Thomas Gibbs jun.	2	—	—	Mrs Lucas	1	—	—
Richard Gibbard	10	—	—	Thomas Rush	1	—	—
Widdow Hicks	2	—	—	John Hancox, sen.	—	10	—
Richard Kerby	4	—	—	Sarah Glendall	1	—	—
Sarah Mayo	3	—	—	John Foster	1	—	—
Mary Overton	8	—	—	William Cornwell	—	10	—
Ann Preston	7	—	—	Edward Cornwell	—	10	—
Job Rainsford	5	—	—	John King	2	—	—
Elizabeth Sanford	4	—	—	Thomas Bartlemew,			
Timothy Simpkins	1	—	—	jun.[2]	—	10	—
Hannah Tuckey	4	—	—	Martha Keen	—	10	—
Edward Venor	1	—	—	Sarah Blith	1	—	—
John Welton	9	—	—				
Dorothy Welch	—	10	—		58	10	—
Ann Webb	1	—	—	William Taft	—	10	—
Mrs Wagstaffe	5	—	—	Margaret Clemens	4	—	—
				Richard Bromley	2	10	—
	147	—	—	Thomas Marriott	2	—	—
				John Burton	4	—	—
The 6th Distribucion ordered				Job Rhodes	2	—	—
the 4th Feb. 1694[/5]				Mrs Bird	1	—	—
William Cook	6	—	—	Thomas Lane, barber	1	10	—
Widdow Hopkins	6	—	—	Robert Tayler	2	—	—
Widdow Clemens	4	—	—	William Newberry	2	—	—
George Flower	3	—	—	John Butler	1	—	—
Thomas Claridge	2	—	—	Samuel Parsons	2	—	—
George Watts	5	—	—	John Hicks, smith	3	—	—
John Watts	5	—	—	Thomas Moore	2	—	—
Robert Watts	5	—	—	Henry Butler	2	—	—
Martin Taylor	2	—	—	Widdow Matthews	—	10	—
John Cakebread	3	—	—	Abigall Rider	1	—	—
Sarah Stanleigh	2	—	—	Whinnock, Elizabeth[3]	2	—	—
Sarah Mayo, baker[1]	1	—	—	Shusanna[4] Hancox	—	10	—

[1] 'baker' added in another hand.
[2] 'jun.' added in another hand.
[3] 'Elizabeth' added in another hand.　　　[4] 'Shus.' in MS.

	£	s.	d.
Abraham Cumin	2	—	—
Josiah Drake	1	—	—
Richard Sharp	2	10	—
John Miles	1	10	—
John Tatnald	1	—	—
Thomas Dixson	3	—	—
Matthew Perry	1	10	—
Edward Angrave	2	—	—
Francis Odhams	1	—	—
John Twycross	1	—	—
John Sherley	1	10	—
Ann Eades, widow	1	10	—
Mr Stratford	2	—	—
John Welton	2	—	—
Thomas Gibbs, sen.	5	—	—
Mrs Cautherne, widdow	5	—	—
Mary Martin	1	—	—
Alexander Nicholls	5	—	—
Francis Power	3	—	—
Ann Harris, widow	2	—	—
Mrs Askell	4	—	—
Robert Cole	1	—	—
Benjamin Powers	2	—	—
George Taylor	1	—	—
	143	10	—

The 7th Distribucion [1]

	£	s.	d.
John Foster	2	—	—
Edward Deacon	2	—	—
John Twycross	1	6	—
Alice Dire	—	10	—
Richard Eborall	2	—	—
John Hancox	—	10	—
Ann Dunn	—	10	—
Susanna Maule	1	10	—
Edward Green, sen.	—	12	—
Edward Green, jun.	2	13	—
Martha Keene	—	10	—
Mary Yardley	1	10	—

	£	s.	d.
Judith Dunn	1	6	—
Sarah Blyth	1	—	—
William Taft	—	6	—
Samuell Willis	—	5	—
John Cole	1	—	—
Richard Hadley	2	—	—
Abraham Symons	2	—	—
Thomas Glendall	2	—	—
Richard Harris	1	6	—
Nicholas Stiles	—	5	—
Thomas Leeke	1	—	—
Richard Hands	1	—	—
Mary Busby	—	3	6
Mary Taylor	—	16	—
William Francis	—	10	—
William Kerby	2	13	—
Elizabeth Burt	2	—	—
William Muntford	2	—	—
Charles Watts	3	—	—
Edward Wall	1	—	—
Mary Bolton	2	—	—
Mary Cakebread	—	4	—
Elizabeth Farr	3	6	—
Alice Hyatte	2	15	—
Edward Cornwell	1	—	—
Elizabeth Glendall	2	—	—
Thomas Bartlemew, jun.	1	5	—
Edward Birk[b]eck	4	—	—
Stephen Allen	2	13	—
Katherine Drewry	1	—	—
William Nobury	1	10	—
Job Burt	2	—	—
Richard Berry	—	8	—
	65	2	6
Ann Cattle	—	7	—
Sarah Asplin	3	6	—
Sarah Bucknill	2	6	—
Amphillis Woodward	—	5	—
Elizabeth Lee	3	—	—

[1] A rough draft gives the date 20 May 1695.

	£	s.	d.		£	s.	d.
Thomas Scarlett	—	11	—	William Horn not paid	—	13	—
William Hadley	—	6	—				
Mary Overton	—	13	—		117	8	6
Dorothy Welch	1	10	—	Thomas Shatswell trans-			
Nathaniel Gilstrup	2	10	—	ferr'd	1	6	—
Jonathan Sturt	—	16	—				
John Burnill	1	17	—		118	14	6
Samuell Drake	—	5	—				
Jacob Dunkley	2	—	—	**A Distribucion of 2s. 6 per lib.**[1]			
Shusanna Gibbs	—	8	—	**July the 15th 1695**			
Shusanna Hancox	—	2	—	Mrs Allott per William			
Robert Ashby	4	—	—	Purefef[2]	7	2	6
Shusanna Wright	—	10	—	Widow Ashwin per			
Samuell Cooke	1	—	—	Thomas Perce	7	—	—
Sarah Hill	2	10	—	Mary Nicholls	3	10	—
William Allen	1	—	—	Samuel Parsons	1	17	6
Ann Eades	1	—	—	Thomas Hicks	3	—	—
Hanah Aris	5	—	—	Richard Hurst	3	5	—
Mary Ash	—	5	—	George Flower	6	—	—
Margarett Clemens	2	—	—	Thomas Arps	5	—	—
Thomas Lynes	1	—	—	Mary Stratford	10	17	6
Matthew Drewry	—	4	—	John Banbury	1	—	—
Hannah Eyres	2	2	—	Henry Rogers	9	5	—
Mary Gibbs	—	6	—	George Harris Quaker's			
Elizabeth Paine	—	6	—	house	6	5	—
Elizabeth Rands	—	13	—	Robert Taylor	4	12	6
William Cornwell	2	—	—	Zachiry Sharp	—	7	6
Ann Southam	—	5	—	Henry Wilson	2	2	6
Elizabeth Field	1	—	—	Judith Farr	3	10	—
Ann Newton	2	6	—	Sarah Edwards	—	15	—
William Jackson	—	7	—	John King	—	15	—
Mrs Lucus	1	—	—	Elizabeth Martin	19	5	—
Sarah Stanley	1	10	—	Joshua Perks	5	—	—
Mary Tuttle	—	10	—	John Atterbury	8	12	6
Mary Goodale	—	6	—	Dorothy Hopkins	16	10	—
Mary Carter	—	11	—	William Smith	1	15	—
				Francis Power	10	7	6
	116	15	6	Matthew Busby	6	17	6

[1] i.e. 2s. 6d. in the £1.
[2] Clearly written, presumably a miswriting of 'Purefoy'.

	£	s.	d.		£	s.	d.
Richard Kerby	11	12	6	Sarah Ryder	2	7	6
John Watts	30	5	—	George Chesley	1	15	—
Katherine Bird	—	2	6	John Welton	18	10	—
Mary Smiths	1	17	6	Ann Ainge	1	17	6
Sarah Atkins	1	12	6	John Bradshaw	2	10	—
Rebekah Bromley	—	10	—	Richard Sharp	2	10	—
John Averne	8	2	6	John Williams	23	17	6
Timothy Simpkins	2	12	6	Richard Hands	18	15	0
Mary Overton	31	—	—	Thomas Gibbs sen.	2		
Sarah Mayo	4	—	—	Thomas Gibbs jun.	19	12	6
John Bunter	41	10	—	Thomas Lane	—	2	6
Elizabeth Pyewell	2	2	6	Mary Martin	—	2	6
Thomas Rush	—	17	6	William Roe	1	17	6
Charles Hicks, Mayor	20	5	—	Mariana Duckett	1	—	—
Matthew Perry	—	5	—	Mary Dickins	1	10	—
Mrs Eades[1]	—	5	—	Mrs Tuckey	3	10	—
Mr Eades	13	15	—	Richard Green	21	5	—
Ann Belton	4	15	—	Elizabeth Murcott	2	5	—
For Mr Charnock per				Richard Gibbard	31	5	—
Mr Whadcock	51	—	—	Thomas Arps	15	—	—
				Thomas Norberry	1	7	6
	371	7	6	Alice Baylice and Mary			
Joseph Willis	—	5	—	Sayle	17	10	—
Richard Crane and John				Sarah Low	—	9	6
Bunter	35	—	—	Stephen Nicholls	10	17	6
George Barton	2	—	—	Thomas West	2	10	—
Mrs Palmer per Mr				Thomas Roberts	3	10	—
Challenor	21	5	—	Mr William Fetherston	30	—	—
John Howell	6	5	—	William Parston	7	10	—
John Evitts	1	10	—	George Tongue	2	10	—
George Watts	20	5	—				
William Reeve	4	—	—		774	2	6
Mr Stoaks per John				James Rainbow	3	15	—
Mitchener	10	15	—	Jane Dale	3	10	—
James Yardley	3	10	—	Elizabeth Sandford	13	—	—
Hannah Doolittle	4	7	6	Mrs Bree per Mrs			
Samuell Barber	3	6	—	Sandford	4	7	6
Joseph Heming	6	17	6	To Mr Jematt 11 6			
Mr Jame[s] Prescott	35	—	—	and 7 6	—	19	—
Francis Comander	—	12	—	Abigall Ryder	1	—	—

[1] Added later.

	£	s.	d.
Mr Dolphin	14	—	—
Thomas Mayo	2	5	—
B.[1] Isaac Tomkys	147	2	6
B. Mr Weale	68	15	—
B. John Holyoake	5	—	—
Mr Brooks per ditto	3	5	—
Mr Grimes, Richard	13	15	—
B. Mr Norton, Edward	64	5	—
George Chinn	2	10	—
Richard Good	6	17	6
B. Mr Joseph Blissett	45	—	—
B. Mr Robert Blissett	81	5	—
Mr Rainsford, Job	9	—	—
Henry Butler	1	12	6
B. Mr Heath	142	—	—
B. Mr Whatcoate	12	10	—
B. Mr Tarver, William	145	12	6
Elizabeth Roberts per Mr Whadcock	6	5	—
Thomas Bromwich	15	15	—
Thomas Edwards	1	15	—
Mr Cooke per Mr William Hunt	29	—	—
Richard Harris	1	5	—
Mrs Askell per Mr Heath	12	—	—
Mr Webb, George	22	10	—
Mr Boyce	25	—	—
Elizabeth Carr per Thomas Care and Joseph Hemings	26	5	—
Charles Emes and John Hicks	15	12	6
George Chinn	1	10	—
Mr Hopkins per Mr Jephcott	10	—	—
Mrs Lucas per Mr Tarver	5	—	—

	£	s.	d.
Mr Ayleworth	2	5	—
Thomas Spencer per Thomas Lea	12	—	—
Sarah Mayo	1	—	—
	1749	11	6
	649	8	3
	2398	19	9

An order for the paying for ground in the High Street[2] the 9th September 1695

	£	s.	d.
Thomas Dixon	1	10	9
William Perks	42	6	—
James Fish	2	11	—
John Atterberry	20	—	6
Mr Tarver	2	18	6
Mr Weale	8	2	6
Mr Nicholas Stephen[3]	10	5	6
Richard Good	5	2	9
Mrs Cawthern per Mr Jemmatt	5	17	—
Crabmill house[4] per Mr Tarver	5	18	6
Mr Okens house per ditto	34	2	6
Mr Welton	7	3	9
Mr Tarver for Mrs Lucas house	4	4	—
Corporacion ground in Jury Street	4	14	6
Thomas Wall	4	19	—
Nicholas Paris	7	5	6
Mrs Palmer	13	10	—
Mr Fish	8	—	—
	158	11	3

[1] Presumably for 'Builder'.
[2] Not all these are in the High Street.
[3] Probably Stephen Nicholes.
[4] Perhaps the house of Richard Bromley, *see* p. 155.

	£	s.	d.		£	s.	d.
4s. in the pound to Builders				Thomas Dadley	15	—	—
Mr Fish	21	—	—	Alexander Nicholls	87	—	—
John Tatnall	1	4	—	Thomas Griffin	1	2	—
Edward Aston	—	14	—	Mrs Cawthern per			
Widow Williams	2	4	—	John Davis	47	7	6
William Perks	40	—	—				
John Jarvis	53	12	—		649	8	3
Thomas Wall	15	—	—	Brought over	2398	19	9
John Burton	32	10	—	Thomas Shatswell per			
Thomas Bartlemew	1	14	—	Samuel Dunkley	2	12	—
Samuel Ainge	26	12	—	Thomas Watts	49	16	—
Joseph Ainge	29	16	—	Nicholas Paris	29	12	—
Thomas Dixon	8	8	—	Richard Hadley	96	—	—
John Hicks	11	4	—	John Watts	28	—	—
Mary Man	7	10	—	George Chesley per			
Thomas Clemens	26	—	—	Edward	38	4	—
Edmund Wilson	63	—	—				
					2643	3	9

Receipts

	£	s.	d.
From Gentlemen and Forreigne Towns	2877	16	$1\frac{1}{2}$
Hemlingford Hundred	375	7	4
Barlichway	299	14	2
Kineton	211	7	8
Knightlow Hundred	288	13	0
	4052	18	3

STATEMENT OF THE TREASURER'S ACCOUNTS

The State of the Book of Receipts and Disbursements October the 12th 1695[1]

An Account of what Monies have been received and paid for the use of the Sufferers by the late fire in Warwick; stated the 12th day of October 1695.

Receipts

Hemlingford Hundred	375	7	4
Barlichway Hundred	299	14	2
Kineton Hundred	212	6	2
Knightlow Hundred	288	13	0
From nobility and gentry	2921	0	10
Received per advance of guineas sent up to London	36	7	9
Mony refused by Oxford Register	2	18	0
Money from Mr Tongu, Coventry	7	0	2
Overwerton breif	1	11	8
	4144	19	1

Payments

1st Distribucion	523	0	0
2nd Distribucion	54	10	0
3rd Distribucion	146	10	0
4th Distribucion	69	0	0
5 Distribucion	147	0	0
6th Distribucion	143	10	0
7th Distribucion	117	8	6
9th Distribucion to builders att 4s. per lib.	587	2	0
8 Distribucion att 2s. 6d. per li.	1123	4	6
10th Distribucion	110	9	6
11 Distribucion	47	19	6
12 Distribucion	32	5	9
An order to Mr Tarver	108	14	1
An order to Mr Newsham	176	8	3
An order to Mr Webb	149	5	6
13 A Distribucion	2	18	6

[1] This heading is taken from an endorsement. The book referred to in it is lost.

An order to Mr Gerrard	4	7	6
An order to Mr Mayor	100	0	0
	3643	13	7

The whole charges as received is	4144	19	1
The whole discharge as appears above is	3643	13	7
Then their remains in the hands of the Treasurers	501	5	6

AN ORDER TO MAKE UP PAYMENTS TO
CERTAIN SUFFERERS TO 4s. IN THE £1

An Order made this 16th day of May '98 by the Trustees of the Breif Monies given for the use of the Sufferers by the late fire in Warwick for the payment of 1s. 6d. in the pound to the severall sufferers hereunder named, to make up what they have already received 4s. in the pound according to their severall losses by the said fire.

	£	s.	d.
Mr Tomkys			
That Mr Isaac Tomkys be paid 1s. 6d. in the pound for the loss of his house and goods as reduced to £1177, to make up what he hath already received, by an order dated the 16th day of December 1695, 4s. in the pound	88	5	6
Mr Norton			
That Mr Edward Norton be paid 1s. 6d. in the pound for the loss of his house and goods as reduced to £514 to make up what he hath already received by the aforesaid order 4s. in the pound	38	11	—
Mr Norton			
That he be paid 1s. 6d. in the pound for the loss of Richard Kerbys house in the Highstreet as the same is reduced to £140 he haveing rebuilt the same	10	10	—
Mr Joseph Blissett			
That Mr Joseph Blissett be paid 1s. 6d. in the pound for the loss of his house and goods as reduced to £360 to make up what he hath received by the aforesaid order 4s. in the pound	27	—	—
Mrs Dorothy Weale			
That Mrs Weale be paid 1s. 6d. in the pound for the loss of £550 as the same is reduced to make up what she hath already received by the aforesaid order 4s. in the pound	41	5	—
Mrs Heath			
That Mrs Heath be paid 1s. 6d. in the pound for the loss of the house and goods in the Church Street as reduced to £1136, to make up what hath been already received by the abovesaid order 4s. in the pound	85	4	—
	290	15	6

Mr Blissett
That Mr Joseph Blissett be paid 1s. 6d. in the pound for the
loss of Mr Grimes his house in the Highstreet as the same is
reduced to £110 he haveing rebuilt the same   8   5   —

                                                              _____

                                                              299   —   6

To the Treasurers of the   Brooke[1]   H. Puckering
Monies received for the use of   Wm. Colmore   Richard Grimes, Mayor
the Sufferers by the late fire of Wm. Bolton
Warwick

[1] These names are signatures.

JAMES FISH'S BILL FOR SURVEYING

An Account[1] of what business has been done in surveying at the Commissioners desire by James Fish since the Town Surveyors were sworne is as follows viz.

	£	s.	d.
For projecting and drawing the ground plott of the Church by a large scale for the Surveyors	0	10	0
For measuring, projecting and drawing the ground plott of the square and the houses adjoyning the Swan lane and many other places of the Town and attending the Surveyors many court days	3	0	0
For measuring and casting up the contents in yards of all the wainscott and the square work of all the seats in the church and allso the content in money of what the work came to per yard	1	0	0
For drawing a designe for the top of the tower and writing a petition for the £1000 granted by her sacred Majestie the Queen	0	10	0
The summ is	5	0	0

[1] The whole account is in the distinctive handwriting of James Fish jun.

TREASURER'S ACCOUNT BOOK

A Book of Receipts and Payments for the use of the Trustees of the Brief Moneys collected for the use of the Sufferers by the late Fire in Warwick by Mr Thomas Newsham, one of the Treasurers of the said Brief.

1698	Receipts	£	s.	d.
Dec. 23rd.	Imprimis received of Mr Joseph Blissett being lent him by the Trustees upon bond delivered up to him	100	—	—
[1698/9] Jan. 11.	Received of Mr Whadcock for the use of Trustees being in part of £150 lent to Mr William Tarver and to him	22	—	—
	Received of Mr Edward Norton in part of £100 lent him by the Trustees as per bond	40	—	—
16th.	Received of George Chinn per order of the said Trustees in full monies lent him upon mortgage	40	—	—
Feb. 2nd.	Received of Mr Stephen Nicholls in part of £100 lent him by the Trustees as per bond	50	—	—
24th.	Received of Mr James Fish in part of £50 lent him by the Trustees as per bond	10	—	—
		262	—	—

1698	Payments	£	s.	d.
Dec. 23rd.	Imprimis paid to Mr Joseph Blissett 1s. 6d. in the pound for the loss of his house and goods as reduced to £360 according to an order dated the 16th May 1698	27	—	—
	Paid to Mr Joseph Blissett 1s. 6d. in the pound for the loss of Mr Grimes his house in the High Street as reduced to £110 according to the aforesaid order	8	5	—
	Paid to William Smith and Francis Smith in part for work done att and towards rebuilding the Church of St Maryes	64	15	—

		£	s.	d.

'98/9 Paid to Thomas Masters and John Phillips in
Jan. 12th. part of monies due to them for frameing and
raiseing the timber roof of the Church of St
Maries per an order dated the 11th of Jan.
'98/9 — — — 50 — —

17th. Paid to Sir William Wilson Kt. in part for surveying the building of the Church of St Marye
per an order dated the 16th day of Jan. '98/9,
he haveing before received of Mr Tarver £62 — 20 — —

Feb. 4th. Paid to Mr William Smith and Francis[1] in farther part for work done towards rebuilding the
Church of St Maries — 25 — —

Jan. 28th. Paid to Thomas Masters in farther part for
frameing and raiseing the timber roof of St
Mary — 10 — —

26. Paid to John Prescott for filling up the wayes
and levelling the ground in the Butts — — 12 —

Feb. 17. Paid to Thomas Masters in farther part for
frameing roof and work done in and about the
Church of St Mary — 30 — —

18. Paid to Samuell Dunkley and Francis Smith in
farther part for work done in and rebuilding
the Church of St Maryes — 20 — —

25th. Paid to Samuell Dunkley and Francis Smith in
farther part for work done in and about the
rebuilding the Church of St Maryes — 20 — —

March 1st. Paid to William Marshall and Nicholas Paris to
pay Mr Archer in part for iron used about the
Church — 20 — —

                                        295 12 —

1698/9   Receipts
        Brought over   262 — —
March 10th. Received of Mr Stephen Nicholles a farther
        part of the £100 lent him by the Trustees   20 — —
    25. Received of Mr Brooke Bridges £300 for which
        was sent him 2 orders for £200 each, both

---

[1] 'and Francis' interlineated.

	£	s.	d.

drawn upon Mr Hoar payable to Mr Bridges or
order upon Mr Bridges promise as by his letter
to pay the other £100 within a fortnight | 300 — —

                                              582 — —

1698/9   Payments
        Brought over   295 12 —
March 8th. Paid to John Phillips and Thomas Masters per
        J. Phillips which with £305 received before of
        Mr Tarver and £90 of John Mitchener is in full
        of the bill for timber boards, etc., amounting to
        £296 12s., and of the bill for frameing and lay-
        ing the roof of St Maryes Church amounting to
        £115 2s., both given in to the Commissioners
        at the Court held the 28th Feb. last.   16 14 —
    10. Paid to Thomas Hoggins by the direction of
        Mr Jephcott for his goeing to desire the com-
        pany of severall Commissioners liveing in the
        country att the Court held the 8th inst.   — 5 —
                            more another jorney   — 2 —
    11. Paid to Samuell Dunkley and Francis Smith in
        farther part for work done in and about
        rebuilding the Church of St Maryes   30 — —
        Paid to Thomas Masters his bill for covering
        the walls of St Mary's Church as allow'd by an
        order of Court of the 28th Feb. last   5 10 —
        Paid to Thomas Masters in part for the timber
        for the braggetting[1] of the Church of St Maryes 5 — —
    17. Paid to William Marshall and Nicholas Paris in
        farther part for iron and workmanshipp of the
        same for the Church of St Maryes   10 — —
    18. Paid to Samuel Dunkley and Francis Smith in
        farther part for work done as aforesaid   30 — —
    25. Paid to Samuell Dunkley and Francis Smith in
        farther part for work done as aforesaid   30 — —
        Paid to William Marshall and Nicholas Paris in
        farther part for iron, etc., as aforesaid   5 — —

[1] Bracketing, wooden framework to which plaster was applied.

	£	s.	d.

Paid the 26th December last for horse hyre to
Sir John Clopton's for his hand to an order for
the return of money from London — 1 —

Paid Feb. the 7th a messenger to Mr Palmer to
desire his company att the Court — 1 6

Paid to John Prescott for removeing the rubbish against the church and the church wall in
the Church Street 1 8 —

429 13 6

1699 Receipts

Brought over 582 — —

Aprill 1st. Received of the feoffees of Mr Thomas Oken in
full of monies lent them by the Trustees of the
Brief Monies being the summ of 300 — —

15th. Received of Mr Fish in farther part of the £50
lent him by the Trustees of Brief Monies 6 — —

June 3rd. Received of Mr Brooke Bridges by Mr Stanley
being in full of £400 return'd by him as mencion'd the 25th of March last 100 — —

Received of Mrs Elizabeth Heath sen. and Mrs
Elizabeth jun. in part of £200 lent Mr Edward
Heath by bond 50 — —

1038 — —

1699 Payments

Brought over 429 13 6

March 28. Paid to William Marshall in farther part for
iron and work for the Church of St Mary 1 1 6

30th. Paid to Nicholas Paris in farther part for iron
and work for the Church of St Marys 5 — —

Aprill 1st. Paid to Samuell Dunckley and Francis Smith in
farther part for work done in and about
rebuilding the Church of St Mary in Warwick 50 — —

6th. Paid Thomas Masters in farther part for timber
used about braggetting the Church of St Mary 15 — —

8th. Paid Nicholas Paris in farther part for iron and
work for the Church of St Marys 10 — —

	£	s.	d.
Paid to Samuell Dunckley and Francis Smith in part for work done in and about digging and laying the foundacions of the Church of St Marys	50	—	—
15. Paid to Samuell Dunckley and Francis Smith in farther part for digging and laying the foundacions of St Marys Church	50	—	—
Paid to Mr Phillipps in part for the braggetting work of St Maryes Church, the workmanshipp thereof	10	17	—
22. Paid to Samuell Dunkley and Francis Smith in farther part for digging and laying the foundacions of St Marys Church	50	—	—
Paid to Thomas Dixon being lent him out of the brief monies per order of Mr Colmore and Mr Thomas Newsham as per bond	20	—	—
28. Paid to Samuell Dunkley and Francis Smith in farther part for digging and laying the foundacions of St Mary's Church	30	—	—
May 1st. Paid to Thomas Masters in farther part for the timber used in and about the tower of St Marys Church	20	—	—
4th. Paid to John Whitehead per order of Mr Colmore and Mr Thomas Newsham for altering the break att the house next the Vicarage in the new square from plaine work to stone coyns	—	13	4
	742	5	4
6th. Paid to Samuell Dunkley and Francis Smith in farther part for digging and laying the foundacions of St Marys Church	40	—	—
Paid to Samuell Acock per Mr Jephcott per order of Sir Henry Puckering in part for colouring the windows, etc., about the Church of St Marys	8	19	6
9th. Paid to Sir William Wilson in farther part monies given him for surveying the rebuilding of the church of St Maryes	10	—	—
10. Paid to Thomas Masters in part for the timber used in and about braggetting the roof of St Mary Church	30	—	—

	£	s.	d.
13. Paid to Samuell Dunkley and Francis Smith in farther part for digging and laying the foundacions of the Church of St Maryes	30	—	—
18. Paid to Nicholas Paris and William Marshall per Paris in farther part for iron used in and about rebuilding the Church of St Maryes	5	—	—
26. Paid to Francis Battson in part for 2000 foot of paveing stone for the Church of St Maryes	3	—	—
27. Paid to Thomas Masters in farther part for timber used in and about the tower of St Maryes	5	—	—
31st. Paid to Francis Battson in farther part as aforesaid	2	—	—
Paid to William Marshall in farther part for iron for the Church of St Maryes	5	—	—
June 3rd. Paid to Francis Battson in farther part as aforesaid	6	—	—
Paid to Samuell Acock in part of his bill for work and tarr used about the tower of St Maryes	6	—	—
10th. Paid to James Walker in part for paveing stone brought in for the Church of St Maryes	10	—	—
13. Paid to Thomas Masters in farther part for timber used about braggetting the Church of St Maryes for plaistering	5	—	—
	908	4	10

1699	Receipts			
	Brought over	1038	—	—
July 21st.	Received of Mrs Elizabeth sen. and Mrs Elizabeth jun. in full of the £200 lent Mr Edward Heath dec. by bond by the Trustees	159	—	—
		1188	—	—

1699	Payments			
	Brought over	908	4	10
June 14th.	Paid to Mr Richard Lane, Mayor, in part for 10 fudder[1] of lead bought att Darby for the			

[1] Or fother. A fother of lead = 19½ cwt or 2184 lbs.

	£	s.	d.
Church of St Maryes and for the carriage of 20 fudder from thence to Warwick	155	—	—
19th. Paid to Thomas Adams for throwing rubbish into the quarry in the church yard from Mr Colmor's wall	—	2	—
Paid to Nicholas Paris and William Marshall by Mr Palmer for Mr Downing in full for a tunn of iron from Ipsley for the tower of St Maryes	17	10	—
Paid labourers removeing rubbish out of the new square			1
26. Paid to Francis Smith and Samuell Dunkley in part for lime and haire provided for the plaistering work of St Maryes Church	15	—	—
Paid to Thomas Masters in farther part for timber for the braggetting[2]	20	17	—
Paid for work in braggetting the roof of St Maryes Church	29	3	—
Paid to Francis Battson in farther part as aforesaid	1	3	6
Paid to Mr Thomas Hicks for 264 foot of ground taken from him att the Red Lyon ground in the Swan Lane att 2d.$\frac{1}{2}$ per foot allow'd him by the jury the 4th of Aprill last	2	15	—
27. Paid to John Phillips, carpenter, in part for the workmanshipp of the braggetting the roof of the Church of St Maryes	20	—	—
July 15. Paid to Francis Battson in farther part as aforesaid	11	11	6
21st. Paid to Mrs Elizabeth Heath[3] one shilling and six pence in the pound for the loss of the house in the Church Street as reduced to [ ][4] as per an order sign'd the 16th day of May 1698	85	5	—
Paid to Samuell Acock in part for work and materialls used and done in and about St Marys Church	6	—	—
	1272	10	10

---

[1] The sum of money is left blank.
[2] 'timber for the braggetting' interlineated.
[3] 'Heath' interlineated.
[4] A space, not filled in.

	£	s.	d.

1699	Receipts			

Brought over — £1188 — —

July 22nd. Received per return being an order drawne upon Sir Francis Child payable to Mr William Newsham or order by Trustees of the Brief Monies dated 22nd day of July 1699 — 500 — —

1688 — —

1699	Payments			

Brought over — 1272 10 10

July 22nd. Paid to Thomas Masters in part for the pewing to be done and putt up in the Church of St Maryes — 60 — —

Paid to William Smith, Samuell Dunkley and Francis Smith in full for the extraordinary work in railes and banisters over the windows of St Marys Church — 25 — —

Paid to William Smith, Samuell Dunkley and Francis Smith in part for getting stone to be used about the tower of St Marys Church — 10 — —

28. Paid to Mr Lane in part for the glazeing work to be done in glazeing the windows of the Church of St Marys — 25 — —

Aug. 3. Paid to Joseph Willis for 48 foot of ground taken from him in the Sheep Street to enlarge the same as per an order dated 2nd of August — 1 4 —

Paid to John Fosters 1s. 6d. in the pound for the loss of the house mencioned in an order dated the 2nd day of August instant — 3 7 6

Paid to Moses Halloway for goeing to severall Commissioners in the country to desire their company to the Court — — 5 —

Paid to John Prescott filling up the well in the square — — — 6

19. Paid to Thomas Masters and Nicholas Kington in farther part for and towards the seateing for St Marys Church — 5 — —

Sept. 2. Paid to Thomas Masters in farther part for braggetting the roofe of St Marys Church — 8 — —

	£	s.	d.

4. Paid to Richard Hurst, plasterer, in part for plastering work done and to be done in and about the said church — 20 — —

1450 7 10

1699   Receipts

Brought over — 1688 — —

Sept. 7. Received of William Colmore, Esq., by Mr George Webb being in part of an order of £500 drawne by the Trustees on Sir Francis Child — 100 — —

15. Received of William Colmore, Esq., in full of the order of £500 drawne as above — 400 — —

Received of Mr Thomas Fothergill, Rector of Culmington in com. Salop being brief monie collected in the said parish upon the Warwick brief as appears by an indorsment on the said brief and a paper of the collections — 1 9 7

2189 9 7

1699   Payments

Brought over — 1450 7 10

Sept. 9th. Paid to Thomas Masters and Nicholas Kington in farther part towards the seateing for the Church of Saint Maryes — 50 — —

Paid to James Walker in farther part for stone laid down att the Church of St Maryes for paveing the same — 10 — —

Paid to Reddle Mason of Henley 2 jorneys to Warwick to waite on the Commissioners upon business — — 17 6

12th Paid to John Burton for 147 foot of ground taken from him according to an order of Court of the 16th day of January last, 5d. per foot — 3 1 3

Paid to Mr Lane in part towards leading the Church of Saint Maryes and work done in and about the said church — 100 — —

23rd. Paid to Thomas Masters in part for timber used in and about the tower and for the timber now lying in the square of the said use — 20 — —

	£	s.	d.
Paid as per a particular paper of disbursments to severall labourers for filling rubbish in the square when carryed away to Serjeant Hadleys pitt with John Hawkurns team July 23rd. '99[1]	2	5	6
Paid John Hawkurn 11 dayes with his team carrying rubbish out of the square 5s. per day	2	15	—
15. Paid labourers as by the said paper of disbursments for levelling part of the church yard and removeing rubbish there	1	12	7
Paid John Haukurn 6 dayes with his team carrying the rubbish out of the square 5s. per day	1	10	—
Paid as per the particular paper of disbursments to severall labourers about removeing rubbish out of the square	1	11	—
Paid Job Heath the 3rd of August for goeing to Commissioners to desire their companys att Warwick upon some business relateing to the Church of St Marys	—	5	—
30. Paid to James Walker in farther part for paveing stone laid down att the Church of St Marys	6	—	—

	1650	5	8

	£	s.	d.
Oct. 12. Paid to William Marshall per Capt. Williams in farther part for the iron work used about the Church of St Maryes	5	5	—
14. Paid to Thomas Masters and Nicholas Kington in farther part towards the seateing for the Church of St Maryes	30	—	—
20. Paid to Mr Smith in farther part towards the stone dugg and now lying in the church yard for the use of the said church	30	—	—
28. Paid to Francis Battson in farther part towards the stone laid down att the Church of St Marys towards paveing the same	2	—	—
Nov. 4. Paid to William Marshall in part towards the iron skreen for the Church of St Marys being to be fixed between the church and chancell there	4	6	—
Paid to Richard Hurst in farther part for and towards plaistering the Church of St Marys in Warwick	20	—	—

[1] 'July 23rd. '99' added in a space.

	£	s.	d.
Dec. 2. Paid to William Marshall in farther part for and towards the iron skreen for the Church of St Marys	7	3	—
6. Paid to Thomas Masters in farther part towards the seats for the Church of St Marys	20	—	—
Paid to William Marshall per Mr Saunders for Mr Archers use being in farther part towards the iron skreen for the Church of Saint Maryes	40	—	—
Paid formerly to Job Heath for goeing to Sir William Wilson per order of the Trustees	—	2	6
Paid October 18th for a letter from Mr Hoar about business relateing to the Brief Monies	—	1	6
14. Paid to Thomas Masters and Nicholas Kington per Mr Stephen Nicholls in farther work towards the seates aforesaid	16	5	—
15. Paid to William Marshall in farther part for the skreen	7	—	—
21st. Paid to Mr Hurst, plaisterer, in farther part as aforesaid	30	—	—
23rd. Paid to Thomas Masters and Nicholas Kington in farther part towards the seateing for the Church of St Maryes	14	—	—
	1876	8	8

1699/1700   Receipts

Brought over	2189	9	7
Jan. 25. Received from Mr Fetherston of Packwood which he received from Upholand in the parish of Wigan in com. Lancaster, being collected there upon the Warwick brief as per the said brief and paper of contributors	1	15	7
Received per ditto from St Oswalds in Chester as indorsed upon the abovesaid brief paid by Mr Henry Prescott per Mr Bourchier	6	11	11
	2197	17	1

1699   Payments

Brought over	1876	8	8

	£	s.	d.

23. Paid to William Smith in part for the 500 ft of paveing stone to be by him provided towards paveing the Church of St Maryes — 3 — —

Jan. 7th. Paid to Thomas Masters and Nicholas Kington per Nathaniel Nicholls in farther part towards the seateing for the Church of St Maryes — 8 — —

10. Paid to Mr Marshall in farther part towards the iron skreen per Mr Saunders for Mr Archer — 23 12 —

Paid to Thomas Masters and Nicholas Kington per Nicholas Kington in farther part towards the seateing for the Church of St Maryes — 2 — —

Paid to Mr Marshall in farther part towards the iron skreen made for the Church of St Marys — 8 4 6

Paid to John Prescott goeing to Sir William Wilson's, Mr Archer and other Commissioners to desire their companys att a meeting held the 25th January inst. to consult Mr Strong, a surveyor from London, about matters relateing to the failure in the pillars of the tower of St Marys Church — — 5 —

Paid to William Clarridge goeing to Sir William Underhill and other Commissioners to desire their companys att the meeting aforesaid — — 2 6

Paid Job Heath goeing to Sir Charles Holts, Sir Clement Fisher and other Commissioners to desire as aforesaid — — 5 —

Paid to Frank Dunn goeing to Mr Feildings, Sir William Boughtons and other Commissioners to desire as aforesaid — — 5 —

Feb. 3rd. Paid to Thomas Masters and Nicholas Kington in farther part towards the seateing for the Church of St Maryes — 30 — —

Paid to Francis Dunn for removeing rubbish from before Mr Bromich his ground in the Markett Place — — 5 —

Paid to John Prescott for filling up the quarry in the church yard att the chancell end[1] — — 10 —

16. Paid to Mr Edes, Vicar, being allow'd him by an order of Court of the 25th January last for the damage he hath already and shall sustaine by

[1] 'att the chancell end' inserted in a space.

	£	s.	d.

reason of the digging stone and laying rubbish
in the church yard .... 5 — —

22nd. Paid to Mr Marshall in farther part toward the
iron skreen .... 4 — —

—————

1961 17 8

1699/'700   Receipts

Brought over 2197 17 1

Feb. 20. Received of Mr Stephen Nicholls in farther
part for the £100 lent him by the Trustees .... 15 — —

1700
May 15th. Received of the Trustees of the Warwick Brief
Monies one order on Sir Francis Child payable
to Mr Thomas Newsham or order for .... 300 — —

—————

2512 17 1

1699/'700   Payments

Brought over 1961 17 8

March 23rd Paid to Mr Marshall in farther part towards the
iron skreen .... 5 — —

Aprill 2nd. Paid to Thomas Masters and Nicholas Kington
in farther part towards the seateing for the
Church of St Maryes .... 15 — —

Paid to Thomas and Samuell Wright per order
of Mr Colmore, etc., one $\frac{1}{2}$ of the 1s. 6d. in the
pound for the loss of Mr Bromich his house in
the Markett Place as the same is reduced to
£230 .... 8 12 6

Paid Samuell Wright per order as aforesaid the
whole one shilling and six pence in the pound
for the loss of Mr Okens house wherein
Matthew Busbie liv'd as the same is reduced to
90 .... 6 15 —

Paid Mr Marshall in farther part towards the
iron skreen per Mr Whadcock .... 3 — —

8th. Paid to John Gardner sen. in part for the 200
load of Shrewley stone to be deliver'd to the
Commissioners for the use of St Marys parish
att 4s. per tunn .... 5 — —

	£	s.	d.
Paid to a labourer for removeing rubbish from Mr Rainsford's wall in the church yard	—	5	—
13th. Paid to Mr Marshall in farther part towards the iron skreen	3	—	—
May 4th. Paid to Mr Marshall in farther part towards the iron skreen	6	—	—
Paid to Mr Marshall per Mr Tarver in farther part towards the iron skreen	4	13	—
11th. Paid to John Gardner sen. in farther part for the stone to be deliver'd as aforesaid	5	—	—
20. Paid to Mr Marshall in farther part towards the iron skreen	1	—	—
Paid to Mr Pritchett being one shilling and 6d. per £1 for the loss of the Corporacion house in the Sheep Street as the same is reduced to £150, according to an order of Court of the 11th of October 1697	11	5	—
24th. Paid to Thomas Masters in farther part towards the seating for the Church of St Marys	30	—	—
	2066	8	2

1700
June 22nd. Paid to John Gardner in farther part towards stone to be delivered as aforesaid — 5 — —

Paid to 2 messengers goeing to the Commissioners to desire them to meet to consult about matters relateing to the failures in the pillars of the tower of St Maryes Church — 9 —

Paid for horse hyre to speak to the Commissioners by John Mitchener — 4 —

25. Paid to Mr Marshall in farther part towards the iron skreen 3 — —

28. Paid to John Gardner sen. in farther part towards Shrewley stone to be delivered as aforesaid 5 — —

29th. Paid to Samuell Dunckley in part towards digging and to lay the foundacions for the tower of St Marys 8 — —

July 12. Paid to Thomas Lea for 160 ft of ground taken away from him to enlarge the street leading to the pillory, according to an order dated the 2nd of August '99 and an order of Court of the 16th day of January 1698[/9] being 5d. per ft.[1] 3 6 8

[1] 'being 5d. per ft.' inserted in a space.

	£	s.	d.

13. Paid to Richard Hancox for 32 ft of ground to enlarge the said street as per ditto orders — 13 4

Paid to James Wilson for 48 ft of ground taken away to enlarge the said street per ditto orders I — —

Paid Samuell Wright for 560 ft of ground to enlarge the said street taken from the ground late of Mr Bromich per the order of Mr Colmore, etc., being 5d. per ft. II 13 4

Paid to Samuell Dunkley and Francis Smith in farther part towards laying the foundacions for the new tower 20 — —

20th. Paid to Samuell Dunckly and Francis Smith in farther part towards laying the foundacions for the new tower 20 — —

1700

2144 14 6

Paid to Richard Overs for the carriage of 14 tun 11ft and 6 inches of Shrewley stone from the quarry to St Maryes Church to build pillars for the new tower att 3s. per tunn[1] 2 4 11

Paid to William Balemay for the carriage of 13 load 16 ft. 2 1 5

Paid to John Masters for the carriage of 4 load — 12 —

Paid Richard Spicer for the carriage of 5 load 17 ft — 17 6

Paid Edward Horley for the carriage of six load and 6 ft. — 18 11

Paid Samuell Fairfax for the carriage of 4 load and 4 ft. — 12 7

Paid to James White for the carriage of 22 load 12 ft. 3 7 9

Paid Thomas Palmer for the carriage of 4 load and 4 ft. — 12 6

23rd. Paid to George Tompson for the carriage of 7 load and 2 ft of stone I I I

Aug. 3rd. Paid to Samuell Dunckley and Francis Smith in farther part towards the foundacion work for the new tower and work about the pillars of Shrewley stone for the same 17 — —

17. Paid to George Flowers for the carriage of 5 load and 5 ft. of Shrewley stone — 15 9

[1] 'att 3s. per tunn' inserted in a space.

	£	s.	d.
Paid to Joseph Budd for the carriage of 5 load and 18 ft of Shrewley stone	—	17	9
Paid to John Gardner sen. in farther part towards Shrewley stone to be deliver'd as aforesaid	5	—	—
Paid to Samuell Dunckley and Francis Smith in farther part as aforesaid for new tower	30	—	—
19th. Paid to James Walker in farther part for paveing stone brought in for the use of St Marys Church	7	—	—
Paid to Richard Huss in farther part towards plaistering in the Church of St Marys	4	—	—

1700

	£	s.	d.
	2221	16	8
20th. Paid to Edward Wall for the carriage of 12 load and 2 ft of stone from Shrewley	1	16	1
Paid to John Prescott for goeing to the Commissioners in order to have a Court about business relateing to the church	—	3	—
24. Paid to James White for the carriage of 12 load and 15 ft of stone from Shrewley	1	18	3
Paid to John Heath for the carriage of 9 load and 17 foot of stone from Shrewley	1	9	5
Paid to Samuell Dunckley and Francis Smith in farther part towards the new tower	12	—	—
Sept. 3rd. Paid to Mr Huss in farther part towards plaistering the Church of St Maryes	10	—	—
Paid to Thomas Palmer for the carriage of 16 load and 12 ft. of stone from Shrewly	2	9	10
Paid Lawrence Eborall for the carriage of 26 load and 3 ft of stone from ditto	3	18	4
Paid to William Balleway for the carriage of 15 load and 10 ft. of stone from ditto	2	6	6
Paid to the Widow Cooper per Francis Acock for the carriage of 21 load and 10 ft from ditto	3	4	6
Paid to George Flower for the carriage of 2 load and 5 ft. of stone from ditto	—	6	9
Paid to John Gardner in farther part for stone as aforesaid	2	—	—
7th. Paid to Mr Dunckley in farther part towards the new tower	22	—	—
12. Paid to Mr Richard Lane in farther part on the account of lead for St Marys Church 5 gns.[1]	5	7	6

[1] '5 gns.' inserted in a space.

	£	s.	d.
14. Paid to Mr Dunckley and Francis Smith in farther part towards the new tower	15	—	—
	2305	16	10

1700	Receipts	£	s.	d.
	Brought over	2512	17	1
Oct.	Received of Mr Paxton, gardiner, being in part of the £100 lent by the Trustees of the Brief Monies unto Samuell Acock upon mortgage of his new house in the High Street	50	—	—
12.	Received of Mr Fish in farther part of monies lent him by the Trustees	5	—	—
		2567	17	1

1700	Payments	£	s.	d.
	Brought over	2305	16	10
Sept. 14.	Paid to John Overton for the carriage of 4 load and 5 ft of stone from Shrewley	—	12	9
	Paid to James White for the carriage of 4 load and 3 ft.	—	12	3
	Paid to [ ]¹ for the carriage of 2 load and 10 ft.	—	7	6
17.	Paid to Mr Frogley per order of Lord Brooke, Sir Henry Puckering, etc., being for his paines in waiteing on the Commissioners severall times about the seats for the church 5 gns	5	7	6
21st.	Paid to Mr Dunckley being in further part towards the new tower	12	—	—
24.	Paid to Sir William Wilson per order of Sir Henry Puckering, Mr Colmore and Mr Thomas Newsham, being for carveing work done in and about the Church of St Marys	20	—	—
28.	Paid to Mr Dunckley and Mr Smith in farther part towards the new tower	15	—	—
	Paid to Richard Saunders for the carriage of 11 load and 3ft. of stone from Shrewley	1	13	4

¹ Blank in MS.

	£	s.	d.
Paid to Richard Lane in farther part towards lead for the Church of St Marys	50	—	—
Oct. 5th. Paid to Thomas Masters and Nicholas Kington in farther part towards the seating for the Church of St Marys	15	—	—
Paid to Samuell Dunckley and Francis Smith in farther part towards the new tower	12	—	—
12th. Paid to Richard Casemore for the carriage of 2 load and 19 ft. of stone from Shrewley	—	8	11
Paid to William Smith and Samuell Dunckley in farther part towards the new tower	10	—	—
1700	2448	19	1
Paid to Mr Huss in farther part towards plaistering work done in the Church of St Marys	6	—	—
19th. Paid to Samuel Dunckley and Francis Smith in farther part towards the new tower	15	—	—
23. Paid to Francis Badson per his son in farther part towards paveing for the Church of St Marys	1	—	—
26. Paid to Thomas Masters being the one shilling and six pence in the pound for the loss of the White Lyon Inn burnt down as the same is reduced to £180	13	10	—
Paid to John Gardner sen. in farther part towards Shrewley stone	9	2	8
Paid to Thomas Masters being his bill for timber and work done and used in and about the additionall part of the roof of St Marys Church as the same was measured and estimated by Mr Jephcott[1]	45	12	—
Paid to William and Francis Smith in farther part towards the new tower	12	—	—
Paid to Mr Huss in farther part towards plaistering the church	10	—	—
Nov. 2nd. Paid to Samuell Dunckley and Francis Smith in farther part towards the new tower	10	—	—
7th. Paid to Francis Badson per his son in farther part as aforesaid	1	—	—
9th. Paid to John Gardner per John Walter £9 and			

---

[1] 'as ... Mr Jephcott' added after writing this item, but before continuing with the next.

	£	s.	d.
per Mr Whadcock 10s. 4d. being in full of monies due to him for Shrewley stone	9	10	4
Paid to Mr Dunckley and Francis Smith in farther part as aforesaid for the new tower	10	—	—
	2592	8	6

Receipts

	£	s.	d.
Brought over	2567	17	1
Received of Samuell Paxton, gardner, in full of the £100 lent unto Samuell Acock upon mortgage of his new house in the High Street	50	—	—
	2617	17	1

Payments

1700

	£	s.	d.
Brought over	2592	8	6
16. Paid to Mr Dunckley in further part towards the new tower	5	—	—
23. Paid to Mr Dunckley in further part towards the new tower	3	—	—
Paid Francis Badson per his son in farther part as aforesaid	1	—	—
29th. Paid to Thomas Masters in part of a bill delivered in for the use of the Trustees for braggetting the middle arch att the west end of the church, and for other extraordinary work about takeing down the floors of the 1st built tower and laying the same in the new built tower at the west end	20	—	—
30th. Paid to Mr Dunckley in farther part towards the new tower	3	—	—
Paid to Mr Huss in farther part towards the plaistering work in St Marys Church	20	—	—
Dec. 7th. Paid to Mr Dunckley and Mr Smith in farther part towards the new tower	23	13	—
Paid to Mr Dunckley in farther part towards the new tower	2	10	—
Paid to Mr Marshall in part towards extraordinary work in and about the new tower	3	12	6

	£	s.	d.

9th. Paid to Richard Hands and John Vernon the
1s. 6d. in the pound for the loss of Mr Oken's
alm houses burnt down in the Pibble Lane and
reduced to £70, the same being by them rebuilt[1] — 5 5 —

11th. Paid to Thomas Masters and Nicholas Kington
per Nicholas Kington in farther part towards
pewing for the church — 4 — —

14th. Paid to Francis Badson per his son in farther
part towards paveing stone for the church — — 10 —

1700 — 2683 19 —

Paid to William Marshall in farther part towards the extraordinary work done in and
about the new tower and church — 5 — —

Paid to Samuell Dunckley and Francis Smith in
farther part towards the new tower — 5 — —

17. Paid to Mr Huss in farther part towards plaistering work done in the Church of St Mary — 50 — —

21st. Paid to Francis Badson in farther part for paveing stone laid and to be laid in the Church of St
Mary — 11 10 —

Paid to Samuell Dunckley and Francis Smith in
farther part towards the new tower — 20 — —

Paid William Smith in farther part towards
paveing stone laid and to be laid in the Church
of St Marys — 5 — —

Jan. 7th. Paid to Samuell Acock in part of the 40s. as
mencioned to be oweing to him in the account
stated and sent up to the Lord Brooke to London — 1 10 —

9. Paid to Thomas Masters and Nicholas Kington
in farther part towards the pewing for the
church — 20 — —

10. Paid to Samuell Dunckley in farther part towards the new tower, etc. — 2 10 —

17. Paid to William Smith, Samuell Dunckley and
Francis Smith in farther part towards work
done and to be done in and about the rebuilding and finishing the church and tower of St
Mary — 250 — —

---

[1] This refers to the ground in Pebble Lane, not to the new almshouses built by the charity in 1696 on the Backhills.

	£	s.	d.

18th. Paid Evan Floyd 12 dayes work about cleaning the place behind the Ladys Chappel, sorting and helping to weigh out the old iron out of the bone house, and leveling the ground under the pews in the church — 12 —

3055 1 —

1700/1   Receipts

Brought over 2617 17 1

Jan. 17. Received of Mr Francis Chernock in full of two orders drawn on Sir Francis Child by the Trustees and payable to the said Mr Chernock or order, for £300 300 — —

Received of Thomas Newsham, Esq., in full of an order drawn att the same time on Sir Francis Child made payable to Mr William Newsham or order 200 — —

Received of Mr Francis Chernock in full of the bill of £250 drawn on Sir Francis Child made payable to him or order 250 — —

Received of Thomas Newsham, Esq., in full of the order of £150 drawn on Mr Hoar made payable to him or order 150 — —

3517 17 1

1700/1   Payments

Brought over 3055 1 —

Feb. 1st. Paid to Thomas Masters in farther part for timber, etc., used about the church and tower of St Marys 12 — —

15th. Paid to Thomas Masters and Nicholas Kington in farther part towards pewing aforesaid 15 — —

27th. Paid to Samuell Dunckley and Francis Smith in farther part towards work done and to be done in and about the church and tower of St Marys 10 — —

March 8th. Paid to Thomas Masters and Nicholas Kington in farther part towards pewing aforesaid 12 — —

	£	s.	d.

1701

April 15. Paid to Samuell Wright per order of Mr Colmore, etc., in full of the 1s. 6d. in the pound for
the loss of Mr Bromich his house in the Markett Place as the same is reduc'd to £90 — 8 12 6

19th. Paid per Samuell Dunckley in farther part towards work done and to be done in and about
the rebuilding and finishing the church and
tower of St Marys — 7 — —

Paid to three men for helping to weigh the bell
mettall — — 3 —

Paid to Thomas Masters and Nicholas Kington
in farther part towards pewing the Church of
St Marys — 20 — —

28th. Paid to Mr Lane in full for the glazeing of the
south window att the west end of St Marys
Church — 3 9 8

May 3rd. Paid per Samuell Dunckley in farther part towards work done and to be done as aforesaid — 3 — —

2nd. Paid to George Perry in part of his bill for
hinges used in the pewing of the Church of St
Marys — 13 — —

5. Paid to Richard Hancox, glazier, being (with
£20 paid him the 27th of July '99) in full for one
half of the glazeing done about the church — 17 16 6

3177 2 8

Receipts

Brought over — 3517 17 1

Received of the Feoffees of Mr Thomas Oken
deceased for 1697ft. of back ground att 1d.$\frac{1}{2}$ per
ft. and for 72ft of front ground att 2d$\frac{1}{2}$ per ft.
taken from the ground call'd the church
ground in the Church Street, and added to the
ground belonging to the said Oken's house in
the possession of Thomas Newsham, Esq.,
being settled by an order of Court and a jury
the 12th of May '99[1] — 11 7 1$\frac{1}{2}$

Received of the Widow Atterbury in full for the
fee simple of a peice of the church ground

---

[1] 'being settled . . . '99' added after writing this item, but before continuing with the next.

	£	s.	d.
abovesaid sold unto her by the Commissioners by decree the 12th of May last	5	—	—
Received of Mr Fish in farther part of the £50 lent him by the Trustees	10	—	—
	3544	4	$2\frac{1}{2}$

Payments

	£	s.	d.
Brought over	3177	2	8
May Paid to Evan Floyd a bill for levelling the ground att the east end of the chancell	1	10	6
10. Paid a messenger to severall Commissioners in the country to desire a meeting the 12 inst. to consider of matters relateing to the church and tower of St Marys	—	4	6
Paid to Phillips and Phenix out of the money received for the church ground on the other side[1] being for the party wall built by them on the north side of the said ground, principall and interest	8	4	—
For measureing the said party wall[2]	—	2	—
Paid to the Widow Atterberry for the party wall built by her on the south side of the said church ground, this being over the summ charg'd received on the other side	9	7	—
Memorandum when the Commissioners sold the church ground to Mr Robbinson and Cook they agreed to pay for party walls.			
31st. Paid to Samuell Dunckley in farther part as aforesaid	5	—	—
June 7th. Paid to Richard King, carpenter, the 1s. 6d. per £1 for the loss of Mrs Lucas house in the High Street as reduced to £40	3	—	—
21st. Paid to Samuell Dunckley and Francis Smith in farther part towards the church, etc., as aforesaid	10	—	—
28. Paid to Samuell Dunckley and Francis Smith in farther part as aforesaid	15	—	—

[1] On the facing page in the original layout.
[2] This item inserted in a space.

	£	s.	d.
Paid to John Gardner for 61 load of Shrewly stone at 4s. per load and 7s. for loading	11	19	—
Paid to Thomas Palmer for the carriage of 5 load of Shrewley stone at 3s.	—	17	9
July 5. Paid to Samuell Dunckley and Francis Smith in farther part as aforesaid	10	—	—
12th. Paid to Samuell Dunckley and Francis Smith in farther part as aforesaid	15	—	—
1701	3267	7	5
19th. Paid to George Perry in farther part towards his bill for hinges for the seats in the church and of locks for the church doores	2	13	—
20. Paid to Samuell Dunckley and Francis Smith per Francis Smith in farther part towards work about the church and tower of St Marys	10	—	—
Paid to Edward Wall for the carriage of 14 load and 2 ft of Shrewley stone att 3s. per load	2	2	—
26. Paid to Samuell Dunckley and Francis Smith in farther part as aforesaid	10	—	—
Aug. 2nd. Paid to Samuell Dunckley and Francis Smith in farther part as aforesaid	15	—	—
Paid to James White for the carriage of 11 load and six foot of stone from Shrewley	1	13	10
9th. Paid to Samuell Dunckley and Francis Smith in farther part as aforesaid	10	—	—
16th. Paid to John and Richard Edwards for the carriage of 10 load and 16 ft of Shrewley stone from Shrewley	1	12	3
Paid to Edward Horley for the carriage of 5 load and 16ft of Shrewley stone	—	17	3
Paid to Samuell Dunckley and Francis Smith in farther part as aforesaid	10	—	—
23. Paid to George Nicks of Birmingham, one of the witnesses att the Assizes against Sarah Clark relateing to bell mettall stol'n out of the bone house	—	2	6
25. Paid to Francis Smith in farther part as aforesaid	10	—	—
26. Paid to Mr Huss, plaisterer, in full ballance of accounts due to him for plaistering work and other work done in and about the Church of St Marys	21	—	—

	£	s.	d.
Paid Mr Huss a bill for work about finishing the mouldings between the church and chancel by the iron skreen and for materialls used about the same, and for whiteing 13 capitalls of the pillars	3	2	—
	3365	**10**	**2**

1701

Sept. 3rd. Paid to Francis Badson in full of 2011 ft of paveing stone laid by him in the Church of St Mary att 5d.$\frac{1}{2}$ per ft. — 3 5 —

13. Paid to Samuell Dunckley in farther part towards work done as aforesaid — 15 — —

Paid to William Clements one other witness att the Assizes aforesaid against Sarah Clark — — 2 6

20th. Paid to William Smith and Samuell Dunckley in farther part as aforesaid — 10 — —

Paid a tayler sewing some ruggs together to hang up over the iron skreen for a tryall to fix the pulpitt — — — 8$\frac{1}{2}$

Paid to Francis Badson in full for another parcell of paveing stone laid by him in the church — 4 7 6

Oct. 22. Paid to Edward Wall for the carriage of one load and 10ft of Shrewley stone — — 4 6

25th. Paid to the Widow Cooper for the carriage of 12 load and 17 ft of Shrewley stone to the church for the tower — 1 18 6

Paid to Francis Smith in farther part towards work done as aforesaid — 10 — —

Nov. 1st. Paid to William Smith in full for paveing stone laid att the church by him, 483 ft laid[1] — 3 1 —

21st. Paid to Mr Henry Jephcott for the draught of a pulpitt for the Church of St Marys drawn in London — — 10 —

Dec. 13th. Paid to labourers Evan Floyd, etc., for remove-ing rubbish out of the church for the paviours to finish there work, and about cleaneing the leads upon the flatt of the church for the plumber to finish, and for makeing a trench to carry

---

[1] '483 ft laid' inserted in a space.

	£	s.	d.
the water into the quarry from the north wall of the church, 9 dayes	—	9	—
	3414	8	11½

1701 — Receipts

	£	s.	d.
Brought over	3544	4	2½
Nov. 21st. Received of Mr Fish in farther part of the £50 lent him by the Trustees	5	—	—
Dec. 16th. Received of Mr Francis Chernock being in full of a bill drawn by the Trustees on Sir Francis Child payable to Mr Chernock or order, drawn in August[1]	250	—	—
Jan. 31st. Received of Thomas Newsham Esq. being in full of a bill drawn by the Trustees on Sir Francis Child payable to the said Thomas Newsham or order	100	—	—
	3899	4	2½

1701 — Payments

	£	s.	d.
Brought over	3414	8	11½
Paid to George Chinn being the 1s. 6d. in the pound for the loss of the Bear Inn as reduced to £280 per order of Mr Colmore	21	—	—
Dec. 20th. Paid to Samuell Dunckley and Francis Smith in farther part towards the church and tower of St Marys	5	—	—
Paid to James Walker being in full with £33 paid before for 1803 ft of paveing stone att 5d.½ per ft, 144 ft of half pace stepps att 12d. a ft and 3 load carriage of the stepps £1	16	10	—
Jan. 31st. Paid to Thomas Masters and Nicholas Kington in farther part toward peweing the Church of St Marys	16	—	—
Paid to Evan Floyd 6 dayes doeing up and removeing rubbish before the church	—	6	—
Paid him 3 days and ½ for makeing holes for the bolts to fasten the church doors	—	3	6

[1] 'drawn in August' added in a space.

	£	s.	d.

Feb. 6th. Paid labourers weighing up the bell mettall in the bone house — — 3 —

21st. Paid to John Pinley being the 1s. 6d. in the pound for the loss of the Dolphin Inn as reduced to £90 — 6 15 —

Paid to Samuell Dunckley being towards building the tower of St Marys — 5 — —

March 7th. Paid Mr Samuell Dunckley in farther part toward building the tower of St Marys — 1 — —

21st. Paid Samuell Dunckley and Francis Smith in farther part — 5 — —

1702

April 18th. Paid to Samuell Dunckley and Francis Smith in farther part — 7 — —

25th. Paid Samuell Dunckley and Francis Smith in farther part — 8 — —

May 1st. Paid to Richard King, carpenter, the 1s. 6d. in the pound for the loss of the Crabbmill ground as reduced to £60 — 4 10 —

2nd. Paid to Samuell Dunckley and Francis Smith in farther part — 10 — —

1702 — 3520 16 5½

9th. Paid to Samuell Dunckley and Francis Smith in farther part toward building the tower — 12 — —

16th. Paid to Samuell Dunckley and Francis Smith in farther part as aforesaid — 15 — —

Paid to Thomas Masters being lent to him by the Trustees of the briefe upon mortgage of a messuage or tenement in the Highstreet in Warwick built upon the Swan ground, etc., dated the 10th of February 1701[/2] — 100 — —

23. Paid to Samuell Dunckley and Francis Smith in farther part toward the work aforesaid — 20 — —

30th. Paid to Samuell Dunckley and Francis Smith in farther part as aforesaid — 10 — —

June 6th. Paid to Samuell Dunckley and Francis Smith in farther part as aforesaid — 10 — —

13. Paid to Samuell Dunckley and Francis Smith in farther part as aforesaid — 16 — —

22nd. Paid to Samuell Dunckley and Francis Smith in farther part as aforesaid — 30 — —

	£	s.	d.
27. Paid to Samuell Dunckley and Francis Smith in farther part as aforesaid	12	—	—
July 4th. Paid to Samuell Dunckley and Francis Smith in farther part as aforesaid	20	—	—
11th. Paid to Francis Badson earnest upon his make-ing a bargaine with the Commissioners to find 1400 ft of paveing stone to pave the chancel in the same manner as the church is done att 5d.$\frac{1}{4}$ per ft., and to finish about a month after All-saints[1] next per order of Mr Colmore and Mr Newsham	—	5	—
Paid to Samuell Dunckley and Francis Smith in farther part as aforesaid	25	—	—
	3791	1	5$\frac{1}{2}$
18th. Paid Samuell Dunckley and Francis Smith in farther part for work as aforesaid	15	—	—
25th. Paid to Samuell Dunckley and Francis Smith in farther part as aforesaid	12	—	—
27th. Paid to Francis Badson per order of Mr Col-more in part for the paveing stone brought in and to be provided for the chancel according to the agreement made the 11th inst.	—[2]	—	—
Paid Job Heath for goeing to Laxton nere Uppingham to Mr Baxter the bell hanger there for him to come to Warwick	—	8	—
Paid to Mr Woodward of Birmingham per George Masters, being for to redeem 82 li. and $\frac{1}{2}$ weight of bell mettall which was stolen from Warwick and sold by one Ann Clark of Lucin-ford to the said Woodward for 5d.$\frac{1}{2}$ per lib., and for bringing it to Warwick	2	—	—
Aug. 1st. Paid to Samuell Dunckley and Francis Smith in farther part as aforesaid	13	—	—
8th. Paid to Samuell Dunckley and Francis Smith in farther part as aforesaid	12	—	—
Paid the same per Mr Dunckley which is to be included in the next receipt[3]	1	—	—
12th. Paid to Mr Baxter the bell hanger being for his			

---

[1] 'Als^ts' in MS.
[2] '£5' has been erased.
[3] Altered from 'which is included in one receipt for ...'.

	£	s.	d.

jorney comeing to Warwick to treat with the Commissioners about hanging the bells, this paid by order of Mr Colmore and Mr Thomas Newsham — 1 10 —

15th. Paid to Samuell Dunckley and Francis Smith for which and for the £1 paid before I have one receipt — 8 — —

1702

3855[1] 19 5½

22. Paid to Samuell Dunckley and Francis Smith in farther part as aforesaid — 20 — —

28. Paid to Samuell Price, bargeman, for the carriage of three tunn of bell mettall from Stratford to Gloucester att 12s. per tunn[2] — 1 16 —

Paid Fletcher of Stratford for the carriage of the bell mettall from Warwick to Stratford — — 18 —

Paid for the carriage of 26 cwt of bell mettall and barrells viz. tare to Stratford — — 7 —

29. Paid to Samuell Dunckley and Francis Smith in farther part as aforesaid — 22 — —

Sept. 5. Paid to Samuel Dunckley and Francis Smith in farther part as aforesaid — 13 — —

Paid Edward Wall for the carriage of 25 load and 12 ft of Shrewley stone to the church viz. for the use of the tower — 3 16 8

Paid Henry Smith for the carriage of 16 load and 3 ft of Shrewley stone for ditto use — 2 8 6

12. Paid to Samuell Dunckley and Francis Smith per Mr Blissett in farther part as aforesaid — 20 — —

19. Paid to Samuell Dunckley and Francis Smith in farther part — 20 — —

Paid John Gardner jun. his bill for Shrewley stone for the tower of St Maryes, being 41 load 15 ft att 4s. per load viz. large parpin stone, one load of parpin stone allow'd in[3] — 8 3 —

26th. Paid to Samuell Dunckley and Francis Smith in farther part as aforesaid — 20 — —

Oct. 3rd. Paid to Samuell Dunckley and Francis Smith in farther part — 15 — —

---

[1] Altered from '3860'.
[2] 'at 12s. per tunn' added in a space.
[3] Parpen: a large stone which passes through a wall from side to side, having 2 dressed faces.

	£	s.	d.
10th. Paid to Samuell Dunckley in farther part as aforesaid, etc.	10	—	—
14. Paid Henry Smith for 19 dayes carriage of rubbish in the church yard to fill up the quarry, with his team	4	15	—
	4018	3	$7\frac{1}{2}$

Receipts

1702

	£	s.	d.
Brought over	3899	4	$2\frac{1}{2}$
July Received of Thomas Newsham, Esq., being an order drawn on Mr Hoar in July last payable to Mr William Newsham or order by the Trustees of the Brief Monies	100	—	—
Received of Mr George Webb in part of a £200 bill drawn by the Trustees on Mr Hoar payable to the said Mr Webb or order, being parte of the £217 3 $4\frac{3}{4}$ ballance of Sir Richard Hoare's account[1]	190	—	—
	4189	4	$2\frac{1}{2}$

Payments

1702

	£	s.	d.
Brought over	4018	3	$7\frac{1}{2}$
Oct. 17th. Paid to Mr Dunckley and Francis Smith in farther part as aforesaid	10	—	—
Paid to Nicholas Kington January 1700/1 in farther part towards the seateing in the church	3	18	—
Paid to Thomas Masters in farther part towards seates	1	1	6
Paid to Mr Marshall a bill for things used about the draw out seates in the church, 2nd Feb. last[2]	1	10	—
Paid to Mr Marshall att severall times being in farther part of work done in and about the church as by the particulars in his account	14	17	—
Paid to George Chinn in part for 180 ft of ground taken from the ground called the Bear Ground to enlarge the High Street	5	—	—

[1] 'being parte ... account' added in a space in another hand.
[2] '2nd Feb. last' added in a space in another hand.

	£	s.	d.
Nov. 14th. Paid to Mr Marshall in part towards the iron band putt up last upon the tower as in his account	5	—	—
14. Paid to Samuell Dunckley being towards getting stone, etc.	3	—	—
21st. Paid to Samuell Dunckley in farther part as aforesaid	2	10	—
28. Paid to Samuell Dunckley in farther part as aforesaid	3	—	—
Dec. 5. Paid to Samuell Dunckley and Francis Smith in farther part	3	—	—
12th. Paid to Samuel Dunckley and Francis Smith in farther part	5	—	—
19. Paid to Samuell Dunckley and Francis Smith in farther part	3	—	—
25. Paid to Samuell Brice for carriage of bell mettall from Stratford to Gloucester 26 c. 21 lb wt att 12s. per tunn	—	15	6
28. Paid to Samuell Dunckley and Francis Smith in part of their bill being extraordinary charges in getting stone att the Pryory quarry and Humbridge Downe, etc., paid per order of Mr Colmore and Mr Newsham	20	—	—
Jan. 16th. Paid to Samuell Dunckley and Francis Smith in farther part for work about the tower	5	—	—
30. Paid to the same in farther part as aforesaid	5	—	—
	4109	15	$7\frac{1}{2}$

Receipts

	£	s.	d.
Brought over	4189	4	$2\frac{1}{2}$
Received of Mr Whadcock which with £22 received of him 11th of January 1698 is £50 in part of the £150 lent unto Mr Tarver and him upon bond	28	—	—
Received of Mr Robert Heath per Mr Whadcock in part of the £100 lent him by the Trustees	35	—	—
1702			
Nov. 14. Received of Thomas Dixon in part of the £40 lent him by the Trustees	30	—	—

	£	s.	d.
March 24. Received of Mr Blissett being a summ of £150 lent him by bond	150	—	—
1703			
Aprill 5th. Received of Mr Weale in part of monies lent him by the Trustees	29	15	—
10. Received of Samuell Ainge in part of £50 lent him by the Trustees	20	—	—
24th. Received of Thomas Masters being in part of £100 lent him	50	—	—
	4531	19	$2\frac{1}{2}$

	Payments	£	s.	d.
1702/3	Brought over	4109	15	$7\frac{1}{2}$
Feb. 13th.	Paid to Mr Dunckley in farther part as aforesaid	5	—	—
March 5th.	Paid to Mr Marshall in farther part of iron and work about the tower of St Maryes, etc.	5	—	—
13.	Paid to Mr Masters in part for timber about the tower, etc.	12	—	—
25th.	Paid to Mr Marshall in farther part of iron work, etc.	2	—	—
26th.	Paid Mr Robert Blissett one shilling and six pence in the pound for the loss of £650	48	15	—
Aprill 3rd.	Paid to Mr Smith, etc., per the quarry men for digging stone, being in part towards work about the tower, etc.	—	8	—
10th.	Paid ditto by the quarry men	—	16	—
17th.	Paid ditto by the quarry men	—	15	—
13th.	Paid to Mr Rudhall, bellfounder, in part for the new bell mettall by him provided for the 8 bells for St Maryes Church, this paid by Mr Harper of Rughby per his order	70	—	—
24th.	Paid to the quarry men for Mr Smith, etc., being towards work about the tower, etc.	—	15	—
	Paid to Mr Marshall in farther part towards iron work, etc.	—	6	—
	Paid to Mr Dunckley in farther part as aforesaid	5	—	—
25th.	Paid to Mr Lane being charges with Mr Prescott, Mr Holyoak and Mr Howell to see the			

	£	s.	d.

bells weigh'd att Gloucester, the particular
weight of which are as follows   2   10   —

Tuns : c.   qrs li

The 1st bell is in weight	— : 6 2 —
The 2nd bell	— : 6 2 8
The 3rd bell	— : 8 2 —
The 4th bell	— : 10 — 22
The 5th bell	— : 12 1 —
The 6th bell	— : 14 3 —
The 7th bell	1 : — 2 14
The 8th bell	1 : 10 — —

5 : 9   1   16

30th. Paid to Mr Marshall for which and for the 6s.
paid as above I have his acquittance   2   4   —

May 1st. Paid to Samuell Burford in part of the one shilling and 6d. per £1 for the loss of the house in
the Sheepstreet formerly one Ashwins   2   —   —

4267   4 $7\frac{1}{2}$

1703   Receipts

Brought over   4531   19 $2\frac{1}{2}$

May 8th. Received of Mr William Tarver towards monies
oweing from him to the Trustees   72   17   8

Received of Samuell Ainge in farther part of
the £50 lent him   5   —   —

June 5th. Received of Mr Blissett in part of a 2nd £150
lent   20   —   —

Received of Mr Weale in farther part of monies
lent him   10   —   —

21st. Received of Sir Francis Child in old moneyes
by tale £279 8 . 8d., in weight 674 oz. 10 dwt[1]
which was carryed to the refiners out of which
was return'd as bad money
    93 oz. 5 dwt soe there remain'd in good money
    581   5   sold for 5s. 2d.$\frac{1}{4}$ per oz. being   150   15   2

    674   10

---

[1] Pennyweight, used in Troy-weight.

	£	s.	d.
Note the 93 oz. 5 dwt lost in melting 15 dwt so that there remain'd but 92 oz. 10 dwt which was assay'd and came to 4s. 4d. per oz. being	20	—	10
Received of Sir Francis Child 7 guineas more	7	10	6
	4818	3	4½

1703   Payments

Brought over		4267	4	7½
May 1st and 15th.	Paid to Mr Dunckley and Francis Smith in farther part towards work about the church and tower, this order'd the 8th of April by an order of Court	100	—	—
1st.	Paid to Mr Dunckley, etc., in further part for work	8	—	—
5th.	Paid to Mr Lane in part towards lead for the church and tower of St Maryes, etc.	55	—	—
8th.	Paid to Mr Dunckley and Smith in farther part	12	—	—
15th.	Paid to Mr Dunckley and Smith in farther part	20	—	—
22nd.	Paid to Mr Smith in farther part	7	—	—
	Paid to Mr Marshall in farther part for iron and work about the tower	—	10	—
June 5th.	Paid to Mr Smith in farther part as aforesaid	23	—	—
	Paid to Mr Ruddhall, bell founder, in farther part for bell mettall and casting bells per Mr Blissett	20	—	—
	Paid to Mr Dunckley and Mr Smith per Mr Weale being in farther part as aforesaid	10	—	—
July 3rd.	Paid to Mr Dunckley and Mr Smith in farther part	20	—	—

Paid coach hyre with old money to the refiners
from Sir Francis Childs 0 2 6
    paid att the refiners 0 1 0
    paid with Mr Jephcott ...... 0 1 5½   — 8 11½
    paid att the tavern with ditto,
    Mr Morses, Mr Bavand, Sir
    Francis Child's men 0 4 6

June 21st. Paid to Sir Francis Child being the ballance
due to him upon account with the Trustees of
the Brief   83 5 5½
Paid to Mr Ruddhall per the hands of Mr John

	£	s.	d.

Lane, etc., in farther part towards casting the
bells and new bell mettall found by him — 50 — —

Paid to Mr Marshall in farther part towards
work about the tower — 1 — —

July 6. Paid him more in farther part — 1 10 —

10. Paid to Mr Dunckley and Mr Smith in farther
part — 10 — —

13. Paid to Mr Masters in farther part of timber
about the tower — 14 — —

4702 19 $\frac{1}{2}$

1703   Receipts

Brought over — 4818 3 4$\frac{1}{2}$

July 20th. Received of Mr Webb in full of the £200 mencioned before being a bill drawn on Mr Hoare
(in further parte of Sir Richard Hoares ballance)[1] — 10 — —

Received of Mr Fish in farther part of monyes
lent unto his father — 4 — —

31st. Received of Mr Robert Heath in farther part of
the £100 lent unto him — 15 — —

Aug. 7th. Received of Mr Blissett in farther part of the
£150 lent him by the Trustees — 10 — —

14th. Received of Mr Robert Heath in farther part as
aforesaid — 20 — —

16th. Received of Mr Bavand by the hands of Mr
Nicholas Kington haveing drawn 2 bills on him
sign'd by Mr Colmore and Mr Newsham, one
payable to Mr John Roger or order, the other
to Mr David Saunders or order — 28 — —

17. Received of Samuell Ainge in farther part of
moneys lent unto him — 10 — —

Received of Mr Fulk Weale in full of the £100
lent him by the Commissioners — 60 5 —

23rd. Received of Mr Joseph Blissett in farther part
towards money lent as aforesaid — 20 — —

Received of Mr Robert Heath being in farther
part of moneys oweing to the Trustees — 20 — —

Received of him in full of the £100 lent — 10 — —

---

[1] 'in further . . . ballance' added in a space in another hand.

	£	s.	d.
Received of the Corporacion of Warwick in full of moneys lent unto them by the Trustees	200	—	—
	5225	8	$4\frac{1}{2}$

		£	s.	d.
1703	Payments			
	Brought over	4702	19	$\frac{1}{2}$
	Paid to Mr Dunckley and Mr Smith 26th June per Doctor Holden	20	—	—
July 17th.	Paid to Mr Dunckley and Mr Smith in farther part for work about the tower	15	—	—
24th.	Paid to Mr Dunckley, etc., in farther part of ditto	15	—	—
31st.	Paid to Mr Dunckley, etc., in farther part of ditto	15	—	—
	Paid unto ditto per Mr Francis Smith in farther part of the tower	10	—	—
Aug. 3rd.	Paid to Nicholas Paris and Mr Marshall in part towards the iron bands of the tower per Mr Wheeler of Stratford	20	—	—
7th.	Paid to Mr Dunckley and Mr Smith in farther part	10	—	—
14th.	Paid to Mr Dunckley, etc., in farther part as aforesaid	20	—	—
	Paid to Mr Masters in farther part towards timber, etc., for the tower	11	16	6
	Paid to Mr Marshall per Mr Weale in farther part of iron about the tower	2	9	5
21.	Paid to Mr Dunckley, etc., in farther part	26	—	—
28.	Paid to them more	15	—	—
Sept. 4th.	Paid to them more	10	—	—
11.	Paid to them more	15	—	—
	Paid to Mr Rudhall jun. not enter'd before, being in part towards casting bells and new bell mettall	10	15	—
	Paid him more in money in farther part	1	10	—
	Paid Aug. 17th to Mr Fulk Weale being the 1s. 6d. in the pound for his losses as reduced to [ ][1]	41	5	—

---

[1] Space not filled in.

	£	s.	d.
Paid Job Heath goeing to Binton to Badson, paviour	—	1	6
Paid to Mr Rudhall by Price the bargeman in farther part the 21st Aug. towards bells, etc.	4	10	—
Paid Price, bargeman, for carriage of the last bell to Gloucester	—	4	—
	4966	10	$5\frac{1}{2}$

1703   Receipts

	£	s.	d.
Brought over	5225	8	$4\frac{1}{2}$
Sept. 25. Received of Mr Joseph Blissett in farther part of monies due to the Trustees	10	—	—
Oct. 2. Received of Joseph Ainge in part of £20 lent to him by the Trustees	8	—	—
Received of Mr Blissett in farther part of monies lent him by the Trustees	12	—	—
9th. Received of him in farther part as aforesaid	20	—	—
	5275	8	$4\frac{1}{2}$

1703   Payments

	£	s.	d.
Brought over	4966	10	$5\frac{1}{2}$
Aug. 28th. Paid to Nicholas Paris in part towards the iron bands for the tower	4	—	—
Paid to Mr Whadcock for cloth used under the wall plates of the roof of the tower, being tarr'd	—	12	—
Sept. 3rd. Paid to Nicholas Paris in farther part toward the band	1	—	—
9. Paid to Mr Rudhall, bell founder, in farther part towards the bells etc.	7	15	—
Paid to Mr Marshall in farther part towards work about the tower	—	0[1]	—
Paid him more in farther part	2	—	—
Paid to Mr Paris and Marshall in farther part (by the carryer) of iron, etc.	1	2	6
18. Paid to Samuell Dunckley and Francis Smith in further part per Mr Colmore	15	—	—
25th. Paid to them more in farther part	10	—	—

[1] '5' altered to 'o', presumably as a way of cancelling the entry.

		£	s.	d.
	Paid to Henry Smith for the carriage of rubbish in the church yard to the quarry	—	10	—
	Paid to Samuell Dunckley and Francis Smith which with £26 paid to them the 21st of August is £30, for which I have there note	4	—	—
Oct. 2nd.	Paid to William Smith, Samuell Dunckley, etc. , in farther part	12	—	—
9.	Paid to them more in farther part of moneys, etc.,	12	—	—
16.	Paid to them more in farther part	13	—	—
25.	Paid to George Perry in full for the locks and keys for the church and for hinges for the seat doors	—	15	—
Nov. 6.	Paid to Mr Paris and Marshall in farther part of iron, etc., by Mr Wheeler	20	—	—
	Paid to Mr Dunckley and Smith in farther part per order of Mr Colmore	10	—	—
13.	Paid to them more in farther part per order of Lord Brook and Mr Colmore	10	—	—
	Paid to Mr Wrothwell for 400c.[1] of leaf gold for the fans to be putt on the great pinacles, etc.	1	17	3
		5092	2	$2\frac{1}{2}$

1703	Receipts			
	Brought over	5275	8	$4\frac{1}{2}$
Nov. 6th.	Received of Mr Joseph Blissett in farther part of moneys oweing to the Trustees	20	—	—
18th.	Received of Mr Blissett in full of moneyes oweing as aforesaid	38	—	—
	Received of Mr Stephen Nicholls in full of moneys oweing to the Commissioners	15	—	—
		5348	8	$4\frac{1}{2}$

1703	Payments			
	Brought over	5092	2	$2\frac{1}{2}$
Nov. 16th.	Paid to John Gardner for Shrewley stone used in the tower	—	12	6

[1] Gold leaf also came in books costing 2s. 6d. (see 26 April 1704 below); these may be single leaves.

	£	s.	d.
18th. Paid for the carriage of the said Shrewley stone	—	9	—
Paid to Mr Marshall in farther part of iron, etc.,	1	—	—
19. Paid to Samuell Acock for 400c. of leaf gold bought att Coventry for the guilding the fanns	1	17	6
27th. Paid to Mr Phillips by his man Edward Bentley in part for hanging the bells	1	—	—
29. Paid to Mr Rudhall in farther part towards bells	6	—	—
Dec. 4th. Paid to Mr Paris and Marshall by Francis Smith which he paid unto Mr Arden Banner for iron bought of Mr John Jennings for the use of the tower, being in farther part of iron delivered by them	30	4	6
10th. Paid to Nicholas Paris for rings for the draw out seats in the church and rivetting them	1	10	—
Paid to Mr Rudhall, bell founder, in farther part for bells, etc., by Mr George Webb	9	16	11
18. Paid to Mr Paris in farther part for iron about the tower and bells	3	—	—
24th. Paid to Thomas Masters upon the account of timber for the roof of the tower, etc.	2	—	—
Paid to Mr Phillips by Ned Bentley in farther part towards hanging bells	1	10	—
Jan. 12. Paid to Mr Phillipps in farther part	2	—	—
18th. Paid to Samuell Burford in full of the 1s. 6d. in the pound for the loss of the house in the Sheep Street formerly Ashwins as reduced to £300	5	10	—
Paid to Mr Marshall in farther part towards iron, etc.	—	10	—
Paid to Mr Phillips in farther part of hanging bells, etc., by his man Bentley	1	10	—
Feb. 5th. Paid to Mr Masters upon the account of timber for the roof of the tower, etc.	2	—	—
Paid to Mr Masters upon the account of moneys oweing to him upon severall bills and upon account of timber, etc.	18	11	6
	5181	4	1½
Feb. 26th. Paid to Nicholas Paris in farther part for iron, etc.	2	—	—
Paid to William Cattell and Barnett for the carriage of bells from Stratford	—	8	6

	£	s.	d.
Paid to Mr Masters on account of timber, etc.	1	5	—
Paid to Mr Whadcock for cloth which was putt under the side peices of the tower after pitch and tarr putt upon the same	—	12	—
March 17. Paid to Mrs Atterberry for 13c. of coales used about the melting lead for the pinacles upon the tower	—	13	—
18th. Paid to Mr Masters in farther part upon the account aforesaid	1	5	—
20. Paid to him more upon account	—	5	—
25. Paid to him in farther part	2	3	—

1704

April 3rd. Paid to Richard Hancox for 100wt of lead used in the pinacles of the tower	—	14	—
Paid him for takeing down part of the glass and mending it	—	2	6
Paid to John Bullock for brass used about the fanns on the tower	—	16	—
Paid Evan Lloyd for goeing to Stratford for bells	—	2	—
Paid him for goeing to Coleshill, Col. Marriotts, etc. to desire the company of my Lord Digby and others about matters relateing to the church	—	5	—
10th. Paid fees att the Treasury upon procureing her Majesties hand to an order for £1000 being her Majesties gift to the Towne of Warwick and for other orders relateing to the same from the Treasury	20	—	—
Paid to the carryer for the carriage of bells to Stratford the 4th and 1st	—	4	—
8th. Paid to Mr Dunckley and Mr Smith per Mr Lanyon	5	—	—
15. Paid to Mr Dunckley, etc. upon account	6	—	—
8th. Paid to John Bullock for more brass for the fanns	—	2	6

short cast 5s. 5222 16 7½

1704   Receipts

Brought over   5348 8 4½

	£	s.	d.

April 26th. Received of the Rt. Honourable the Lord Brooke by order of Mr Chernock by the hands of Mr Fairefax, being part of his Lordshipps gift towards finishing the Church of St Maryes ... 80 — —

Received of Mr Chernock by the hands of Nicholas Paris, being in full of his Lordshipps gift ... 20 — —

5448 8 $4\frac{1}{2}$

1704   Payments

Brought over ... 5222 16 $7\frac{1}{2}$

April 15th. Paid to labourers in part towards levelling church yard ... 1 6 2

15. Paid to Thomas Masters upon the account of the Trustees ... 2 — —

18th. Paid to Mr Arkesden a bill for copper, etc., for the fanns putt upon the tower ... 4 10 —

Paid to Thomas Copland being for putting up the fanns upon the tower ... — 4 —

21st. Paid to the labourers about levelling in the church yard ... 1 1 —

26. Paid to Nicholas Paris upon the account of the Commissioners ... 5 — —

Paid him for 8 books of leaf gold used about gilding the fanns ... 1 — —

29th. Paid to Richard Williams for stone brought in for the church yard mound[1] ... 6 1 —

Paid to Mr Dunckley and Mr Smith upon account ... 10 — —

Paid to Mr Francis Smith in farther part upon account ... 2 — —

Paid to severall labourers levelling in the church yard ... 1 14 $5\frac{1}{2}$

May 1st. Paid to Mr Marshall upon the account of the Commissioners ... 1 10 —

Paid Hadley, labourer, one day about the foundacion of the church yard mound ... — 1 —

8th. Paid to Nicholas Paris in part towards the clock for the church ... 10 — —

[1] i.e. the boundary wall.

	£	s.	d.

Paid Zachary Sharp upon the account of bell ropes — — 15 —

9th. Paid Robert Knib, etc., 4 dayes work in church yard — — 4 —

Paid Robert Wilson one day there — — 1 —

13th. Paid to Mr Smith and Mr Dunckley in farther part upon account of the Commissioners — 5 — —

Paid to Knib, etc., work in the church yard — — 5 —

19th. Paid to Mr Marshall upon account of the Commissioners — — 5 —

20. Paid to John Glendall a dayes work cleanseing the chancell — — 1 —

Paid to William Smith for lime used about church yard wall — 1 8 —

———

5277 3 3

1704   Receipts

Brought over   5448 8 4½

July 7th. Received then of Mr Norton being in farther part of moneys he ow'd to the Commissioners — 8 — —

8th. Received of Mr Joseph Ainge in part of moneys oweing to the Commissioners — 3 — —

24th. Received of Samuell Ainge in farther part of moneys oweing to the Commissioners — 2 — —

———

5461 8 4½

1704   Payments

Brought over   5277 3 3

Aug. 20. Paid to Mr Dunckley upon the account of the Commissioners — 5 — —

24. Paid to Mr Dunckley and Mr Smith upon ditto account — 6 — —

Paid to Mr Masters upon account of the Commissioners — 5 7 6

June 24. Paid to Richard Williams in part of a bill for stone — 1 10 —

Paid to John Glendall for burying bones, etc., in the church yard — — 3 —

	£	s.	d.
Paid to Nicholas Paris in farther part upon account	1	10	—
Paid to Mr Masters upon account of the Commissioners	—	5	—
July 3rd. Paid to Evan Lloyd for work for the Commissioners	—	2	—
Paid for bricks to Samuell Burford used by Mr Huss about the dialls	—	8	6
8th. Paid to Nicholas Paris upon the account aforesaid	1	10	—
Paid to William Smith for 85 strike of lime used about the church yard wall	2	2	6
Paid to Mr Dunckley and Mr Smith in farther part	6	—	—
Paid to Richard Williams in farther part for stone delivered to the church wall	1	10	—
Paid to the Widow Walker for 41 strike of lime per ditto	1	—	6
14. Paid to George Watts a bill for coale, etc., upon the account of melting lead for the pinacles of the tower	—	9	5
Paid for the carriage of two bells from Gloucester to Stratford	—	8	—
Paid for the carriage of the same to Warwick	—	6	—
19th. Paid Thomas Greenway for hair had by Mr Huss for the use of the church	—	6	6
22nd. Paid to severall labourers levelling in the Church Street and Sheep Street	1	6	6
Paid to Evan Lloyd for ½ a dayes work	—	—	6
29th. Paid to Mr Paris in farther part upon account	2	—	—
Paid to the men in earnest for undertaking the paveing of the streets	—	1	—
	5314	10	2
Paid for two scuttles to be used by the paviors of the street	—	1	2
29th. Paid [ ]¹ Green, etc., in part for their pitching work in the streets about the church	1	—	—
Paid to John Prescott in part towards pibbles² brought in for the pitching the streets and square	1	10	—

¹ Space left blank.   ² Altered from 'pipples', and so on 3 other occasions.

	£	s.	d.
Paid to Mr Dunckley in farther part towards work	2	—	—
Paid to Robert Wilson for 6 dayes work for Commissioners	—	6	—
Paid to Mr Masters upon account of the Commissioners	—	5	—
31st. Paid John Prescott in farther part for pibbles	—	5	—
Paid him more in farther part for ditto	—	5	—
Paid to Mr Marshall upon account of the Commissioners	—	5	—
Paid to John Glendall one day in the church yard	—	1	—
Aug. 1st. Paid for 3 load of pipples from Norton	—	16	6
4th. Paid to Mr Marshall which with the 5s. paid above is £2 5s. for which I have an acquittance	2	—	—
Paid to John Prescott in farther part for pibbles	—	5	—
Paid to Richard Williams in farther part for stone for the church yard mound	—	4	—
5th. Paid to Mr Dunckley in farther part on account	2	10	—
Paid to John Prescott in farther part for pibbles	1	10	—
Paid to John Prescott in farther part	—	1	—
Paid to Richard Green in farther part towards pitching	2	10	—
Paid Robert Wilson for 5 dayes skreening sand, etc.	—	5	—
Paid William Prescott for 6 dayes about ditto	—	6	—
7. Paid for a load of pipples from Norton	—	6	—
Paid John Prescott in farther part	—	—	6
8th and 10. Paid him more in farther part	—	7	6
8th. Paid for a load of pipples from Norton	—	6	—
Paid Evan Lloyd for one weeks work for the Commissioners	—	6	—
12. Paid John Prescott in farther part towards pibbles	3	8	6
Paid for 3 load of pipples from Norton	—	18	—
Paid to Thomas Masters upon account of the Commissioners	2	—	—
	5338	8	4

		£	s.	d.

	£	s.	d.
Brought over	5461	8	$4\frac{1}{2}$

Aug. 19th. Received of the Honourable the Lady Bowyer
being the gift of Sir Henry Puckering dec. towards building the church

	20	—	—

	5481	8	$4\frac{1}{2}$

1704   Payments

	£	s.	d.
Brought over	5338	8	4

Aug. 12th. Paid to Mr Dunckley in farther part upon
account ... 2 10 —

Paid him for 6 dayes work for his boy about
levelling ground, etc., about the church ... — 6 —

Paid for 29 strike of pibbles to Phillip Dale, etc.,
at 3d.$\frac{1}{2}$ per strike ... — 9 $5\frac{1}{2}$

Paid Robert Wilson 5 dayes work about levelling ... — 5 —

Paid to Evan Lloyd 12 dayes work about ditto ... — 12 —

14th. Paid to John Prescott in full for 627 strike of
pibbles laid downe about the church att 3d.$\frac{1}{2}$ ... 1 10 $5\frac{1}{2}$

Paid to the paviors in farther part towards
pitching the streets ... 1 — —

Paid to Mr Phillips by Edward Bentley upon
account of the Commissioners ... — 10 —

Paid to Mr Masters upon the account of the
Commissioners ... 5 — —

Paid to Evan Lloyd 28 dayes work about levelling in the chancell for the paviors. Badson[1] ... 1 8 —

Paid to Robert Wilson for 25 dayes work there ... 1 5 —

Paid to Evan Lloyd and Wilson being there
bargaine for filling up the quarry on the south
side of the church, removeing stone and for
extraordinary work there ... 4 2 —

19th. Paid Phillip Dale for 88 strike of pibbles att 3d. ... 1 2 2

Paid to Mr Dunckley for 2 dayes work, his boy ... — 2 —

Paid to James[2] Green and his sons in further
part for pitching streets ... 2 10 —

Paid to William Smith, limeman, for lime for
the church yard wall, 20 strike ... — 10 —

---

[1] 'Badson' inserted in a space.   [2] Altered from 'Richard'.

	£	s.	d.
Paid to Mr Dunckley in farther part upon account	2	10	—
Paid Robert Wilson for 6 dayes work about levelling	—	6	—
Paid to William Prescott 5 dayes $\frac{1}{2}$ for ditto	—	5	6
Paid to Richard Ward for 7 dayes work about ditto	—	7	—
Paid to Evan Lloyd for 6 dayes work about ditto	—	6	—

1704	5365	4	11
Paid Evan Lloyd for chercoale for to melt lead to fasten the dyall	—	—	8
24th. Paid to John Garfeild for projecting the sun diall and drawing the lines on the same	2	—	—
Paid to Mr Robbinson the 3 guineas order'd him by the Commissioners	3	4	6
Paid a labourer 2 dayes work	—	2	—
Paid to Nicholas Paris by Mr Chernock in part towards the church clock, etc.	20	—	—
26th. Paid to John Hill for pibbles 40 strike	—	11	6
Paid Perry one day filling rubbish, etc.	—	1	—
Paid to Mr Dunckley in farther part	1	10	—
Paid Green pitchers in the streets in farther part	1	10	—
Paid to Dunckleys boy 4 dayes filling rubbish	—	4	—
Paid Robert Wilson 5 dayes and $\frac{1}{2}$ about ditto	—	5	6
Paid Ward, labourer, 6 dayes work	—	6	—
28th. Paid to John Gardner in part for Shrewley stone deliver'd for the use of the church	3	—	—
Paid to Mr Masters on account of the Commissioners the 6th of November last	5	—	—
Paid to Mr Masters the 4th of December last short cast in page (32)[1]	—	5	—
Paid to Mr Masters May 13th not enter'd before	1	—	—
29th. Paid to Samuell Acock in part towards painting the dialls, etc.	6	—	—
Paid to Richard Huss and Phillip Dale for 55 strike of pibbles	—	13	10

[1] See p. 469.

	£	s.	d.
Paid to Mr Marshall upon account of the Commissioners	—	5	—
Paid Zachary Sharp in farther part upon the account of bellropes	1	10	—
Sept. 2nd. Paid to John Prescott in full for 403 strike of pibbles used in the streets att 3d. a strike	5	—	9
Paid him for diggin 7 load of gravell	—	7	—
Paid John Prescott for 18 strike of pibbles	—	4	6
	5421	6	2

1704

	£	s.	d.
Paid to Thomas Masters upon the account of the Trustees	1	—	—
Paid to James Green in farther part towards paveing of the streets	2	10	—
Paid to Richard Ward 6 dayes levelling in the square, etc.	—	6	—
Paid to William Prescott 5 dayes there	—	5	—
Paid to Sherborn of Norton 3 load of pibbles	—	19	6
Paid for mending the sckuttles used about paveing	—	—	2
Paid to Mr Dunckley in farther part upon account	1	—	—
Paid Robert Wilson for 6 dayes work	—	6	—
Paid Evan Lloyd 6 dayes work about ditto	—	6	—
Paid to Phillip Dale in full for 191 strike of pibbles	2	7	9
Paid to Thomas Copland as he paid for the use of a stall cloth used about the dialls	—	1	—
9. Paid to Richard Ward for 4 dayes work and ½ about the streets	—	4	6
Paid William Prescott 8 dayes work	—	8	—
Paid to Mr Dunckley in farther part	—	10	—
Paid the paviors boy keeping teams off the pavement	1	10	1
16th. Paid Sherborn of Hampton for a load of pibbles	—	6	—
Paid John Webb for two load of pibbles	—	13	—
Paid to the paviors viz. James Green in farther part for paveing	3	10	—
Paid to Mr Masters in farther part	1	5	—
Paid for flakes[1] used in doeing of the dialls	—	5	10
Paid for a load of pibbles from Hampton	—	6	6

[1] Hurdles. The abstract of the account has 'for flacks used about sheltering the dials'.

	£	s.	d.
Paid for two load of pibbles from thence	—	13	—
Paid to Mr Dunckley in farther part	1	10	—
Paid for 3 load of pibbles from Norton, to Sherborne[1]	1	1	—

1704 — 5442 10 6

16	Paid to Robert Wilson for 5 dayes work	—	5	—
	Paid to Richard Ward 5 dayes	—	5	—
	Paid to Samuell Acock in farther part for dialls, etc.	3	—	—
23rd.	Paid for the carriage of sand, 6 load	—	6	—
	Paid to Richard Ward 6 dayes work	—	6	—
	Paid to James Green the paviors in farther part	2	3	—
	Paid to Mr Dunckley in farther part	2	3	—
	Paid to Thomas Masters in farther part	1	1	6
29th.	Paid to Mr Marshall a bill for takeing downe and setting up the iron gates	—	19	—
30th.	Paid Robert Wilson for 12 days work	—	12	—
	Paid William Prescott for 15 dayes and ½ work	—	15	6
	Paid to Richard Ward for 6 dayes work	—	6	—
	Paid to Thomas Copland for 17 dayes work makeing scaffold in order for to paint dialls and for takeing down the same[2]	1	2	8
	Paid for the use of two hair cloths used about sheltering the sun[3] dialls	—	2	—
	Paid to Mr Dunckley in farther part	2	—	—

5458 7 2

1704   Receipts

	£	s.	d.
Brought over	5481	8	4½
Aug. 29th. Received of Mr Thomas Young being in part of the £60 lent unto Sergt. Hadley upon bond	50	—	—
Oct. 12th. Received of Mr Knight of Slapton being by order of Mr Wilcox, Surveyor Generall of the Queens Woods, in part of the £1000 her Majestyes gift to the Towne of Warwick	400	—	—

5931 8 4½

---

[1] 'to Sherborne' [the carter] added in a space.
[2] '5 dayes, 12 dayes' added in the margin.   [3] 'sun' interlineated over a caret.

		£	s.	d.
1704	Payments			
	Brought over	5458	7	2
Oct. 2.	Paid to Mr Marshall in further part	—	10	—
7.	Paid to John Hill for a load of pibbles	—	5	6
	Paid to John Prescott for 80 strike of pibbles used in Swann Lane against Red Lyon wall	1	15	—
	Paid to Robert Wilson 3 dayes work there	—	3	—
	Paid Richard Ward for 2 dayes work there	—	2	—
	Paid to Mr Francis Smith upon account	5	—	—
	Paid to Mr Masters upon account of Commissioners	4	—	—
	Paid Robert Wilson 1 day and $\frac{1}{2}$ in Swan Lane	—	1	6
21st.	Paid to Mr Masters upon account of the Commissioners	2	—	—
	Paid to Mr Marshall upon ditto account	2	—	—
	Paid to Mr Dunckley upon ditto account	2	10	—
23rd.	Paid to Samuell Burford for 66 ft. of ground taken from him to enlarge the Sheep Street	1	13	—
28th.	Paid to Nicholas Paris upon account of Commissioners	3	—	—
	Paid to Mr Masters upon ditto account	10	—	—
	Paid to Mr Nicholls in part of a bill for the Commissioners for pitch, etc.	5	—	—
Nov. 3rd.	Paid to Samuell Acock in part of his bill	10	—	—
4.	Paid to Mr Dunckley upon account	2	10	—
Oct. 30.	Paid to Richard Green, pavior, for pitching in the Swan Lane against Red Lyon wall	—	17	—
	Paid Zachyry Sharp for bell ropes in full	—	5	—
	Paid to Mr Chesley which is the gift of the Commissioners towards building his ground in the Square, by order of Court of the 31st of March 1704[1]	25	—	—
31st.	Paid to Mr Phillips by Thomas Wall in farther part towards hanging bells	3	—	—
	Paid to Mr Marshall upon account	—	10	—
Nov. 1st.	Paid to Robert Taylor the 1s. 6d. in the pound for the loss of the house in the Butts burnt downe in the late fire in the possession of			

---

[1] 'by order ... 1704' added in a space in another hand.

	£	s.	d.
Henry Wilson as the same is reduced to £25 by order of Court of the 21st of September last	1	17	6
	5539	11	8

1704	Receipts	£	s.	d.
	Brought over	5931	8	4½
Nov.	Received att the Church of St Maryes for pews sold in the said church for the use of the Trustees, in part	78	10	—
23.	Received of Mr Young in farther part of the £60 lent unto Serjt. Hadley	7	—	—
	Received of Mr Jemmatt and the Steward of the Hospitall for 2 seates in St Maryes Church	4	10	—
		6021	8	4½

1704	Payments	£	s.	d.
	Brought over	5539	11	8
Nov.	Paid to Smith, limeman, for a quarter of lime for the church yard mound wall	—	4	—
8th.	Paid to Samuell Acock upon account of the Commissioners bill	1	—	—
	Paid to Moses Hollaway for goeing to Sir William Underhills and other Commissioners to desire their companyes at the Court	—	2	6
11.	Paid to Mr Dunckley upon account	1	10	—
	Paid to Mr Acock upon account of his bill	5	—	—
	Paid to Mr Masters upon account	3	5	—
16.	Paid to Mr Masters upon account of the Commissioners by Mr Hands, maulster	42	10	—
18th.	Paid to Thomas Mayo in full of the 1s. 6d. in the pound for the loss of houses burnt downe in the Joyce Pool	—	16	—
	Paid to Mr Dunckley and Mr Smith in farther part upon account of the Commissioners	100	—	—
16th.	Paid to Richard Williams per Henry Smith in full for carriage of stone for the church wall	5	—	—
	Paid to Thomas Geasey in full for dayes works			

	£	s.	d.
for the Commissioners about cleaning tower floors, etc.	—	5	—
18. Paid to Nicholas Paris upon account	2	—	—
Paid to John Prescott for 5 load of sand laid down in the Swan Lane	—	3	4
Paid Zachary Sharpe for cords had by Nicholas Paris for the church clock	—	13	—
23rd. Paid to Mr Rudhall upon account of casting bells, etc., this being in full of monies due to him except £10	28	7	7
25th. Paid to Mr Masters in part for the stuffe provided for the stalls in the chancell per order	20	—	—
Paid to Thomas Masters upon account, this in acquitance of the 23rd December[1]	—	5	—
26th. Paid to Marshall upon account of work, etc.	1	—	—
25th. Paid to Nicholas Paris upon account of the clock, etc.	5	—	—

	5756	13	1

1704	Receipts			
Brought over		6021	8	4½
Dec. 8th. Received of Mr Fetherston sen. for his part of a seate in St Maryes Church		3	—	—
9th. Received of the Rt. Honourable the Lord Brooke by Mr Chernock for seates in the said church		28	10	—
Received of Mr Edward Norton and Mr Rogers for a seate in the church		6	10	—
Received of Mr Cumming for a seate in the said church		6	—	—
13. Received of Joshua Perks and [ ][2] Reppingall for a seate in the church		1	5	—

	6066	13	4½

1704	Payments			
Brought over		5756	13	1

---

[1] 'this ... December' added in a space in another hand.
[2] Space left blank.

	£	s.	d.
Dec. 2nd. Paid to Robert Wilson for 6 dayes work about setting up posts for trees in the church yard	—	6	—
Paid to Thomas Copland for 4 dayes work about the tower in putting up scaffolds for to cutt the inscription, etc.	—	5	4
Paid Samuell Acock upon account of his bill	3	—	—
5th. Paid to Henry Smith a bill for the carriage of stone from Shrewley quarry to the church, 20 load and 6 ft at 3s. a load	3	—	11
Paid to him a bill for carriage of rubbish from the church, etc., and for sand laid downe for the pavement	9	16	—
4th. Paid to Mr Lane being a bill of his for repaireing the chancell	47	—	—
Memorandum the summ of £15 charged paid to Mr Lane att the other end of the book in the account of chancell work is to be towards Mr Lane's next bill upon the account of the Commissioners £15.			
Paid to William Wright, chandler, a bill for pitch, tarr and tallow for the tower, etc.	2	8	—
Paid to Mr Huss by Serjt. Harris in farther part of his bill about repaireing monuments, etc.	4	1	—
Paid to Mr Lane being in farther part of his next bill	3	8	—
Paid to Thomas Copland 4 dayes and ½ about makeing scaffolds to hang up curtaines between the chancell	—	6	—
Paid to Thomas Wright about the same work 13 dayes and ½	—	12	3
Paid for chercoale to melt lead to fasten irons in for to hang curtaines	—	—	2
Paid to James Green in full for work about pitching about the tower	1	6	10
Paid to Richard Ward for 10 dayes work about helping ditto	—	8	4
	5832	11	11

1704	Receipts			
Brought over		6066	13	4½

	£	s.	d.

Jan. 20th. Received of Mr Robert Heath for his seate in the Church of St Maryes — 7 — —

Received of John Evitts in farther part for Mr Young of the £60 lent unto Serjt. Hadley — 2 — —

6075 13 4½

Payments

	£	s.	d.
Brought over	5832	11	11

Dec. Paid for digging 4 load of gravell for the pavement about the tower — — 2 —

22nd. Paid for a parcell of pibbles to Mr Chesley bought of him for pavement under the tower — — 16 —

Paid to Mr Dunckley for 30 strike of pibbles — — 7 6

Paid to him for horse hyre to Oxford to the Bishopp about the faculty for fixing the pulpit — — 4 6

Paid to Thomas Wright for 6 dayes work about levelling the ground under tower and setting up posts, etc. — — 7 —

Paid to Thomas Masters upon the account of the Commissioners — 2 — —

Paid to John Burton by order of Commissioners being to be in part — 1 10 —

23. Paid to Richard Williams a bill for stone laid downe to be used in the church yard mound — 1 15 9

Paid to William Smith in part for stone steps to be used about the font and att the church doors — 1 10 —

26. Paid to [   ]¹ Butler a bill for work about helping downe bells, etc., to put them in order — — 10 —

Paid to Richard Ward ½ a dayes work about removeing rubbish — — — 5

Jan. 2nd. Paid Samuell Acock upon account of the Commissioners — 1 — —

Paid to Thomas Standish for the carriage of trees that are sett in the church yard [   ]²

12th. Paid to Mr Rudhall in full of moneys due to him from the Commissioners about casting bells, etc. — 10 — —

---

¹ Space left blank.   ² Sum of money left blank.

	£	s.	d.
31st. Paid the Widow Farr for a lock for the door att the bottom of the tower staires	—	8	—
Feb. 2nd. Paid to Mr George Watts for horse hyre to London and to Mr Knights to receive £400 of the Queens money, part of her Majestyes gift to the Towne of Warwick, etc.	—	10	—
Paid him for ale that was allow'd att the putting up the fanns upon the pinacles of the tower	—	1	6
	5853	14	7
2nd. Paid to Mr Phillips by his man upon account of hanging the bells, etc.	1	—	—
3rd. Paid to Mr Phillips upon account aforesaid by the hands of Mr Deakins the Lord Coventry's steward	17	10	—
Paid to the apparator for bringing the faculty about fixing pulpit, etc.[1]	—	1	—
Paid to Marshall upon account of the Trustees	—	10	—
Paid to Richard Ward one dayes work about removeing rubbish, etc., from the tower	—	1	—
5th. Paid to Ward more for 13 dayes and ½ helping the pavior about pitching under the tower	—	11	3
Paid to James Green, pavior for pitching under the tower and about it	1	6	6
3rd. Paid to Samuell Acock upon account of the Commissioners bill for work	2	3	—
Paid to Mr Lane upon account of his next bill, paid it him att the Mayors Parlour[2]	2	—	—
8th. Paid to Mr Gardner for horse hyre to Worcester about the faculty for fixing pulpit, etc.	—	5	—
9. Paid to Mr Masters upon account	—	5	—
10th. Paid to Mr Paris being for the great bell claper made new	2	3	—
Paid to William Smith in further part of a bill for the stepps about the font and church doors	3	10	—
12. Paid to Mr Masters upon account	—	10	—
15th. Paid to Mr Huss being sent by Walter Grascome to be paid to Jonathan Reading for his use to Coventry in part of moneys oweing to him	7	10	—

[1] 'about . . . etc.' interlineated over a caret.
[2] 'paid . . . Parlour' added in a space.

	£	s.	d.

Paid to the pavior James Green a dayes work pitching a gutter below the tower in Church Street — £— 1 6

17. Paid to Mr Dunckley upon account of the Commissioners — 2 — —

Paid to Nicholas Paris upon account — 2 — —

Paid to Mr Chettle per the apparitor for the faculty, etc. obtained from the Court at Worcester for fixing pulpit, etc. — 3 12 —

5900 13 10

1704/5 **Receipts**

Brought over — 6075 13 4½

Received formerly of Mr Henry Heath att the Woolpack for two seates in the church — 5 10 —

Feb. 13th. Received of Thomas Masters being in full for the £100 lent him — 50 — —

6131 3 4½

1704/5 **Payments**

Brought over — 5900 13 10

Feb. 17. Paid to William Smith by his apprentice in farther part for the stepps aforesaid — 1 — —

Paid to Thomas Masters upon account of work, etc. — 50 — —

Paid to Evan Lloyd for 27 dayes work and a half about helping in the streets when the same were paved, the same not enter'd before[1] — 1 7 6

17. Paid to him 5 dayes when he went to London for the bill upon Mr Knight of Slapton of £400, part of the gift of Queen Ann, charged as received on the 12th day of August last — — 5 —

Paid him for horse hyre to Lord Digbys — — 1 6

Paid Evan Lloyd expences to London when he went for the aforesaid bill — — 11 9

Paid to Samuell Paris for horse hyre to London with Evan Lloyd when he went with the

[1] 'October' written in the margin against this item.

	£	s.	d.

Decree Booke to have it sign'd by Lord Brooke,
etc. — — 10 —

Paid to Evan Lloyd being a bill to the 7th of December for 20 dayes work about makeing scaffolds for to make the inscripcions about the tower, cleaning clock roome, digging holes for to sett trees, scaffolding in the chancell, etc. — 1 — —

Paid him 2 dayes for horse hyre to Lord Digbys and other Commissioners — — 2 —

Paid Evan Lloyd for 2 jorneys to Worcester and one to Oxford, himself horse hyre and charges — 1 10 —

Paid to him for his own charges, his trouble and horse charges to and from London with the Decree Book to gett Commissioners to sign it — 1 1 6

Paid him goeing to some of the Commissioners and charges — — 2 9

Evan Lloyd his bill comes to 3 16 3.

Paid Evan Lloyd a bill being for 18 dayes about setting up posts and railes, scaffolding in the chancell for the curtaine, and levelling in the church porch — — 18 —

Paid him for 4 dayes setting up the gibletts[1] under tower and ½, about digging the foundacions of the church yard walls 4 dayes, and about levelling the church yard 4 dayes, in all 12 dayes and ½ — — 12 6

| | 5959 | 16 | 4 |

Receipts

Brought over — 6131 3 4½

Brought over as received att the other end of the booke of the Corporation[2] — 50 — —

| | 6181 | 3 | 4½ |

Payments

Brought over — 5959 16 4

[1] The abstract of the account has 'gibbets', probably cranes or pullies.

[2] See pp. 506–7.

	£	s.	d.
Brought over as paid att the other end of the book being chancell work[1]	201	14	7
Brought over as paid for severall matters att the other end of the booke	10	12	9
Paid to Marshall upon account of the Trustees per his wife	—	5	—
Feb. 24th. Paid to Mr Masters in farther part towards stuffs bought for to make the stalls in the chancell	10	—	—
Paid to William Smith being in farther part for stepps aforesaid	1	—	—
Paid to Thomas Masters upon account of etc.	1	—	—
25th. Paid to Marshall by Mr Smith upon account	1	—	—
Paid to Samuell Acock in farther part upon account, etc.	6	—	—
Paid to Thomas Standish for the carriage of trees that were sett in the church yard	—	12	—
March 2nd. Paid to Marshall upon account	—	2	6
3rd. Paid to Henry Mellars a bill for ceileing the belfrey floor	2	7	—
Paid to William Smith which with £1 10s. paid the 23rd of December, £3 10s. the 10th of February, £1 the 17th of February and £1 the 24th of February is in full for a bill of £8 14s. for stepps att the font, steps att the middle door and south door, and for bordering stones under the tower in the pavement	1	14	—
6. Paid to Mr Masters in farther part upon account	—	10	—
Paid to Mr Robbinson for 10 ew trees that were sett in the church yard and charges in fetching of them	3	8	—
3rd. Paid to Mr Dunckley in part of a bill	3	—	—
8. Paid to John Glendall for 2 dayes work in the church yard and a half day	—	2	6
	6203	4	8

1704[/5]   Receipts
Brought over   6181 3 4½

[1] See p. 508.

		£	s.	d.

Feb. 21st. Received by Mr Newsham of Sir Richard Hoar in farther part of the £1000 given by her Majesty to the Towne of Warwick ... 200 — —

Received by ditto of Mr Bavand being some arrears of brief monies received by him ... 20 — —

6401 3 4½

1704[/5]	Payments			

Brought over ... 6203 4 8

March 8th. Paid to Mr Paris by Mr Crow in farther part upon account ... 3 10 —

Paid Mr Marshall upon account ... — 15 —

14. Paid John Prescott for getting 6 load of gravell to spread about the church upon the pavement ... — 4 —

Paid to Mr Marshall upon account of the Commissioners the 15s. above and ... 1 10 —

16. Paid to Mr Masters upon account ... 1 — —

Paid to the Widow Walker a bill for lime used about the church wall ... 1 7 6

Paid to James Green for 6 dayes work about new ramming the pavement and mending some part of it ... — 10 —

Paid to William Dawson, labourer, 6 dayes about the same work ... — 6 —

Paid Robert Wiggs one days work in the church yard ... — 1 —

Paid John Marriott 2 dayes work there ... — 2 —

Paid to John Prescott 2 dayes work there ... — 2 —

Paid to Thomas Lucas 3 dayes work there ... — 3 —

Paid to Evan Lloyd 2 dayes work there ... — 2 —

Paid to John Glendall 2 dayes work there ... — 2 —

31st. Paid to Mr Dunckley in full for makeing the urns upon the pillars by the church yard gates ... 4 10 —

31st and Paid to John Dreyton a bill for gravell and car-
March 7th. riage to the walk in the church yard ... 1 4 —

Paid for the gravell which was spread about the pavement by the church ... — 5 —

	£	s.	d.

Aprill 6th. Paid to Mr Robbinson for a ew tree sett in the church yard ... 1 — —

1705 ... 6219 15 2

    7. Paid to Nicholas Wrothwell for John Gardner being for Shrewley stone brought in for the church yard mound ... 3 5 6

Paid to Nicholas Paris per his wife per Trustees upon account of work ... 3 — —

Paid to Francis Dunn 2 dayes work spreading gravell in the church yard walk ... — 2 —

  10. Paid to Mr Marshall upon account of the Commissioners ... 1 — —

18th. Paid to Mr Phillips upon account ... 3 — —

Paid to William Allen and another man for bringing home the last ew tree bought by Mr Robbinson ... — 3 —

Paid to Mr Marshall upon account ... — 2 6

Paid to Thomas Masters upon account of Trustees ... 1 — —

21st. Paid to Mr Masters upon account of etc. ... 2 3 —

28th. Paid to Evan Lloyd 6 dayes about the church yard ... — 6 —

May 1st. Paid to Mr Masters and Kington in part towards the new pulpitt ... 2 3 —

5th. Paid to Mr Masters upon account ... 1 1 6

11th. Paid to Mr Paris upon account ... 2 — —

12th. Paid to Mr Dunckley a bill for takeing downe the old glass in the chancell window and pointing the same new, and for pulling down the old wall att the chancell and the scaffold att the chancell window ... 3 17 —

Paid Robert Wilson 6 dayes levelling in the church yard ... — 6 —

1705 ... 6243 4 8

Paid to Francis Dunn 6 dayes about levelling at the church yard ... — 6 —

Paid Evan Lloyd 2 dayes about ditto ... — 2 —

19th. Paid to Robert Wilson for 6 dayes levelling in the church yard ... — 6 —

	£	s.	d.
Paid John Glendall for 3 dayes work about ditto	—	3	—
Paid by Mr Newsham to Mr Hurlbert for Mr Nost, stone cutter, for the font sett up in St Maryes Church	30	—	—
Paid for 15 firr trees bought att London by Mr Newsham for the church yard att 2s. each	1	10	—
Paid to Mr Whadcock his bill for the curtaines, rodds and rings for the same curtaines between the church and chancell	17	1	6
Paid for Mr Hunt 53 bushell of pibbles bought and used about the pavement by the church	—	13	—
22nd. Paid to Thomas Masters and Nicholas Kington towards work about the pulpitt by Thomas Jackson	4	—	—
June 2nd. Paid to Evan Lloyd for 16 dayes work in levelling in the church yard	—	16	—
Paid Robert Wilson for 10 dayes work there	—	10	—
Paid to John Glendall for 5 dayes and ½ there	—	5	6
Paid to Mr Lane upon account of the church	10	—	—
9th. Paid to Mr Dunckley in part towards the new work in railes and ballasters of stone on the side walls of the chancell	6	—	—

	£	s.	d.
	6314	17	8

		£	s.	d.
1705	Receipts			
Brought over		6401	3	4½
Received being 15s. 6d. twice charged as paid to William Smith for lime att the other end of the book in the account of chancell work[1]		—	15	6
		6401	18	10½

		£	s.	d.
1705	Payments			
Brought over		6314	17	8
June 12th. Paid to John Hadley being order'd to be paid to Richard Hadley his father for 273 foot of ground taken from him to enlarge the Sheep				

[1] See p. 507.

	£	s.	d.

Street, as by Order of Court of the 30th of March last — 6 16 6

Short cast in page 47[1] — — 5 —

6321 19 2

1705   Receipts

Brought over — 6401 18 10$\frac{1}{2}$

June 15th Received of the Rt. Honorable the Lord Digby, being his Lordship's gift towards business about the church — 30 — —

6431 18 10$\frac{1}{2}$

1705   Payments

Brought over — 6321 19 2

June 20th. Paid to Mr Bendish which, with £20 paid him the 10th Aprill 1704, is £30 upon account of fees due upon getting her Majestyes gift of £1000, this paid by Mr William Newsham — 10 — —

Paid to Mr William Newsham charges in waiteing on Surveyor Generall and Mr Bendish about the Queen's gift — — 1 11

15th. Paid to Thomas Masters upon account — 3 4 6

17. Paid to Mr Paris for leaf gold to gild the iron work over the canopy of the pulpitt — 1 13 —

Paid to Mr Lane upon the account of work done — 80 — —

July 14. Paid to Mr Dunckley upon account of rayles and ballasters — 5 — —

17. Paid to Mr Paris upon account — 5 — —

21st. Paid more to Mr Paris upon account — 5 — —

Paid to Mr Masters upon account — 2 — —

Paid to Samuell Acock upon account — — 10 —

Paid to William Smith for lime per rayles, etc., about the chancell — — 4 —

Paid to Mr Masters and Kington by Thomas Jackson upon account of pulpitt — 6 17 —

30th. Paid to Richard Williams in part for stone for rayles and ballasters about chancell — 5 — —

[1] See pp. 487–8.

		£	s.	d.
28th. Paid to Mr Masters upon account		1	1	6
Paid to Mr Dunckley upon account of rayles, etc.		2	3	—
Paid to William Smith for lime for ditto		—	8	—
Aug. 1st. Paid to Mr Paris upon account		10	—	—
Paid to Mr Phillips upon account per Mr Whadcocke[1]		1	1	6
11th. Paid to Mr Dunckley upon account of rayles		5	—	—
Paid to Mr Paris upon account		5	—	—
		6471	3	7

1705   Receipts

	£	s.	d.
Brought over	6431	18	$10\frac{1}{2}$
July 18th. Received of Sir Richard Hoar being an order drawn upon him for £150 in further part of the Queen's gift lying in his hands	150	—	—
	6581	18	$10\frac{1}{2}$

1705   Payments

	£	s.	d.
Brought over	6471	3	7
Aug. 15th. Paid to Mr Masters per Mr Norton upon account	2	12	—
3rd. Paid to the Widow Walker for lime for rayles and ballusters	—	12	—
4th. Paid to Mr Acock upon account of work	1	—	—
Paid to Robert Wilson 2 dayes and $\frac{1}{2}$ work about levelling in the church yard	—	2	6
18th. Paid to Mr Masters upon account	3	—	—
25. Paid to Mr Dunckley upon account of rayles	6	—	—
Paid to Evan Lloyd for watering trees in the church yard, and for a day and half about the ladder to reach the roof of the church to make a hole in the arch for to put in the iron to carry the canopy	—	6	—
Sept. 8. Paid to Mr Dunckley upon account of rayles	5	—	—
Paid to Robert Wilson for watering trees in the church yard 19 nights att 3d. a night and 3d. over for one other night	—	5	—

[1] 'per Mr Whadcocke' added in a space.

	£	s.	d.
Paid to William Smith for lime for rayles and ballasters about the chancel	—	6	—
15. Paid to Mr Dunckley upon account	1	—	—
Paid to Mr Masters upon account	2	7	—
13th. Paid to Mr Paris upon account	4	—	—
14th. Paid to Samuell Acock upon account by Cole[1]	2	—	—
Oct. 6th. Paid to Mr Masters upon account	1	—	—
Paid to Mr Dunckley upon account	1	—	—
	6501	14	1

Receipts

Brought over	6581	18	10½
Received of William Colmore, Esq., being his gift towards rebuilding the church and repaireing the chancel of St Maryes in Warwick	10	—	—
Received of William Colmore, Esq., for his seats in the Church of St Marys	15	10	—
	6607	8	10½

Memorandum to be deducted 10s. which I have over charged my self with in the summ of £78 10s. charged received for seates the [   ]² day of November last, Mrs Adams being charged for her seate in that summ £4 when her seate is valued but att £3 10s. and soe sold for.   — 10 —

6606 18 10½

1705   Payments

Brought over	6501	14	1
Oct. 9th. Paid to Samuell Acock upon account by Mr Cummins	7	—	—
Paid to Mr Dunckley more	1	10	—
Paid to Robert Wilson 10 dayes levelling in the church yard and putting up the canopy in the church (1 day and ½)	—	10	—

¹ 'by Cole' added in a space in another hand.
² Space left blank. See p. 479.

	£	s.	d.
Paid to Evan Lloyd 5 dayes and ½ levelling in the church yard	—	5	6
Nov. 22. Paid for a ew tree to sett in the church yard	—	5	—
23. Paid for another ew tree to sett there	—	5	—
Paid to Mr Masters upon account of the work done by bill, etc.	2	—	—
Paid to Mr Dunckley upon account of rayles, etc.	3	10	—
Dec. 1st. Paid for land and water carriage of a bell from Warwick to Gloucester, etc.	—	15	—
Paid to Mr Richardson for weighing the said bell	—	1	—
Paid to Mr Smith and Mr Dunckley by William Colmore, Esq.	10	—	—
Paid to Francis Badson by Mr Colmore upon account of paving the church	2	—	—
Paid to Mr Kington upon account of pulpitt	4	—	—
Paid to Mr Marshall not enter'd before, by his wife	—	10	—
30 Oct. 1703. Paid to Mr Smith and Mr Dunckley upon account	10	—	—
27 Nov. 1703. Paid to them more upon account	5	—	—
	6554	5	7

1705 Receipts	£	s.	d.
Brought over	6606	18	10½
Sept. 6th. Received of Mr Simpkins for a seate in the church	2	5	—
March 1st. Received of Mrs Stanton for her seate in the church	7	—	—
	6616	3	10½

1705 Payments	£	s.	d.
Brought over	6554	5	7
Dec. 8th. Paid to Evan Lloyd for 3 dayes work about takeing down the scaffolds from the topp of the tower and other work	—	3	—
Paid to Thomas Wright for the same	—	3	—

	£	s.	d.
Paid to Robert Kington 3 dayes about the same	—	3	—
12. Paid to Mr Richardson for crabb tree and leather used in fitting the bell clapers	—	4	6
Paid to Francis Badson by Mr Colmore, I haveing charged but £2 before when the same should have been £4	2	—	—
Paid for a ew tree bought by Mr Robbinson of one Rawlins of Stoneleigh	—	5	—
Paid for 2 ew trees bought by ditto of Mr Fetherstons man of Packwood	—	8	—
Paid Mr Robbinsons horse hyre for the same	—	1	—
15. Paid to the Widow Walker for lime used about the rayles and ballasters round the topp of the chancell	—	3	—
24th. Paid to Richard Williams in farther part for stone for railes and ballasters aforesaid	3	6	—
Jan. 15th. Paid to Nicholas Paris upon account by John Fulks	1	1	6
21st. Paid to the Widow Standish for the carriage of the font	2	6	—
Nov. 28th. Paid to Nicholas Kington a bill formerly on account	1	1	—
Feb. 10th. Paid to Richard Williams by Henry Smith in full for a bill for stone as aforesaid	6	6	—
Paid Henry Smith for the carriage of ew trees	—	10	—
Paid to John Sharley upon account of his loss given in by the fire of £15 which was left out of the book of losses by Mr Lanyon's mistake	2	—	—
23rd. Paid John Glendall for a dayes work setting trees	—	—	10
28. Paid to Evan Lloyd for 4 dayes work about fenceing the trees in the church yard	—	4	—
March 2nd. Paid to Mr Dunckley being for poles cutt to fence trees with	—	5	6
9. Paid to Mr Evitts and Mr Robbinson for ew trees bought and sett in the church yard	3	9	—
	6578	5	11

1706   Receipts

Brought over   6616   3 $10\frac{1}{2}$

	£	s.	d.
June 5th. Received of Mr Arkesden, etc., for a seate in the church	3	—	—
Received of Thomas Newsham, Esq., being for one half of a seate in the church	3	5	—
Received of the Corporacion of Warwick for their seates in the church	29	—	—
	6651	8	$10\frac{1}{2}$

1705[/6] Payments			
Brought over	6578	5	11
March 16. Paid to Mr Masters by the Widow Farr upon account	10	—	—
Paid to the Widow Farr for a lock for the steeple door	—	8	—
23rd. Paid to the Church Wardens of the parish of St Marys in full of their right to a toft of poor's ground in the High Street, mencioned in a decree made to Mr Tarver beareing date the 8th day of November 1704	7	6	10
Paid to the Church Wardens of the parish of St Nicholas being in full as order'd by the decree before mencioned	7	6	10
1706			
26th. Paid to Mr Phillips in full for the Commissioners about the bells hanging	—	10	3
Paid to Mr Phillips in full for the Commissioners being allowed him by order of Court the 30th of March 1704 as Surveyor	1	10	—
Paid to Serjt. Parker for his oppinion about matters relateing to the burnt ground	1	1	6
16th. Paid to Mr Dunckley upon account of the work done	5	—	—
24th. Paid to Mr Dunckley in farther part upon account	10	—	—
30th. Paid to Mr Corpson 4s. in the £1 for his loss of £15 (as reduced) by the late fire	3	—	—
Paid to Mr Marshall in full of all accounts between him and the Commissioners and Nicholas Paris as partners	3	15	—
May 10th. Paid to Mr Paris upon account of the Trustees	6	—	—

	£	s.	d.
13. Paid to Mr Dunckley in part upon account	6	—	—
18. Paid to Mr Paris upon account	10	—	—
Paid Samuell Burford for pibbles used about paveing the streets	—	1	6
June 15. Paid to Mr Paris upon account being a note under his hand 1st March 1700	5	—	—
Paid to Mr Paris more upon account	20	—	—
22nd. Paid to Mr Horton for Sir William Wilson in part for work done by Sir William's men about the church	5	6	—
Paid Richard Crook a bill for things used about the bellfrey for the ropes to goe through	—	5	—
	6680	16	10

1706	Receipts			
Brought over		6651	8	$10\frac{1}{2}$
July Received of Sir Richard Hoar being in full of the Queen's gift of £1000 given to the Towne of Warwick		250	—	—
		6901	8	$10\frac{1}{2}$

1706	Payments			
Brought over		6680	16	10
July 1st. Paid to Thomas Copland for work about the pinacles, building scaffolds, etc.		—	15	—
Paid Evan Lloyd for work about ditto		—	14	8
Paid to Robert Williams for work the same		—	2	8
Paid to Thomas Ward for elm boards bought for the scaffolds		—	8	—
Paid Mr Greeneway for 42 poles for the scaffolds		—	3	6
5. Paid to Nicholas Paris upon account		1	—	—
26th. Paid to Mr William Smith upon account		3	—	—
Paid to Capt. Williams for a jorney to Leicester formerly to apprehend a person that went about as a cheat relateing to the briefes		—	12	—
Paid to Mr William Smith, etc., by Mr Masters upon account of masons work		3	—	—

	£	s.	d.

1705[/6]

	£	s.	d.
Feb. 27. Paid to Mr Wilcox, Surveyor Generall, his fee for the Queen's gift, etc.	20	—	—
March 12th. Paid to Mr Bendish his fee for the same	5	—	—
Paid fees in passing the Surveyors account before the two Auditors relateing to the Queens gift	1	6	8
Aug. 17. Paid to Mr Masters upon account	5	—	—
21st. Paid to Mr Masters upon account of stalls in the chancell for to pay for timber	20	—	—
Oct. 2. Paid to Mr Smith and Mr Dunckley per Thomas Wall on account	4	—	—
12. Paid to Mr Masters (per Kington) upon account of stalls	1	—	—
Nov. 11. Paid to Mr Kington in farther part for ditto stalls	1	5	—
Paid to Mr Henry Jephcott being a bill of £10 8s. 6d. for rayles and balasters to goe round the communion table and £1 1s. 6d. for Mr Hurlberts trouble in buying the same	12	—	—
15. Paid to Nicholas Kington for raysing the pulpitt desk	—	5	—
13th. Paid to Nicholas Kington upon account of stalls	1	—	—
Paid to Thomas Masters upon account of ditto	2	—	—
23. Paid to Thomas Masters and Nicholas Kington in farther part	10	—	—
	6773	9	4

1706[/7]

	£	s.	d.
Jan. 3rd. Paid to Thomas Masters upon account of stalls	2	—	—
4. Paid to Bevor Standish for the carriage of planks and rayles and balasters for communion table	3	3	6
Paid to Mr Masters and Kington upon account of stalls	8	—	—
27. Paid to Evan Lloyd for 17 dayes work and ½ in the chancell	—	17	6
Feb. 8. Paid to Nicholas Kington upon account of stalls	2	—	—
12. Paid to Mr Masters upon the same account	1	—	—
Paid to Samuell Acock upon account of a bill	1	—	—

		£	s.	d.
15.	Paid to Mr Masters upon account of the stalls	1	—	—
17.	Paid to Masters and Kington upon the same account	2	—	—
20.	Paid to Mr Nicholles being for goods fetcht by Mr Dunckley and Mr Smith's order and us'd about the church. Note this bill to be settled whether it be the Commissioners account or the workmen's own (the bill come to £9 15s.)	4	15	—
March 1st.	Paid to Mr Masters and Kington in farther part towards the stalls	2	—	—
22nd.	Paid to Mr Masters more upon the same account	2	—	—
	Paid to Nicholas Kington upon the same account	—	10	—
	Paid to Evan Lloyd ½ a day in the chancell	—	—	6

1707

		£	s.	d.
April 21st.	Paid to Nicholas Kington upon account of stalls	1	—	—
May 3rd.	Paid to Richard Williams being for stone for the urns	—	6	3
5.	Paid to Marshall upon account of iron to be us'd about the urns	1	—	—
	Paid to Mr Dunckley upon account of the urns about the chancell, viz. of £9 15s.	2	10	—
10.	Paid to Mr Paris for iron cramps about the tower viz. in fastning the pinacles	3	2	—
	Paid to Mr Masters the 22nd of Dec. 1705 by Simpkins upon account of work. March 9th.[1]	2	10	—
24.	Paid to Mr Dunckley in farther part about the urns	5	—	—

	£	s.	d.
	6819	4	1

1707   Receipts

		£	s.	d.
	Brought over	6901	8	10½
	Received of Mrs Paris for part of a seat in the church next to Gardner's	2	10	—
May 26th.	Received of the executrix of Mr Hodges dec. late Register of the Diocess of Worcester upon			

[1] 'March 9th' added in a space.

	£	s.	d.
account of moneys collected in the said Diocess upon the account of the Warwick brief	10	—	—
	6913	18	$10\frac{1}{2}$

		£	s.	d.
1707	Payments			
	Brought over	6819	4	1
July	Paid to Mr Paris in full of all accounts, viz. old account	3	—	—
2.	Paid to Mr Webb of Sherborne for 85 ft of ground taken away from him to enlarge the Sheepstreet	2	2	6
5.	Paid to Mr Dunckley in farther part for the urns, etc.	1	—	—
12th.	Paid to Mr Lane upon account of a bill for chancell	3	—	—
16.	Paid to him more upon ditto account.	10	—	—
	Paid to Mr Masters Jan. 22nd 1705 not enter'd before	1	1	6
	Paid to him the 7th of March not enter'd before	—	5	—
22nd.	Paid to Mr Masters upon account	1	—	—
24th.	Paid to Mr Lane in farther part for the bill about the chancell work	2	10	—
31st.	Paid to Mr Dunckley in full for the urnes	1	5	—
	Paid to Mr Marshall in full of a bill for iron work about the urns sett over the chancell	—	6	4
Oct. 4th.	Paid to Mr Acock upon account	—	5	—
	Paid to Sir William Wilson in part of £20 order'd him by Mr Colmore and Mr Newsham	5	—	—
	Paid to Henry Smith for the carriage of ew trees to the church yard	—	10	—
	Nov. 15th 1706. Paid to Mr Francis Smith by Mr Masters in part towards work	2	—	—
	Paid to Mr Francis Smith per Mr Yardly Feb. 12th 1706	—	10	—
	Paid to the Widow Farr a bill for cords and ale and nailes when the pinacles were mended	—	8	6
	Paid for matting the firr trees charged the 19th of May 1705 and for portridge	—	4	6

	£	s.	d.
Dec. 13th. Paid to Mr Huss, plaisterer, in full of his work about the church	—	13	—
17th. Paid to Mr Paris in part of his bill about the chancell, viz. the iron and scrus about the comunion rayles	1	1	6
22nd. Paid to Edward Gambold his bill for setting trees in the church yard, by the direction of Mr Colmore	1	—	—
	6856	6	11

1707[/8]   Receipts

	£	s.	d.
Brought over	6913	18	10$\frac{1}{2}$
Feb 23. Received of Mr Edward Norton in full of all money lent unto him	52	—	—
Received of the Honourable Francis Grevile, Esq., being his gift to the Church of St Marys finishing	20	—	—
1708			
June 17th. Received of the Bishop of Worcester being his Lordship's gift towards the church	10	—	—
Dec. 11th. Received of Thomas Dixon in part of £10 due to the Trustees as lent	1	—	—
March 21st. Received of Thomas Dixon in full of the £10 he ow'd	9	—	—
1709			
Aprill 14th. Received of Mr Rainsford for his part of a seat in the church	3	—	—
May 21st. Received of George Masters his part of a seat in the church	1	5	—
June 3rd. Received (by the hands of Docter Hodges) of Dr Ward, Minister of Willian nere Hitchen in Hartfordshire, being collected upon the Warwick brief and not called for	—	14	—
Aug. 12th. Received of Mrs White being one half of the £1 5s. which Mr White was to pay for part of a seate in the church	—	12	6
Received of Samuell Ainge in full of moneys due from him to the Commissioners as lent	13	—	—
	7024	10	4$\frac{1}{2}$

	£	s.	d.

1707[/8]   Payments

Brought over   6856   6   11

Jan. 31st. Paid to Mr Paris in full of his bill for iron, etc.,
about the rayles in the chancell   —   8   6

Feb. 12 and 21st. Paid to Sir William Wilson in full of £20
order'd to be paid him by Mr Colmore, etc.   15   —   —

24. Paid to Francis Badson, pavior, in full of all his
work about paveing the chancell and church of
St Maryes in Warwick   7   —   —

23rd. Paid to Mr Norton the one shilling and six in
the pound for his loss by the fire according to
his loss   49   1   —

March 22nd. Paid to Mr Wills a bill by order of the Trustees
being for charges in prosecuting a bill in Chancery against Doctor Corley and above 30 more
persons for moneys collected upon the War-
wick brief   40   7   —

1708
June 22nd. Paid to Mr Kington a bill for work about the
rayles att the comunion table, etc.   6   —   —

Paid to Mr Lane in full of his bill about the
chancel   7   —   —

Paid to Mr Horton a bill for ale, etc., when the
bell mettall was refin'd and when the bells
came   1   15   8

1709
Nov. 11. Paid to Widow Farr a bill for nailes and ale for
the men when the pinacles of the tower were
fastned   —   8   8

Paid to Old Green and his sons which made in
full of his work for pitching the streets as
appears in the book of the abstracts of this
account page (50),[1] this summ not enter'd
before   8   1   6

Querie if the owners of the pavement in the
square must not repay their shares for pitching before the door.

Paid to Mr Dunckley per two notes being upon
account between Mr Smith and him   6   10   —

---

[1] The abstract brings together 12 payments to them at 2½d. per yard, total £26 5 6.

	£	s.	d.
Paid to Thomas Wall for Mr Smith and Mr Dunckley	7	10	$4\frac{1}{2}$
	7005	9	$7\frac{1}{2}$

Receipts

	£	s.	d.
Brought over	7024	10	$4\frac{1}{2}$
Received of Mr Young in full of the £60 lent unto Serjt. Hadley	1	—	—
Received as att the other end of the book of the Widow Perks by Timothy Simpkins in part of £60 lent unto her husband William Perks deceased after payments deducted[1]	47	1	8
	7072	12	$\frac{1}{2}$

Payments

	£	s.	d.
Brought over	7005	9	$7\frac{1}{2}$
Paid to Evan Lloyd by himself 1s. 6d. and by Mr Marshall 14s. being for his cleering of rubbish out of the chancell and about the church 15 dayes and $\frac{1}{2}$	—	15	6
Paid charges and expences att Tocester when I went to receive £400 of the Queen's gift from the Queen's Surveyor Generall with Mr Smith and Lloyd	1	1	6
Paid to the Widow Atterberry for ale allow'd to the teames and paviors att the time the streets were pav'd	—	18	6
Paid to Mr Teonge for a parchment book, bought to enter orders and decrees made by the Commissioners in, 18s 6d. and for stamping the same and carriage 1 6 6	2	15	—
Paid to Mr Francis Smith, being the one shilling and six pence in the pound for the part of burnt ground by him built in Sheepstreet, according to order the 21st of September 1704	10	—	—

Paid to Mr Francis Smith being for 38 ft of ground in length and four ft in breadth as taken

[1] 'after ... deducted' added in a space.

	£	s.	d.
away from the ground built upon according to the said order, 6d. per ft. for 152 ft.	3	16	—
Paid to Nicholas Kington which was answer'd unto him by me by direccion of Thomas Masters, not enter'd before	—	8	10
Paid to Mr Acock, painter, before and on Jan. 8th 1708	2	3	6
Paid to Serjt. Harris upon the account of the Commissioners for attendance	1	2	—
	7028	10	$5\frac{1}{2}$

	£	s.	d.
By this account there is received by John Mitchener the summ of	7072	12	$\frac{1}{2}$
And paid by this account	7028	10	$5\frac{1}{2}$
Then remaines due from this accomptant	44	1	7

We whose names are hereunto subscribed, Trustees of the Moneys raised by vertue of the Brief for the Towne of Warwick and mett att the Mayors Parlour on Thursday the 6th day of September 1711, haveing consider'd this account, doe hereby agree to and allow of the same, and doe hereby order and allow that John Mitchener the accomptant be allowed the said summe of fourty four pounds one shilling and seven pence for his many years service done upon account of the said Trustees relateing to the sufferers by the said fire, and agree that this accompt shall be and is hereby fully ballanced.

Symon Biddulph	Thomas Newsham	Geo: Lucy
J. Shukburgh	W. Bromley	Mordaunt
Ri: Lane, Mayor	Digby	Wm Colmore

[At the back of the book, book reversed]

Monies paid about refineing Bell Mettall, etc., upon the Account of the Trustees

		£	s.	d.
	Paid to Fell, cooper, and Acock, painter, about hoopeing of barrells and figureing them when the bell mettall was sent to Gloucester	—	1	6
	Paid for barrells for to putt the bell mettall in and charges there att the sending of it away	—	10	2
	Paid men weigheing the mettall	—	1	—
	Paid for water to wash the mettall	—	2	6
	Paid George Tipping for washing the bell mettall and the rubbish in the bone house	2	10	—
	Paid Evan Lloyd 3 dayes about washing bell mettall	—	3	—
	Paid the Stratford carryer for bringing a parcell of bell mettall from Perk, brazier	—	1	—
	Paid for a new tew iron[1] used about refineing mettall	—	2	6
	Paid for pipe clay used about the refineing furnace	—	—	6
	Paid charges about refineing	—	1	6
1702	Paid 3 men helping about the refineing in the night	—	3	—
Aug. 28th.	Paid loading the bell mettall after refin'd when carryed to Stratford	—	—	10
	Paid weighing bell mettall att Stratford	—	1	—
	Paid horse hyre and expences about delivering and weighing the mettall att Stratford	—	2	6
	Paid for 2 c. and ½ of brick for refineing furnace	—	5	—
	Paid for a letter from Mr Rudhall about bell mettall	—	—	5
	Paid to Mr Willmore of Stratford for a lime barrell to putt the bell mettall in	—	4	—
	Paid William Rawbone for ale and bread had att the refineing of the bell mettall	—	11	9
	Paid to Mr Brookes for 60 baggs of chercoale to refine mettall	3	10	—
	Paid to Thomas Copland workeing night and day about refineing bell mettall	—	6	—

[1] A tuyère, the tube through which the blast of air enters a furnace.

	£	s.	d.
Jan. 30th. Paid for a letter from Gloucester about bells	—	—	5
	8	18	7
March 15. Paid for a letter from Gloucester about bells	—	—	5
Aprill 8. Paid for ditto	—	—	5
21. Paid for ditto	—	—	5
May 15. Paid for ditto	—	—	5
June 7. Paid for ditto	—	—	5
July 9. Paid for ditto	—	—	5
Sept. 31st. Paid for ditto	—	—	5
Paid to William Tayler, wheelright, for mending a waggon which broke in bringing home bells from Stratford	—	3	6
Oct. 25. Paid to Thomas Davis of Leek Wootton for the carriage of 2 bells from Warwick to Stratford	—	5	—
Nov. 8th. Paid to Robert Grey a bill for ladles used in refineing bell mettall	—	5	9
Paid Evan Lloyd and Wilson helping up with the bells from Hortons and into the tower	—	1	8
Jan. 18. Paid Samuell Burford for bricks to build furnace for the refineing bell mettall	—	11	6
Paid Geasey for helping 2 dayes about the bells in getting them up, etc.	—	2	—
Paid for bringing one of the bell clapers to Warwick	—	1	—
July 29. Paid for a letter from bell founder	—	—	5
Paid for a letter from ditto	—	—	5
Carry'd to the other end of the book and entered page (46)[1]	10	12	9

An Account of moneys paid about new repaireing the Chancell

1702

	£	s.	d.
July 27. Imprimis paid to Francis Badson in part towards paveing stone to be used in and about paveing the chancell	5	—	—
Sept. 25th. Paid to him in farther part towards the stone pro ditto	7	—	—

[1] See p. 486.

	£	s.	d.
Oct. 3rd. Paid to Zachary Sharpe for 128 lb. of ropeing for to tye the scaffolding there	3	4	—
Paid to William Smith for 11 quarter and 2 strike of lime deliver'd to Mr Huss for the same use, 6d. strike	2	5	—
9. Paid to Evan Floyd for haire for the same	—	3	6
24. Paid to Mr Huss, plaisterer, in part towards work	5	—	—
Nov. 3rd. Paid to William Marshall in part towards iron work about the chancell	1	10	—
14th. Paid to Mr Huss in farther part about plaistering work	6	—	—
Paid to Mr Masters for flakes for scaffolding	1	11	4
21st. Paid to Mr Masters in part of his bill towards work repaireing the chancell, etc.	10	—	—
28. Paid Mr Marshall in farther part as aforesaid	—	10	—
Paid William Smith for 3 quarter of lime for the said work	—	12	—
Dec. 1st. Paid to Mr Marshall in farther part as aforesaid	—	10	—
9. Paid to him in farther part as aforesaid	—	14	—
22nd. Paid to Mr Huss in farther part as aforesaid	20	—	—
23rd. Paid to Mr Marshall in farther part as aforesaid	2	10	
Paid to William Smith for 12 bushell of lime for ditto	—	6	—
26th. Paid to Francis Badson per order of Mr Colmore, etc., in farther part towards paveing stone	4	—	—
Jan. 23rd. Paid to William Smith for 3 quarter and 1 strike of lime pro ditto	—	12	6
Feb. 3rd. Paid to Mr Huss in farther part as aforesaid	2	3	—
Paid to him in farther part as aforesaid	2	17	—
13. Paid to Mr Marshall in farther part of his bill about ditto	1	—	9
20. Paid to Mr Huss in farther part as aforesaid	2	—	—
Paid William Smith for 3 quarter and 7 strike of lime pro ditto	—	15	6
	80	4	7

Received of the Corporacion of Warwick towards moneys laid out in repaireing and

	£	s.	d.
beautifying the chancell	50	—	—
Carried to the other end of the booke to page (46)			

		£	s.	d.
1702[/3]	Brought over	80	4	7
March 4th.	Paid to William Smith for 3 quarter and 7 strike of lime[1]	—	15	6
	Paid for a load of sand for plaisterer	—	2	—
1703 25th.	Paid to Mr Huss in farther part towards work	7	—	—
27.	Paid to Francis Badson towards paveing stone	1	—	—
Aprill 10th.	Paid to Samuell Acock for painting the shields in the chancell	5	12	—
	Paid to William Smith for 2 quarter of lime	—	8	—
23.	Paid Mr Huss in farther part	5	—	—
May 1st.	Paid to Mr Dunckley in full of his bill	3	4	—
13th.	Paid to Mr Huss by his man in farther part	10	—	—
	Paid to Mr Huss the 15th of December last not enter'd before	4	—	—
July 19.	Paid to Mr Yeates for water for the use of the chancell	—	5	—
	Paid to Mr Huss in full for doeing the chancell	12	—	—
	Paid to Mr Reeve for whiteing for the chancell	—	7	6
	Paid Matthew Perry and Richard Burnill for poles for scaffolding the chancell	1	10	—
	Paid to Mr Marshall in farther part	—	5	—
Sept. 25th.	Paid to him more	1	15	—
	Paid to Charles Watts his bill for candles used att the time of repaireing the chancell	1	—	—
Oct. 11.	Paid to Mr Richard Lane towards leading work and spouts done and made att the repaireing of the chancell	15	—	—
Dec. 10.	Paid to Mr Greeneway for hair for the chancell	—	9	4
18.	Paid Evan Lloyd goeing to Binton about stone for paveing the chancell	—	2	—
21st.	Paid Francis Badson in farther part for stone as above	3	—	—
	Paid Evan Lloyd and Wilson 5 dayes each in the chancell levelling it for the pavior	—	10	—
	Paid to Mr Masters which with £10 paid him the 21st of Nov. last is in full of a bill for work about the chancell, etc.	3	15	—

[1] 'charged twice' written above in another hand.

	£	s.	d.
Paid to Mr Masters a bill for makeing molds for Mr Huss, takeing the scaffold downe in the chancell, etc.	1	—	—
	158	4	11

Receipts

	£	s.	d.
Brought over	50	—	—
Received of Evan Lloyd for 2 strike of lime sold out of the chancell[1]			
Carry'd to the other end, page 46.			

Payments

	£	s.	d.
1703[/4] Brought over	158	4	11
Feb. 26th. Paid to Francis Badson per his son in farther part for stone about the chancell	2	10	—
March 14. Paid to ditto in farther part	3	10	—
17. Paid for 8 strike of lime used in the chancel	—	4	8
1704 31st. Paid to Robert Wilson 3 dayes about levelling in the chancell	—	3	—
April 21st. Paid to Mr Huss about repaireing the monument in the chancell, etc.	7	—	—
29. Paid to Mr Huss in farther part for ditto	3	—	—
Paid William Smith for lime used by ditto there	1	10	—
May 13. Paid to Mr Huss about ditto in farther part	5	—	—
20. Paid John Glendall cleanseing the chancell 1 day	—	0[2]	—
Paid to William Smith for lime delivered to Mr Huss	—	12	—
24th. Paid to Mr Huss in farther part	10	—	—
Aug. 5th. Paid to Francis Badson in farther part towards stone, etc., mencion'd as aforesaid	8	—	—
Sept. 2. Paid to Francis Badson in farther part	2	—	—
	201	14	7

Carryed to the other end of the booke page 46[3]

---

[1] Sum of money left blank. This item is not entered elsewhere.
[2] '1' altered to '0', to cancel this item.
[3] See p. 486.

HOARE'S BANK ACCOUNTS[1]

[LEDGER E. FOLIO 9]

**The Right Honourable the Lord Brooke, Lord Digby and others
Trustees for the Sufferers by fire at Warwick:**   Drs

1695

Aprill 3rd.	To money paid John Tuffnell per note from the Lord Digby	£6 0 0

Per Contra   Crs

1694[/5]   £   s.   d.

February 25.	By money received of John King, Minister of Trinity Minores in Middlesex	5 5 10
March 4.	By Mr Pead, Minister of St James Clerken Well in Middlesex	9 4 9
9.	By John Adams, Minister of St Olaves, Silver Street, London	3 14 —
	By ditto, Minister of St Albans, Wood Street, London	5 10 6
19.	By Wm. Bassett, Minister of St Swithins, London Stone, per the hands of Thomas Holmes	8 1 —
23.	By James Lacey, Minister of Sherburn in Dorsetshire	15 13 3
29.	By Thomas Brice, Curate of St Leonards, Foster Lane, London	3 16 —
	By Tho. Brice, Curate of Christs Church, London	16 6 1
	By Dr Timothy Halton, Archdeacon of Oxon., per the hands of Dr William Lancaster 109 gs[2]	140 — —
Aprill primo	By Wm. Bassett, Minister of St Mary Bothaw, London	4 19 6
	By Thomas Rogers, Churchwarden of St Mildred Poultrey, London	6 — —
	By Wm. Jones, Churchwarden of St Mary Cole Church, London	5 10 —

[1] The Trustees' account with Hoare's Bank is contained in the Bank's ledgers E. and F. A copy was sent to the Trustees at Warwick in about September 1698, although the account at the Bank is not finally closed until 1721. For this transcript the original ledgers have been preferred, though, for the period covered by the copy, a few words have been taken from it, usually proper names when they appear in less abbreviated forms.

[2] Guineas. Where guineas are noted, they sometimes constitute the whole sum, and sometimes only that part of the sum which was paid in gold.

2. By Richard Guy, Church Warden of St Mary Woolnoth, London	7	9	—
By Thomas Dacres, Churchwarden of St Mary Woolchurch Haw, London	4	—	—
3. By Marmaduke Hobkins, Minister of St Michael Le Querne, London	7	19	6
8. By Dr William Beveridge, Minister of St Peters Cornhill, per the hands of Simon Lynch	11	1	2
13. By Thomas Tillot, being collected in the peculiars of the Arch Bishop of Canterbury	43	14	$10\frac{1}{2}$
By Dr Zachary Isham, being collected in the parish of St Botolphs Bishopsgate, London	17	5	9
17. By Charles Trumball, Minister of Hadleigh in Suffolk	4	4	1
By Dr Thomas Plume, Archdeacon of Rochester	49	—	—
By ditto being collected in the parish of Greenwich	18	12	1
22. By John Grant, Minister of St Dunstans in the West, London	35	8	3
By Ofspring Blackall, Rector of St Thomas Apostles, London	3	12	9
25. By N. Bradey, Minister of Cree Church, London	19	10	—
By Wm Fleetwood, Minister of St Austens, London	15	6	$10\frac{1}{2}$
By ditto, Minister of St Faiths, London	3	7	2
By Dr Thomas Hecking, Minister of St Botolph Aldersgate	18	2	—
29. By Mr Whitfield, Minister of St Martins Ludgate	8	10	$6\frac{1}{2}$
May 6. By bill on John Kirkman from Manchester	120	—	—
8. By John Knight, Register to the Archdeacon of Essex, per the hands of John Hall	60	—	—
17. By Joshua Richardson, Minister of Alhallows on the Wall, London	8	4	6
18. By Dr Green, Vicar of St Martins Ironmonger Lane	6	17	6
By ditto, Vicar of St Olave Old Jury	5	—	—
20. By Richard Haywood, Register of Buckingham, per the hands of Joseph Churchill	30	—	—
21. By Thomas Holmes of Wm Fashion, collected in the Archdeaconry of Yorke	100	—	—

27.	By Dr Thomas Plume, Archdeacon of Rochester	34	16	10
	By ditto	4	8	10
30.	By Charles Armitt, collected in the Archdeaconry of Surrey	69	17	4
June primo	By the Bishop of Worcester, being given by Mr Brownlow and his lady	20	—	—
	By Robert Blake, Minister of the united parishes of St Andrew Wardrobe and St Ann Blacke Fryers	4	16	3
5.	By Edward Bowerman, Minister of Caddington, Bedfordshire 4 gs.	11	1	11
8.	By Richard Wynne Esq. being given by him to the Sufferers	5	—	—
10.	By Stephen Pearce, Rector of Claworthy in the county of Somerset and Deanary of Dunstar	—	16	—
11.	By Dr Beveridge of Phillip Betts, collected in the Archdeaconry of Colchester	43	15	—
	By Dr Cory of Philip Betts, collected in the Archdeaconary of Middlesex	56	5	—
12.	By Wm Baker, Rector of Monk Eleigh in Suffolke, per the hands of Dr Charles Trumball	2	8	—
15.	By Mathew Disney, Rector of Bletching in the county of Bucks.	2	18	7
	By William May, Churchwarden of St Giles in the Fields, Middlesex 15 gs.	154	10	$11\frac{1}{2}$
	By Thomas Shepard per the hands of John Shepard, collected in the Diocess of Peterborough	170	—	—
18.	By bill on John Pilkington of John Hutton, Archdeacon of Stow in the Diocess of Lincolne	40	—	—
19.	By Henry Rix, Minister of Newport Pond in Essex	2	14	6
20.	By Thomas Tillott, being collected in the peculiars of the Archbishop of Canterbury 10 gs.	61	3	4
	By John Knight, Register of the Archdeacon of Essex	25	—	—
28.	By Dr Thomas Lynford, collected in the parishes of St Edmond the King and St Nicholas Acorns	15	5	—
29.	By Francis Atterbury, Minister of Bridewell, per the hands of Anthony Heardson	2	2	3

July primo. By Charles Armitt, collected in the Archdeaconry of Surrey	52 10	—
By Dr Thomas Carter, Rector of Debden and Wichen Bonnet in Essex	2 17	6½
2. By Phineas Rothwell, Vicar of Broxborne, Hertfordshire	5 1	2½
By Charles Heron, Register of Exon., per the hands of Edward Shaw	54 10	4
3. By Dr Thomas Plume, Archdeacon of Rochester	7 6	11
5. By John Hutton, Archdeacon of Stow in the Diocess of Lincolne	15 11	5½
10. By John Cocke, Vicar of Thatcham in Berkshire	2 6	0½
16. By Thomas White, Clark of Stratford le Bow in Middlesex	6 4	4
22. By Dr Thomas Copping, Minister of St Olaves Hartstreet, London	5 12	7½
24. By bill on John Huggett per order of Joseph Tucker, Register of the Archdeaconry of Barnstaple	50 —	—
27. By Thomas Shepard per the hands of John Shepard, collected in the Diocess of Peterbrough	45 —	—
29. By bill on John Kirkman from Manchester 7gs.	12 —	2
Aug. 1. By Jacob Merchant, Minister of Cappell in Surrey	1 18	4
6. By Dr Thomas Plume, Archdeacon of Rochester	3 4	1½
7. By Dr Charles Alston, Archdeacon of Essex	2 15	6
By Lilly Butler, Minister of St Mary Aldermanbury, London	7 17	3
8. By Richard Haywood, Register of Aylesbury, collected in the Archdeaconry of Bucks.	40 —	—
21. By John Knightbridge, Register to the Archdeacon of Essex	20 —	—
By Adam Froggat of Lichfield per the hands of John Baskett, collected in the county of Stafford 14 gs.	50 —	—
24. By Wm Lancaster per order of Timothy Halton, Archdeacon of Oxfordshire 33 gs.	50 —	—
	1983 2	6½

Vide folio 10

[folio 10]
The Rt Honourable the Trustees for the Sufferers by Fire at Warwick: **Drs**
1695

		£	s.	d.
	To money paid as brought from folio 9	6	—	—
Nov. 6.	To William Newsham per order of the Lord Brook and 6 other Commissioners	2000	—	—
15.	To Thomas Bedford for himself, the Apparitors and returning the money	7	10	—
Dec. 3.	To Mrs Eyre per order of Mr Newsham	5	—	—
7.	To Thomas Newsham per order of the Lord Brooke and 5 other Commissioners	190	—	—
9.	To Mrs Eyre per order of Mr Newsham	5	—	—
12.	To ditto per order of ditto	5	—	—
13.	To ditto per order of ditto	5	—	—
20.	To Thomas Bavand per order of the Lord Brooke	10	—	—
		£2233	10	—

Per Contra **Crs**
1695

		£	s.	d.
	By money received as brought from folio 9	1983	2	6½
Sept. 4.	By Dr Lewis Atterbury collected in the parish of Highgate in Middlesex	7	3	11
6.	By bill on Robert Horner per order of Thomas Parker collected in Cleveland	40	—	—
17.	By bill on Edward Bird per order of Charles Heron, Register of Exon. Archdeaconry	50	—	—
19.	By Richard Heywood, Register of Bucks. collected in that Archdeaconry	32	—	—
21.	By Dr Thomas Sawrey, Archdeacon of Surrey 13 gs and £10 10s.	30	—	—
	By bill on Wm Browne per order of Nicholas Browne, Register of Norwich	100	—	—
26.	By Dr Richard Hollingworth collected in the parish of St Botolph without Aldgate	12	3	7
	By Dr Plume, Archdeacon of Rochester, collected in Yalding parish in Kent	3	7	—
30.	By Henry Hankey, Rector of Wansted in Essex	6	2	4

Oct. 12. By bill on Robert Horner per order of Wm Mawde, collected in the East Riding of Yorkshire   40 — —

15. By Thomas Derby, Rector of Gratley in the county of Southampton and Diocess of Winton   — 3 10

By ditto Vicar of Damerham South in the county of Wilts and Diocess of Sarum   1 6 2

17. By Dr Thomas Plume, Archdeacon of Rochester, 4 briefs   2 1 11

19. By Dr Thomas Sayer, Archdeacon of Surrey, per the hands of Charles Armitt   10 gs.   71 5 6

By Thomas Tyllott collected in the Peculiars of the Archbishop of Canterbury   7 gs.   23 10 —

22. By Richard Hatch, Minister of Stonistratford in the county of Buckes   4 4 —

23. By John Clerke per the order of Thomas Shepard, Register of Northampton   66 gs.   99 — —

28. By Dr Thomas Risbury, Rector of St Pauls Shadwell, per James Dighton   7 gs.   10 15 —

Nov. 6. By a bill on William Leigh per order of Thomas Holmes, collected in Yorke Archdeaconry   50 — —

15. By Wm Portman per order of John Wright, Vicar of Stepney in the county of Middlesex   16 gs.   32 16 10

By John Skelton per the hands of Thomas Bedford, collected in Bedford Archdeaconary   26 gs.   200 13 1

20. By William Bedford collected in the parish of St George Botolph Lane   1 13 —

23. By Samuel Harris, Rector of the parish of St Ethelburg   6 5 8

By Thomas Holmes for the Archdeaconry of Yorke   50 — —

28. By Dr Sayer, Archdeacon of Surrey, per the hands of Charles Armitt   8 gs.   41 10 —

29. By James Lomax, Vicar of Epping, Essex   2 7 6

30. By Dr William Lancaster for St Marttins in the Fields   30 gs.   60 7 9

Dec. primo. By Dr Beveridge per Phillip Betts, collected in the Archdeaconry of Colchester   45 — —

By Dr Thomas Cory per ditto, collected in the Archdeaconry of Middlesex   53 gs.   35 — —

4.	By Dr Timothy Halton, Archdeacon of Oxon.	50	—	—
5.	By Thomas Merry for the parish of New Windsor, Archdeaconry of Berks.	7	1	9
9.	By Dr Saywell, Archdeacon of Ely, per the hands of Edward Purver per order of Richard Pyke	113	17	11
10.	By Dr Sayer per the hands of Charles Armitt, Archdeacon of Surrey	10	13	6
11.	By Thomas Newsham given by Mr Fawkner	1	—	—
17.	By Lord Digby per the hands of Thomas Newsham, given by the Lord Leinster	1	—	—
18.	By bill on William Brown per order of Nicholas Brown, Archdeaconry of Norwich 34 gs.	55	2	—
23.	By Thomas Wotton, Curate of the united parishes of St Lawrence Jury and St Mary Magdalen Milk Street	14	6	7
28.	By Nicholas Davies, Vicar of Compton in the county of Berks.	—	5	—
31.	By Richard Leach, Rector of St Peters Poore	25	5	6
Jan. primo.	By Thomas Holmes for the Archdeaconry of Yorke	70	—	—
7.	By Thomas Tyllot for the peculiars of Canterbury	5	—	—
11.	By Charles Heron, Register for the Archdeaconry of Exon.	23	10	—
14.	By John Strype, Vicar of Low Layton in Essex	3	13	—
	By Edmond Sylvester, Vicar of Cheeveley etc., 4 briefs, Archdeaconry of Berkes	4	1	11
	By Dr Thomas Plume per the hands of Phillip Stubbs, Archdeaconry Rochester, 5 briefs	8	7	11
20.	By Charles Armett for the Archdeaconry of Surrey	5	—	—
21.	By Richard Nurse, Rector of Chiddington in Kent	2	16	11
	By Dr Lancaster per order of Dr Halton, Archdeacon of Oxon. 13 gs.	20	—	—
22.	By Thomas Shepard per the hands of Benjamin Raye, collected in the Diocess of Peterborough	12	—	6
24.	By John Coles, Archdeacon of St Albans, per the hands of John Turner	37	18	3
25.	By John Crofts, Vicar of Winslowe in Buckinghamshire	5	4	2

27. By Henry Hankey, Rector of Wansted, given by the Lady Emma Child	5	—	—
Feb. primo. By Jonathan Bayley, Curate of Murseley in Buckinghamshire	—	12	1
By John Denham for the parrishes of Rogate and Ipring cum Chithurst in Sussex	1	4	9
By John Southey, Register to Dr Edward Waple, Archdeacon of Taunton	20	—	—
By John Shepard per order of Thomas Shepard, Register of the Diocese of Peterborough 42 gs	69	9	—

520 guineas £3614 10 4½

To folio 11

[folio 11]

The Trustees for the Sufferers by Fire at Warwick: Drs
1695[/6]

To money paid as brought from folio 10	£2233	10	—
Feb. 15. To Mrs Eyre per order of Thomas Newsham	5	—	—
18. To John Newsham	315	—	—
28. To Isaac Tompkis per order of the Lord Brooke and 3 others	100	—	—
March 27. To Thomas Newsham 10 guineas	15	—	—
May 26. To ditto 552 guineas per order of the Lord Brooke and 6 other Commissioners	828	—	—
July 1. To Thomas Bavand 8½ guineas	9	6	5
4. To Thomas Newsham 59 guineas	64	18	—
14. To Thomas Bavand 18 gns	20	—	—
Aug. 27. To Samuel Green 50 guineas	55	—	—
Sept. 16. To Emanuel Langford 9 gns.	10	—	—
Oct. 22. To William Newsham	100	—	—
31. To William Parker paid all the inclosed in new	260	—	—
Nov. 21. To Thomas Newsham money and guineas	50	—	—
Dec. 14. To Thomas Bavand	21	—	—
21. To the carrier of Chester for money sent by Mr Prescott	—	16	8
Jan. 30. To ditto for money sent by Mr Prescott	1	—	6
Feb. 4. To Thomas Bavand	20	—	—

£4108 11 7

8. To Monmouth carrier for money sent by Mr Morgan	—	5	4

18. To money paid on account of tallies	1294	14	5
	£5403	11	4

Per Contra

1695[/6]

		£	s	d
	By money received as brought from folio 10			
	520 gs.	£3614	10	$4\frac{1}{2}$
Feb. 8.	By John Marshall, Vicar of Pancras alias Kentish Towne	2	12	8
11.	By Richard Haywood, Register for the Archdeaconry of Buckes 20 gs	137	13	$4\frac{1}{2}$
13.	By Dr Timothy Halton, Archdeacon of Oxon., per the hands of Samuel Rush	116	10	—
14.	By William Nicholson, Archdeacon of Carlisle, per the hands of Samuel Clarke	22	3	8
19.	By Mr Spencer, Chancellor of the Diocess of Sarum, collected in the said Diocess	17	16	$2\frac{1}{2}$
Mar. 4.	By Nicholas Brown, Register of Norwich			
	10 guineas	85	6	2
13.	By Thomas Woodward, Register in Lincoln Diocess, per the hands of Edward Dennester			
	14 gs.	68	—	—
16.	By Mathew Mead, Rector of St Thomas Southwarke	3	3	3
17.	By John Turton, Curate of St Margaretts Lothbury	6	3	—
1696				
April 15.	By John Gaskarth, Minister of Alhallows Barking in London	6	11	6
21.	By Richard Hayward, Register of Aylesbury in the county of Buckes	10	—	—
22.	By Jeremy Wheat, Curate of Barford St Michael in the county of Oxon.	3	4	1
24.	By Anthony Hornecke for the precinct of the Savoy	1	17	5
29.	By Thomas Holmes for the Archdeaconry of Yorke	19	—	—
May primo.	By John Coles, Archdeacon of St Albans	14	14	1
2.	By Dr Saywell, Archdeacon of Ely, per order Richard Pyke per the hands of William Martinn	10	19	6

4. By John Knight, Register to the Archdeacon of Essex	19	2	1
11. By Doctor Plume, Archdeacon of Rochester	10	18	8
12. By Thomas Newsham as paid him the 27 March last 10 gs.	15	—	—
13. By Joseph Tucker, Register for the Archdeaconry of Barnstaple	21	11	3
22. By John Southey, Register of Taunton	20	—	—
27. By Thomas Newsham as paid him the 26th instant 552 guineas	607	4	—
June 5. By Thomas Sheppard, Register of Northampton, collected in Peterborough Diocess	8	14	3
8. By J. Sambee, Curate of Soulbury, Buckes	1	11	2
By Charles Armitt for the Archdeaconry of Surrey	3	9	2
By Samuell Warner, collected in the parish of St Benedict Pauls Wharfe	12	2	—
13. By Nicholas Brown, Register of Norwich	19	6	3
18. By Charles Armitt, collected at Battersea in Surrey	9	13	6
July 3. By Richard Heywood, Register of Aylesbury	1	16	1
4. By Phillip Betts, collected in the Archdeaconrys of Colchester and Middlesex	30	—	—
25. By Edmund Nuboult, Rector of Chiddington, Buckes	1	10	8
Aug. 8. By William Martin per order of Richard Pike, Archdeaconry of Ely	7	12	—
13. By Doctor Plume, collected in the Archdeaconry of Rochester	1	1	10
17. By Charles Heron, Archdeaconry of Exon.	10	10	—
28. By William Ward, Vicar of Hanslop, Buckes	3	14	8
Sept. 28. By Thomas Berrow, Rector of St Marttins Outwich, London	5	6	—
Nov. 7. By Robert Nevile, Rector of Newton Blossomvile, Buckes	—	13	—
11. By Abraham Kenyon, Vicar of Warfield, Archdeaconry of Reading	—	17	—
14. By Samuel Musgrave, Vicar of Brayfield and Lavenden, Buckes	1	5	4
20. By Isaac Gwinnett, Minister of Ashton Keynes, Wilts.	—	19	6
By Josia Lambert, collected in the Archdea-			

conrys of Kendall, Lensdale, Copeland and Turnes in the Archdeaconry of Richmond	42	—	—
21. By William Nicholson collected in the Archdeaconry of Carlisle	5	3	$4\frac{1}{2}$
Dec. 21. By Henry Prescott, Register of Chester	100	—	—
Jan. 8. By William Lamplugh, Vicar of Dagenham in Essex	1	16	9
14. By Anthony Close, Deputy Register of the Archdeaconry of Richmond	44	9	10
30. By Henry Prescott, Register of Chester	112	18	4
Feb. 6. By John Southey, Register of the Archdeaconry of Taunton	10	12	3
8. By Nathaniel Morgan and Thomas Powell, Registers of the Archdeaconrys of Carmarthen, Cardigan and Meneven	27	4	$1\frac{1}{2}$
By Mr Stephens, Register of Leicester	100	—	—

£5398 8 5

To folio 64

[folio 64]
The Trustees for the Sufferers by Fire att Warwick: Drs
1697

To money paid as brought from folio 11	£5403	11	4	
July 6 To George Webb	200	—	—	
9 To Sir John Burgoyne	1050	—	—	
Oct. 6 To William Tarver	100	—	—	
12 To Brooke Bridges	200	—	—	
Nov. 25 To Thomas Newsham	11	—	—[1]	
Feb. 17. To Edward Wills	200	—	—	
March 24. To Thomas Bavand	20	—	—	
1698				
May 10. To Charles Egerton Esq.	1500	—	—	
13. To Thomas Woodhall	110	—	—	
June 4. To Richard Lane	198	15	—	
18. To Brooke Bridges	300	—	—	

Paid £9293 6 4

[1] This item is omitted in the Trustees' copy. The clerk began to write it, then changed to the item following, presumably because he was aware that the sum had been repaid on 17 Sept. following.

Oct. 4.	To money paid William Tarver	110	— —
14.	To ditto	500	— —[1]
Aprill 3.	To Brooke Bridges Esq.	200	— —
	To ditto	200	— —
Feb. 7.	To Edw. Strong	12	18 —
Jan. 30.	To Thomas Newsham Esq.	150	— —
July 22.	To Wm. Newsham	100	— —
Sept. 15.	To Geo Webb	200	— —
Octo. 10.	To Wm. Newsham as received of Edw. Wilcox	400	— —
Feb. 22.	To ditto	200	— —
July 10.	To ditto	150	— —
Octo. 28.	To Thomas Newsham	250	— —
Nov. 10.	To the loss of 11 5 9 received the 20 April 1697 in old mony which weigh'd 30 oz. 8 which at 5s. 2d. per oz. comes to £9 8s.	1	17 9
		2474	15 9

Per Contra   **Crs**
1696[/7]

	By money received as brought from folio 11	£5398	8 5
March 11.	By money received from the Mint	1406	5 —
Aprill 20.	By Thomas Madocks, Register of Landaffe Diocess £2 in new money, £11 5 9 old money[2]	13	5 9
22.	By Dr Timothy Halton, Archdeacon of Oxon.	5	13 —
May 21.	By Dr Cawley, Archdeacon of Illington, Lincolnshire	15	— —
Sept. 3.	By 6 months interest of two orders on the 3s. Aid	60	— —
Oct. 9.	By 6 months interest of £1300 on the 3s. Aid	52	— —
11.	By Samuel Symonds, Curate of Clapham	5	10 10
	By Thomas Tyllot, Register for the peculiars of Canterbury	4	10 —
21.	By £93 15 in Exchequer bills received for the 4d. per ounce on hammer'd money discounted for	87	8 —
Nov. 9.	By Thomas Woodward, Register for the Archdeaconry Huntington	16	— —

---

[1] These two items have been added in another hand in the Trustees' copy, which records no further payments.
[2] '£2 in new money, £11 5 9 old money' added in another hand in the Bank ledger only.

Dec. 17. By principall and interest of an order on the 3s. Aid	517	3	—
By Edward Tenison Esq.	166	17	—
Jan. 24. By Thomas Cooke, Curate of St Dionis Back-church	19	10	—
Feb. 17. By principall and interest of an order on the 3s. Aid	1045	8	—
21. By Francis Swanton one of the trustees of Dr Ward deceased	55	—	—
March 4. By principall and interest of an order on the 3s. Aid	106	17	—
Aprill 6. By principall and interest of two orders on the 3s. Aid	841	19	8
14. By William Whiner, Curate of Boxgrove in Sussex	5	—	—
18. By principall and interest of an order on the 3s. Aid	316	4	—
19. By principall and interest of two orders on ditto	210	15	—
June 17. By J. M. de Langley the Curate of Steventon, Berks.	1	15	—
July 27. By Dr Woodward, Deane of Saram	19	19	6
Sept. 17. By Thomas Newsham as paid him the 25 November	11	—	—[1]

Paid	10381	9	2
Received	9293	6	4
Remaines	1088	2	10[2]

1699

May 30. By Dr Saywell per the hands of Edward Pyke collected in the Dioces of Ealey	3	8	6
June 17. By Thomas Barrett collected in the Archdea-conry of Lewis in Sussex	8	—	—
Sept. 5. By Dr John Cawley	50	—	—
22. By ditto per the hands of Francis Milles	50	—	—
Oct. 1. By Dr John Cawley	100	—	—
Feb. 14. By ditto	46	6	6

1700

May 14. By ditto	50	—	—

[1] This item is omitted from the Trustees' copy.
[2] The Trustees' copy ends at this point.

June 22. By John Eglestone collected at Bristoll	30	—	—
July 30. By Dr John Cawley	50	—	—
Nov. 28. By Charles Heron of Exiter £6 7s. new money £2 12s. old money weighed 7 oz. 9dwt at 5s. 2 per oz. 1 18 6	8	5	6
Feb. 4. By Thomas Maddox of Landalf	—	15	—

1701

April 19. By Mr Prescot of Chester 7 15 6 in old mony comes to	5	3	—

1704

Oct. 10. By a bill drawn per Edward Wilcox on Tho. Knight	400	—	—
Feb. 12. By Edward Wilcox	200	—	—

1705

May 25. By ditto per hands of Hemes Pooler	150	—	—
Aug. 9. By ditto	100	—	—
Feb. 28. By ditto	150	—	—

1706

Sept. 13. By William Alexander	3	10	—
Aug. 20. By course old mony melted down weighing 139 oz. 10	30	4	6
	2523	15	10

Transferr'd to Ledger F. folio 345

[Ledger F. folio 345]

The Trustees for the Sufferers at Warwick: **Drs**

1718

Money paid and brought from Ledger E. f. 64.	£2474	15	9

1721

May 27. To William Colemore	80	—	—

Per Contra   **Crs**

By money received as brought from Ledger E. f. 64	£2523	15	10

1721

May 27. By Henry Hoare	30	19	11[1]

[1] This is the amount by which the account failed to balance.

CHILD'S BANK ACCOUNTS[1]

Moneys Received on Account of the Warwick Briefe per Sir Francis Child and Mr John Rogers

1694[/5]

		£	s	d
Feb. 16.	Rec. of St Anns Aldersgate and St John Zachery	5	12	1
22.	Rec. of Falmough order Mr Quarn per John Dyer	8	14	$\frac{1}{2}$
Mar. 23.	Rec. of Hamsted	5	—	6
1695				
30.	Rec. of St Alphage within Cripplegate	2	13	7
Apr. 5.	Rec. of St Mary Abchurch and St Lawrence Pountney	12	5	$7\frac{1}{2}$
11.	Rec. of Mr Mugg for Inkbro' Worcestershire	6	14	—
15.	Rec. of St Magnus and St Margarets, New Fishstreet	7	18	1
16.	Rec. of St Mildret and Margaret, Bread Street	8	3	6
19.	Rec. of St Anns Westminster	21	10	1
29.	Rec. of St Mary Magdelen, Old Fishstreet	1	19	7
	Rec. of St Gregory, Old Fishstreet	13	7	—
May 1.	Rec. of St Bennet Grace Church	7	19	—
	Rec. of St Leonard, East Cheap	2	2	—
3.	Rec. of St Stephen, Colman Street	12	17	10
	Rec. of Dr Wolsley collected in Dioces of Peterboro'	35	5	—
	Rec. of Thomas Serocold order Francis Eger	130	—	—
6.	Rec. of St Margarets Westminster	42	4	$0\frac{1}{2}$
8.	Rec. of Dr Battely, Archdeacon of Canterbury	30	—	—
15.	Rec. of Dr Hyde collected Dioces Glocester	50	—	—
17.	Rec. of Waltham Abby, Essex	5	1	1
	Rec. of Nazing in Essex	1	6	—
21.	Rec. of Dr Clutterbuck, Archdeacon, Winton	36	17	—
23.	Rec. of Alhollows Staining per Mr Fogg	10	9	$1\frac{1}{2}$
25.	Rec. of Mr Woodward, Archdeacon of Huntindon	20	—	—
30.	Rec. of Dr Wolsey Dioces of Peterborogh	9	19	9
	Moneys Received	£ 487	18	11
	Rec. of Mr Teringham Stephens, Archdeaconry Lester	200	—	—

[1] The Trustees' account with Child's Bank exists only in a copy at Warwick made for the Trustees in about December 1695, as far as can be ascertained until the Bank permits access to its early records. The account still had £971 3 $7\frac{3}{4}$ in it at that date.

31. Rec. of St Pauls Covent Garden	51 11	3
June 1. Rec. of Thomas Burgis order Dr Hyde Archdeaconry Glocester	30 —	—
4. Rec. of Mr King and Neve for the Rolles Liberty	10 1	7
8. Rec. of Henry Goodwin Archdeaconry Sodbury Dioces Norwich	50 —	—
Rec. of the hamblet of Popler, Middlesex	7 7	6
11. Rec. of William Skinner Archdeaconry Darbyshire	100 —	—
12. Rec. of St Michael Woodstreet, London	6 2	8
Rec. of St Mary Stainings, London	1 4	—
13. Rec. of Dr Wolsly, Dioces Peterborough	9 15	—
Rec. of S. Richards Archdeaconry Salop Dioces Coventry and Lichfield	100 —	—
27. Rec. of Aden Forroget Archdeaconry Lichfield & Coventry	100 —	—
29. Rec. of Ra.[1] Gerrard order E. Draw Archdeaconry Cornwall	82 —	$9\frac{1}{2}$
July 3. Rec. of St James's Westminster	79 3	—
4. Rec. of Henry Goodwin Register Bury St Edmunds Archdeaconry Sudbury	29 12	—
11. Rec. of Dr Clutterbuck per Daniel Small	295 17	4
16. Rec. of Dr Batteley Archdeaconry Canterbury per Francis Grevell	100 —	—
20. Rec. of Dr Hyde Archdeaconry Glocester per Thomas Burges	150 —	—
22. Rec. of St Margarets White Chappell	11 14	6
23. Rec. of Mr Exton Register of Archdeaconry of London and Middlesex	108 8	$5\frac{3}{4}$
24. Rec. of St Clements Danes parish	56 18	4
30. Rec. of Henry Goodwin Archdeaconry Sudbury	40 —	—
Aug. 3. Rec. of Dr Battely Archdeaconry Canterbury per John Oliver	20 —	—
5. Rec. of John Greenway Archdeaconry Berks.	94 8	8
Moneys Received carried over	2222 4	$0\frac{1}{4}$
Aug. 26. Rec. of William Pearson Archdeaconry Nottingham	144 —	—
Sept. 3. Rec. of Mr Cater order Dr Battely Archdeaconry Canterbury	50 —	—

---

[1] Probably 'Radcliff'.

		£	s	d
7. Rec. of Mr Wakeford Archdeaconry Chichester		28	8	$11\frac{1}{2}$
Rec. of Sparsholt and Kingston Lisle Berks		1	5	$4\frac{1}{2}$
10. Rec. of St Nicholas Cole Abby & St Nicholas Olive, London		4	2	—
19. Rec. of Mr Wade for Hamersmith		7	11	9
Rec. of Mr Barry for Fulham		12	—	8
Oct. 1. Rec. of John Atherton Register Archdeaconry Totnes		50	—	—
Nov. 7. Rec. of William Robinson Archdeaconry Coventry		100	—	—
13. Rec. of Tockinham, Middlesex	15g.	23	13	10
22. Rec. of Dr Wolsey Archdeaconry Northampton	14g.	23	—	—
Rec. of Archdeaconry of Hereford & Salop 66g. at 30s.		100	—	—
26. Rec. of William Robinson, Archdeaconry of Darby		100	—	—
Rec. of Thomas Barret Archdeaconry of Lewes in Sussex		135	—	—
28. Rec. of Dr John Blagrave of Longworth Berks		2	6	—
29. Rec. of St John Evangelist London		3	15	6
Dec. 4. Rec. of St Bartholomew per the Exchange	3g.	5	11	—
Rec. of the parish of Hampton Middlesex	$2g.\frac{1}{2}$	3	10	—
Rec. of Hampton hamlet parish ditto	$\frac{1}{2}$g.	—	14	3
14. Rec. of Mr Exton Register of London & Middlesex 14g.		72	—	$3\frac{1}{2}$
		3088	3	$7\frac{3}{4}$

1695

		£	s	d
Nov. 6. Paid Mr William Newsham per order of my Lord Brooke and 6 other Commissioners		2000	—	—
Dec. 7. Paid Mr Thomas Newsham		117	—	—
23.[1] Paid cariage of 60 li. from Lecister		—	10	—
Jan. 10. Paid cariage of 60 from Wells		1	—	—
21. Paid cariage of 103:18:9 from Sarum		—	2	6
25. Paid cariage of 59:14:7$\frac{1}{2}$ from Suffolk		—	8	6
29. Paid cariage of money from West Drayton, Berks		—	1	6
Feb. 8. Paid cariage of 20:15:3		—	4	$4\frac{1}{2}$
17. Paid cariage of 9:12:10$\frac{1}{2}$		—	1	3
19. Paid Mr John Newsham course money[2]		938	—	—

[1] The Trustees' copy ends here, but the account is continued in another copy made in connection with the Chancery suit brought by some of the sufferers and preserved in the Warwick Castle MSS. (CR 1886/9151).

[2] Added in another hand.

1696

	£	s	d
Apr. 7. Paid cariage 51:8	—	17	—
May 25. Paid cariage 4:15:10	—	1	—
26. Paid Mr Thomas Newsham 250 g. at 30s.	375	—	—
Nov. 3. Paid Dr Feelding charges he layd out in bringing up 78:10 from Dorsetshire paid mild[1] money[2]	1	5	—
Feb. 5. Paid cariage of 44:13:7 mild money[2]	—	13	—
	£3435	4	1½

	£	s	d
1695 Brought over Rec.	£3088	3	7¾
Dec. 23. Rec. of Mr Stephens Archdeaconry Lecester	60	—	—
Rec. of Mr Exton 7g. 30s.	20	10	—
24. Rec. of Dr Batteley Archdeaconry Canterbury	63	2	9
Rec. of ditto	7	9	11½
27. Rec. of Frumpton & Fryer collectors in Wapping	10	14	7
31. Rec. of St Mathew Fryday Street & St Peter Cheapside	6	11	9
Rec. of William Pearson Archdeaconry Nottingham	46	7	—
Rec. of St Giles's without Cripple geate	24	5	2
Jan. 4. Rec. of Dr Hyde Archdeaconry Glocester	50	—	—
8. Rec. of Archdeaconry Taunton per John Dyer g.30	50	—	—
Rec. of St Mary in Bury St Edmonds	11	9	—
Rec. of Moses Gill for Archdeaconry Berkes	95	—	5½
10. Rec. of John Payne Deputy Register Archdeaconry Wells	60	—	—
Rec. of John Merret Register Huntingdon	44	—	—
11. Rec. of Dr Thomas Hyde Archdeaconry Glocester	14	—	—
21. Rec. of Mr Joseph Kelsey Archdeaconry Sarum	103	18	9
Rec. of Dr Clutterbuck Archdeaconry Winton	73	3	7
	£3828	16	7¾
25. Rec. of the parish of Eveslegh, Hantshire	—	19	3
Rec. of Francis Edgar Archdeaconry Suffolk	59	14	7½
28. Rec. of West Drayton com. Berks 1g.	1	10	—
29. Rec. of Shipston } com. Worcester	3	4	7
Rec. of Tidington }		13	3
31. Rec. of Harmondsworth } com. Meddx	1	2	9
Rec. of West Drayton }	3	3	7
Feb. 3. Rec. of Gernborough[3] com. Berks	2	1	6

[1] i.e. milled.   [2] Added in another hand.   [3] Altered from 'Greenborough'.

Rec. of St Andrew Holborne 9g.$\frac{1}{2}$	49 14	3
6. Rec. of Ightam com. Kent	— 13	—
7. Rec. of Henry Goodwin Register Archdeaconry Sudbury	17 10	6
8. Rec. of J. Wakefield Deputy Register Chichester	20 [	][1]
10. Rec. of Dr Thomas Wolsey Archdeaconry Peterborough 35g.	57 17	—
Rec. of St Dunstons in the East, London 5g.	19 2	4
17. Rec. of Dr Ashenhurst Archdeaconry Darby 6g.	9 12	10$\frac{1}{2}$
Rec. of Dr Thomas Wolsey Archdeaconry Peterborough	28 6	9$\frac{3}{4}$
Rec. of Aden Forroget Archdeaconry Coventry & Lich.	142 5	6
18. Rec. of parish Clousley com. Berks. 1g.	1 12	—
	£4248 15	4$\frac{1}{2}$
18. Rec. of the parish of Moulstoe, Berks.	8	4
19. Rec. of parish of New Brentford, Meddx.	7	6
29. Rec. of Dr Johnson Archdeaconry Hereford	61 12	5$\frac{1}{2}$
Mar. 10. Rec. of the Sub Dean of Sarum per Woodford order Mr Nash	17 6	6
1696		
Apr. 7. Rec. of Griff. Vaughan Archdeaconry Salop.	51 8	—$\frac{1}{2}$
14. Rec. of Dr Horneck collected in the Savoy.	11 2	6
21. Rec. of Mr Hawkins churchwardens of Kimbolton	2 18	3
30. Rec. of Dr Batteley per Paul Lukus	8 14	9
Rec. of parish Finchley, Midx.	2 16	—
Rec. of St Christophers, London	5 16	6
May 9. Rec. of Mr Smith Register of Durham	49 18	10$\frac{1}{2}$
21. Rec. of parish Kandigley com. Radner	5	10
22. Rec. of Dr Johnson Archdeaconry Hereford	27 15	1
Rec. of John Payne Register Wells 2g.$\frac{1}{2}$ & post 30s.	18 —	—
25. Rec. of Dr Wolsly Archdeaconry Peterborough	4 5	10
June 4. Rec. of Dr Hyde Archdeaconry Gloster	10 10	—
20. Rec. of Aden Forrogat Archdeaconry Coventry & Lichfield 8g.	70 2	5
22. Rec. of hamlet Hunsted, Hertfordshire, diocese Lincoln	4 11	0$\frac{1}{2}$
25. Rec. of St Brides parish, London	13 4	—
29. Rec. of William Pearson Archdeaconry Nottingham	2 4	3

[1] Edge of document missing.

July 14. Rec. of parish St Bartholomew the Less	2	6	5
28. Rec. of Dr Thomas Clutterbuck Archdeaconry Winton	15	18	6
Aug. 14. Rec. of Griff. Reynolds diocese Hereford clipt & bad money[1]	92	1	—
29. Rec. of Dr Hyde Archdeaconry Glocester ditto[1]	63	—	—
Nov. 3. Rec. of Dr Fielding Archdeaconry Dorsett ditto[1]	78	10	—
6. Rec. of ditto bad money[1]	2	12	8
20. Rec. of Dr Drew Archdeaconry Cornwell bad money[1]	11	12	4
24. Rec. of Francis Edger Register Ipswich clipt & bad money[1]	4	15	11
2[ ]. Rec. of the parish of Aberfield, Berks.		11	1
Dec. 7. Rec. of John Wakefield Deputy Register for Chichester clipt money[1]	12	15	8½
23. Rec. of St Katherine Colman Fenchurch Street	4	8	—
Jan. 19. Rec. of parish of Alesbury, Bucks.	4	15	—
21. Rec. of Thomas Barret Archdeaconry Lewis, Sussix	8	4	4
Feb. 5. Rec. of John Payne Register Archdeaconry Wells old money[1]	9	8	7
Rec. of Francis Evans Archdeaconry Bathe ditto[1]	35	5	—

	£4965	6	6¾
8. Rec of Dr Wolsey Archdeaconry Peterborough		8	8½
1697			
Apr. 1. Rec. of Cor. Yeate collected parish of St Maryes Marlborough milled money[1]	7	4	—
May 18. Rec. of the parish of Ohney, Bucks. per tale 10 oz. per weight[2]	4	19	0¼
July 2. Rec. of Dr John Morton Archdeaconry Northumberland 206 oz.[3] per tale	75	11	4¾
Rec.[4] of Mr Richard Hoare 3400 oz. of old money at 5/1d.¼ per oz.	867	14	2
Aug. 24. Rec. of Mr Thomas Kelsey Archdeaconry Sarum 4g. 30s.	22	11	9½
Rec. of ditto administrator to Dr Ward 3g. at 30s.	51	16	7
Oct. 28. Rec. of Archdeaconry Coventry & Stafford per John Barrett in money	14	17	6

---

[1] Added in another hand. [2] '10 oz. per weight' added in another hand.
[3] '206 oz.' added in another hand. [4] A pointing hand in the margin against this entry.

		£	s	d
Nov. 27.	Rec. of Smith Register of Archdeaconry Durham 26[1] oz. per tale	12	6	$4\frac{1}{2}$
Dec. 9.	Rec. for a tally on the 3s. aid principal 1000 interest 71:2	1071	2	—
Mar. 3.	Rec. for a tally on 3s. aid principal 100 interest 8:17	108	17	—
12.	Rec. for a tally on 3s. aid principal 50 interest 4:9	54	9	—
21.	Rec. for 4 tallys on 3s. aid principal 400 interest 36:7	436	7	—
1698 30.	Rec. for a tally on 3s. aid principal 500 interest 44:7:6	544	7	6
		£8237	18	$7\frac{1}{4}$
Oct. 24.	Rec. 6 months interest of 2200 due 30th Sept.	88	—	—
Nov. 28.	Rec. of Francis Edger Deputy Register Deocess Norwich	6	5	6
Mar. 3.	Rec. 4 orders No. 1263, 1264, 1265 & 1266	2065	16	8
8.	Rec. 2 orders No. 1411 & 1412	206	15	—
1699				
June 10.	Rec. of the minister & churchwardens of Bazingshaw, London, interest £18	6	5	6
	Rec. a tally on the Disbanding Act[2]	1048	12	—
1703				
June 21.	Rec. of Mr Jephcott & Mr Mitchener to ballance the account	83	5	$5\frac{1}{4}$
		£11742	18	$8\frac{1}{2}$
1696	Brought over paid	£3435	4	$1\frac{1}{2}$
Feb. 16.	Paid 3388 oz. 6dwt which at 6s.2d$\frac{3}{8}$ bought tallys for £1050 on 3s. aid per tale	1363	1	3
	Paid 3400 oz. rec. of Mr Hoare in part for a tally of £1000	867	14	2
	Paid to make up £900 for a tally of 1000 on the 3s. aid 126 oz. 11dwt at $5/1\frac{1}{4}$ £32:5:10 per tale	42	10	—
1698				
Apr. 19.	Paid for 6 tallys on 2nd 3s. aid No. 1263, 1264, 1265, 1266, 1411 & 1412 dated 30 Mar. last principal £2200 at 3 per cent discount	2134	—	—
		7842	9	$6\frac{1}{2}$

---

[1] '26 oz.' added in another hand.   [2] 10 & 11 W.III cap. 9.

1699

Apr. 26. Paid into the Exchequer on the Disbanding Act transfered to 3rd 3s.	1000	—	—
May 18. Paid John Hutchinson for lead	112	10	—
Aug. 11. Paid Mr William Newsham	500	—	—
Sept. 18. Paid William Colemore Esq.	500	—	—
Paid per letters etc.	1	—	—

1700

May 15. Paid Thomas Newsham Esq.	300	—	—
July 15. Paid Richard Lane	100	—	—
Oct. 2. Paid Francis Chernock	175	—	—
4. Paid ditto	125	—	—
14. Paid Mr William Newsham	200	—	—
Jan. 23. Paid Francis Chernock	250	—	—
Sept. 11. Paid ditto	250	—	—
Feb. 7. Paid Thomas Newsham Esq.	100	—	—

1703

June 21. Paid Mr Jephcot & Mr Mitchener	7	10	6
Paid[1] ditto 674 oz. old money which was taken for	279	8	8
	£11742	18	$8\frac{1}{2}$

[1] A pointing hand in the margin against this entry.

STREET DIAGRAMS

STREET DIAGRAMS OF WARWICK

These diagrams are not maps of the town. The map nearest to the time of the fire is the map of 1711 by James Fish, on which the maps reproduced as end-papers are based. These diagrams of the burnt areas are designed to show conjecturally the relative positions of the houses in the streets at the time of the fire. They are derived from internal evidence in the fire documents, but also from deeds, rentals, and particularly from the commoners' rolls from 1698 onwards. Mr Stephen Wallsgrove very kindly allowed his researches into the commoners' records to be incorporated. Post-fire houses did not always coincide with pre-fire sites, and caution is needed in identifying a site with a present-day house. In the poorer parts of the town, especially Joyce Pool and the Butts, for which few deeds survive and which apparently had no common rights, only a minority of houses have so far been located. Many sufferers are known to have lived in those areas, and their names have been added in panels, with arrows indicating only the approximate location of their dwellings.

IN THESE DIAGRAMS,
occupiers are in bold type
owners are in italics and
MESNE TENANTS in italic capitals

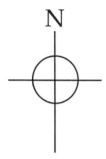

N

Mrs Townsend	**Thomas Roberts**	RED LION INN				
William Tarver	**—— Drake**		KING & QUEEN'S HEAD	**Matthew Busby**		
William Tarver	**Edward Owen**			**Edward Deacon** *George Chinn*		
	George Tongue			**John Avern** **Joseph Avern** **Richard Rawbone** *John Avern*		
William Tarver	**Samuel Brierley**			**John Stokes** *William Tarver*		
	Thomas West					

SWAN LANE

FORMER BELL INN

SWAN INN

HIGH

SALTISFORD

JOYCE POOL

NORTHGATE

WALL   DYKE

John
Hopkins

WATER
HOUSE

		Robert Watts sen.	
	The County	John Williams	GAOL
	The County		SHIRE HALL
	Corpn.	John Pritchard	
		John Pritchard	
	Eleanor Ashwin	Joseph Willis	
	John Hawks	Thomas Arps	BLACK RAVEN INN

STREET

SHEEP

GREEN DRAGON INN

CROWN INN

Richard Harris	*Elizabeth Cawthern*		
Martin Taylor	*Elizabeth Cawthern*		
Richard Hadley			
John Butler	*WILLIAM GERARD*	*Mary Wagstaffe*	
Thomas Rush	*Mary Wagstaffe*		
Samuel Parsons	*John Watts*		
John Burnill	*John Watts*		
Thomas Wise			
Job Rainsford	*Anne Prescott*		

PEBBLE   LANE

		Oken's Charity	John Atterbury	BIRD IN HAND INN
			William Edes	PARSONAGE
	Mary Murcott	William Fetherston	Mary Murcott	
		George Chesley	Edward Chesley	
			James Fish sen.	
Oken's Charity	*JOHN BIKER*	John Cakebread	Sarah Edwards	
	Church	*JOHN DOLPHIN*	Sarah Mayo	
		Church	Joseph Hemmings	
			Elizabeth Carr	
			William Perks	
		Anne Palmer	Robert Taylor	
	John Weale	Stephen Nicholls	Alexander Nicholls	
		Elizabeth Cawthern	Thomas Claridge	
		Fulke Weale	Henry Smith	
		Thomas Dadley	John Hands	
		William Tarver	Devereux Whadcock	

STREET

CHURCH

CHURCH YARD

CHURCH OF SAINT MARY

Beauchamp Chapel

CHURCH YARD

John Jarvis	John Cole	Ann Webb	John Jarvis
Edward Heath			
Thomas Lane	*Hannah Tuckey*		
Samuel Ainge			
Joseph Ainge			
Robert Blissett			

STREET

JURY   STREET

COW LANE

Edward Venor — John Holyoak

Mary Overton

Sarah Hicks — Edward Clopton — **DOLPHIN INN**

Sarah Bunter — Richard Crane & Sarah Bunter — **BEAR INN**

Thomas Stratford

Thomas Stratford

Thomas West — Samuel Brierley — George Tongue — William Tarver — **FORMER BELL INN**

SWAN LANE

John Stokes — William Tarver — **SWAN INN**

Joseph Blissett

George Taylor — Thomas Moore — John Gibbs — Richard Grimes

Edward Norton

Richard Kerby

Thomas Watts

Thomas Dadley

Thomas Dadley — John & the Weale poor

HIGH STREET OR HIGH PAVEMENT

SAUNDERS ROW

Mr Corpson — Thomas Russell — Joshua Perks — John Banbury

Mr Corpson — George Harris

Corpn. — Richard Sharp

Ann Lucas

Corpn. — Richard Bromley

Dorothy Weale — Abraham du Commun — Sarah Rider

Dorothy Weale — Humphrey Carter

Thomas Dixon

Dorothy Hopkins — George Watts

Corpn. — Thomas Gibbs

Isaac Tomkiss

QUAKERS HOUSE

WHITE LION INN

FOXES LANE

John Welton — John Langton

John Welton — William Eborall

Anne & James Prescott — Elizabeth Sandford

Anne & James Prescott — Elizabeth Askell

Richard Green — Thomas Maunder

Richard Green — George Barton — Councillor Smith

Thomas Archer — George Smith

Thomas Archer — Charles Harrison

Edmund Wilson — Henry Rogers

William Cooke — Richard Hands

William Cooke — Thomas Tipping — Oken's Charity

Fulke Weale — Dorothy Weale

Thomas

(534)

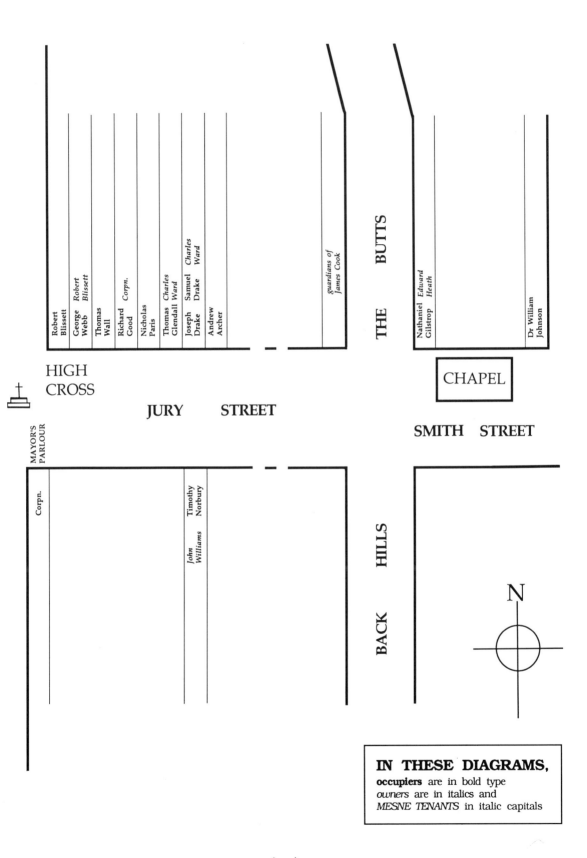

HIGH
CROSS

THE BUTTS

CHAPEL

JURY STREET

SMITH STREET

Robert Blissett

George Webb *Robert Blissett*

Thomas Wall

Richard Good *Corpn.*

Nicholas Paris

Thomas Glendall *Charles Ward*

Joseph Drake Samuel Drake *Charles Ward*

Andrew Archer

guardians of James Cook

Nathaniel Gilstrop *Edward Heath*

Dr William Johnson

MAYOR'S PARLOUR

Corpn.

John Williams Timothy Norbury

BACK HILLS

N

IN THESE DIAGRAMS,
occupiers are in bold type
owners are in italics and
MESNE TENANTS in italic capitals

(535)

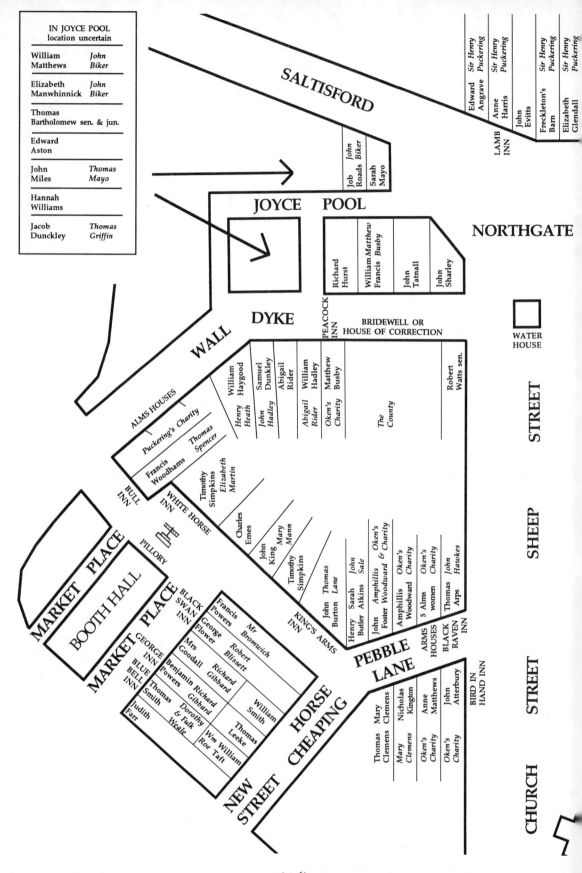

IN JOYCE POOL
location uncertain

William Matthews	John Biker
Elizabeth Manwhinnick	John Biker
Thomas Bartholomew sen. & jun.	
Edward Aston	
John Miles	Thomas Mayo
Hannah Williams	
Jacob Dunckley	Thomas Griffin

SALTISFORD

Edward Angrave — Sir Henry Puckering
Anne Harris — Sir Henry Puckering
John Evitts
Freckleton's Barn — Sir Henry Puckering
Elizabeth Glendall — Sir Henry Puckering
LAMB INN

Job Roads — John Biker
Sarah Mayo

JOYCE POOL

NORTHGATE

Richard Hurst
William Matthew — Francis Busby
John Tatnall
John Sharley

DYKE

WALL

PEACOCK INN

BRIDEWELL OR HOUSE OF CORRECTION

WATER HOUSE

STREET

William Haygood
Samuel Dunkley
Abigail Rider
William Hadley
Matthew Busby

ALMS HOUSES

Puckering's Charity

Henry Heath
John Hadley
Abigail Rider
Oken's Charity

Thomas Spencer

Francis Woodhams

Robert Watts sen.

The County

Timothy Simpkins
Elizabeth Martin

BULL INN

WHITE HORSE INN

PILLORY

Charles Emes

John King
Mary Mann
Timothy Simpkins

Henry Butler
Sarah Atkins
John Sale
John Amphillis Foster Woodward
Oken's Woodward & Charity
Amphillis Woodward
Oken's Charity
5 Alms women
Oken's Charity
Thomas Arps
John Hawkes

SHEEP STREET

MARKET PLACE

BOOTH HALL

MARKET PLACE

John Burton
Thomas Lane

KING'S ARMS INN

PEBBLE LANE

ARMS HOUSES
BLACK RAVEN INN

BLACK SWAN INN

Francis Powers
George Flower
Mr Bromwich
Robert Blissett

GEORGE INN

Mrs Goodall
Richard Gibbard
William Smith

BLUE BELL INN

Benjamin Powers
Richard Gibbard

Thomas Smith
Dorothy & Fulk Weale
Thomas Leeke

Judith Farr
Wm William Roe Taft

HORSE CHEAPING

BIRD IN HAND INN

STREET

NEW STREET

Thomas Clemens
Mary Clemens
Nicholas Kington
Anne Matthews
John Atterbury

Mary Clemens
Oken's Charity
Oken's Charity

CHURCH

(536)

PRIORY LANE

THE PRIORY

N

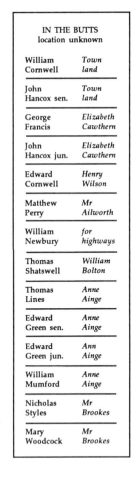

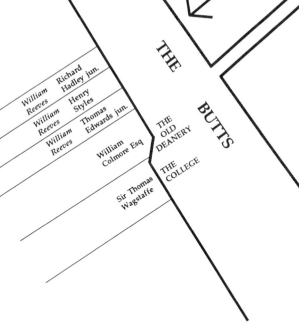

William Reeves *Richard Hadley jun.*

William Reeves *Henry Styles*

William Reeves *Thomas Edwards jun.*

William Colmore Esq

THE OLD DEANERY

Sir Thomas Wagstaffe

THE COLLEGE

THE BUTTS

IN THESE DIAGRAMS,
occupiers are in bold type
owners are in italics and
MESNE TENANTS in italic capitals

(537)

GENERAL INDEX

In this index, people are assumed to be of Warwick unless otherwise stated; brief biographical details and dates of death are given, if known. Contemporary street names are used, with cross-references from modern names if different. Houses are identified by the names of occupants at the time of the fire, and inns by their signs. (Houses were not numbered in Warwick until after 1870.) A few glossary entries are included.

fire court: officers: (*cont.*)

surveyors: Sam. Dunckley, Thos. Master, Jas. Fish sen. appointed, xv, 19–20; Sam. Dunckley, John Phillips, Wm. Smith elected, duties defined, 26; to view and report irregularities against Act and orders of crt., 30; schemes of ground added to or taken from proprietors, 22–4, 75; drafts of Swan La., new square and new street, 28, 33–4; scheme of all roofs by Phillips, 37; Jas. Fish jun. paid for survey of the town and plans, 41, 429; cartway across Pigwells staked out and viewed, 46–8, 61–2; to order wells, privies, cellars to be covered, 48; to re-stake out Swan La., 59; to survey ground taken in new street from pillory to new square, 81; to regulate paving, 61, 63, 78; individual sites measured or viewed, 39–40, 55–7, 68, 78n., 346; party walls measured, work valued, 66, 285, 310, 351; Red Lion wall rebuilt, 83; Smith and Dunckley paid 'for care and pains in office', 76; Phillips paid, 107, 320, 495; Moses Robinson appointed surveyor and director of earth and rubbish, 45, to report negligences in clearing streets, 47

treasurers: Wm. Tarver ordered, from money in his hands, to pay for sending briefs, 17, and distribution to rebuilders, 19; distribution by treasurers to sufferers ordered, 26, to be entered in book of receipts and disbursements, 28; distributions ordered, 26–9, 35, 37–8, 51–3; distribution lists, 415–24; distributions adjusted, 28–9, suspended, 30; distributions at the Mayor's Parlour, 35, day appointed, 40; treasurers to lay statements of a/c before crt., 30, 56, 63, 67, 82, 86, 88; specimen statement of a/c, 425–6, treasurers named, 47–8; brief money stored in chest in Castle, 29, 51, bad money from London to be mixed with it, 52–3; Wm. Tarver ordered to pay in money retained for loss of his goods, disallowed, and to deliver up all books and papers, 105, 107

procedure: style of the crt. fixed, 13; Northampton town clerk paid for advice on proceedings in fire court there, 15; copies of orders to be posted on County Hall, Market Hall and Mayor's Parlour, 17, 24, 'most public places in borough', 74–5; Monday to be crt. day, 17; parties to approach crt. by petition, xvii, 28; lost estimate to be re-submitted, 35, allowed, 42; witnesses to be heard, 38–9; 2 commissioners to view garden wall, 68; 3

coms. to hear dispute, 43, or view ground, 55; 5 coms. to approve securities for loans, 53–4; parties to withdraw while matters debated, 52

fire-fighting, payment to 34 men for putting out an earlier fire, ix; payment to Sam. Dunckley for 30 men 'as put out the fire at Hall', and to Jas. Fish for 4 men at Beauchamp Chapel, x, 412; fire buckets lost by Chas. Harrison, 166, and by Saddlers' and Shoemakers' Companies, 202–3; ho.s demolished, xi, of Na. Gilstrop in Jury St., 374–6, of John King nr. the pillory, 355–6, of Geo. Chinn in Swan La., 341, of Tim. Norbury in Jury St., 333; of Thos. Leeke, 227; of Jas. Cook an infant in Jury St., 294; town water engine burnt, ix, 77n., 229, 242, 298

fire insurance, in London, ix–x

fire, separate, petn. of Marg. West, widow, *re* separate, later fire in Brittaine La. or Saltisford, 359

Fish:

Jas., sen., parish clerk, d. 1702, payment to 4 men that put out fire at the [Beauchamp] chapel, x, 412; appointed a surveyor, 20, not reappointed, 26; ho. in Church St., estimate, 138, 182–3, 235, 246, 254; distributions to, 27, 417, 418, 424; paid for ground taken, 423; encroachment by, 78n., 296; paid for party wall, 81, 350–1; approved with Jas. jun. as security for loans, 54; loan to, repaid, 86, 93, 430, 433, 446, 452, 455; timber bldgs. in Church St., thatched bldgs. in High St. & Mkt. Pl. ward, 271, 275

Jas., jun., surveyor, b. 1673, loan to Jas. sen. repaid in part by, xxi, 464; paid for drawing survey of town and other surveying for crt., 41, 111, 429; Thos. Clements's ground measured by, 319; draft of Wm. Cook's ground by, 28, and attorney for, 28, 326, 377–9; put forward by sufferers to inspect Mitchener's a/cs., xxxi

Fisher:

Sir Clement, Bt., commissioner named in Brief, 119, and Act, 121; summoned *re* failure of tower, 441

Francis, Esq., commissioner named in Brief, 119, and Act, 122

Mr., payment to, by John Burton, 352

Flamstead [?] (Hunsted) (Herts.), brief money from, 527

flax, 145–6, 154, 159, 174, 176, 182, 192, 196, 213–14, 217, 222, 226, 229; wick yarn, 230; swingle ho., 154; flax barn, 279; *and see* trades: flaxdresser

Gerrard (Garrett, Jarrett):

Radcliff [?], brief money from, 524

Wm., of Henley-in-Arden or Worcester, gent., tenant of ho. in Sheep St., Mary Wagstaffe owner, sub-let to John Butler, estimate, 199, 238; petn. against, 29, 32, 328-9

Mr., payment to, 426

Gerrard St. *see* Gaolhall La.

Gibbard (Giberd, Gibbert, Gibert), Ric., maltster, owner of George Inn in Mkt. Pl., Benj. Powers tenant, estimate, 142, 212, 229, 239, 251; a rebuilder, 29; dispute with Mrs. D. Weale *re* gutter, 38-40, 42, 332-3; distributions to, 419, 422; juror *re* encroachment, 287; owner of ho. in Mkt. Pl., let to Mrs. Goodhall [?], estimate, 142, 229, 240; owner of ho. in New St., let to Mr. Dodd, estimate, 143, 229, 242; dispute with Wm. Smith adj., *re* quarrying, encroachment, 55, 60, 61, 267, 339

Gibbins, Clement, thatched ho. in Saltisford ward, 276

Gibbs (Gibbes):

Ann, sister of Thos., goods in his estimate, 159

Eliz., servant to John Stokes at the Swan, estimate, 230, 242

John, tailor, ho. in High St., Ric. Grimes owner, estimate, 145, 147, 231; distributions to, 412, 416; thatched barn in Bridge End, 283

Mary, distribution to, 421

Susannah (Shusanna, Susance), servant to Sam. Ainge in Church St., estimate, 169, 234; distribution to, 421

Thos., sen., alderman, ho. in High St. [?], estimate, 168; distributions to, 420, 422

Thos., sen. or jun., shoemaker, ho. in High St., corpn. owner, estimate, 136, 159, 160, 233, 244, 364; ground to be taken from street and added to site, 23; lease to be inspected 37*n.*; dispute with I. Tomkiss *re* side windows, 258; decree of site to John Williams, carpenter, 311-12, 399-400; distributions to, 416, 418, 419, 422

Thos., jun., juror to view encroachment, 287, 305; distributions to, 419, 422

Gill, Moses, brief money from, 526

Gilstrop (Gilstop, Gilstrup, Guilstrop), Nathan or Nathaniel, labourer, d. 1701, ho. in Jury St. nr. Eastgate, Edw. Heath owner, estimate, 143, 188-9, 236, 252, pulled down by Dr. Johnson, xi, 49, 374-6; distributions to, 416, 421

Glendall (Glendell, Glendole):

Eliz., d. 1711, w. of John, ho., barns, etc., in

Saltisford, Sir H. Puckering owner, estimate, 221, 241; distributions to, 418, 420

John, cleaning chancel, work in churchyard, 471-2, 486-7, 494

Sarah, servant to widow Edwards in Church St., estimate, 180, 235; distribution to, 419

Steph., security for Wm. Holmes, brickmaker, 66; coals of, taken, 67; thatched bldgs. in Jury St., 271, 277

Thos., shoemaker, ho. in Jury St., Mr. Ward of Barford owner, estimate, 142, 186, 236, 250; distributions to, 415, 420

Mrs., thatched bldgs. in Bridge End, 283

nurse, distribution to, 416

Gloucester, bells re-cast at, *see* Rudhall, Abraham

archdeaconry, brief money from, 524, 526-8

dioc., brief money from, 523

Glover:

John, juror to view encroachment, 288, 305; thatched ho. in High St. ward, 274, barn in Coten End, 282

Wm., thatched bldg. in Bridge End, 283

widow, thatched bldgs. in Coten End, 281

Good (Goode, Goods):

Jerome or Jeremiah, baker, of Baginton, malt lost with J. Hemmings, wheat lost with G. Flower, 178, 211-12, 239, 253

Ric., tallow chandler, ho. in Jury St., corpn. owner, estimate, 142, 186, 236, 254, 364; distributions to, 415, 423; paid for ground taken into street, 423; site decreed to N. Paris and T. Wall, 372; to desist from building chandlery nr. A. Archer, 47-8; to be paid as builder for Mr. Ward's ho., 74; signs petn. *re* Swan La., 354

Goodall (Goodalle, Goodale):

Mary, servant of Sam. Ainge in Church St., estimate, 169, 234; distribution to, 421

Mrs., ho. adj. George Inn in Mkt. Pl., owner Ric. Gibbard, estimate, 229

Goodwin, Hen., registrar, Sudbury archdeaconry, 524, 527

Goodwyne, Mr., bishop's letters printed by, 411

Grant, John, min. of St Dunstan's in the West, London, 510

Grascome, Walter, money for Mr. Huss *via*, 483

Green (Greene):

Edw., sen., labourer, ho. in Butts, Mrs. Ainge owner, estimate, 222, 241, 253; distribution to, 416, 420

Edw., jun., flaxman, in Butts, loss in flax, estimate, 222, 241; distribution to, 420

Eliz., of Abingdon, w. of Ric., owner of ho. in High St. from mother, let to Thos. Maunder, decree to him, 70, 290-1

Hadley: (*cont.*)

Ric., serjt.-at-mace, innkeeper, bur. 5 Feb. 1705, notice against timber-framing to be given by, 16; chosen crt. beadle, 17; precepts to, 287, 304-6; petn. to excise coms., 10; owner of Green Dragon in Sheep St. incl. prison ho., estimate, 141, 198, 237, 240; to remove rubbish, 84; ground taken to enlarge street, 106, 489-90; allowed break in ho. front, 57, 59; distributions to, 27, 415-17, 420, 424; loan to, 82, repaid *via* alderman Young, 107, 477, 479, 482, 502; petns. of John and Geo. Watts, Elias Webb, against, *re* watercourse, 101, 103, 354-5, 362; rubbish to his quarry, 342, 439; thatched work-ho. and ho. in Saltisford ward, 276-7

Ric., jun., fellmonger and woolcomber, at Green Dragon, estimate of goods, 198, 237

Ric., jun., flaxdresser or labourer, ho. in Butts, Wm. Reeves owner, estimate, 140, 224, 241, 248

Wm., shoemaker, ho. in Joyce Pool adj. Peacock, Mrs. Rider owner, estimate, 219, 241; distributions to, 416, 421; ho. formerly of, in Joyce Pool, 365-6

Mr., thatched bldgs. in Saltisford ward, 276-7

—, labourer, churchyard wall foundations, 470

Halford, widow, with Isaac Tomkis in High St., estimate, 233

Hall:

John, brief money from, 510

John, thatched bldgs. in Bridge End, 282

Halton, Dr. Tim., archdeacon of Oxon., 509, 512, 515, 517, 520

Hammersmith (Mdx.), brief money from, 525

Hampe, Wm., thatched barn in Bridge End, 282

Hamper, Wm., of Birmingham, antiquary, fire documents lent to, xxxiii

Hampstead (Mdx.?), brief money from, 523

Hampton (Mdx.), brief money from, 525

Hampton[-on-the-Hill], pebbles from, 476-7

Hancox (Hancocks, Hancock):

John, sen., herder, ho. in Butts, surveyors of highways owners, estimate, 140, 223-4, 241, 248; distributions to, 45, 419

John, distributions to, 416, 420

John and Cath., petn. for aid to finish ho. in Butts, xxi, 363

John, jun., labourer, ho. in Butts, Mrs. Cawthern owner, estimate, 224, 241; distribution to, 417

John, glazier, 384-6, error for Ric. *q.v.*

Ric., glazier, contract for glazing church, xxvi, 93-4; paid for glazing, 451; paid for lead for pinnacles, 469; witness for Mrs. D. Weale, 39; toft of Eliz. Martin [White Horse] in Mkt. Pl. decreed to, 71, 384-6; paid for ground taken into new street, 90, 317, 444; paid as rebuilder, 2 ho.s, 78, 298, 300; thatched bldg. in Mkt. Pl. ward, 275

Susanna, widow, d. 1713, goods in Pebble La., 206, 239; distributions to, 419, 421

Thos., 45, error for John, *q.v.*

Hands:

Geo., thatched bldg. in Saltisford ward, 276

John, glover, ho. in Church St., Thos. Dadley owner, estimate, 138, 144, 173, 234; distribution to, 415; signs petn. *re* Swan La., 354, Jury St. petn. *re* thatch, 315

Ric., maltster, alderman, mayor 1696-7, 1708-9, d. 1716, present at crts., 74, 76-7, 79, 81-2; bearer of letters of request, 2; expenses in Hemlingford Hundred, 412; to regulate estimates, 21, 252; signs petn. *re* Swan La., 354; signs Oken's char. petn. as feoffee, 355; signs boro. order *re* ground sold, 258; payment to T. Masters *via*, 479; juror to view encroachment, 287; decree to, as mortgagee, of J. Pritchard's ho. in Sheep St., 29, 31-2, 38, 57, 72, 256, 384; site bought by J. Willis, petns. for ground to be set out, 295, 342; distributions to 415, 420, 422

Ric., baker ('baker Hands'), tenant of 1 of 2 ho.s in High St. of Wm. Cook of London, 367-7; estimate, 135, 166, 234; site decreed to Hands, 261-2, 378-9, sold to Thos. Dadley and Edw. Chesley, 303

Ric., joiner, goods lost in Jury St., estimate, 187, 236, 252; builder on land of Thos. Clements in new square, petns. for valuation, 101, 103, 362; paid as builder of Oken's almshouse site in Pebble La., 449; petns. to buy Bell ground, and *re* chief rent, 110, 315-16, 362; petn. against foreign joiners, 348; timber-framed barn in High St., 271, thatched barn in Jury St., 277

Thos., thatched bldgs. in Saltisford ward, 276

Hankey, Hen., rector of Wanstead (Essex), 513, 516

Hanks, John, thatched bldgs. in Coten End, 281

Hanslope (Bucks.), brief money from, 518

Harmondsworth (Mdx.), brief money from, 526

Rainsford (Ransford), Job (*cont.*)
 ground bought from Wm. Holmes and
  rebuilt, 74, 76; to be paid by Cole for
  party wall, 87; seat in church, 500
Rands:
 Eliz., servant to Mrs. Overton in High St.,
  estimate, 167, 234; distribution to, 421
 Jos., thatched ho. in Saunders Row, 274
Raning, John, thatched ho. in Saunders Row,
 274
Rawbone (Rabonn):
 Ric., butcher, ho. in Swan La., John Avern
  owner, estimate, 209–10, 239; distribu-
  tion to, 416; thatched bldgs. in Friar La.,
  273
 Wm., paid for bread and ale at refining, 504;
  thatched barn in Smith St., 279
 —, in poss. of the Black Boy [or Raven] in
  Sheep St., 398–9
Rawlins:
 Sam., thatched bldgs. in Bridge End, 283
 Thos., serjeant at law, J.P., commissioner
  named in Brief, 119; signs Q.S. cert. of
  losses, 9, 116
 —, of Stoneleigh, yew tree bought from, 494
Raye, Benj., brief money rec. *via*, 515
Reading (Redding):
 Edw., mason, petn. with Wm. Holmes *v.*
  Wm. Perks, whose ho. they undertook to
  rebuild, 57, 265
 Francis, thatched barn in Bridge End, 283
 John, thatched bldgs. in Coten End, 281
 Jonathan, money to Mr. Huss sent *via*, in
  Coventry, 483
 Miles, thatched bldgs. in West St. ward, 272
recoinage *see under* money: debased
Redding *see* Reading
reductions of estimates, 244–54
Reeves (Reeve):
 Edw., signs book of reductions of goods, 254
 Wm., owner, 2 ho.s, 1 barn in Butts, estimate,
  225; decreed to Wm. Colmore, 57,
  390–1; owner of ho.s of Ric. Hadley jun.
  and Hen. Styles in Butts, estimates, 224,
  241; owner of barn in Butts where timber
  of Thos. Edwards jun. lost, 241; distribution to, 422
 Mr., owner of barn, Thos. Masters tenant,
  estimate, 140, 249
 Mr., paid for whitewashing chancel, 507
Reppingale (Reppingall):
 Wm., thatched bldgs. in Bridge End, 283
 widow, thatched bldg. in West St. ward, 272
 —, seat in church, 480
Reynolds (Reignolds), Griff., collector of brief
  money employed at Hereford, xxiii;
  money rec. from, 528
Rhodes *see* Roades

Richards, S., registrar, Shropshire arch-
 deaconry, 524
Richardson:
 John., thatched bldg. in Smith St., 279
 Joshua, min. of Allhallows on the Wall,
  London, 510
 Mr., bell weighed by, 493; paid for wood and
  leather for clappers, 494
Richmond archdeaconry, brief money from,
 518–19
Rider (Ryder):
 Abigail, d. 1712, husb. 'gone for a soldier', 2
  ho.s in Joyce Pool, 1 let to Wm. Hadley,
  estimate, 219, 241; distributions to, 68,
  419, 422
 Sarah, widow, midwife, ho. in High St., 23,
  F. and Mrs. D. Weale owners, estimate,
  136, 156, 167, 232, 253; distributions to,
  416–19, 422; site still unbuilt, 108,
  decreed to J. Mitchener, 111–12
Right *see* Wright
Risbury, Dr. Thos., rector of St Paul's, Shadwell, London, 514
Rix, Hen., min. of Newport Pond (Essex), 511
Roades (Roads, Rhodes, Rohds, Roods, Rodes),
 Job, innkeeper, ho. in Joyce Pool, J.
  Biker owner, estimate, 140, 179, 215,
  240, 254; distributions to, 415, 418–19;
  petn. to excise coms., 10; thatched bldg.
  in Saltisford ward, 277
Roberts:
 Eliz., widow, apothecary, sub-tenant of part
  of Eliz. Askell's ho. in High St., esti-
  mate, 163, 233, 253; distribution to, 423
 Thos., innkeeper, bearer of letter of request,
  1; expenses in Hemlingford Hundred,
  412; to regulate estimates, 21, 252, 254;
  witness to agreement between Lane and
  Burton, 311; tenant of outho. of John
  Avern and barn of Mr. Hicks in Swan
  La., estimates, 143, 209–10, 239, 251;
  distribution to, 422; petn. as tenant of
  Red Lion [not burnt] *re* Swan La. and
  paving of ground taken, 109, 321, 326–7;
  Red Lion garden wall forms boundary
  with Geo. Chinn, 392–3; thatched bldg.
  in Friar La., 273
 Tim., draper, petn. with Thos. Wall, as
  owners of 2 ho.s built on ground late Mr.
  Welton's, for reduced chief rent, 110,
  320–1
Roberts *alias* Burford, Sam., brickmaker and
  innkeeper, paid for bricks used about
  dials, 472, for refining furnace, 505; paid
  for pebbles for paving, 496; site at corner
  of Horse Cheaping and Pebble La.
  bought from John Sale and rebuilt, 77*n.*,
  295–6, 391–2; plan of exchange with

Shire Hall *see under* Warwick county; Warwick
   streets: Sheep St.
Shoemakers' Company *see under* Company
shop-books:
   of Ric. Sharp in High St., 155
   of Wm. Eborall in High St., 161
   of Ann Edes in Sheep St., 195
   of Sarah Hill's dec. husb. in Sheep St., 200
Short, Sam., son-in-law of Wm. Clements,
   323-4
Shotteswell:
   Steph., thatched ho. in St Nich. Church St.,
      280
   Thos., thatched bldg. in Bridge End, 283
Shrewley, stone from, *see under* quarries
Shropshire (Salop) archdeaconry, brief money
   from, 524-5, 527
Shuckburgh   (Shughburg,   Shugberg,
   Shugburg):
   Sir Chas., Bt., J.P., of Shuckburgh, d. 1705,
      present at cttee., 7; signs Q.S. cert of
      losses, 9, 116
   John, J.P., signs Mitchener's a/c book, 503
Silk, Wm., son-in-law of Wm. Clements, 323-4
Silvester, Kath., lodger with Thos. Lane, 344
Simmonds (Simonds, Symons):
   Abraham, surgeon, goods in High St., esti-
      mate, 164, 233; distributions to, 417, 420
   Sam., cur. of Clapham, 520
Simpkins (Simkins), Tim., innkeeper and malt-
      ster, petn. to excise commissioners, 10;
      tenant of White Horse in Mkt. Pl., Eliz.
      Martin owner, estimate, 142, 228, 242,
      251, 253-4; owner 1 bay, part burnt, 142,
      251; flaxseed of Job Burt lost, 213; shop of
      Sarah Blythe part of his ho., 226; distri-
      butions to, 416, 418-19, 422; timber-
      framed bldgs. in Mkt. Pl., 272; payment
      to T. Masters *via*, 498; loan to widow
      Perks repaid *via*, 502; seat in church, 493
Skelton, John, archdeacon of Bedford, 514
Skidmore *see* Scudamore
Skinner, Wm., [registrar?], Derbyshire arch-
   deaconry, 524
Slye, Thos., thatched bldgs. in High St., 271,
   and Mkt. Pl. ward, 275
Slyer, Nic., thatched bldg. in Saltisford ward,
   276
Small, Dan., brief money rec. *via*, 524
Smart, Francis, owner of Sarah Mayo's
   [rebuilt] ho. in Church St., petn. *v.* Nic.
   Wrothwell that window in new stable on
   part of Swan garden is a nuisance, 101,
   104-5*n.*, 318, 362
Smith (Smyth, Smiths):
   Francis, mason, mayor 1713-14, 1728-9, d.
      1738, digging and laying church founda-
      tions, 434-5; with Sam. Dunckley and

Wm. Smith, contract for stonework of
   church and tower, xxv; paid for getting
   stone, 437, 461; paid for work unspecified on church and tower, 103, 430-1,
   433, 449-50, 453-4, 470, 478, 499, 501;
   paid for balustrade round church and
   over windows, 90-1, 437; with other
   masons, contract for laying foundations
   of new tower and building Shrewley
   stone pillars, 98; paid for tower foundations and pillars, 444-5; for getting stone
   at Priory and Humbridge Down quarries, 460; for work unspecified on new
   tower, 446-72 *passim*; to add coats of
   arms and block windows, 106; paid in
   full, 106; detail of final a/c, 107*n.*; to have
   extra £40 on completion, 110; warned *re*
   unbuilt ground in Sheep St., 108; paid as
   rebuilder of part and for ground taken,
   109, 502-3; unbuilt ground decreed to
   Mitchener, 111-12, 406-7; date of conveyance from Cawthern, 112
   Geo., barber, and jun., ho. in High St., Thos.
      Archer, Esq. owner, estimate, 165, 233;
      ground sold to Thos. Mann of Kenil-
      worth, xviii-xix; overpaid on first dis-
      tribution, 30; signs petn. *re* Swan La.,
      354; tenant of new ho. of Thos. Wall in
      Jury St., 372
   Hen., butcher, ho. in Church St., Mrs. and F.
      Weale owners, estimate, 138, 173-4, 235,
      246, 251; distribution to, 415; tenant of
      new ho. of G. and J. Watts in Sheep St.,
      322, 354-5; no watercourse from his ho.,
      103; timber-framed slaughterho. in Mkt.
      Pl., 272
   Hen., paid for carriage of Shrewley stone,
      458, 481, of rubbish, 459, 467, 481;
      payment to Ric. Williams *via*, 479, 494;
      carriage of yew trees, 494, 499
   Israel *see* Susanna
   John, Esq., of Frolesworth (Leics.), baron of
      the Exchequer 1702, d. 1726, paid for
      drawing up the Act, xiii, 413; present at
      crt., 107
   John, gent., 'at the Cross', contributor to
      letter of request, 2; to list sufferers, 3;
      signs petns. for paying old money into
      Exchequer, 266, *re* John Atterbury's
      encroachment, 287, against thatch, 315;
      guardian of Jas. Cook, infant, 294;
      thatched bldg. in Saltisford ward, 276
   Jonathan, hatter, goods broken and lost in
      Castle St., estimate, 190, 237, 252
   Mary, distribution to, 422
   Rog., signs Jury St. petn. against thatch, 315
   Susanna or Israel, clothes lost with Thos.
      Moore [?] in High St., estimate, 146, 231

Warwick streets: (cont.)

Backhills: thatched barns on, 277, 279

Back La. see Fox's La.

Bridge End: thatched bldgs. and great tithe barn in, 282-3

Brook St. see Cow La.

Brittaine La.: thatched bldgs. in, 270, 278-9

Butts: total losses in, 243; rubbish to be laid in hollows, 39, 45, 54, filled and levelled, 431

College, Sir Thos. Wagstaffe, no damage claimed, 242

Colmore, Wm., barn, coach ho. and land decreed to, 395

Cornwell, Edw., ho. of, Hen. Wilson owner, 45, 225-6, 241

Cornwell, Wm., ho. of, town land, 223, 241

Edwards, Thos., barn of, Wm. Reeves owner, 225, 241

Francis, Geo., ho. of, Mrs. Cawthern owner, 224, 241

Green, Edw. sen., ho. of, Mrs. Ainge owner, 222, 241

Hadley, Ric. jun., ho. of, Wm. Reeves owner, 224, 241

Hancox, John, sen., ho. and new bldg. of, town land, 223-4, 241

Hancox, John, jun., ho. of, Mrs. Cawthern owner, 224, 241

Lines, Thos., ho. of, Mrs. Ainge owner, 222, 241

Mumford, Wm., ho. of, Mrs. Ainge owner, 223, 241

Newbury, Wm., ho. of, surveyors of highways owners, 220-1, 241

Perry, Mat., ho. of, Mr. Ailworth owner and rebuilder, 81, 220, 241, 310

Shatswell, Thos., ho. of, Wm. Bolton owner, Shatswell paid as rebuilder, 27, 30, 221-2, 241, 424

Styles, Hen. ho. of, widow Rider or Wm. Reeves owner, 224, 241

Styles, Nic., ho. of, Mr. Brooks owner, rebuilt by Wm. Bolton, 72, 223, 241

Wilson, Hen. ho. of, Rob. Taylor owner and rebuilder, 110, 478-9

Woodcock, Mary, ho. and barn of, Mr. Brooks owner, 223, 241

Cape Rd. see Priory La.

Castle St.: total losses in, 243; no tallow chandler permitted in, 111; thatched bldgs. in, 270, 278; petn. of Jury St. inhabitants against thatch in, 315

Ashby, Rob., goods burnt in church, 189-90, 237, 252

Bradshaw, John, corner ho. of, see under High St.

Cumberlidge, Joan, goods lost, 190, 237, 252

Fowkes, Wm., to pull down or tile a thatched bldg., part of his ho., 94n.

Fox, Sam., to tile a thatched back bldg., 94n.

Jackson, Wm., goods lost, 190, 237, 252

Marriott, Thos., ho. of, part burnt, Oken's char. owner, 142, 189, 236

Mayor's Parlour or Court Ho., part burnt, 143, 236, 252, 364; and see under Jury St.

Smith, Jonathan, 'things broke and lost', 190, 237, 252

Church St.: destruction in, 1, 4; total losses in, 243; power to widen in Act, 124; building line on W. side staked out, 15; surveyors to view and set out E. side, 31; price for ground taken on W. side, 50; to be cleared of rubbish 40 ft. wide, 47; proprietors on W. side must pave to gutter, 61; new survey ordered of ground taken, 69; descents to be aligned for better paving, 78; rubbish against church wall to be removed, 90; paving belonging to church to be considered, 94n.; timber-framing in, since fire, 271; no tallow chandler permitted in, 111

Ainge, Jos., ho. of, 169-70, 234; paid as rebuilder, 424

Ainge, Sam., ho. of, 169, 234; a rebuilder, 29, 33n.; exchange of ground with Thos. Lean, 39-40

Asplin, Sarah, goods lost in church porch chamber, 183, 235

Blissett, Rob., corner ho. of, 168, 234; ground from Jury St. added to, 24; to be 3 storeys matching others at Cross, xviii, 18, 34, 36, 65; to pull down upper row of dormers, 37

Cakebread, John, ho. of, sub-let by John Biker, Oken's char. owner, 181-2, 235

Canon Row, opposite church, x

Carr, Eliz., ho., barns, stables of, 177, 235; toft bought and rebuilt by J. Atterbury, 49, 74, 379-80, encroaching on church ground, 286-7; encroachment sold to widow Atterbury, 451-2

Chesley, Edw., ho. of, 183, 235; ground taken into Church St. and new square, 34, 79-80; Jas. Fish paid for party wall, 81

Claridge, Thos., ho. of, Mrs. Cawthern owner, 174, 235; to be rebuilt by Eliz. and Thos. Cawthern, 331

Cole, John, ho. of, John Jarvis owner, 172, 234

Dolphin, John, 2 ho.s of, as exec. of Edm. Aylesbury, churchwardens owners, 1 sub-let to Sarah Mayo, 178, 235

RECORD PUBLICATIONS
(Main Series)

*Copies of the Society's Record Publications and Occasional Papers marked with an asterisk * are still available. They are obtainable from the Honorary Secretary, The Dugdale Society, The Shakespeare Centre, Stratford-upon-Avon, Warwickshire, CV37 6QW.*

OCCASIONAL PAPERS